British Television

COMPILED FOR THE BRITISH FILM
INSTITUTE BY

TISE VAHIMAGI

AN ILLUSTRATED GUIDE

British Television

OXFORD UNIVERSITY PRESS

Oxford University Press, Walton Street, Oxford OX2 6DP

Oxford New York

Athens Auckland Bangkok Bombay
Calcutta Cape Town Dar es Salaam Delhi
Florence Hong Kong Istanbul Karachi
Kuala Lumpur Madras Madrid Melbourne
Mexico City Nairobi Paris Singapore
Taipei Tokyo Toronto

and associated companies in
Berlin Ibadan

Oxford is a trade mark of Oxford University Press

Published in the United States by
Oxford University Press Inc., New York

First published 1994

British Library Cataloguing in Publication Data
Data available

Library of Congress Cataloging in Publication Data
Vahimagi, Tise.
British television : an illustrated guide / by Tise Vahimagi.
1. Television broadcasting—Great Britain—History. I. Title.
PN1992.3.G7V34 1994
791.45'75'0941—dc20 94–6981

ISBN 0–19–818336–4

3 5 7 9 10 8 6 4 2

Printed in Great Britain
on acid-free paper by
Butler & Tanner Ltd.
Frome and London.

At low moments during my twenty years' career in television, I have avoided sleepless nights by telling myself, head on pillow, 'for goodness sake, it's only television'. Contrast that with the politicians' oft expressed view that 'television is the most powerful influence in the world'. Who is right? The answer, I suspect, must be left to future scholars, for although television is taken for granted by the present generation, it is still in its infancy.

This volume is intended both as an entertaining flick through the first sixty years of the whole of British television programming, and as a resource for future historians and scholars. The author has miraculously and meticulously uncovered still photographs, originally for publicity purposes, of programmes going back to the 1930s.

The book itself attempts to answer no questions; rather it lays out all the available data and leaves the reader to discern the cultural and social trends either reflected or even suggested by television over the years. What is clear is that television started very much as a derivative medium. It took what existed—theatre, West End cabaret, concert hall, and, when technology allowed, actual live events—and attempted, somewhat crudely by today's standards, to relay them to the home. It was certainly an élitist's medium to begin with. No regional accents, dinner jackets seemed *de rigueur*, programmes and speech were all 'very naice'. Apart from the technological novelty, there was nothing original in the programme mix.

But, as you turn the pages, as the years roll by, the reader will quickly spot television breaking out of its cocoon. Suddenly original drama, created for television, begins to appear. The new generation of producers, trained only in television (or radio) and not products of other disciplines like the theatre, begin to push at the barriers and create formats that are *sui generis*. Magazine shows, current affairs, documentaries, soap operas, and yes, quiz programmes. Personalities begin to emerge as household names, both actors and actresses and, of course, figures of authority like Richard Dimbleby. He was one of the few to make the transition from radio to television, rather like Hollywood stars moving from silent to talking film. Television begins, tentatively, in the 1950s to create its own culture and not simply to rely on the repertoire.

The foundation for all this, of course, was the BBC with its strong, public service ethic laid down by its first Director-General, Lord Reith. You will see from the pictorial evidence of the period that the BBC, although maturing, was still reflecting the world through very refined (in every sense) filters. It took the arrival of Independent Television in 1955 to break the class and regional barriers. Nothing was ever the same; light entertainment moved from *Café Continental* with its evening dress, to *Sunday Night at the Palladium*, with 'Beat the Clock' and a £1,000 jackpot. Drama moved from the drawing-room of Noel Coward and Terence Rattigan to *Armchair Theatre*, with Pinter, Mercer, Owen, *et al*. And ITN invented newscasters, moving pictures—news *programmes* as opposed to the BBC's rather staid bulletins.

The BBC had been in danger of losing touch with the mood of the nation. In theatre, in literature, in politics, in newspapers, in universities, the old pre-war assumptions were being challenged. The advent of the iconoclastic ITV ensured that television did not miss the 'wind of change'—and the BBC grew up. In short, the advent of ITV was, in my personal view, the reason television viewing became the nation's most regular leisure habit.

It is for history to judge whether society has benefited from this change, whether television has enhanced the lives of the present generation of television addicts, watching an average of 25 (approx.) hours per week. The conveyor belt of images, information, and occasional inspiration that now passes into 20 million homes each day is handsomely recorded in this volume.

All sides of this debate will agree, however, that television is important. The argument begins

MICHAEL GRADE

when you try to evaluate how. This unique volume will provoke and stimulate the combatants. It will make a significant contribution to the debate.

Apart from which, it is a glorious and indispensable exercise in nostalgia. For me, personally, the illustrations serve to remind me that it is only television—or is it? I do expect a few sleepless nights now—reading and rereading it.

This book does two things. First, it offers an overview of British television from its very beginnings in 1936 up to the early 1990s. Within that framework it provides descriptions of over one thousand programmes, with dates, notes on content, and production credits for over fifty years of dramas and documentaries, sitcoms and soaps, game shows and talk shows. Secondly, it offers a unique collection of still photographs which are, in many cases, the only remaining visual record of programmes which were transmitted live (and not recorded) or have subsequently been wiped. Many of the rarest images come from the archives of the BBC's Photographic Library; access to this collection was a valued privilege.

Considerations of length, of course, have made it impossible to include every single programme since 1936; instead we have set out to provide a perspective on the totality of British television from the earliest days. The book privileges neither the silly nor the serious, but attempts to survey the strands of programming which together have made British television such a richly textured totality. In so doing, we have presented a wealth of information not only on fondly remembered favourites but on many programmes which are now, perhaps, largely forgotten. Given that the archaeology of television is still in its infancy, hard information on the past in the form of detailed production credits, transmission dates, etc., is difficult to come by. We believe this provides the most useful one-volume reference work on British television programmes yet published.

A number of criteria governed selection. Since we have accorded the visual record equal status with the written, where no picture could be discovered, no entry was included. It also proved virtually impossible to include the details of local and regional programming, and so we have confined ourselves to networked programmes, together with those Anglo-American productions transmitted in most ITV regions. A selection of imported American series has been included simply because they have always been part of the viewers' experience of British television, and especially so during the early years of ITV.

Programmes have been listed alphabetically within the year of transmission, thus allowing the reader to form a sense of television's historical development. However, in order to make relevant connections, additional programmes have whenever possible been added to an initial entry. For instance, the Richard Gordon *Doctor in the House* (LWT, 1969–70) sitcom series was followed by *Doctor at Large* (LWT, 1971), *Doctor in Charge* (LWT, 1972–73), *Doctor at Sea* (LWT, 1974), *Doctor on the Go* (LWT, 1975–77), the Australian-produced *Doctor Down Under* (1981), and *Doctor at the Top* (BBC-1, 1991); as well as the Gordon-related *Doctors' Daughters* (ATV, 1981). A complete index allows both programmes and personnel to be quickly located.

The same format has been used for each entry. The programme title is followed by the production company (co-producers are connected by a rule; commissioning companies are separated by an oblique [/] symbol), then the première transmission date (day/month/year for single-part screening; d./m./y. to d./m./y. for limited-run screening; year to year for multiple series transmission). The dates (except where noted) are based on première UK transmission (tx); BBC TV tx is generally for network transmission; the ITV programme tx is based on the London area listings guide, for the most part, and other London-located sources.

BBC TV references indicate the distinctions between the two BBC channels from the première of the second channel in 1964; programmes from 1936 to 1949, all BBC TV, are simply given as tx —/—/—; BBC programmes from 1950 to 1964 (November) are given as BBC-tv; from 1964 onwards it is indicated whether the programme appeared on BBC-1 or BBC-2.

Unlike American TV, which generally adheres to set seasons for their programming (roughly September through to April) with the summer season given over to specials and re-runs, British television maintains no such strict seasonal corridors of programme presentation. Although British TV schedulers and programmers make a habit of premièring most of their popular or prestigious products during the onset of the autumn season (September / October onwards; for the obvious purposes of greater audience attendance during the winter nights), series as well as other forms of programming can and do emerge at any time throughout the year, regardless of climate and condition. Therefore, it would be misleading to refer to blocks of episodes of a continuing programme in the American form as, say, the first or second season. More accurately these are referred to as 'series' (packages of episodes), regardless of the programmes' ultimate episode-count. The totality of a series usually comes under the general term of 'programme'.

The reference period for this work ended in early 1993 and where tx dates have an open date-span it simply means that at the time of writing the programme / series appeared to be continuing. For the imported programmes (American, Australian, Canadian TV, etc.) we have only listed the date at which they first started being shown on British television (again, from a London-located reference source).

Abbreviations have been used to preserve space and these are as follows in the individual entries: Prod. / Production(s); pr. / producer; dir. / director; wr. / writer; eps. / episodes; mins. / minutes; an ampersand [&] used for writing collaboration means that the writers worked on the script together as a team (Galton & Simpson, for instance).

ITV companies are abbreviated as follows: A-R / Associated Rediffusion; ABC / Associated British Picture Corporation; ATV / Associated Television; C4 / Channel Four Television; HTV / Harlech Television; LWT / London Weekend Television; S4C / Sianel Pedwar Cymru (Channel Four Wales); TVS / Television South; TSW / Television South West; TWW / Television Wales and West; YTV / Yorkshire Television; ITC / Incorporated Television Company.

This book would not have been possible without the generous and unfailing help of Margaret Kirby, Miranda Pollock, Debbie Florsham, and the other friendly and highly efficient staff of the BBC Photograph Library (formerly Harlesden); Adam Lee; Ian McGarry and Equity; the various ITV regional companies (Anglia TV, Border TV, Central TV, Grampian TV, Granada TV and Susan Hayes, HTV, LWT, Scottish TV, Southern TV; S4C, TV-am, TVS, TSW, Thames TV, Tyne Tees TV, Ulster TV, Yorkshire TV); ITC; Bill Harvey (*TVTimes*); Production Design Company; and the good folks at Channel Four Television. The above individuals and organizations certainly helped make the long and at times complicated journey though picture research a passage of pleasure.

Special thanks are also due to Colin MacCabe, Wilf Stevenson, Anne Hanford, Richard Paterson, and Roma Gibson; and particularly Channel Four chief executive Michael Grade for not only delighting me with his personal knowledge of British TV history but also for taking time out to compose the foreword to this work. But a special debt of gratitude must go to my editor Ed Buscombe, who continually resparked enthusiasm during my periods of procrastination. Tana Wollen, Veronica Taylor, and the esteemed team of the BFI Television Unit also deserve more memorable mention than I can possibly relate here.

I should like also to thank the following colleagues and friends who kindly gave their time and their knowledge: Aileen Cook, Gillian Hartnoll, David Sharp, and the staff of the BFI Library and Information Services; Olwen Terris, Simon Baker, and the extremely crucial crew of the NFTVA Cataloguing Department; and Bridget Kinally, Evelyn Shepherd, Colin Rattee, Louise Balls, and the staff of the NFTVA Stills, Posters and Designs Department. I would also like to say a personal thank-you to the ever-patient and always supportive staff of the National Film and Television Archive (Clyde Jeavons, Anne Fleming, Elaine Burrows, Steve Bryant and Pam Logan, James Patterson and Sue Woods, and Bryony Dixon).

The assistance and support of the following individuals indeed helped convert smugness into madness (always preferable): Tony Mechele, Martin Page, Markku Salmi, Richard Dacre, Manuel Alvarado, Jacintha Cusack, Alan Gregory, Jim Cook, David Meeker, Phil Crossley, Tim Courtney, Dave Kent, Jayne Pilling, Dick Fiddy, Sue Bobbermein, Kathleen Luckey, Rosy Wolfe, and Anita Miller; plus the various lost legionnaires of the A&Q and 25 Rathbone Place W1.

T.V.

Published sources include:

ABRAMSON, ALBERT, *The History of Television, 1880 to 1941* (Jefferson, NC: McFarland & Company Inc., 1987);

ALVARADO, MANUEL, and STEWART, JOHN, *Made for Television: Euston Films Limited* (London: British Film Institute, 1985);

BROOKS, TIM, and MARSH, EARLE, *The Complete Directory to Prime Time Network TV Shows* (New York: Ballantine Books, 1979);

DAVIS, ANTHONY, *Television: The First Forty Years* (London: Severn House Publishers, 1976);

FULTON, ROGER, *The Encyclopedia of TV Science Fiction* (London: Boxtree, 1990);

HALLIWELL, LESLIE, with PURSER, PHILIP, *Halliwell's Television Companion* (published as *Halliwell's Teleguide* by Granada Publishing, 1979; retitled and published (3rd edition) London: Grafton Books, 1986);

KINGSLEY, HILARY, *Soap Box: The Papermac Guide to Soap Opera* (London: Papermac, 1988);

—— and TIBBALS, GEOFF, *Box of Delights: The Golden Years of Television* (London: Macmillan, 1989);

MOSS, NICHOLAS, *BBC TV Presents: A Fiftieth Anniversary Celebration* (London: BBC Data Publications, 1986);

PASSINGHAM, KENNETH, *The Guinness Book of Television Facts and Feats* (Enfield: Guinness Superlatives Ltd., 1984);

ROGERS, DAVE, *The ITV Encyclopedia of Adventure* (London: Boxtree, 1988);

SHULMAN, ARTHUR, and YOUMAN, ROGER, *How Sweet It Was* (New York: Bonanza Books, 1966);

SMITH, ANTHONY, *British Broadcasting* (Newton Abbott: David & Charles, 1974);

25 Years on ITV (compiled and produced by ITV Books and *TVTimes*; London: ITV Books and Michael Joseph, 1980);

BBC Handbooks (London: BBC, 1928–);

ITV Yearbooks, Guide to Independent Television (London: ITA/IBA, 1955–).

Magazines and periodicals:

Broadcast (International Thomson Business Publishing, 1973–)

Campaign (Haymarket Publications, 1968–)

Daily Variety (Daily Variety, 1933–)

Emmy (Academy of Television Arts & Sciences, 1979–)

Film Dope (Film Dope, 1972–)

Hollywood Reporter (Billboard Publications, 1930–)

L.A. Weekly (Los Angeles Weekly Inc., 1978–)

Listener (Listener Pubs. Ltd., 1929–91)

Primetime (Wider Television Access, 1981–)

Radio Times (BBC Magazines, 1923–)

Spectator (Spectator (1828) Ltd, 1828–)

Television—The Journal of the Royal Television Society (Royal Television Society, 1927–)

Television Mail (Television Mail Ltd., 1959–1972)

TVTimes (Independent Television Publications, 1955–)

Variety (Reed Publishing, 1905–)

Village Voice (VV Publishing Corporation, 1955–)

1930s 1940s 1950s 1960s

Contents

1970s

1980s

1990s

The chronicle of British television over the past sixty years is indissolubly linked with the story of BBC Television. The Corporation gave the public a sample of things to come when Cecil Madden as programme organizer and senior producer presented a number of closed-circuit test transmissions at the Radiolympia Exhibition in August 1936. Although there were barely 300 receivers available to pick up the transmissions, the service was formally launched on 2 November 1936 from a small studio in north London's Alexandra Palace. This is generally regarded as the world's first high-definition transmission service and, in the intervening half-century, BBC TV has pioneered several major developments in electronic broadcasting, ranging from the first cross-Channel link between Dover and Calais to the opening up of the Eurovision Network and the direct photographic cable between Britain and Canada.

The actual history of television in Britain dates back to 1924, when Scotsman John Logie Baird began his first serious experiments in broadcasting sound and vision. Within two years he was able to demonstrate the results of his experiments to the press and eminent scientists, and the results were so impressive that he received backing from several influential sources who could, even at that time, gauge the commercial prospects of television, even though the image Baird achieved was roughly the size of a postcard and the pictures were somewhat crude and blurred.

With money coming in from speculative sources Baird moved out of his small laboratory in London's Soho area into more suitable premises in Long Acre, Covent Garden, in 1927 and, later, began experimenting with colour transmissions. With encouragement from the press and continued help from his backers, he continued to make substantial progress in black-and-white transmissions and a few prominent people ordered sets to be installed in their homes. One of the earliest owners of a receiver was the Prime Minister of the day, Ramsay MacDonald.

As a result of constant pressure from the press, which naturally regarded Baird and his invention as an exciting news story, the BBC, at that time concerned only with sound broadcasting, was forced into announcing that television was still too experimental to be adopted as a public service. In 1929, however, Sir John Reith, the BBC's first Director-General, agreed to allow Baird to use one of the BBC's main transmitters for a demonstration to BBC engineers and other experts. Thus the government, while declining to accept the idea of a TV service, offered Baird facilities for more ambitious experiments. The BBC continued to support Baird's experiments and, during the trial period, registered an impressive list of 'firsts'. One of the outstanding achievements of that period was the televising of the Derby, and, a year later, it was to be repeated on a giant 8 ft. × 10 ft. cinema screen. Another milestone was the first successful transmission to an express train, and this was followed by broadcasts which were received on board ship and on a plane in flight.

By late 1931 more experimental programmes were beginning to emanate from the BBC's own studios. On 22 August 1932, the BBC decided to set up its own television studios using its own technicians and producers, and this involved buying a substantial amount of TV equipment from the Baird group. A former radio dance orchestra studio in Broadcasting House was set aside to house the new infant and this became the world's first real TV studio. At around the same time the BBC made its first technical appointments. A key scientist appointed was Douglas Birkinshaw and two other technical experts brought in at the time were D. R. Campbell and D. H. Bridgewater. This triumvirate subsequently decided that the future of television lay in a higher-definition system than the 30-line system they were then using.

Meanwhile, other countries were experimenting with their own television systems. Research centres opened in the United States and Europe and in Britain a noted British scientist, Campbell Swinton, was quietly developing alternative forms of transmission for Marconi EMI. While developing the Baird group's ideas, the BBC also decided to carry out experiments with the rival

THE 1930S

Marconi EMI system. Baird, however, remained the primary news source for journalists and his new developments were always widely publicized, while Marconi EMI under Isaac Shoenberg's leadership, though competing vigorously in the battle for supremacy, kept a low profile about their technical achievements. The BBC's tactic of playing off the two competing factions bore fruit in the improved definition of a system that increased the original 30 lines to more than 100 lines.

Baird and Marconi EMI continued to compete to improve quality as the government stepped in and announced the appointment of a committee headed by Lord Selsdon to make recommendations for a public television service. In January 1935, the committee recommended the immediate introduction of a public service to be administered by the BBC with the two rival systems broadcasting alternately on a weekly basis for a trial three-month period. Temporary transmissions ceased while the apparatus was being installed in an allocated corner of Alexandra Palace, which housed the world's first TV network.

In these formative days BBC TV had a staff of some fifty people at Alexandra Palace. The first director of television was Gerald Cock and Cecil Madden was in charge of programming. His first and immediately popular on-screen staff were announcers Jasmine Bligh and Elizabeth Cowell and the only male announcer, Leslie Mitchell. One of Madden's earliest experiences was to receive a message from Gerald Cock that an eleventh-hour decision had been taken to programme from Radiolympia during the Radio Manufacturers' Association annual show, which was due to open in ten days. Starting from scratch Madden had just those ten days in which to find twenty programmes. The schedule was filled with a combination of short films and studio broadcasts, setting the BBC off to a flying start in television broadcasting. Radiolympia 1936 proved to be the first serious market-place for TV receivers and sets were retailed at prices ranging up to £100. After the exhibition there was a six-week shutdown and BBC TV press officer E. C. Thompson later recalled that it was during that 'dark' period that the idea of **Picture Page** as a programme was conceived. This popular programme continued until the service was forced to close down at the outbreak of the Second World War, but it came back in 1946, when it ran for another 300 editions. Canadian Joan Miller, its presenter, became one of Britain's best-known TV personalities.

The Baird system was used for the initial transmission of 26 August 1936 and thereafter it was alternated with the Marconi EMI equipment. To purists, that date rates as the real start of the world's first public TV service, though historians still adhere to the official date of 2 November when the service formally started.

A key feature was the continuing struggle between the rival Baird and Marconi EMI systems, and it soon became apparent that the latter was winning the race. It was certainly preferred by programme-makers but fate probably decided the issue when much of the Baird apparatus was destroyed by fire. Three months after the inauguration date, the Postmaster-General favoured the Marconi EMI 405-line system, using 50 frames per second, a bitter blow to Baird and his financial backers, who had after all been the first in the field.

Experts who recall the pioneering days maintain that, after the choice of system had been made, programme production became simplified and standards of presentation showed substantial improvements. New presentation techniques were gradually developed which initially owed little to either theatre or cinema, but were evidence that TV was becoming an entertainment medium in its own right and in its own way.

Although films were broadcast each morning as a service to retailers, the emphasis was on live presentation. In line with that policy, the TV service bought its first mobile unit early in 1937 and that led to one of the historic turning-points in public acceptance of the new medium. The mobile unit came into its own by filming King George VI's Coronation that year and it was estimated that more than 10,000 viewers saw the royal procession passing Hyde Park Corner as recorded by three cameras. The adventurous spirit in Outside Broadcasting, encouraged by the response to its first endeavour, grew in subsequent months in its coverage of tennis championships at Wimbledon and other sporting events, the Lord Mayor's Show, the Armistice Day Service at the Cenotaph, as well as visits to

Pinewood and other studios, and to Pets Corner at London Zoo. The mobile unit was also used for local broadcasts from Alexandra Palace, and in that way provided BBC TV with an outdoor studio.

While making substantial strides in technical improvements and gaining public acceptance, BBC TV was nevertheless finding itself starved of cash with which to develop the system. The BBC itself regarded television as a poor relation to radio and the cost of running the TV service in its first year was shared equally by the Treasury and the BBC. Subsequently, the government made a grant out of radio licence revenue, from which the BBC had to meet the entire cost of the television service.

Though hampered by lack of finance, television output was gradually increasing and, as most of the programming was live, this represented a tremendous strain on the limited production, technical, and acting staffs who were turning out about 150 minutes of live programmes every day and had to work at a terrifying pace to maintain the schedule. Every hour of screen time needed six or seven hours of rehearsal, and rehearsals went on from morning until night in the studios at Broadcasting House and Maida Vale, in music rooms and odd corners of Alexandra Palace, and occasionally even in the homes of the producers. Camera rehearsals were frequently limited to an hour or two immediately preceding the transmission.

As television approached its first anniversary, there were clear signs that it was becoming organized into two distinct groups, one concerned with engineering and the other with programming. The programme department was again subdivided with one section responsible for programme organization and the other for programme management. The programme organizer headed a team of producers which had now swollen to the grand total of fourteen, while the productions manager oversaw the presentation side, taking care of announcers, stage managers, and stage staff. Major strides were being made on the technical side and as a result television began to be regarded as a serious competitor to other forms of entertainment. It was during this time that Cecil Madden established the principle of a Sunday night TV drama, beginning on 28 March 1938 with Pirandello's **Henry IV**.

Ominous signs from Europe were beginning to have an effect on TV programming. By October 1938 television was transmitting such military-minded fare as **Balloon Barrage** (tx 27/10/38; by permission of the Air Ministry and No. 30 (Balloon Barrage) Group of the RAF), showing viewers the inflation and ascent of a barrage balloon, and **ARP** (tx 28/10/38), a demonstration of the methods of dealing with an incendiary bomb.

The outstanding success of those pioneering days was **Picture Page**. This magazine show, which had a running time of an hour, with two editions each week, was one of the first TV programmes to receive major acclaim. Madden employed a team of scouts who were on a seven-day-a-week look-out for subjects. There were on average about twenty items in each edition. Joan Miller (while presenting **Picture Page**) became, through a weather freak, the first person ever to cross the Atlantic via TV. In November 1938, some New York radio engineers who were playing around with a British television receiver were able to pick up pictures of Miller as she was presenting her programme.

Public interest in the new medium increased throughout 1938 and by the beginning of the following year there were an estimated 11,000 receivers in regular use. Responding to this growing number of viewers, Gerald Cock extended the service by the introduction of Sunday matinées and at the same time decided to step up drama production.

The fledgling unit was developing so rapidly that it was outgrowing its limited space at Alexandra Palace. Outside help was brought in by using more films and by more regular use of the remote mobile unit. Another consequence of the overcrowding was the use of the mobile unit for a full transmission of a West End musical, **Magyar Melody**, starring Binnie Hale, direct from His Majesty's Theatre.

Throughout 1939, with the threat of war overshadowing all else, producers carried on as normally as possible. Among the major events covered that year were the University Boat Race, the

Derby, and the golf tournament between Bobbie Locke and Reg Whitcombe. Another innovation of that year was the introduction of 'Children's Hour' as a regular feature on the network.

The BBC continued its normal services up to and including 31 August, but on the following day—the day on which German troops invaded Poland—the government gave TV executives exactly 10 minutes notice to shut down. Thus, the world's first TV service came to an abrupt end, in the middle of a Mickey Mouse cartoon. The government clamp-down in 1939 was, of course, for security reasons. It was feared the air waves might provide valuable information for Nazi bombers, but, equally important, the engineers were considered too valuable to the armed forces to continue in what was still a luxury entertainment service. It was almost another seven years before the BBC's television service could be resumed.

The BBC was not unique in its development of a television service during this period. Other pioneers in television had been making great strides in the development of TV technology and provided a number of television 'firsts'. For instance, the XI Olympic Games, held in Berlin in July/August 1936, were covered by television for the first time in history, in this case by the German Post Office (DRP) using equipment provided by Telefunken. The first German television experiments were open to the public at the Berlin radio and television exhibitions in 1929 and 1930, and the first German transmission of high-definition TV (240 lines) began in 1935 when the term *Volksfernsehempfänger* (people's television receiver) was coined. The Games were seen in 'TV parlours' and theatres, and in the Olympic village, transmitting on 180 lines at 25 pictures per second. Eight hours of programming were transmitted every day into twenty-five 'parlours' in Berlin, one in Potsdam, and two in Leipzig and were seen by over 162,000 viewers, the highest ever TV audience figure in Nazi Germany—all this under the leadership of Dr Goebbels and the German Propaganda Ministry. However, the standard used for the 1936 Berlin Radio Exhibition (August–September) after the Olympics was on 375 lines. The television units covering the Berlin Olympics, incidentally, were given greater access to the events than the official film crews under acclaimed German film-maker Leni Riefenstahl.

Meanwhile, in Japan, the Japan Broadcasting Corporation (NHK) had been extending its television research to enable direct viewing of the 1940 Olympic Games due to be held in Tokyo. Sadly, this technology was forced into a less positive route with the outbreak of the Second World War on both the European and Pacific fronts.

The USA had begun experimenting with non-commercial television during the early 1930s at the State University of Iowa, Kansas State College, and Purdue University, but development was slow. In 1932 NBC started a TV station based in the Empire State Building (343 lines). By 1939 RCA was showcasing television at the New York World's Fair. A commercial television service was premièred in 1941, and CBS and NBC demonstrated colour TV in 1946.

The first Russian television programme was broadcast from Moscow on 5 November 1934 (a 25-minute programme with actor Ivan Moskvin reading Chekhov's *The Criminal*), with a very limited broadcasting range. A superior television system was started in Moscow in March 1939 and in Leningrad around the same time, and in 1940 programming included news bulletins read by TV announcers. The Second World War impeded development but TV Moscow was the first station in Europe to resume regular programming (on 15 October 1945) with only 420 TV sets in Moscow homes. The standard 625-line image began with an experimental programme in November 1948.

The French PTT (Postes, Télégraphes, et Téléphones) started an experimental 60-line, 25 frames per second service on 26 April 1935 using the apparatus of Réné Barthélemy of the Compagnie pour la Fabrication des Compteurs et Matériel d'Usines à Gaz. In the same month Barthélemy demonstrated his low-definition television system of 60 lines at 25 frames/sec, at L'Exposition Universelle et Internationale in Brussels.

Picture Page
(BBC tx 1936–39; 1946–52)

Was a hugely popular magazine programme of topical and general interest, presented or, rather, connected by Joan Miller (known as 'The Switchboard Girl'). The programme was devised and edited by Cecil Madden and produced by George More O'Ferrall and Royston Morley; it was later produced by Harold Clayton and John Irwin. Studio guests during the first few months of transmission included such popular figures of the time as aviator Jim Mollison, tennis champion Kay Stammers, film director Alexander Shaw, author Algernon Blackwood, 'poster model and film artist' Dinah Sheridan, German novelist Vicki Baum, cartoonist David Low, actor Will Hay, and film-maker Robert Flaherty with Sabu, 'the Elephant Boy'.

Radiolympia
(BBC tx 26/8–5/9/36)

During this period of further experimentation and commercial showcasing, the BBC's high-definition TV programmes were transmitted from the Alexandra Palace television studios in north London specially for reception at Radiolympia (the Radio Show held at the Olympia exhibition halls) on weekdays. Transmission time alternated the Baird (240-line) and Marconi EMI (405-line) systems. The programme items included feature film excerpts, Gaumont British News(reels), GPO film shorts, variety with Helen McKay (*pictured*) singing *Here's Looking at You*, and the first (albeit accidental) television outside broadcast: the departure of comedy performer Leonard Henry from the Television Station at Alexandra Palace.

Theatre Parade
(BBC tx 1936–38)

Presented scenes from popular London theatre productions of the time. The first television presentation of Lewis Carroll's 'Alice Through the Looking Glass' (22/1/37; 25 mins.) was produced by George More O'Ferrall under the **Theatre Parade** banner, with scenes from Nancy Price's Little Theatre production featuring Ursula Hanray (*left*; as Alice), Esme Percy (Humpty-Dumpty), Andrew Leigh (Tweedledum; *right*), Ernest Butcher (Tweedledee; *left*), Elizabeth Maude (White Queen), and Fred O'Donovan (White Knight); More O'Ferrall went on to produce 'Alice in Wonderland' (29/4/37 and 1/5/37, re-presented with various alterations and additions on 26/12/37; 25 mins.) with Hanray again playing Alice, supported by Walter Tobias (as the March Hare), Earle Grey (the Mad Hatter), Fred O'Donovan (the King of Hearts), and Alban Blakelock (the White Rabbit). On 7 May 1937, O'Ferrall presented Act II of Eugene O'Neill's 'Anna Christie' (20 mins.), as produced at the Westminster Theatre, with Flora Robson (as Anna Christopherson) and Edward Rigby (as Christopherson); the setting was on a barge at anchor off Provincetown, Mass. 'Hassan', the colourful story of Hassan of Bagdad and how he came to make the Golden Journey to Samarkand, was one of the most elaborate and complex productions undertaken by producer O'Ferrall in 1937. The play, by James Elroy Flecker, starred a young Greer Garson (*pictured overleaf left*; as Yasmin), Frank Cellier (Hassan; *right*), John Wyse, D. A. Clarke-Smith, and Ivan Samson; performed in two parts (8/6/37, 40 mins. and 14/6/37, 35 mins.), the production was accompanied by the BBC Television Orchestra, conducted by Hyam Greenbaum, with incidental music by Delius which had been composed for the original stage production in 1923 at His Majesty's Theatre; dances were arranged by Marion Wilson; décor was by Peter Bax. The first television broadcast of an Agatha Christie mystery came on 28 June 1937, with O'Ferrall's 25-minute production of a hitherto unpublished and unperformed play, 'The Wasp's Nest', starring Francis L. Sullivan (*pictured overleaf left*; with D. A. Clarke-Smith, Antoinette Cellier, and Wallace Douglas) as the famous detective Hercule Poirot, a role with which Sullivan had been closely identified in

stage productions since 1931. Early 1938 saw the presentation of Act I of the Shaftesbury Theatre production of 'Thank You, Mr Pepys' (6/1/38), adapted for television by W. P. Lipscomb, with Barry K. Barnes (as King Charles II), Edmund Gwenn (Pepys), Douglas Matthews (James, Duke of York), and Henry Oscar (Earl of Shaftesbury); television production was again by George More O'Ferrall.

The Coronation of King George VI
(BBC tx 12/5/37)

The Coronation Procession was televised from the north and south faces of the main arch of Apsley Gate, Hyde Park Corner, using three Emitron cameras linked by means of a special coaxial cable connection with the Alexandra Palace transmitter (as a stand-by, there was also a van equipped with an ultra-short-wave transmitter for feeding the programme to Alexandra Palace). Frederick Grisewood supplied the commentary for the Wednesday afternoon transmission (2.00 p.m. to 3.00 p.m.); it marked the first televised coronation.

The Disorderly Room
(BBC tx 17/4/37)

Featured Tommy Handley (*2nd right*) and Company (*l. to r.* Fred Hudson, Harry Cranley, Doug Verne, and Len Maxwell), before Handley's famous *ITMA* radio show, as the Officer in Eric Blore's popular wartime (First World War) variety musical sketch about army life. The 15-minute programme was presented on television regularly until the outbreak of the Second World War.

For the Children
(BBC tx 1937–39; 1946–50)

Introduced the first television programme specially designed for children of school age. The series was premièred at three o'clock in the afternoon of Saturday, 24 April 1937, with a performance by Zenora the Clown. Initially broadcast in a 10-minute slot, it expanded to 20 minutes when reintroduced in 1946 (on Sunday, 7 July). One of the early programmes presented Paul Leyssac, author, lecturer, actor, and broadcaster, reading stories by Hans Andersen; his Danish mother, apparently, had read the fairy tales to him as a youngster as she had heard them told by Andersen himself. Presentation was by Mary Adams. In 1946 the programme was broadcast on Sunday afternoons, featuring among the items Commander A. B. Campbell and his 'sea chest of treasures' of interest for children; and L. N. and M. Williams, of the Junior Philatelic Society, showing young collectors commemorative stamps (from the then newly issued Victory stamp to the Penny Black); the programme was by then presented by Andrew Miller Jones. The edition of 4 August 1946 presented a musical story by Annette Mills (sister of actor John Mills) in her TV début with puppet Muffin the Mule. For her 5-minute slot Annette Mills (working with puppeteer Ann Hogarth) told a story from a seat at a grand piano while Hogarth, standing on the piano top behind a curtain, manipulated Muffin's strings; the idea for this simple but effective set-up came from producer Andrew Miller Jones. Mills/Hogarth's original puppet repertory company consisted of Peregrine the Penguin, Louise the Lamb, and Oswald the Ostrich. Other animal-related segments included 'Friends from the Zoo', and Nat Allen and his Musical Menagerie with songs about animals. Annette Mills is pictured with Muffin the Mule in a 1947 broadcast.

The Ghost Train
(BBC tx 20/12/37)

Was performed in front of Emitron cameras by (l. to r.) John Counsell, Joan Lawson, Don Gemmell, Alex McCringle, Clifford Benn, Arthur Young, S. E. Reynolds, Hugh Dempster, Rani Waller, Philip Thornley, and Daphne Riggs. This 40-minute presentation of Arnold Ridley's famous play was produced by Jan Bussell. In the West End stage version, Laura Smithson, playing the part of Miss Bourne, spent a good deal of time asleep on the table of a railway station waiting-room; concealed in the table, out of audience vision, was a comfortable mattress. She had to do without the comfort on TV when it was discovered that the Emitron close-ups would immediately reveal the mattress.

How He Lied To Her Husband
(BBC tx 7/7/37)

Starring Greer Garson (left) and D. A. Clarke-Smith (centre; with Derek Williams), was the first George Bernard Shaw play to be televised from Alexandra Palace. Production was by George More O'Ferrall. At the time the BBC stressed that *How He Lied To Her Husband* was the only play that Shaw had allowed to be seen in the cinema; the 1931 film, produced by British International Pictures, was directed by Cecil Lewis who had also been a TV producer. One of Greer Garson's first professional roles on the stage had been in Shaw's *Too True to be Good*. The second television production of a Shaw play was on 4 July 1938, when Desmond Davis produced **Androcles and the Lion** in a 60-minute broadcast with Esmé Percy as Androcles.

1937

Journey's End
(BBC tx 11/11/37)

By R. C. Sherriff, was given an entire evening's presentation (9.00–10.00 p.m.), the first time that the limited evening programme period had been filled by a single play. George More O'Ferrall's Alexandra Palace production managed to condense the script without ruining continuity and rhythm. It was reported that a few film sequences were used from G. W. Pabst's 1930 feature film *Westfront 1918*. The cast included Reginald Tate (*right*; as Stanhope), Basil Gill (Osborne), Norman Pierce (Trotter), Wallace Douglas (Raleigh), J. Neil More (*left*; the Colonel), R. Brooks Turner (the Company Sergeant-Major), Alexander Field (Mason), Reginald Smith (Hardy), and Olaf Olsen (a young German soldier).

Night Must Fall
(BBC tx 21/10/37)

Starred Esmond Knight (*pictured*; Vivienne Bennett *in background*) in the famous Emlyn Williams psychological drama, produced (in a 30-minute broadcast) by George More O'Ferrall.

The School for Scandal
(BBC tx 19/5/37)

Another **Play Parade** presentation, featured Greer Garson and Campbell Gullan (*pictured*), and Denis Blakelock and Earle Grey in scenes from the play by Richard Brinsley Sheridan; *School for Scandal* was first performed in 1777. Produced for television by George More O'Ferrall.

Sports Review
(BBC tx 1937)

Was broadcast in 20-minute editions and compèred by Howard Marshall (*left*) from the second broadcast (he was, in the term of the day, 'indisposed' for the first edition on 30/4/37). The series presented a survey of the outstanding sporting events that had occurred during the month. Marshall, who was well known to radio listeners, conducted interviews (pictured here with New Zealand cricketers J. L. Kerr, D. A. R. Maloney, and A. W. Roberts) and showed film extracts.

Starlight
(BBC tx 1937–39; 1946–49)

A variety programme that presented Gracie Fields (*pictured*) in her first appearance at Alexandra Palace, with accompanist Harry Parr-Davies and the BBC Television Orchestra conducted by Hyam Greenbaum. In March of 1938 Richard Hearne, with Lily Palmer and George Nelson, appeared in the comedy sketch 'Moving Furniture'.

Tele-Ho!
(BBC tx 14/12/37)

Billed as an intimate revue for television, the presentation was written by John Paddy Carstairs with music by William Walker. The programme featured Nelson Keys (*centre*; father of director-screenwriter John Paddy Carstairs), Valerie Hobson (*left*), Cyril Fletcher, Nugent Marshall, Peter Bull (*right*), the Van Thal Girls, and the BBC Television Orchestra (leader Boris Pecker) conducted by Hyam Greenbaum. The 20-minute production was by Dallas Bower.

Twelfth Night
(BBC tx 14/5/37)

Featured the second television appearance of Greer Garson (*left*) in scenes from the play, presented as a part of the **Play Parade** series. The 30-minute broadcast was produced by George More O'Ferrall and included performances by Henry Oscar, Hilary Pritchard, and South African actress Dorothy Black (*right*).

Ann and Harold
(BBC tx 12/7–9/8/38)

The first television serial presented a five-part series of short romantic interludes in the lives of a London Society couple, played by Ann Todd (as Ann Teviot) and William Hutchison (Harold Warden) (*both pictured*), written by Louis Goodrich. The story took them from (ep. 1) 'Their First Meeting' to their grand Society wedding (the narrative spanned a period of over ten months). Guest players included David Smith-Dorrien (ep. 2); Louis Goodrich (ep. 3); Halliwell Hobbs, Bryan Powley, Buena Bent, Mary Godwin, Louis Goodrich, A. Bromley Davenport, and Fred Rivenhall (ep. 4, 'Their Wedding'); the final instalment (ep. 5) was set at Lord's cricket ground (but a topical cricketing event planned to have them crossing the river to the Oval cricket ground). The programme was premièred on Tuesday, 12 July, at 9.15 p.m.; 3 eps. × 20 mins. and 2 eps. × 15 mins. were produced by Lanham Titchener. Goodrich's serial was first broadcast on sound in 1932, with Ann Trevor in the part of Ann.

The Breadwinner
(BBC tx 7/11/38)

The first W. Somerset Maugham play to be televised. The comedy play, first produced in 1930 at the Vaudeville, featured (*l. to r.*) Margaret Vines, Nicholas Hannen, D. A. Clarke-Smith, Lewis Shaw, Athene Seyler, Ena Moon, Laura Cowie, and Guy Verney. The 90-minute broadcast was produced by Stephen Thomas.

The Case of the Frightened Lady
(BBC tx 12/7/38)

Was produced at Wyndham's Theatre in 1931 and filmed in 1932 as *The Frightened Lady*, with Cathleen Nesbitt playing the sinister Lady Lebanon in both productions. When Michael Barry produced Edgar Wallace's play for television, in a 75-minute broadcast, he cast Nesbitt (*left*) again in her familiar role, supported by Andrew Osborn (*right*), Walter Hudd, Terence de Marney, Frederick Piper, William Fox, Rachel Kempson, George Cross, George Pughe, John M. Moore, John Rudling, Kenneth Eaves, Michael Nono, Denis Shaw, John Fraser, and Robin Wentworth. BBC-2 produced a new 75-minute version for 28/12/83, with Virginia McKenna as Lady Lebanon, supported by Warren Clarke, Tim Woodward, and Elizabeth Carvie; Victor Pemberton adapted and Chris Menaul directed for producer Cedric Messina.

Checkmate
(BBC tx 8/5/38)

Was a 'ballet in one scene with a prologue', the story of Death conquering Love depicted symbolically by chess-piece figures performed by the Vic-Wells Ballet. The 50-minute broadcast featured Joy Newton and Frederick Ashton (as the Two Players), June Brae (the Black Queen), Pamela May (the Red Queen), and Robert Helpmann (the Red King). The music was by Arthur Bliss; the BBC Television Orchestra was conducted by Constant Lambert. Costumes and decor were by E. McKnight Kauffer and the choreography was by Ninette de Valois. The programme was presented by D. H. Munro. The production was repeated on 13 May 1938 with the same cast except that Joy Newton and Alan Carter took the parts of the Two Players and Frederick Ashton the part of the Red King.

Clive of India
(BBC tx 19/2/38)

Was specially rewritten and prepared for television by scenario writer W. P. Lipscomb; he had written the original stage play (filmed by 20th Century-Fox in 1935) in collaboration with R. J. Minney. Working with producer George More O'Ferrall, Lipscomb wrote the 60-minute television version to suit the Alexandra Palace studio, adding several scenes that were not included in the stage or screen productions. Colin Keith-Johnston (as Clive; *pictured centre*) and Gillian Lind (as Margaret Maskelyne) headed the cast.

Comedy Cabaret
(BBC tx 28/2/38)

Was the title billing for this 35-minute broadcast of music and humour presented by Harry Pringle. Featured were compère Charles Heslop, the Music-Hall Boys, comedian Émile Boreo, comedy juggler Gaston Palmer, comedian Ed Morelle, and George Robey (*pictured*) as the German Professor.

The Constant Nymph
(BBC tx 31/5/38)

Was presented in a 90-minute broadcast with Victoria Hopper (*pictured*; with Eric Portman) in her original 1933 film role as Tessa. Producer George More O'Ferrall shortened the play for studio purposes by reducing the number of Tessa's relatives. He also used extracts from the film version for some of the exterior scenes. Margaretta Scott, Dorothy Hyson, Tony de Lungo, Alexander Field, Andrea Melandrinos, Molly Hamley Clifford, Ronald Shiner, and H. G. Stoker made up the cast for the Margaret Kennedy and Basil Dean play.

Cyrano de Bergerac
(BBC tx 30/10/38)

Was a major 90-minute production starring Leslie Banks (as Cyrano; *3rd right*), Constance Cummings (Roxane), and James Mason (Christian de Neuvillette; *right background*); also Kenneth Villiers (*left*), André Morell (*centre*), and John Stobart (*centre right*). Adapted from the version compiled by Robert Loraine, the Edmond Rostand story was produced by George More O'Ferrall; Hyam Greenbaum conducted the BBC Television Orchestra.

The Emperor Jones
(BBC tx 11/5/38)

By Eugene O'Neill, was a 60-minute broadcast featuring Robert Adams (*left*; as the Emperor Jones), Frederick Burtwell (*right*; as the Cockney Trader), and Irene Howe in the production by Dallas Bower.

FA Cup Final
(BBC tx 30/4/38)

The televised England v. Scotland international match two weeks earlier had proved a successful test run for televising what was at the time regarded as 'almost the biggest television broadcast of the year'—the Cup Final from Wembley between Preston North End and Huddersfield Town. Only two outside broadcast vans (for the scanning and the transmitting) were in attendance; with a conveniently nearby substation supplying the transmitter (instead of the usual generator). The aerial was placed on the flat roof of the stadium between the two domes on the north side. The link at Highgate received messages from the aerial and transmitted them by land-line to Alexandra Palace. Picture shows a Super-Emitron camera 'in action'. (The result: Preston NE 1, Huddersfield Tn. 0.)

The Last Voyage of Captain Grant
(BBC tx 1/11/38)

A narrative of the Arctic based upon Robert Flaherty's novel *The Captain's Chair*, the 45-minute television production was adapted and produced by Denis Johnston. The cast featured (*l. to r.*) Douglas Allen, John Thompson, John Laurie, Guy Glover, and Ian Aylmer; David Marsh, Basil Cunard, Cyril Gardiner, William Heilbronn, and Micheline Patton were also in the cast.

Lord's—Test Cricket
(BBC tx 24–25, 27/6/38)

The BBC Outside Broadcast department televised the first two days at Lord's on Friday, 24 June (tx 11.30 a.m.–12.30 p.m.; then at 2.30 p.m. and 3.50 p.m.) and Saturday, 25 June (tx 11.30 a.m–12.30 p.m.; 2.30 p.m.; 3.50 p.m.), and continued transmission on Monday, 27 June, but announced that if there was no doubt about the result by the third day and the finish seemed 'unlikely to be exciting', the mobile unit would leave Lord's to prepare for the forthcoming Wimbledon transmission on the Thursday. Second Test Match: Drawn, England, 494 and 242 for 8 wkts. dec.; Australia, 422 and 204 for 6 wkts. The picture shows the television camera, *far right*, on hotel roof overlooking the ground.

Love From a Stranger
(BBC tx 23/11/38)

Was a 90-minute psychological thriller written by Frank Vosper from a short story by Agatha Christie. Featured players were Edna Best (*left*), Henry Oscar (*right*), Bernard Lee, Eileen Sharp, Esma Cannon, Miles Otway, Morris Harvey, Beatrice Rowe, and Sam Lysons. Production was by George More O'Ferrall. In 1947 O'Ferrall restaged the play in a 75-minute broadcast (tx 25/5/47) with Joy Harington, Henry Oscar, Arthur Wontner, and Elizabeth Kirkby.

On The Spot
(BBC tx 2/7/38)

This Edgar Wallace play about gangster warfare in prohibition Chicago was first performed on stage at Wyndham's Theatre in 1930, with Charles Laughton as gangster Tony Perelli. The 90-minute television version, produced by Royston Morley, featured Arthur Gomez (who had been Laughton's understudy on stage), Gillian Lind, Percy Parsons, Edmund Willard, Queenie Leonard, Alan Keith, Richard Newton, Harry Hutchinson, Thornton Bassett, Adrian Byrne, Alex McCrindle, and Peggy Stacey. For the first time in British television drama two studio cameras were taken outside the building, their cables trailing down two flights of stairs, to televise exterior scenes (*pictured*). **On The Spot** was revived for broadcast on 30 May 1948, with Reginald Tate as Perelli and screen actress Christine Norden making her TV play début as the gangster's girlfriend; Douglas Allen produced.

1938

R.U.R.
(BBC tx 11/2/38)

Karel Čapek's prophetic 1921 science fiction play, showing how technological progress (in this case Rossum's Universal Robots) can dominate man and threaten him with extinction, was produced by Jan Bussell in this 35-minute presentation. The cast featured Harvey Braban, Cherry Cottrell, Desmond Davis, Annie Esmond, Judith Gick, Stephen Jack, Gordon McLeod; and (*l. to r.*) Connaught Stanleigh, Derek Bond, Larry Silverstone, and (*front*) Evan John. Costumes were designed by Mary Allan.

Smoky Cell
(BBC tx 31/10/38)

Presented another Edgar Wallace play, with George Pughe, John Lothar, Richard Newton (*centre*), Jon Farrell, Richard George, and Bernard Miles; also (*l. to r.*) Francis R. Mann, Cecil Parker, Frank Sutthony, and Jon Farrell. The 90-minute broadcast was produced by Michael Barry. This was followed up by Wallace's **The Ringer**, broadcast at the end of the year (BBC tx 23/12/38), with Cecil Parker, Gina Malo, Henry Oscar, Garry Marsh, Wally Patch, and Marjorie Rhodes; the 90-minute production was by Royston Morley.

Telecrime
(BBC tx 1938–39; 1946)

Irregular series of 10- and 20-minute whodunits in which the viewers were given sufficient evidence to enable them to solve the problem confronting the detectives. The première story was 'The Back-Stage Murder' (10/8/38) written by Mileson Horton and H. T. Hopkinson, followed by 'Poetic Justice' (24/10/38; wr. Arthur Phillips), 'The Fletcher Case' (24/2/39; wr. Horton; with, *l. to r.*, Shelagh Furley, Richard George, and J. B. Rowe), 'The Almost Perfect Murder' (15/4/39; wr. Horton), 'Circumstantial Evidence' (25/7/39; wr. Horton). Twelve more stories, of 15 minutes each, were performed under producers Gordon Crier, Stephen Harrison, and Douglas Mair and written by Mileson Horton, for tx 22/10–25/11/46; by which time the series was known as **Telecrimes**.

Villa for Sale
(BBC tx 10/11/38)

Starred Rex Harrison (*right*) in the Sacha Guitry comedy (translated by Virginia and Frank Vernon) with Cathleen Cordell (*left*) and Pauline Vilda. The 25-minute broadcast was produced by Stephen Harrison.

The White Chateau
(BBC tx 11/11/38)

Was first broadcast on sound in 1925, and was specially written for radio by Reginald Berkeley. It was produced on the London stage in 1927 and this television version marked its second translation into a new medium. The 90-minute broadcast starred Antoinette Cellier and Andrew Osborn (*left*), with A. R. Whatmore, Edward Lexy (*2nd left*), Harold Scott, William Hutchison, Bernard Miles, George Woodbridge, and Erik Chitty. The setting of a front-line trench was constructed in the studio but, for added effect, in the grounds of Alexandra Palace were two 6-inch howitzers and about thirty men of the Territorial Army. Production was by Royston Morley; music from Sibelius's Second Symphony.

White Secrets
(BBC tx 5/7/38)

Presented a 75-minute drama of the Antarctic by R. E. Earp. Based on Maurice Browne's production from the Fortune Theatre, the broadcast featured D. A. Clarke-Smith, David Hawthorne (*pictured*), Colin Keith-Johnston, Barrie Livesey, Peter Osborn, Alexander Field, John Laurie, and Arthur Young. Produced for television by George More O'Ferrall.

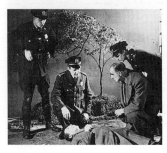

The Anatomist
(BBC tx 2/6/39)

Presented a 90-minute black comedy about body-snatchers Burke and Hare, their mentor Dr Knox, and the West Port murders of the early nineteenth century. Written by James Bridie and produced by Moultrie R. Kelsall, the cast featured Andrew Cruickshank as Dr Knox, W. G. Fay as Burke, and Harry Hutchinson as Hare.

Cabaret Cruise
(aka **S.S. 'Sunshine'**) (BBC tx 1939; 1946)

Subtitled 'All Star "Cabaret Cruise" ', this was a popular song and dance variety show drawing on radio and local-circuit cabaret artistes. The 2/9/46 show featured Jean Kent, George Robey, and The Beverley Sisters (*pictured*, *centre*, in a July 1946 broadcast); directed by Stanley Andrews for producer Harry Pringle. Master of Ceremonies was Commander A. B. Campbell.

Condemned To Be Shot
(BBC tx 4/3/39)

Was a play in the first person specially written for television by R. E. J. Brooke. It was the first time the TV camera became one of the characters, the central figure in the play. This invisible character, with its own 'voice off', was by the end of the play looking down the rifle barrels of a firing squad. Producer Jan Bussell's 20-minute broadcast featured Reginald Brooke (*right*), Zoe Davies, Olga Edwardes, Wilfred Fletcher (*left*), Neil Porter, Hilary Pritchard (*2nd right*), Henry Belling (*2nd left*), and Ben Soutten.

The Fame of Grace Darling
(BBC tx 9/7/39)

Took up the whole of the evening's transmission (9.05 p.m. to 11.05 p.m.) and starred Wendy Hiller in the title role, her first television appearance. Yvette Pienne's play, based on fact and concerning sensation-mongering in the early nineteenth century, was set in Northumberland and covered the period 1838 to 1842. The cast also featured Mark Dignam, Marie Ault, Norman Claridge, Viola Lyel, Jack Lambert, William Hutchison, and Michael Brennan. Décor was by Malcolm Baker-Smith; Fred O'Donovan produced.

Gas Light
(BBC tx 19/3/39)

'A new play by Patrick Hamilton' was how **Gas Light** was billed at the time of the broadcast. The television presentation of the psychological Victorian thriller was based on Gardner Davies's production then running at London's Apollo Theatre. Gwen Ffrangon-Davies (*right*) starred, with Milton Rosmer, Dennis Arundell (*left*), Elizabeth Inglis, and Beatrice Rowe. The 95-minute television presentation was by Lanham Titchener. The play was filmed in 1940 by Thorold Dickinson and by George Cukor for MGM in 1944. Producer Stephen Harrison restaged the play, under the title **Gaslight** (BBC tx 24/7/47; 100 mins.), with Anthony Ireland, Catherine Lacey, and Jennifer Gray; Beatrice Rowe and Milton Rosmer appeared again.

1939

Magyar Melody
(BBC tx 27/3/39)

This mammoth presentation was one of BBC Television's high spots of 1939. The 175-minute direct outside broadcast from His Majesty's Theatre, via the TV mobile unit, became the first full-length musical play to be seen on television. Billed as 'a musical romance', composed by Eric Maschwitz, Fred Thompson, and Guy Bolton (with lyrics by Harold Purcell and Maschwitz), the production starred Binnie Hale (*centre*, in Act II, Scene i) and included Arthur Margetson, Roger Treville, Lawrence Anderson, Stella Arbenina, Allan Bourne, and Peter Mosley. Walford Hyden directed his Magyar Symphonic Orchestra with music by George Posford and Bernard Grun; dances and ensembles were arranged by Joan Davis and Cleo Nordi. Production was by William Mollison.

Marco Millions
(BBC tx 8/1/39)

Eugene O'Neill's satire about the thirteenth-century traveller Marco Polo was presented by Lanham Titchener in a 90-minute broadcast. The cast featured Griffith Jones (as Marco; *centre left*), Catherine Lacey (Princess Kukachin; *centre right*), and Robert Harris (Kublai Khan), supported by Stephen Murray, George Woodbridge, Max Adrian, Michael Denison (*kneeling*), and Robert Emhardt. The TV version was taken from Michael Macowan's Westminster Theatre production. Décor was by Peter Goffin and Malcolm Baker-Smith designed the sets.

Prison Without Bars
(BBC tx 29/7/39)

Peggy Barwell adapted the play by Gina Kaus and Otto & Edgar Eis (from an idea by Hilde Koveloff) which became the basis of a successful 1933 French film, *Prison sans barreaux*, and the 1938 British remake. The television version of the play (very different from the films) tells the story of a girls' reformatory inmate (played by Nova Pilbeam, *left*, in her first TV appearance) falling in love with the school's young doctor (Sebastian Shaw; *right*) and competing for his affection with the new superintendent (Jill Esmond). The 85-minute broadcast was produced by Moultrie R. Kelsall.

Private Lives
(BBC tx 12/8/39)

Billed as 'an intimate comedy in three acts' by Noel Coward, this television version of the famous play (first performed on stage in 1930) featured (*l. to r.*) Guy Verney, Diana Churchill, Denis Webb, and Molly Rankin; Jane Ingram also appeared. Malcolm Baker-Smith designed the settings; Reginald Smith produced the 75-minute broadcast.

The Tell-Tale Heart
(BBC tx 4/1/39)

Was Michael Hogan's television adaptation of the Edgar Allan Poe chiller, featuring (*l. to r.*) Olaf Olsen, Basil Cunard, Stuart Latham, and Ernest Milton; Harding Steerman also appeared. Décor was by Edmund Hogan; music by James Hartley and the BBC Television Orchestra, conducted by Hyam Greenbaum. Dallas Bower produced the 25-minute broadcast.

14

About a year after the end of the Second World War the BBC reopened its television service, at 3.00 p.m. on 7 June 1946. One of the original 1930s announcers, Jasmine Bligh, smiled into the camera on the terrace at Alexandra Palace and, accompanied by a Television March specially composed by Eric Coates, made the first post-war announcement: 'Hello, remember me?' A few moments later, at the inaugural ceremony in Studio A, the Postmaster-General, the Earl of Listowel, formally declared the service open.

In September 1943, the government had appointed a committee to prepare plans for the reinstatement and development of the television service following the end of the war. Special consideration was given to extending the service to 'at any rate the larger centres of population within a reasonable period after the war', to research and development, and to the question of exporting television equipment. Under the chairmanship of Lord Hankey, the committee consisted of representatives from the General Post Office, the Department of Scientific and Industrial Research (DSIR), the Treasury, and the BBC. Among this respected group were the very distinguished scientists Sir Edward Appleton, who represented the DSIR, and Professor Cockcroft, who retained his interest in the committee's proceedings even after his energies were diverted to the atomic bomb.

The committee's report was presented in December 1944, and the government indicated agreement with its main recommendations in October 1945, giving the BBC the go ahead to prepare to resume the television service. When the service reopened in 1946 the range of transmission was within a radius of about forty miles from Alexandra Palace. The technical standards were the same as used in 1939: 405 lines, 50 frames interlaced, giving 25 complete picture frames per second (today's television in the UK is 625 lines / 25 frames per second).

Less than twenty hours after reopening, the service was put to a supreme test. For the Victory Parade (tx 8/6/46) television cameras were mounted on a stand in the Mall opposite the Royal saluting base to present a view of the complete Parade, the arrival of Their Majesties, the long procession itself, and even some of the aircraft in the fly-past. Alongside the television cameras the BBC Film Unit took pictures for televising later that evening. Richard Dimbleby and Freddie Grisewood were on hand for this major TV outside broadcast. It proved to be a great success.

More spectacularly successful outside broadcasts followed, the final Wightman Cup matches from Wimbledon, the first England v. India Test Match at Lord's, a whole week at Wimbledon for the International Tennis Championships, and the first post-war visit to a theatre, the Garrick, for the Beatrice Lillie revue *Better Late*. The first televised church service, held in St George's Chapel on Battle of Britain Sunday, was televised on 15/9/46. In the studio plays by Shakespeare, Shaw, Oscar Wilde, and Edgar Wallace were very popular, but transmissions also included a number of plays specially written or arranged for TV, among them J. B. Priestley's **The Rose and Crown** (tx 27/8/46) and the well-known stage play and film, **Thunder Rock** (tx 29/10/46). **For the Children** premièred on 7 July 1946 as the first children's TV programme, and in August Richard Hearne appeared as Mr Pastry (in the comedy sketch 'The Village Store'); October saw Annette Mills introduce Muffin the Mule and friends such as Oswald the Ostrich.

Picture Page recaptured its pre-war audience while new television personalities emerged: Philip Harben established himself as the doyen of televised cookery, and Fred Streeter enlivened horticulture in the **Television Garden** (tx 1946–51). Unfortunately, permission had not yet been obtained from the film industry to televise newsreels so the BBC's own Film Unit was active recording such events as the liner *Queen Elizabeth*'s sea trials off the west coast of Scotland, the Lord Mayor's Show, the Cenotaph Service, and the Procession for the Opening of Parliament. Just how many television sets were in operation at this time is still a matter of conjecture, but estimates vary

1940s

between 15,000 and 25,000. Despite the 1946 introduction of the combined TV and Radio licence at double the previous figure (£2) the demand for receivers began to exceed supply. Among the many inevitable post-war problems to beset the BBC and delay development, one of the most serious was the fuel and power crisis in early 1947 which meant a daytime shutdown of all TV transmission from February to March. In June 1947 the country-wide extension of television was brought nearer when the BBC ordered equipment for the Birmingham Television Station. In August the Corporation announced that it was preparing to start its own weekly newsreel service to supplement outside broadcasts. Later it promised a twice-weekly service, and finally a change of newsreels every day.

The number of outside broadcasts soared throughout 1947, with the 'panorama of actualities' culminating in the Royal Wedding of Princess Elizabeth and Lt. Philip Mountbatten RN in November (tx 20/11/47). The Outside Broadcast Unit covered the Trooping of the Colours, the Royal Drive at Ascot, and the Service at the Cenotaph; viewers were also present for the first time at the Cambridge Theatre for opera and at Covent Garden for ballet. For variety the highlight of the year was the **Ici Paris** programme on France's National Day, 14 July, when the French Ambassador and his wife joined the studio audience at Alexandra Palace for an all-French entertainment show presented by Jacques Pauliac of Radiodiffusion Française.

Picture Page, edited and introduced by Joan Gilbert, continued its popularity, and the magazine programme **Kaleidoscope** premièred and was televised every second Friday. Television was evolving its own documentary technique with **I Want To Be a Doctor**, tx 20/5/47; written and produced by Michael Barry; while visual talks included **Film History** recounted by Roger Manvell. The showing of films on television was still hampered by an industry which feared competition and so banned TV showings of film newsreels and feature films, but viewers were given a showing of D. W. Griffith's classic *Birth of a Nation* (tx 7/7/47), with an orchestral accompaniment from the original musical score.

The Outside Broadcast Unit and studio production teams collaborated for the first post-war Radiolympia exhibition in October 1947. From the BBC's specially created studio at the exhibition a mobile unit relayed TV programmes to the thousands watching at home, to the visitors watching in the galleries, and to the screens on stands at the exhibition and in a darkened avenue at Olympia. A 90 × 90 ft. triple stage was built into a studio at Radiolympia and from this were produced **Café Continental**, an exotic spectacle derived from a wartime show in Cairo, **Stars in Your Eyes**, with Gillie Potter and Maudie Edwards, **Sepia**, an 'all-coloured' show of black song and dance down the years, and **Variety**, a showcase for 'stars of the stage, television, and radio'. Visitors also had a chance to take part in **Come and Be Televised** as well as in two of the most popular radio programmes of the day, *ITMA* and *Merry Go Round*.

By 1948 the number of television licences had risen to some 54,000 and among the leading events covered by television that year were the XIV Olympiad from Wembley Stadium and the first direct broadcast by a Prime Minister (Clement Attlee) from his official residence at 10 Downing Street.

The 1948 Olympic Games presented a planning and operational problem which had never before been encountered by any broadcasting organization. The first requirement was a building near the Wembley Stadium, and it was initially thought that a special building would have to be erected, but the Managing Director of Wembley Stadium Ltd. offered to lend the BBC an old building which had been the Palace of Arts for the 1924 British Empire Exhibition. Thirty-two (sound) channels in the Wembley studio (now known as the Broadcasting Centre) were needed and so were fifteen commentary boxes, together with seventeen open positions at the Stadium; the Empire Pool had sixteen commentary positions and took delivery of the latest Outside Broadcast Unit cameras. These cameras used a new design of pick-up tube which had only been used experimentally in prototype form on two previous broadcasts. The control equipment for these cameras was located in a vehicle outside the building and connected by coaxial cable to the vision control room in the

Broadcasting Centre. The older television cameras were used in the Stadium, as they required much more light to obtain a satisfactory image. In a small production room the producer had three monitors which showed the actual picture as broadcast, together with previews of pictures from the Stadium and Empire Pool.

The 1948 Olympiad television transmission engaged some 200 engineers and used twenty-five venues, with 130 commentary positions, which of course included sound broadcasting. The whole project took twelve months to plan, building and installation work took six months, and three months were required to dismantle and return to normal. The public's caution about buying new receivers soon faded and sales began to rise; TV licences increased from 61,000 in August 1948 to over 90,000 by late 1949.

In 1949 the Postmaster-General announced the standardization of the 405-line transmission system and it could be seen that television was fast approaching semi-national status. The first provincial transmitter opened in Sutton Coldfield that autumn to bring TV to the midlands, and a site for a north of England station was located at Holme Moss, near Huddersfield. Coverage of the Olympic Games gave television a triumphant boost.

Technical improvements also leaped in 1949 with the introduction of new cameras equipped with rapidly interchangeable telephoto lenses mounted on turrets, the zoom lens, and the use of kinescopes, a new system enabling direct recording from the TV screen. Outside broadcasts benefited greatly from these technical advances and continued to present some of the year's TV highlights, including the transmission of the entire University Boat Race, for the first time using a battery of cameras spaced at strategic points along the river bank as well as a camera following the crews in a launch.

Among the television favourites of 1949 were Jack Hulbert and Cicely Courtneidge, Bobby Howes and Binnie Hale, Richard Hearne, and Jean Kent. It was also in 1949 that the BBC acquired the Lime Grove studios from Gaumont-British and was given the green light by London County Council to proceed with its Television Centre at White City.

Alice
(BBC tx 21/12/46)

Was the first of two George More O'Ferrall productions of the Lewis Carroll fantasy, with this presentation subtitled 'Some of her Adventures in Wonderland'. This 40-minute television broadcast was taken from Clemence Dane's dramatized version (adapted by O'Ferrall), for which Richard Addinsell composed the music. Vivian Pickles (*pictured*) played Alice, with Erik Chitty, Desmond Walter-Ellis, John Baker, Gwyneth Lewis, Dorothy Stuart, John Roderick, and, further along the cast, young Miriam Karlin as Cook. Settings were by James Bould.

The Dark Lady of the Sonnets
(BBC tx 7/6/46)

Was broadcast on the afternoon of BBC TV's reopening of the television service. George More O'Ferrall's production, by George Bernard Shaw, featured Henry Oscar as Shakespeare, Lesley Deane (*centre*) as the Dark Lady, Dorothy Black (*right*) as Queen Elizabeth, and Alban Blakelock as the Beefeater. The programme was followed by a visit to the Mall for the preparations for the following day's Victory Parade. Denis Webb is pictured (*left*) as Shakespeare in this March 1947 rehearsal on closed circuit for a restaging of the play.

Frieda
(BBC tx 7/7/46)

The complete cast from the Westminster Theatre production reassembled at Alexandra Palace to perform the 90-minute broadcast for producer Harold Clayton. Valerie White appeared as Frieda, the German wife of an RAF officer whom he brought home to his family in a small English town during the closing days of the Second World War. Barbara Everest (as Mrs Dawson, the mother), Barbara Couper, Ursula Howells, Richard Warner, Jack Allen (as her husband Robert Dawson), and Carl Jaffe appeared. The Ronald Millar play was filmed in 1947 by Basil Dearden for Rank (with Mai Zetterling in the title role). **Frieda** was re-presented on 24/10/48 with a new cast: Moira Lister played Frieda, Derek Bond (in his TV debut) was the husband, and Albert Lieven repeated his film role of Richard Mansfield. Harold Clayton again produced.

Jeannie
(BBC tx 2/7/46)

Was the story of a young Scottish girl, played by Barbara Mullen (*left*), who inherits some money and decides to take the holiday of a lifetime. The 90-minute comedy by Aimée Stuart was produced by Eric Fawcett, with John Laurie (*right*), Eve Lynd (*centre*), Julian Orde, Christine Cherrill, and Carl Bernard supporting. Stuart's play had been filmed by director Harold French in 1941, with Barbara Mullen in the title role.

Kaleidoscope
(BBC tx 1946–53)

Began as a fortnightly magazine programme (every other Friday; 30 mins.), presenting such viewer-interest material as Iris Brooke describing antique treasures in 'Collector's Corner'; 'Word Play', a game of charades, played by members of J. Arthur Rank's Company of Youth (aspiring young film stars); Leslie Welch, the 'Memory Man'; and the comedy 'Watch that Faux Pas' with Max Kester (*pictured*) as the Lecturer. 'Be Your Own Detective', a short thriller by Mileson Horton testing the viewers' powers of observation, started in 1947 with a theme along similar lines to **Telecrime**. The programmes were introduced by McDonald Hobley; edited and produced by John Irwin.

1946

The Man With the Cloak Full of Holes
(BBC tx 20/8/46)

Was a new play by W. P. Lipscomb about Christopher Columbus; the story was set in 1492, the year in which he sailed to find the New World. The 90-minute broadcast featured F. Wyndham Goldie as Columbus, with Abraham Sofaer, James Dale, and Oriel Ross supporting. The programme was produced by George More O'Ferrall.

Morning Departure
(BBC tx 1/12/46)

Kenneth Woollard's play about the survivors of a sunken submarine and the efforts of a salvage ship to raise her was stunningly presented (via the Alexandra Palace studio set, complete with giant rockers to effect an underwater swaying motion) in this 90-minute broadcast produced by Harold Clayton. Members of the crew of trapped Submarine S14 were (*l. to r.*) John Baker, Alban Blakelock, Anthony Hudson, Cameron Hall, Nigel Patrick, Ronald Adam, Derek Elphinstone, and, not shown, John Stevens and Patrick Macnee. The Royal Navy rescue team included Michael Hordern, Robert Raglan, and Fred Groves. Settings were designed by James Bould. The play was restaged on 26/2/48, with Michael Rennie as Lt.-Cmdr. Stanford (the original Nigel Patrick role) and again produced by Harold Clayton. The play was filmed by Roy Baker in 1949.

Pinwright's Progress
(BBC tx 29/11/46–16/5/47)

Was a fortnightly comedy series alternating on Fridays with **Kaleidoscope**. Written by Rodney Hobson and edited by *ITMA*'s scriptwriter Ted Kavanagh, the 10 eps. × 30 mins. series followed the misadventures of J. Pinwright (played by James Hayter; *pictured*), proprietor of the 'smallest multiple store in the world'. Clarence Wright, Doris Palmer, Daphne Maddox, Jill Christie, Charles Irwin, and Sam Hinton also appeared. John Glyn-Jones produced.

The Playboy of the Western World
(BBC tx 9/8/46)

By J. M. Synge, featured Arthur Sinclair, Phyllis Ryan, Tom Warden, Joyce Chancler, and J. Edward Byrne in this classic Irish drama where 'the action takes place in a shebeen near a village on a wild coast of Mayo, Ireland'. The 90-minute broadcast was produced by Fred O'Donovan.

Reopening of the BBC Television Service

On Friday, 7 June 1946, at 3.00 p.m. the Postmaster-General, the Earl of Listowel, reopened the television service with a programme that included a *pas seul* by Margot Fonteyn, the harpist John Cockerill, and the cartoonist David Low giving a talk illustrated with his drawings. Philip Bate produced. Also broadcast was Disney's 1933 *Mickey's Gala Première* cartoon, the last item transmitted before the TV service was interrupted on Friday, 1 September 1939.

The Rose and Crown
(BBC tx 27/8/46)

Presented a one-act play written for television by J. B. Priestley, and set in the private bar of The Rose and Crown, a small public house in north-east London. D. A. Clarke-Smith (*left*), Phyllis Morris (*right*), Carl Bernard, Jane Barrett (*2nd right*), Muriel George (*2nd left*), John Slater (*centre left*), and Mark Dignam appeared in the 35-minute broadcast produced by John Glyn-Jones.

19

The Shop at Sly Corner
(BBC tx 21/7/46)

The St Martin's Theatre production of Edward Percy's story of blackmail and murder was presented in a 90-minute broadcast featuring Keneth Kent (as Descius Heiss), Kenneth Griffith (blackmailer Archie Fellowes), and Jean Colin (as daughter Margaret Heiss). S. E. Reynolds produced. George King Productions filmed the play in 1947 (with Griffith repeating his Archie Fellowes role).

Toad of Toad Hall
(BBC tx 29/12/46),

The play from Kenneth Grahame's *The Wind in the Willows*, dramatized by A. A. Milne, was adapted for TV and produced by Michael Barry. Alan Reid was Toad, Kenneth More was Mr Badger, Andrew Osborn was Water Rat, and Jack Newmark was Mole; Victor Woolf and John Thomas played Alfred the horse, while Jon Pertwee played the Judge. The 90-minute broadcast also featured music by H. Fraser-Simson and settings designed by Barry Learoyd.

The Amazing Dr Clitterhouse
(BBC tx 3/8/47)

Barre Lyndon's comedy-thriller about a doctor who carries his medical research into the criminal world was adapted and produced in a 90-minute broadcast by John Glyn-Jones. Harold Warrender played Dr Clitterhouse, supported by Marjorie Mars, Alex Mango, Charles Farrell, Eleanor Summerfield, Richard Caldicot, and Henry Oscar.

The Bad Man
(BBC tx 24/6/47)

Was an updated (though studio-bound) Western, along the old rancher's-daughter-trying-to-raise-the-mortgage-in-time lines. Porter Emerson Browne's plot also involved a war veteran, a wealthy stockbroker, possible oil on the property, and a murderous Mexican bandit. Cast featured (*l. to r.*) Charles Irwin, Robert Ayres, Charles Farrell, Ben Williams, and Charles Rolfe. Carla Lehmann, Zena Foster, and Richard Molinas (as bandit Pancho Lopez) were also featured. Eric Fawcett produced the 90-minute broadcast.

The Birth of a Nation
(BBC tx 7/7/47)

This was a shortened version (in a 60-minute transmission) of D. W. Griffith's classic 1915 adaptation from Thomas Dixon's novel (published 1905) and play (performed 1906) *The Clansman*. The special musical score, composed and arranged by Joseph Carl Breil to accompany the original presentation of the film, was used by courtesy of the Film Department of the Museum of Modern Art, New York, and played in the studio by Louis Voss and his Orchestra. Narration was written and spoken by Roger Manvell. A. Miller Jones produced for television; he also arranged for the print to be shown at the 'correct speed'. Later cinema presentations included **The Blue Angel (der Blaue Engel)** (tx 1/12/47), billed 'to be screened in its entirety of ninety-eight minutes'; **Alexander Nevsky** (tx 21/5/48, 9.15 p.m. to 10.15 p.m.), with a warning that 'the version for television is rather shorter than the original'; and the two-part showing of **Les Enfants du paradis** (tx Tuesday, 3/8/48, 8.30 p.m. to 10.00 p.m.; Wednesday, 4/8/48, 8.30 p.m. to 9.40 p.m.). Also, during this period, there were multiple screenings of the *Renfrew of the Mounties* and Tex Ritter B-movies scattered among the schedules. Cinema films had on occasion been a part of TV programming during the late 1930s (Michael Powell's 1937 drama **The Edge of the World**, for instance, had been transmitted on 22/3/39, 9.25 p.m. to 10.35 p.m., and was reshown on 1/4/39).

Boys in Brown
(BBC tx 27/7/47)

Was set in a Borstal Institution, and followed the lives of an assorted group of inmates: the tough, the weak, and 'the morons'. Nigel Stock (as Jackie Knowles) and André Morell (as the Governor) led the cast; John Carol, Alwyne Whatsley, Tony Halfpenny, Jordan Lawrence, and Michael Ripper also appeared. Michael Barry presented the 105-minute broadcast. Reginald Beckwith's play was filmed by Gainsborough Pictures in 1949.

Busman's Honeymoon
(BBC tx 2/10/47)

Was up until that time the only play based on the adventures of Dorothy L. Sayers's famous amateur detective, Lord Peter Wimsey (co-authored with M. St Clare Byrne). The 90-minute TV play, adapted and produced by John Glyn-Jones, offered the viewer a true 'detective problem', in which every clue was shown at the same time to the audience and to the detective so that both of them had an equal chance to solve the problem. Harold Warrender played Wimsey and Ruth Lodge was Harriet Vane; they were supported by Ronald Adam, Patric Curwen, Joan Hickson, and Sidney Tafler.

Café Continental
(BBC tx 1947–53)

Premièred as a spectacular, 45-minute cabaret show with Al Burnett as master of ceremonies; the introductory billing announced to the viewer that 'your table has been reserved by the Maître d'hôtel' (played by Claude Frederic, *left*; with guests Sally Anne Howes and her father, Bobby Howes, *centre*). The programme had been devised and produced by Henry Caldwell; a variety format he had first produced for ENSA in the Middle East. A 1948 programme featured the Italian comedy singing quartet, Quatuor Cetra, three men and a girl who burlesqued everything from opera to swing and who in their own country dubbed all the sound tracks for Walt Disney cartoon films. Perhaps one of the biggest scoops and attractions for **Café Continental** during the late 1940s (BBC tx 26/6/48) was presenting Josephine Baker (*pictured*), famous star of the Folies Bergères, who appeared with bandleader husband Jo Bouillon as a curtain-raiser for a special show on the following Tuesday (BBC tx 29/6/48) with Eric Robinson and his Orchestra; the programme was presented by Henry Caldwell.

Cry Havoc
(BBC tx 9/2/47)

This BBC TV presentation was the first performance of Allan R. Kenward's play to be seen in Britain (excluding the slightly altered 1943 MGM feature film version). The tense story told of a group of army nurses, raw recruits, who volunteered for work on the Bataan Peninsula during the Japanese advance across the Philippines in 1942. The scene was exclusively in their living quarters, a converted gun emplacement (the original BBC set design still is shown). The all-female cast included Joyce Heron, Elizabeth Hunt, Diana Decker, Sally Rogers, Pax Walker, Mary Martlew, and Aletha Orr. George More O'Ferrall produced the 90-minute broadcast.

The Green Pack
(BBC tx 31/8/47)

The first of Edgar Wallace's thrillers to return to the television screen, this time with the action set in Portuguese West Africa among the gold prospectors. Gordon Littman, Alan Lawrance, and Lawrence O'Madden led the cast, supported by Philip Leaver and Gabrielle Brune. The 90-minute broadcast was produced by Ian Atkins, with sets designed by Stephen Bundy.

The Happiest Days of Your Life
(BBC tx 4/2/47)

John Dighton's comical farce in which the Ministry mistakenly billets a girls' private boarding school with a boys' school was produced by Stephen Harrison in a 90-minute broadcast. Cast featured (*close to camera*) Nigel Stock and Hilary Liddell; (*l. to r., background*) Richard Goolden (as Pond, head of the boys' school) and Jane Henderson (as Miss Whitchurch, head of the girls' school), Brian Oulton and Marjorie Gresley, Edward Lexy and Una Venning, Graveley Edwards and Hilda Davies. Dighton's play was filmed by Frank Launder in 1950.

Larry the Lamb
(BBC tx 11/5/47)

Was one of the more popular programmes in radio's *BBC Children's Hour*; created in the late 1920s by S. G. Hulme Beaman. Hendrik Baker, a writer friend of Beaman, turned four of the radio plays into a stage play called *The Cruise of the Toytown Belle* and it was this production that was presented in a 60-minute broadcast by producer Alex McCrindle. The cast featured (*l. to r.*) Betty Blackler (as Larry the Lamb), Malcolm Thomas (as Dennis the Dachshund), and Roger Trafford (as Peter Brass). Fred Essex, Raymond Rollett, and Van Boolen were also among the members of the original stage show.

The Man Who Came to Dinner
(BBC tx 23/3/47)

Following the success of Moss Hart and George F. Kaufman's stage and film productions, BBC TV presented a 90-minute broadcast featuring (*l. to r.*) Macdonald Parker (as Dr Bradley), Jean St Clair (as Miss Preen), Felicity Gower (as Maggie Cutler), Frank Pettingell (as Sheridan Whiteside), Hal Thompson (as Mr Stanley), Helen Miller (as June Stanley), and Janet Morrison (as Mrs Stanley). June Clyde (as Lorraine Sheldon) and Alan Keith (as Banjo) also appeared. Joel O'Brien produced. O'Brien later produced another famous Hart and Kaufman play for television, **You Can't Take It With You** (BBC tx 18/5/47), starring Finlay Currie (as Martin Vanderhof), with Bessie Love, William Kemp, Diana Decker, and Connie Smith.

New Faces
(BBC tx 16/8/47)

Presented a 45-minute variety show, featuring the Eric Maschwitz Revue; with Zoe Gail, Bill Fraser, Charles Hawtrey, Hazel Bray, Peggy Willoughby, John Bentley, Ian Carmichael, Gordon Murray, and Eric Robinson and his Orchestra. The settings were designed by Barry Learoyd; Henry Caldwell produced. A contemporary critic noted that 'Fraser and Hawtrey gave an enthusiastic rendering of "Mother O'Mine"'.

Rebecca
(BBC tx 19/1/47)

Taking place in the Hall at Manderley, the home of Maxim de Winter, in 1939, Harold Clayton's 105-minute production of Daphne du Maurier's story emphasized a suitable atmosphere of mood and suspense, albeit in some very theatrical surroundings. Dorothy Gordon (*right*) played the new Mrs de Winter, Michael Hordern (*2nd right*) was Maxim de Winter, and Dorothy Black (*2nd left*) was Mrs Danvers. Mackenzie Ward (*left*) as Jack Favell and Eric Messiter (*seated*) as Colonel Julyan also appeared.

The Two Mrs Carrolls
(BBC tx 6/2/47)

Martin Vale's suspense drama about a husband, Geoffrey Carroll (played by William Fox), planning his wife's murder through slow poisoning. Tatiana Lieven was Sally, the wife; also appearing were Ilona Ference, Howard Douglas, and Beryl Ede. The 90-minute broadcast was produced by Ian Atkins; James Bould designed the sets. The Warner Bros. feature film version, made in 1945, was released in 1947.

The BBC Television Newsreel
(BBC tx 1948–54)

Premièring on 5/1/48, **Newsreel** gave viewers initially four opportunities to see the regular weekly service (Mondays, Wednesdays, Saturday evenings, and Saturday afternoons for children) which generally followed the newsreel pattern of the cinema. But unlike the commercial newsfilms, the programme ran for about 15 minutes, instead of the customary ten minutes, and contained fewer items than the commercial reels. The producer was Harold Cox, at one time with Gaumont-British and later an Outside Broadcast Unit manager with the Television Service; D. A. Smith was the editor; chief cameraman was Alan Lawson; and J. K. Byer was head of sound recordists. The **Newsreel** also covered events on the other side of the Atlantic, under a film exchange agreement with NBC-TV. From 1951 Sunday evenings began with a 15-minute **Newsreel Review of the Week**, using selected items and important moments from the previous week's newsreels presented by Edward Halliday, who for the reviews appeared from time to time on the screen.

The Front Page
(BBC tx 15/8/48)

Ben Hecht and Charles MacArthur's classic comedy, set in the Press Room of a criminal court in Chicago, was presented in a 90-minute broadcast by producer Joel O'Brien. Sidney James (*centre*) led the cast as Hildy Johnson, supported by Henry Gilbert (as editor Walter Burns), Ivan Vander (as Diamond Louie), Marjorie Gordon (as Molly Molloy), and Michael Balfour (*far right*; as Woodenshoes Eichhorn).

I Killed the Count
(BBC tx 14/3/48)

Alec Coppel's comedy-thriller celebrated the use of flashbacks in its unravelling of the mystery of who killed Count Victor Mattoni (played by Philip Leaver). The story-line also offered various confessional flashback moments for Det. Insp. Davidson (Frank Foster) to analyse; instead of using pre-shot film to effect the flashback sequences, producer Ian Atkins continued the play live, so the cast had to get around from set to set with only split seconds to spare.

Kid Flanagan
(BBC tx 1/8/48)

Moody, psychological drama set in the boxing world featured a young Michael Medwin in his first television role as boxer Johnny Flanagan, with Sidney James (as promoter Sharkey Morrison), Lewis Stringer, and Jenny Laird. The 90-minute play by Max Catto was produced by Joel O'Brien. The story was filmed by Exclusive in 1953; James repeated his role of Sharkey.

Men of Darkness
(BBC tx 21/3/48)

The first British production of an English version of the play *Les Nuits de la colère* by Armand Salacrou, adapted and produced by Royston Morley, about the dividing-line created between occupied and unoccupied France in 1940, separating friend from friend, resister from collaborator. Roger Livesey and Joyce Redman were featured with George Woodbridge (*left;* as Resistance leader Rivoire) and Raymond Huntley (*right;* as Pisancon, a member of the Vichy Militia) in this 90-minute production.

Opening Ceremony of the Olympic Games
(BBC tx 29/7/48)

The XIV Olympiad, held in London, was televised from 29 July to 14 August 1948 and amounted to more than fifty hours of programmes, an average of three and half hours a day. A special television cable was laid from the centre of London to Wembley and two new mobile units were brought into service using, for the first time, the up-to-date cameras with turret lenses. Commentary teams consisted of: Richard Dimbleby and Michael Henderson (opening and closing ceremonies); Roy Moor, Pat Lansberg, and Jack Crump (athletics); Fred Milton and John Webb (swimming); Peter Wilson and Dudley Lister (boxing); James Jewell (football); Michael Henderson (hockey); Col. Allenby and Peter Dimmock (riding). The Olympiad represented the most ambitious series of BBC TV programmes ever undertaken. The march past of the contingent of competitors from Great Britain during the opening ceremony is shown.

Pygmalion
(BBC tx 8/2/48)

Presented the TV débuts of Margaret Lockwood and Gordon Harker in the Bernard Shaw play produced by Royston Morley. This television version was presented exactly as it was in the original stage production and, with a 150-minute broadcast time, was transmitted for longer than any previous television play. Lockwood (*right*) played Eliza Doolittle, Ralph Michael (*centre*) was Professor Henry Higgins, Arthur Wontner (*left*) was Colonel Pickering, and Gordon Harker took the role of Alfred Doolittle. Sets were designed by Barry Learoyd.

Television Dancing Club
(BBC tx 1948–62)

Began as a half-hour programme and for many years featured the popular dance music of Victor Sylvester and his Ballroom Orchestra. Its première producer was Richard Afton. The equally popular stable-mate programme **Come Dancing** started the following year. In the early 1960s the programme became **Dancing Club** (BBC-tv, 1963–64).

By Candlelight
(BBC tx 27/11/49)

Cinema actress Luise Rainer (*centre*) made her BBC TV début in this frothy European-set comedy translated from the German (of Siegried Geyer) by Harry Graham; (*l. to r.*) Anthony Shaw, Clive Morton, Rainer, and Robert Flemyng appeared in the 105-minute broadcast, produced by Harold Clayton.

Come Dancing
(BBC tx 1949–)

This venerable programme has been described variously as an odd mixture of fashion parade and exhibition dancing and, in more recent times, competitive showbiz. Developed from an original idea by showman Eric Morley, **Come Dancing**'s television world of ladies wrapped in yards of sequinned tulle and gents rigidly outfitted in tails performing extravagant quicksteps as representatives of the Penge Formation Dance Team (or some such) began from the floor of the Ritz Ballroom, Manchester, in October 1949. During the early years the BBC outside broadcast cameras simply televised events from various dance-halls with the added attraction of dance lessons given by World Champions Syd Perkins and Edna Duffield. The now familiar interregional competitions were not introduced until 1953. Among the many presenters the programme has had over the years, Peter Dimmock, Mary Malcolm, Sylvia Peters, Peter West, Terry Wogan, and Angela Rippon remain the most memorable for their off-dance-floor enthusiasm. Early 1960s presenter Brian Johnston is pictured (*centre*) participating in the general dancing.

Miranda
(BBC tx 25/12/49)

By coincidence, followed closely on the BBC's purchase of Lime Grove studios where Glynis Johns had made the famous 1948 film. This 100-minute television production, adapted from Peter Blackmore's play, featured Peggy Simpson (*pictured*; as Miranda), Emrys Jones, Peter Williams, Anne Crawford, and David Tomlinson. Tomlinson, on loan from the Rank Organisation, was kept busy filming *The Wooden Horse* during the day and had to rehearse the TV play almost by instalment. The production was designed by Barry Learoyd and produced by John Glyn-Jones.

The Time Machine
(BBC tx 25/1/49)

Billed as 'a fantastic voyage into the future', the 60-minute play featured Russell Napier (*pictured, right*) as H. G. Wells's time traveller who projected himself into the year AD 802,701, and journeyed onwards into the twilight of the world. The story was adapted and produced for television by Robert Barr. The production was designed by Barry Learoyd. A revised production (with a partly rewritten script) was presented on 21/2/49 (also 60 minutes).

Triple Bill
(BBC tx 10/6/49)

Was a 75-minute broadcast featuring a crime play ('Witness for the Prosecution', adapted by Sidney Budd from the story by Agatha Christie), an Irish comedy ('The Call to Arms', adapted by John Glyn-Jones from the story by Denis Johnston), and a short play that was set in the confines of a telephone box ('Box for One', an original story for television by Peter Brook, featuring Marius Goring (*pictured*)). John Glyn-Jones produced.

Television's growing popularity in all sections of society as the 1950s began was reflected by noticeable changes in the social habits of viewers and by the medium's influence on people in general. This popularity was both the cause and the effect of an increase in the amount of television available. The Beveridge Committee's report on broadcasting recommended renewal of the BBC's charter (continuing its monopoly) with no fixed time-limit but with a review of its workings in five years. More regional autonomy was suggested and further development of the television service, with an increased licence fee. One of the most important proposals in the government's statement on Beveridge's report referred to the possibility of an alternative television service provided by private enterprise.

With independent television still some five years away BBC TV, in 1950, continued scoring successes, particularly with their outside broadcast programming: the 1950 University Boat Race was at that time one of the biggest outside broadcasts ever attempted in Britain. Almost all of the BBC's resources in equipment and personnel were engaged and some of the technology was especially developed and used for the first time: microwave radio transmission links, 200 Mc/s portable radio links, a VHF two-way communication link, and a mobile central control unit. Expanding on the 1949 coverage of the Boat Race, BBC TV used a mounted camera in the bow of a launch following the boats as before but increased the number of cameras stationed along the shore (to twelve) and offered a separate TV sound commentary from the launch carrying the camera.

During May 1952 the BBC carried out a test programme in six Middlesex secondary schools to evaluate the use of films in schools. It helped children by televising discussions on current affairs by people whose opinions were regarded as worth hearing and who through television were seen by the children as real people. However, it was still believed that television could only aid teaching and that it would never be an adequate teaching method by itself. The BBC hoped to start a second series of school television programmes, this time available to the whole country, at the end of 1953 depending on the results of the first experiment. However it was not until the autumn of 1957 that BBC TV inaugurated an experimental school television service. The BBC TV schools service began in September 1957 (with a programme called **Living in the Commonwealth**, aimed at 11 to 12 year olds) and broadcast afternoon programmes during the autumn term. In July 1959 BBC TV announced that from September of the following year it would double its existing expenditure of £200,000 a year on school television; the service, which had up until that time still been regarded as somewhat experimental, was now to be considered permanent and greatly expanded.

The summer of 1952 saw the first occasion on which the television system of one country was able to broadcast to another, when television programmes from France were shown by the BBC (as a **Paris Panorama**, tx 8–14/7/52). A special type of convertor was necessary to change the pictures from the definition standard of the Radiodiffusion et Télévision Française to the British Standard. The images were carried over radio links and coaxial cable in eight stages, Paris–Villers Cotterêts–Péronne–Lille–Cassel–Alembon–Dover–Wrotham–London. The programmes, hosted by Richard Dimbleby along with Sylvia Peters and RTF's Jacqueline Joubert, included a travelogue of street scenes, visits to the Louvre and to a sculptor's studio, a fashion show on board a boat in the Seine, sports events, and a military tattoo in the Palais des Sports.

The televising of the Coronation was a significant factor in the increase of TV sets in public use, and in March 1953 figures for combined sound and television licences were given as 2,142,452, compared with 1,457,000 a year previously. The (tx 2/6/53) Coronation broadcast lasted for seven hours and viewers saw the whole service except for the Anointing, the Communion prayers, and the administration of the Sacrament. Taking into account large-screen presentations in cinemas, church halls, hospitals, and other public venues, it was estimated that no fewer than 20 million people watched the service in the UK alone. The Coronation programme was also relayed to the Continent, with clear pictures received in France, Belgium, Holland, and West Germany. Telefilms of the service were flown immediately to Canada (reaching Goose Bay, Labrador, at 6.45 p.m.) and were seen by viewers in Montreal that same evening. America's NBC and CBS networks chartered aeroplanes which flew directly to New York, with the films being processed during the journey; they were shown that same evening in New York and Boston.

Another 'first' in television development in 1953 was the first BBC television broadcast from a ship at sea during the Naval Review at Spithead. During the same year the BBC decided to replace transmission from Alexandra Palace with a new and more powerful transmitting station situated in the grounds of the old Crystal Palace. Meanwhile, the transfer of various activities from Alexandra Palace to the Lime Grove studios in Shepherd's Bush continued and a small part of the proposed television centre at the White City was also brought into use. Having achieved some measure of centralization, the BBC launched a five-year development plan which included the establishment of an alternative BBC TV channel and the introduction of colour. On the latter project, an agreement was announced on 15 June 1954 between Thorn Electrical and the American company Sylvania Electric Products Inc., to set up a UK-based company for the development of colour television.

Sports broadcasts managed to present many Rugby Union and Rugby League club matches during the early to mid-1950s but Football League matches and Rugby Union internationals were still absent from television. Some of the Lawn Tennis Championships at Wimbledon and county and Test Match cricket were shown, with the televising of the Test Matches proving particularly popular with viewers. It was not until May 1959 that the MCC announced that a contract had been signed between the MCC and the BBC allowing unlimited televising of Test matches by the BBC for the next three years. The BBC also acquired around that time the exclusive rights for the touring side's matches for 1959/1960/1961.

The Conservative Government's Bill proposing the introduction of a commercial television service aroused a storm of debate in Parliament in early 1954. The Bill provided for the establishment of a public corporation to operate the new service, the Independent Television Authority (ITA), which would consist of a chairman, a deputy chairman and from five to eight other members, of whom three would represent Scotland, Wales, and Northern Ireland. The programmes were to be 'predominantly British in tone and style and of high quality, and nothing was to be included which offended against good taste or decency or which was likely to encourage or incite to crime or to lead to disorder or to be offensive to public feeling'. Religious television programmes would be permitted on the advice of a religious advisory committee but religious and political bodies would not be permitted to advertise. Nothing was to be included in any programme or advertisement shown in the service which would imply that any part of any programme broadcast by the ITA had been supplied or suggested by any advertiser.

During the summer of 1954, two independent bodies were formed with opposing views on the question of commercial television. The National Television Council was opposed to commercial television in any form, and wished to encourage far-reaching development of public service television, including the early provision of an alternative BBC television channel. The Popular Television Association was founded to oppose the BBC monopoly in television and aimed 'to awaken the national conscience to the dangers, social, political, and artistic, of monopoly in the rapidly expanding field of television, to provide the public at the earliest possible moment with alternative programmes'.

The controversy and debate about the desirability of commercial television raged throughout the early 1950s. Clement Attlee, in a speech in June 1953, had actually stated that if the government introduced commercial television the Labour Party, if returned to power, would have to alter it. Nevertheless the Television Bill became law at the end of July 1954 and the ITA service, transmitting from its station at Norwood, was inaugurated on 22 September 1955 when, after a 5-minute documentary film, the opening speeches made at a Guildhall dinner by the Lord Mayor, the

Postmaster-General, and ITA chairman Sir Kenneth Clarke were broadcast. Independent Television had finally arrived in Britain.

During late October 1954 the ITA had decided to offer station contracts to three contractors: Broadcast Relay Services and Associated Newspapers, who had made a joint application, Granada Theatres Ltd. (under the helm of Sidney Bernstein and partner Alfred Hitchcock), and the Kemsley-Winnick group. A fourth contractor was later added, the Associated Broadcasting Development Company (later ATV). Broadcast Relay Services and Associated Newspapers then formed a subsidiary company to carry out their contract and this company became Associated Rediffusion.

The first stage in the development of commercial television was completed in November 1956 when the ITA's new transmitter at Emley Moor near Huddersfield was opened and brought an additional 5 million viewers within reach of ITV programmes. In July 1957 the ITA announced the application of a group formed by the Rank Organisation, Associated Newspapers, and the Amalgamated Press to provide all programmes for the southern region. It was estimated, around the end of March 1957, that the adult television public numbered about 19.5 million and that viewers spent on average nearly 40 per cent of each evening watching television. Those who had a choice of programmes spent one-third of the time devoted to television in watching BBC programmes and two-thirds in watching ITV programmes.

The première transmission companies, for their respective regions and tx periods, were as follows: Associated Rediffusion began transmitting on 22 September 1955 for the London area (on weekdays); ATV began on 24 September 1955 for London (weekends) and later for the midlands (weekdays) on 17 February 1956; the Associated British Picture Corporation (generally known as ABC TV) started on 18 February 1956 for the midlands (weekends), later for the north of England (weekends) on 5 May 1956; and Granada TV premièred on 3 May 1956 to supply the north-west of England (weekdays).

Joining these early ITV regional companies during the latter years of the decade were Scottish Television (which opened on 31 August 1957 with an estimated viewing public of 400,000) to service central Scotland; Television Wales and West (TWW, from 14 January 1958) for South Wales and the west of England; Southern Television for the south of England which began broadcasting from its new TV centre at Southampton on 30 August 1958 and which was generally regarded as the first truly local TV station in Britain; Tyne Tees Television, which began serving the north-east of England on 15 January 1959, and which was created by a group formed by the *News Chronicle*, impresarios George and Alfred Black, and film producer Sidney Box; Anglia Television which started transmission from Norwich on 27 October 1959 for the east of England, thus extending ITV coverage to 90 per cent of the country; and, the final ITV station to begin transmission during the 1950s, Ulster Television, supplying programmes for Northern Ireland from 31 October 1959.

The ITA also announced in 1955 that news programmes would be dealt with by a specialist organization to be known as the Independent Television News Company (ITN) which would supply news broadcasts for all the ITV companies.

From October 1955, at the request of the Television Advisory Committee, BBC TV carried out a series of experimental colour transmissions from the Alexandra Palace Studios which consisted mainly of still images, demonstration colour films, and simple studio shots. Following further experimental colour transmissions in 1956 and 1957 (which included live studio productions and films, transmitted outside normal programme times from the Crystal Palace station), the BBC issued a report on the many problems to be solved before colour television could be considered a viable part of the broadcasting service. The first requirement from the public point of view was the production of a reasonably priced and reliable colour television set. The Postmaster-General, Ernest Marples, pointed out in early 1957 that in the USA, where at that time about 100,000 people owned colour TV sets, the cost of a set was approximately £175. However, extensive research had been carried out with the co-operation of some British radio manufacturers which had adapted the

American NTSC (National Television Standards Committee) system to the 405-line standard used in Britain. The report considered the technical performance of the American system to be adequate to launch a colour television system in Britain in the frequency bands currently used.

From 1953 to 1954 the BBC was developing plans to introduce a second television service when the frequencies became available, even if it meant some reduction of hours for the first channel. In March 1959, almost four years after ITV was established, the government was still refusing to authorize a third television channel until it was decided which line definition system would be adopted permanently in Britain. The principal systems in use were the 405-line system in Britain, the 525-line system in America, the 625-line system available in most of Europe, and the 817-line system in France. While commenting on the proposed third television channel the Postmaster-General stated that a colour television service in Britain was still a long way off.

In April 1958, Sir Harold Bishop, BBC Director of Engineering, demonstrated an early video-recording machine (using magnetic tape) called the Vision Electronic Recording Apparatus and known as 'Vera'. A complete broadcast in vision and sound was reproduced on a TV monitor screen by 'Vera' in one minute whereas the usual method of filmed telerecording would have taken some three or four hours. The BBC announced that the new system would be particularly advantageous for the News and Outside Broadcasting departments.

In December 1959 licences were issued for 10 million combined television and sound receiving sets in Britain, a number exceeded only in the United States, and in a report at the end of the decade Dr W. A. Belson, former psychologist in the BBC research department, explained to the British Association the effect of television on family behaviour. TV viewing either produced a disruption of family affairs during the evening, or brought the family unit together. From the 550 adult viewers questioned for the survey very few thought that TV's influence on the family had been bad; about half said that the total effect had been good for family life. However, many families hurried through meals in time for viewing, and in many cases meals were eaten while watching television. Frequently, people carried on with something else while viewing. In some homes children pleaded to stay up after their bedtime to view and in some households the wife was left to finish various jobs while the family went off to view—the latter two situations, obviously, causing most friction.

The swing of television favourites in the 1950s went from comfortable, cosy programmes such as **Dixon of Dock Green** (drama), **The Good Old Days** (variety), and **What's My Line?** (quiz) to the post-1955 ITV period of **Armchair Theatre** (drama), **Sunday Night at the London Palladium** (variety), and **Double Your Money** (game). The latter part of the decade was particularly influenced by American TV forms and styles: basic trivia quiz shows became money prize-winning game shows, filmed drama series were produced in a style to suit American tastes, TV plays adopted the gritty working-class characters and milieu of such American TV classics as 'Marty' and 'Tragedy in a Temporary Town', and there was a rush of imported US cop shows and Western series to supplement the ITV schedules.

While the 1930s and 1940s standard of Sunday night 'theatre' presentations continued throughout the decade, sharing their popularity with the off-beat successes of the Nigel Kneale-scripted '1984' and the Quatermass serials, it was the half-hour, filmed period–action series that soon became hugely popular on both sides of the Atlantic. This genre of TV swashbucklers was launched by **The Adventures of Robin Hood** in 1955 and this was immediately followed by **The Adventures of Sir Lancelot**, **The Adventures of William Tell**, **The Buccaneers**, **The Count of Monte Cristo**, **Sword of Freedom**, and others.

But it was ITV's **Armchair Theatre**, which had started out in safe theatrical territory, that changed for ever the look and style (in both writing and production) of the British TV play, especially after Canadian producer Sydney Newman took over the programme in 1958. He wisely invested in the work of such writers as Alun Owen and Ray Rigby, Canadian author Mordecai Richler and American Rod Serling, to achieve not only the 'original' TV look to his productions but also to introduce characters and settings with which the ordinary viewing household could identify.

With a generally higher standard of living in Britain than ever before, for which the Conservative Government of the day claimed responsibility, the latter part of the 1950s produced that curious phenomena, the 'Admag'—an advertising magazine programme which was broadcast in the guise of an actual TV programme. Now the ordinary viewing household, with their fatter wage packets, could be entertained while parting with their new-found wealth. Not surprisingly, the Admags were soon among the most popular items on television, until they were banned by Parliament in 1963.

The Admirable Crichton
(BBC-tv, 11/6/50)

Sir James M. Barrie's 1902 play about the butler who becomes the master when his aristocratic employers are castaway on an uninhabited Pacific island was presented by Royston Morley in this 105-minute production. Raymond Huntley (*left*) starred as Crichton, with (*l. to r.*) David Markham (as the Hon. Ernest Woolley), Geoffrey Wearing (the Reverend John Treherne), Harcourt Williams (the Earl of Loam), Joan Hopkins (Lady Mary Lasenby), Alvin Maben (Lady Agatha Lasenby), and Jean Compton (Lady Catherine Lasenby). The play was later filmed (1957; after the 1913, 1918, 1919, and 1934 versions) by Lewis Gilbert.

Adventure Story
(BBC-tv, 30/7/50)

Presented Terence Rattigan's historical drama, first seen at the St James's Theatre in 1949, of Alexander the Great (played by Andrew Osborn; *left*). The 105-minute dramatic study of the Macedonian conqueror was set in Greece and various parts of Asia during the period 336 BC to 323 BC and featured Gladys Cooper, in her television début (as the Queen Mother of Persia; *right*), Patrick Troughton, Terence Longdon, John Slater, and Michael Hordern. Production was by Michael Barry. Rattigan's play was produced again by BBC TV on 12/6/61 by Rudolph Cartier, starring Sean Connery, Margaretta Scott, William Russell, and Lyndon Brook.

Andy Pandy
(BBC-tv, 1950–57; BBC-1, 1970)

The little string-puppet baby clown dressed in rompers and a hat was the creation of schoolteacher Maria Bird following a conversation with the then Head of TV's Children's Programmes, Freda Lingstrom, who was looking for a programme specially to entertain the pre-school toddlers. Bird devised the character, wrote the scripts, and composed the music. She then recruited singer Gladys Whitred to sing the songs (although Janet Ferber also performed on the early recordings). To help puppeteer Audrey Atterbury pull the strings, Molly Gibson was also brought in. (This same team later created Bill and Ben, **The Flowerpot Men**.) The first four filmed programmes were regarded as experimental and BBC TV welcomed comments from mothers before embarking on a full series, in which Andy was later joined by Teddy and rag doll Looby Loo. The 15-minute episodes were run and re-run for many years. Thirteen new colour episodes were produced in 1970, written and produced by Freda Lingstrom.

Children's Television
(BBC-tv, 1950–59)

Together with **Watch With Mother**, formerly **For the Children**, presented such daytime programmes for the toddler and junior set as: **Toad of Toad Hall** (2/1/50), adapted and produced by Michael Barry, with Kenneth More (as Mr Badger), James Hayter (Toad), Sam Kydd, Patrick Troughton, and Harry Secombe; 1930s cinema serials in two or three chapters per afternoon (*Custer's Last Stand* (1936), for example); Muffin the Mule (until 1955) and Prudence Kitten with Annette Mills (Prudence later with Molly Blake); **Under the Sea** (1950) with Commander Jacques Cousteau; **Children's Newsreel** (from 23/4/50), introduced by Huw Wheldon and edited by Cliff Michelmore; **Little Grey Rabbit** (from 8/9/50) from stories by Alison Uttley, arranged and told by Ann Hogarth and Jan Bussell with their glove puppets; the daytime version of Armand and Michaela Denis's **Filming in Africa**; Charlie Drake and Jack Edwardes in **The Adventures of Mick and Montmorency**; **The Appleyards**, reaching its eleventh series in 1957; **Sooty** (from 1953)

with Harry Corbett; the US Western series **The Cisco Kid** and **The Range Rider**; the BBC Puppet Theatre presenting legends of Gordon Murray's **Rubovia** (*pictured*); Lenny the Lion with Terry Hall; **Toytown** with Larry the Lamb; and Mikki the Martian with Ray Alan (from 1958). The fortnightly children's variety magazine series **Whirligig** began in November 1950 and featured presenter Humphrey Lestocq, assisted by a puppet called Mr Turnip (created by Joy Laurey); also **The Adventures of Hank**, an animated strip cartoon series (later a string puppet) created by Francis Coudrill, assisted by Alfred Wurmser, about a happy-go-lucky cowboy character; Steve Race, at the piano, and Rolf Harris (his début) also appeared on **Whirligig**. Michael Bentine's **The Bumblies** (filmed by Richard Dendy and Associates) also made its début in 1954 (from 14/2/54).

Cookery Lesson
(BBC-tv, 1950)

Philip Harben, bearded and striped apron clad, was BBC's great post-war TV chef. He first appeared in June 1946 with his 20-minute **Cookery** (BBC-tv, 1946–51) programme which must have been intended as more of a tantalizing TV display showcasing Harben's culinary prowess than an actual kitchen instructional, given that the country was still under ration-book rule at the time; the series was followed by various one-off versions during 1952–53. In **Cookery Lesson** Harben introduced a series of twelve lessons on the basic principles of cooking; the programme was produced by S. E. Reynolds. **Philip Harben** (BBC-tv, 1956), again with producer Reynolds, and **What's Cooking?** (BBC-tv, 1956) continued Harben's entertaining kitchen presence on BBC TV. For ITV, **Headway** (ABC TV, 1964), subtitled 'The Grammar of Cookery', featured Harben in thirteen programmes on the craft and theory of cooking. (Coincidentally, and confusingly, around the same time ATV's 1964–65 adult education psychology series bearing the same title was also being transmitted.) Harben's last television show was **The Tools of Cookery** for Thames TV (1968–69), presenting an afternoon series of 20-minute programmes about making the best use of a modern kitchen; Harben also co-produced with Pamela Lonsdale.

General Election Results
(BBC-tv, 23/2/50)

The first TV election results production went out at 10.45 p.m., Thursday evening, with commentators R. B. McCallum (Fellow of Pembroke College, Oxford, and author of *The British General Election of 1945*; *centre*), David Butler (research student of Nuffield College, Oxford; *left*) and radio journalist Chester Wilmot (*right*); Richard Dimbleby was for over two hours the 'television guide' to the proceedings. The political positions were painstakingly inked in by hand on the State of the Parties' board as the results came in (*background*). McCallum, Butler, and Wilmot also supplied an illustrated survey as an **Election Analysis** (BBC-tv, 24/2/50) at 8.15 p.m. the following evening.

Mr Pastry's Progress
(BBC-tv, 1950–51)

Mr Pastry, the slapstick character complete with walrus moustache and flapping coat-tails, was the popular creation of actor-acrobat-dancer Richard Hearne and was a great success for many years with juvenile viewers. Hearne's character was also a big hit with general audiences on ATV's **Sunday Night at the London Palladium** and American CBS TV's **The Ed Sullivan Show**; he had also appeared on pre-1950 BBC TV in guest performances transmitted live from the Alexandra Palace television studios. Later children's series included **Leave It to Mr Pastry** (BBC-tv, 1960), **Ask Mr Pastry** (BBC-tv, 1961), and **Mr Pastry's Pet Shop** (BBC-tv, 1962). For cinema, Hearne starred as his TV character in *Method and Madness* (1950; a 29-minute Gas Council short), *Mr Pastry Does the Laundry* (1951; a 27-minute short), *Madame Louise* (Nettlefold Films, 1951), *What a Husband* (1952; a 20-minute short), *The Time of His Life* (Shaftesbury Films, 1955), and *Tons of Trouble* (Shaftesbury Films, 1956). Richard Hearne as Mr Pastry (*right*) is pictured with guest Jack Warner.

1950

Rope
(BBC-tv, 8/1/50)

Patrick Hamilton's 1929 play, a psychological thriller about two Oxford undergraduates who murder a fellow student, was first presented on British TV in 1939 with Ernest Milton, Oliver Burt, and Basil C. Langton and then in 1947 with David Markham and Dirk Bogarde. This 1950 version, produced by Stephen Harrison (who had also produced the 1947 one), starred (*l. to r.*) Peter George (as Kenneth Raglan), Shelagh Fraser (as Leila Arden), Alan Wheatley (as Rupert Cadell), and David Markham (as Wyndham Brandon). Peter Wyngarde, not shown, also appeared as Charles Granillo. Harrison used the television close-up technique effectively, making sure that the reaction of the characters was as important as their action and speech. Harrison produced yet another version (tx 8/12/53), featuring Alan Wheatley as Cadell, David Peel as Brandon, and Kenneth Fortescue as Granillo.

The Scarlet Pimpernel
(BBC-tv, 5/2/50)

Margaretta Scott (*centre*; as Lady Marguerite Blakeney, née St Just) and James Carney (*left*; as Sir Percy Blakeney) starred in this 110-minute production of Baroness Orczy's famous 1905 adventure novel about the languid English fop who outwitted the villainous agents of the French Revolution. John Witty (*right*) co-starred in Fred O'Donovan's production; James Bould was the designer. The same company repeated the performance on 14/1/51.

Television Crosses the Channel
(BBC-tv, 27/8/50)

On 27 August the BBC televised (a 60-minute outside broadcast) the celebrations of the centenary of the laying of the submarine cable between England and France. For the first time in history a programme was transmitted across the Channel, as viewers saw the town of Calais *en fête*, with a torchlight procession, dancing in the square, and a firework display. Richard Dimbleby and Alan Adair gave commentaries on the festivities and interviewed local personalities in front of the cameras. The picture shows a television camera facing the Clock Tower of the Hotel de Ville, Calais.

Television Sports Magazine
(BBC-tv, 1950–51)

Presented a fortnightly programme catering not only for the great body of knowledgeable sports fans but the thousands of viewers who had been introduced to sports through television and whose knowledge was as yet limited. The aim of the programme was to focus on some topical aspect of a game, a point of technique or a point of procedure or rule, and call in the experts to find out what lay behind a particular problem. The Wednesday evening programme was introduced by Max Robertson. The picture shows Berkeley Smith (*left*) interviewing Ken Cameron, the winner of the 1951 Open Amateur Golf Tournament.

Watch With Mother
(BBC-tv, 1950–80)

Led on from **For the Children** and was shown under the **Children's Television** daytime programming banner. Produced by Freda Lingstrom, the stripped-across-the-week series featured **Picture Book** (BBC-tv, 1955–63) on Mondays, with Patricia Driscoll and later Vera McKechnie turning the pages; **Andy Pandy** on Tuesdays; **The Flowerpot Men** on Wednesdays; **Rag, Tag, and Bobtail** on Thursdays; and **The Woodentops** on Fridays. From 1980 the programming slot came under the heading of **See-Saw** when BBC TV felt that children of the 1980s did not necessarily share their TV viewing habits with their parents.

Albert
(BBC-tv, 12/8/51)

The setting of this play, based on a true story, was a prison camp for Allied naval officers in Germany during 1944. The title character was a life-size dummy (*seated in foreground*) constructed by the POWs to 'stand in' during roll-call for an escaping officer when the prisoners were taken out of the camp to a communal bath-house. The play told the story of Albert's creation and 'his' subsequent fooling of the German guards, leading up to the first escape. Adapted for television by Edward Sammis and Guy Morgan, the 100-minute play featured (*l. to r.*) Warren Stanhope, Gerald Metcalfe, Bill Travers, Michael Gough (*seated*), Harold Ayer, and Douglas Hurn; Ferdy Mayne also appeared. Stephen Harrison produced. The story was later filmed by director Lewis Gilbert for Dial Films in 1953 and released as **Albert, RN**.

The Black Arrow
(BBC-tv, 20 and 27/5/51)

Robert L. Stevenson's 1888 medieval melodrama concerning action and adventure during the Wars of the Roses was presented as a two-part (40-minute each) serial adapted for television by John Blatchley and producer Naomi Capon from the original production for the Young Vic Company by Michel St Denis. The Young Vic Company TV cast included (*l. to r.*) Dennis Clinton, John Garley, Powys Thomas, Keith Michell, and Derek Godfrey; Denis Quilley (as Richard Shelton) and Tarn Bassett (as Joanna Sedley) also appeared. Scenery and costumes were by Joseph Carl; original music by Henry Boyes. A few years later BBC TV presented a six-part adaptation of Stevenson's unfinished **St Ives** (30/10–4/12/55; adapt. and pr. Rex Tucker), later completed by Sir Arthur Quiller-Couch; with William Russell, Roger Delgado, Anthony Sharp, and Joan Sanderson appearing.

1951

The Charlie Chester Show
(BBC-tv, 1951; 1955)

The seaside trouper/radio performer of music-hall gags and song-and-dance spots was, following on from his air wave popularity of the war years, something of a BBC TV fixture throughout the 1950s. Unfortunately, 'Cheerful Charlie' and his limited repertoire of quick-fire patter faded into virtual obscurity during the mid-1960s. Nevertheless, his place in British TV history is ensured through his numerous appearances on variety shows and his **Educated Evans** (BBC-tv, 1957–58) and **The Charlie Chester Music Hall** (BBC-tv, 1961–62) series. **The Charlie Chester Show** was produced by Walton Anderson (Albert Stevenson for the series of monthly shows in 1955) and written by Chester (pictured, *right*) who appeared with regulars Ingeborg Wells, Deryck Guyler, Arthur Haynes (*left*), and Mischa Auer.

The Final Test
(BBC-tv, 29/7/51)

Was specially written by Terence Rattigan as part of **Television Festival Drama** (BBC-tv, 1951), a monthly series of plays celebrating the Festival of Britain. The play, with its cricket background, was noted as being Rattigan's first work for the medium. The performers were Patrick Barr (*right*), John Witty, Harold Siddons, Campbell Singer, Violet Gould (*left*), Gordon Whiting (*2nd left*), Stanley Rose (*centre*), and Jane Barrett (*2nd right*); Brian Johnston, John Arlott, Rex Alston, W. J. Edrich, Alec Bedser, Jack Robertson, Cecil Day Lewis, Jill Balcon, Pat Butler, Franklin Engelmann, and Frank Phillips appeared as themselves. The 125-minute production was by Royston Morley. Rattigan also wrote the screenplay for Anthony Asquith's feature film version, released in 1953.

The Inch Man
(BBC-tv, 1951–52)

Was the adventure-drama story of a house detective, Stephen Inch (played by Robert Ayres; *left*, with Lana Morris), working in a busy London hotel, the Imperial Crescent. Written by Lester Powell, the half-hour programme moved between the behind-the-scenes activities of hotel life and the sleuthings of our hero. Producers over the two series of stories were Ronald Waldman and T. Leslie Jackson, and Douglas Moodie.

Sherlock Holmes
(BBC-tv, 20/10–1/12/51)

Influential *Observer* film critic C. A. Lejeune adapted six **Sherlock Holmes** (BBC-tv, 20/10–1/12/51) stories for producer Ian Atkins for the first British television Holmes series; the six 35-minute plays were presented live and billed under their individual titles: 'The Empty House' (20/10/51), 'A Scandal in Bohemia' (27/10/51), 'The Dying Detective' (3/11/51), 'The Reigate Squires' (17/11/51), 'The Red-Headed League' (24/11/51), and 'The Second Stain' (1/12/51). The series was aimed to tie in with the Festival of Britain celebrations held that year and the corresponding Sherlock Holmes Exhibition in Baker Street during the summer. The scene shown, from 'The Red-Headed League', features (*l. to r.*) Bill Owen (as Inspector Lestrade), Arthur Goulett, Alan Wheatley (Holmes), and Raymond Francis (Dr Watson). An American-produced, European-filmed syndicated series, **The Adventures of Sherlock Holmes** (Guild Films-MPTV, 1954–55), starring Ronald Howard in the lead role with support from H. Marion Crawford as Dr Watson, was also seen via the various ITV companies during the mid-1950s.

What's My Line?
(BBC-tv, 1951–62; BBC-2, 1973–74; Thames TV, 1984–90)

Was one of the first British TV panel games (derived from the popular CBS TV programme) and featured four personalities trying to discover the profession or occupation of a guest contestant. The original programmes were chaired by Eamonn Andrews, starting his TV career (David Jacobs took over the chair in the 1970s), and featured Gilbert Harding (*right*), Barbara Kelly (*2nd right*), Lady Isobel Barnett (*2nd left*), and David Nixon (*left*) on the panel. Thames TV revived the programme for a series of runs in 1984, with Andrews (later Angela Rippon) back in the chair for producer Maurice Leonard. Another early 1950s half-hour quiz show with a similar theme, **Guess My Story** (BBC-tv, 1953–54), chaired by Peter West, had a panel trying to guess the identity of people in the news; an early panel consisted of Pat Kirkland, Helen Cherry, and Michael Pertwee.

Treasure on Pelican
(BBC-tv, 2/9/51)

Presented a satirical comedy specially written for television by J. B. Priestley and transmitted under the **Television Festival Drama** series of programmes. The 125-minute play, about a private expedition in search of buried treasure on Pelican Island in the Caribbean, featured (*l. to r.*) Clive Morton, Julien Mitchell, Eileen Beldon, Roger Snowdon, Barbara Kelly, Barbara Couper, and Basil Sydney. Harold Clayton produced.

Animal, Vegetable, Mineral?
(BBC-tv, 1952–59)

Popular, fortnightly quiz programme in which a panel of experts were challenged to identify an unusual object selected from a museum and to explain briefly how they came to do so. Natural History museums, Science museums, and Art museums were drawn upon for the items and, as a form of cultural showcase, pointed up the wealth of 'our national inheritance'. Picture shows (*l. to r.*) chairman Glyn Daniel, Sir Mortimer Wheeler, Dr W. E. Swinton, and Professor Thomas Bodkin.

The Appleyards
(BBC-tv, 1952–57)

Lightweight, domestic series about the trivial ups and downs of the rosy Appleyard family, consisting of Mr and Mrs Appleyard (played by Constance Fraser, *3rd left*, and Frederick Piper, *right*; later by Douglas Muir) and their four children, teenagers John (David Edwards, *2nd left*; with Robert Dickens, *left*) and Janet (Tessa Clarke, *3rd right*), younger brother Tommy (Derek Rowe, *2nd right*), and Margaret (Pat Fryer, *centre*). Transmitted as a part of the **Children's Television** slot, the series was something of a junior version of the adult-market **The Grove Family** serial which was running during the same period. Philip Burton scripted the 20-minute stories. A special reunion edition, 'Christmas With the Appleyards' (wr.-pr. Kevin Sheldon), was screened on 24/12/60.

1952

Billy Bunter of Greyfriars School
(BBC-tv, 1952–61)

The plump career of Billy Bunter started out in a pre-1914 magazine called the *Magnet*, created and written by Frank Richards (Charles Hamilton). Bunter's adventures revolved around food and the fluent acquisition of it, which, in most instances, led him into sticky situations either with his peers or the formidable form master Mr Quelch (played originally by Kynaston Reeves). The half-hour children's series of prankish schoolboy stories was produced by Joy Harington and featured Gerald Campion as Bunter (*seated, centre*).

The Flowerpot Men
(BBC-tv, 1952–54)

The second **Watch with Mother** programme created after **Andy Pandy** was the work of the same team: scripts, music, and manipulation was by Maira Bird, Audrey Atterbury, and Molly Gibson. The general format was that Bill and Ben, the Flowerpot Men, lived in flowerpots near a shed at the bottom of a garden: their playthings were man-sized. The characters were designed as identical twins, their bodies shaped like flowerpots, their legs made of small pots stacked one on top of the other. They had big garden gloves and well-worn garden boots. They were comics who did not play *with* children as did Andy Pandy, but who were busy about their own affairs. Their companion was a weed who grew between the flowerpots, telling them when it was safe to come out and play or when the gardener was returning. The voices of Bill and Ben, who talked rubbish (under the impression that there was a Flowerpot language), were provided by Peter Hawkins, and Gladys Whitred and Julia Williams sang or squeaked as desired. The series was re-run for many years. **Rag, Tag, and Bobtail** (BBC-tv, 1953–55) was another of the classic **Watch with Mother** programmes, this time featuring the adventures of a trio of wildlife characters: Rag the hedgehog, Tag the fieldmouse, and Bobtail the rabbit. The glove-puppet creatures were made and operated by Sam and Elizabeth Williams. The stories were told by Charles E. Stidwill from scripts by Louise Cochrane, and re-run for many years.

The Howerd Crowd
(BBC-tv, 1952)

Presented comedian Frankie Howerd in his first television series, an hour-long lightweight entertainment of comedy and music. Eric Sykes wrote the scripts and Bill Lyon-Shaw produced. Pictured are (*l. to r.*) Jean Kent, Howerd, and Marjorie Holmes. Later the same year Howerd starred in a special, **Frankie Howerd's Korean Party** (BBC-tv, 9/12/52), televised from the Nuffield Centre, in which he performed with Eve Boswell, Eddie Arnold, Clifford Kirkham, and Vera Jessop before an audience of Service men and women; the programme was presented by Kenneth Carter. **Frankie Howerd in Ulster** (BBC-1, 14/3/73), recorded during his tour of military camps in Ulster, presented a similar entertainment; Terry Hughes produced.

38

Markheim
(BBC-tv, 28/12/52)

A visually eerie television adaptation, by Winston Clewes, of R. L. Stevenson's short story. A sinister curio shop stuffed with statues and clocks was the setting of this 30-minute, minimum-dialogue play, featuring Douglas Wilmer (*left*; as the troubled Markheim) and Eric Chitty (*right*; as the Dealer). The play was produced by Christian Simpson and Tony Richardson; the atmospheric settings were designed by Stephen Taylor. Among later TV adaptations of the story were the Scottish TV production (tx. 24/12/74; dir. Tina Wakerell) featuring Derek Jacobi as Markheim, and the BBC Bristol presentation (3/1/90; dir. Derek Dodd) under the title of **10 × 10** with James Vaughan as the title character.

Asian Club
(BBC-tv, 1953–61)

Was first introduced on television to commemorate the twenty-first year of BBC's General Overseas Service, via which the radio version of *Asian Club* had been broadcast for ten years. The exciting feature of the TV programmes, at that time, was the lively, free-for-all question time when the invited studio audience (exotically clad in the national costumes of India, Pakistan, Ceylon, China, Japan, Indonesia, and Burma) talked freely about their problems with a studio guest speaker. These speakers included Bertrand Russell, Lady Violet Bonham Carter, Sir Christopher Hinton, and actor Kenneth More. The picture shows hostess Miss Rosemary Sands holding out the microphone while an audience member speaks. **Eastern Eye** (C4/LWT, 1982–85), over a quarter of a century later, presented a lively and topical news magazine reporting on the Asian community in Britain in the 1980s. Reporters were Dippy Chaudhary, Ziauddin Sardar, and Karan Thapar; Samir Shah produced.

Before Your Very Eyes
(BBC-tv, 1953–55)

Was a fortnightly comedy series starring Arthur Askey (*right*), aided and abetted by Dickie Henderson and Diana Decker (*left*). The 30-minute series was produced by Bill Ward; Sid Colin, Talbot Rothwell, and David Climie supplied the scripts. In 1955 Askey moved over to ITV and starred in a five-part sitcom called **Love and Kisses** (A-R, 4/11–2/12/55), written by Glenn Melvyn and directed by Richard Bird (the series was actually Askey's Blackpool summer show, filmed and edited into five instalments for TV). Askey also transferred his **Before Your Very Eyes** show to ITV in 1956, under the A-R banner for producer-director Kenneth Carter, where it went out live until 1958. **The Arthur Askey Show** (ATV, 11/3–22/4/61) was a six-part sitcom featuring Askey, June Whitfield, Arthur Mullard, and Patricia Hayes; Dave Freeman scripted for producer Josephine Douglas. The following year he co-starred in **Raise Your Glasses** (BBC-tv, 1962) with Alan Melville (who also scripted) in what was billed as 'a series of unusual spectacles'; Bryan Sears produced.

1953

Coronation of Queen Elizabeth II
(BBC-tv, 2/6/53)

BBC Television embarked on the most complicated and prolonged outside broadcast in television history when they televised, live, the events of this day. The broadcast proper began at 10.15 a.m. with the first pictures from mobile units (using up to sixteen cameras) at the Victoria Memorial (with commentators Chester Wilmot and Berkeley Smith), on the Embankment (with Max Robertson), and outside the Abbey (with Mary Hill and Michael Henderson). The Coronation Service, starting at 11.20 a.m., was described for TV by Richard Dimbleby from a position high up in the Triforium; five television cameras were used in the Abbey. The State Procession was then televised, first at a point in Hyde Park just north of Grosvenor Gate, with commentary by Bernard Braden and Brian Johnston, and then again at the Victoria Memorial. Throughout the morning and afternoon two sets of equipment were used to make telerecordings of the Coronation broadcast, the first to make possible the broadcast at eight o'clock that night of an edited version of the Westminster Abbey ceremony, and for transmission that same night in Canada, the USA, and several European countries of a 2-hour edited telerecording; Canberra jet bombers were used to fly the films across the Atlantic. The second set of equipment recorded the whole outside broadcast for archive purposes. The Queen's broadcast to her peoples was carried in sound only and the Coronation Day transmissions ended with the firework display staged on the South Bank of the Thames between County Hall and the Royal Festival Hall. The marathon outside broadcast was transmitted from 10.15 a.m. to 5.20 p.m. It was estimated that over 20 million people in Britain watched the Coronation on television, in churches, shops, halls, and homes.

The Good Old Days
(BBC-tv, 1953–83)

A televisual nostalgia variety series that included the Edwardian era costumed audience (transmitted from the Leeds City Varieties Theatre) as an additional element of the entertainment. The old-time music-hall format, presided over by the pompously polysyllabic Chairman Leonard Sachs (originally Don Gemmell), scored as much success with the memory-lane viewers as the sing-something-simple stablemate programme **The Black and White Minstrel Show**. Barney Colehan was the driving force behind the production. **The Good Old Days** format was springboarded from an earlier (that year) programme called **City Varieties** (BBC-tv, 1953), also produced by Colehan, with Kenneth Carter, and was ringmastered by Derek Guyler as a sartorially and tonsorially old-style narrator of proceedings.

Our Marie
(BBC-tv, 8/2/53)

The story of the undisputed Queen of the British music-hall, Miss Marie Lloyd, was presented in **Our Marie** (BBC-tv, 8/2/53), scripted by Alfred Shaughnessy and Christopher Barry and directed by Peter Graham Scott. The 105-minute musical biography featured Pat Kirkwood in the title role in which, as the story took her from the age of 16 to 52, she had to effect no fewer than fifty changes of costume, sing fifteen different songs, and appear in almost all the hundred-odd scenes in the show, which spanned the period 1886 through to Marie Lloyd's death in 1922. Michael Mills produced under the 'famous Victorians' series banner of *The Passing Show*. A second performance was presented on 12/2/53.

Panorama
(BBC-tv, 1953–)

Remains the oldest-established current affairs programme on television. It started as an ordinary fortnightly magazine programme, with guide and interviewer Max Robertson and critics Nancy Spain (on books), Denis Mathews (on art), and Lionel Hale (on theatre), before it was overhauled and relaunched as the incisive investigative flagship presented at first in weekly editions, then nightly. Richard Dimbleby (*pictured*) headed the 1950s team, which included athlete Christopher Chataway and John Freeman; during the 1960s Michael Barratt, Robin Day, Michael Charlton, Trevor Philpott, and Leonard Parkin were among the reporters and interviewers. Dimbleby continued as anchorman. During the early 1960s period it was regarded as the most powerful, respected TV programme of its type on British television.

The Quatermass Experiment
(BBC-tv, 18/7–22/8/53)

Was the first of TV playwright Nigel Kneale's classic Quatermass serials of the 1950s (a fourth was produced for ITV in 1979). This 6 eps. × 30 mins. cliff-hanger told of the mysterious lone survivor of a three-man experimental rocket crew who slowly mutates into an enormous vegetable-like creature, due to infection by an alien organism, and is pursued eventually to Westminster Abbey where it takes its final refuge. Broadcast live, with some filmed inserts, the serial's clever blending of science fiction and horror elements virtually terrified viewers of the time. Reginald Tate (*left*) played Professor Bernard Quatermass, supported by (*l. to r.*) Moray Watson, Isabel Dean, W. Thorp Devereux, Paul Whitsun-Jones, and Duncan Lamont (*seated*) as Victor Carroon, the surviving crew member. Rudolph Cartier produced. Hammer Films remade the story as a feature film in 1955.

Robin Hood

(BBC-tv, 17/3–21/4/53)

Presented under the *Children's Television* programming banner, **Robin Hood** (BBC-tv, 17/3–21/4/53) was a 30-minute serial in six parts written by Max Kester and based on the traditional medieval story. Patrick Troughton (*pictured*) starred as Robin, with Kenneth Mackintosh as Little John, Wensley Pithey as Friar Tuck, and David Kossoff as the Sheriff of Nottingham. The serial was produced by Joy Harington. Twenty-two years later BBC TV produced **The Legend of Robin Hood** (BBC-1, 23/11–28/12/75), again in a six-part serial form (× 55 mins.). Martin Potter appeared as Robin in this colourful version, with Diane Keen as Maid Marian. Alistair Bell scripted for producer George Gallaccio.

Worzel Gummidge Turns Detective

(BBC-tv, 10/2–3/3/53)

Was a four-part, half-hour comedy series written for TV by Worzel-creator Barbara Euphan Todd and programmed as a part of the **Children's Television** slot. Pamela Brown was the producer of the series which starred Frank Atkinson as the animated scarecrow Worzel (pictured with Mabel Constanduros). Some twenty-five years later the character would return in the popular Southern TV series, **Worzel Gummidge**, with Jon Pertwee in the title part.

Wuthering Heights

(BBC-tv, 6/12/53)

Screen actor Richard Todd appeared as Heathcliff in this Nigel Kneale-adapted version for producer Rudolph Cartier. The picture features (*l. to r.*) Todd, John Kidd (as Doctor Kenneth), Rene Ray (Isabella), Peter Bryant (Edgar Linton), and (*centre*) Yvonne Mitchell (as Cathy). Richard Addinsell supplied the ballad music; settings were by Barry Learoyd. The first BBC TV version of Emily Brontë's *Wuthering Heights* was broadcast on 7/3/48 (dramatized by John Davison with additional dialogue by Alfred Sangster, adapted and produced by George More O'Ferrall) with Kieron Moore as Heathcliff and Katharine Blake as Cathy. Kneale and Cartier produced a new version for BBC tx 11/5/62, starring Keith Michell and Claire Bloom. Five years later Peter Sasdy directed a four-part BBC-2 version (28/10–18/11/67; pr. David Conroy) with Ian McShane and Angela Scoular in the lead roles. Yet another BBC-2 version was produced in 1978 by Jonathan Powell as a five-part story (24/9–22/10/78; dramatized by Hugh Leonard and David Snodin), featuring Ken Hutchison and Kay Adshead as the doomed lovers.

BBC Television News
(BBC-tv, 1954–)

Was first broadcast at 7.30 p.m. on 5/7/54 and presented by Richard Baker as 'an illustrated summary of the news'. In the pioneer days BBC television news was simply a re-run of the radio bulletins and, even when TV news arrived in its own right, it was a cautious compilation of stills, interviews, maps, and newsreels. Visible newsreaders were originally forbidden (in case their change of expression threatened impartiality) but in September 1955 the BBC put newsreaders into vision. Kenneth Kendall, Robert Dougall, and Richard Baker were the early on-screen newsreaders. These were the days before Autocues and Teleprompters, with the newsreaders reading directly from a script. Video overtook filmed reports eventually and news-gathering technology leaped into the new world of speed and access; pictures by satellite—first used on a large scale for covering the funeral of Kennedy in 1963—became a part of the TV news routine. The **Nine O'Clock News** programme developed from this form in 1963.

The Bespoke Overcoat
(BBC-tv, 17/2/54)

Based on Gogol's *The Cloak*, Wolf Mankowitz's one-act, half-hour play was produced by Eric Fawcett in the form of a modern Jewish folk-tale featuring Alfie Bass (*left*) as Fender, a poor warehouse clerk in need of a new overcoat, and David Kossoff (*right*) as Morry, the tailor. Arnold Diamond (as Ranting, the employer) and Oscar Quitak (as a clerk) supported. Mankowitz's play was filmed in 1955 by Jack Clayton and went on to win the best short film prize at the Venice Festival.

Fabian of Scotland Yard
(BBC-tv/Anthony Beauchamp Prods.–Trinity Prods., 1954–56)

Bruce Seton's Inspector Fabian (*pictured, right*) was, for many of the first British TV generation, *the* small-screen detective. Through thirty-nine half-hour episodes Fabian stalked the wrongdoers and unravelled mysteries with quiet competence, pursuing his Scotland Yard cases with painstaking work and a singular dedication to seeing justice done. The series was based on the career of celebrated former Scotland Yard detective Robert Fabian, who usually appeared briefly before the final fade-out to wind up the story. John Larkin and Anthony Beauchamp produced. Among the teleplay contributors was Arthur La Bern, later to be author of the novel *Goodbye Piccadilly, Farewell Leicester Square* from which came the 1972 Alfred Hitchcock thriller *Frenzy*. The series was also known as **Inspector Fabian of Scotland Yard** and **Fabian of the Yard** in some TV markets. Two feature films consisting of re-edited episodes were released to cinemas: *Fabian of the Yard* (1954) and *Handcuffs, London* (1955).

The Grove Family
(BBC-tv, 1954–57)

Was the first real British TV soap serial, featuring a lower middle-class, post-war family in stories, more naïve than dramatic, dealing with simple social issues and consumerist concerns. The family group consisted of (*l. to r.*) Daphne (Margaret Downs), Mrs Grove (Ruth Dunning), Gran (Nancy Roberts), Lennie (Christopher Beeny); (*standing*) Jack (Peter Bryant), Pat (Carole Mowlam; earlier Sheila Sweet), and Mr Grove (Edward Evans). Michael & Roland Pertwee wrote the 15/20-minute scripts for producer John Warrington. A 71-minute feature film version, *It's a Great Day*, was produced (by Warrington) in 1955 and starred the TV line-up.

Nineteen Eighty-Four
(BBC-tv, 12/12/54)

George Orwell's doom-laden foretelling of a totalitarian state was produced by Rudolph Cartier as a stunning and, for its time, horrifying view of a future Britain. The story takes place in London, the chief city of Airstrip One, now a Province of the State of Oceania, featuring the strange population pyramid of the Proles, the Outer Party, and the Inner Party, all headed by the infallible figure of Big Brother. Despite a generally outraged and alarmed reaction to the initial presentation (transmitted live), the 120-minute play was restaged four days later (16/12/54)—again live! Responding against complaints about the production one original viewer remarked, 'Surely the right to switch off one's television set is not reserved for "inner party members" only!'; (*l. to r.*) Yvonne Mitchell (as Julia), Peter Cushing (Winston Smith), and André Morell (O'Brien) were the principal players. The television play was adapted by Nigel Kneale.

The Promised Years
(BBC-tv, 23/5–15/8/54)

Iain MacCormick's cycle of four full-length plays, **The Promised Years** (BBC-tv, 23/5–15/8/54), was the first of its kind in this format for British television. The core of the plays was the proposed Allied destruction of a small Italian town in early 1945 in order to impede the withdrawal of the German army in that sector. The decision as to whether the town should be evacuated prior to the bombing was left in the hands of a young British officer. The first play, 'The Liberators' (85 mins.), was set in Italy in 1945, with (*pictured l. to r.*) Paul Carpenter, Owen Holder as the British officer, Douglas Blackwell, and Patrick Allen; the second play, 'The Good Partners' (85 mins.), took place during the Berlin Air-Lift; the third, 'The Small Victory' (100 mins.), was set in 1951 Korea; and the final play, 'Return to the River' (75 mins.), brought the wartime officer back to the Italian town in 1954. Julian Amyes and Alvin Rakoff produced.

Sportsview
(BBC-tv, 1954–68)

One of the earlier TV sports magazine programmes, introduced for many years by Peter Dimmock (followed by Brian Johnston) and, originally, produced by Dennis Monger, later by Cecil Petty. The programme's more memorable items included Roger Bannister's 4-minute mile, the Pirie–Zatopek duel at the White City, coverage of the Olympic Games in Melbourne, and an exhibition bout in the **Sportsview** studio by the then reigning world heavyweight champion, Floyd Patterson. **Junior Sportsview** (BBC-tv, 1957–62) was presented by Danny Blanchflower and Billy Wright; Cliff Michelmore introduced. Picture shows Dimmock (*right*) with October 1955 guest Sir Stanley Rous, Secretary of the Football Association. Michelmore, with David Coleman and Kenneth Wolstenholme, also reported highlights of the weekend's sport in **Sports Special** (BBC-tv, 1956–61; 1964).

The Three Musketeers
(BBC-tv, 24/11–29/12/54)

Was brought to television as a six-part cloak-and-dagger adventure by producer Rex Tucker and adapted for TV by Felix Felton and Susan Ashman. (In America, an unsold series pilot on the same theme had been produced by Hal Roach Jr. but was subsequently released to cinemas as **The Sword of D'Artagnan** in 1952.) The BBC's seventeenth-century derring-do was performed by (*l. to r.*) Paul Whitsun-Jones (as Porthos), Paul Hansard (Aramis), Roger Delgado (Athos), and Laurence Payne (D'Artagnan), for both the early evening children's audience and (via a repeat) the mid-evening adult viewers. Some twelve years after, Alexandre Dumas's adventure was again presented on the small screen with **The Three Musketeers** (BBC-tv, 1966–67; 10 eps. × 25 mins.) portrayed by Brian Blessed (Porthos), Jeremy Young (Athos), Gary Watson (Aramis), and a young Jeremy Brett as D'Artagnan. The series was written by Anthony Steven and produced by William Sterling. Producer Sterling returned with the **Further Adventures of the Musketeers** (BBC-tv, 1967; 16 eps. × 25 mins.), this time the swashbuckling line-up featuring Joss Ackland as D'Artagnan and John Woodvine as Aramis; Alexander Baron scripted. The following year Campbell Logan produced the nine-part **The Man in the Iron Mask** (BBC-tv, 1968; wr. Anthony Steven, dir. Hugh David): with Edwin Richfield (as D'Artagnan), Jack Gwillim (Athos), Noel Willman (Aramis), and Roger Livesey (Porthos).

War in the Air
(BBC-tv, 1954–55)

Presented a documentary series of fifteen half-hour films made in conjunction with the Air Ministry telling the story of air power and its impact on the world during the previous twenty years. The series was written and produced by John Elliot (*right*) and directed by Philip Dorte (*2nd right*); with narration by Robert Harris. Air Chief Marshal Sir Philip Joubert was the series adviser. The title music was specially composed by Sir Arthur Bliss (*2nd left*), played by the London Symphony Orchestra, and conducted by Muir Mathieson (*left*).

Zoo Quest
(BBC-tv, 1954–61)

Was a 30-minute report of zoological expeditions jointly sponsored by the London Zoo and the Television Service to film and collect rare birds and animals from various regions of the world; from quests for the Komodo Dragon in south-east Asia to armadillos in Paraguay. The première edition, for instance, saw producer David Attenborough, BBC cameraman Charles Lagus, Jack Lester, and Alfred Woods of the London Zoo on an expedition to the West African forest in search of a rare bird (the Picathartes).

1955

The Adventures of Robin Hood

(ABC TV/Sapphire Films Prod.–ITP, 1955–59)

This popular action series was a rousing success on both sides of the Atlantic and helped unleash a score of filmed costume adventures series on to British (and American) TV screens. Richard Greene (*centre*) played the title role; the more memorable players supporting him during the series' early years were Bernadette O'Farrell (as Maid Marian; later played by Patricia Driscoll), Alexander Gauge (Friar Tuck), Archie Duncan (Little John), and Alan Wheatley (Sheriff of Nottingham). Donald Pleasance and Hollywood actor Ian Hunter also appeared in the series, as Prince John and King Richard, respectively. From the series' production base at Nettlefold Studios, Walton-on-Thames, series executive producer Hannah Weinstein favoured using blacklisted US writers (such as Ring Lardner Jr. and Ian McLellan Hunter) behind various 'front' names. Directors Terence Fisher, Lindsay Anderson, and Robert Day also contributed to the series. The Saxon outlaw's fight against Norman injustice was told in 143 half-hour stories.

The Adventures of the Scarlet Pimpernel

(Towers of London Prod./ITP, 1955–56)

Marius Goring starred as Sir Percy Blakeney in Baroness Orczy's tales of the late eighteenth-century aristocrat who presented himself as a weakling and a dandy to fashionable London society but was the daring Scarlet Pimpernel to the persecuted aristocracy in Robespierre's revolutionary France. Marius Goring co-produced (with Dennis Vance and David Macdonald) as well as appeared in this 39 eps. × half-hour adventure series. The Pimpernel's regular associates were Sir Andrew Ffoulkes (played by Patrick Troughton) and Lord Richard Hastings (Anthony Newlands); Stanley Van Beers was the sinister Chauvelin. Goring had previously been heard on BBC radio between July and August 1949 playing the Blakeney role in the six-part serial *The Scarlet Pimpernel*; he also recorded fifty-two radio adventures for NBC radio (1954).

The Benny Hill Show

(BBC-tv, 1955–57; 1961; BBC-1, 1964–66; ATV, 1967; BBC-1, 1968; Thames TV, 1969–89)

British television's infamous saucy comedian with a flair for smutty jokes, slapstick routines, and some inventive impersonations and characterizations. His early TV work included some hilarious on-target spoofs of contemporary TV shows and personalities, mercilessly caricaturing such popular figures of the time as Hughie Green (of **Opportunity Knocks** fame) and globe-trotting journalist Alan Whicker. The later **Benny Hill** (BBC-tv, 1962–63) series presented a collection of self-contained comedy plays with such wacky themes and settings as the 'Shooting of Willie the Kid', the 'Time Bicycle', and the 'Secret of Planet Seven'. Duncan Wood produced. **Eddie in August** (Thames TV, 3/6/70), written by and starring Hill, featured him in a half-hour silent TV film about a love-smitten loser in search of the girl in his dreams. The one-off was produced-directed by John Robins & Benny Hill, with the latter also credited for the music.

The Brains Trust

(BBC-tv, 1955–61)

Second only to *ITMA* in wartime radio national popularity, this programme of lively conversation pieces came to television in 1955 with some of the most eminent people of the time, to answer, spontaneously and without advance knowledge of the questions, some of the things viewers wanted to know (discussing such broad themes as 'What is civilization?'). The original question-master was Hugh Ross Williamson. Peter Brook produced and John Furness directed the series. Pictured (*l.* to *r.*) are question-master Michael Flanders, the Most Reverend Joost de Blank, Archbishop of Cape Town, Elspeth Huxley, novelist and critic, Oliver Woods, Colonial Editor of *The Times*, and Dr J. Bronowski in a 1958 edition.

The Children of the New Forest

(BBC-tv, 5/4–10/5/55)

Captain Frederick Marryat's 1847 children's classic **The Children of the New Forest** (BBC-tv, 5/4–10/5/55), a tale set during the English Civil War, was first produced for BBC TV as a 6 eps. × 30 mins. series by Douglas Hurn, featuring Warren Mitchell (as Cromwell), Colin Douglas, Robert Hewitt, Jon Rollason, John Charlesworth, Shirley Cooklin, Anthony Valentine, Gillian Gale, and Barbara Hicks. Tom Twigge adapted the story. Nine years later Anthony Coburn dramatized the novel as a six-part serial (BBC-1, 23/8–27/9/64) starring Bernard Archard as the Roundhead Heatherstone; the production, with exteriors filmed in the original location, was directed by Brandon Acton-Bond. In 1977 another serial version of Marryat's story was produced by Barry Letts (BBC-1, 13/11–11/12/77) and adapted by William Pointer. Five 30-minute episodes were presented, with John Carson (as Heatherstone) and Artro Morris (as Cromwell); John Frankau directed.

Colonel March of Scotland Yard

(Panda Prods., 1953–54; first shown via the ITV companies in 1955)

Was based on the Carter Dickson (John Dickson Carr) collection of short stories, *The Department of Queer Complaints*, published in 1940. The series starred Boris Karloff (*centre*) in 26 eps. × 25 mins. as the urbane, eye-patched sleuth whose mystery-solving ranged from the unnatural to the supernatural. Ewan Roberts and Richard Wattis (*left*) supported. Producer Hannah Weinstein's company also released the three-episode compilation *Colonel March Investigates* as a feature film in 1953. Also pictured, guest player Sonya Hana.

1955

Crackerjack
(BBC-tv, 1955–84)

Long-term children's programme with resident compère and master of ceremonies Eamonn Andrews (later Michael Aspel), presented from the BBC Children's Television Theatre. Original producer was Johnny Downes and early resident performers included Leslie Crowther (also as host) and Peter Glaze with their outrageous puns, Pip Hinton, and Jillian Comber; Richard Hearne's Mr Pastry was a regular guest. The scene pictured is from the popular 'Double or Drop' quiz game (devised by Andrews; *holding microphone*) in which the junior contestants either won a **Crackerjack** pencil or lost to receive the booby prize of a cabbage. In later years Ed Stewart and Stu Francis hosted the programme.

Dixon of Dock Green
(BBC-tv, 1955–76)

The brainchild of Ted Willis (from his original screenplay and play of the film, in partnership with Jan Read), **Dixon** still ranks as the longest running police series on British television, having notched up some 367 episodes (30 mins., then 40/45 mins.). The setting was the fictitious Dock Green neighbourhood of London's East End and the central character, the paternal and avuncular PC George Dixon, was played effortlessly by Jack Warner; Dixon was promoted to Sergeant in 1964. The series' early mixture of everyday suburban station life, petty larceny, and homely moralizing rarely strayed from its reassuring, never-never world of hearts-of-gold coppers and 'cor, blimey!' crooks. PC Dixon (Warner) was originally seen in the 1949 Ealing film *The Blue Lamp*, at the end of which the Dixon character was killed off, but Willis decided to bring the character back in a six-episode TV series (initially) and the Dixon myth grew from there. In 1962 the programme presented a two-part story ('A Special Kind of Jones', 10/2/62, and 'The Cruel Streak', 17/2/62; wr. Willis, pr. Douglas Moodie) featuring a flashback to 1938 when Dixon (played by Desmond Davies) and the later-to-be Sergeant Flint (Cavan Malone in flashback; Arthur Rigby in regular series) were raw recruits. The series was originally produced by Douglas Moodie and televised from Lime Grove studios. Peter Byrne (originally as PC Andy Crawford) and Arthur Rigby (as Flint) repeated their roles from the play; Dixon's daughter, Mary, was played by a young Billie Whitelaw during the early series. Pictured are (*l. to r.*) Warner, Rigby, Moira Mannion (as Sergeant Grace Millard), Byrne, and Jeannette Hutchinson (as Mary, in the later series).

Double Your Money

(A-R, 1955–68)

Was, along with A-R stablemate **Take Your Pick**, one of the fledgling ITV's first quiz shows. The pre-filmed programme was hosted by Hughie Green over its thirteen-year network run. The idea was that contestants chose their own subject from fifty available areas and every time they answered correctly their money was doubled, leading up to the Treasure Trail prize of £1,000 (the contestants by then ushered into a soundproof booth for the climactic questions). The general format was based on American CBS TV's **The $64,000 Question**, which had also been premièred in 1955; a British version, **The 64,000 Question** (ATV, 1956–58), hosted by Jerry Desmonde, racked up the prize money in units of sixpence instead of the US top-dollar prize. **Double Your Money** was an Arlington Television and Radio Ltd. programme devised by John Beard. Hughie Green (*right*) and hostess Nancy Roberts are pictured with a lucky contestant.

Douglas Fairbanks Presents

(Douglas Fairbanks Prods.; ITV tx 1955–59)

Anticipating the demand and subsequent rush into production of short films for television in the early 1950s, Douglas Fairbanks Jr. reopened the British National Studios at Elstree and embarked on an ambitious series of half-hour films using British performers, directors, and technicians. He started out with a contract to supply thirty-nine telefilms to NBC TV, which the American network transmitted from January 1953, while for the British cinema market his company supplied features made up of these re-edited TV episodes (three eps. per feature released as *The Triangle* (1953), *Three's Company* (1953), *Thought to Kill* (1953), and *The Red Dress* (1954), for example). Fairbanks hosted and often appeared in the stories of this internationally popular anthology series. Among the British directors he recruited were Lance Comfort, Leslie Arliss, Terence Fisher, Lawrence Huntington, and Bernard Knowles. Various segments of the package were also seen in ITV regions under the headings of **Play Gems**, **Saturday Playhouse**, and **Crown Theatre** during 1956. Fairbanks, *centre*, is pictured in a scene from the episode 'A Lodging for the Night'.

Dragnet

(Mark VII–MCA; ITV tx 1955–)

Producer-director-actor Jack Webb's introduction of the 'from the files of . . .' TV crime action series featured the daily police routines of two Los Angeles detectives, Sgt. Joe Friday (Webb; *pictured*) and Officer Frank Smith (Ben Alexander; during the 1960s, Harry Morgan as Officer Bill Gannon) as they investigated various crimes ranging from hold-ups to prison escapes. Friday's trade-mark patter immortalized him with 'Just the facts, ma'am' and the half-hour episodes always wrapped up with 'The story you have just seen is true; only the names have been changed to protect the innocent.' Dum-de-dum-dum! (US tx 1952–59; 1967–70)

Gardening Club

(BBC-tv, 1955–67)

Had begun from the roof garden above Lime Grove studios with Percy Thrower serving the nation with his gardening facts and techniques as well as introducing guests from allotment societies around the country. **Gardening Club** developed into **Gardeners' World** (BBC-2, 1968–), also with Percy Thrower, which further broadened the scope of interest for the British gardener, from orchid-breeding to showbench onion-polishing; professional and top amateur guests shared programme time with filmed visits to National Trust and private gardens. Percy Thrower is pictured, *left*, with guests D. E. P. Dunne and R. C. Balfour.

I Love Lucy
(Desilu Prod.; ITV tx 1955–)

One of the great American sitcoms of the 1950s, and one of the first to be shown when Britain's commercial television began, **I Love Lucy** starred Hollywood contract player Lucille Ball and her Cuban musician husband Desi Arnaz in this half-hour (× 179 eps.) series. The stories revolved around Ball's crazy antics (in the Lucy-gets-a-new-job, Lucy-tries-to-make-Desi-jealous mode) with straight-man Arnaz displaying a quaint Latin flair for comedy, supported by William Frawley and Vivian Vance as their neighbours Fred and Ethel Mertz. The programme was an instant success when it premièred on CBS TV in 1951 and remained a top-rated show even after it ceased production in 1957; rather cleverly, the programme was filmed (by veteran Hollywood cinematographer Karl Freund) instead of broadcast live thus permitting the series a whole new lease of life in re-runs and international sales. Jess Oppenheimer was the original producer (as well as a contributing writer). A later long-running series in a similar style was **The Lucy Show** (aka **The Lucille Ball Show**; Desilu Prod., 1962–68) with Ball this time playing a widow with two children (Lucy and Desi having parted company in 1960); Vance once again appeared as Lucy's neighbour-friend and Gale Gordon was her perplexed bank manager employer. The series was retitled **Here's Lucy** in 1968 and ran through to 1974.

It's Magic
(BBC-tv, 1955–58)

'A thirty minute mixture of mystery and music' was the log line billing for actor-magician-entertainer David Nixon's popular 1950s series in which the prepossessing host was accompanied by illusionist Al Koran. The sleight-of-hand / variety showcase was televised from the BBC TV studios in Edinburgh and Birmingham. Nixon (*pictured*) was also a regular panellist on **What's My Line?** and **My Wildest Dream** (Granada TV, 1956–57) before moving into the role of resident host in **Showtime** (BBC-tv, 1959–61) and **Comedy Bandbox** (ABC TV, 1964). His own series include **Nixon at Nine-Five** (BBC-1, 1967), **Now for Nixon** (BBC-1, 1967–68), **The Nixon Line** (BBC-1, 1968), **David Nixon** (BBC-1, 1967–68), **Tonight With David Nixon** (ATV, 1969), and **The David Nixon Show** (Thames TV, 1972–77).

Kitchen Magic
(BBC-tv, 1955)

Featured famed tele-chefs John (Johnnie) and Phyllis (Fanny) Cradock (*pictured*) in this series in which they performed their unique brand of cookery to a studio audience; the series was produced by Alan Sleath. **Fanny's Kitchen** (A-R, 1955; 1957; 1961), **Chez Bon Viveur** (A-R, 1956), and **The Cradocks** (A-R, 1962) followed. Years later they were still appearing on television with such programmes as BBC TV's **Giving a Dinner Party** (BBC-2, 1969), **Fanny Cradock Invites** (BBC-2, 1970), and **Fanny Cradock Cooks for Christmas** (BBC-1, 1975).

Life With the Lyons
(BBC-tv, 1955–56; A-R, 1957–60)

Was a popular domestic sitcom featuring the real-life family group of (*l. to r.*) Ben Lyon, Bebe Daniels, Barbara Lyon, guest Richard Bellaers as Robin, and Richard Lyon. They first appeared in a fortnightly series of shows (following their success on BBC radio with *Hi, Gang!* and *Life With the Lyons*) for BBC TV, produced by Bryan Sears, before moving over to ITV in 1957 and continuing in pretty much the same format (fortnightly family sitcom) until 1960. Scottish actress Molly Weir, who had been with them on their BBC TV show also appeared in the later Associated-Rediffusion series.

Look
(BBC-tv, 1955–67)

A series of early wildlife programmes introduced by naturalist Peter Scott which gave a new depth and variety to the study of natural history on television. A children's edition was also shown during the **Children's Television** slot. From 1959 special editions under the title **Faraway Look** presented film of Scott's own travels in Australia and in the Galapagos Islands of the Pacific. The programme was produced from the BBC's West of England TV studios. Picture shows Peter Scott with Mme Michèle Rebel, Programme Planner for Radio Television Française, standing by the lake outside Scott's house in the grounds of the Severn Wildfowl Trust.

Mick and Montmorency
(A-R, 1955–57)

Started out for its first few months of transmission as **Jobstoppers**, and featured comedians Charlie Drake (as Mick) and Jack Edwardes (Montmorency) as a couple of inept jack-of-all-trades workmen in this 'children's slot' programme. Drake then moved over to BBC TV to appear in **Laughter in Store** (BBC-tv, 1957) with Irene Handl and, later that same year, **Drake's Progress** (BBC-tv, 1957), his first starring TV series, also with Handl and Warren Mitchell; the latter half-hour series was created and produced by George Inns and scripted by George Wadmore and Drake. The 30-minute comedy series **Charlie Drake** (BBC-tv, 1958; 1960) followed, with the 1960 series, under producer G. B. Lupino, featuring spoofs of the cinema: 'We Diet at Dawn' and 'March of the Movies', for example. Drake, David Cummings, and Derek Collyer shared the scripts.

Portrait of Alison
(BBC-tv, 16/2–23/3/55)

Television suspense thriller writer Francis Durbridge's fourth BBC TV serial starred Patrick Barr (*left*; with Elaine Dundy) as Tim Forester, a well-known portrait painter, whose brother was killed in an apparently straightforward motor accident in Italy; Alan Bromly produced the six half-hour episodes. Durbridge's **The Broken Horseshoe** (BBC-tv, 15/3–19/4/52; 6 eps.) was TV's first thriller serial, produced live in a tiny studio at Alexandra Palace. Durbridge, who had been a radio writer since the 1930s (and in 1938 had created for radio *Send for Paul Temple*), followed with **Operation Diplomat** (BBC-tv, 25/10–29/11/52; 6 eps.), **The Teckman Biography** (BBC-tv, 26/12/53–9/1/54; 3 eps.), **Portrait of Alison** (1955, above), **My Friend Charles** (BBC-tv, 10/3–14/4/56; 6 eps.), **The Other Man** (BBC-tv, 20 and 27/10/56), **A Time of Day** (BBC-tv, 13/11–18/12/57; 6 eps.), **The Scarf** (BBC-tv, 9/2–16/3/59; 6 eps.), **The World of Tim Frazer** (BBC-tv, 1960–1), **The Desperate People** (BBC-1, 24/2–31/3/63; 6 eps.), **Melissa** (BBC-2, 26/4–31/5/64; 6 eps.), **A Man Called Harry Brent** (BBC-1, 22/3–26/4/65; 6 eps.), **A Game of Murder** (BBC-2, 26/2–2/4/66; 6 eps.), **Bat Out of Hell** (BBC-2, 26/11–24/12/66; 5 eps.), **Paul Temple** (BBC-1, 1970–1), **The Passenger** (BBC-1, 23/10–6/11/71, 3 eps.; plus compilation 5/10/73), **Melissa** (BBC-1, 4–18/12/74; 3 eps.; remake of 1964 serial), **The Doll** (BBC-1, 25/11–9/12/75; 3 eps.), **Breakaway: A Family Affair** (BBC-1, 11/1–15/2/80; 6 eps.), and **Breakaway: The Local Affair** (BBC-1, 22/2–28/3/80; 6 eps.).

Quatermass II
(BBC-tv, 22/10–26/11/55)

John Robinson (*pictured*) was
Professor Quatermass in this the
second of Nigel Kneale's
'Quatermass' serials, 6 eps. × 30
mins., produced by Rudolph
Cartier. This one was a creepy,
alien invasion story set around a
sinister chemical plant in a remote
part of the country. Discovering
that alien entities are infiltrating
members of the government,
Quatermass and his companions
(played by Hugh Griffiths, John
Stone, and Rupert Davies) set
about destroying the creatures
which are located in chambers
within the plant. This was also
remade as a feature film by
Hammer in 1956.

Sailor of Fortune
(ATV/Michael Sadlier Prod.–Mid-Ocean
Films, 1955–56)

Canadian actor Lorne Greene
starred in this 25-minute
action–drama series as Captain
Grant Mitchell, an adventurer
who steered his American motor
freighter through twenty-six
episodes with the assistance of
shipmates Alfonso (played by
Rupert Davies) and Sean (Jack
MacGowran). Ted Holliday was
associate producer. The scene
pictured is from the episode
'Desert Hostages' with (*l. to r.*)
Betty McDowell, Greene, and
Martin Benson.

Sunday Night at the London Palladium
(ATV, 1955–67; 1973–74)

The undisputed highlight of
weekend programming during
the 1950s and early 1960s
(alongside **Armchair Theatre**),
transmitted from London's
première variety theatre and
presenting top international talent
as well as the cream of local
artistes. Gracie Fields, Guy
Mitchell, Bob Hope, Dorothy
Dandridge, and Johnnie Ray were
among the top-billers during the
early years. In addition to the
headline performers, the show
also included the American
parlour game 'Beat the Clock'
which gained popularity through
the ad libbing and high-speed
patter of the programme's first
master of ceremonies Tommy
Trinder; later masters of
ceremonies included Dickie
Henderson, Bruce Forsyth
(*pictured*), Norman Vaughan, and
Jimmy Tarbuck. Filling out the
show's traditional format were the
high-kicking Tiller Girls and the
revolving-stage finale. Producer
Val Parnell had pioneered the
presentation policy which gave
the Palladium its unique world-
wide status.

Sunday-Night Theatre
(BBC-tv, 1955–59)

Presented a long-running series of
prestigious plays for television
that included such proven
successes as 'Mrs Patterson'
(17/6/56; wr. Charles Sebree and
Greer Johnson, pr. Anthony
Pelissier) with Eartha Kitt, Estelle
Winwood, and Elisabeth Welch
(Kitt had first performed in the
play on Broadway in 1954); 'The
Cold Light' (29/7/56; wr. Judith
Kerr from Elizabeth Montagu's
translation of the Carl Zuckmayer
story, pr. Rudolph Cartier) with
Marius Goring; 'Clive of India'
(30/12/56; adapted from the play
by W. P. Lipscomb and R. J.
Minney and pr. Cartier) starring
Marius Goring and Jeannette
Sterke (*pictured*; with producer
Rudolph Cartier); and 'The Small
Back Room' (5/4/59; adapted by
John Hopkins from the novel by
Nigel Balchin, pr. Harold Clayton)
with John Gregson and Ursula
Howells. ATV reintroduced the
programme as *The London
Palladium Show* in 1969 (Jan.–Feb.).

Take Your Pick
(A-R, 1955–68)

Companion (and friendly rival) quiz show to **Double Your Money** in which resident question master Michael Miles (*pictured*) put contestants through a series of minor obstacles, including a 60-seconds spot where the player had to answer questions without the use of the words 'yes' or 'no', and finally three straight questions which led up to the prizes (announced by the voice of Bob Danvers-Walker). Then the fast-talking Miles would enter into some cash bidding for the keys to the boxes selected by the players; three out of the ten boxes contained dud prizes. The pre-filmed programme was produced by Arlington Television and Radio Ltd. The programme was revived by Thames TV in 1992 and hosted by Des O'Connor (assisted by Jodie Wilson); Brian Klein produced.

This is Your Life
(BBC-tv, 1955–64; Thames TV, 1969–92; Thames TV–Central TV/ Carlton TV, 1993–   )

Factual, emotional show which was derived from an American original (first seen on NBC TV in 1952) and which became a heart-tug tradition of British TV. Theme and format was that an unsuspecting celebrity was accosted by master of ceremonies Eamonn Andrews (in the early days; Michael Aspel in later years), drawn into a TV studio in front of an audience, and made to endure publicly a retelling of his or her life via sundry 'surprise' guests/memories from their pre-celebrity lives. Footballer Danny Blanchflower was among those who tossed the 'surprise' format on its head by walking off in a mixture of embarrassment and anger at the invasion of personal privacy. **This is Your Life** started out on American radio in the late 1940s, devised by Ralph Edwards. Richard Todd, pictured with Andrews, was the subject of the 7/3/60 edition.

Thunder Rock
(BBC-tv, 17/5/55)

Robert Ardrey's 1939 play, **Thunder Rock** (BBC-tv, 17/5/55), was brought up to date in this 60-minute television adaptation and starred (*l. to r.*) Stephen Murray (as Charleston), Finlay Currie, Walter Rilla, and Margo Lorenz. The story of the disillusioned and cynical Charleston who had become keeper of a lonely lighthouse where he had withdrawn into a world of his own imagination was produced by Rudolph Cartier. John Clements designed the moody setting. Some years earlier, Jan Bussell had produced a 90-minute version (tx 29/10/46), adapted by radio writer Peter Sims, featuring Robert Sansom (as Charleston). Charles Dance starred as Charleston in director Mike Vardy's 6/10/85 remake.

The Woodentops
(BBC-tv, 1955–58)

Rounded up the Monday through to Friday **Watch With Mother** programming and featured the string-puppet country-life family of Mummy, Daddy, and baby Woodentop, twins Willie and Jenny, Mrs Scrubit the daily help, Sam the farmhand, Buttercup the cow, and (the munchkin market's favourite character) Spotty dog. Once again Audrey Atterbury and Molly Gibson were on the creative end of the strings, while Eileen Brown, Josephina Ray, and Peter Hawkins produced the voices. Script and music were by Maria Bird.

The Adventures of Champion

(Flying 'A' Prods.; BBC tx 1956–)

Early children's adventure series imported from the USA featuring the stories of Champion, the 'Wonder Horse' and leader of a herd of wild horses, and his 12-year-old friend Ricky (played by young Barry Curtis); assisted frequently by Ricky's German shepherd dog Rebel. Set in the late nineteenth-century West, the episodes also featured Ricky's cowboy-ranch owner Uncle Sandy (Jim Bannon) and comic-relief character Will Calhoun (Francis McDonald). The 26 eps. × half-hour series was geared to promote Western star Gene Autry's famed horse (it was Autry's production company) but as there just were not enough things a horse could do by itself the stories relied mainly on the boy-and-his-dog formula. The highly popular theme song, performed in the 1950s Frankie Laine shout style, was played for many years. (US tx 1955–56)

The Adventures of Sir Lancelot

(Sapphire Films, 1956–57)

Handsomely mounted, for its time, costume series following the gallant exploits of Queen Guinevere's champion during the days of King Arthur and the Round Table at Camelot. William Russell (left; with Ballard Berkeley and David Morrell) appeared in the title role with Ronald Leigh-Hunt as King Arthur (played in early episodes by Bruce Seton), Jane Hylton as Queen Guinevere, and Cyril Smith as Merlin. Executive producer Hannah Weinstein once again employed US blacklisted writers Ian McLellan Hunter & Ring Lardner Jr. (among others) to supply scripts behind 'front' names; Sidney Cole, Dallas Bower, and Bernard Knowles produced the 30 × half-hour episodes from the Nettlefold Studios, Walton-on-Thames. The story of King Arthur and his Knights of the Round Table appeared again in **The Legend of King Arthur** (BBC-1–Time Life–ABC (Australia), 7/10–25/11/79) serial with David Robb cast in the Lancelot role and Felicity Dean as Guinevere; Rodney Bennett directed Andrew Davies's dramatization for producer Ken Riddington.

Armchair Theatre

(ABC TV, 1956–69; Thames TV, 1970–4)

This long-running series of live and taped drama represented ITV's Golden Age of writing and production, especially after Canadian producer Sydney Newman joined the Teddington-based team in 1958. Among the many powerful plays presented in the famous Sunday-evening slot were Ted Willis's 'Hot Summer Night' (1/2/59), F. Scott Fitzgerald's 'The Last Tycoon' (27/12/59), adapted by Don Mankiewicz, 'The Picture of Dorian Gray' (22/1/61) with John Bethune scripting the Oscar Wilde story, and Canadian author Mordecai Richler's own teleplay for his 'The Apprenticeship of Duddy Kravitz' (30/7/61). In June 1962 **Armchair Theatre** produced John Wyndham's 'Dumb Martian' which acted as an introduction to the science fiction anthology **Out of This World**. John Moxey, Philip Saville, Charles Jarrott, and David Greene were among the directors working for **Armchair Theatre** during the early years; players like Joan Greenwood, Gracie Fields, Tyrone Power, Flora Robson, and Donald Pleasance graced the stages; and designers such as Bertram Tyrer and Voytek embellished the sets. During the summer stretches in the mid-1960s the series was alternatively known as **Armchair Summer Theatre** and **Armchair Mystery Theatre** (1960–65). Thames TV inherited the programme during the franchise change-over in the late 1960s from ABC Television and returned to the format during 1974 as **Armchair Cinema**, a short-lived series of filmed works, one of which—Ian Kennedy Martin's 'Regan' (4/6/74; dir. Tom Clegg)—served as a pilot programme for the later Flying Squad series **The Sweeney**. During 1973 Thames TV ran a late night series of half-hour stories under the heading of **Armchair 30** (**Thirty**), produced by Joan Kemp-Welch. Some four years later Thames TV also developed the series **Armchair Thriller** (1978–80).

'Wolf Pack' (13/4/58) featured Ian Bannen (centre) in a taut submarine drama about a captured German U-boat manned by British sailors in German uniform who are hunted by both enemy and Allied forces. Richard Gale, David Davies, Anthony

Wager, and William Fox co-starred. Wilfrid Eades directed the Jon Manchip White teleplay.

'The Lodger' (**Armchair Mystery Theatre**: 25/7/65): Charles Gray and Brenda Bruce starred in Anthony Skene's adaptation of the Mary Belloc Lowndes story about a strange gentleman-lodger in London's East End during the late nineteenth century. Angela Douglas and Victor Platt co-starred. The play was produced by Leonard White and directed by Don Leaver; novelist Norman Bogner was the story editor.

'Lena, O My Lena' (25/9/60) was Alun Owen's third TV play and starred Billie Whitelaw (*below left*) and Peter McEnery in a pithy story of a Liverpool student who falls in love with a factory girl. Scott Forbes and Colin Blakely supported. William T. Kotcheff directed Sydney Newman's production.

The Arthur Haynes Show
(ATV, 1956–66)

Was a comedy favourite for ten years and brought fame and frustration to one of Haynes's (*left*) favourite foils: Nicholas Parsons (*right*); Patricia Hayes, Graham Stark, and Dermot Kelly were also present. The shows were generally a lightweight mixture of comedy sketches (from scripts by Johnny Speight) and musical interludes; but it is the comedy skits that are most fondly remembered. The two most popular routines consisted of Arthur Haynes's famous tramp character manipulating Parsons's bewildered official and Haynes's tramp philosophizing on a park bench with cohort Dermot Kelly in a sort of lower-case 'Pete and Dud' (Peter Cook & Dudley Moore) fashion.

The Billy Cotton Band Show
(BBC-tv, 1956–65)

A highly popular variety show starring exuberant, all-purpose entertainer Billy Cotton in what seemed like an inexhaustable 50 minutes of non-stop song, dance, and comedy. Cotton's resident team of entertainers included Alan Breeze, Kathie Kay, Doreen Stephens, and pianist Russ Conway. His son Bill Cotton Jr. produced. The programme developed from the earlier variety show **Wakey Wakey!** (BBC-tv, 1956) featuring Cotton and his regulars and produced by Brian Tesler, which in turn had originated from **The Tin Pan Alley Show** (BBC-tv, 1956) with Cotton, Dennis Lotis, Shani Wallis, and the Kentones; it was based on an idea by Stanley Black who also conducted the music. Following on from **The Billy Cotton Band Show** he featured in the similarly themed **Billy Cotton's Music-Hall** (BBC-1, 1965–68). On the ITV side, earlier, Cotton and his Band, with Doreen Stephens and Alan Breeze, had a brief spell in producer-director Bill Ward's **Saturday Showtime** (ITP, 5/11–10/12/55). Cotton is pictured with dancers The Silhouettes.

Boyd QC
(A-R, 1956–65)

Michael Denison (*pictured*) was the suave legal-eagle barrister, Richard Boyd, whose confident courtroom methods offered fascinating observations of British justice at work (in an Anglo-Perry Mason sort of way). Charles Leno acted as Boyd's clerk and narrator. Jack Roffey was the main author of the half-hour stories under executive producer Caryl Doncaster; Michael Currer-Briggs directed the early episodes.

The Buccaneers
(Sapphire Films, 1956–57)

One of the earliest of the ITV swashbuckling series, set around the port of Nassau in New Providence, an island of the Bahamas, in 1722, this also saw the television series début of Robert Shaw. Once Shaw's pardoned ex-pirate Captain Dan Tempest was established (he did not come into the series until the third story) the seafaring adventures ranged from battles with Blackbeard (George Margo, later Terence Cooper) to missions along the South Carolina coast with all the cannon fire and swordplay expected from the genre. The première episode ('Blackbeard', written pseudonymously by Ring Lardner Jr. & Ian McLellan Hunter) set up the series's basic theme: a former privateer, appointed as the new Governor of Nassau, offers a pardon to all the pirates who will help rid the province of roving cutthroats. Alec Clunes played Governor Woodes Rogers and Peter Hammond was his Lieutenant Beamish. Sidney Cole produced the 39 eps. × half-hour series for executive producer Hannah Weinstein; Robert Day also contributed as director and second-unit director. Shaw is pictured (*right*) with guest players Jane Griffiths and John Harvey.

Cool for Cats
(A-R, 1956–61)

Was a shop-window record show aimed strictly at the teenage set, designed to introduce newly released discs and backed by novel dance routines (the latter directed by Douglas Squires). Kent Walton (*pictured*) and Ker Robertson introduced the (originally) 15-minute doses of rock 'n' roll and other contemporary rhythmic music. The programme, devised and directed by Joan Kemp-Welch, went out Mondays, Wednesdays, and Fridays.

The Count of Monte Cristo
(Vision Prods.–TPA, 1956)

The nineteenth-century sword-wielding adventures of Alexandre Dumas's hero Edmund Dantes were again whipped into action for this 39 eps. × half-hour action series. George Dolenz (*right*; with guest Alastair Hunter) starred as Dantes and the series presented episodes in his life after his discovery of fame and fortune as Cristo. His two regular companions were played by the acrobatic Nick Cravat, as a bearded mute, and the stout Fortunio Bonanova. Leon Fromkess produced the series, which was filmed and shown first on American TV in 1955; famed Hollywood Western director Budd Boetticher was credited for the première episode, 'Affair of the Three Napoleons'.

Diving to Adventure
(BBC-tv, 6/4–11/5/56)

Presented a series of six 30-minute films featuring the undersea explorations of husband-and-wife team Hans and Lotte Hass; Dr Hans Hass was the director of the International Institute for Submarine Research. This series, produced by Geoffrey Baines, saw the photogenic aquanauts submerged beneath the Caribbean, the Aegean, and the Red Sea. They returned with **Undersea World of Adventure** (BBC-tv, 6/8–10/9/58, 6 eps. × 30 mins., pr. Tony Soper) and later **Adventure** (BBC-tv, 8/5–19/6/59, 7 eps. × 30 mins.; 7/1–11/2/60, 6 eps. × 30 mins.), three series of documentaries in which Hans and Lotte and a team of scientists on board the marine research vessel *Xarifa* explored underwater life in the Indian Ocean. Hans Hass directed the 1959 series for producer Nicholas Crocker; Hass directed and produced the 1960 series in association with the BBC Natural History Unit.

Errol Flynn Theatre
(Inter-TV Prods., 1956–57)

British-produced anthology series of thirty-nine half-hour episodes, hosted by former Hollywood swashbuckler Flynn, who also featured in half a dozen or so stories. The series was presented along similar lines to **Douglas Fairbanks Presents**, another former Hollywood screen adventurer with TV production ties in England, with themes and settings ranging from domestic melodramas to court intrigues in tsarist Russia. Notable guest players included Patrice Wymore (Mrs Flynn), Glynis Johns, Herbert Lom, Paulette Goddard, Lilli Palmer, Mai Zetterling, Patricia Roc, and Jean Kent. Norman Williams produced the trans-Atlantic market series at Bray Studios.

Frontiers of Science
(BBC-tv, 1956–60; BBC-2, 1968–69)

'Popular science' was the theme of this informative without being baffling series, originally produced by James McCloy. The 30-minute series looked at such (mid-1950s) items as the work of the doctors and scientists of the Royal Air Force Institute of Aviation Medicine as men reached out towards space; the scientific basis of intelligence tests and their value in selection for education and career; the effects of atmospheric pollution by chemicals and germs; and the possibilities of space travel. The series was revived for two brief periods during the late 1960s. Pictured are W. A. Clegg (*left*) and Dr G. R. Richards, of the Royal Aircraft Establishment, Farnborough, with their model of a satellite on a parapet of Lime Grove roof; the signals from it were received in Riverside 2 Studio during the programme.

Gunsmoke
(CBS TV; ITV tx 1956–)

Originally transmitted as **Gun Law** in Britain, this famous half-hour Western series was one of the first to stampede on to the ITV schedules in the commercial network's early days. James Arness (*2nd left*) starred as Marshal Matt Dillon of Dodge City, assisted by Deputy Chester Goode (Dennis Weaver, *2nd right*; later Ken Curtis as Festus), Doc (Milburn Stone; *right*), and Long Branch saloon keeper Miss Kitty (Amanda Blake; *left*). The series later became an hour-long programme. It was also acquired by BBC TV for transmission in 1972. (US tx 1955–75)

Hancock's Half-Hour
(BBC-tv, 1956–60)

Started out in 1954 as a radio show starring Tony Hancock, supported by Moira Lister, Bill Kerr, and Sid James. For the television series Hancock's guests and foils included Kerr and James as well as Patricia Hayes, Irene Handl, Valentine Dyall, Hermione Baddeley, Warren Mitchell, Kenneth Williams, and Hattie Jacques. The skilful comedy patter and timing of Hancock (teamed with Sid James) was perfectly in tune with the superb scripts supplied by Alan Simpson & Ray Galton and Duncan Wood's production. The scene pictured is from 'The Missing Page' with James (*left*), Hancock (*centre*), and guest Hugh Lloyd (*right*). On 23/12/57 Wood produced a 43-minute special called (what else?) 'Hancock's Forty-Three Minutes' as a Christmas show featuring an 'all-star cast' from the East Cheam Repertory Company; written by Galton & Simpson. **Hancock** (BBC-tv, 1961) was the seventh series of Hancock shows to be put out by BBC TV where, now minus Sid, the black homburg, and the astrakhan collar, the Galton & Simpson plots became solid situation comedy, producing some of the great Hancock moments: getting trapped in a lift, turning to amateur radio, and, generally considered his finest moment, becoming a blood donor. The 25-minute episode series was again produced by Duncan Wood. Then on the ITV side, **Hancock** (ATV-MacConkey Presentation, 1963) saw him as a pompous and bumbling outsider who was drawn into situations beyond his ability. The initial half-hour was scripted by Terry Nation from an original story by Ray Whyberd; other episodes were written by Godfrey Harrison, Richard Harris, and Dennis Spooner. Alan Tarrant produced. Four years later, in one of his last TV appearances, he starred in **Hancock's** (ABC TV, 1967), a half-hour show in which he emerged as Swinging Tony Hancock, owner of a night club in 'Swinging' London. His staff and associates included June Whitfield, Joe Ritchie, Edward Evans, Bernadette Milnes, Bob Todd, and Harry Davis, as well as guest players. Scripts were by John Muir and Eric Geen; Mark Stuart produced. Hancock's first-ever TV series was **The Tony Hancock Show** (A-R, 27/4–1/6/56; 16/11/56–25/1/57), tx under the *Jack Hylton Presents* banner, a 6 eps. × half-hour comedy (in two series) produced and directed by Eric Fawcett; the later shows alternated weekly with Arthur Askey's **Before Your Very Eyes**.

Highway Patrol
(Ziv–UA TV; ITV tx 1956–)

Highly popular police action-drama starring Broderick Crawford (*left*) as Highway Patrol Chief Dan Matthews and featuring the half-hour crime-busting stories and techniques employed by the California Highway Patrol division. Furious chases and shoot-outs were the mainstay of this terse drama; Crawford's clipped call-sign response 'Ten-Four' became a part of contemporary dialogue. (US tx 1955–59)

Men in Battle
(BBC-tv, 1956–57)

Consisted of two popular monthly series of programmes in which Lieutenant-General Sir Brian Horrocks drew upon his memories (along with various wall charts) of the great battlefields of the Second World War; each military manœuvre was described with the solemnity of an actual pre-offensive battle plan. The series was produced by Huw Wheldon, as were later ones. Horrocks followed up this tactic analysis series with the self-explanatory **Epic Battles** (BBC-tv, 1958), the forward-looking **Battle in Space** (BBC-tv, 1958), **Men of Action** (BBC-tv, 1959–60), **Great Captains** (BBC-tv, 1960–61), and **Tunes of Glory** (BBC-tv, 1963), the latter a series about the men and music of famous regiments.

The Norman Wisdom Show
(BBC-tv, 1956)

Presented three hour-long variety shows under the 'Saturday Comedy Hour' banner, produced by Ernest Maxin, starring popular cinema comedian Norman Wisdom (*pictured*) with Marion Keene, Eddie Leslie, and the George Mitchell Singers. Despite scores of TV appearances, mainly in a variety format, Wisdom later starred in only three television series (all situation comedies): **Norman** (ATV, 2/4–7/5/70), his first TV sitcom, written by Ray Cooney and John Chapman, and produced and directed by Alan Tarrant; **Nobody is Norman Wisdom** (ATV, 26/6–7/8/73), based on an idea by Watt Nicoll and John Sichel and produced by John Scholz-Conway; and **A Little Bit of Wisdom** (ATV, 1974–76), produced by Scholz-Conway and Les Chatfield.

Opportunity Knocks!
(A-R, 1956; ABC TV, 1964–67; Thames TV, 1968–78)

Adapted from a successful radio format which the effusive host Hughie Green pioneered many years before and presented as a viewer-participation TV programme in which the home audience was invited to vote for the best acts on each show while the studio audience registered their votes via an applause 'Clapometer'. BBC TV picked up the format some years later and produced **Bob Says Opportunity Knocks** (BBC-1, 1987–89), featuring Bob Monkhouse at the helm and produced by Stewart Morris; the title reverted to **Opportunity Knocks** in 1990 when Les Dawson took over as master of ceremonies. **Search for a Star** (LWT, 1979–81) was an ITV attempt to revive the potential-star show with presenter Steve Jones conducting the nation-wide search; Tony Cornford and David MacMahon produced. The scene, picturing Hughie Green, is from a late 1960s show.

Picture Parade
(BBC-tv, 1956–62)

One of the early weekly magazine programmes about the world of cinema and new cinema releases, with star or director guests in the studio and reviews of upcoming features in a form that would be popularized by presenter Barry Norman in the 1970s. Founder presenters were Peter Haigh and Derek Bond; Robert Robinson (pictured, *left*, with studio guest director John Schlesinger) took over in 1959.

A Show Called Fred
(A-R, 27/4–30/5/56)

Goonish humour and lunacy from the pen of Spike Milligan (*right*), and performed by Peter Sellers (*left*), Valentine Dyall, Kenneth Connor, Graham Stark, Patti Lewis, and Max Geldray, filled the half-hour episodes of this Dick Lester-directed comedy. The team returned later the same year with **Son of Fred** (A-R, 17/9–5/11/56), with the above line-up continuing their goofy pranks; Cuthbert Harding and Johnny Vyvyan also joined the ranks. **Idiot Weekly, Price 2d.** (A-R, Febr.–Mar. 1956) was perhaps the origin of the comedy package, featuring Sellers as the editor of a tatty Victorian weekly paper which was used as the convenient link between music (by Patti Lewis) and sketches. Eric Sykes, June Whitfield, and Spike Milligan contributed alongside Dyall, Connor, and Stark; Dick Lester directed. In a similar vein, **Yes, It's the Cathode-Ray Tube Show!** (A-R, 11/2–18/3/57) featured a half-hour of craziness from Peter Sellers and Michael Bentine, devised and written by Bentine and David Nettheim; Kenneth Carter directed-produced. For ITV's first Christmas holiday period transmission Associated-Rediffusion presented a half-hour comedy programme called **The Dick Lester Show** (tx 23/12/55) in which Lester played the piano, the guitar, sang, and performed Goon-like skits; Patti Lewis and Alun Owen also appeared in the Philip Saville & Dick Lester-devised show, directed by Douglas Hurn.

Spot the Tune
(Granada TV, 1956–62)

Was an early musical quiz game in which contestants had to beat a time-limit in coming up with a correct song title after hearing only a few bars of a melody. Central to the proceedings was sunny songstress Marion Ryan (*pictured*), backed by the Peter Knight Orchestra; Ryan's teenage sons, Paul and Barry, achieved their own recording fame during the late 1960s. Ken Platt, Ted Ray, and Canadian entertainer Jackie Rae were among the masters of ceremonies during the show's run of 209 half-hour episodes. The musical quiz format was later revived by Tom O'Connor (and later Lionel Blair) for **Name That Tune** (Thames TV, 1983–84) which came out of Thames's **London Night Out** (1978–83) variety show.

This Week
(A-R, 1956–68; Thames TV, 1968–)

A public affairs series that has maintained a high level of both interest and enterprise over the years, originally produced by Caryl Doncaster and introduced first by Rene Cutforth, and then by Michael Westmore, Ludovic Kennedy, and Daniel Farson during the 1950s. The programme's news editor Peter Hunt went on to replace Doncaster as producer. The series went out under the press tag-line of 'A window on the world behind the headlines'. The scene pictured shows members of the **This Week** team working in the heart of Salisbury, Southern Rhodesia, in 1965: *l. to r.*, Ron Osborne (camera), Peter Robinson (director), and Stan Clarke (sound).

Whack-O!
(BBC-tv, 1956–60; BBC-1, 1971–72)

One of the more famous (if not legendary) 1950s situation comedies, starring film and stage comedian Jimmy Edwards (*2nd from right*) in his popular role of the conniving, cane-thrashing, horse-betting (and often drunken) Headmaster of Chiselbury public school. Arthur Howard (*right*) was his simple-minded assistant, Mr Pettigrew, during the early series; Julian Orchard was Pettigrew when the programme was revived in the early 1970s (13 eps. × 30 mins., pr. Douglas Argent). Frank Muir & Denis Norden were the main authors throughout. A feature film version, *Bottoms Up!*, was produced by Associated-British in 1960.

What the Papers Say
(Granada TV, 1956–68; 1970–82; C4/Granada TV, 1982–89; BBC-2/Granada TV, 1990–)

Headlines of the world's news of the past week formed the basis of this topical, controversial (at times), and informative series. The main function of the programme was to indicate a particular bias of individual papers in their handling of the main happenings of the week. When the series was first shown, it was presented alternately by Kingsley Martin (then editor of the *New Statesman*) and Brian Inglis (*pictured*) (then assistant editor of the *Spectator*); Inglis went on to present the first twelve years of the programme. Then, for five weeks (1/8–19/9/68), the programme became **What the Weeklies Say**, produced for Granada TV by David Boulton; this was followed by **The Papers** (Granada TV, 1968–69), introduced by Stuart Hall. Channel Four has networked the programme since November 1982; BBC-2 from March 1990.

The White Falcon
(BBC-tv, 5/2/56)

Was presented, essentially, as a love story, a romantic, light-hearted treatment of the well-known Henry VIII and Anne Boleyn story but divested of all the 'historical costume drama' heaviness. Paul Rogers (*left*) starred as Henry VIII, with Jeannette Sterke (*centre*) as Anne Boleyn, Margaretta Scott as Catherine of Aragon, and Patrick Troughton as Cardinal Wolsey; Eric Lander, Marius Goring (*right*; as Dr Cranmer), and Ruper Davies also appeared. Incidental music was by Elisabeth Lutyens; Stephen Taylor designed the sets. Neilson Gattey and Jordan Lawrence wrote the 90-minute play (which was shown under the **Sunday-Night Theatre** series banner) for Rudolph Cartier's production.

Zoo Time
(Granada TV, 1956–68)

Introduced an entertaining and educational animal behaviour programme from the London Zoo-based GTV Film Unit presented by zoological expert Desmond Morris (pictured with some of his students). In all 331 half-hour editions were produced. Director and cinema documentary pioneer Harry Watt introduced the programme during 1960; Chris Kelly presented (from Chester Zoo) from 1967, for producer Peter Mullings. **Animal Story** (Granada TV, 1960–62), also with Dr Morris, was another series featuring animal life and was made at London and Whipsnade Zoos; Milton Shulman and, later, Derek Twist produced the twenty-three half-hour episodes. **A to Zoo** (Granada TV, 1960–61), also produced by Twist, was a series of films through the alphabet in the world of animals; the commentary was by Harry Watt for the twenty-six half-hour episodes.

The Adventures of Long John Silver
(transmitted via the ITV companies in 1957)

Enjoyably noisy Australian-made skull-and-crossbones adventure series, **The Adventures of Long John Silver** was based on Robert Louis Stevenson's *Treasure Island* and starred Robert Newton (*pictured*) in the rollicking title role; supported by Kit Taylor as Jim Hawkins and Connie Gilchrist as Miss Purity Pinker. The series was filmed (in colour) in Sydney by producer Joseph Kaufman for Isola del'Oro Prods.; twenty-six half-hour episodes were produced. A feature film version, in CinemaScope, was released in 1954. Some thirty years later HTV produced **John Silver's Return to Treasure Island** (HTV, 5/7–23/8/86), a sequel to the original adventure, starring Brian Blessed in the title role; John Goldsmith scripted the eight episodes (1 × 115 mins., 7 × 60 mins.) for producer Alan Clayton. BBC TV produced a nine-part serial of **Treasure Island** (BBC-1, 3/11–29/12/68) featuring Peter Vaughan as Silver and Michael Newport as Jim Hawkins; Peter Hammond directed David Turner's script for producer Campbell Logan. A few years later Anglia TV produced another version, as a six-part serial (tx 10/7–14/8/72), told in a series of colour illustrations by adapter-narrator-producer Paul Honeyman; John Worsley did the artwork, John Salway directed.

Alfred Hitchcock Presents
(Shamley Prod.–Revue; ITV tx 1957–)

Crime-mystery-fantasy anthology series hosted by famous film director Alfred Hitchcock and shown, initially, in half-hour episodes. The series featured nerve-gripping stories usually about shady characters who harbour some sort of guilty secret (wife / husband murderers, blackmailers, serial killers) and who ultimately become victims of their own devilry. Hitchcock's excellent though offbeat blend of cynicism and black humour in announcing the final come-uppance of the story's villain at the episode's close was only matched by his sarcastic remarks relating to the programme's US sponsor (referring particularly to the intrusion of the commercial breaks; *pictured*). After 265 half-hours, under producer Joan Harrison, the episodes were lengthened and became **The Alfred Hitchcock Hour**, with a further ninety-three episodes produced again by Harrison. Hitchcock himself took the director's chair for eighteen stories during the programme's original ten years. (US tx **Presents** 1955–62, **Hour** 1962–65)

Alma Cogan Show
(BBC-tv, 1957; 1962)

Considered to be British television's First Lady of popular music during the late 1950s and early 1960s, Alma Cogan was top of the bill of almost all the notable variety shows then running on TV (**Max Bygraves Entertains**, **Saturday Spectacular**, **Val Parnell's Startime**, **Sunday Night at the London Palladium**, among numerous others). Although she favoured playing the variety theatres her appearances on television—conveying charm and a pleasant song delivery with an outsize presence in extravagant dresses—made her one of the great (and much sought after) TV personalities, rivalled only by such similar songbirds of the period as Joan Regan and Ruby Murray.

The Army Game
(Granada TV, 1957–61)

A highly popular ITV series of the late 1950s about a gang of peacetime soldiers in constant pursuit of easy money and ways of outwitting their fiery Sergeant-Major. Based at Hut 29 of the Surplus Ordnance Depot at Nether Hopping, the original bunch of privates consisted of Pte. 'Excused Boots' Bisley (played by Alfie Bass), Pte. 'Professor' Hatchett (Charles Hawtrey; *2nd right*), Pte. 'Cupcake' Cook (Norman Rossington; *2nd left*) and Pte. 'Popeye' Popplewell (Bernard Bresslaw, *centre*, who soon became a national favourite with his 'I only arsked' catchline); Cpl. Springer (Michael Medwin) was their Bilko-like ring leader, Sgt.-Maj. Bullimore (William Hartnell; *right*) their regular taskmaster, and the scatterbrained Major Upshot-Bagley (Geoffrey Sumner; *left*) the camp commandant. The series was transmitted fortnightly (live at first) for the first six months then became a weekly programme. Bill Fraser (as CSM Claude Snudge) replaced Hartnell for the 1958–60 series prior to embarking on the spin-off **Bootsie and Snudge**. With some of the original cast having moved on to other things by 1960, the new characters recruited into Hut 29 were Cpl. 'Flogger' Hoskins (Harry Fowler), Pte. Bone (Ted Lune), Pte. 'Chubby' Catchpole (Dick Emery), and L / Cpl. 'Moosh' Merryweather (Mario Fabrizi); Hartnell returned as the Sgt.-Maj. The 153 eps. × half-hour were produced by Peter Eton and directed by Milo Lewis and (later) Max Morgan-Witts; Larry Stephens, Maurice Wiltshire, Sid Colin, Barry Took, and Marty Feldman contributed to the script department. Bernard Bresslaw's popular 'Popeye' character inspired the Hammer Films-produced feature film of the series, *I Only Arsked*, in 1958. **Bootsie and Snudge** (Granada TV, 1960–63; initial tag-on title was **in Civvy Street**; 100 eps. × half-hour) featured the spin-off characters of Alfie Bass as the wily little fellow and Bill Fraser the pompous, blustering one now working together in an upper-class London club. They were later joined by Clive Dunn and Robert Dorning. Peter Eton produced the scripts by Barry Took, Marty Feldman, and John Antrobus; Milo Lewis and Eric Fawcett directed. Granada revived the series in 1974 for 6 × half-hour episodes written by

David Climie and Ronnie Cass, with Bootsie now as a £1,000,000 prize pools winner and Snudge the man from the pools company; director-producer was Bill Podmore. Following the original **Bootsie and Snudge** series during the early 1960s the Bass–Fraser duo appeared in 8 × half-hour episodes of **Foreign Affairs** (Granada TV, 1964), in which they entered the diplomatic service and took up positions as the same bumbling pair at the British Embassy in Bosnik. Once again Peter Eton produced and Milo Lewis directed.

Chelsea at Nine
(Granada TV, 1957–60)

Was Granada TV's venture into the variety show with the aim of featuring some of the world's headline artists (usually American), broadcast direct from their newly converted Granada theatre in London's Chelsea. The show celebrated such varied performers as ventriloquist Edgar Bergen, singer-actor Eddie Constantine, American pianists Ferrante and Teicher, 17-year-old guitarist John Williams, comedians Alan Young and Larry Storch, 15-year-old classical pianist Daniel Barenboim, and group comedy sketches performed by Mai Zetterling, Dennis Price, and Irene Handl; and Hermione Baddeley and Stanley Baxter in 'Dinner for One'. The resident song-and-dance line, The Granadiers, were also on hand for high kicks and harmonies. Jazz and blues singer Billie Holiday (*pictured*) was the guest star on the 18/3/59 show. The programme was retitled **Chelsea at Eight** in early 1958 (due to an evening scheduling shift) and during the summer months, from the same year, was known as **Chelsea Summertime**. Sixty programmes were produced by Denis Forman.

Criss Cross Quiz
(Granada TV, 1957–67)

Was the British TV version of America's **Tic Tac Dough** (NBC TV, 1956–59) in which two contestants competed against each other to complete a line diagonally, vertically, or horizontally with either noughts or crosses; for each correct answer the value of the game (worth up to £100 in the early days) increased. Actor Jeremy Hawk (pictured with contestants) was the original quiz-master of this three-times-a-week game show; 342 episodes were produced. **Junior Criss Cross Quiz** (Granada TV, 1957–67; 391 eps.), aimed at the 12–14 year olds, was introduced just a few months later and slotted into early-evening Wednesday programming.

Emergency—Ward 10
(ATV, 1957–67)

Was ITV's first long-running, twice-weekly soap opera, following the professional and personal lives of the doctors and nurses, as well as patients, of Oxbridge General Hospital. Created by writer Tessa Diamond originally as a six-week serial about the life of a probationary nurse (**Calling Nurse Roberts**), ATV broadened the format, switched the title, and the series soon soared through the ratings with its half-hour Tuesday and Friday prescriptions of romantic entanglements and medical dramatics. Jill Browne's Nurse (later Sister) Carole Young (*2nd right*) became an immediate hit with the viewers, as did such other early series regulars as Charles Tingwell (*left*), Richard Thorp, Ray Barrett, Glyn Owen, and Desmond Carrington; a young John Alderton came on board as Dr Richard Moone in the latter part of 1963. Antony Kearey produced and directed the early series. In 1961 producer Rex Firkin and writer Diana Morgan spun off **Call Oxbridge 2000** (ATV, 1961–62), removing Richard Thorp's Dr Rennie from the wards and placing him in private practice with local GP Dr Richard Graham

1957

(Noel Howlett); the 45-minute programme went out on Sunday afternoons. When this series ended, **24 Hour Call** (ATV, 1963) was brought in to supply the private practice medico interest, in this case the group practice of four doctors (Godfrey Quigley and Geoffrey Frederick from the previous series and newcomers Scott Forbes and Andrew Downie) sharing the same headquarters and working on a rotating system. Philip Dale was the producer. The scene pictured also shows Rosemary Miller (*2nd left*), Frederick Bartram (*centre*), and John Paul (*far right*). A spin-off feature film, *Life in Emergency Ward 10*, was produced in 1958 (dir. Robert Day).

Eurovision Song Contest
(BBC-tv, 1957–)

A long-running and still popular annual musical event in which a collection of European countries compete for the best popular song of the year. In the first UK-transmitted event (3/3/57) ten countries were entered; now there are some twenty-two European countries in competition. The first Eurovision Song Contest was seen on the Eurovision network in 1956 but Britain did not enter until the following year. From 1956 BBC TV had been presenting Britain's own **Festival of British Popular Songs**, a series of monthly contests between songwriters performed by such 1950s favourites as Shirley Abicair, Frankie Vaughan, and Ronnie Hilton. The winner of the **Festival** contest, and subsequently Britain's first Eurovision entry, was *All*, written by Reynell Wreford and Alan Stranks, and sung by Patricia Bredin (who finished in seventh place). Britain's initial interest arose from the idea that to stem the flood of American songs sweeping the country home-grown talent should be encouraged, almost as an act of nationalism. The scene is from the 1960 contest, with Jacqueline Boyer singing the winning French song; Katie Boyle (*centre, background*) hosted for many years.

Gay Cavalier
(A-R/George King Prod., 1957)

Veteran British film producer George King entered the TV series field with this costume action series set during the English Civil War and starring French actor Christian Marquand as the dashing swashbuckler Captain Claude Duval. Directors Terence Fisher and Lance Comfort shared the 13 eps. × half-hour series.

Hawkeye and the Last of the Mohicans
(Normandie Prods.; ITV tx 1957–)

This Canadian-produced (eastern) Western series was set in pre-Revolutionary USA and Canada and starred John Hart (*left*) as James Fenimore Cooper's hero Hawkeye, with Lon Chaney Jr. (*right*) as his blood-brother, Chingachgook. Produced by Sigmund Neufeld, the thirty-nine half-hour episodes were originally syndicated in early 1957 and, in presenting a straight heroes-and-villains treatment, supplied sufficient late afternoon thrills for the junior set. Four telefeatures were later made available from re-edited episodes: *Along the Mohawk Trail, The Long Rifle and the Tomahawk, The Pathfinder and the Mohican*, and *The Redmen and the Renegades*.

Hour of Mystery
(ABC TV, 1957)

Was a series of thirteen hour-long fantasy-suspense plays presented and linked by Donald Wolfit (*pictured*) who portrayed a connoisseur and private collector of crime objects. The series began with Mary Hayley Bell's 'Duet for Two Hands' (7/6/57) and went on to present productions of Barre Lyndon's 'The Man in Half Moon Street' (22/6/57), with star Anton Diffring playing the role some two years before appearing in Hammer Films' *The Man Who Could Cheat Death*, Emlyn Williams's 'Night Must Fall' (19/7/57), and Ivan Goff & Ben Roberts's 'Portrait in Black' (30/8/57). John Nelson Burton produced.

Jim's Inn
(A-R, 1957–63)

Was perhaps the most famous and popular of the British TV rush into the Admag form (a TV programme specially built around commercials). This particular advertising magazine cast Jimmy and Maggie Hanley as a couple who ran a village pub in a place called Wembleham and had them discussing the price and quality of various domestic products with their customers (the latter pictured: Jack Edwards, *left*, and Ron Sherlock, *right*). Before they were outlawed in 1963 by Parliament, the Admags covered almost every consumer subject: **About Homes and Gardens** (ATV, 1956) featured Noele Gordon on the title items; **Where Shall We Go?** (ABC TV, 1956), with Peter Butterworth and Janet Brown, and **Over the Hills** (A-R, 1956–57) dealt with holiday planning; **What's in Store** (ABC TV, 1956) helped viewers with their Christmas gift buying; **What's New** (A-R, 1957) had the latest ideas in furnishing; while John **Slater's Bazaar** (ATV, 1957–59) appeared to present everything.

The Kilt Is My Delight
(BBC-tv, 1957–63)

Was a jolly programme of Scottish songs and dances which presented a traditional yet somewhat dated half-hour series celebrating north-of-the-border nationalism via such variety turns as the Clan Hay Dancers and the Royal Scottish Country Dance Orchestra. The kilt-swirling showcase was broadcast parallel to **The White Heather Club** (BBC-tv, 1957–68), basically another traditional New Year's Eve party backdrop programme which highlighted the talents of Andy Stewart, Jimmy Logan, Jimmy Shand and his Band, Moira Anderson, Duncan Macrae, and Roddy McMillan. Both were BBC Glasgow-based productions; **The Kilt Is My Delight** was produced by Alan Rees, while **The White Heather Club** was for many years produced by Iain MacFadyen.

Lenny the Lion Show
(BBC-tv, 1957–58; 1960)

Began under the **Children's Television** banner and presented ventriloquist Terry Hall and his lion dummy in a series of shows usually supported by contemporary pop groups as guest stars; Johnny Downes was the programme's original producer. This was followed by a series of 10-minute shows called **Lenny's Den** (BBC-tv, 1959–61) and, later on, **Pops and Lenny** (BBC-tv, 1962–63), which continued to be popular with the family audience.

The Lone Ranger
(Apex/Jack Chertok/Clayton Moore/Jack Wrather Corp.; BBC tx 1957–)

Was another of the early children's adventure imports from the USA, starring Clayton Moore (*pictured*) as the masked champion of Western justice and Jay Silverheels as his Indian sidekick Tonto (John Hart played the Ranger for a while in the early 1950s). Together they galloped across the early frontier capturing rather than shooting the bad guys. The long-running half-hour series was based on the original radio stories by Fran Striker from the format created by George W. Trendle and Striker. The 'Hi-Yo, Silver!' duo also appeared in two spin-off feature films: *The Lone Ranger* (WB, 1955) and *The Lone Ranger and the Lost City of Gold* (UA, 1958). (US tx 1949–57)

Mark Saber
(Danzigers, GB tx 1957–62)

With possibly one of the most complicated television histories for a single TV character, Mark Saber first appeared in the suave form of Tom Conway as a quasi-British police inspector working for an American police department in a US series called **Mystery Theatre** (Roland Reed Prods., US tx 1951–52). Conway returned as Saber when the series was retitled **Inspector Mark Saber—Homicide Squad** (Roland Reed Prods., US tx 1952–54). In 1955 Saber returned once more but this time the character was played by one-armed actor Donald Gray and the series (produced in England) was called **The Vise** (Danzigers, US tx 1955–57); Saber was now a former Scotland Yard man turned private investigator based in London. The Saber **Vise** was a continuation of a Danzigers-produced anthology series, **The Vise** (US tx 1954–55), which had been for some sixty-five episodes hosted by Ron Randell before the title was taken over for the Saber series. In the UK this series was transmitted as **Mark Saber** from 1957 while in America it was presented as **Saber of London** (US tx 1957–60); to complicate matters further the series was also known in the UK from 1959 as **Saber of London**. Some ITV areas later ran the latter title until 1965. The supporting cast for the various series were: James Burke as Conway's sidekick Sgt. Tim Maloney during **Mystery Theatre** and **Inspector Mark Saber—Homicide Squad**; Michael Balfour, Teresa Thorne, and Diana Decker as Gray's associates during Saber's **The Vise** days; and Neil McCallum, Gordon Tanner, Robert Arden, and Colin Tapley for the later UK series.

The New Adventures of Charlie Chan
(ITC/TPA, 1957–58)

Created by author Earl Derr Biggers in his 1925 novel *The House Without a Key*, Chinese Det.-Insp. Charlie Chan (of the Honolulu Police Department) finally made his television début in this mainly British-produced series—some episodes were produced and filmed in the USA—that presented a heavily made-up J. Carrol Naish affecting an uncomfortable Oriental accent as Chan. Sadly, the plots were standard fare, with Chan pursuing various and unusual clues before finally solving the mystery despite the over-eager antics of his 'number one son' Barry Chan (played by James Hong). Rupert Davies and Hugh Williams supported as Inspectors Duff and Marlowe. The 39 eps. × half-hour series was produced by Rudolph C. Flothow and Sidney Marshall; Leon Fromkess served as executive producer. Colin Garde applied the make-up.

On Safari
(BBC-tv, 1957–59; 1961–65)

A series of exotic wildlife films exploring, mainly, African animals in their natural surroundings produced by the husband-and-wife team of Armand and Michaela Denis (*pictured*); the couple's home and centre of operations was in Nairobi. Their on-camera treks across Uganda, Kenya, etc., with Michaela's shapely form constantly darting in front of the lens and Armand's relaxed, almost domestic manner when soft-shoeing after dangerous creatures established the couple as TV favourites during the 1950s. The duo had scored an earlier hit with **Filming Wild Animals** (BBC-tv, 1954–55) and **Filming in Africa** (BBC-tv, 1955) and then, about the same time on the ITV channel, with the similar **Michaela and Armand Denis** (ATV, 1955–58) before embarking on **Safari to Asia** (BBC-tv, 1959–61). Another mid-1950s African wildlife series was **The Michaels in Africa** (BBC-tv, 1955–56) which followed the adventures of a real family (from Pretoria) on safari with a camera, featuring (producer) George Michael, his wife Marjorie, and daughters Carole and June; commentary was written by James Leasor.

O.S.S.
(ITV/Buckeye–LSQ Prods.–Flamingo Films–ITP, 1957–58)

Stories from the files of America's Office of Strategic Services (the wartime predecessor of the CIA) were the basis for this Second World War cloak-and-dagger adventure. The Anglo-American series, based at the National Studios at Elstree under producer Jules Buck, featured Ron Randell (*right*; with Lyndon Brook in the 'Operation Orange Blossom' ep.) as OSS agent Major Frank Hawthorne who undertook clandestine missions into occupied Europe for purposes of sabotage, rescue, contact, and information. Filmed in moody, night-time black and white (several episodes were directed by ace *film noir* maker Robert Siodmak), in England and France, each of the stories dramatized apparently had a basis in actual Second World War history; executive producer on the programme was Colonel William Eliscu, one-time aide to real-life OSS Chief General 'Wild Bill' Donovan. Lionel Murton was Hawthorne's Chief back at headquarters and Robert Gallico played their assistant, Sgt. O'Brien. In all 26 × half-hour episodes were produced.

The Phil Silvers Show
(CBS TV; BBC tx 1957–)

A classic situation comedy series featuring Phil Silvers (*centre*) as the fast-talking, money-hungry Master Sergeant Ernie Bilko who was continually looking to make the fast buck, either from his less-than-bright Motor Pool platoon or the cautious residents of nearby Roseville, Kansas (Bilko was stationed at the fictitious Fort Baxter, Kansas; later at Camp Fremont, California). Bilko's accomplices were usually Corporals Barbella (Harvey Lembeck; *2nd left*) and Henshaw (Allan Melvin); his on-base foils were slovenly Pte. Duane Doberman (played with absurd confidence by Maurice Gosfield; *foreground with helmet*) and Bilko's superior, the dithery Colonel Hall (Paul Ford). The series was created by producer-writer Nat Hiken and directed by Al DeCaprio; the (earlier) half-hour series also presented scripts written by Neil Simon. The series began in America as **You'll Never Get Rich** but then became **The Phil Silvers Show** after two months; also known as **Sgt. Bilko** in syndication. (US tx 1955–59)

1957

Pinky and Perky
(BBC-tv, 1957; 1962–66; Thames TV, 1968–70)

Czech puppeteers Jan and Vlasta Dalibor's dancing pig puppets (Perky wore the hat!) were long-time TV favourites with their amusing cabaret of string-puppet struttings to contemporary pop music. Their additional BBC TV series were **Pinky and Perky's Pop Parade** (1960), **Pinky and Perky's American Journey** (1963), **Pinky and Perky's Island** (1967), and **Pinky and Perky Times** (1968); the early programmes originated from the BBC's north of England studios. Picture shows the Dalibors operating their puppets Pinky and Perky on the studio paddle steamship set.

Roving Report
(ITN, 1957–64)

Presented and produced by the Independent Television News team, this documentary series attempted to distil contemporary ideas and the way of life of a city or a country or a group of people into a forthright, fair-minded, and occasionally offbeat film on a foreign country in the news. ITN editor Geoffrey Cox was the founder of **Roving Report** and, under producer Michael Barsley (later Robert Verrall), his early team consisted of chief rover Robin Day, George Ffitch, Reginald Bosanquet, Tim Brinton, Huw Thomas, and Lynne Reid Banks. Their 16mm-filmed travels took them from America (where the first programme, on 19/3/57, came from the top of the Empire State Building) to Zanzibar (prog. of 8/5/58). The politically headstrong Archbishop Makarios III of Cyprus, during the 1950s, was one of their favourite targets/subjects (*pictured*). Since 1967, news agency Worldwide Television News has produced **Roving Report** for syndication as a weekly current affairs magazine programme to international broadcasters.

The Royalty
(BBC-tv, 1957–58)

Stories about the grand guests and staff at the Royalty Hotel in London's St James made up the episodes in this serialized programme starring Margaret Lockwood (*right*; as the owner, Mrs Mollie Miller), assisted by receptionist Joan Hickson, chef Ferdy Mayne, and the bar staff Richard Pearson and Lana Morris. A. E. Matthews, Hugh Sinclair, Frances Rowe, and Margaret's daughter, Julia Lockwood (*left*), also appeared. The half-hour programme was created and written by Donald Wilson and Michael Voysey; Campbell Logan produced. **The Flying Swan** (BBC-1, 1965) was set along similar lines (the title hotel now being by the Thames) and also featured the mother-and-daughter team of Margaret and Julia Lockwood (the former as ex-actress Mollie Manning and the latter as her air-hostess daughter); with Wendy Hall, Tom Watson, Nerys Hughes, and Molly Urquhart. Donald Wilson scripted the opening 45-minute story and Harold Clayton produced.

Six-Five Special
(BBC-tv, 1957–58)

First of the popular teenager television shows featuring a jiving studio youth audience with such skiffle group guests as Tommy Steele and his Steelmen and Don Lang's Frantic Five (the latter generally on hand for supporting guest solo artistes). Peter Murray and Josephine (Jo) Douglas were the mainline presenters; Douglas also co-produced with Jack Good (the show's originator). A special New Year's Eve show, called **Twelve-Five Special**, was produced by Good, Dennis Main Wilson, and Dennis Monger in 1957, presenting The Jazz Couriers, with Tubby Hayes and Ronnie Scott, and Wee Willie Harris, among others. Jo Douglas, Pete Murray, and former boxer Freddie Mills introduced the 40-minute show which was presented from a London Airport restaurant. The show also branched off into other things, including a feature film version (*6.5 Special*, Anglo Amalgamated, 1958), and producer Good went on to ABC TV's **Oh Boy!**, **Boy Meets Girls**, and **Wham!!**. Pictured are skifflers Adam Faith and, in foreground, Jon Pertwee in a November 1957 show.

The Sky at Night
(BBC-tv, 1957–)

Began some six months before the space-race launching of Sputnik I and was presented, as it still is, by Dr Patrick Moore, the doyen of television astronomers. With his terse diction and generally wind-swept appearance Moore has explored, charted, explained, and analysed the great astronomical events for over a quarter of a century for the benefit of the late-night TV viewer. For young star-gazers there was also **Seeing Stars** (BBC-1, 1970), a junior version with 8 eps. × 4 mins. scheduled in the early evening children's slot, presented by Moore.

Tonight
(BBC-tv, 1957–65; BBC-1, 1975–79)

A week-nightly news magazine programme that offered a competent and amiable diversion for the early evening audience, providing follow-ups to news items of the day, not always of the profoundest import but still holding some modest element of controversy wherever possible. Early editions were produced by Donald Baverstock and directed by Alasdair Milne (*left*). Cliff Michelmore (*2nd left*) was the unruffled anchorman supported by various reporters and link-men: Derek Hart (*right*), Geoffrey Johnson Smith, Alan Whicker, Fyfe Robertson, Trevor Philpott, Macdonald Hastings, Julian Pettifer, Kenneth Allsop, Brian Redhead, and Magnus Magnusson; *2nd right* is Mrs Grace Wyndham Goldie, Assistant Head of Talks, Television. Robin Hall and Jimmie MacGregor usually provided the folk-song finale. The general format and title was revived in a late night slot in 1975 with Sue Lawley, Denis Tuohy, and Donald MacCormick as co-presenters. From 1965 most of the **Tonight** team were transferred to **Twenty-Four Hours** (BBC-1, 1965–72), a new format news and current affairs magazine that looked back on the day's world events from a late-night (10.30 p.m.) viewpoint.

The Trial of Mary Lafarge
(BBC-tv, 15/12/57)

Featured Yvonne Mitchell (*pictured, centre*) in the title role as the attractive widow, charged with the murder of her husband at the famous trial which took place in 1840 Paris. The 90-minute production was presented under the **Sunday-Night Theatre** banner. Freda Jackson, John Le Mesurier, George Murcell (*right*; as Lafarge), Annabelle Lee (*left*; as her maid Clementine), Maxwell Shaw, and Avril Elgar also appeared. Judith Kerr translated and adapted (from Marcelle Maurette) for producer Stuart Burge.

The Wharf Road Mob
(BBC-tv, 28/3/57)

Presented a dramatized documentary look at the young men of the rock 'n' roll era who found a new and more adventurous club for themselves in the Teddy Boy fraternity instead of the church-organized community youth clubs. Written by Colin Morris and produced by Gilchrist Calder (almost as a seamy-side forerunner to Karel Reisz's 1959 documentary *We Are the Lambeth Boys*), the 60-minute production featured Anthony Newley (*2nd left*) and Melvyn Hayes (*right*). Douglas Wolfe was the film cameraman.

The Adventures of William Tell
(ITC–NTA, 1958–59)

A costumed action-adventure series set in fourteenth-century Switzerland when it was under the tyrannical rule of Emperor Rudolph of Austria. Conrad Phillips (*pictured*; with guest Brian Rawlinson) starred in the title role with Jennifer Jayne as his wife Hedda and Richard Rogers his young son (from whose head the legendary apple was shot in the opening story); the splendidly bulky Willoughby Goddard played the hero's main protagonist, Landburgher Gessler, and Nigel Greene turned up in a few episodes as Tell's uneasy ally, a robber known as 'The Bear'. The 39 eps. × half-hour were filmed at National Studios and on location among the snow-clad mountains in Wales for producer Ralph Smart. An international co-production (Britain, France, USA) series, **William Tell** (Crossbow Films–FR3–Cinecom–Centre National de la Cinématograph–Robert Halmi–Hal Roach Studios, 1989–90), was produced in the late 1980s with Will Lyman as Tell and Jeremy Clyde as the sinister Gessler; Conrad Phillips even turned up as guest.

African Patrol
(Gross-Krasne Prods.–Kenya Prods., 1958–59)

Policing the East African territory of Kenya was the theme and setting for this rather uninspired action-adventure series. John Bentley (*pictured*) played Patrol Inspector Paul Derek, a straight-arrow safari sheriff who marched almost robot-like through the exotic scenery (filmed on location in the Kenya game reserve) and the sub-par plots; a single note of quality being the impressive African wildlife photography injected into the scenes. Thirty-nine half-hour episodes were produced.

The Black and White Minstrel Show
(BBC-tv, 1958–78)

Was devised and produced by George Inns, and featured the Mitchell Minstrels (with solo performers Tony Mercer, Dai Francis, and John Boulter), conducted by George Mitchell, and the Television Toppers dance troupe. Lightweight moments were provided in the 45-minute, non-stop format by Leslie Crowther, George Chisholm, and Stan Stennett during the early years. The mainstay was the singalong medley of tunes, ranging from Mississippi melodies to Country-and-Western ditties, that were possibly pensionable at the birth of the horseless carriage. A year before the show was first shown George Inns had produced the **1957 Television Minstrels** (BBC-tv, 2/9/57) as a part of the 1957 National Radio Show at the Earls Court Exhibition Hall, London, with George Mitchell's Minstrels and the Television Toppers filling the hour broadcast. **The George Mitchell Glee Club** (BBC-tv, 1957–58) also featured the powerful vocals of Tony Mercer and Dai Francis. **The Black and White Minstrel Show** drew to a close when it became obvious, if not offensive, that the Minstrels' black-face performance was becoming increasingly outmoded in a multiracial culture. Pictured are the Mitchell Minstrels and the Television Toppers.

Blue Peter
(BBC-tv/BBC-1, 1958–)

Originally listed under the **Children's Television** banner, this highly popular magazine programme for junior school-aged children was devised and produced as a 15-minute programme by John Hunter Blair and, in its early years, was presented by Christopher Trace and Leila Williams (*pictured*). It later became a half-hour series, with presenter Valerie Singleton joining Trace (following Williams's departure) in 1962; Peter Purves replaced Trace in 1967. More than a dozen other presenters have appeared on the programme since that time. Petra, the programme's famous showcase pet dog, came on board in 1962 and was one of its most popular fixtures until 1977. Hyperactive co-presenter John Noakes appeared in 1965 and took on almost every hazardous and madcap assignment the producers could dish out, usually in the bounding company of his TV pet dog Shep. He left the series in 1979 after doubling as presenter with his own spin-off series, **Go With Noakes** (BBC-1, 1976–80). 'Biddy' Baxter was the long-term guiding spirit behind the programme as series editor until her retirement in 1988.

Cheyenne
(Warner Bros. TV; ITV tx 1958–)

The post-Civil War adventures of fast-on-the draw drifter Cheyenne Bodie (Clint Walker; *pictured*) was the thread running through this 'adult' Western drama. Walker's contractual disagreement with his WB studio bosses saw him walk out on the series and have the programme slot replaced by **Bronco** (WB TV; BBC TV tx 1959) in which Ty Hardin starred as another drifter, Bronco Laine. (**Cheyenne** US tx 1955–62; **Bronco** US tx 1958–62).

Dial 999
(Towers of London Prod.-Ziv TV, 1958–59)

Streets-of-London crime drama with Canadian actor Robert Beatty (shown getting a slugging from Raf de la Torre) as Det. Insp. Mike Maguire, a Canadian Mountie assigned to Scotland Yard to study detection methods. Filmed on location around London and at the Associated British Film Studios at Elstree, this *policier* came across as a fairly rough and rugged detective story with plots suggesting that it takes a clenched-fist Canadian copper to clean up London's underworld. Harry Alan Towers produced the 39 eps. × half-hour series.

Dick and the Duchess
(A-R/Sheldon Reynolds, 1958–59)

Made-in-England filmed sitcom series featuring the tribulations of a young American insurance investigator, Dick Starrett (Patrick O'Neal; *right*), assigned to his company's London office and married to Jane (Hazel Court; *left*), the daughter of a British peer. Richard Wattis appeared as his London colleague. Hollywood screenwriter Harry Kurnitz supplied the half-hour scripts for producer-director Reynolds. Guest Eugene Deckers is centre.

Dotto
(ATV, 1958–60)

Early ITV quiz show presenting a game in which two contestants each face a screen which conceals, in fifty dots, the portrait of a personality. When the contestant gives the correct answer the appropriate number of dots is filled in. The contestant who first identified the personality received £5 for every dot *not* filled in. Robert Gladwell (*pictured, centre, with two contestants*) presided; later hosted by Shaw Taylor. John Irwin produced.

Educating Archie
(A-R, 1958–59)

Brought long-time radio personality Archie Andrews (a ventriloquist's dummy; *centre*) and his human partner Peter Brough (*left*) to ITV with this half-hour comedy series written by Marty Feldman & Ronald Chesney and Barry Pevan. Irene Handl, Dick Emery, and Freddie Sales (*right*) were the series regulars. The programme was shot on film to safeguard the effects that gave Archie the illusion of movement. Christopher Hodson directed. BBC TV had earlier presented **Here's Archie** (BBC-tv, 1956), featuring Archie and Peter Brough in a series of 15-minute comedies scripted by Ronnie Wolfe and John Waterhouse, with guests Ronald Chesney and Irene Handl; the programme was produced by John Warrington.

1958

The Government Inspector
(BBC-tv, 9/2/58)

Was a 75-minute play produced under the **Television World Theatre** (BBC-tv, 1957–58) banner and featured Tony Hancock (*right*) in his first straight role as Hlestakov, the man mistaken for the Government Inspector when he comes to a backwoods village in Russia. The play was adapted by Barry Thomas from the English version by D. F. Campbell of the Nikolai Gogol novel and produced by Alan Bromly; (*l. to r.*) Susan Maryott, Helen Christie, and John Phillips also appeared. **Television World Theatre** also presented productions of 'The Life of Henry the Fifth' (29/12/57; pr. Peter Dews) with John Neville and Bernard Hepton; 'The Cherry Orchard' (5/1/58; pr. Harold Clayton) with Nora Swinburne and Paul Rogers; and 'The Dark is Light Enough' (26/1/58; wr. Christopher Fry, pr. Stuart Burge) with Edith Evans.

Grandstand
(BBC-tv, 1958–)

Remains the world's longest-running live sports series presenting a non-stop Saturday afternoon sports service, including football news flashes, half-time scores, and up-to-the-minute racing service and starting prices. Originally, the various outside broadcasts were linked from Lime Grove studios by Peter Dimmock who was the presenter for only two weeks, deputizing for David Coleman (*pictured*) who introduced the programme until Frank Bough took over in 1968. Peter O'Sullevan and Clive Graham were the commentating team on horse-racing, Tim Gudgin read the racing results, and Leonard Martin read the football results. The première studio presentation was by Bryan Cowgill and programme editor was Paul Fox. **Sunday Grandstand** started in 1981 on BBC-2.

The Invisible Man
(Official Films–ITP, 1958–59)

Dr Peter Brady is a scientist conducting experiments regarding the refraction of light when a laboratory accident results in his becoming invisible. Following the authorities' initial suspicion and puzzlement he is allowed to continue his experiments (still invisible) to reverse the situation while acting as an unseen do-gooder for various government and police departments. The stories were usually gossamer thin and the series depended on the novelty value of its special effects: the sight of a driverless car in motion, doors opening and closing themselves, an unseen hand dialling a phone number, and the obligatory fist-fight with the impact felt rather than seen. His regular companions were his widowed sister (Lisa Daniely) and his young niece (Deborah Watling); the part of Brady was anonymous in the credits (Tim Turner supplied the voice). The 26 eps. × half-hour were produced by Ralph Smart; Aida Young was the production supervisor. On-screen titles were given as **H. G. Wells' The Invisible Man** (suggested for TV by Larry White). The scene pictured is from 'The Rocket' episode with guest Jennifer Wright.

Ivanhoe
(Sydney Box Prods.–Screen Gems/ITC, 1958)

Roger Moore made his British TV series debut in this costume action-adventure featuring the noble exploits of Sir Walter Scott's Ivanhoe during the reign of Prince John. The series, filmed at Beaconfield Studios, had all the rousing ingredients for this type of programme, with well-handled swordfight scenes and stunts, an energetic hero, and above-average outdoor photography. Robert Brown (as the squire Gurth) and John Pike (the squire's son Bart) were the hero's regular companions; Andrew Keir played the recurring villain Prince John. The 39 eps. × half-hour series was produced by Bernard Coote and Herbert Smith. Moore (*right*) and Brown (*left*) are pictured with guest villain Anthony Dawson. A BBC TV serialization, in ten 25-minute parts, was presented in 1970, under the title **Ivanhoe** (BBC-1, 4/1–8/3/70), featuring Eric Flynn in the title role; David Maloney directed Alexander Baron's script for producers Campbell Logan and John McRae.

Land of Song
(TWW, 1958–64)

A Welsh-styled music programme featuring baritone Ivor Emmanuel and soprano Mary Thomas, with Marian Davies, Janice Thomas, and Sian Hopkins, usually accompanied by the Pontcanna Children's Choir or a male-voice choir. Christopher Mercer produced the popular Sunday evening series for the TWW Welsh Language Network. Emmanuel is pictured with Pontcanna Children's Choir.

The Larkins
(ATV, 1958–60; 1963–64)

Were the rumbustious cockney family full of farcical situations, headed by the henpecked, but cunning, husband, Alf (played by David Kossoff; *2nd right*), and the burly, bossy wife, Ada (Peggy Mount; *seated right*). The other regulars were Shaun O'Riordan (*2nd left*) as son Eddie, Ronan O'Casey (*centre*) as son-in-law Jeff Roger, Ruth Trouncer (*left*) as daughter Joyce Roger, and Hilary Bamberger as girl-next-door Myrtle Prout (Barbara Mitchell also appeared as snooping neighbour Hetty Prout). The highly popular-for-the-period sitcom was created and written by Fred Robinson and produced by Alan Tarrant. A feature film spin-off, *Inn for Trouble*, was produced by Film Locations in 1959.

Martin Kane, Private Investigator
(Towers of London–Ziv TV; ITV tx 1958–59)

This private detective character first appeared on live American TV in 1949, played by William Gargan, and set his base of operations in New York. Lloyd Nolan, Lee Tracy, and Mark Stevens, respectively, played the role between 1951 and 1954 before Gargan (*pictured*) returned to the part for a syndicated, European-filmed series in 1957. Originally titled **The New Adventures of Martin Kane**, Kane now did his sleuthing from a London base assisting Scotland Yard Supt. Page (Brian Reece) for thirty-nine half-hour cops-and-robbers chase adventures. Harry Alan Towers produced.

Monitor
(BBC-tv, 1958–65)

A long-running minority-audience programme that took in all the arts though it is best remembered, perhaps, for its series of TV film biographies of classical composers by director Ken Russell. 'Elgar' (11/11/62), written and directed by Russell, was the first of the full-length biographies and also marked the 100th edition of **Monitor**. Later there came 'The Debussy Film' (18/5/65), with Oliver Reed and Vladek Sheybal, co-scripted with Melvyn Bragg; also a film about artist-painter Henry 'Douanier' Rousseau, 'Always on Sunday' (29/6/65), again co-scripted with Bragg. In addition, Russell put his mark on 'Cranks at Work' (24/4/60), about John Cranko, choreographer, 'The Miner's Picnic' (brass band carnival), 'Shelagh Delaney's Salford', 'Prokofiev', 'Pop Goes the Easel', 'Watch the Birdie' (photographer David Hurn), and 'Bela Bartok' (24/5/64). Director John Schlesinger's 'Circus' (2/2/58) premièred the series; Schlesinger also worked on the editions 'Benjamin Britten', 'Innocent Eye', 'The Class', and others between 1958 and 1960. The programme was, for the most part, hosted by Huw Wheldon, whose studied relaxation became a part of the series image. Peter Newington was the original producer. The programme's general format was later revived in the shape of **Omnibus**. Pictured (*l. to r.*) are Huw Wheldon, Ken Russell, and Peter Cantor (film editor).

1958

Oh Boy!
(ABC TV, 1958–59)

Was a half-hour powerhouse of non-stop 1950s rock 'n' roll presented, initially, from the stage of the Wood Green Empire in front of a live and suitably hysterical audience. The early resident line-up consisted of the groups the John Barry Seven and Lord Rockingham's XI, the vocal groups the Dallas Boys and Neville Taylor's Cutters, and the dancing-singing Vernons Girls. Popular guest performers of the time included Marty Wilde, Cliff Richard, (*pictured*) and the Drifters (the latter soon to become the Shadows), Vince Eager, tenor sax player Red Price, 'Cuddly' Dudley, and Emile Ford. **Oh Boy!** creator-producer Jack Good went on to present the equally lively sequels **Boy Meets Girls** (ABC TV, 1959–60), with Marty Wilde (who also presented), Terry Dene, Gene Vincent, Little Tony, Freddy Cannon, Adam Faith, and Joe Brown; and **Wham!!** (ABC TV, 1960), adding the likes of Jess Conrad, Billy Fury, Johnny Kidd and the Pirates, and Dickie Pride to the on-stage rockers. The Vernons Girls, in various forms and line-ups, appeared throughout all the programmes; Keith Fordyce introduced the latter series. The original 1950s format was revived some twenty years later, again as **Oh Boy!** (ATV, 1979–80), with the regulars now including Joe Brown, Les Gray, Freddie 'Fingers' Lee, Alvin Stardust, Shakin' Stevens, and Fumble. Richard Leyland and Ken O'Neill produced the rockin' half-hours.

Private Investigator
(BBC-tv, 1958–59)

Was a series of dramatized documentaries about the work of an English detective agency and the fictitious private investigator John Unthank (Campbell Singer; *left*). Written and produced by Arthur Swinson, the 9 eps. × 30 mins. series featured the various cases (with clients ranging from wealthy company directors to an official of the National Canine Defence League!) of the smart and polished Unthank as he tracked down the missing and the lost, unmasked the villainous, and cleaned out the corrupt. Writer Swinson carried out his research into areas of police procedure and other legal territories through the help of a group called Q-Men, an organization of ex-Scotland Yard detectives. Unthank's team of regulars were played by Ursula Camm, Douglas Muir (*back to camera*), Ian White (*2nd left*), and Allan McClelland (*right*). David Graham (*centre*) also appeared in 'The Latin Triangle' episode.

Quatermass and the Pit
(BBC-tv, 22/12/58–26/1/59)

The third and last of the 1950s Quatermass serials was perhaps the spookiest of them all. The 6 eps. × 30/35 mins. serial, starring André Morell (*left*) as Professor Quatermass, centred on the discovery of a buried, 5 million-year-old Martian spacecraft and its long-dead inhabitants, from which an evil influence still exudes. Written by Nigel Kneale as a combination of supernatural hysteria and science fantasy ancestry, the mood-drenched drama excelled in eerie sound and visual effects. Cec Linder, Christine Finn, John Stratton, Anthony Bushell (*right*) and Michael Ripper also appeared; Rudolph Cartier produced.

Sammy
(BBC-tv, 26/3/58)

A gripping one-man play written and produced by Ken Hughes featuring Anthony Newley as Sammy Ellerman, a flat-broke character who, alone in his room, has three hours in which to raise £200 to pay off his debts to a menacing bookie or end up in the casualty ward. Starting from scratch, he sets about making the money through a series of complicated transactions over the telephone, eventually building up to the required total but with only a short time for the cash to reach him before the heavies arrive. A nerve-stretching 40-minute drama, laden with breaking-point tension but laced with appropriate pathos and humour, and a masterful solo performance by Newley. Later in the same year American NBC TV presented 'Eddie' (via **Alcoa Theatre** ep. 17/11/58), co-scripted by American Alfred Brenner and Hughes (and dir. Jack Smight), starring Mickey Rooney in the Newley/Sammy role.

Saturday Playhouse
(BBC-tv, 1958–61)

Was a popular showcase for such theatre-originated works as 'Britannia of Billingsgate' (15/2/58), by Sewell Stokes and Christine Jope-Slade, produced by Adrian Brown, and starring Hermione Baddeley and George Coulouris; and Emlyn Williams's 'The Corn is Green' (1/3/58), starring Joan Miller and produced by David J. Thomas from the BBC's Welsh TV studio. The scene pictured is from Terence Rattigan's 'French Without Tears' (7/6/58), produced by Ronald Eyre and featuring Denholm Elliott (as the Hon. Alan Howard) and Patricia Raine (as Diana Lake).

Sea Hunt
(Ziv-UA TV; ITV tx 1958–)

Lloyd Bridges (*pictured*) starred in this underwater adventure series as Mike Nelson, a freelance aquanaut who was hired on research expeditions, rescue missions, in fact anything below sea-level. Extremely popular at the time, this half-hour series was to coral what **Highway Patrol** was to asphalt. (US tx 1958–61)

Sword of Freedom
(Weinstein Prods./Sapphire Films, 1958–60)

Florence during the period of the Renaissance was the setting for this swashbuckling adventure series produced by Sidney Cole for executive producer Hannah Weinstein. American actor Edmund Purdom (*far right*) appeared as artist-freedom fighter Marco del Monte, assisted by his model Angelica (played by Adrienne Corri) and sturdy companion Sandro (Rowland Bartrop), who gets involved in all manner of intrigue in his constant battle to outwit the evil influences of the wicked de Medicis and Machiavelli. American writers Ring Lardner Jr. and Ian McLellan Hunter wrote the pilot episode 'Francesca' under the name of Lewis Ishart; they also composed the episode 'Choice of Weapons' in which Leonardo da Vinci displays his latest invention, the world's first machine-gun! In all 39 eps. × half-hour were produced; the series was originally to be called **The Florentine**. The scene pictured is from 'The Value of Paper' episode with (*foreground, l. to r.*) Brian Haines, Jennifer Jayne, John Longden, and Purdom.

This Wonderful World
(Scottish TV, 1958–65)

Fascinating human observation and documentary series arranged and presented by documentary film pioneer John Grierson (*pictured*). Originally produced by Rai Purdy. Grierson later introduced **John Grierson Presents** (Scottish TV, 1966), showing the work of new film producers from home and abroad.

1958

Wagon Train

(Revue/MCA; ITV tx 1958–)

The action-drama stories involving the journey of a wagon train from St Joseph, Missouri, to California in the late 1860s was the theme of this 'Wagons Ho!' series. Ward Bond starred as wagon master Major Seth Adams (later John McIntire as Chris Hale), with Robert Horton as trail scout Flint McCullough, Frank McGrath as cook Charlie Wooster, and Terry Wilson as assistant wagon master Bill Hawks. Indian raids, outlaws, and various natural disasters made up the multiple plot elements; two episodes of note were 'A Man Called Horse' by Dorothy M. Johnson (starring Ralph Meeker) and 'The Colter Craven Story' (directed by John Ford and featuring John Carradine and John Wayne as guests). BBC TV acquired the series in 1962. The scene pictured shows (*l. to r.*) guest Ricardo Montalban, Horton, and Bond in 'The Jean LeBec Story' episode. (US tx 1957–65).

White Hunter

(Beaconsfield Prods.–ITP, 1958–60)

The adventurous life of John A. Hunter (big-game hunter and author of *African Safari* and *Hunter's Tracks*) formed the basis for this jungle trek action drama. Filmed, like **African Patrol**, in East Africa, the series starred Rhodes Reason in the title role, acting as safari guide and game warden to various wayward travellers; when the stories started to flag there was always a charging rhino, a prowling lion, or a group of dancing natives to boost the excitement (39 eps. × half-hour). Reason is pictured (*left foreground*) with Howard Lang (*centre*) and Harry Baird (*right*).

Yesterday's Enemy

(BBC-tv, 14/10/58)

Featured a straggling British unit who stumble across a vital piece of military information in an enemy compound in the heart of the Burmese jungle in 1942 when the British army was retreating before the Japanese advance. Gordon Jackson (*left*) played Sgt. Ian McKenzie and Alex Scott (*right*) was the Captain; supporting players included Barry Foster, Alan Rowe, Terence Brook, Burt Kwouk, and Lee Montague. Peter R. Newman's script was produced by Chloe Gibson; John Cooper was the designer. The story was filmed by Hammer Films in 1959, with Jackson repeating his original role.

Your Life in Their Hands

(BBC-tv, 1958–64; BBC-2, 1980–86; 1991)

A controversial series of 30-minute programmes that took viewers inside hospitals and, in particular, operating theatres. Intended as an update on the techniques of modern medicine and as a kind of PR job for the medical profession, the BBC used up to six cameras (recording on video tape by a mobile unit) to observe everything from the treatment of gallstones to open heart surgery (the latter in alarming close-up). Consultant physician for the early programmes was Dr Charles Fletcher. Bill Duncalf, Peter Bruce, and Humphrey Fisher were the original producers; John Mansfield and Fiona Holmes produced the BBC-2 series. The 1980s series, originally with narration by Robert Winston under producer Fiona Holmes, was shown in heart-warming colour! An additional 5 eps. × 50-mins. were shown in 1991 (26/4–24/5/91), produced by Stephen Rose.

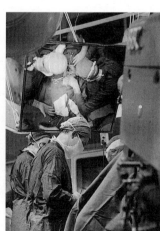

Drumbeat
(BBC-tv, 1959)

Was another early teen show following on from **Six-Five Special** which tried to keep in touch with the changing flow of popular music. **Drumbeat** was announced as 'thirty fast-moving minutes of music in the ultra-modern manner . . . Off- and On-Beat singers, Pop-Beat disc stars, and Down-Beat bands will all be there at 6.30 every Saturday'. Hosted by Gus Goodwin and later by Trevor Peacock, the show featured performances by such contemporary favourites as Bob Miller and the Millermen, the John Barry Seven (*pictured*, with John Barry, *left foreground*), Adam Faith, Vince Eager, and Marty Wilde. The programme was produced by Stewart Morris.

Face to Face
(BBC-tv, 1959–62)

Presented one of the most searching interview programmes on British television, with John Freeman as the permanent inquisitor. Among the more memorable guests who were subjected to the 15-minute (later 30-minute) grilling were Adam Faith (11/12/60; *pictured*), Dame Edith Sitwell (6/5/59), Dr Martin Luther King (29/10/61), Professor Carl Jung (22/11/59), Tony Hancock (7/2/60), and, perhaps the most famous interview, Gilbert Harding (18/9/60), who nearly broke down due to Freeman's relentless probing. Hugh Burnett produced; many editions opened and closed with distinctive charcoal drawings of the week's subject drawn by Feliks Topolski.

The Four Just Men
(Sapphire Films, 1959–60)

Based on the novel by Edgar Wallace, first published in 1906, and produced by Hannah Weinstein, this action-drama series featured the crime-busting exploits of four former wartime colleagues who once again banded together to combat evil and fight injustice as self-styled crusaders of law and order. Reunited at the bequest of their late wartime commander (played in an opening flashback by Anthony Bushell), the just four consisted of Tim Collier (Dan Dailey; *2nd right*), a Paris-based US correspondent, Ricco Poccari (Vittorio De Sica; *2nd left*), a wealthy Italian hotelier, Jeff Ryder (Richard Conte; *right*), a prominent New York attorney, and Ben Manfred (Jack Hawkins; *left*), an independent Member of Parliament. Their adventures were spread across the principal characters' home bases (Paris, Rome, New York, London) with each of the four stars appearing in separate episodes; John Collier, T. E. B. Clarke, and Leon Griffiths contributed scripts, but much of the writing was done behind 'front' names by Ring Lardner Jr. and (an unofficial story consultant) Ian McLellan Hunter. Basil Dearden, Don Chaffey, and Harry Watt were prominent among the directors for the 39 eps. × half-hour series.

Garry Halliday
(BBC-tv, 1959–62)

Was a pilot of a commercial airline company who, like Biggles, flew from one aeronautical adventure to another. Terence Longdon starred as the able-bodied aviator of the title, assisted by Ann Gudrun and Terence Alexander. Real-life Silver City Airways assisted in the production of the series, transforming part of their Ferryfield Airport at Lydd, Kent, into suitable location settings. The half-hour series was produced by Richard West. Pictured are (*l. to r.*) Alexander, Juno Stevas, and Longdon.

1959

Interpol Calling
(Rank-Wrather Corp./ATV, 1959–60)

A highly charged crime series based on the files of the International Criminal Police Organisation with Charles Korvin (*pictured, right*; followed by Richard Leech) as Inspector Duval and partner Edwin Richfield (Inspector Mornay) involved in, largely, European murder, robbery, forgery, and narcotics busting. Signalling the action to come, the series always opened with the subjective viewpoint of a speeding driver crashing a checkpoint and being fired upon by border guards. The stories usually did not let up from there. The Rank co-production made the most of its vast European facilities, placing the series several notches above similar programmes of the period. The 39 eps. × half-hour series was produced by Anthony Perry and Connery Chapel.

Juke Box Jury
(BBC-tv, 1959–67; BBC-1, 1979; BBC-2, 1989; BBC-2/Noel Gay Production, 1990)

Devised by Peter Potter, this popular, contemporary music series featured a celebrity panel of guests giving their verdict to David Jacobs (*pictured* 'in the chair') on a selection of the latest pop releases; Jacobs's ring on a bell signalled a hit, a rasping hooter registered a miss. Starting originally on Mondays but soon switching to its famous Saturday slot, the programme's première panel consisted of singer Alma Cogan, DJ Pete Murray, singer Gary Miller, and young Susan Stranks (as 'a typical teenager'; she later became presenter on Thames TV's **Magpie**); Katie Boyle was a regular panel guest during the 1960s and, in a 1963 edition, all four Beatles made up the jury. The show has been revived for short stints in more recent years; chaired by Noel Edmonds (1979) and later Jools Holland (1989–90).

Jungle Boy
(Gross-Krasne Prod., 1959)

An adventure series filmed in East Africa by producer-director George Breakston about a boy (played by Michael Carr Hartley) who had been orphaned when his parents failed to return from a trip into the jungle. He lived in a tree-top hut made of bamboo cane and leaves. His companions included Simba, a lion cub, Quaggo, a young zebra, and Cheetah, a sleek, fully grown jungle cat. Thirty-nine half-hour episodes were produced. Also known as **Adventures of a Jungle Boy**.

The Ken Dodd Show
(BBC-tv, 1959–63; BBC-1, 1966)

Liverpudlian comedian Ken Dodd, like Hill, Drake, Howerd, and others, was largely a product of 1960s TV comedy specials and series through which he made popular his trademark mop of unruly hair, tombstone teeth, and a gallery of bizarre characters, supposedly cute, called the 'Diddy' people. Also, like later comedian Des O'Connor, Dodd punctuated his comedy routines with sentimental ditties that usually went on to become record chart-toppers. Among his other TV appearances were **Ken Dodd** (BBC-1, 9/1–27/2/72), **Ken Dodd in 'Funny You Should Say That . . .'** (ATV, 8/4–13/5/72), **Ken Dodd's World of Laughter** (BBC-1, 1974–76), **The Ken Dodd Laughter Show** (Thames TV, 8/1–12/2/79), and **Ken Dodd's Showbiz** (BBC-1, 13/3–17/4/82). Dodd also appeared (out of his usual idiot character) as Tollmaster in the three-part **Doctor Who** serial 'Delta and the Bannermen' (2–16/11/87). Pictured are (*l. to r.*) Dodd's guest judo expert and TV personality Alex Mackintosh, Ken Dodd, and judo tutor Senta Yamada.

78

Knight Errant '59
(Granada TV, 1959)

An adventurer-for-hire drama series in the Thin Man mould featuring the mystery-solving exploits of Adam Knight (played by John Turner) and his original two partners, Liz Parrish (Kay Callard) and Peter Parker (Richard Carpenter). Changing with the times, the series became **Knight Errant '60** (Granada TV, 1960) and later **Knight Errant Limited** (Granada TV, 1960–61), with the final format front-lined by investigators Hugh David, Wendy Williams, and Kay Callard (reintroduced in her original newspaper woman role). Warren Jenkins and Kitty Black produced. John Turner is pictured in an early publicity shot.

Maverick
(Warner Bros. TV; ITV tx 1959–)

The tongue-in-cheek Western misadventures of gambler Bret Maverick (played by James Garner; *left*) were immortalized in this hour-long drama series. Bret alternated weekly capers with brother Bart (Jack Kelly; *right*); later replaced by another brother Brent (Robert Colbert) and English cousin Beau (Roger Moore). Garner's almost artistic less-than-heroic hero persona, however, reached fruition with his 1974–80 private eye series, **The Rockford Files** (tx BBC TV). (US tx 1957–62)

Morning in the Streets
(BBC-tv, 25/3/59)

Producer Denis Mitchell was probably the outstanding TV documentarist of his day, heading up an educational and informational collection of highly regarded programmes of which his impressionistic observation of a northern industrial town at dawn was, reputedly, his personal favourite. The basic production team for this BBC TV Northern Film Unit documentary consisted of film editor Donald James and photographers Roy Harris, Gerry Pullen, Graham Turner, and Ted Wallbank; the dawn-of-day soundtrack melody on solo harmonica was by Tommy Reilly. Mitchell and Harris directed. Among his many non-fiction TV programmes and series, whether using the technique of sound applied to unrelated visuals or straight married sound, Mitchell excelled with such works as **A Soho Story** (BBC-tv, 22/4/59), focusing on London's most cosmopolitan quarter, **Wind of Change** (BBC-tv, 10–11–12/4/60), featuring three filmed reports on Africa, **Chicago—Portrait of a City** (BBC-tv, 21/2/61), made with the collaboration of the American ABC TV network, **A Wedding on Saturday** (Granada TV, 1/4/64), set in a Yorkshire mining community, and **Seven Men** (Granada TV, 1971), a seven-part series of profiles on Michael Burn, Quentin Crisp, Rene Cutforth, Douglas Glass, Ivor Montagu, Frank Shaw, and Commander Charles Drage; the 'Quentin Crisp' part was originally produced as a segment (tx 6/7/70) of Granada's **World in Action**.

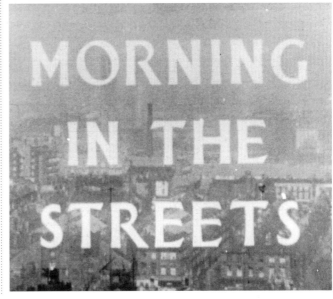

No Hiding Place
(A-R, 1959–67)

Was perhaps ITV's best-known early police drama series, starring Raymond Francis (*left*) as Chief Det. Supt. Lockhart. Lockhart's popularity with the TV audience had grown from two earlier series. **Murder Bag** (A-R, 1957–59) introduced Francis's Lockhart (then a Det. Supt.) in this 55 eps. × half-hour series of formula police investigation casebooks created by Glyn Davies and produced by Barry Baker. This series developed a follow-up in the form of **Crime Sheet** (A-R, 1959) in which Lockhart was promoted and his activities broadened to encompass a wider range of criminal investigation; Barry Baker produced the seventeen half-hour episodes. **No Hiding Place** followed. During the course of Lockhart's 236 hour-long cases he was assisted by Det. Sgt. Baxter (Eric Lander), Det. Sgt. Russell (Johnny Briggs), Det. Sgt. Perryman (Michael McStay), and Det. Sgt. Gregg (Sean Caffrey; *pictured right*). One particular episode, 'The Most Beautiful Room in the World' (25/9/62; wr. Peter Miller and James Kelly, dir. Richard Doubleday), brought together Francis/Lockhart, Lander/Baxter, Russell/York, and **Top Secret**'s counter-espionage chief Miguel Garetta, played again by Patrick Cargill. Francis's Lockhart also turned up in a holiday season play called *Deep and Crisp and Stolen* (Rediffusion, 21/12/64), a 90-minute comedy about a plot to rob a department store on Christmas Eve; Ronald Marriott directed Dave Freeman's script. Ray Dicks, Richard Matthews, Johnny Goodman, Peter Willes, Geoffrey Nugus, and Michael Currer-Briggs produced the series, respectively. As a footnote, Eric Lander's Det. Sgt. Baxter moved over to another London police division (using unmarked patrol cars) and became Det. Insp. Baxter, assisted by Det. Sgt. York (Geoffrey Russell), for **Echo Four-Two** (A-R, 1961) in ten half-hour episodes produced by Richard Matthews.

Para Handy—Master Mariner
(BBC-tv, 1959–60)

This BBC Scotland comedy series became a popular Friday night item with viewers for its simple humour and colourful characters. Para Handy of the title (portrayed by Duncan Macrae; *far left*) was the skipper of a 'puffer,' a small cargo boat that operated as a merchantman along the West Coast of Scotland, called the *Vital Spark*. The half-hour stories followed the slightly less-than-legit adventures of her crew (*2nd l. to r.*, John Grieve as Macphail, Roddy McMillan as Dougie, Angus Lennie as Sunny Jim) as they plied their coasting trade. The stories, scripted by Duncan Ross, were based on a 1905 *Glasgow Evening News* series written by Neil Munro under the pen-name of 'Hugh Foulis'; Pharic Maclaren produced. Five years later **Comedy Playhouse** presented a revival episode called 'The Vital Spark' (12/8/65; wr. Bill Craig, pr. Pharic Maclaren) which launched another series, **The Vital Spark** (BBC-1, 1966–67; 1974) featuring Roddy McMillan as Para Handy (son of Sandy), John Grieve, Walter Carr (as Dougie; played by Robert Urquhart in the pilot episode), and Alex McAvoy (as Sunny Jim). An additional six episodes (× 30 mins.) were made in 1974 and transmitted on BBC-2.

Probation Officer
(ATV, 1959–62)

Spotlighted the drama of the men and women who give service to the welfare of those people put in their charge by the courts. The 55-minute stories dealt with themes ranging from teenage drug users to the racial problems then making the headlines in London's Notting Hill and still managed to project a documentary flavour into the activities. The original three principal characters were played by John Paul, David Davies, and Honor Blackman; the later series featured Jessica Spencer as a stalwart probation woman. Antony Kearey and Royston Morley produced the early series. **Hard Cases** (Central TV, 1988–89) also presented dramas revolving around the probation service; Phillip Bowman (later Andrew Benson) produced. John Paul (*right*) is pictured with guest offender Melvyn Hayes.

Rawhide
(CBS TV; ITV tx 1959–)

The 'head 'em up, move 'em out'
action-drama Western chronicles
of a band of drovers, led by trail
boss Gil Favor (Eric Fleming;
right), herding cattle along the
1870s Sedalia Trail. Favor's men
included ramrod Rowdy Yates
(Clint Eastwood, pictured with
guest Ruta Lee), trail-hand Pete
Nolan (Sheb Wooley), Wishbone
the cook (Paul Brinegar), and
cook's assistant Mushy (James
Murdock). Frankie Laine belted
out the title song ('Git those
doggies rollin' . . .'). (US tx
1959–66)

Redgauntlet
(BBC-tv, 11/10–15/11/59)

Six-part half-hour children's
adventure serial, adapted by E. J.
Bell from the novel by Sir Walter
Scott, was set in Scotland in the
days following Bonnie Prince
Charlie's defeat at the battle of
Culloden, and starred Tom
Fleming (*pictured*) as Redgauntlet
with John Cairney as Alan
Fairford; Kevin Sheldon produced.
Scottish TV later produced a
colour version, **Redgauntlet**
(Scottish TV, 7/1–25/2/70),
adapted by Ian Stuart Black and
featuring Jack Watson as the hero,
Redgauntlet, harrying the red
coats for the Stuart cause; these 8
eps. × half-hour were produced-
directed by Clarke Tait.

The Saga of Noggin the Nog
(BBC-tv, 1959–65; BBC-2, 1982)

The 10-minute per episode
cartoon adventures of Noggin the
Viking, Prince (later King) of the
Nogs and heir to the throne of the
Northlands, was the creation of
writer Oliver Postgate and artist
Peter Firmin (under their
Smallfilms company banner); told
by Ronnie Stevens and Postgate.
The amusing stories of Noggin's
voyages, his meeting with the not-
so-ferocious Ice Dragon, and the
dark deeds of his wicked uncle,
Nogbad the Bad, were popular
with the moppet masses. Postgate
and Firmin revived the character
for a short, colour-filmed series in
the early 1980s. Music was by
Vernon Elliott.

Skyport
(Granada TV, 1959–60)

Presented half-hour dramas set
against the background of a large
airport which tried to encompass
as many airline/airport elements
as possible. George Moon
(*pictured*) starred as an airport
travel agent, supported by Lisa
Gastoni, Gerald Harper, and
Barry Foster; fifty-two episodes
were produced.

Spycatcher
(BBC-tv, 1959–61)

Was based on the published wartime experiences of Allied counter-espionage wizard Lt.-Col. Oreste Pinto. The theme of the series was that with the German occupation of Europe there was a steady flow of refugees into Britain, all of whom had to be screened by Col. Pinto and his team of interrogators to prevent the infiltration of enemy spies. Bernard Archard (*left*) played Pinto as the relentless spycatcher who, generally through a bit of verbal psychological warfare, usually got his man; in one particular episode forcing a confession out of a spy by the simple means of using Hitler's portrait as a dartboard! The 19 eps. × 30-mins. series were produced by Terence Cook and written by Robert Barr. Harvey Hall (*right*) played a traitor in the episode 'Game, Set, and March'. On the ITV side, **Man Trap** (A-R, 17/9–29/10/56) was a half-hour series presenting tales of espionage from the Second World War with based-on-fact stories scripted, generally, by Jan Murray (one of the episodes, 'Phantom Refugees', was from a story by Pinto); Caryl Doncaster served as executive producer. **Secret Mission** (A-R, 5/11–17/12/56), with scripts by Robert Barr, featured more half-hour true stories this time about a group of women who served during the war in SOE.; Doncaster continued as executive producer.

Tell It To The Marines
(Jack Hylton TV Prod./A-R, 1959–60)

The traditional rivalry between the Royal Navy and the Marines provided the background for this early Jack Hylton-produced comedy series starring Alan White (*right*; as Leading Seaman White), Ronald Hines (Marine Cpl. Surtees), Ian MacNaughton (Dalrymple), Ian Whittaker (Whittle), Henry McGee (*left*; as Lt. Raleigh), and Jack Allen (Major Howard). The half-hour sitcom was written by Eric Paice and Malcolm Hulke; Ted Willis devised.

The Third Man
(Third Man Corp.–BBC-tv–NTA–British Lion, 1959–60)

An Anglo-American co-production derived from Graham Greene's original screenplay for the 1949 Carol Reed/Orson Welles film, it presented episodes filmed and produced in both Britain and the USA. The series went on to shuttle new episodes in and out of the BBC TV schedules (following its initial 1959–60 run) between 1962 and 1965. Michael Rennie was Harry Lime, not the cold-as-ice villain depicted in the film version but a well-tailored, wealthy businessman-adventurer who globe-trotted from one international intrigue to another on behalf of the underdog; he was assisted, for the most part, by his delightfully impassive personal secretary Bradford Webster (played by Jonathan Harris). As an episodic adventure/hero yarn the series was average for its type but its only true hold-over from the Greene-Reed-Welles original was the zither theme music. The TV format was generally based on the style of the 1951 Harry Alan Towers/Orson Welles-produced radio series, *The Adventures of Harry Lime*, with Welles in the title role playing it as a romantic rogue for the radio audience. The picture shows (*l. to r.*) guests Onslow Stevens and Robert Wilke with Rennie in the 'Trouble at Drill Hill' episode.

Whicker's World
(BBC-tv, 1959; BBC-1, 1965–68; Yorkshire TV, 1975–80; BBC-1, 1982; 1984–85; 1988)

Began as a 'quick look' back over the subjects of the series of films that travelling journalist Alan Whicker (*right, with microphone*) made for the **Tonight** programme during the 1950s with cameraman Cyril Moorhead and recordist Freddie Downton. Whicker's multiple other global travel reports included **Whicker Down Under** (BBC-tv, 1961), **Whicker on Top of the World** (BBC-tv, 1962), **Whicker Down Mexico Way** (BBC-tv, 1963), **Whicker's New World** (Yorkshire TV, 1969), **Whicker in Europe** (Yorkshire TV, 1969–70), **Whicker's Walkabout** (Yorkshire TV, 1970), **The World of Whicker** (Yorkshire TV, 1971), **Whicker's Orient** (Yorkshire TV, 1972), **Whicker Within a Woman's World** (Yorkshire TV, 1972), **Whicker's South Seas** (Yorkshire TV, 1973), **Whicker Way Out West** (Yorkshire TV, 1973), and **Around Whicker's World in 25 Years** (Yorkshire TV, 1982). One of his most famous reports came when he was allowed to interview the dictatorial 'spiritual leader' Dr François 'Papa Doc' Duvalier, then President of Haiti, for **Papa Doc—The Black Sheep** (Yorkshire TV, 17/6/69; pr.-dir. Michael Blakstad). In more recent years, he has presented **Whicker's World: A Taste of Spain** (BBC-1, 3/5–5/7/92) and the four-part **Around Whicker's World: The Ultimate Package!** (Yorkshire TV, 24/7–14/8/92).

Who, Me?
(BBC-tv, 15/10/59)

This programme reached the heights of great documentary drama, and was the outcome of the creative partnership of writer Colin Morris and producer-director Gilchrist Calder. The 55-minute play followed the interrogation of three robbery suspects by a shrewd Liverpool CID sergeant, resulting not only in a conviction but *en route* engaging in an amusing psychological confrontation between the policeman and his suspects. The featured players were (*l. to r.*) Lee Montague (as Det. Sgt. Tom Hitchin; based on retired Liverpool Det. Sgt. Bill Prendergast) and suspects (*foreground*) Maxwell Shaw, Jack Rodney, and Neil McCarthy. Brewster Mason and Lawrence James are in background.

World Theatre
(BBC-tv, 1959)

Presented a series of fortnightly plays (Tuesdays) designed primarily to catch the flavour of international playwriting. 'Julius Caesar' (5/5/59; 105 mins.), edited and produced by Stuart Burge, with Eric Porter (*right*), Michael Gough (*left*), and William Sylvester, launched the second series; 'Danton's Death' by German writer Georg Buechner, 'Blood Wedding' by Lorca, Ben Jonson's 'Volpone', Bertolt Brecht's 'Mother Courage', 'Henry IV' by Pirandello, and 'The School for Scandal' by Sheridan followed.

In the early 1960s the Pilkington Committee reported on the future of broadcasting. The committee, chaired by industrialist Sir Harry Pilkington, criticized the existing structure of ITV and recommended that it should be reorganized so that the independent companies should produce and sell programmes to the Authority and that the ITA should in turn schedule the programmes and sell advertising time. The report also proposed that the BBC should be authorized as soon as possible to provide a third television channel. Among its other recommendations were that the line definition standard in Britain should be changed from 405 lines to 625—the general standard used in Europe—and that a service of colour television on 625 lines, also in the ultra high frequency (UHF) bands, should be introduced as soon as possible.

In July 1962 the government published a White Paper on the Pilkington Report which approved a number of its recommendations. It was agreed that by 1964 the BBC should launch a second TV channel on 625 lines in UHF; the channel would be available first to the London area only, but it was expected to cover the whole of Britain by the year 1970. The go-ahead was also given for the development of colour television, and the BBC was authorized to establish a self-contained, distinctive Welsh TV service, to extend its broadcasting hours, and for the production of more educational programmes for adults.

The government published a second memorandum on the Pilkington Report in December 1962 outlining its views on the future of the ITA. The paper stated that statutory powers would be taken to strengthen the ITA's control over contracting companies, and that responsibility for approval and supervision of the buying and selling of programmes, and for the content and quality of the service as a whole would pass to the Authority. The government's view was that there was little evidence of public demand for a fourth channel, as a second commercial channel, and it was not satisfied that there would be sufficient advertising revenue to sustain two such channels adequately.

Three new ITV stations came into being during 1961; with Westward Television (from 29 April) serving south-west England, Border Television (from 1 September) for the Border region, and Grampian Television (from 30 September) for north Scotland. Channel Television, for the Channel Islands, followed on 1 September 1962; Wales-West and North from 14 September 1962. Border Television also serviced the Isle of Man from 26 March 1965.

In January 1964, Lord Hill of Luton, chairman of the ITA, announced administrative changes which ensured a tighter watch over ITV programmes and advertising and made clear that no changes would be made to the existing contractors from 1964 to 1967, when it was expected that a second ITV channel would be launched. The programme schedules of the companies would from then on be drawn up in consultation with the ITA. The ITA would have access to all advertisements before transmission, and all doubtful cases would be settled by a new committee under the chairmanship of the Authority. In February 1965 the government decided to end the advertising of cigarettes on television; in March the Postmaster-General announced that the ban would take effect from 1 August. In August 1965 also the ITA instructed the ITV companies that between 8.00 p.m. and 8.55 p.m. from Monday to Friday there should not be more than two out of five programmes of American origin, and not more than three should be crime dramas or Westerns.

The summer of 1967 saw the ITA announce the new independent television companies awarded contracts for six years as from July 1968. Three new ITV companies came into existence at this time: the London Television Consortium (to become London Weekend Television from 2 August 1968) which would take over weekend programming for the London area, Telefusion Yorkshire (to become Yorkshire Television from 29 July 1968), and the Harlech Consortium (to become HTV from 4 March 1968) which would replace TWW in Wales and part of the west of England. The London weekday contract went to a company, to be called Thames Television from 29 July 1968, formed by the amalgamation of Rediffusion and ABC TV, with ABC having the controlling interest. ATV, which had been serving the midlands during weekdays and London at weekends, received the full week contract for the midland region. All the other ITV companies had their contracts renewed.

Following the 1962 White Paper, BBC chairman Sir Arthur fforde announced in August 1962 that although cameras of 625 lines would first have to be installed, and an important series of UHF tests completed, it was hoped to start operating BBC's second channel, on 625 lines, in the London area by the beginning of April 1964. Trial transmission started in January 1964 with the intention of starting the full service in London and the south-east in April. The second channel was expected to be available for the midlands region, from the Sutton Coldfield Station, in April 1965, and by the end of that same year there would be ten UHF television stations providing the new programme to 60–70 per cent of the population of Britain.

The end of September 1963 saw the BBC launch a campaign to familiarize viewers with the new BBC-2 network, symbolized by an illustrated kangaroo character which appeared in a series of short trailers giving information about the new service. The second channel, BBC-2, opened on the 625-line system in the London area on 21 April 1964—twenty-four hours later than announced due to a power failure which effectively blacked out the launch of the infant channel. The delayed BBC-2 launch programmes included the 95-minute musical **Kiss Me, Kate** (a BBC TV production), with Patricia Morison and Howard Keel, and a programme featuring Soviet comedian Arkady Raikin.

The provisions within the 1962 White Paper for more educational television programmes echoed a growing interest in this field. The Institute for Educational Television had been formed in November 1961 with the aims of bringing together experts and teachers interested in visual aids to education, of becoming a reference bureau for the uses to which educational television had been put in Britain and overseas, and of encouraging various experiments.

The Glasgow Corporation educational television scheme, the largest closed circuit service of its kind in Europe at that time, began on 30 August 1965, with the first telerecorded programmes in French, geometry, arithmetic, and algebra transmitted to 300 schools. The relay was by direct cable to the schools with each receiver modified to show Glasgow ETV on 625 lines and BBC and ITV programmes on 405 lines.

Discussions on proposals for a 'University of the Air' led to a government announcement in September 1967 that it would create a new university institution to provide courses leading to degrees and other qualifications through a combination of television, radio, correspondence, tutorials, and local audio-visual centres. It was hoped that this **Open University** would be launched by autumn 1970 via BBC-2.

The advent of colour television, encouraged by the 1962 White Paper, was heralded by advances later that year. Following some two months of tests in their 625-line experimental service, radiating purely engineering information from Crystal Palace, BBC TV began in November 1962 to add full colour to some transmissions, broadcasting for 7½ hours a day, Monday to Friday. Although the American NTSC system was initially used, the BBC, in April 1963, began testing the French Secam colour system, in co-operation with the GPO, the ITA, and the radio industry. There was also interest in the PAL system, which was a modified version of the NTSC system produced by the Telefunken Company in Germany.

By early 1964 delegates from nineteen countries, after a ten-day meeting as the International Radio Consultative Committee (CCIR), were still undecided on the colour system standard for Europe; the British delegation had come out in favour of adopting the US NTSC system but most of the European representatives pressed for further study before they committed themselves. The BBC were disappointed they were unable to plan for colour television starting in 1965 as had been hoped. Various test transmissions and demonstrations were carried out in 1965 and 1966 but even so the European television representatives still failed to agree on a unified European colour system.

Meanwhile discussion and controversy continued on the allocation of colour television in Britain. Reviving an earlier technical proposal (described as 'sound on synchronized pulses'), the BBC planned to introduce a standardized 625-line system using the German PAL colour system which, it was hoped, might help to transfer BBC-1 and ITV from 405 lines to 625 thereby facilitating the provision of colour television on all channels. Following a limited colour service on BBC-2 from 1 July 1967 (5 hours a week), the colour service began officially on Saturday, 2 December 1967, with some 27 to 29 hours of colour per week. The 2 December launch of colour on BBC-2 included a visit to Billy Smart's Circus, the première episode of the serial **Vanity Fair**, **Whicker's World**, a couple of sports items, and **Late Night Line-Up**.

The programming trends of the 1960s ranged in popularity from the heights of drama (**The Wednesday Play**) to the extremes of escapism (**The Avengers**), with a new television comedy form (**Till Death Us Do Part**) edging in somewhere between the two.

The 'new wave' television drama area was represented, for the most part, by **The Wednesday Play**, BBC TV's controversial series of original plays written specifically for TV by new writers. Although **The Wednesday Play**'s ground-breaking inheritance came indirectly from **Armchair Theatre** (and the latter programme's Sydney Newman years in particular), the presentation of such outstanding plays as Jeremy Sandford's 'Cathy Come Home', Dennis Potter's 'Vote, Vote, Vote for Nigel Barton', and Nell Dunn's 'Up the Junction' won BBC TV both kudos and condemnation. Directly-to-the-point drama series such as **Z Cars**, **The Power Game**, and the later **Callan** offered weekly instalments of gritty, realistic, and perhaps at times overly negative characters and plots. A North Country-based twice-weekly serial, **Coronation Street**, took the so-called 'Kitchen Sink' drama style to new television dimensions and maintained a faithful audience at the top of the ratings for over thirty years.

The escapist element arrived in the mid-1960s, inspired by the sudden popularity of the spy/espionage genre, especially following the cinema success of the James Bond novels. One of the earliest and most bizarre of these was **The Avengers**, which had started out as a straightforward government agent drama (in a somewhat similar vein to **Danger Man**) before it became the inspiration for similar series that followed: **The Champions**, **The Prisoner**, **The Corridor People**.

Comedy and humour also reached a new peak with the programming of **That Was the Week That Was** (introducing satire to the general audience) and the controversial sitcom series of Galton & Simpson, **Steptoe and Son**, and Johnny Speight's **Till Death Us Do Part**. The mid-1960s off-the-wall comedy skits, **At Last the 1948 Show**, **Do Not Adjust Your Set**, and others, led to a new turning-point of TV comedy represented by **Monty Python's Flying Circus** at the end of the decade.

It may be significant to note that this new-found freedom of expression and creativity flourished under the Harold Wilson Labour Government (1964–70), which also heralded the 'Swinging London' years and its related youth industries (fashion, music, photography, design; itself fused into programmes like **Adam Adamant Lives!**).

An Age of Kings
(BBC-tv, 28/4–17/11/60; 15 parts × 60 mins.)

The opening play, 'Richard II', marked the sixtieth production of Shakespeare for BBC TV since the presentation of a 15-minute scene from **Henry V** in February 1937. Transmitted as a serial in fifteen parts, the five plays between them covered eighty-six years of British history and chronicled the rise and fall of seven monarchs before the overthrow of the last Plantagenet, Richard III, on Bosworth field. The serial began with the production of the first half of 'King Richard II'. A fortnight later the remainder of the play was shown, followed two weeks later by the beginning of 'Henry IV' (*pictured*; with Sean Connery and, *right*, Robert Hardy) and so on. Shakespeare's five plays 'Richard II', 'Henry IV', 'Henry V', 'Henry VI', and 'Richard III' put together this way told a continuous story, broken only by a short gap in time between the end of the play of 'Henry V', and the beginning of 'Henry VI'. The serial was produced by Peter Dews, directed by Michael Hayes, with title music by Sir Arthur Bliss.

All Our Yesterdays
(Granada TV, 1960–73; 1987–89)

The idea of this documentary series was to show newsreels from the same week twenty-five years ago, and to link them with a commentary by noted foreign correspondent James Cameron; Brian Inglis later took over and presented the programme throughout the 1960s. During the early, 20-minute per episode series the programme edited together the two weekly editions of the 1930s cinema newsreels to make a portrait of the week. Tim Hewat was the original producer. When the programme resumed in 1987, under producer Mike Murphy, it was presented by Bernard Braden and used footage from the film archives of Granada, ITN, and Pathe Newsreel. Inglis (*right*) is pictured with studio guest Terry Ashwood, a wartime newsreel cameraman.

Biggles
(Granada TV, 1960)

Was primarily a children's adventure series, transmitted in an early evening slot in twenty-eight half-hour episodes. Created by author Captain W. E. Johns as a sort of flying adventurer for the Air Police, Inspector Bigglesworth—better known as Biggles (Nevil Whiting; *centre*)—and his companions, Bertie and Ginger (played by David Drummond (*left*) and John Leyton (*right*), respectively), were conventional, old-style crook chasers whose adventures amused and excited the younger set. Harry Elton and Kitty Black produced.

Bonanza
(NBC TV; ITV tx 1960–)

Tales of the vast, sprawling Ponderosa Ranch near Virginia City during the 1860s with the all-male Cartwright clan, featuring Lorne Greene (*2nd left*) as father Ben and sons Adam (Pernell Roberts; *2nd right*), Hoss (Dan Blocker; *left*), and Little Joe (Michael Landon; *right*). The close-knit, Western family-ranch format also appeared in such later imported series as **The Big Valley** (via ITV), **Lancer**, and **The High Chaparral** (the latter two via BBC TV). (US tx 1959–73)

Bonehead
(BBC-tv, 1960–62)

Featured the 'silliest and least successful gang in the underworld' in a 25-minute comedy series written and produced by Shaun Sutton. The gang, whose efforts at forgery, smuggling, smash-and-grab, etc., all went disastrously wrong, consisted of (*l. to r.*) the mournful Happy (Douglas Blackwell), the dim-witted Bonehead (Colin Douglas), and the bulky Boss (Paul Whitsun-Jones).

The Charlie Drake Show
(BBC-tv, 1960–62; BBC-1, 1967–68)

The diminutive Drake's (*pictured*) fine line in slapstick and pathos continued in this half-hour series (after the 1959–60 **Charlie Drake** show), scripted by Drake and Richard Waring for producer Ronald Marsh. On the ITV side meanwhile, Drake was also featured in the comedy-music series titled (what else?) **The Charlie Drake Show** (ATV, 1963) under producer Colin Clews with scripts by Drake and partner Lewis Schwarz; a very young Olivia Hussey also appeared in some of the routines. For the early 1970s there was **Slapstick and Old Lace** (ATV, 4/3–15/4/71) in which Drake involved viewers in singalong songs and madcap sketches in his Imperial Vaudeville House at Elstree for seven half-hour episodes, produced-directed by Shaun O'Riordan with script and songs by Drake.

Citizen James
(BBC-tv, 1960–62)

After the demise of **Hancock's Half-Hour** Sidney James (*left*) branched out on his own in a Alan Simpson & Ray Galton-scripted comedy series called **Citizen James** (BBC-tv, 1960–62) in which he reprised his character role of the growling, fast-talking Cockney layabout, aided this time by girlfriend Liz Fraser and sidekick Bill Kerr; the series later changed format so that James became less of a layabout and more of a social do-gooder, assisted now by Sydney Tafler (*right*). The second series was written by the Sid Green & Dick Hills team. Duncan Wood produced the half-hour series.

Coronation Street
(Granada TV, 1960–)

Has been the most successful soap opera in the history of British prime-time television. The twice-weekly (three times a week from late 1989) half-hour instalments of continuing stories in the lives of working-class folk in a gloomy street in the north of England started out as a limited thirteen-episode series originally called 'Florizel Street' by the programme's creator Tony Warren. But with the rise of interest in northern-based drama during the early 1960s (popularized by such social realist films of the time as *Saturday Night and Sunday Morning*) the matter-of-fact characters and their gritty setting of **Coronation Street** became an instant hit. The original cast line-up included Violet Carson (*centre*; as Ena Sharples), Doris Speed (Annie Walker), Arthur Leslie (*background*; as Jack Walker), Pat Phoenix (Elsie Tanner), Philip Lowrie (Dennis Tanner), Lynne Carol (*right*; as Martha Longhurst), Margot Bryant (*left*; as Minnie Caldwell), Peter Adamson (Len Fairclough), William Roache (Ken Barlow), Jack Howarth (Albert Tatlock), Betty Alberge

(Florrie Lindley), and Jennifer Moss (Lucille Hewitt); later came Bryan Mosley (Alf Roberts), Arthur Lowe (Leonard Swindley), Kenneth Cope (Jed Stone), Eileen Derbyshire (Emily Nugent), Bernard Youens and Jean Alexander (as Stan and Hilda Ogden). During the second decade of the series such cast members/characters as Anne Kirkbride (Deirdre Langton), Betty Driver (Betty Turpin), Julie Goodyear (Bet Lynch), and Geoffrey Hughes (Eddie Yeats) grew to fame and took the series into its third and, eventually, fourth decade. H. V. Kershaw charted the early scripts and producers Stuart Latham and, later, Bill Podmore oversaw the (Mondays and Wednesdays) episodes.

Danger Man
(ATV/ITC, 1960–61; 1964–67)

Patrick McGoohan's solo-starring TV series début was a fast-paced, no-nonsense espionage action series that brought him to public attention and fame. John Drake (McGoohan) was a special security man/troubleshooter for NATO's secret service department whose hazardous assignments took him to all points of the compass. Adept at slugging it out with the bad guys, he rarely resorted to gunplay and, although always in the proximity of delectable damsels, it was never even implied that he locked limbs with the ladies. Excellent scripts (by such writers as Brian Clemens, Ralph Smart, Philip Broadley, David Stone, Donald Johnson), deft direction (by Seth Holt, Clive Donner, Charles Crichton, Robert Day, Philip Leacock, Peter Yates; and a couple by McGoohan himself),

and the cool, forceful performance and clipped delivery of McGoohan made this one of the more notable British spy-drama series. The early series (39 eps. × half-hour) was produced by (format creator) Ralph Smart; the mid-1960s series (45 eps. × hour) were produced by Aida Young (1964–65) and Sidney Cole; Edwin Astley supplied the music. Two hour-long, colour-filmed episodes ('Koroshi' and 'Shinda Shima', 1967) were re-edited and issued as a 93-minute TV feature called *Koroshi*. The hour series was transmitted in America under the title **Secret Agent** with rockabilly Johnny Rivers wailing a new musical signature tune to open and close the CBS TV networked programme. McGoohan is pictured in a scene from the 'Colonel Rodriguez' episode.

Deadline Midnight
(ATV, 1960–61)

The news-gathering pursuits of the staff of the *Daily Globe* were the focal point of this Fleet Street-located drama series featuring Peter Vaughan as the news editor and his team of intrepid reporters (Bruce Beeby, Jeremy Young (*left*), James Culliford, and Mary Law). With the technical assistance of ex-*Daily Express* editor Arthur Christiansen the series managed to maintain an air of Fleet Street authenticity despite a rather under-populated-looking newsroom. Glyn Houston (*right*) took over the role of editor for the 1961 series. The 39 eps. × 60-mins. series was produced by Hugh Rennie (1st series) and Rex Firkin (2nd series).

The Dickie Henderson Show
(A-R, 1960–65; 1968; 1971)

Domestic-comedy series, modelled closely on the American style, featuring a family threesome, with the addition of a guest star. Dickie Henderson (*centre*) was the centre-of-it-all entertainer father, June Laverick (*left*) the lively wife, and John Parsons was their 10-year-old son. Lionel Murton (*right*) also appeared as Henderson's musical manager buddy. Bill Hitchcock directed the half-hour scripts by Jimmy Grafton, Jeremy Lloyd, Eric Newman, Stan Mars, and others. This series was a lead-on from **The Dickie Henderson Half-Hour** (A-R / Jack Hylton TV Prods., 1958–60), a similar sitcom series in which he co-starred with Anthea Askey playing his 'wife'. Peter Frazer-Jones produced-directed the later **A Present for Dickie** (Thames TV, 1969–70) comedy series with Henderson starring once again as an easy-going entertainer, this time supported by Fabia Drake as his constantly suspicious mother-in-law and, of all things, a baby elephant. The 6 eps. × half-hour series was devised by Jimmy Grafton and co-scripted by Grafton and Johnny Heyward. Earlier, Henderson had starred in a variety show, **The Dickie Henderson Show** (ATV, 1957), which went out under the *Val Parnell's Saturday Spectacular* billing (prod.-dir. Brian Tesler).

The Flying Doctor
(ABC TV, 1960–61)

Stories based on the real-life activities of the Royal Flying Doctor Service serving the Australian Outback were presented in this 39 eps. × half-hour action drama; filmed at Associated British Studios, Elstree, and on location in Australia. American actor Richard Denning (*pictured*) played Dr Greg Graham, a US medic on leave from a San Francisco research institute who took over the duties of a blind doctor colleague (played by Peter Madden), with the help of nurse Mary Meredith (Jill Adams) and pilot Charley Wood (Alan White). Their medical service, covering an area of around 2,000,000 square miles, ranged from dealing with mine disasters to effecting Outback rescue missions. David Macdonald was the producer-director; Mike Noonan acted as principal writer / story editor.

Four Feather Falls
(Granada TV/AP Films, 1960)

An early string-puppet series from producer Gerry Anderson, featuring Tex Tucker (*left*; voiced by Nicholas Parsons; sung by Michael Holliday), a wandering cowboy who becomes Sheriff of the small town of Four Feather Falls. His companions were Rocky, his talking horse, Dusty, his talking dog, and his magic six-guns. Other regular characters were Pedro the bandit and his sidekick Fernando, friendly Indians Chief Kalamakooya and his son Makooya, and townspeople Martha Jones, Grandpa Twink, and Little Jake. Kenneth Connor, Denise Bryer, and David Graham supplied the other voices; 39 eps. × 15 mins. were produced.

1960

Glencannon

(Gross-Krasne Ltd., 1960)

A near slapstick comedy series based on the *Glencannon* stories by Guy Gilpatrick about a rascally chief engineer on the world-travelling tramp steamer *Inchcliffe Castle*. Instead of translating Gilpatrick's roguish character to the screen intact the producers decided to make him something of a Chaplinesque clown, despite the casting of impish American actor Thomas Mitchell (*right*) in the title role, therefore making the series a shallow romp through predictable plots. Supporting Mitchell were Patrick Allen (*left*; as his Bos'n buddy), Charles Carson (the Captain), with Barry Keegan, Georgie Wood, Peter Collingwood, and Kerry Jordan. Executive producer Donald Hyde developed thirty-nine half-hour episodes.

Here's Harry

(BBC-tv, 1960–65)

A comedy series built around the well-meaning though muddle-headed Harry Worth (*pictured*) television character and his ineffectual attempts to do the right thing. Contributing writers included Eddie McGuire, Vince Powell, and Harry Driver; John Ammonds produced. This popular series developed from the Ronnie Taylor-scripted/Ammonds-produced sitcom **The Trouble With Harry** (BBC-tv, 1959–60), produced from the BBC north of England studios. Worth's later series include **Harry Worth** (BBC-1, 1967–70; pr. Eric Fawcett), **Thirty Minutes Worth** (Thames TV, 1972–73; dir.-pr. Les Chatfield), **My Name is Harry Worth** (Thames TV, 1974; dir.-pr. William G. Stewart), and the 6 eps. × 30-mins. **Oh Happy Band!** (BBC-1, 3/9–8/10/80; pr. David Croft), written by Jeremy Lloyd and Croft.

How Green Was My Valley

(BBC-tv, 1/1–19/2/60; 8 eps. × 30 mins.)

Richard Llewellyn's famous novel was brought to television as an eight-part serial by producer Dafydd Gruffydd and broadcast from the BBC's Welsh Television Studios. Barry Thomas adapted the epic story chronicling the fortunes of the Morgan family in a small Welsh mining valley at the turn of the century, from the last decade of Victoria's reign until just before the First World War. Playing the Morgan family were Eynon Evans (the father), Glyn Houston (the eldest son), Islwyn Maelor Evans (*left*; youngest son), Rachel Thomas (*right*; the mother), and Sulwen Morgan (the daughter). The production was designed by Alan Taylor; Bill Greenhalgh was the film cameraman. BBC TV produced a new version fifteen years later (BBC-2, 29/12/75–2/2/76; 6 eps. × 50 mins.) starring Stanley Baker (as the father) and Sian Phillips (the mother). Elaine Morgan dramatized the new serial for producer Martin Lisemore; Ronald Wilson directed.

International Detective

(Delry–A. Edward Sutherland–Associated British–Pathe, synd. 1959–60; shown via the ITV companies in 1960)

Featured Arthur Fleming (as private eye Ken Franklin) in this action-drama series based on the files of the American William J. Burns International Detective Agency. Former Hollywood director Eddie Sutherland acted as sometime producer-director of the thirty-nine half-hour episodes. The scene pictured is from 'The Santeno Case' episode with guest Derek Sydney and Fleming (*right*).

It's a Square World
(BBC-tv, 1960–64)

One of BBC TV's top comedy-satire shows of the early 1960s, with the programme's leading writer-performer Michael Bentine (*pictured, seated on car front*) and his team (Dick Emery, Clive Dunn, Benny Lee, Frank Thornton, Leon Thau, Anthea Wyndham, Louis Mansi, Janette Rowselle, and John Bluthal) moving the gags and sketches along with a visual activity based on cartoon and silent-movie techniques. A capsule gag, for instance, had a couple of ships-in-bottles opening fire on each other and one of them sinking. The programme, devised by Bentine, was produced by G. B. Lupino and John Street. Bentine returned with **All Square** (ATV, 1966–67) on ITV, supported by most of his usual team, for producer Jon Scoffield. He returned again in 1977 for a 30-minute special, **Michael Bentine's Square World** (BBC-1, 19/4/77), which also featured Jack Haig, Jan Hunt, Barrie Manning, and Stuart Fell; the programme was written by Bentine and John Ennis for producer Jim Franklin.

A Life of Bliss
(BBC-tv, 1960–61)

Had been a BBC radio favourite for many years before being transferred to television. George Cole carried over his role of the shy, young bachelor, David Bliss, who was always likely to put his foot in it up to his neck or take the wrong end of the nearest stick. Also from the radio version came Bliss's bachelor flat companion and sympathetic ear, Psyche, a wire-haired fox terrier (played by 'Mady', with 'assistance' from sound vocalist Percy Edwards); other regular members of the TV cast were Colin Gordon (as his brother-in-law), Sheila Sweet (*right*; his girlfriend), and Isabel Dean (his sister Anne). The second series saw Bliss move in with his sister (now played by Frances Bennett) and her husband (Hugh Sinclair) where his natural talent for verbal gaffes was allowed to run riot again. The half-hour programme was written and produced by Godfrey Harrison.

Maigret
(BBC-tv–Winwell Prod., 1960–63)

Was first introduced to BBC TV as a part of their **Sunday-Night Theatre** presentations with 'Maigret and the Lost Life' (6/12/59), written by Giles Cooper from a 1954 novel by Georges Simenon and produced-directed by Campbell Logan. Basil Sydney played Commissioner Maigret in the 75-minute production, supported by Henry Oscar, Patrick Troughton, Mary Merrall, and Andre Van Gyseghem. The actual series began in October 1960, the first of what would eventually become four series totalling 51 eps. × 45/55 mins. The BBC had acquired the rights, with Simenon's blessing, against worldwide competition, making it their most ambitious series production to that date. The casting of Rupert Davies (*right*; with guest player Delena Kidd) as Maigret greatly pleased Simenon at the time; supporting players included Ewen Solon (as his assistant Lucas) and Helen Shingler (as Madame Maigret). An intuitive detective, Maigret often investigated his cases by watching and listening, moving slowly through his list of suspects until someone made a slip or broke down and confessed. Davies's Maigret was a man of infinite patience. Andrew Osborn steered the series as executive producer, with Giles Cooper as script editor/writer; the settings and overall French atmosphere was created by designer Eileen Diss. The music was composed by Ron Grainer, including the memorable Paris street accordion accompanying the opening shot of a match being struck on a wall and the light flickering across Rupert

Davies's face as he lights his pipe. Davies returned as Maigret to host the introductions to the 1964 series **Detective** and later revived the role in the 90-minute production 'Maigret at Bay' (9/2/69; wr. Donald Bull from a 1964 novel by Simenon, dir. William Slater), with Helen Shingler playing Madame Maigret again, for **Play of the Month**. In 1988 HTV presented a 2-hour telefilm, **Maigret** (21/5/88), with a rather haggard-looking Richard Harris sprinting about as Jules Maigret; the film was written by Arthur Weingarten and directed by Paul Lynch for the international market. The character was revived in **Maigret** (Granada TV, 1992–) with Michael Gambon in the title role, supported by Geoffrey Hutchings as Sgt. Lucas and Ciaran Madden (Barbara Flynn from 1993) as Mme Maigret; Jonathan Alwyn (1992) and Paul Marcus (1993) produced.

On Trial
(Granada TV, 1960; 10 eps. × 60 mins.)

The re-enactment of famous British trials was the theme of this well-documented and to-the-point series. It was something of a forerunner to the courtroom drama documentaries that would become popular in the 1980s, including the use of an 'outside' narrator (Andrew Faulds) and commentator (Brian Inglis) to draw references on the proceedings. The series opened with the trial of 'Sir Roger Casement' (8/7/60; dir. Cliff Owen), with Peter Wyngarde (*shown*) in the title role, and continued with the trials of other well-known figures in history such as 'The Trial of Oscar Wilde' (5/8/60; dir. Silvio Narizzano) and 'Sir Charles Dilke' (12/8/60; dir. Cliff Owen). Peter Wildeblood produced.

Our House
(ABC TV, 1960–61)

This comedy series about nine ill-assorted people who pool their funds to buy and share a ramshackle house was written by Norman Hudis, screenwriter of the early *Carry On* film successes. Very much in keeping with the pratfalls and belly-laughs of the big screen versions, the major share of the humour during the first series (13 eps. × 55 mins.) was handled by Hattie Jacques, Charles Hawtrey (*left*), Joan Sims, and Norman Rossington (supported by Ina de la Haye, Frank Pettingell, Trader Faulkner, Leigh Madison and Frederick Peisley). For the second (7 eps. × 45 mins.) series, still running with the oddballs-under-same-roof format, Hattie Jacques, Bernard Bresslaw (*right*), and Hylda Baker carried most of the fun until the falling, tripping, and collapsing of furniture comedy grew tiresome. Ernest Maxin produced.

77 Sunset Strip
(Warner Bros. TV; ITV tx 1960–)

This sophisticated private-eye series first started in the USA in 1958 and its immediate popularity created dozens of similar series (**Hawaiian Eye**, **Bourbon Street Beat**, **Surfside 6**, etc.). Based at the then swanky Hollywood address were freelance gumshoes Stuart Bailey (Efrem Zimbalist Jr.), Jeff Spencer (Roger Smith), and, at the next-door diner, their parking-lot attendant, the jive-talking Kookie (Edd Byrnes). Pictured (*l. to r.*) are Richard Long (as Rex Randolph, on a visit from **Bourbon Street Beat**), Zimbalist Jr., Jacqueline Beer (secretary Suzanne), Smith, Louise Quinn (gambler Roscoe), and Byrnes. (US tx 1958–64)

94

Siwan
(BBC-tv, 1/3/60)

Was set in the thirteenth century, and presented the historically factual story of the arranged marriage of King John's daughter, Siwan, to the Welsh Prince Llywelyn in order to seal the uneasy peace between them. The essence of the 90-minute play was the clash between the private and public lives of the powerful, and the nature of married love and infidelity. Siwan was played by Sian Phillips (*right*) and her then real-life husband Peter O'Toole (*left*) was her adulterous lover Gwilym De Breos. The play, transmitted on St David's day, was written for television by Welsh dramatist Saunders Lewis and translated from the Welsh and produced by Emyr Humphreys.

SMS
(A-R, 1960)

Subtitled 'Somerset Maugham Stories', this series embarked on thirteen straight dramatizations of Maugham tales, introduced by Daniel Farson. Moira Lister (as Vesta Grange; *pictured*) appeared in the opening play 'Flotsam and Jetsam' (3/2/60), later followed by Ernest Thesiger in 'The Happy Couple' (18/2/60), Donald Pleasence in 'Episode' (10/3/60), and Dulcie Gray in 'Winter Cruise' (28/4/60). Another Maugham story-based programme, in two series, followed: **Somerset Maugham Hour** (A-R, 1961–62). Hugh Williams introduced the 1961 series, Ian Hunter the 1962 series. At the end of the 1960s **W. Somerset Maugham** (BBC-2, 1969–70) appeared, presenting 26 eps. × 50 mins. stories (including 'The Letter', 24/6/69; and 'Rain', 7/5/70) produced by Verity Lambert.

Soldier, Soldier
(BBC-tv, 16/2/60)

John Arden's morally ambiguous play about an imperious army sergeant who descends on an emotionally vulnerable family and psychologically intimidates them into submission stirred some critical interest at the time. Andrew Keir (*pictured left*) was the Scottish soldier who tricks his way into a family home by claiming he knows their missing son, having served in the same regiment. Finally, after having elicited several favours, as well as making love to the missing son's wife, he tells them that he had made the whole thing up to show them what fools they were and moves on, piping his tin whistle. The gullible family group consisted of Maurice Denham, Frank Finlay (*right*), Anna Wing, Edna Petrie, and Margaretta D'Arcy (*centre*) as the young wife. The 60-minute play was produced by Stuart Burge.

The Splendid Spur
(BBC-tv, 28/2–4/4/60)

A Civil War adventure set in the year 1642, when King Charles I had moved his court to Oxford and the whole country was in confusion. Patrick Troughton (*pictured*) starred as Captain Luke Settle, with Michael Balfour, Victoria Watts, and Kenneth Farrington. The 6 eps. × 30 mins. serial was adapted by David Tutaev from Sir Arthur Quiller-Couch's story. David Goddard produced.

1960

The Strange World of Gurney Slade
(ATV, 1960; 6 eps. × 30 mins.)

Was exactly that, an almost surrealistic landscape of characters and situations seen through the eyes or via the mind of a timid and overly imaginative young man, played by Anthony Newley (*pictured*). The short-lived series was written by Sid Green and Dick Hills, for producer Alan Tarrant, and had Newley wandering (and wondering) his way through the bizarre stories, talking to himself, talking to trees, and fantasizing about the ideal woman. The haunting music was composed by Max Harris and conducted by Jack Parnell. One of TV's weirder offerings.

The Sunday-Night Play
(BBC-tv, 1960–63)

Presenting a series of new plays specially written for television, premièred with John Whiting's 'A Walk in the Desert' (25/9/60; pr. Naomi Capon), featuring Lawrence Harvey, Nigel Stock, and Tracy Lloyd. Other notable plays in the series included Alun Owen's 'The Ruffians' (9/10/60; pr. John Jacobs) with (*pictured l. to r.*) James Booth, Patrick Magee, Margaret D'Arcy, and Thomas Heathcote; John Osborne's 'A Subject of Scandal and Concern' (6/11/60; pr. Tony Richardson) with Richard Burton and Rachel Roberts; Clemence Dane's 'Marriage Lines' (14/5/61; pr. Alan Bromly) with Stephen Murray and Ann Castle; and David Mercer's 'A Suitable Case for Treatment' (21/10/62; pr. Don Taylor) with Ian Hendry and Moira Redmond (remade as a feature film, *Morgan, A Suitable Case for Treatment*, by Karel Reisz in 1966). David E. Rose came on board as series producer in 1961.

Sykes
(BBC-tv, 1960–65; BBC-1, 1971–79)

A long-running, popular sitcom led by one of Britain's superior comedy performers and scriptwriters, Eric Sykes. Although the programme was structured in the form of a domestic comedy the series (alternatively titled **Sykes and a . . .**, or whatever the theme was of that week's episode) rang the changes on contemporary TV sitcoms and characters, mostly due to Sykes's writing originality and his creative manipulation of the television format. The springboard was always the new 'toy' (such as a newly delivered telephone) or bizarre idea (such as running a bus route that stopped at individual people's homes) that Sykes and his sister Hattie explored, usually to the frustration and annoyance of arrogant neighbour Richard Wattis and local-beat policeman Derek Guyler. Dennis Main Wilson, Sydney Lotterby, and Roger Race were among the producers over the series' span. The scene pictured is from 'Sykes and a Plank' (3/3/64), with Hattie Jacques and Eric Sykes (Associated London Films produced a 54-minute cinema-release version of *The Plank* in 1967 and Thames TV presented a 30-minute television version on 17/12/79; both wr.-dir. Sykes).

Tales of the Riverbank
(BBC-tv, 1960; 1963; BBC-1, 1971)

Canadian-produced children's series (featuring real animals) about the adventures of two animal friends: Hammy, a hamster, and Roderick, a white rat. Both animals lived along a riverbank and shared adventures with their neighbours: a guinea pig, a racoon, a squirrel, a chipmunk, a frog, a toad, and various weasels and skunks. They were shown to move around in miniature boats, cars, balloons, and aeroplanes; and their homes were fully furnished (rodent size, of course). The 15-minute films were shot at double the normal camera speed to slow down the movements of the animals. All the writing, directing, editing, set designing, and construction was done by the team of Dave Ellison & Paul Sutherland. Photography was by Josef Seckeresh, formerly of Budapest Studios in Hungary. An additional twenty-six half-hour colour episodes were produced in the 1970s. Commentary was spoken by Johnny Morris.

Target Luna
(ABC TV, 1960)

Was the first of seven children's science-fantasy series produced by ABC TV using a blatant comic-book approach of placing a youngster in the central role usually populated by adults. **Target Luna** (6 eps. × half-hour), featuring a trip around the Moon, was written by Malcolm Hulke and Eric Paice and starred David Markham, Michael Hammond, Sylvia Davies, and Michael Craze; Sydney Newman produced. Writers Hulke and Paice and producer Newman went on to **Pathfinders in Space** (1960; 7 eps. × half-hour), **Pathfinders to Mars** (1960–61; 6 eps. × half-hour), and **Pathfinders to Venus** (1961; 8 eps. × half-hour), with Peter Williams, Stewart Guidotti, Gerald Flood, Pamela Barney, and George Coulouris appearing in the various serials. **Plateau of Fear** (1961; 6 eps. × half-hour), set around a nuclear power station in the Andes, was written by Malcolm Stuart Fellows and Sutherland Ross and produced by Guy Verney; John Barron, Jan Miller, Gerald Flood, and Stewart Guidotti led the cast. **City Beneath the Sea** (1962; 7 eps. × half-hour), about a voyage in an atomic submarine to an underwater city, was written by John Lucarotti and produced by Verney; Flood and Guidotti once again starred. **Secret Beneath the Sea** (1963; 6 eps. × half-hour) was a sequel to the 1962 serial with the same leading players, writer, and producer. The scene pictured is from the sequel **Pathfinders in Space**, with (*l. to r.*) Stewart Guidotti, Gillian Ferguson, and Gerald Flood.

Torchy
(A-R/AP Films, 1960–61)

'The battery boy', was the creation of children's author Roberta Leigh and his string-held adventures in the 52 eps. × 15 mins. series took place in the fairy-tale Topsy Turvy Land, populated by such nursery-rhyme characters as Old Mr Bumble-Drop, a girl called Bossy Boots, a dog called Pompom, and the memory-free King Dithers. Since Torchy was a toy that had been given a form of life his character and some of the elementary plots were not too far removed from Pinocchio-like fables. Roberta Leigh also supplied the music and lyrics, Gerry Anderson co-produced, and Vivian Milroy directed. Anderson's first TV puppet project (as director) had been **The Adventures of Twizzle** (A-R, 1957–60), written and produced by creator Roberta Leigh, and featuring Twizzle, a peculiar toy child who ran away from a toyshop and became friends with a black cat called Footso.

Whiplash
(ATV-ITC, 1960–61)

Australian-filmed, American West-style action series featuring Peter Graves (*pictured*) as stagecoach-line boss Christopher Cobb in his struggle to maintain law and order along the route of Australia's first passenger/freight stage line during the turbulent 1850s. Thirty-four half-hour adventures were produced.

The World of Tim Frazer

(BBC-tv, 1960–61)

Was presented under the *Francis Durbridge Presents* banner, and was, up until that time, the longest serial transmitted by BBC TV. Three Tim Frazer adventures (in individual six-part series) were shown in a straight run of 18 eps. × 30 mins. Jack Hedley (*pictured*) played the title role, an easygoing structural engineer who gets involved with a secret government department and is recruited as an undercover agent. Durbridge collaborated with three writers for the programme: Clive Exton for the première series (produced by Alan Bromly); Charles Hatton for the second series ('The Salinger Affair'; pr. Terence Dudley); and Barry Thomas for the third series ('The Mellin Forest Mystery'; pr. Richmond Harding).

A for Andromeda

(BBC-tv, 3/10–14/11/61); 7 eps. × 45 mins.)

A high-brow science fiction serial composed by astronomer Fred Hoyle and writer John Elliot about a mysterious signal picked up from the Andromeda galaxy via a powerful radio telescope which instructs a group of scientists on how to build a super-computer. The computer then created an artificial girl who was controlled by it; the girl was played by newcomer Julie Christie (*left*). Esmond Knight, Peter Halliday (*right*), Mary Morris, and Frank Windsor were the scientists. Michael Hayes and Norman James produced; photography was by Peter Sargent. Following the success of the first serial BBC TV produced a sequel, **The Andromeda Breakthrough** (BBC-tv, 28/6–2/8/62; 6 eps. × 45 mins.), where two of the scientists from the earlier story (Halliday and Morris) trail the girl, known as Andromeda (and now played by the young Susan Hampshire), to the Middle East and discover the real meaning of the strange messages from space. The sequel was also written by Hoyle and Elliot, with the latter doubling as producer.

Anna Karenina

(BBC-tv, 3/11/61)

Written by Marcelle-Maurette and adapted for television by Donald Bull, Tolstoy's 1873 classic novel was presented for the first time on TV in a 105-minute production. The massive novel was simplified to the essence of its dramatic story, namely Anna's adultery with Count Alexis Vronsky. Producer Rudolph Cartier saw it not so much as a love story set in 1880 but rather as a modern psychological drama. Claire Bloom played Anna and Sean Connery was Count Vronsky (*shown*); Valerie Taylor, June Thorburn, Albert Lieven, and Patricia Laffan supported. A. A. Englander was the film cameraman.

The Avengers

(ABC TV, 1961–69)

An enjoyable, fantasized espionage series that started out as a straight crime drama headed by two daredevil crime-busters, Dr David Keel (played by Ian Hendry) and the mysterious undercover agent John Steed (Patrick Macnee); Leonard White produced twenty-six hour-long episodes. In 1962 the Steed character, bowler hatted, charmingly insolent, and always unruffled, took centre stage (after the departure of Hendry's Keel) and was joined by the cucumber-cool, leather-clad agent Cathy Gale (Honor Blackman); Macnee and Blackman are pictured. Producers Leonard White and, later, John Bryce led them through fifty-two hour-long adventures; Julie Stevens as nightclub singer Venus Smith came in occasionally to assist Steed. But perhaps the most memorable period of **The Avengers** took off in 1965 with the introduction of Diana Rigg as Steed's new partner, the freelance adventuress Emma Peel, and a positive format swing in the direction of fantastic plots and diabolical villains. Their fifty hour-long, high-velocity operations

were produced by Julian Wintle and later Albert Fennell & Brian Clemens (the latter also responsible for charting the main course of offbeat action). For the final series of thirty-three hour-long episodes (still under Fennell & Clemens's production eye) Rigg's Mrs Peel handed over her half of the partnership to fledgling agent Tara King (Linda Thorson); in the sixth series, in the opening 'The Forget-Me-Knot' episode (25/9/68), Patrick Newell (as their chief, called Mother) and Rhonda Parker (as his secretary) also appeared. Some six years later **The New Avengers** (Avengers (Film and TV) Enterprises Ltd. Prod.–IDTV TV Prod., Paris, 1976–77) hit the screen starring Macnee once again as Steed, now in charge of two spitfire agents, the slim Purdey (played by Joanna Lumley) and the cool Gambit (Gareth Hunt). Fennell & Clemens again produced the

twenty-six hour-long episodes (with filming locations shared between France, Canada, and Britain).

Cliff!
(ATV, 1961)

Some four years after scoring a hit on the **Oh Boy!** show young rock 'n' roller Cliff Richard, supported by his backing group The Shadows, appeared in his own TV series. The half-hour shows, produced by Dinah Thetford, tried to aim for an all-age audience but somehow managed to dilute the interest in all sectors. Supported by the all-purpose musical backing of Jack Parnell and his Orchestra, Richard's line-up of guests over the shows included Petula Clark, Marty Wilde, Dickie Valentine, and Alma Cogan, assisted by the coy choreography of the Vernons Girls.

Comedy Playhouse
(BBC-tv, 1961–74)

BBC TV's première showcase for comedy writers and a celebrated launch pad for many popular series, inaugurated by Tom Sloan (then Head of BBC TV Light Entertainment) and piloted by the writing team of Alan Simpson & Ray Galton (their episode of 5/1/62, 'The Offer', became **Steptoe and Son**). Such successful series as **Till Death Us Do Part**, **All Gas and Gaiters**, **Me Mammy**, **Not in Front of the Children**, **The Liver Birds**, **The Last of the Summer Wine**, **Happy Ever After**, and **Open All Hours** originated from the show. A later series with a similar aim, **Comedy Special** (BBC-1, 1977), helped introduce John Sullivan's **Citizen Smith**. The scene pictured is from 'The Liver Birds' (14/4/69) with Pauline Collins and Polly James. In 1993 ITV locked on to the comedy showcase/potential series idea and produced **Comedy Playhouse** (Carlton, 23/2–13/4/93), a collection of eight half-hour comedy try-outs, one of which, 'Brighton Belles', was an anglicization of Susan Harris's **Golden Girls** (NBC, 1985–92).

Drama '61
(ATV, 1961–64; 1966–67)

Associated TeleVision's Sunday evening play series that alternated with ABC TV's **Armchair Theatre**. The umbrella title changed accordingly for each year of presentation, with **Drama '67** covering the final two years. The series began with Reginald Rose's 'The Cruel Day' (19/3/61; prod.-dir. Herbert Wise), starring Marius Goring, Peter Arne, and Margot Van Der Burgh in a story of moral conflict during the Franco-Algerian war. This was followed by such compositions as Frederic Raphael's 'The Executioners' (30/4/61), Harold Swanton's 'The Machine Calls It Murder' (25/6/61), Tad Mosel's 'The Morning Face' (3/9/61), and Anthony Thorne's 'So Long at the Fair' (29/10/61). The scene pictured is from 'Miss Hanago' (22/11/64), during **Drama '64**, with Anthony Quayle (*left*; as Lord Moritsugu) and Senta Yomada (*right*; as a samurai warrior).

Ghost Squad
(Rank-ATV, 1961–63)

The clandestine activities of undercover Scotland Yard agents was the central theme of this 39 eps. × hour drama series; based on Scotland Yard's International Investigation Division and inspired by Det. Supt. John Gosling's book of the same name. The series starred Sir Donald Wolfit (*left*; as the squad's chief Sir Andrew Wilson; seen with Angela Browne) and Michael Quinn (as agent Nick Craig). Connery Chappell produced. The programme returned in 1964 (for thirteen hour-long episodes) as **G.S.5**, with Ray Barrett as the new undercover agent Peter Clarke; he was assisted by Neil Hallett who continued his role from the earlier series. **The Men from Room 13** (BBC-tv, 1959–61) was also based on Scotland Yard's post-war 'Ghost Squad' department. Presented in two weekly parts and produced by Gerard Glaister, John Warrington, and Terence Dudley, the series starred John Welsh as Supt. Halcro; later played by Brian Wilde. The programme was created and written by Michael Gilbert, with some of the stories loosely based on the novel *Men from the Shadows* by Stanley Firmin.

Harpers West One
(ATV, 1961–63)

The back-room young executives and shop-floor sales staff were the central figures in this soap drama series about the running of Harpers, a large West End department store. Created and written by John Whitney and Geoffrey Bellman, the series ranged from high to low narrative threads combining the activities of eager-beaver public relations men with sales counter sympathy and psychology. With the hour-long stories featuring a 'family' of regular characters in an authentic setting, the programme soon developed the same audience interest as the similarly constructed ATV series **Emergency-Ward 10** and **Deadline Midnight**. Pictured are Vivian Pickles (*left*) and Jan Holden.

Jacks and Knaves
(BBC-tv, 16/11–7/12/61)

A mini-series of four 45-minute comedy/drama documentaries built around the cases of famed Liverpool Det. Sgt. William Prendergast. The four episodes, 'The Master Mind' (16/11/61), 'The Interrogation' (23/11/61), 'The Great Art Robbery' (30/11/61), and 'It Was Doing Nothing' (7/12/61), were written by Colin Morris and produced by Gilchrist Calder. The programme became the inspiration for **Z Cars**, which premièred the following year. Pictured (*l. to r.*) are John Barrie (as Det. Sgt. Tom Hitchin), Philip Stone (Sgt. Harry Frost), and Leonard Williams (Det. Con. Bert Hoyle) in 'The Master Mind' episode.

Journey of a Lifetime
(ABC TV, 1961–62)

The rather idealistic Bible-based holiday travels of Anne Lawson and John Bonney (playing a honeymooning couple; *pictured*) through a conveniently televisual Holy Land formed the basis of this religious-slot travelogue-with-a-message. The couple moved between Nazareth and the Sea of Galilee and the Tomb of King David and discovered a strong conflict of views in their relationship as well as picture-postcard scenes of New Testament ruins, hills, and fig trees. Lloyd Shirley directed the 39 eps. × 15 mins. series which was shown during the early evening Sunday period.

The Morecambe and Wise Show
(ATV, 1961–64; 1966–68; BBC-2/BBC-1, 1968–76; Thames TV, 1980–83)

Perhaps Britain's funniest and most popular TV comedy team, Eric Morecambe and Ernie Wise ruled small-screen comedy variety for almost a quarter of a century on both ITV and BBC TV channels. In the early 1960s they appeared in a series of comedy music shows, produced by Colin Clews, in which they shared their Sid Green & Dick Hills-scripted gag time (Eric striding around singing 'Boom Oo Yatta Ta Ta' off-key and grabbing straight man Ernie by the throat demanding 'Get outta that!') with Jack Parnell and his Orchestra, trad bands, and popular artistes of the day; writers Green & Hill had their own show for a while in 1967 called **Those Two Fellers** on ABC TV. But it is from the 1970s and 1980s that they are most likely to be remembered for their spectacular Christmas shows: the BBC-1 specials guest-starring Glenda Jackson and André Previn (1972), Vanessa Redgrave, Laurence Olivier, and Previn (1973), Diana Rigg and Des O'Connor (1975), Angela Rippon (1976); the Thames TV specials with guests such as former Prime Minister Harold Wilson (1978), Peter Cushing and Glenda Jackson (1980), and Diana Dors, Denis Healey, Jackson, and Previn (1982). Their first TV appearance had been in September 1951 in BBC-tv's **The Youth Parade**; they later headlined a fortnightly comedy variety show called **Running Wild** (BBC-tv, 1954) which also featured the young Alma Cogan as the resident singer. The duo's last TV work together was a 90-minute comedy thriller, **Night Train to Murder** (Thames TV, 3/1/85), written by them and the programme's producer-director Joe McGrath. Picture shows (*l. to r.*) Ernie Wise, guest Glenda Jackson, and Eric Morecambe in their 1972 Christmas show.

One Step Beyond
(A-R/Collier Young Prod.–Lancer Films, 1961–62)

This series of case histories concerning supernatural phenomena and the occult started out on American television as **Alcoa Presents** (subtitled 'One Step Beyond') in 1959. Although some of the American episodes were shown in the various ITV regions, Associated-Rediffusion networked a series of thirteen half-hour stories that had been produced in England. The programme was, as in America, hosted by actor-director John Newland ('Explain it? We cannot. Disprove it? We cannot.'); Peter Marriott produced. The scene pictured is from 'The Stranger' episode, showing Harold Kaskett (with three children he has saved from an earthquake).

1961

Points of View
(BBC-tv, 1961–)

Started as a 5-minute filler between programmes and went on to become 'a little piece of democracy' as a sounding-board for the public's opinions of BBC programmes. The majority of the complaints over the years have concerned bad language, nudity, sex, too much football, and **Grange Hill** during its early years. Presenters over the programme's span, so far, have been Robert Robinson (*pictured*), Kenneth Robinson (from 1965), RR again in the late 1960s, Barry Took (in 1979), and, in more recent years, Anne Robinson. Robert Robinson also presented **Junior Points of View** (BBC-tv, 1963–70).

The Pursuers
(ATV/Crestview Prod., 1961–62)

Fading Hollywood actor Louis Hayward (*pictured*) was Det. Insp. Steve Bollinger who 'walks the lonely streets of London with his police dog' (Ivan) in this standard join-the-dots Scotland Yard drama. Even the rapid-fire editing could not disguise the snail's-pace plotting and dialogue and the audience soon tired of this cop and his canine caper. Thirty-nine half-hour scamperings were produced.

The Rag Trade
(BBC-tv, 1961–63)

The dressmaking workshop of Fenner Fashions was the setting for this early 1960s comedy hit, created and written by Ronald Wolfe and Ronald Chesney (their first series for TV). The abrasive humour revolved around the rivalry between Fenner (Peter Jones; *standing, centre*), the workroom boss, and Paddy (Miriam Karlin; *far left*), the belligerent shop steward who was always on the alert when it came to protecting her co-workers' rights. By tele-recording the series on Sundays producer Dennis Main Wilson managed to cast almost exclusively from top West End theatre players who were not generally available for TV work. The first series' line-up also included Reg Varney (*5th right*), Esma Cannon (*2nd left*), Sheila Hancock (*far right*), Ann Beach (*3rd right*), Barbara Windsor (*4th right*), Toni Palmer, Judy Carne (*2nd right*), and Rita Smythe; three series (35 eps. × 30 mins.) were produced. Wolfe and Chesney revived the series in the late 1970s on ITV for director/producer Bryan Izzard (the 2nd series was dir./prod. William G. Stewart) under the original title, **The Rag Trade** (LWT, 1977–78; 22 eps. × half-hour), with Peter Jones and Miriam Karlin repeating their earlier roles; part of the new workshop staff were Christopher Beeny, Anna Karen, Gillian Taylforth, and Diane Langton.

Rashomon
(BBC-tv, 3/3/61)

This TV production was based on the 1959 stage version by American playwrights Fay and Michael Kanin who had added to Ryunosuke Akutagawa's original short story, *In the Bushes*, another of the author's *1,000 Tales of the 12th Century* called *Rashomon*, from which the title of the classic 1951 Japanese film was taken. The 90-minute play featured Lee Montague (*right*) as the bandit Tajomaru, whose trial for assault and murder is conducted (and shown) in multiple narrative with each witness recounting the incident from their own point of view. Japanese actress Yoko Tani (*left*) played the murdered man's wife; Robert Hardy was the Husband, Cyril Shaps the Wigmaker, Roy Patrick the Bailiff, and Richard Pearson the Woodcutter. Laurence Rosenthal composed the music and Clifford Hatts designed the rustic setting for producer Rudolph Cartier.

The Seven Faces of Jim
(BBC-tv, 16/11–28/12/61)

A 30-minute comedy series written by Frank Muir & Denis Norden that featured Jimmy Edwards (shown with June Whitfield) in a variety of eccentric characters and situations. Two further series followed: **Six More Faces of Jim** (BBC-tv, 15/11–20/12/62), featuring the TV première of the Glum family of radio's *Take It From Here* with Edwards as Mr Glum, Ronnie Barker as Ron, and June Whitfield as Eth (later reintroduced in LWT's **Bruce Forsyth's Big Night**), and **More Faces of Jim** (BBC-tv, 1963). Latter two series also written by Muir & Norden. James Gilbert produced.

Sir Francis Drake
(ATV–ABC TV, 1961–62)

A costume drama series set during the reign of Queen Elizabeth I, with Drake (Terence Morgan; *pictured*) and the *Golden Hind* battling the Spaniards all the way from the English Channel to the West Indies. Roger Delgado's villainous Mendoza was there to oppose him, while Queen Elizabeth I (Jean Kent; *pictured*) quietly supported his sea-hawk adventures through twenty-six episodes. The series was produced by Anthony Bushell; several episodes were re-edited and issued as TV features in America: *The Flame and The Sword*, *Marauders of the Sea*, *Mission of the Seahawk*, and *Raiders of the Spanish Main*, all 1962.

Songs of Praise
(BBC-tv, 1961–)

Early evening Sunday series of congregational hymn-singing presented from churches around the country. The première programme was presented from the Tabernacle Baptist Chapel in Cardiff; the programme has been hosted by various presenters, including Jimmy Savile, Eddie Waring, Cliff Richard, and Russell Harty. The series has, however, a somewhat artificial air with the camera-panned sea of hymn-singing faces sporting their best Sunday clothes and hats and being rather self-conscious about the BBC camera presence. The scene pictured is at Westminster Abbey during a 1966 recording.

Storyboard
(BBC-tv, 28/7–1/9/61)

Producer James MacTaggart presented six half-hour plays that were billed as exhibiting the key elements of characterization and atmosphere and the ability to tell the story in visual terms. The series premièred with John Dickson Carr's 'The Gentleman from Paris' (28/7/61; dramatized by Troy Kennedy Martin and Michael Imison) (Carr's story had been filmed in 1951 by MGM as *Man With a Cloak*); and was followed by Bernard Malamud's 'The Magic Barrel' (4/8/61; scr. Martin), 'The Middle Men' (11/8/61; scr. Martin), John Wyndham's 'The Long Spoon' (18/8/61; scr. Martin), Raymond Chandler's 'I'll Be Waiting' (25/8/61; scr. Martin and Imison; *pictured*; with Patricia Moffatt and Richard Lupino), and Ken Wlaschen's 'Tickets to Trieste' (1/9/61; scr. Martin).

1961

Supercar
(ATV/AP Films Prod./ITC, 1961–62)

Featured the science-fantasy adventures of a 'super car' that could speed above the ground, fly like a jet or a helicopter, hover, and also travel on and under water. Test pilot of this spectacular vehicle and series hero was Mike Mercury (voiced by Graydon Gould); assisted by inventor Prof. Popkiss (voice by George Murcell, later Cyril Shaps), 10-year-old Jimmy (Sylvia Anderson), British boffin Dr Beeker, and Mitch the monkey (latter voices by David Graham). The Supermarionation series of thirty-nine half-hour gear shifts were produced by Gerry Anderson.

Survival
(Anglia TV, 1961–)

A long-running and internationally successful wildlife programme originally produced and presented by naturalist Aubrey Buxton (as a co-production with Associated-Rediffusion); the programme's writer-producer Colin Willock has been associated with the series since it first began. Pictured is the late German cameraman G. Dieter Plage trying to escape from a charging Asian elephant in 'The Last Round-Up' (1984) edition. **World of Survival** was a syndication title used for overseas sales. **Survival Special** was an unofficial title used when the programme/episode was an hour (rather than the regular half-hour) length. **Animals in Action** (Anglia TV, 1980–83; 1986) presented a half-hour 'children's slot' programme in similar form; produced originally by Malcolm Penny.

Tales of Mystery
(A-R, 1961–63)

Suspense and the supernatural were the key elements in this half-hour series of stories based on the work of occult-obsessed author Algernon Blackwood. The episodes were introduced by John Laurie (*pictured*) in a rather theatrical, eyeball-rolling manner and involved all kinds of ghostly happenings and psychic phenomena—similar in theme and presentation to another early 1960s A-R programme of spooky stories, **One Step Beyond**. The series of twenty-nine episodes was produced by Peter Graham Scott. From January to August 1948, and April to October 1949, Algernon Blackwood appeared on BBC TV in a programme called **Saturday-Night Stories**, a series of 15-minute episodes produced by Robert Barr, in 1948, and Stephen McCormack, 1949, in which he told original, spine-chilling stories direct to camera.

Tempo
(ABC TV, 1961–67)

A counter to BBC TV's **Monitor**, this omnibus programme labelled itself as a 'fortnightly magazine programme which measures art in terms of enjoyment'. Originally hosted by Lord Harewood (later by Leonard Maguire and others) and edited by Kenneth Tynan, the 50-minute then 25-minute series presented what was considered the best in drama, film, music, painting, sculpture, ballet, and literature in the years preceding LWT's **Aquarius**. A March–April 1962 'Tempo Special' series of five programmes premièred with a report on the impact of the Irish on the Arts, featuring playwright Brendan Behan, theatre producer Sir Tyrone Guthrie, and stage designer Sean Kenny. Pictured are (*l. to r.*) Kenneth Tynan, Lord Harewood, co-editor Clive Goodwin, and director Reginald Collin.

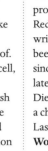

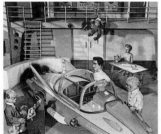

Thank Your Lucky Stars
(ABC TV, 1961–66)

Current pop disc themed show that started out as a rival to BBC TV's **Juke Box Jury** (early Saturday evenings) hosted by Keith Fordyce and later joined by Brian Matthew. From mournful ballads, sung by anguished crooners like John Leyton, to raging rhythm and blues (Bo Diddley's 'Pretty Thing'), the teenaged viewers lapped up every second. Disc jockey Don Moss cornered a weekly panel of youngsters for their views on new record releases and unearthed a minor studio celebrity in the form of west midlands-accented Janice Nicholls. In 1964 ABC TV premièred **Lucky Stars Summer Spin** as the show's mid-year Saturday replacement. Picture shows regular guest rock 'n' roller Billy Fury shimmying up a storm at an early session.

The Valiant Years
(BBC-tv, tx 1961)

Award-winning 26 eps. × 25 mins. documentary series based on Sir Winston Churchill's wartime memoirs (published as *The Second World War*), produced in New York by America's ABC TV network, under the leadership of Robert D. Graff and Ben Feiner Jr. Millions of feet of newsreel film were drawn from British, American, Soviet, French, German, Italian, and Japanese sources, including extensive wartime recordings made by the BBC. Special music was composed by Richard Rodgers to accompany the series. Recordings of Churchill's speeches were used along with his words read by Richard Burton; narrative links were spoken by Gary Merrill.

Where the Difference Begins
(BBC-tv, 15/12/61)

The first of playwright David Mercer's trilogy, written specially for television and dealing with social and political themes. **Where the Difference Begins** featured Leslie Sands, Nigel Stock (*right*), Pauline Letts (*left*), Barry Foster, and Hylda Baker in the 95-minute story about two brothers who, following the death of the mother, meet for the first time in many years when even death cannot paper over their differences. **A Climate of Fear** (BBC-tv, 22/6/62), the second of the trilogy, launched itself with the premiss of a nuclear scientist who found himself confronted with the fact that his children were members of the CND. Pauline Letts, John Stratton, Geoffrey Bayldon, Tony Garnett, and Douglas Wilmer starred in the 90-minute production. The last of the three plays, **The Birth of a Private Man** (BBC-tv, 8/3/63), continued the self-questioning theme (and characters) established in the previous play and closed Mercer's attempt to show the rise and fall of socialist idealism in the country over the previous sixty years, as seen through three generations of a family. Overall production was by Don Taylor.

Animal Magic
(BBC-tv, 1962–84)

Long-running children's zoology programme presented in whimsical fashion by Johnny Morris (*pictured*) as he observed the various creatures at Bristol Zoo (and later at more exotic locations like Frankfurt Zoo, Miami Seaquarium, etc.) and added his own, distinctive voice-overs to the animals on view. Assisting him during the early years were wildlife film-maker Tony Soper, showing extracts from his films, and naturalist Gerald Durrell giving tours of his own zoo in Jersey. Première producer for BBC West was Winwood Reade. Earlier, Johnny Morris had been **The Hot Chestnut Man** (BBC-tv, 1953–61), a teller of humorous stories for the junior audience.

1962

Brothers in Law
(BBC-tv, 1962; 13 eps. × 30 mins.)

Was based on the best-selling book by Henry Cecil (filmed by the Boulting Brothers in 1956) and brought to television by producer Graeme Muir. The series moved around the farcical legal predicaments of a pupil barrister, Roger Thursby, during his first year in Chambers. Thursby was played by 27-year-old Richard Briers (*far right*) in his first leading role in a series; Richard Waring (*second from right*), as a barrister friend, and June Barry (*centre*), as his girlfriend, supported; John Glyn-Jones (*left*) also appeared. The stories were written by Frank Muir and Denis Norden, with additional material by Henry Cecil. Producer Muir returned the following year with **Mr Justice Duncannon** (BBC-tv, 1963), featuring Andrew Cruickshank, on a break from his **Dr Finlay's Casebook** saga, as the stern but humane judge who was introduced in a guest appearance in the final episode of **Brothers in Law**. Scripts were once again provided by Muir & Norden, with Henry Cecil.

The Cheaters
(Danziger Prod., 1962–63)

Eastern Insurance Company investigator John Hunter (John Ireland; *pictured*) was the focus of this early 1960s drama series. The shabbily dressed Hunter was the man who decided which were the fraudulent cases and which were genuine, with some by-the-numbers dramatics involving cases of heavily insured fires, double indemnity cases, and insurance scams in sports events. Edward J. & Harry Lee Danziger produced.

Compact
(BBC-tv, 1962–65)

Emerged around the time that the ITV soap dramas were grounded by an Equity strike, giving this twice-weekly (Tuesdays and Thursdays) series a head start with the mid-evening, serial-seeking audience. The setting was the editorial offices of a women's magazine, *Compact*, staffed by a diverse group of editors, art directors, photographers, and secretaries, all of whom wrangled and romanced more than the fictional story subjects of their magazine. The original principal players were Jean Harvey (as Editor Joanne Minster), Nicholas Selby (Features Editor), Moray Watson (Art Director), Gareth Davies (*right*; Fiction Editor), and Leo Maguire (photographer); with an assortment of secretaries, Sonia Graham, Monica Evans, Anna Castaldini. The series later took on Clinton Greyn, Dawn Beret, and Ronald Allen (*2nd right*) as the magazine's second Editor and chairman of their publishing house Harmon Enterprises. Created by writers Hazel Adair and Peter Ling (before they went on to launch ATV's **Crossroads**), the series was originally scheduled to run for only three months but by December 1963 it was notching up its 200th episode and celebrating the 'hundredth edition' of the magazine. Three directors—Joan Craft, Vere Lorrimer, and Christopher Barry—worked in rotation on each week's two episodes when the series began; 50-minute omnibus editions were shown from April 1964. The 373 eps. × 30 mins. were produced by Alan Bromly (1962), Douglas Allen (1962–63), Morris Barry (1963–64; 1964–65), Bernard Hepton (1964), Joan Craft (1964), Harold Clayton (1965), and William Sterling (1965). The scene pictured also shows Frances Bennett (*left*) and Robert Flemyng (*2nd left*).

Dial Rix
(BBC-tv, 1962–63)

Produced a series of popular, 50-minute farces by Brian Rix's Whitehall Company that were shown at monthly intervals during the winter. Writers John Chapman, Ray Cooney, Kenneth Horne, and Tony Hilton contributed. Two further programmes in a similar vein followed: **Laughter from Whitehall** (BBC-tv, 1963–64) and **Laughter from the Whitehall** (BBC-1, 1965). The scene pictured shows (*l. to r.*) Carole Shelly, Brian Rix, and Elspet Gray in the première play 'Between the Balance Sheets'.

Dr Finlay's Casebook
(BBC-tv, 1962–71)

Long-running BBC TV medical series set in Scotland (in and around the village of Tannochbrae) during the late 1920s and based on A. J. Cronin's stories *The Adventures of a Black Bag*. Andrew Cruickshank (*right*) played the crusty Dr Cameron, a former surgeon who had moved into general practice, Bill Simpson (*left*) was the young, dedicated Dr Alan Finlay, and Barbara Mullen (*centre*) played their no-nonsense housekeeper Janet. While the two different generations of doctors clashed over various medical opinions they usually learned something from each other and succeeded in solving the problem at hand, from an outbreak of smallpox to a case of epilepsy. The series immediately caught the viewers' attention (despite opposition from US imports **Dr Kildare** and **Ben Casey**) and remained a firm favourite for many years. Producers across the thirteen series of 200 eps. × 50 mins. were Campbell Logan (1962–63), Andrew Osborn (1964–65), Gerard Glaister (1965–66), Douglas Allen (1966–67), Royston Morley (1967–69), and John Henderson (1970–71). **Doctor Finlay** (Scottish TV, 1993–) revived the character and setting with David Rintoul playing Finlay, returning home to Tannochbrae after service in the Second World War; housekeeper Janet was played by Annette Crosbie and Ian Bannen portrayed Dr Cameron. Peter Wolfes produced.

Electra
(A-R, 28/11/62)

Joan Kemp-Welch adapted and directed Sophocles' 2,500-year-old play featuring the Piraikon Greek Tragedy Theatre Company (under Piraikon Theatre producer Dimitrios Rondiris). Aspassia Papathanassiou (*right*) performed as Electra, one of the daughters of Queen Clytemnestra (Georgia Saris; *left*), supported by Dimitri Malavetas, Dimitri Veakis, and Anthi Kariofili. The hour-long production was designed by Michael Yates. BBC TV's **Play of the Month** presented a translation by E. F. Watling, directed by Michael Lindsay-Hogg, on 24/10/74; Eileen Atkins, Rosalie Crutchley, and Julian Glover were featured.

1962

Fireball XL5
(AP Films–ATV/ITC, 1962–63)

Science fiction marionette adventures from the Gerry and Sylvia Anderson stable, featuring (*l. to r.*) Robert the Robot (voiced by Gerry Anderson), Venus (Sylvia Anderson), and the futuristic hero Steve Zodiac (Paul Maxwell). The straightforward plots, out-of-this-world characters, and mechanical effects made this one of the more popular series of the period for the moppet market. Filmed in Supermarionation, with special effects created by Derek Meddings, **Fireball XL5** rocketed through thirty-nine half-hour missions.

Hugh and I
(BBC-tv, 1962–67)

Was the first television comedy of Whitehall farce writer John Chapman (he had written the successful plays *Dry Rot* and *Simple Spymen*) and the first coupling and co-starring of the small and fretting Hugh Lloyd (*left*) and plump and know-all Terry Scott (*right*). Produced by David Croft, the **Hugh and I** format located the two characters in suburbia where Lloyd was a lodger in Scott's mother's house and the unwitting accomplice in Scott's various fortune-making schemes. The series then developed into **Hugh and I Spy** (BBC1, 1968; 6 eps. × 30 mins.), under producer Croft with Chapman writing, where the Laurel and Hardy-like duo were given more adventurous situations to muddle through each week. The following year they appeared in the oddball, Jimmy Perry-scripted **The Gnomes of Dulwich** (BBC2, 1969; 6 eps. × 30 mins.) playing a couple of stone garden gnomes who observe the foibles of the (unseen) human race while competing in snobbery with the plastic gnomes in an adjacent garden.

The Largest Theatre in the World
(BBC-tv, 1962; 1965; 1967; 1970–71)

The idea for this programme originated at a gathering of television professionals for the award of the Italia Prize in 1960. By way of overcoming the language barrier nations were invited to commission from a leading author, whose reputation bridged all frontiers, a play which would be simultaneously produced in each country in its own language, so that the audience for the performance would truly represent the largest theatre in the world. The United Kingdom was invited to be the first member country of the European Broadcasting Union (of some nine countries) to commission a play for the series. This first play, 'Heart to Heart' (6/12/62), was specially written by Terence Rattigan for two actors: Kenneth More (*right*) as a cynical and hard-drinking Grand Inquisitor of the TV programme Heart to Heart, and Ralph Richardson (*left*) as the newly appointed Minister of Labour in whose past the interviewer finds evidence which could destroy him politically. Alvin Rakoff produced. The second British production under the EBU scheme was Harold Pinter's 'Tea Party' (25/3/65), starring Leo McKern, Vivien Merchant, Jennifer Wright, John Le Mesurier, and Charles Gray. Charles Jarrott directed Sydney Newman's 75-minute production.

Man of the World
(ATV, 1962–63)

Gave globe-trotting photo-journalist Mike Strait (played by Craig Stevens) licence to forage for action in all the colourful corners of the world, usually assisted by his svelte sidekick Maggie (Tracy Reed). Plot locations ranged from Indo-China to Mexico to the Amazon, with the adventurous hero supplying the cool or the conflict as the situation demanded. Several episodes were re-edited as TV features: *Dangerous Hideaway* (1962), *Double Exposure* (1962), *The Fanatics* (1962), *Flashpoint* (1962), *Love Me—Love Me Not* (1962). The twenty hour-long episodes were produced by Harry Fine; music was supplied by Henry Mancini. An early episode, 'The Sentimental Agent' (wr. Jack Davies, dir. Charles Frend), concerning a rather shady import–export agent (Carlos Thompson), became the source of the series **The Sentimental Agent** (ATV, 1963) with Thompson reviving the role for producer Fine in thirteen hour-long episodes. (*Pictured*) Guest Patrick Troughton levels the gun at Stevens in the 'Death of a Conference' episode.

The Monsters
(BBC-tv, 8–29/11/62; 4 eps. × 45/50 mins.)

The writing collaboration of Evelyn Frazer and Vincent Tilsley produced this four-part cliff-hanger of murky goings-on in the Lakelands. Plot concerned a Professor of Zoology (William Greene), on honeymoon with his new wife (Elizabeth Weaver), becoming involved in the mysterious death of a security agent, the dangerous activities of a bizarre scientist (Robert Harris; *right*, with Gordon Whiting) and some lurking Loch Ness-type monsters. More a serial of mood and mystery than (as the title suggests) monstrous mayhem, the producers however did come across with the science fantasy goods in the form of special effects by Bernard Wilkie and Stewart Marshall; photography was by John McGlashan. Mervyn Pinfield directed for George R. Foa.

The Odd Man
(Granada TV, 1962–63)

Suspense serial interplaying political intrigue, domestic dissent, and crime-caper sleuthing starred Edwin Richfield (*left*), Moultrie Kelsall, Sarah Lawson (*right*), Christopher Guinee, and Keith Barron. William Mervyn (*centre*) entered the ongoing story during the second series as the supercilious Chief Insp. Rose. The programme was created and for the most part written by Eddie Boyd; Stuart Latham produced the twenty-four hour-long episodes. Mervyn's Rose character and Keith Barron's Det. Sgt. Swift moved on to feature in **It's Dark Outside** (Granada TV, 1964–65), a crime thriller series also featuring John Carson, June Tobin, and Oliver Reed. Derek Bennett produced and directed the sixteen hour-long episodes. William Mervyn then starred as the now-retired Chief Insp. Rose in **Mr Rose** (Granada TV, 1967–68), settling down to write his memoirs but being constantly sidetracked by characters and incidents from his past. Gillian Lewis, Donald Webster, Jennifer Clulow, and Eric Woolfe supported. The twenty-five hour-long episodes were produced by creator Philip Mackie and (later) Margaret Morris.

Oliver Twist
(BBC-tv, 7/1–1/4/62; 13 eps. × 25 mins.)

BBC TV's long association with Dickens's adaptations in its early evening Sunday slot was brought to a pitch with this grim and psychologically dark version, produced by Eric Tayler and dramatized by Constance Cox. The production, designed by Stephen Bundy, was suitably gloomy and colourless, portraying the desolation and depravity of the early nineteenth-century London underworld. Thirteen-year-old Bruce Prochnik (*right*) played Oliver, with Max Adrian (*left*; as Fagin), Melvyn Hayes (the Artful Dodger), Peter Vaughan (Bill Sykes), and Carmel McSharry (Nancy). The final episode, in which Bill Sykes brutally murders Nancy, brought forth a storm of protest from shocked viewers, parents, and TV monitoring groups.

On the Braden Beat
(ATV, 1962–67)

Was one of the first of the then new topical consumer-affairs programmes, presented by Canadian actor-writer Bernard Braden (*left*; with guest American humourist S. J. Perelman). The late night Saturday show, with its investigations into public services and man-in-the-street-level analyses of current affairs, was something of a forerunner to **That's Life**. The programme was originally produced by Jock Watson, later by Francis Coleman. **Braden . . . On the Box** (ATV, 7–28/7/68) followed as a four-part programme about television itself: how a TV programme was planned, rehearsed, the finished programme, and finally an examination of the third week's show. Nevile Wortman produced; photography by Chris Menges.

Out of This World
(ABC TV, 1962)

An hour-long series of science fiction adaptations that preceded BBC-2's more famous **Out of the Unknown** fantasy anthology; the ABC TV story editor Irene Shubik went on to become the early producer for the BBC TV anthology. Under producer Leonard White, **Out of This World** presented TV dramatizations of such works as Isaac Asimov's 'Little Lost Robot', Philip K. Dick's 'Imposter', Raymond F. Jones's 'Divided We Fall', and two stories by Clifford Simak, 'Immigrant' and 'Target Generation'. Terry Nation contributed 'Botany Bay' as well as adapting the teleplays for 'Imposter' and 'Immigrant'. The introductory episode, John Wyndham's 'Dumb Martian' (24/6/62; pr. Sydney Newman, dir. Charles Jarrott), was transmitted a week before the series opened as a part of Newman's **Armchair Theatre** play collection. Horror star Boris Karloff was the rather unlikely series host for the thirteen episodes. The scene pictured is from Tom Godwin's 'Cold Equations' episode, with Jane Asher and Peter Wyngarde.

Police Five
(ATV, 1962–69; LWT, 1970–90)

A long-running series of 5-minute (later extended) crime prevention programmes presented by New Scotland Yard in conjunction with ATV and introduced by Shaw Taylor which was designed to help the public combat crime on their own doorsteps. The early series were produced by Stephen Wade. **Junior Police Five** (LWT, 1972–78) was later introduced so that kids could become local neighbourhood snoops and informers.

The Saint
(ATV–New World–Bamore Prod./ITC, 1962–69)

Basing the format on The Saint stories that Leslie Charteris had been writing since the late 1920s, Robert S. Baker and Monty Berman produced one of the 1960s' most (internationally) popular and longest-running action adventure series: 185 (black and white and colour) hour-long episodes. The adventurer-hero, Simon Templar (played with Brylcreemed dash by Roger Moore), was a freelance 'instrument of justice', slugging it out with the heavies and dallying with the dames in exotic, international locations. His Scotland Yard contact, and perpetually frustrated ally, was Insp. Claude Eustace Teal (Ivor Dean). Two telefeatures were produced from re-edited, two-part episodes: *The Fiction-Makers* (1967, dir. Roy Baker) and *Vendetta for the Saint* (1968, dir. Jim O'Connolly). Harry H. Junkin was script supervisor (and regular contributor); Edwin Astley composed the haunting music. John Paddy Carstairs, Peter Yates, Leslie Norman, Freddie Francis, and Roger Moore (for nine eps.) contributed from the director's chair. **Return of the Saint** (ITC, 1978–79) starred Ian Ogilvy as Simon Templar in twenty-four hour-long episodes produced by Anthony Spinner; Robert S. Baker was executive producer. Templar reappeared again (in the form of Simon Dutton) in a short-run series of 100-minutes-plus adventures in **The Saint** (Saint Prods.–LWT, 1989–90). The scene pictured is from 'The Latin Touch' episode with Suzan Farmer, Moore, and Peter Illing.

Steptoe and Son

(BBC-tv, 1962–65, 26 eps. × 30 mins.; 1970, 7 eps. × 30 mins.; 1972, 7 eps. × 30 mins.; 1974, 6 eps. × 30 mins.)

This series was one of the comedy highlights of 1960s BBC TV. It was created by the scriptwriting team of Alan Simpson and Ray Galton from a half-hour playlet, 'The Offer' (5/1/62), presented as a part of the series **Comedy Playhouse**. For the most part, **Steptoe and Son** was a superior two-actor show featuring a couple of junk men and their run-down junkyard; Wilfrid Brambell (*right*) was the quarrelsome and grubby Albert and Harry H. Corbett (*left*) was his restless son Harold. While Harold continually fought to better himself and escape his junkyard life the wily, old Albert always managed to turn the situation around not only to restrain Harold's rebellious nature but also suit his own selfish, and lonely, existence. The partnership of Brambell and Corbett clicked immediately, allowing the writers to weave an undercurrent of pathos into the humour; the comedy element appeared to rise naturally from the interplay between the characters they played. They were, and remain, the original 'odd couple'. In the early 1970s American producer Norman Lear purchased the series format and turned it into the successful **Sanford and Son** for NBC TV; Dutch television, meanwhile, translated the BBC series into **Stiefbeen en Zoon**. Producers for the BBC TV series were Duncan Wood, John Howard Davies (1972), Douglas Argent (1974). There were also two special Christmas shows (24/12/73 × 45 mins., pr. Graeme Muir; 26/12/74 × 40 mins., pr. Douglas Argent). MGM–EMI released two feature film spin-offs, *Steptoe and Son* (1972) and *Steptoe & Son Ride Again* (1973).

1962

Studio 4
(BBC-tv, 1962)

A series of 50-minute programmes largely based on adaptations of modern novels, beamed out of Television Centre's modern Studio 4. The programme premièred with Roger Smith's adaptation of Albert Maltz's 'The Cross and the Arrow' (22/1/62; pr. James MacTaggart); later productions included Roy Fuller's 'The Second Curtain', Muriel Spark's 'Ballad of Peckham Rye', and Graham Greene's 'Stamboul Train' (*pictured*; with Ivor Salter, *left*, and Richard Warner). Arthur Hailey's 'Flight into Danger' was one of the few pieces originally written for TV.

Take a Letter
(Granada TV, 1962–64)

Was a game show based on the crossword principle in which contestants had to get the clues provided by a display board and via a verbal clue supplied by host Bob Holness (*pictured*) to fill in the blanks. The cash prize (maximum of around £34 when the show began) depended on the number of letters turned up before the correct solution was given. The programme of 130 editions was produced by John Hamp.

That Was the Week That Was
(BBC-tv, 1962–63)

Influential Saturday night satire show presented by David Frost (*left*) and his team (*2nd l. to r.*, Roy Kinnear, Kenneth Cope, Lance Percival, William Rushton; with David Kernan, Al Mancini, and Bernard Levin) as they pounced on the oddities and idiocies of the Week that Was, leaving it shredded on the studio floor. Millicent Martin warbled the near-libellous lyrics and Ned Sherrin produced the 30-minute programme. In 1964 America's NBC adopted the format and title, also featuring David Frost, although styled to suit American tastes. **Not So Much a Programme, More a Way of Life** (BBC-1, 1964–65) followed, filling the gap left by **TW3** on Saturday nights as well as Fridays and Sundays. The 45-minute series, also under producer Sherrin, was presided over by Frost, Rushton, and P. J. Kavanagh.

University Challenge
(Granada TV, 1962–87)

A quiz show with a difference: the competing teams, ranged in tiers, were made up of four full-time university students and the questions were chosen to test quick reaction, fluency, and general knowledge. The emphasis was placed on speed. The opening match was between the Universities of Leeds and Reading. Bamber Gascoigne (*pictured*) was the quiz-master, and the producers over the years were Barrie Heads, Douglas Terry, and Peter Mullings.

William
(BBC-tv, 1962)

Adapted for television by C. E. Webber in 25-minute episodes (titled 'William and the Wonderful Present', 'William and the Leopard Hunter', 'William Finds a Job', etc.) from the stories by Richmal Crompton, the series featured a young Dennis Waterman (*pictured*) as leader of the Outlaws: Douglas (played by Carlo Cura), Henry (Kaplan Kaye), and Ginger (Christopher Witty). Gillian Gostling was Violet Elizabeth Bott. Denis Gilmore played William in the second series. Leonard Chase produced. Fifteen years later **Just William** (LWT, 1977–78) appeared with Adrian Dannatt as the title character in 27 eps. × 30 mins. for producer John Davies; Keith Dewhurst adapted the stories.

Z Cars
(BBC-tv, 1962–78)

Probably the most authentic if not finest police drama series to have appeared on British television in the 1960s. The series, originated by writer Troy Kennedy Martin for producer David E. Rose, focused squarely on the professional activities of the policemen of a new north of England overspill estate called Newtown. It was a TV first in its presentation of grim and gritty police procedure. The original cast who established the policemen as ordinary men who drank, backed horses, and even vented their frustrations on their wives were Jeremy Kemp (as PC Steele), James Ellis (as PC Bert Lynch, later Det. Con.), Joseph Brady (as PC Jock Weir), Brian Blessed (as PC 'Fancy' Smith), and Terence Edmond (as PC Sweet); later joined by Colin Welland as PC Graham. Stratford Johns's Det. Chief Insp. Barlow and Frank Windsor's Det. Sgt. John Watt were also part of the original cast; they were later promoted to the spin-off series **Softly, Softly** and **Barlow at Large**. The programme was made with the co-operation of the Lancashire Police and with casebook material provided by former CID Sgt. Bill Prendergast and former CID Chief Supt. Cecil Lindsay. Scripts during the formative years were supplied by Elwyn Jones, John Hopkins, Allan Prior, and Alan Plater. Directors included Shaun Sutton, John McGrath, and Ken Loach. Under producers Rose, Colin Morris, Ron Craddock, and Roderick Graham, respectively, the Liverpool flutes and drums signature tune (called *Johnny Todd*) heralded over 667 45-, 50-, then 25-minute episodes; becoming a twice-weekly (occasionally more) serial in 1967.

Zero One
(MGM TV–BBC-tv, 1962–65)

Was the call sign for the International Air Security Board, based at London Airport, and featured Nigel Patrick (*right*) as their chief investigator covering all air transport services; his powers permitted investigation into all areas short of air crashes and disasters. He was assisted by Jimmy Delaney (played by American actor Bill Smith) and secretary Maya (Katya Douglas). The 39 eps. × 25 mins. series was produced in England by Lawrence P. Bachmann. Episode 'Fly Away Peter' (*shown*) also featuring Jack Watson (*left*) and Peter Halliday (*centre*).

Citizen 63
(BBC-tv, 28/8–25/9/63)

This five-part documentary series, produced by John Boorman for BBC West (Bristol), observed the day-to-day lives of five different people in an attempt to capture the mood and flavour of life in 1963 Britain. The five subjects profiled by the pursuing cameras were shown as being typically representative of people confronting, conforming, and simply reacting to the problems and pressures of life at the time. Boorman's cameras recorded, in turn, the world of a young businessman, the world of a police inspector, the story of a rebellious girl at a secondary-modern school, the story of a shop steward, and the life of a scientist (Frank George; *pictured*). There were 5 eps. × 30 mins. produced; Ewart Needham was the senior cameraman. Boorman returned the following year to produce **The Newcomers** (BBC-2, 30/4–4/6/64), a 6 eps. × 30 mins. series recording a six-month period in the lives of a young married couple as they await the birth of their first child. Michael Croucher was associate producer; Arthur Smith and Jim Saunders the cameramen. Eleven years later producer Paul Watson would take this TV life-study form to almost epic proportions with **The Family**.

Corrigan Blake
(BBC-tv, 1963)

Was first introduced in a single, 70-minute play, **You Can't Win 'Em All** (BBC-tv, 2/2/62; pr. John Jacobs), written by Alun Owen, with Jack Hedley as a open-for-offers Cockney seaman. Hedley's Blake became involved with a rebel group in a Latin American country, with him ending up deeper in the turmoil than he had wished. In April of the following year, when the series premièred, Blake was played by John Turner (*left*; after his stint as ITV's **Knight Errant**) as a 'Cockney hipster and travelling man'. This time he had a sidekick in the form of the aristocratic Wallace St John Smith (Paul Daneman; *right*) while the Alun Owen-scripted series developed a certain situation comedy flavour. With the series subtitled 'the adventures of a bird fancier', Blake roistered through the stories maintaining a dangerously keen eye on the distaff domain. The series was produced by Elwyn Jones and directed by James MacTaggart.

Crane
(A-R, 1963–65)

Was a Moroccan-based smuggler who owned a run-down café near Casablanca and a boat that was available for various assignments, including running cargoes of illicit cigarettes and liquor; he steered clear of narcotics and guns. Patrick Allen (*pictured*) played the smuggler, always a couple of steps ahead of Mahmoud (Gerald Flood), the elegant chief of police; his partner in the 'import–export' business was a colourful beachcomber called Orlando O'Connor (Sam Kydd) while Halima (Laya Raki), a sultry Arab girl, looked after his café bar. The series was created by Patrick Alexander and Jordan Lawrence (the latter also produced). Sam Kydd's Orlando character later went on to his own series, **Orlando** (Rediffusion, 1965–68), but in the diluted format of a serialized children's programme.

The Dick Emery Show
(BBC-tv, 1963–81)

As the comic master of the extravagant impersonation, Dick Emery excelled in the broad art of larger-than-life comedy. His mimicry of bizarre males and females produced such screwy characters as Old Lampwick, the wily Mr Crump, Farmer Finch, and the street-interview subject, the Dumb Blonde, which eventually led to the feature film *Ooh . . . You Are Awful* (produced by Quintain Prods. in 1972). Pictured (*l. to r.*) are Emery with singer Gary Miller, co-star Joan Sims, singer Mary Millar, and dancer-actress Una Stubbs. Emery's holiday specials, **The Dick Emery Christmas Show** (BBC-1, 24/12/72, 35 mins.; 24/12/77, 45 mins.; 27/12/80, 50 mins.), were always extremely popular with viewers; all were produced by Harold Snoad. He followed with **Emery** (BBC-1, 16/2–23/3/82; 3/6–15/7/83), two light-hearted thriller series featuring him as Bernie Weinstock, a small-time private detective. The two series were written by John and Steven Singer and produced by Harold Snoad (1982) and Stuart Allen (1983).

Doctor Who
(BBC-tv, 1963–)

Originally intended for the undiscriminating junior viewer, this often wild and imaginative science fiction series (made up of multiple, self-contained mini-serials) has outlived every other SF-orientated television programme to enjoy deservedly one of the great TV cult followings. The time and space adventures of the alien Time Lord, known simply as The Doctor, have been represented in the title role by, respectively, William Hartnell, Patrick Troughton, Jon Pertwee, Tom Baker, Peter Davison, Colin Baker, and, the last to date, Sylvester McCoy. A 50-minute spin-off, **K9 and Company** (BBC-1, 28/12/81), featuring Elisabeth Sladen and robo-dog K9, was written by Terence Dudley and directed by John Black for long-time **Doctor Who** producer John Nathan-Turner. Two feature film spin-offs were also produced during the 1960s: *Dr Who and the Daleks* (1965) and *Daleks—Invasion Earth 2150 A.D.* (1966) with Peter Cushing cast as the Doctor in both films. Pictured are (*l. to r.*) William Russell, Hartnell, Jacqueline Hill, and Carol Ann Ford in the 'Keys of Marinus' story.

Epitaph for a Spy
(BBC-tv, 19/5–9/6/63)

Eric Ambler's third novel (1938), about an innocent photographer arrested for espionage in France in 1937, was presented as a four-part 30-minute Sunday serial dramatized by Elaine Morgan and produced-directed by Dorothea Brooking. Colin Jeavons (*pictured*) featured as photographer Vadassy, with Janet McIntire, Peter Ducrow, and Barry Shawzin. The story had been serialized ten years earlier, BBC-tv, 14/3–18/4/53, as a six-part 30-minute serial starring Peter Cushing, Yvonne Andre, Ferdy Mayne, and Philip Leaver; Giles Cooper dramatized the novel for producer Stephen Harrison; Patrick Harvey directed.

Espionage
(Plautus Prods.–ITC, 1963–64)

Presented an above-average anthology series of European-filmed suspense dramas dealing with undercover agents and their activities, ranging in period from the American Revolution politics of the eighteenth century to contemporary Cold War capers. Twenty-four hour-long episodes were produced by George Justin. The scene pictured is from a Second World War story, 'The Weakling' (wr. by Arnold Perl and dir. Stuart Rosenberg), starring Patricia Neal (*left*) and Dennis Hopper (*right*).

Festival
(BBC-tv, 1963–64)

Introduced a programme of dramatic plays to 'entertain the intelligent viewer'. It premièred with Noel Coward's 'Fallen Angels' (9/10/63) and went on to present productions of 'The Human Voice' (6/11/63), the first Jean Cocteau play to be shown on BBC TV, starring Anouk Aimée (*pictured*); Samuel Beckett's 'Krapp's Last Tape' (13/11/63) with Cyril Cusack (*pictured*); 'Stalingrad' (4/12/63), written by Claus Hubalek from the novel by Theodore Plievier, adapted from the German and directed by Rudolph Cartier; Dylan Thomas's 'Under Milk Wood' (4/3/64) with Donald Houston; 'Murder in the Cathedral' (25/3/64) by T. S. Eliot; and 'Bloomsday' (10/6/64), based on *Ulysses* by James Joyce, dramatized by Allan McClelland and directed by Henric Hirsch, starring Milo O'Shea (*left*; as Leopold Bloom) and June Tobin (*right*; as Molly Bloom). Peter Luke was series producer.

1963

First Night
(BBC-tv, 1963–64)

Presented a series of new plays written expressly for television with the emphasis on action and conflict. The series premièred with Alun Owen's 'The Strain' (22/9/63; dir. William T. Kotcheff; *l. to r.*, Michael Coles, Neil McCarthy, Glyn Owen, John Junkin, Jack MacGowran, and Ray Barrett); Nigel Kneale's 'The Road' (29/9/63; dir. Christopher Morahan) followed. Later came Simon Raven's 'The Scapegoat' (15/2/64; dir. Prudence FitzGerald) starring Kenneth More.

Five O'Clock Club
(A-R, 1963–66)

Held its Tuesday and Friday meetings for the under-12 year olds for three years, with hosts Muriel Young and Howard Williams (later Wally Whyton) handling the small-fry set-up of pop stars and weekly guests as well as playing stooge to puppet characters Ollie Beak and Fred Barker. Special spots were given to Grahame Dangerfield (dealing with pets), Jimmy Hanley (discussing hobbies), and Bert Weedon (on guitar). The series evolved out of **Lucky Dip** (A-R, 1958–61), which even had a 'Happy Cooking' segment presented by Fanny and Johnnie Cradock, when in turn that series became **Tuesday Rendezvous** (A-R, 1961–63) and featured pretty much the same studio line-up (Williams, Young, Weedon, etc.) that presented **Five O'Clock Club**. The programme was also known as **Ollie and Fred's Five O'Clock Club** from 1965; that same year Marjorie Sigley introduced the **Five O'Clock Funfair** (Rediffusion, 1965) series with the help of Ollie and Fred. Associated-Rediffusion's midday children's slot **Small Time** started in 1955 (running through to 1966), originally produced-directed by Pat Baker as 'a programme for children of five and under'. The early series, devised by Eric Spear, was presented by Susan Spear; Muriel Young and Wally Whyton presented the early evening version of the show from 1959, which included Fred Barker's first appearance (in a segment called 'Dogwatch') and was also the TV showcase for popular puppet Pussy Cat Willum during 1959–64. Weedon and Young are shown on the set of **Tuesday Rendezvous**.

Hornblower
(BBC-tv–Collier Young Associates, 3/6/63)

Produced at Elstree Studios as a colour-filmed, 50-minute pilot for a possible US/GB series, the C. S. Forester-derived story starred David Buck (*right*) as Lt.-Commander Horatio Hornblower. The Donald Wilson-scripted plot saw Hornblower quell a mutiny on a British man-of-war while outfoxing Napoleon's navy at the same time. Also appearing were Terence Longdon (*left*; as Lt. Bush), Nigel Green, Sean Kelly, Jeremy Bulloch, and Peter Arne. John Newland directed for producer Julian Plowden; executive producer was Collier Young. The programme was originally produced for, and first scheduled on, **Alcoa Première**. (US tx 28/2/63)

116

The Human Jungle
(Independent Artists Prod./ABC TV, 1963–65)

Herbert Lom was Dr Roger Corder in this addictive and fascinating series concerning the world of psychiatry. Corder's practice, patients, and his domestic life, with teenage daughter Jennifer (played by Sally Smith), provided the stories for the often moody twenty-six-episode series. When the doctor was not involved with a private case he was called on as a consultant to a public clinic. The series was created by Julian Wintle, who co-produced with Leslie Parkyn; the suitably hypnotic music was composed by Bernard Ebbinghouse and played by John Barry. Joan Collins (pictured with Lom) guested in the episode 'Struggle for a Mind'. A later series, called **The Inside Man** (LWT, 1969), featured Frederick Jaeger as doctor-psychiatrist-criminologist Dr James Austen in a 12 eps. × hour drama series produced by Derek Granger.

Love Story
(ATV, 1963–67; 1969; 1972–74)

An anthology series of plays about love in the 1960s and 1970s, originally produced by Antony Kearey, Dennis Vance, Josephine Douglas, Rex Firkin, and others. The specially written plays included 'The Habit of Loving' (17/6/63) adapted from her own novel by Doris Lessing, 'Some Grist for Mervyn's Mill' (12/8/63) by Mordecai Richler, and 'The Kiss of Truth' (2/9/63) by Jacques Gillies. Lewis Greifer was script consultant for the series during the 1960s. Dudley Moore appeared in a straight role for the Roman Polanski-scripted 'The Girl Opposite' (1/11/65), directed by John Cooper. Pictured are Julia Foster and Rodney Bewes in 'The Wedding of Smith Seven-Nine' (1/7/63).

The Marriage Lines
(BBC-tv, 1963–66)

Former actor Richard Waring created and scripted this comedy series specially for ex-**Brothers in Law** acting partner Richard Briers, and brought in the producer-director of the earlier series, Graeme Muir, to launch the new programme. Briers (*left*; as George Starling) and Prunella Scales (*right*; Kate Starling) were the young couple trying to adjust to married life in the confines of their Earl's Court flat; he was a city clerk and she had been his secretary. Ronald Hines and Christine Finn played their neighbours, Peter and Norah, during the first series. The fourth series introduced a third Starling, a baby daughter, adding to their already chaotic domestic life; the end of this series saw George fly off to start a new job in Lagos, appearing to bring the programme to an end when writer Waring thought that the fourth would be the last series. The fifth and final series had George return to England because Kate (and actress Prunella Scales) was pregnant and did not want to follow him out to Lagos. An endearing and sprightly series that helped launch Brier's amiable, light-comedy TV persona. Graeme Muir produced the first three series and Robin Nash produced the final two; a total of 43 eps. × 30 mins.

Maupassant
(Granada TV, 1963)

France in the 1880s was the setting for this series of theme-linked plays based on the tales by the master of the short story, Guy de Maupassant. The first episode was 'Wives and Lovers' (20/6/63; dir. Silvio Narizzano, adapt. Doris Lessing). Later plays were also dramatized by Lessing, with Stanley Miller and Hugh Leonard. Philip Mackie produced. Scene shows Leonard Rossiter and Angela Morant in 'The Story of a Farm Girl'.

Moonstrike
(BBC-tv, 1963)

Told the story of the men who flew the agile little Lysander aircraft into enemy-occupied Europe to deliver or pick up agents during the Second World War. The stories concerned not only the pilots of the special duties squadrons but also the individual agents of the special operations executive (SOE) and their undercover work after they were landed. Producer Gerard Glaister and creator-writer Robert Barr furnished the series with as much authenticity as possible, at times to the point where any dramatic impact faded in the face of over-earnest accuracy. A. A. Englander photographed the film sequences; Dudley Simpson composed the music. Lyndon Brook, *left*, and George Roderick appeared in the 'Unwelcome Guest' (11/4/63) episode.

Our Man at St Mark's
(A-R, 1963–65)

The amusing and often sentimental incidents in the day-to-day activities of a country vicar made up the content of this coy situation comedy. Leslie Phillips (*pictured*) filled the title role for the first series, supported in his rural ramblings by his girlfriend (played by Anne Lawson) and housekeeper (Joan Hickson). Donald Sinden took over as the parish parson in 1964, retaining Hickson's housekeeper but now assisted by a Sam Weller-style Harry Fowler as a reformed ex-crook; while the stories started to develop into a sort of soft-boiled clergy comedy. The series was created and written by James Kelly & Peter Miller and produced by Eric Maschwitz. The twelve-episode 1966 series was retitled **Our Man from St Mark's** when the Sinden character was promoted to archdeacon and went on to perform his duties in the precincts of a cathedral.

The Plane Makers
(ATV, 1963–65)

A taut drama series focusing on all aspects of the aviation industry, from the workshop floor to the boardroom, produced by Rex Firkin and script-edited by John Whitney and Geoffrey Bellman, and Wilfred Greatorex. However popular this early series was, it did not hit its high-water mark until it reappeared as **The Power Game** (ATV, 1965–66; 1969), specifically structured around the ambitious and ruthless tycoon character of John Wilder (played with easy menace by Patrick Wymark). The executive boardroom was now the main backdrop with Wilder scheming, lobbying, and bulldozing his way in the battle for power. Co-starring were Clifford Evans (as Caswell Bligh), Peter Barkworth (as Caswell's son Kenneth), Jack Watling (as sales director Don Henderson), and, continuing her earlier **The Plane Makers** role, Barbara Murray as Lady Wilder, the attractive yet neglected wife; Ann Firbank took over the part for the final series of **The Plane Makers**. Rex Firkin (1965–66) and David Reid (1969) produced the spin-off series. The scene shows (*l. to r.*) Barbara Murray, Patrick Wymark, and Michael Jayston in **The Power Game**.

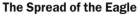

Ready, Steady, Go!
(A-R, 1963–66)

'The weekend starts here' Friday rock–pop show presented by Keith Fordyce and (perhaps more fondly remembered by the mid-1960s TV viewer) Cathy McGowan. The disco scene studio setting, bouncing with swinging teenagers, first of all featured such contemporary acts as The Springfields, The Beatles, and Johnny Kidd and the Pirates before the Mod fashion and its subculture set the programme up as the prime showcase for musicians like Little Stevie Wonder, Steam Packet, and The Rolling Stones. The programme had a title change to **Ready Steady Goes Live!** from April 1965 for a while.

Sergeant Cork
(ATV, 1963–66)

Was a meticulous Victorian policeman (played by John Barrie, *pictured*) operating in the early days of the CID when scientific forms of crime detection were just being developed. Created by the prolific Ted Willis, the series rivalled the familiar London setting of Sherlock Holmes with its dense Victorian atmosphere of opera cloaks and top hats combined with hansom cabs clattering along foggy, cobblestoned streets, but from a police procedural perspective. William Gaunt was Cork's young and eager assistant, Bob Marriott. The series producer was Jack Williams; designer Tom Lingwood created the appropriate mood-drenched settings. In the early 1980s Granada TV revisited the period and the genre with Peter Lovesey's **Cribb**.

Space Patrol
(National Interest Picture Prod./Wonderama Prods., 1963–64)

Featured the string-puppet adventures of Captain Larry Dart (*right*) of the United Galactic Organization, aided and assisted by a variety of colourful characters, including Husky the Martian, Slim the Venusian, and the Gabbler Bird (*left*). The thirty-nine half-hour episodes were written by creator Roberta Leigh, who also co-produced with Arthur Provis.

The Spread of the Eagle
(BBC-tv, 1963)

A nine-part cycle, based on three Roman plays by William Shakespeare, was producer Peter Dews's follow-up to his earlier, successful linking of Shakespeare's history plays, **An Age of Kings**. This time he packaged the Roman plays 'Coriolanus', 'Antony and Cleopatra', and 'Julius Caesar' into a nine-week saga emphasizing the plays' belief in Rome as an ideal. Keith Michell played Mark Antony, Peter Cushing (*2nd right*) was Cassius, Roland Culver was Menenius Agrippa, Beatrix Lehmann was Volumnia, Paul Eddington (*right*) was Brutus, Barry Jones (*left*) was Julius Caesar, Robert Hardy was Coriolanus, and Mary Morris appeared as Cleopatra.

1963

Stars and Garters
(A-R, 1963–66)

Traditional pub entertainment variety series heralded as a return to the music-hall, hosted by Ray Martine (with material written by Dick Vosburgh and Marty Feldman) and featuring the resident singers Clinton Ford, Kathy Kirby (*pictured*), Tommy Bruce, Julie Rayne, and Vince Hill. A one-off, hour-long programme called **Time, Gentlemen, Please!** (A-R, 5/12/62; dir. Rollo Gamble), with Daniel Farson taking a documentary look at the pub entertainment scene in London, was perhaps the format source of this series. The programme was retitled **The New Stars and Garters** for a few weeks during October–November 1965 and was introduced by actress Jill Browne, with assistance from William Rushton. A similar-themed show, **Wheeltappers' and Shunters' Social Club** (Granada TV, 1974–76), was produced by John Hamp featuring performers and audience in a northern working-men's club setting; comedians Bernard Manning and Colin Crompton hosted the 39 eps. × 45 mins.

The Sunday Play
(BBC-tv, 1963)

A series of television plays on contemporary themes–comedies, social dramas, love stories, and the occasional tragedy, all by modern authors. Plays were based on original scripts by Stewart Love, Henry Livings, Michael Gilbert, Bernard Kops, Thomas Murphy, Errol John, David Turner, Alan Plater, and several new young dramatists. The series also presented TV premières of contemporary stage and radio plays by James Saunders, Willis Hall, and Keith Waterhouse, and the Swedish writer Stig Dagerman as well as an American teleplay by Richard Nash. Producer of the series was John Elliot. **The Sunday Play** opened with Stewart Love's 'The Big Donkey' (31/3/63; dir. Herbert Wise), featuring Tom Bell (*left*) and Joseph Tomelty (*right*).

Taxi!
(BBC-tv, 1963–64)

The stories of a London cab driver, Sid Stone (played effortlessly by Sid James; *left*), made this Ted Willis series a rather lukewarm attempt at creating a social Dixon-on-wheels. Sid was an owner-driver who was always getting involved in other people's problems when not dealing with those of his partner Fred Cuddell (Bill Owen; *right*) or young driver Terry Mills (Ray Brooks). Drama and comedy interweaved throughout the stories but, ultimately, there appeared to be little excuse to mix the plot action with the world of cabbies. Michael Mills produced.

The Telegoons
(BBC-tv–Grosvenor Films, 1963–64)

TV puppet adventures of the immortal Goons (Neddy Seagoon, Major Bloodnok; Eccles, *right*; Bluebottle, *left*; Brigadier Gritpype-Thynne; Henry Crun; Minnie Bannister) whose weekly radio exploits were extremely popular during the 1950s. Harry Secombe, Spike Milligan, and Peter Sellars were temporarily reassembled to record new material where necessary, but basically the new visual version was made up from the classic radio scripts edited into 15-minute films. Tony Young produced. There had been two earlier Goon-like shows, **Trial Gallop** (BBC-tv, 13/2/51; 45 mins.) and **Goonreel** (BBC-tv, 2/7/52; 45 mins.), devised and written by Michael Bentine and Jimmy Grafton. A one-off, half-hour reunion show, **The Goon Show** (Thames TV, 8/8/68), featuring Sellers, Secombe, and Milligan (assisted by John Cleese and John Hamilton), was written by Milligan and directed by Joe McGrath; Peter Eton produced.

The Victorians

(Granada TV, 1963; 8 plays × 60 mins.)

Was a series of self-contained plays representing slices of nineteenth-century life, covering the period of the 1830s to the 1880s. The series was produced by Philip Mackie and performed by a TV repertory company consisting of Geoffrey Bayldon, Michael Barrington, Patricia Garwood, Ingrid Hafner, Barrie Ingham, Charles Kay, and John Wood. The eight plays were: 'The Rent Day' (31/5/63; by Douglas Jerrold, dir. Herbert Wise), 'London Assurance' (7/6/63; by Dion Boucicault, dir. Stuart Latham), 'Society' (14/6/63; by T. W. Robertson, dir. Graeme McDonald; *pictured* are players Ingham, *left*, and Kay), 'The Ticket of Leave Man' (21/6/63; by Tom Taylor, dir. Stuart Latham), 'Two Roses' (28/6/63; by James Albery, dir. Richard Everitt), 'The Silver King' (5/7/63; by Henry Arthur Jones and Henry Herman, dir. Herbert Wise), 'Still Waters Run Deep' (12/7/63; by Tom Taylor, dir. Cliff Owen), and 'Sweet Lavender' (19/7/63; by Arthur Wing Pinero, adapt. Gerald Savory and dir. Graeme McDonald). Granada TV followed up with similar revivals

from the Edwardian period in **The Edwardians** (Granada TV, 1965; 4 plays × 90 mins.), exhuming plays originally written and produced between 1901 and 1910. The four were: 'The Walls of Jericho' (3/5/65; by Alfred Sutro, dir. Howard Baker) with Patrick Allen, Diana Fairfax, and Fulton Mackay, 'Mid Channel' (10/5/65; by Arthur Pinero, dir. Howard Baker), 'Olive Latimer's Husband' (17/5/65; by Rudolf Besier, dir.-pr. Claude Whatham) with Barbara Jefford, Robin Bailey, and Mark Dignam, 'The Madras House' (24/5/65; by Harley Granville-Barker, dir. Julian Amyes) with Gerald Flood (*pictured*, *left*; with John Westbrook and Joan Heath), Gene Anderson, and Clifford Evans. The series was produced by Stuart Latham and the stories adapted by Gerald Savory. BBC TV also produced a series called **The Edwardians** (BBC-2, 21/11/72–9/1/73; 8 eps. × 80 mins.) which were dramatizations of famous people of the time; for example, the première episode, 'Mr Rolls and Mr Royce' (21/11/72; wr. Ian Curteis, dir. Gerald Blake), featured Michael

Jayston and Robert Powell as the founders of the famous motor firm.

World in Action

(Granada TV, 1963–)

A highly regarded public affairs programme presenting hard-news stories (usually before others), anticipating news and interpreting shifts and changes in society, and in the political scene. The original production team of the half-hour series consisted of Bill Grundy, Tim Hewat, Stephen Peet, Alex Valentine, Louis Wolfers, and Mike Wooller. The programmes were narrated by Derek Cooper and Wilfred Thomas. An irregular series of **World in Action Specials**, ranging in running time from half-hour to 90 minutes, began in 1973. **WIA** cameraman George Turner is pictured in Saigon, Vietnam, filming for a programme in November 1964.

1964

Baxter on Travel
(BBC-tv, 1964)

Featured comedian Stanley Baxter in a fortnightly series in which he took a jaundiced eye view of topics of national interest, such as deep sea diving (Baxter, *pictured*, with June Whitfield). The following episodes presented 'Baxter on Television', 'Baxter on Law', 'Baxter on Theatre', 'Baxter on Sex'. Michael Mills produced.

The Beat Room
(BBC-2, 1964–65)

Was billed as 'twenty-five minutes non-stop beat and shake' (later expanded to 30 mins.) and introduced by Pat Campbell. Early guests on the show were The Animals, Inez Foxx, Long John Baldry, Georgie Fame, Manfred Mann, Memphis Slim, and Lulu (*pictured*: The Beat Girls dancers). The programme was produced by Barry Langford. When this show ended **Gadzooks! It's All Happening** (BBC-2, 1965) took over with presenters Alan David and Christine Holmes introducing Marianne Faithfull, the popular The Animals, and other mid-1960s rock/pop acts; The Beat Girls also continued in this half-hour show. Then it was retitled **Gadzooks! It's the In Crowd** after five months, with Alan David co-presenting with Lulu, and eventually became plain **Gadzooks!**.

Beyond the Fringe
(BBC-2, 12/12/64)

A special farewell performance of the famous revue by the original cast: (*l. to r.*) Jonathan Miller, Alan Bennett, Dudley Moore, and Peter Cook. The 60-minute programme included highspots from the original show, plus some newer items, with such delights as Moore's classical pianist who could never find the last chord, Bennett performing his mad sermon, and Cook as the deadpan miner with literary ambitions; and their joint final take-off of Shakespearian absurdities. The theme music was by the Johnny Dankworth Seven; Duncan Wood directed for producer Don Silverman.

The Caves of Steel
(BBC-2, 5/6/64)

Peter Cushing (*pictured*) starred as Elijah Baley, the Deputy Commissioner of Police in the New York of some 200 years in the future. He was assisted in his investigation of the murder of a top scientist by a detective named R. Daneel Olivaw (played by John Carson). The 'R' stood for Robot. Isaac Asimov's 1954 science fiction novel was dramatized by Terry Nation; Peter Sasdy directed the 75-minute play for producer Eric Tayler (as a part of BBC-2's **Story Parade** series). Asimov's 1957 novel featuring the Elijah Baley character, *The Naked Sun*, later turned up as an episode (same title, tx 18/2/69) of **Out of the Unknown**, adapted by Robert Muller and directed by Rudolph Cartier.

122

Cinema

(Granada TV, 1964–75)

A half-hour, weekly film magazine programme (of some 534 eps.) that shuffled between clips of new releases, star interviews, and retrospective extracts. The première presenter was Bamber Gascoigne (for 3 months), followed in succession by Derek Granger, Michael Scott (2½ years), Mark Shivas (6 months), Michael Parkinson (2 years), Clive James (35 progs.), and Brian Trueman. Granada later introduced the junior-slanted **Clapperboard** (1972–82; 254 eps. × 25 mins.) with Chris Kelly as host; Muriel Young was the original producer. **Clapperboard North West**, taking in the history of film-making in the north-west, appeared briefly during 1978–79, again with Kelly as host. Lee Marvin (*shown*) was a guest in a 1969 **Cinema** edition.

Cluff

(BBC-tv, 1964–65)

Leslie Sands (*left*) played the North Country sleuth Sergeant Caleb Cluff as a sort of Maigret of Yorkshire in this series written by Gil North (Geoffrey Horne), author of the original novels. **Cluff** was a spin-off from the anthology series **Detective**, episode 'The Drawing' (6/4/64; wr. North, dir. Terence Dudley, with Sands as Cluff). The stolid Cluff moved through the stories in an almost casual way, unmasking the villain or solving the crime purely by waiting and watching until the culprits gave themselves away. The series was produced and directed by Terence Dudley; cameraman Ewart Needham made good use of the Yorkshire locations. Pictured are Sands and John McKelevey.

Crossroads

(ATV, 1964–88)

Began as a late afternoon domestic soap serial set in the fictitious midlands' King's Oak Crossroads Motel and was, originally, built around the character of Meg Richardson (played by Noele Gordon; *left*), the motel's owner. The other regular characters during the early years were Meg's daughter Jill (Jane Rossington; *standing*) and son Sandy (Roger Tonge; *right*), their cousin Brian Jarvis (David Fennell), Meg's sister Kitty Jarvis (Beryl Johnstone), her husband Dick (Brian Kent), the motel's Spanish chef Carlos (Anthony Morton), waitress Marilyn Gates (Sue Nicholls), and receptionist Diane Lawton (Susan Hanson). The undemanding serial followed typical TV-style soap opera life in a midlands halfway-house motel (ATV had originally titled it **The Midland Road**) but the cosy antics of the characters and the rather hurried production schedule soon became the butt of endless jokes, culminating, perhaps, in Victoria Wood's wonderful 'Acorn Antiques' pastiche. The serial's foundation character, Noele Gordon's Meg Richardson, was written out of the story in 1981 (Meg sailed off on the *QE2* to a new life) and the motel was then run by a succession of characters (John Bentley's Hugh Mortimer, Ronald Allen's David Hunter, Gabrielle Drake's Nicola Freeman, Terence Rigby's Tommy Lancaster) until Nicola's stepson Daniel Freeman (Philip Goodhew) finally took over the motel, leaving the last original, Jill, to zoom off in a sports car toward new horizons with another character, John Maddingham (Jeremy Nicholas). Over the 4,510 episodes the motel sheltered the likes of such quirky and/or engaging characters as motel cleaner Amy Turtle (Ann George), the dim-witted Benny (Paul Henry), and the personable Barbara Brady (Sue Lloyd). **Crossroads** was based on an original idea by writers Hazel Adair and Peter Ling; the producers over the years included Reg Watson, Jack Barton, Phillip Bowman, and William Smethurst. The easygoing theme music was provided by Tony Hatch & Jackie Trent; later rearranged by Paul McCartney and Wings.

1964

Culloden
(BBC-1, 15/12/64)

The battle of Culloden outside Inverness in 1746 was the last battle to be fought on British soil. It was here that the Scottish Jacobites made their one final attempt to restore the Royal Stuarts to the thrones of Scotland, England, and Ireland, and to sever the Union with England. In creating this stupendous 70-minute documentary reconstruction writer-producer Peter Watkins used a newsreel camera technique to stunning, and at times horrific, effect; working on a shoestring budget, also, he could only afford the use of twenty-five redcoat uniforms and fifteen Highland costumes. The real battle engaged some fifteen thousand soldiers. Watkins's cast of soldiers consisted of plasterers and students, teachers and solicitors. John Prebble was historical adviser (it was based on his book); stuntman Derek Ware was the battle co-ordinator; photography was by Dick Bush; and the film was edited by Michael Bradsell.

Detective
(BBC-tv, 1964; BBC-1, 1968–69)

In this packaged anthology series BBC TV aimed to showcase, in novel-to-teleplay form, examples of the best literary detectives in the world of crime fiction. The first series of 18 eps. × 60 mins. was introduced by Rupert Davies in his role as Maigret, for producer David Goddard. The series premièred with 'The Moving Toyshop' (30/3/64; scr. John Hopkins from the novel by Edmund Crispin, dir. Shaun Sutton) featuring Richard Wordsworth as Professor Gervase Fen. Other stories that followed included 'Trent's Last Case' (13/4/64; from the 1913 novel by E. C. Bentley, dir. Peter Duguid), with Michael Gwynn as Philip Trent, 'The Judas Widow' (27/4/64; scr. Dick Sharples from the novel by Carter Dickson, dir. Edgar Wreford), with David Horne as Sir Henry Merrivale, 'Death in Ecstasy' (8/6/64; from the 1936 novel by Ngaio Marsh, dir. Shaun Sutton), with Geoffrey Keen as Det. Chief Insp. Alleyn, and 'The Quick One' (27/7/64; scr. Clifford Witting from the story by G. K. Chesterton, dir. Gilchrist Calder), with Mervyn Johns as Father Brown. The anthology was a natural springboard for potential series, three of which later appeared: 'The Drawing' (6/4/64) became **Cluff**, 'The Speckled Band' (18/5/64) became **Sherlock Holmes** in 1965, and 'The Case of Oscar Brodski' (6/7/64) became **Thorndyke**. Four years later producer Verity Lambert returned **Detective** for seventeen episodes, starting off with 'The Deadly Climate' (17/5/68; scr. George F. Kerr from the novel by Ursula Curtiss, dir. John Frankau), with Dudley Sutton as reporter/investigator Robert Carmichael. This was followed by such stories as 'Born Victim' (5/7/68; scr. William Emms from the novel by Hillary Waugh, dir. Alan Bridges), with Lee Montague as Police Chief Fellows, 'The Murders in the Rue Morgue' (1/9/68; scr. James MacTaggart from the story by Edgar Allan Poe, dir. James Cellan Jones), with Edward Woodward (*right*) as Auguste Dupin and Charles Kay (*left*) as Poe, 'Prisoner's Plea' (7/9/69; scr. William Emms from Hillary Waugh's novel, dir. Jonathan Alwyn), with Lee Montague again as Fellows, and 'Hunt the Peacock' (12/10/69; scr. Hugh Leonard from the novel by H. R. F. Keating, dir. Ben Rea), with Zia Mohyeddin as Inspector Ghote. The third series (Sept.–Nov. 1969) was produced by Jordan Lawrence.

Diary of a Young Man
(BBC-1, 8/8–12/9/64)

Presented a six-part (× 45 min.) story of two young northerners and their experiences as they arrive in London and observe the people, places, and contemporary attitudes across the city. (*l. to r.*) Victor Henry, Nerys Hughes, and Richard Moore headed the cast. The often shrewd, sometimes cynical scripts were by Troy Kennedy Martin and John McGrath; Kenneth Loach and Peter Duguid directed; James MacTaggart produced.

The Eamonn Andrews Show
(ABC TV, 1964–69; Thames TV, 1979)

Was a late night (Sundays) medley of talk and music, hosted by the ever-smiling Andrews as he guided his celebrity guests through 45 minutes of painless patter. The early ABC TV production team included Roy Bottomley, Tom Brennand, Tom Clegg (as director), Malcolm Morris, and Lloyd Shirley. The revived Thames TV series (of thirteen hour-long eps.) was produced by Stella Richman. Shown, with Andrews, *left*, are guests Dora Bryan and Kenneth Williams. There had been an earlier series, **The Eamonn Andrews Show** (BBC-tv, 1956–57), which was shown under BBC TV's *Saturday Comedy Hour* billing; S. C. (Sid) Green and R. M. (Dick) Hills scripted the music-dance-comedy format for producer Ernest Maxin.

Fire Crackers
(ATV, 1964–65)

The work-shy firemen of the forgotten English village of Cropper's End were the focus of **Fire Crackers** (ATV, 1964–65), a comedy series blending Keystone Cops slapstick with the mischievious spirit of Will Hay. On closer inspection, the zany formula appeared to be patterned pretty closely after Hay's 1941 film *Where's That Fire?*, with Alfred Marks, Joe Baker, Cardew Robinson, Ronnie Brody, and Sidney Bromley performing similar incompetent firewatch routines (on or off their turn-of-the-century fire engine, called Bessie). The series was written by Fred Robinson (responsible for creating ATV's hit series **The Larkins** in 1958) and produced by Alan Tarrant.

The Four Seasons of Rosie Carr
(BBC-1, 4–25/7/64)

A cycle of four enchanting though over-sentimentalized plays following the life of an indomitable woman, Rosie Carr (played by June Barry in the first story, Jane Hylton in the last three), from the Edwardian era to the 1950s. The Ted Willis-scripted quartet opened with Rosie working as a lowly tavern barmaid in the spring of 1907 ('Spring at the Winged Horse') and courted by street-trader Tommo (Kenneth J. Warren); the second play showed Rosie in her thirties, married to the unemployed Tommo and trying to bring up a family in a London slum ('Summer in Matlock Street'; (*l. to r.*) Pamela Hewes, Terry Brooks, Gretchen Franklin, Hylton, Rose Hiller, Catherine Finn, Elisabeth Wade); by the third play ('Autumn Near the Angel') she was in her fifties, with a world war about to start, her husband working only occasionally, and her daughter Millie (played by June Barry) about to get married; the fourth and final play ('Long Winter Journey') saw Rosie as a widow in her late sixties, trying to come to terms with life in the strange Welfare State of the 1950s. The series was produced by James MacTaggart and directed by Peter Graham Scott.

Frankie Howerd
(BBC-1, 1964–65)

The improvisation style of Frankie Howerd, linked with his individual gift for nervous, anecdotal patter, had not only helped guide his career through the various currents and face-lifts of British TV comedy but also warmed him to two generations of small-screen viewers (Howerd having originally trodden a similar TV path as Benny Hill and Charlie Drake). Although his highly popular-for-its-time sitcom **Up Pompeii!** tended to overshadow Howerd's other TV performances he still managed to score with **The Frankie Howerd Show** (ATV, 9/8–13/9/69), **The Howerd Confessions** (Thames TV, 2/9–7/10/76), and **Frankie Howerd Strikes Again** (Yorkshire TV, 1/9–6/10/81). Howerd also attempted to launch another bawdy sitcom series with the 45-minute pilot **A Touch of the Casanovas** (Thames TV, 31/12/75), scripted by Sid Colin and Hugh Stuckley from an idea by Howerd. In more recent years he hosted the British pilot version of **The Gong Show** (C4/Gambit Enterprises, 9/12/85) and starred in the children's slot sitcom **All Change** (Yorkshire TV/Childsplay Prod., 15/11–20/12/89).

1964

The Fugitive
(Quinn Martin Prod.; ITV tx 1964–)

Became one of TV's great chase sequences, lasting for almost four years. The basic theme and format (not a million miles removed from Victor Hugo's *Les Misérables*) focused on David Janssen's Dr Richard Kimble, the fugitive of the title who was chasing the one-armed man (played by Bill Raisch) who had murdered Kimble's wife, and for which Kimble took the rap. In constant pursuit of the innocent-on-the-run was the relentless police Lt. Gerard (Barry Morse). (US tx 1963–67)

Gideon's Way
(ATV, 1964–65)

John Gregson starred in this 26 eps. × hour police procedural drama series based on the twenty-one Gideon novels written by John Creasey under the name of J. J. Marric. Gregson's Commander George Gideon (*pictured*) was an easygoing detective whose methods were often in conflict with the scientific approach of his younger assistant, Det. Chief Insp. David Keen (Alexander Davion). Daphne Anderson (as Gideon's wife, Kate) and Ian Rossiter (as Det. Chief Supt. Bell) supported. Robert S. Baker and Monty Berman produced.

Great Temples of the World
(ATV, 1964–66)

Sir Kenneth Clark acted as guide to many of the world's great buildings, choosing them not merely for their artistic virtues, but for the clues they offered to the past in this lengthy, irregularly shown series. The Basilica of St Mark's, Chartres Cathedral, and Karnak were among the locations honoured. Clark's TV forays into international art and artefacts included his series of talks discussing the birth of landscape painting, **Landscape Into Art** (ATV, 1961), talks about the life and work of the great Dutch artist **Rembrandt** (ATV, 21/5–4/6/62), three talks on **Discovering Japanese Art** (ATV, 2–16/12/63), a three-part series on nineteenth-century painters Courbet, Manet, and Degas in **Three Faces of France** (ATV, 18/4–2/5/66), the six-part **Pioneers of Modern Painting** (ATV, 13/11–18/12/71), a fifteen-part look at **Romantic v. Classic Art** (ATV, 13/6–10/10/73), and, once again, **Rembrandt** (BBC-2, 29/6–27/7/76). Clark is pictured at the Basilica of St Mark's, Venice, with an ATV camera crew.

The Great War
(BBC-2, 1964)

A 26 eps. × 40 mins. history of the 1914–18 War written by young historians John Terraine, Correlli Barnett, and Alistair Horne for producers Tony Essex and Gordon Watkins. The multiple award-winning documentary, using the voices of Sir Michael Redgrave, Sir Ralph Richardson, and Emlyn Williams, was produced in collaboration with the Imperial War Museum, the Canadian Broadcasting Corporation, and the Australian Broadcasting Commission. A few years earlier producer John Irwin had presented **First World War** (ATV, 1961), a half-hour series of six lectures by A. J. P. Taylor.

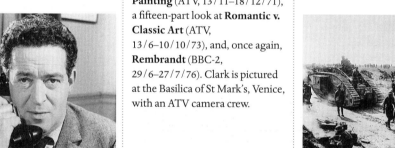

Hamlet at Elsinore
(BBC-tv–Danmarks Radio, 19/4/64)

Was something of a first in British television techniques. It marked the first time that a major full-length play had been televised by outside broadcast cameras working on location. The original suggestion for making the version in the authentic setting came from the Danish Television Service. For director Philip Saville the Danes laid on two of their O.B. units (making ten cameras available) and provided a 200-man force of extras from the Danish army and police forces. A special power cable for lighting was laid from Elsinore to the castle, and nearly 150 lights were used. Christopher Plummer (*centre*; with Peter Prowse, *left*) starred as Hamlet, supported by Robert Shaw, Alec Clunes, June Tobin, Jo Maxwell Muller, and Michael Caine (*right*). Peter Luke produced the 170-minute play.

The Hidden Truth
(Rediffusion, 1964)

Dealt with forensic science and presented the cases—an air crash, arson, drunken driving, forgery, disputed paternity—of pathologists Professor Robert Lazard (Alexander Knox; *left*), Dr Henry Fox (James Maxwell; *right*), Dr Ruth Coliton (Elizabeth Weaver), and Dr Hamavid de Silva (Zia Mohyeddin). It was claimed that every episode illustrated aspects of real-life cases. Four hour-long episodes were produced by Stella Richman. The programme was created by Geoffrey Bellman and John Whitney.

Horizon
(BBC-2, 1964–)

The science magazine programme that presented science not as a series of isolated discoveries but as a continuing and essential part of twentieth-century culture. Each programme revolved around one central theme, focusing on two or three aspects and dealing with them at length. **Horizon** also presented occasional dramatizations of science history: 'Hand Me My Sword, Humphrey' (25/12/66; wr. Richard Wade, dir. Peter R. Smith) cast Dudley Foster as Humphrey Hastings, a fictitious inventor and amateur scientist; 'Dynamo' (23/2/67; wr.-pr. Leo Aylen), with Ian Richardson (*shown*) as Michael Faraday and Richard Bebb as Sir Humphrey Davy. The episode of 25/12/66 developed into a 6 eps. × 30 mins. Christmas special, **A Hundred Years of Humphrey Hastings** (BBC-2, 16/11–21/12/67; wr. Wade, dir. Smith, pr. Ramsay Short), with Dudley Foster playing the generations of amateur scientist Hastings from 1867 through to 1967. **Horizon** began as a monthly series (pr. Ramsay Short and ed. Philip Daly) but in January 1965 became a fortnightly fixture.

Impromptu
(BBC-2, 27/4–15/6/64)

Unscripted comedy show, devised by producer David Croft, in which the five members of the cast (Lance Percival, *foreground*, Victor Spinetti, *right*, Peter Reeves, *left*, Anne Cunningham, *centre*, and Betty Impey) were given cards bearing the characters, situations, and first lines forming the outline of each programme. Jeremy Hawk was the card-giver (called the 'Boss Man') and John Barry supplied the music. In the 1980s Channel Four introduced **Whose Line Is It Anyway?** (C4/Hat Trick Prods., 1988–), a half-hour series of ad-libbed comedy based on studio audience suggestions for club circuit improvisation stars (such as John Sessions, Josie Lawrence, Tony Slattery) to perform, rotating as weekly guests. Former barrister Clive Anderson chaired the games. The programme was devised by Dan Patterson and Mark Leveson.

Jazz 625
(BBC-2, 1964–66)

Was one of the most welcome features of the new BBC-2 channel. Of all the forms of music seen on television, jazz is perhaps best suited to the small screen as TV has the unique ability to capture the spontaneity of a jazz performance, by the use of compelling close-ups to show the musician at work. Each edition of the programme featured a particular facet of jazz, drawing on such talent as Dizzy Gillespie (*pictured*), Duke Ellington and his Orchestra, the Modern Jazz Quartet with guitarist Laurindo Almeida, New Orleans trumpeter Henry 'Red' Allen, the Oscar Peterson Trio, the Dave Brubeck Quartet, Errol Garner, the Woody Herman Band, and the Julian 'Cannonball' Adderley Sextet. British jazz was represented by the Tubby Hayes Quintet, Chris Barber's Jazzband, the Humphrey Lyttelton Fifteen, and others. In November 1964 **Jazz 625** broadcast 'In Memoriam—Charlie Parker', a musical tribute to the great saxophonist featuring J. J. Johnson (trombone), Sonny Stitt (alto-sax), Howard McGhee (trumpet), Walter Bishop (piano), Tommy Potter (bass), and Kenny Clarke (drums). **Jazz 625** was introduced by Steve Race (and later by Humphrey Lyttelton) and produced by Terry Henebery. (A ten-part series of re-edited editions of original **Jazz 625** programmes were shown during the summer of 1991.) Following on, **Commonwealth Jazz Club** (BBC-2, 2–30/9/65) ran for 5 eps. × half-hour under producer Henebery; **Jazz Goes to College** (BBC-2, 1966–67) presented international jazz recorded in concert at various colleges and universities around Britain; and **Jazz Scene** (BBC-2, 1969–70), a weekly series (also produced by Henebery) featured some of Britain's top jazz artists at the Ronnie Scott Club, then celebrating its tenth anniversary in September 1969. The opening of Channel Four also introduced **Jazz on Four** (C4/various, 1982–83) and, later, **Jazz at the Gateway** (C4/Scottish TV, 1987).

Kipling
(BBC-1, 1964)

Lightweight series of Rudyard Kipling anecdotes taken from the 1,200-word sketches he wrote for a Lahore daily during the 1880s. For purposes of continuity two regular characters—newspaper editor William Stevens (Joss Ackland; *left*) and his young assistant James Lockwood (Kenneth Fortescue)—weaved in and out of the stories, two of which were usually combined to strengthen each episode. Several other regular Kipling characters appeared during the series but the most amusing were the *Soldiers Three*: Privates Stanley Ortheris (Harry Landis), Jock Learoyd (Douglas Livingstone; *right*), and Terence Mulvaney (David Burke; *centre*). Their boozing and scrounging adventures were recounted in 'Private Learoyd's Story' (26/7/64; wr. Anthony Read, dir. Peter Cregeen), 'The Madness of Private Ortheris' (30/8/64; wr. A. R. Rawlinson, dir. Shaun Sutton), 'Black Jack' (20/9/64; wr. Pat Dunlop, dir. Peter Cregeen), 'Watches of the Night' (11/10/64; wr. William Emms, dir. Ian Curteis), 'Love o' Women' (1/11/64; wr. William Emms, dir. Max Varnel), and 'His Private Honour' (22/11/64; wr. William Emms, dir. Lionel Harris). David Goddard and John Robins (from ep. 17) produced the 25 eps. × 50 mins. series.

The Likely Lads
(BBC-2/BBC-1, 1964–66)

First-rate Dick Clements & Ian La Fresnais sitcom series centring on a couple of young northern boys-around-town, the extrovert Terry Collier (played by James Bolam; *left*) and the plodding Bob Ferris (Rodney Bewes; *right*), who were continually getting themselves involved in humorous schemes and situations, usually associated with girls, pubs, and their jobs. When this popular series came to the end of its run Bob had a girlfriend, Thelma (Brigit Forsyth), and Terry was off to new pastures. Clement & La Fresnais returned with Bob and Terry in **Whatever Happened to the Likely Lads?** (BBC-1, 1973–74), picking their story up when Terry returned home after five years in the army and Bob was about to marry his boss's daughter, Thelma. Clement & La Fresnais produced the first series of 20 eps. × 25 mins. James Gilbert and Bernard Thompson produced the 1970s series of 27 eps. × 30 mins. Anglo-EMI produced a feature film version in 1976.

Line-Up
(BBC-2, 1964–72)

Began as a 10-minute curtain-raiser to the evening's programmes on the second channel until in September of its première year it was extended, slotted in at the end of the evening, and became **Late Night Line-Up**. It ran six or seven nights a week and eventually marked up more than 3,000 editions, presenting slots for films, books, jazz, folk and progressive rock music and, in October 1965, adding **Line-Up Review**, the first regular programme dealing at length with the world of television, as well as **Plunder**, billed as 'a weekly raid on the archives of BBC Television' (pre-1955 programmes). 'Colour Me Pop' began as a 25-minute 'Saturday diversion' from 7/9/68 (produced by Steve Turner for **Late Night Line-Up**), with the first edition featuring The Hollies; it eventually went out under its own **Colour Me Pop** (BBC-2, 1968–69) banner from 2/11/68 (edited by Rowan Ayers) and presented such popular bands of the time as Jethro Tull, The Nice, The Alan Price Set, Julie Driscoll and The Brian Auger Trinity, and Love Sculpture. **Film Night** (BBC-2, 1969–76) developed out of the **Late Night Line-Up** segment 'The Film World Past and Present' with Philip Jenkinson; **Film Night** was presented by Tony Bilbow (*pictured*) and Jenkinson, and edited by Ayers; in 1975 producer Barry Brown tried out a trio of young presenters, Jane Mercer, David Castell, and Chris Petit, for a short period. **Disco 2** (BBC-2, 1970–71), introduced by Tommy Vance, was also known as 'Line-Up's Disco 2' when it started on 10/1/70. The original **Late Night Line-Up** team consisted of Denis Tuohy, Michael Dean, Nicholas Tresilian, and Joan Bakewell.

Little Big Business
(Granada TV, 1964–65)

Starred David Kossoff (*left*) as the sage, stubborn Marcus Lieberman and Francis Matthews (*right*) as his ambitious, educated son, Simon, who were involved in the furniture business and in father-and-son skirmishes. Writing by Jack Pulman was nicely flavoured with gentle, Jewish humour; Peter Eton produced the half-hour series. Granada TV and producer Eton had earlier tried out a pilot half-hour episode on 8/8/63 with Kossoff and James Maxwell as Simon.

Match of the Day
(BBC-2, 1964–66; BBC-1, 1966–)

Was born when Bryan Cowgill, negotiating for BBC TV, proposed to Alan Hardaker (representing the Football League) that the BBC record 45 minutes of a selected league match and put it out on the infant BBC-2 the same evening. **Match of the Day** moved to BBC-1 the same year as the World Cup was played in England, a watershed event which transformed football from a television sport into a serious television subject. Alan Chivers was the original producer. Kenneth Wolstenholme (*pictured*) was, with Wally Barnes, among the first outside broadcast commentators on the programme.

1964

Meet the Wife
(BBC-1, 1964–65)

Was developed from one of the **Comedy Playhouse** segments ('The Bed', 28/12/63; wr. Ronald Wolfe and Ronald Chesney, pr. John Paddy Carstairs), into an amusing and enjoyable series featuring (as in the original) Thora Hird and Freddie Frinton (*shown*) as a northern married couple, the Blacklocks. Their constant, mutually affectionate bickering and skirmishing (she the bossy wife, he the sometimes rebellious husband) usually over the most trivial of matters always resulted in a cuddlesome reunion at the end, with the Hird–Frinton partnership sparkling to Wolfe & Chesney's crisp dialogue and pacing. Robin Nash produced the 30-minute series.

Miss Adventure
(ABC TV, 1964)

The comfortably contoured Hattie Jacques played the male-hunting Stacey Smith, a confidential investigator for a private-eye agency who gets herself embroiled in various deeds and disasters. The programme was presented as a series of multi-part stories: 'Strangers in Paradise' (6 parts) involved her in murder and blackmail in Greece; 'The Velvet Touch' (4 parts) saw her outsmart a con man; and 'Journey to Copenhagen' (3 parts) where more mystery and intrigue came her way via the title description. Unlike her *Carry On* film and **Sykes** TV characterizations Jacques played it fairly straight for this series, despite her natural, bubbly presence. Peter and Marjorie Yeldham composed the scripts (Peter Yeldham solo for the 3-parter) and Jonathan Alwyn directed; Ernest Maxin produced the 13 eps. × 45 mins. series. Maurice Kaufmann (*left*) and Jacques are pictured disposing of a body in the première serial.

Play School
(BBC-2, 1964–88)

Used all the advantages of television to provide a 'nursery school' for the under-fives, featuring a Pets' Corner, a Play School garden, songs, traditional games, and even at one time George Melly presenting an ABC of jazz. Alongside the toy characters of Humpty Dumpty, Jemima, and Teddy the series also featured presenters Julie Stevens and Terence Holland (*pictured*); later Brian Cant, Miranda Connell, Derek Griffiths, Lionel Morton, and Floella Benjamin. Joy Whitby produced the half-hour, Monday to Friday morning shows.

The Protectors
(ABC TV, 1964)

Were the team that offered protection and security at a commercial rate to prevent crime. The do-good line-up consisted of Ian Souter (played by the bearded and burly Andrew Faulds; *left*) and Robert Shoesmith (Michael Atkinson; *centre*), who headed the outfit, and their breezy secretary Heather Keys (Ann Morrish; *right*). The 14 eps. × hour series was produced by Michael Chapman. A couple of years earlier US television had featured a drama series created by Eric Ambler called **Checkmate** (CBS TV, 1960–62) which presented a group of criminologists engaged in preventing crimes.

R3
(BBC-1, 1964–65)

Title referred to Research Centre Number Three, a fictional establishment connected to the Ministry of Research. The theme of the series was to interweave the lives of the principal scientists with their personal and professional activities, giving the white-coated ones a 'beyond the laboratory door' dimension. Featured players were John Robinson (as Sir Michael Gerrard, head of R3), Elizabeth Sellers (*right*), Richard Wordsworth (*left*), Moultrie Kelsall, and, in the second series, Michael Hawkins and Oliver Reed. Under story editor N. J. Crisp the first series dealt with a wide range of contemporary research, taking in such topics of the times as missiles and drugs, but the second series tended to stray off in the direction of espionage and agents. The first 26 eps. × 50 mins. series was produced by Andrew Osborn and (2nd series) John Robins.

Six
(BBC-2, 12/12/64–16/1/65)

A series in which six film-makers were given freedom to express themselves without compromise, offering them the opportunity to produce work that did not fit into a conventional TV category. The 30- to 60-minute plays were 'Diary of a Nobody' (12/12/64; adapt.-dir. Ken Russell from the novel by the Grossmith Brothers); 'The Chase' (19/12/64; wr. Troy Kennedy Martin and Michael Elster, the latter also dir.); 'Don't I Look Like a Lord's Son' (26/12/64; wr.-dir. Joe Massot); 'The Day of Ragnarok' (2/1/65; wr.-dir. John McGrath); 'The Logic Game' (9/1/65; wr. Philip Saville (also dir.) and Jane Arden); and 'Andy's Game' (16/1/65; wr.-dir. David Andrews). Pictured are Vivian Pickles, Brian Murphy, and Avril Elgar in 'Diary of a Nobody'.

Stingray
(AP Films Prod.–ATV/ITC, 1964–65)

Was producer Gerry Anderson's third string-puppet production, following on from the successful **Supercar** and **Fireball XL5**. The stories were set in the year 2000 and featured the crew of the super submarine Stingray, commanded by Captain Troy Tempest (voiced by Don Mason) with assistance from his First Mate, Phones (voice by Robert Easton), and an underwater-bred beauty called Marina. The organization behind the sub and its crew was the World Aquanaut Security Patrol, headed by Commander Shore (voice by Ray Barrett); his daughter Atlanta (voice by Lois Maxwell) also shared in the adventures. Thirty-nine half-hour submersions were produced.

Studio '64
(ATV, 1964)

Executive producer-director Stuart Burge brought together a group of directors and writers to create six plays with complete freedom to produce whatever kind of TV play each writer and directed wanted. The fortnightly series premièred with Nigel Kneale's 'The Crunch' (19/1/64; dir. Michael Elliott) and followed with Stanley Mann's 'Better Luck Next Time' (2/2/64; dir. Silvio Narizzano), Ken Taylor's 'The Devil and John Brown' (23/2/64; dir. Burge), Giles Cooper's 'A Wicked World' (8/3/64; dir. Donald McWhinnie; with David Buck, *left*, and Peter Sallis, *right*), Keith Waterhouse & Willis Hall's 'The Happy Moorings' (22/3/65; dir. David Greene), and Clive Exton's 'The Close Prisoner' (19/4/64; dir. Ted Kotcheff).

1964

The Sullavan Brothers
(ATV, 1964–65)

Legal drama series featuring four brothers, three solicitors and a barrister, operating as a team. The 55-minute series of twenty-six episodes, created and edited by Ted Willis for producer Jack Williams, starred Anthony Bate (as Paul; *right*), Tenniel Evans (John), Hugh Manning (Robert; *left*), David Summer (Patrick), and Mary Kenton (as John's wife, Beth).

Tales from Europe: The Singing, Ringing Tree
(BBC-1, 19–26/11 and 3/12/64)

Was part of a series of films (generally shown in serial form) from various European sources and was transmitted under the general title of **Tales from Europe**. Perhaps the most famous (or most fondly remembered) film was the 1958 East German production **The Singing, Ringing Tree**, directed and co-written (with Anne Geelhaer) by Francesco Stefani for the DEFA company as **Das Singende Klingende Baumchen**. The BBC TV 3 parts × 25 mins. fairy story told of a Prince who set out to find a magic tree to offer to a bad-tempered Princess. The cast included Christel Bodenstein, Charles-Hans Vogt, and Eckart Dux; the English version was written and presented by Peggy Miller, and told by Antony Bilbow.

Theatre 625
(BBC-2, 1964–68)

Was set up to explore dramatic themes rather more profoundly than had been possible up to that time. Starting just a few weeks after the launch of BBC-2, under project producer Cedric Messina, the programme attempted to use as much original material as possible, though existing plays were adapted when appropriate. Opening play, 'The Seekers' (3–10–17/5/64), was the first of a trilogy written by Ken Taylor and directed by Alvin Rakoff. Among the more outstanding productions over the programme's four-year run were Giles Cooper's trilogy consisting of 'Unman, Wittering and Zigo' (27/6/65; dir. Donald McWhinnie) (filmed by Paramount/Mediarts in 1971), 'Seek Her Out' (4/7/65), and 'The Long House' (11/7/65); and three plays under the subtitle of 'The World of George Orwell', '1984' (28/11/65; scr. Nigel Kneale), 'Keep the Aspidistra Flying' (7/11/65), and 'Coming Up for Air' (21/11/65), all directed by Christopher Morahan. See also separate entries for **Theatre 625** presentations, **Talking to a Stranger**, and **The Year of the Sex Olympics**. Pictured are Peter Blythe and Tamara Hinchco as John and Nadia Ebony in 'Unman, Wittering and Zigo'.

Thorndyke
(BBC-tv, 1964)

Stemming from an introductory episode in the anthology series **Detective** ('The Case of Oscar Brodski', 6/7/64; adapt. Allan Prior from a story by R. Austin Freeman, dir. Richmond Harding), this series featured the scientific sleuthings of Dr John Evelyn Thorndyke in the early days of forensic science (with Peter Copley, *pictured*, continuing his role from the anthology). The stories were based on the works of crime author Richard Austin Freeman whose hero solved his cases via the microscope in his private laboratory. Thorndyke, in a Holmes and Watson style, had two principal associates, Dr Jervis (Paul Williamson) and manservant Polton (Patrick Newell), who acted as the Watson-like foils to Thorndyke's new-fangled lab bench techniques. The 50-minute episodes were produced by John Robins and photographed by David Prosser. Other Thorndyke/Freeman adaptations also appeared in Thames TV's **The Rivals of Sherlock Holmes** in the early 1970s.

Top of the Pops
(BBC-tv, 1964–)

Longest-running British popular music show based on hits from the current week's top twenty or thirty, with studio guest artists miming their songs. The programme was originally shown on Wednesdays but was soon shifted to Thursdays, with première presenter Jimmy Savile (alternating with David Jacobs, Alan Freeman, and Pete Murray during the early days) and original producer Johnny Stewart. The programme was first presented from BBC's Manchester studios with a set made to resemble a coffee bar disco and the DJs sitting at turntables. During the 1970s, under producer Robin Nash, the show featured studio dancers Pan's People and Legs and Co. who performed to records when the artists were not available in person. *Pick of the Pops*, BBC radio's Light Programme record-charts show, was the basic model for the TV programme. Singer Sandie Shaw can be seen (*bottom right*); with Jimmy Savile (*standing in background*).

Victoria Regina
(Granada TV, 13/11–4/12/64)

A four-part series of plays chosen by adapter-producer Peter Wildeblood from playwright Laurence Housman's collection of short plays about Queen Victoria (Housman's plays had been banned by the Lord Chamberlain until 1937). The selected episodes marked the milestones in Victoria's career, starting from when she came to the throne in 1837, covering her choice of Prince Albert for consort, marrying him in 1840, his death of typhoid in 1861, and ending at her diamond jubilee in 1897. Patricia Routledge (*left*; with Barbara Couper) portrayed the four ages of the Queen; Max Adrian played Disraeli, Geoffrey Dunn was the Archbishop of Canterbury, and German actor Joachim Hansen was Prince Albert. Stuart Latham directed.

The Villains
(Granada TV, 1964–65)

Was a crime drama series that concentrated on the criminals themselves with the stories slanted towards criminal lives rather than crimes. These murky underside dramatic studies of criminal elements in the harsh locales of northern England were produced by Howard Baker and H. V. Kershaw; Jack Rosenthal contributed as writer. Pictured are Bryan Mosley and Mary Chester in Jack Rosenthal's 'Bent' (11/12/64; dir. Michael Beckham).

The Wednesday Play
(BBC-1, 1964–70)

Set out to stimulate its audience with seasons of dramas in which the writers had the opportunity both to produce original work and to exercise themselves in dramatizing the original ideas of others. The series became a byword for challenging, left-of-centre drama. The programme premièred with 'A Crack in the Ice' (28/10/64) by Nikolai Leskov, dramatized and directed by Ronald Eyre and starring Bill Fraser, James Maxwell, and Michael Hordern. It was followed by such notable productions as Jean-Paul Sartre's 'In Camera' (4/11/64), adapted and directed by Philip Saville, featuring Harold Pinter and Jane Arden; and Roger Manvell's 'The July Plot' (9/12/64), based on the book by Manvell and Heinrich Fraenkel, directed by Rudolph Cartier, and featuring Cyril Luckham, Joseph Furst, and (*pictured l. to r.*) Michael Anthony, Peter Copley, John Carson, and John Lee. The following year the series presented 'Three Clear Sundays' (7/4/65) by James O'Connor, directed by Kenneth Loach and photographed by Tony Imi; 'The Good Shoemaker and the Poor Fish

Peddler' (28/4/65), about the controversial trial of alleged anarchists Sacco and Vanzetti (played by Bill Nagy, *pictured left*, and John Bailey, *right*), written by Jean Benedetti and directed by John Gorrie; David Mercer's 'And Did Those Feet?' (2/6/65), directed by Don Taylor; Dennis Potter's 'Vote, Vote, Vote for Nigel Barton' (23/6/65) and 'Stand Up, Nigel Barton' (8/12/65) with Keith Barron in the title role; and Nell Dunn's gritty 'Up the

Junction' (3/11/65; Geraldine Sherman, Carol White, and Vickery Turner are pictured, *l. to r. from foreground*), directed by Kenneth Loach (filmed in 1967 by Peter Collinson). 'The Lump' (1/2/67) by Jim Allen, directed by Jack Gold and starring Leslie Sands as a bricklayer by trade and a revolutionary by vocation, and 'In Two Minds' (1/3/67) with Kenneth Loach directing David Mercer's play, continued the tradition.

The Airbase
(BBC-2, 1965)

The setting for this short-lived comedy series was RAF Wittlethorpe, somewhere in rural England. The station was an American Air Force base populated by such Bilko-like types as Staff Sergeant Miller (David Healy; *back right*) and Airman Randy 'Little Wonder' Ricks (Eddie Matthews; *back left*), under the command of Colonel Hoggart (Alan Gifford; *front right*). Brought in as base commander and liaison between the Americans and the local community was Squadron Leader Terence Heatherton (David Kelsey, *front left*) who had to deal with problems that ranged from demonstrations by peace campaigners to capers dreamt up by the American airmen. American writer John Briley wrote the scripts for producer Douglas Moodie.

BBC-3
(BBC-1, 1965–66)

Was an unofficial follow-through to **Not So Much a Programme . . .** with John Bird, Robert Robinson, and Lynda Baron leading the songs, sketches, conversation, and film reports; contributing writers included Christopher Booker, David Frost, Herbert Kretzmer, John Mortimer, Peter Shaffer, and Keith Waterhouse. Also appearing were Patrick Campbell, Denis Norden, Malcolm Muggeridge, Alan Bennett, John Fortune, Roy Dotrice (*right*), Bill Oddie, and Leonard Rossiter. The programme was produced-directed by Ned Sherrin (*left*). The same team later made **My Father Knew Lloyd George** (BBC-1, 18/12/65) which co-producer Sherrin (with Jack Gold) described as 'a fictional documentary film investigating an imagined scandal at the turn of the century'. John Bird, with additional material by the players John Bennett, Eleanor Bron, and John Fortune, wrote the 70-minute programme; directed by Gold. **A Series of Bird's** (BBC-1, 3/10–21/11/67) was another John Bird–John Fortune (written) programme, in eight 25-minute editions; produced by Denis Main Wilson. Terry Jones and Michael Palin supplied additional material.

The Bed-Sit Girl
(BBC-1, 1965–66)

Sheila Hancock (*right*) was the single-girl heroine of the title whose life was a steady stream of doomed love affairs and office failures (she was a secretary). But her dreams of a life of glamour and sophistication never became tarnished. During the first series she was under the influence of her air hostess friend Dilys (played by Dilys Laye; *left*) and attempted to associate herself with the high-flying set. The second series saw her with a boyfriend, David (Derek Nimmo), who lived in the next-door flat, and a new worldly wise friend and adviser, Liz (Hy Hazell). Scripts were supplied by Ronald Wolfe and Ronald Chesney for producers Duncan Wood (1st series) and Graeme Muir (2nd series); 12 eps. × 30 mins. were produced.

Blackmail
(Rediffusion, 1965–66)

The multiple forms, meanings, and nuances of the word 'blackmail' were the basis of this collection of original dramas produced by Stella Richman. Among the star players who illuminated the series were Nigel Green, Joss Ackland, Diane Cilento, Ian Hendry, Bernard Lee, Ronald Lacey, and (*pictured, l. to r.*) Jean Marsh, Ronald Hines, and George Cole in 'The Sound of Distant Guns' (14/11/66).

Blood and Thunder
(Granada TV, 1965; 2 plays × 80 mins.)

Two Jacobean plays by seventeenth-century English dramatist Thomas Middleton. The first, 'The Changeling' (4/1/65), was set in Spain and featured Derek Godfrey (*centre, facing*) and Kika Markham as uneasy partners in a murder plot. Philip Mackie adapted and produced Middleton's play (written in collaboration with William Rowley); Derek Bennett directed. The second production, 'Women Beware Women' (11/1/65), starred Gene Anderson, Diana Rigg, and Clifford Evans as a set of pleasure seekers whose lives erupt in murder and suicide; the setting was Florence in 1620. Mackie again adapted and produced; Gordon Flemyng was the director.

Call My Bluff
(BBC-2, 1965–)

One of the longest running of BBC TV game shows, **Call My Bluff** was a contest of wit and elaboration and the amusement of being verbally seduced by a celebrity guest lying directly to camera. The general format, devised by American game show wizards Mark Goodson & Bill Todman, featured two teams of three who were given one of the more recondite words to be found in the *Oxford English Dictionary*. Each team bluffed a definition in turn, with one of the panellists giving the true meaning while the others offered a false but convincing explanation. The original chairman was Robin Ray (*centre*), while Frank Muir (*right*) and Robert Morley (*left*) headed the teams. Robert Robinson later became chairman and Patrick Campbell led one of the teams; Campbell's place was taken up by Arthur Marshall in the 1980s.

1965

Court Martial
(Roncom Films-ITC, 1965–67)

Produced and filmed in England, **Court Martial** (Roncom Films-ITC, 1965–67) was an Anglo-American production featuring two officer attorneys attached to the US Army Judge Advocate General's department in Second World War Europe. Peter Graves (*left*) played the senior officer Major Frank Whittaker, generally the prosecution officer, and Bradford Dillman (*right*) was Captain David Young, the defender. Usually, during their pre-trial investigations, they were assisted by M/Sgt. John MacCaskey (Kenneth J. Warren) and Sgt. Wendy (Diane Clare), with the search for evidence and witnesses taking them anywhere from back alley dives in Soho to a monastery in Naples to the Belsen concentration camp. The 26 eps. × hour series was produced at Pinewood Studios. The series developed from a two-part story, 'The Case Against Paul Ryker' (US tx 10 and 17/10/63), shown as a part of Universal TV's **Kraft Suspense Theatre**; this was also re-edited and released as the feature *Sergeant Ryker* in 1968.

Deckie Learner
(Granada TV, 16/6/65)

A fascinating eyewitness account of a 15 year old's first trip on a Grimsby fishing trawler during a rugged, 22-day journey to the Arctic Circle and back. John Bratley was the Grimsby lad facing his first trip as 'deckie learner'. The 40-minute film was photographed by Terry Gould (assisted by David Drinkwater) and edited by Robert Vas; soundman was John Purchese. Mike Grigsby produced.

For Whom the Bell Tolls
(BBC-2, 2–23/10/65)

Ernest Hemingway's passionate novel of the Spanish Civil War was dramatized as a 4 part × 45 mins. serial by Giles Cooper for producer Douglas Allen. Taking place in 1937, the story told of American teacher Robert Jordan (played by John Ronane; *pictured*) dispatched on a mission behind the Nationalist lines to destroy a bridge which could affect a forthcoming Republican attack on Segovia. Ann Bell played Maria, the partisan girl with whom Jordan falls in love, Glynn Edwards was the guerilla leader, and Joan Miller the old gypsy, Pilar. It was the first Hemingway novel ever presented on British TV. Rex Tucker directed from the BBC's Glasgow studios.

Front Page Story
(ATV, 1965)

Producer Rex Firkin and script editor Wilfred Greatorex, still glowing from their success with **The Plane Makers**, came up with this Fleet Street newspaper series as a replacement for their earlier hit. An advance from ATV's earlier **Deadline Midnight**, this series took the authentically portrayed reporters out of the office and into the streets. Firkin's production crew used a special mobile self-contained tape and sound recording unit that allowed them to shoot scenes on-the-run anywhere and at almost any time; Thames TV's **The Bill** would later perfect this form of fast-moving, on-location tape shooting. Principal players were Derek Godfrey (*right*), Derek Newark, Harry Towb, and Patrick Mower (as the reporters), and Roddy McMillan (news editor; *left*), John Bennett (editor), and Ivor Dean (editorial director).

Jackanory
(BBC-1, 1965–)

A long-running and popular 15-minute series of children's stories read by various guests and celebrities. A September 1984 edition featured HRH The Prince of Wales telling his own story, 'The Old Man of Lochnagar' (with illustrations by Sir Hugh Casson) especially for **Jackanory**. In 1972 **Jackanory Playhouse** (BBC-1, 17/11–22/12/72) was introduced, presenting six 25-minute plays featuring such performers as Roy Kinnear, James Bolam, Joan Sims, and Hannah Gordon. A later programme, **Spine Chillers** (BBC-1, 1980), was a kind of spooky **Jackanory** for slightly older children but without the illustrations. Actors Freddie Jones, John Woodvine, Jonathan Pryce, and Michael Bryant told stories from the works of H. G. Wells, Saki, and M. R. James. Angela Beeching produced. Nina van Pallandt (then of Nina and Frederik vocal duo fame) appeared in an early edition; she is pictured reading a story to her three children.

Jury Room
(BBC-2, 1965)

Consisted of a series of 12 eps. × 50 mins. plays about famous trials with each case viewed principally through the eyes of the jury and focused on the hypothetical conflicts of the jury room. The series opened with 'The Sandyford Mystery' (11/7/65), based on the 1862 trial, by Alistair Bell and produced-directed by Peter Dews, starring Finlay Currie, Amanda Walker (*pictured*; with John Barcroft), and Robert Urquhart. Later examples included the 1894 case of 'The Lady and the Axe' (8/8/65), written by Robert Storey and directed by Julia Smith, with Bridget Turner (as Lizzie Borden), Robert Beatty, and Glynn Edwards; and 'Traitor' (19/9/65), written by Vincent Tilsley and directed by Derek Martinus, with Michael Gwynn (as Sir Roger Casement), Allan Cuthbertson, and James Urquhart. Peter Dews was producer.
The Verdict is Yours (Granada TV, 1958–59; 1962–63), some years earlier, presented a series of three-day, unscripted trials (Tuesdays, Wednesdays, and Thursdays; the programme later went out on Mondays then Fridays) using actors with legal experience as judge, counsel, and witnesses and recruiting Granada viewers as members of the jury. The half-hour episodes produced by Harry Elton (1958–59), Peter Wildeblood (1962), and Claude Whatham (1963), and featured ex-police prosecutor David Ensor as Mr Justice Ensor. **In Court Today** (Granada TV, 1959) had presented a similar series of unscripted Magistrates' Court cases; Harry Elton produced.

The Magic Roundabout
(BBC-1, 1965–75)

Featured a new puppet technique, a hybrid of animated cartoon and marionettes (in a frame-movement-at-a-time, stop-motion filmed process), to bring to life the amusing and inventive adventures of (*l. to r.*) Dylan, Basil, Brian the snail, Mr Rusty, Dougal, Florence, Paul, Zebedee, and Mr MacLenry in a superb colour setting. Concept and production was by French animator Serge Danot, working out of a studio near Nantes in western France, and the English version was written and told by Eric Thompson (the late father of actress Emma Thompson). The 5-minute première run began on Mondays in the 5.50 p.m. slot and captured the interest of both children and adults. A feature film, *Dougal and the Blue Cat* (*Pollux et le Chat Bleu*, 1970), was released in Britain in 1972.

1965

Man Alive
(BBC-2, 1965–82)

The long-running public affairs programme that focused on ordinary people and the situations that shaped their lives. With the original production team of producer Michael Latham, co-editors Desmond Wilcox and Bill Morton, and reporters Jim Douglas Henry, Angela Huth, Jeremy James, John Percival, and Trevor Philpott, **Man Alive**'s range covered such areas as the subject of child molesting ('What Shall We Tell the Children?'), a report on sufferers from agoraphobia ('The Frightened Ones'), and a candid examination of Britain's marriage bureaux ('The Business of Marriage'). Pictured (l. to r.) are production assistant Esther Rantzen, researcher John Pitman, Huth, Percival, Wilcox, Henry, reporter Harold Williamson, and production assistant Jeanne Le Chard.

A Man Called Harry Brent
(BBC-2, 22/3–26/4/65)

Was writer Francis Durbridge's twelfth serial story for TV. The 6 eps. × 25 mins. serial featured Edward Brayshaw (*right*) as Harry Brent, a travel agent who had wandered into the murder of his fiancée's boss. Gerald Harper (*2nd left*), Jennifer Daniel (*2nd right*), Brian Wilde, and Bernard Brown (*left*) also appeared. Alan Bromly produced and directed; the programme went out under the *Francis Durbridge Presents . . .* banner.

The Man in Room 17
(Granada TV, 1965–66)

A fascinating espionage series with elements of comedy, thriller, and simple adventure about a couple of high-IQ, Ministry-connected types, Oldenshaw (Richard Vernon; *right*) and Dimmock (Michael Aldridge; *left*), who from the seclusion of Room 17 tracked their quarry with the aplomb of a chess player. Denholm Elliott's Defraits replaced the Aldridge character for the second series. Twenty-six hour-long episodes were produced by Richard Everitt; The programme was created by Robin Chapman. **The Fellows (Late of Room 17)** (Granada TV, 1967) was a 13 eps. × hour follow-up reuniting Oldenshaw / Vernon and Dimmock / Aldridge in a new series (and format) of fighting highly intelligent criminals. Chapman and Peter Plummer produced.

Mogul
(BBC-1, 1965; 13 eps. × 50 mins.)

Mogul International was a vast commercial oil corporation with interests world-wide. The stories moved between power play in the boardroom and drilling for oil on the various sites and rigs. Extensive location filming along with sharp and well-defined scripts made this one of the more exciting mid-1960s drama series, with plot settings ranging from desert oil rigs to tankers at sea. Geoffrey Keen and Philip Latham represented the head office top brass while Ray Barrett was the punchy troubleshooter keeping the drilling operations going. For the second series the title was changed to **The Troubleshooters** (BBC-1, 1966–72; 123 eps. × 50 mins.) and the action ranged from Venezuela to Antarctica; Barrett, Latham, and Keen continued in their earlier roles. **Mogul** (and the later **Troubleshooters** format) was created by writer-producer John Elliot and produced by Peter Graham Scott (1966; 1967–68); Anthony Read produced the 1966, 1969–72 series. In a similar vein, producer Gerard Glaister & writer N. J. Crisp's **Oil Strike North** (BBC-1, 1975; 13 eps. × 55 mins.) dealt with the battle for oil in the North Sea; starring Nigel Davenport, Michael Whitney, and Angela Douglas. William Sylvester is pictured as a Mogul driller in the première episode 'Kelly's Eye'.

138

Naked Island
(BBC-2, 11/2/65)

Australian author Russell Braddon turned his experiences as a Japanese prisoner of war during the Second World War into a best-selling novel, which in turn became this 80-minute **Thursday Theatre** production. The story was set in Singapore's Changi Jail in August 1945 and featured a group of Australian POWs who secretly listened to the BBC every night on a home-made radio, passing the information on to other prisoners. Featured (*l. to r.*) are James Bolam, Ray Barrett, and Burt Kwouk. John Gorrie directed Braddon's script for producer Bernard Hepton.

The Newcomers
(BBC-1, 1965–69)

Was the twice-weekly (Tuesdays and Fridays) story of the Coopers, a London family adapting to life in the fictitious country town of Angleton. The Cooper clan consisted of (*l. to r.*) grannie (played by Gladys Henson), young Lance (Raymond Hunt), teenage son (Jeremy Bulloch), mother Vivienne (Maggie Fitzgibbon), teenage daughter (Judy Geeson), and father, Ellis Cooper (Alan Browning). All the pains and pleasures of living on a new housing estate were brought into focus, from the loneliness and boredom that such existence brings to comprehending the local, rural lifestyle. The Robertson family (portrayed by Jack Watling, Deborah Watling, Mary Kenton, Robert Bartlett, and Paul Bartlett) became the central characters from January 1968. The 430 eps. × half-hour series was devised by Colin Morris. Producers over the five-year period were Verity Lambert (1965), Morris Barry (1965–66), Ronald Travers (1966–67), and Bill Sellars (1967–69).

Not Only—But Also . . .
(BBC-2, 1965–66; 1970)

Hailed at the time as 'the new school of TV humour', this showcase for the casual, cynical comedy skits of Peter Cook (*left*) and Dudley Moore (*right*; with the latter also performing some fine jazzy pieces on piano) became popular, for the most part, due to their timeless Pete & Dud routine, pictured, whereby a couple of proletarian characters conducted a casual conversation that would escalate into delusions of grandeur and hilarious flights of fantasy. Scripts for the première series were by Moore, Cook, Robert Fuest, and John Law. Joe McGrath and Dick Clements produced. An additional two episodes (× 30 mins.), produced by the Australian Broadcasting Commission, were shown on 18 and 25/6/71; written by Cook and Moore, with guest Barry Humphries and a Pete & Dud in Australia routine.

199 Park Lane
(BBC1, 3/8–1/10/65)

The fashionable and exclusive London apartment block of **199 Park Lane** was the opulent setting for this twice-weekly serial about the comings and goings of the high-life set. Greek millionaires, politicians, top models, and bankers paraded through the multiple storylines, with all the various strands connected by a snooping gossip column writer (Philip Bond) on the prowl for a keyhole scoop. Brenda Kaye (*right*) played the manageress of the luxury flats, Geoffrey Toone (*left*) the head porter; the high-powered residents included Edwin Richfield, Isabel Dean, and Derek Bond. Main writer and creator of this 18 eps. × 30 mins. window-gazing exercise was William Fairchild; Morris Barry, late of **Compact**, produced.

1965

Out of the Unknown
(BBC-2, 1965–71)

BBC TV's superlative science fiction anthology series, launched by producer Irene Shubik (and produced by Alan Bromly during the 3rd and 4th series), presented the works of such famous SF writers as John Wyndham, Isaac Asimov, Ray Bradbury, J. G. Ballard, Frederick Pohl, Robert Sheckley, Clifford Simak, Nigel Kneale, and John Brunner. The 49 eps. × 50/60 mins. series ran the gamut of science fiction themes (despite the in-house budgetary restrictions) and stands as one of the last, great genre anthologies. Philip Saville and Rudolph Cartier also contributed as directors; Ridley Scott, before SF film fame as director some fourteen years later, was the designer for the 'Some Lapses of Time' (6/12/65) episode. The scene pictured is from 'Get Off My Cloud' (1/4/69) with Peter Jeffrey (*left*) and Donal Donnelly (*right*).

Pardon the Expression
(Granada TV, 1965–66)

Was, in a rather unusual move, a spin-off from soap serial **Coronation Street**, featuring Arthur Lowe (*left*) in his fusspot Leonard Swindley character as an assistant manager with the northern branch of Dobson and Hawks, a national chain store. The 39 eps. × half-hour sitcom also featured Paul Dawkins, Joy Stewart, Robert Dorning (*right*), and Betty Driver. Producer was Harry Driver; Jack Rosenthal and Vince Powell also contributed in the script department. At the end of the sitcom series Lowe's Swindley and Dorning's store manager Walter Hunt were unceremoniously sacked, but they teamed up to become (of all things) amateur ghost hunters in **Turn Out the Lights** (Granada TV, 1967), a comic drama series of 6 eps. × 45 mins. produced by Derek Granger.

Peyton Place
(20th Century-Fox TV; ITV tx 1965–)

Perhaps the first of the big prime-time soap dramas, originally shown twice weekly in half-hour instalments. Based on Grace Metalious's 1957 novel about extra-marital entanglements in a small New England town, the serial became an immediate hit and was avidly followed by viewers during the programme's original five-year run. The central, and original, players were Dorothy Malone as Constance Mackenzie, her daughter Mia Farrow, the town physician Ed Nelson, newspaper editor Warner Anderson, teenage brothers Ryan O'Neal (*pictured*; with Leigh Taylor-Young) and Christopher Connelly, and the town siren Barbara Parkins. (US tx 1964–69) A spin-off series of 500 half-hour episodes under the title **Return to Peyton Place** (20th Century-Fox TV-NBC-TV, US tx 1972–74) was also produced.

Play of the Month
(BBC-1, 1965–79; 1982–83)

Presented a collection of culturally impressive dramas, premièring with John Osborne's 'Luther' (19/10/65; 90 mins.), starring Alec McCowen, Patrick Magee, and Geoffrey Bayldon. Alan Cooke directed Cedric Messina's production. There was also 'A Passage to India' (16/11/65; 110 mins.) by Santha Rama Rau, from the novel by E. M. Forster, adapted for TV by John Maynard; starring Sybil Thorndike (*centre*), Virginia McKenna (*2nd right*), Cyril Cusack (*left*), Michael Bates (*right*), and Zia Mohyeddin as Dr Aziz (*2nd left*). Waris Hussein directed Peter Luke's production (filmed by David Lean in 1984). Robin Maugham's 'Gordon of Khartoum' (18/1/66; 90 mins.), was adapted for TV by David

Benedictus, starring Alan Badel as General Gordon. Rudolph Cartier directed. 'Lee Oswald—Assassin' (15/3/66; 90 mins.) was written by Rudolph Cartier and Reed de Rouen, from a documentary play by Felix Lutzkendorf, and starred Tony Bill as Lee Harvey Oswald (*pictured*). Cartier directed Peter Luke's production. Arthur Miller's 'Death of a Salesman' (24/5/66; 95 mins.) starred Rod Steiger (as Willy Loman), Betsy Blair, Tony Bill, Joss Ackland, Kenneth J. Warren, and Brian Davies. Alan Cooke directed Cedric Messina's production. 'The Adventures of Don Quixote' (7/1/73; 115 mins.) from the novel by Cervantes, screenplay by Hugh Whitemore, starred Rex Harrison and Frank Finlay (as Sancho Panza). The BBC TV-Universal Pictures TV co-production was directed by Alvin Rakoff for producer Gerald Savory; Michel Legrand composed the music. 'A Room with a View' (15/4/73; 120 mins.) by E. M. Forster was adapted for TV by Pauline Macauley, starring Judy Geeson (as Lucy Honeychurch), Charles Gray, Robert Coote, Lally Bowers, and Tom Chadbon. Donald McWhinnie directed Cedric Messina's production (filmed by James Ivory in 1985).

Public Eye
(ABC TV, 1965–68; Thames TV, 1969–75)

This downbeat private detective drama centred on the seedy back-street activities of Frank Marker (played by Alfred Burke), a sullen, cynical anti-hero. The 87 eps. × hour series was based on an idea by Roger Marshall and Anthony Marriott; John Bryce, Don Leaver, Richard Bates, Michael Chapman, Kim Mills, and Robert Love produced over the programme's ten-year run. The Marker character was jailed (after a frame-up) at the end of ABC TV's forty-one episodes but returned after ABC's successor, Thames TV, released him from prison (for story continuity) to pursue a further forty-six cases. The scene pictured is from 'You Can Keep the Medal' episode with Burke (*centre*) and Christopher Sandford (*far left*).

Redcap
(ABC TV, 1965–66)

John Thaw (*pictured*) led this intriguing series about the work of the Special Investigation Branch of the Royal Military Police which took him through a variety of story locations, extending from Germany to Cyprus to Borneo. ABC TV's production budget, however, could not stretch to actual location work so the foreign settings were limited to the studio. While **Redcap** premièred its London networking on 20 May 1965, the series had already been running in the ABC TV midlands region since October 1964. Jack Bell originated the programme for producer John Bryce and Ian Kennedy Martin was story editor; 26 eps. × 55 mins. were transmitted.

Riviera Police
(Rediffusion, 1965)

Sun, sand, and sanguine damsels made up this south of France police drama about a quartet of detectives (rarely seen in the same story together) fighting crime between bouts of chatting up the bikini clad. The principals were played by (*l. to r.*) Brian Spink, Noel Trevarthen, Frank Lieberman, and Geoffrey Frederick. Thirteen hour-long episodes were produced by Jordan Lawrence.

1965

Sherlock Holmes
(BBC-1, 20/2–8/5/65;
9/9–23/12/68)

This programme developed from an episode of the **Detective** anthology series ('The Speckled Band', 18/5/64; adapt. Giles Cooper, dir. Robin Midgley) with Douglas Wilmer as Holmes and Nigel Stock as Dr Watson. When the series premièred, under producer David Goddard, Wilmer (*left*) and Stock (*right*) continued their roles, with Wilmer's Holmes striking the right note of cool and probing composure and Stock's Watson coming across as a commonsensical GP. Peter Madden appeared as Inspector Lestrade and Derek Francis as Mycroft Holmes. There were 12 eps. × 50 mins. produced. The second series, in 1968, was billed as 'Sir Arthur Conan Doyle's Sherlock Holmes' and starred Peter Cushing as Holmes, still aided and abetted by Nigel Stock's Watson; 16 eps. × 50 mins. were produced by William Sterling, including the two-part 'The Hound of the Baskervilles' (30/9 and 7/10/68), scripted by Hugh Leonard and directed by Graham Evans.

Six Shades of Black
(Granada TV, 1965)

Featured a series of six hour-long plays in which the hero of one play was the villain of the next, illustrating both the character's good and bad sides. The following were written and produced by Peter Wildeblood: 'The Good Woman of Chester Square' (30/4/65; dir. Herbert Wise), with Pamela Brown and Thorley Walters; 'A Touch of Uplift'/aka 'Of Men and Angels' (7/5/65; dir. Wise), with Bill Fraser and Ursula Howells; 'The Finer Things of Life' (14/5/65; dir. Stuart Latham), with Ursula Howells (*pictured*; with Richard O'Sullivan), Frederick Bartman, and Clare Kelly; 'A Loving Disposition' (21/5/65; dir. Gordon Flemyng), with Nyree Dawn Porter and Frederick Bartman; 'The Kindest Thing To Do' (28/5/65; dir. David Boisseau), with Faith Brook, David Langton, and Robin Phillips; 'There is a Happy Land . . .' (4/6/65; dir. Boisseau), with Pamela Brown, Agnes Lauchlan, Peter Bull, and Robin Phillips.

The State Funeral of Sir Winston Churchill
(BBC-1; ITV, 30/1/65)

The solemn pageantry of the funeral of 90-year-old statesman Sir Winston Churchill was seen, it was estimated, by over 350,000,000 viewers throughout the world. BBC TV used forty cameras and ITV used forty-five to cover the event: the procession from Westminster Hall, the service in St Paul's Cathedral, then the road and river procession to Waterloo Station, and the departure of the train to the family resting place at the village of Bladon. Honouring Lady Churchill's request, there was no TV or radio coverage after Sir Winston's body left Waterloo. BBC TV's coverage, with Richard Dimbleby as sole commentator, was from 9.20 a.m. to 1.30 p.m. with, later during the day, a recording of the funeral shown simultaneously on both BBC-1 and BBC-2. ITV's coverage was similar (morning to 1.30 p.m.) and had Sir Laurence Olivier introducing the scene at 8.30 a.m.; commentator Brian Connell and three narrators, working from monitor screens at Television House, led the ITV audience along the cortège route. The edited version of the 5-hour ITV outside broadcast, **The Valiant Man**, was awarded the Grand Prix at the first International Festival for Outside Broadcasts at Cannes in May 1965; the hour-long programme was transmitted via Rediffusion on 26/1/66.

Thunderbirds
(ATV/AP Films Prod./ITC, 1965–66)

Gerry and Sylvia Anderson's spectacular Supermarionation series featuring the (usually) explosive missions undertaken by the family-based members of International Rescue. The string-puppet series 'starred' Jeff Tracey and his five sons, Scott (pilot of Thunderbird I), Virgil (Thunderbird II), Alan (Thunderbird III), Gordon (co-pilot Thunderbird II, pilot of Thunderbird IV for underwater work), and John (Thunderbird V space satellite). Voices were supplied by Ray Barrett, Peter Dyneley, David Graham, Christine Finn, David Holliday, Shane Rimmer, Matt Zimmerman, and Jeremy Wilkin; Sylvia Anderson voiced blonde London agent Lady Penelope. Special effects were created by Derek Meddings. Gerry Anderson and Reg Hill produced the 32 eps. × hour series. AP Films also produced two feature film spin-offs, *Thunderbirds Are Go* (1966) and *Thunderbird 6* (1968).

Tomorrow's World
(BBC-1, 1965–)

Raymond Baxter (*pictured*) introduced film, outside broadcasts, and studio reports on the developments which were changing our way of looking at, and living, life. A science–future series embracing all and every invention (madcap and otherwise) as it was publicly premièred, with studio demonstrations and on-location test runs. The original producers were Peter Bruce and Peter R. Smith. A junior-level version was seen in the mid-1970s in the form of **Discovery** (Yorkshire TV, 1975–76), a half-hour early evening programme produced by Simon Welfare and, later, David Taylor.

Undermind
(ABC TV, 1965)

An offbeat psychological science-fantasy series about a sinister element of unknown subversives referred to as the Sixth Column whose aim was to destroy the structure of society by undermining public confidence in the people and institutions that form its backbone. Struggling against this *Invasion of the Body Snatchers*-like threat was a young industrial personnel officer (played by Jeremy Wilkin) and his brother's young widow (Rosemary Nicols). By the eleventh, and final, episode the alien-influenced network of brainwashed subversives was rounded up. The hour-long series was produced by Michael Chapman with Robert Banks Stewart, who had provided the original idea, as story editor. Note: gimmicky title spelling is correct! The scene pictured shows (*l. to r.*) Jeremy Wilkin, Rosemary Nicols, and guest George Baker in the 'End Signal' episode.

United!
(BBC-1, 1965–67)

Premièred the same week as another BBC TV twice-weekly soap drama, **The Newcomers**, and was set in the world of Association Football, featuring the team and staff of the fictional Brentwich FC. The idea of weaving a half-hour soap serial out of a male-dominated sports activity, with the writers trying to overlay the sporting atmosphere with domestic interludes, invited prime-time suicide. The series kicked off with a new manager (David Lodge) being brought in to pull the club out of its lowly position at the bottom of the Second Division; his patchwork of players included Bryan Marshall (*right*), George Layton (*centre*), and Stephen Yardley. Harold Goodwin (*left*) was the trainer. Special facilities, such as a pitch area to play on, were provided by Stoke City Football Club and well-known player Jimmy Hill was recruited as a technical adviser. Bernard Hepton and Anthony Cornish (1965–66), David Conroy (1966), and John McRay (1966–67) produced the 147 eps. × 30 mins. series for BBC Midlands. The series was created by Brian Hayles.

The Walrus and the Carpenter
(BBC-1, 1965)

Developed from a 14/12/63 episode of **Comedy Playhouse** written by Marty Feldman & Barry Took. The 30-minute comedy series starred Hugh Griffith (*left*; as illiterate ex-seaman Luther Flannery) and Felix Aylmer (*right*; as highly literate ex-schoolmaster Gascoigne Quilt) in stories about two septuagenarians who are both preparing for death and whiling away their remaining time by trying to live it up. James Gilbert produced.

1965

The War Game
(BBC TV, [prod; not tx] 1965; BBC-1,
31/7/85)

Writer-producer Peter Watkins's
controversial 1965 drama-
documentary story of a nuclear
attack on Britain in the 1960s was
considered so distressing that the
original planned transmission was
halted by then BBC Director-
General Sir Hugh Greene and the
programme remained off-air until
it was shown as a part of BBC TV's
fortieth anniversary remembrance
of the atomic bomb being
dropped on Hiroshima. In a style
similar to his earlier **Culloden**,
Watkins used mainly non-actors
and an effective range of *verité*
techniques in dramatizing the
preparations for nuclear attack
and, later, the horrendous toll and
after-effect on the population.
Although the 50-minute
programme was made with the
available scientific facts of the time
it still remains a most harrowing
representation of the
consequences of nuclear war. The
suitably grim black and white
photography was by Peter
Bartlett.

The Wars of the Roses
(BBC-1, 1965)

The Royal Shakespeare
Company's cycle of three plays,
shown on three successive
Thursdays, chronicling the Wars
of the Roses. Peter Hall's RSC
production, produced for TV by
Michael Barry, was adapted by
John Barton. Part 1: 'Henry VI'
(8/4/65; 165 mins.), Part 2:
'Edward IV' (15/4/65; 175 mins.),
Part 3: 'Richard III' (22/4/65; 145
mins.). David Warner (*pictured*)
starred as King Henry VI, Roy
Dotrice as King Edward IV, and
Paul Martin as Richard. Michael
Hayes and Robin Midgley directed
for BBC TV.

The Wednesday Thriller
(BBC-1, 1965)

Presented a series of suspense-
racked plays by eight authors,
including some established
novelists. The première play was
the spine-chilling 'The House'
(4/8/65; wr. Peter van Greenaway,
dir. Naomi Capon), with
Denholm Elliott, Nancie Jackson,
Anabel Littledale (*shown*), and
Terence Alexander. Other plays
included William Trevor's 'The
Babysitter' (18/8/65; dir. Silvio
Narizzano), with Kenneth Griffith
and Yootha Joyce, and Patricia
Highsmith's 'The Cellar'
(22/9/65; dir. George R. Foa),
with Ursula Howells and Scott
Forbes. The plays were produced
by Bernard Hepton.

The Worker
(ATV, 1965–70)

Featured comedian Charlie Drake
(*right*) as an unemployed man who
was willing to take on any form of
work, except that he was
incapable of holding down a job
for more than one day, resulting in
his daily haunting of what was
then called the Labour Exchange.
Henry McGee (*left*) played
Exchange official Mr Pugh. The
sitcom was written by Lewis
Schwarz and Drake, and produced
by Alan Tarrant and, later, Shaun
O'Riordan. Drake was also the
little man in search of love, with
assistance from marriage bureau
secretary Kathleen Byron, in **Who
is Sylvia?** (ATV, 1967); the seven-
part comedy was co-written by
Drake (who also created the
series) and Donald Churchill, and
directed by O'Riordan.

World of Sport
(ITV various, 1965–85)

Eamonn Andrews presented 4½ hours of Saturday afternoon sport with support from a battery of tape machines and backed by a staff of Fleet Street sub-editors. The original studio line-up included Peter Lorenzo (of the *Sun*), analysing the latest football news, John Rickman, offering informed selections of the day's televised races, Ian Wooldridge (of the *Daily Mail*) covering cricketing events, Freddie Trueman voicing opinions on controversial issues in sport, and Jimmy Hill commenting on soccer issues; Richard Davies (*pictured*), who later fronted the programme, and Martin Locke were also on the early team.

The World of Wooster
(BBC-1, 1965–67)

This comedy series was billed as **P. G. Wodehouse's The World of Wooster** to enhance the reputation of the author's classic stories about the social misadventures of a young 1920s aristocrat and his gentleman's gentleman. Ian Carmichael (*left*) was the stuttering and dependent Bertie Wooster and the suave Dennis Price (*right*) played the imperturbable, snobbish Jeeves. While both actors were a little past the youthful antics created on the printed page their combined mastery of comic timing and dialogue delivery made the series one of BBC TV's comedy successes. The stories were adapted for TV (after the Corporation had acquired rights for all of the Jeeves–Wooster saga) by Richard Waring and Michael Mills, with the latter also producing in association with Peter Cotes. Actor Derek Nimmo turned up in the 1966 series (as 'silly ass' Bingo Little) prior to his **All Gas and Gaiters** comedy programme.

Adam Adamant Lives!
(BBC-1, 1966–67)

Something of a cross-breed between **Batman** and **The Avengers**, the setting for this series was the 'Swinging London' of the mid-1960s but featuring a hero, Adam Llewellyn de Vere Adamant (Gerald Harper; *left*), from the Edwardian times. Adam Adamant, gentleman-adventurer, was drugged and frozen alive in a block of ice by his arch-enemy 'The Face' (Peter Ducrow) in 1902 where he remained until discovered and thawed out, alive and intact, into the noisy and garish world of 1966. He soon acquired two companions, chirpy girl-about-town Georgina (Juliet Harmer; *right*) and valet Simms (Jack May), and set about swashbuckling his way through modern-day crime and villainy; during the second (Dec. 1966–Mar. 1967) series he again crossed swords with his old enemy 'The Face', now active in Adamant's new time. The 29 eps. × 50 mins. adventure series was created by Donald Cotton and Richard Harris, and produced by Verity Lambert. Tony Williamson, Brian Clemens, Vince Powell, and Harry Driver were among the principal writers; Ridley Scott and Moira Armstrong were among those contributing from the director's chair.

145

Alice in Wonderland
(BBC-1, 28/12/66)

Producer-director Jonathan Miller's haunting and imaginative 80-minute TV version of the Lewis Carroll nursery fantasy, with offbeat musical backing from Ravi Shankar's sitar, was more a peculiar Victorian fantasy for adults rather than a fanciful adventure for youngsters. The impressive cast line-up included Alan Bennett, John Bird, Wilfrid Brambell, John Gielgud, Leo McKern, Malcolm Muggeridge, Michael Redgrave, and Peter Sellars; pictured are (*l. to r.*) Peter Cook (Mad Hatter), Wilfrid Lawson (Dormouse), Michael Gough (March Hare), and Anne-Marie Mallik (as Alice). Some twenty years later two further adaptations were produced, in serial form: Anglia TV's **Alice in Wonderland** (26/3–23/4/85; 5 eps. × 25 mins.) featured Giselle Andrews as Alice in a version where most of the parts were played by puppets; and BBC-1's **Alice in Wonderland** (5–26/1/86; 4 eps. × 30 mins.) with Kate Dorning as Alice, dramatized and directed by Barry Letts. **The Adventures of Alice** (BBC-tv, 23/12/60; 69 mins.) was adapted and produced for TV by Charles Lefeaux with music composed by Antony Hopkins; Gillian Ferguson appeared as Alice. Dennis Potter's 'Alice' (BBC-1, 13/10/65; 75 mins.) was presented as a part of **The Wednesday Play**, starring George Baker as Revd. C. L. Dodgson (Lewis Carroll) and Deborah Watling as Alice Liddell; Gareth Davies directed for producer James MacTaggart. Daphne Shadwell produced a 12 eps. × 15 mins. children's daytime serial of **Alice Through the Looking Glass** (Thames TV, 15/1–2/4/73) with Carol Hollands in the title role. Another Looking-Glass adventure came from MacTaggart (as adapt.-dir.) later that year (BBC-2, 25/12/73; 75 mins.) with the cast including Brenda Bruce, Freddie Jones, and Geoffrey Bayldon; Alice was played by Sarah Sutton.

The Baron
(ATV/ITC, 1966–67)

Was John Mannering (Steve Forrest; *pictured, right*), a wealthy, jet-age antique dealer, who operates the most exclusive shops of their kind in London, Paris, and Washington; he was also an undercover agent for the police and the government when the need arose, using his special knowledge of antiques and his international locations as a front. Assisting in most of his global adventures was the immaculate Cordelia Winfield (Sue Lloyd; *left*), also an intelligence agent. The action-adventure series was based on the character created by prolific author John Creasey (writing under the pseudonym of Anthony Morton); Mannering was a reformed jewel thief and man-about-town in the original novels. The TV Mannering bore little resemblance to Creasey's original concept in the Monty Berman-produced series. Two TV features were produced from re-edited episodes as *Mystery Island* (1966) and *The Man in a Looking Glass* (1968).

Chronicle
(BBC-2, 1966–)

A remarkable and fascinating series of 50-minute, monthly programmes featuring the latest discoveries in archaeology and history. Introducing the programme in the early days were distinguished scholars (and familiar TV faces) Glyn Daniel, lecturer in archaeology at Cambridge, and Magnus Magnusson, former **Tonight** reporter. Paul Johnstone produced the series for many years. On multiple occasions the excellent films were the result of co-productions (with, for example, the Pennsylvania University Museum, KRO Holland, Cyprus Broadcasting Corporation, National Geographic Society, Nova WGBH). The picture shows Magnus Magnusson in the studio with a life-size replica of the Bayeux Tapestry (230 feet long) on the occasion of the 900th anniversary of the Norman Conquest (tx 8/10/66).

The Corridor People
(Granada TV, 1966; 4 eps. × 45 mins.)

The mid-1960s was the prime period for offbeat thrillers and send-up series and this comic-strip yet stylish four-part adventure was one of the weirder ones devised. Created and scripted by Eddie Boyd (who had earlier created **The Odd Man** series for Granada) and produced by Richard Everitt, this series followed the absurd schemes of vamp-villainess Syrie Van Epp (Elizabeth Shepherd; *pictured*) as she attempted to manipulate a peculiar amnesia perfume (in 'Victim as Bird Watcher', 26/8/66); control a scientist who can resurrect the dead ('Victim as Whitebait', 2/9/66); kidnap a defector important to the Soviets ('Victim as Red', 9/9/66); and become involved with eccentric royalty ('Victim as Black', 16/9/66). The other central characters were equally strange: a CID man called Kronk (John Sharp), a private eye called Scrotty (Gary Cockrell), Inspector Blood (Alan Curtis), Sgt. Hound (William Maxwell), and a dwarf called Nonesuch (William Trigger). Unfortunately, the series was too short to develop its own special audience in the cult style of **The Avengers** and **Adam Adamant Lives!**.

Dusty
(BBC-1, 1966–67)

Was Dusty Springfield, formerly of The Springfields trio and, after going solo, perhaps Britain's greatest white female soul singer of the 1960s. A powerful supporter of the then emerging black American record labels Tamla Motown and Stax, the 'sounds' of which were just starting to become popular in Britain, Dusty was regarded by fans and critics as the perfect exponent of this gospel-influenced music. Her own renditions on the show reflected this influence but, unfortunately, her choice of guests was not allowed to be as representative of her musical tastes as she may have wished. Special guests Spanish-American singer Jose Feliciano and Tom Jones appeared to have been the only ones who came close to sharing her gutsy vocal style. Madeline Bell, Lesley Duncan, and Margaret Stredder supplied the back-up vocals. Stanley Dorfman produced her only two TV series (Aug.–Sept. 1966 and Aug.–Sept. 1967).

A Farewell to Arms
(BBC-2, 15, 22/2, and 1/3/66)

Giles Cooper successfully adapted Ernest Hemingway's novel of love and conflict at the Italian front in 1917 into a faithful 3 parts × 45 mins. serial. The story of the emotional development between Lt. Frederick Henry (played by Hollywood actor George Hamilton; *left*), an uninvolved American attached to an ambulance unit, and lonely English nurse Catherine Barkley (Vanessa Redgrave; *right*) was told in flashback, in the context of her pregnancy, against the harsh and sometimes farcical background of the First World War. The television serialization was able to add a dimension to the poignant (and somewhat personal) story that previous dramatizations had missed or restricted, despite a touch too objective an approach to the subject. Rex Tucker directed for producer Douglas Allen.

1966

The Frost Report
(BBC-1, 1966–67)

Continued David Frost's reputation for ruffling feathers while underlining the follies of authority. The regular cast consisted of (*l. to r., back row*) Nicholas Smith, Ronnie Barker, John Cleese, Nicky Henson; (*front row*) Julie Felix, Tom Lehrer, Ronnie Corbett, and Frost. A spin-off, **Frost Over England** (BBC-1, 26/3/67), featuring some of the best items from **The Frost Report** won the Golden Rose at the Montreux Festival in 1967. **The Frost Programme** (Rediffusion, 1966–68; LWT, 1972–73; BBC-1, 1977) presented a series of hard-hitting interviews including the 1967 confrontation with Dr Emil Savundra, former head of a car insurance company who had been charged with conspiracy to defraud his customers; giving rise to the phrase 'trial by television'. **Frost on Friday** (LWT, 1968–70), in tandem with **Frost on Saturday** and **Frost on Sunday**, offered a weekend mixture of current affairs (Fri.), comedy (Sat.), and variety (Sun.). Finally he reached the summit of his interview career with **The Nixon Interviews** (BBC-1/David Paradine Prods., 5–22/5/77), in which he subjected the disgraced former President to a series of in-depth grillings. In the 1990s Frost returned with **The Frost Programme** (Carlton TV/David Paradine Prods., 1993–) as a late night discussion series.

George and the Dragon
(ATV, 1966–68)

The inspired casting of Peggy Mount and Sid James together in this comedy scripted by Harry Driver & Vince Powell produced some excellent comic moments and visual gags. The series theme had Mount being employed as cook-housekeeper in John Le Mesurier's household previously dominated by chauffeur Sid James. It was their humorous clash of characters, with Mount's high-velocity bellowing and James's almost homicidal cunning, that gave the 26 eps. × half-hour series its strength and pace. The first three series were produced by Alan Tarrant; Jack Williams produced the final six episodes (Sept.–Oct. 1968).

How
(Southern TV, 1966–81)

A long-time popular children's education programme that presented a lightweight mixture of facts with fun, using studio stunts and experiments to illustrate a variety of (both fascinating and trivial) science-based subjects. The half-hour series was presented by Bunty James, Fred Dinenage (*2nd right*), Jack Hargreaves (*left*), and Jon Miller (*right*) (Marian Davies later took over from James); presenter Jill Graham is also pictured. Hargreaves also had his own 15-minute series, **Out of Town** (Southern TV, 1963–69; 1972–78), in which he strolled through the English countryside sharing his knowledge of things green and growing with the viewers. **How 2** (TVS, 1990–) returned to the series format for producer Tim Edmunds; presenters included Dinenage, Carol Vorderman, and Gareth 'Gaz Top' Jones.

The Informer
(Rediffusion, 1966–67)

Was Alex Lambert (played by Ian Hendry; *right*), a disbarred barrister with connections in the underworld who acts as an informant for the police. The central set-up had Hendry pursue vital information about criminal activities which he then sold to his special police contact (Neil Hallett) while keeping his wife (Heather Sears; *left*) in the dark about his undercover career and seeking solace and sympathy from the girlfriend (Jean Marsh) of a man he unsuccessfully defended, a case which led to his disbarment. Created by John Whitney and Geoffrey Bellman, the 21 eps. × 55 mins. series was produced by Stella Richman and Peter Collinson and (2nd series) John Whitney. Contributors included directors Michael Lindsay-Hogg and Ridley Scott and writers Richard Harris, Reuben Ship, and Jack Trevor Story.

Intrigue
(ABC TV, 1966)

The pursuit of TV detectives with a difference led to this 12 eps. × 55 mins. industrial espionage drama where the investigator hero, Gavin Grant (Edward Judd; *shown*), was called upon to ferret out industrial spies in the world of big business. Based on an idea by Tony Williamson, the general concept was interesting enough had it been allowed to develop but, unfortunately, the central character failed to come across as anything more than a one-dimensional non-starter; his assistant/girlfriend, Val (Caroline Mortimer), was also a character cut from cardboard. The short-run series was produced by Robert Banks Stewart.

Isadora
(BBC-1, 22/9/66)

Subtitled 'The Biggest Dancer in the World', presented the lively story of flamboyant dancer Isadora Duncan as she shocked the world during the early part of the century. Director-producer Ken Russell, who worked with Sewell Stokes on the screenplay (the latter wrote the dialogue), emphasized Duncan's extravagant life and exotic dances, mixing pathos and absurdity in the director's usual quirky screen style. The striking though bizarre telefilm (running at 65 mins.) rounded out Duncan's peculiar story with her death in 1927 when her scarf was caught in the wheel of a car. Vivian Pickles (*pictured*) starred as the extraordinary Isadora, supported by Peter Bowles, Murray Melvin, and Alex Jawdomikov. Sixteen years later Kenneth MacMillan's ballet **Isadora** (Granada TV, 23/2/82), with music by Richard Rodney Bennett from the Royal Opera House, Covent Garden, featured two Isadoras—Merle Park danced the revolutionary steps and Mary Miller spoke the words. Steve Hawes produced the 2-hour programme for Granada TV. (This latter programme had originally been scheduled for tx in Dec. 1981.)

It's a Knockout
(BBC-1, 1966–82)

Once described as 'a competition to perform the pointless in the quickest possible time', the origins of this TV Olympiad of inter-town rivalry reached back to a 1954 BBC TV programme called **Top Town**, which presented a series of weekly talent contests of amateur and semi-professional variety entertainers from different cities. **It's a Knockout** presented a similar format but this time with amateur athletic teams in crazy costumes competing in absurd games (the French, for instance, had their own TV version in 1963 called **Intervilles**). The international version for European countries, **Jeux sans Frontières**, started in 1967. Commentators for the British programme were Eddie Waring (*pictured, centre*), David Vine (*left*), and Stuart Hall. Barney Colehan was the producer who master-minded all of them.

The Liars
(Granada TV, 1966; 9 eps. × 55 mins.)

Drawing from a broad collection of short stories from the works of such famous names as Stacy Aumonier, Anatole France, Lord Dunsany, William Sansom, Michael Arlen, Oscar Wilde, Saki, and Guy de Maupassant, producer Philip Mackie fashioned a curious showcase for their presentation. He linked the tall tales through four related narrators who try to outdo each other with their enactment of the outrageous yarns; the 'liars' were Nyree Dawn Porter (*left*, with Richard Carpenter), Ian Ogilvy, William Mervyn, and Isla Blair. The scripts were written by Mackie and Hugh Leonard.

1966

Mrs Thursday
(ATV, 1966–67)

Was played by Kathleen Harrison (*pictured*) in this part-comedy, part-human interest series, created by (Lord) Ted Willis, about a Cockney charwoman who came into a fortune, a property empire, and a Rolls Royce as an inheritance from her late employer, a property tycoon. The series became an instant success due, for the most part, to the correct mix of (viewers') wish-fulfilment fantasy and the gritty, common-sense character portrayed by Harrison. Hugh Manning supported as her business-suited right-hand man Richard Hunter. The 25 eps. × 55 mins. series was produced by Jack Williams; Jack Rosenthal also contributed in the writing department.

Mystery and Imagination
(ABC TV; Thames TV, 1966–70)

Spooky stories in Gothic settings were the general theme of this chiller series that featured David Buck (*pictured*) as Victorian adventurer Richard Beckett, the linking narrator and sometime participator. Devised by producer Jonathan Alwyn and script editor Terence Feely, who between them read some four hundred Victorian tales of the supernatural to find material for the first thirteen episodes, the series presented such haunted and horrific works as Robert Louis Stevenson's 'The Body Snatcher' (5/2/66; adapt. Robert Muller, dir. Toby Robertson) with Ian Holm; Poe's 'The Fall of the House of Usher' (12/2/66; adapt. David Campton, dir. Kim Mills) with Susannah York and Denholm Elliott; M. R. James's 'Casting the Runes' (22/3/68; adapt. Evelyn Frazer, dir. Alan Cooke); 'Frankenstein' (11/11/68; adapt. Robert Muller, dir. Voytek); and 'Dracula' (18/11/68; adapt. Charles Graham, dir. by Patrick Dromgoole) with Denholm Elliott. Three series in all, over the four-year period, were produced: 1966, 13 eps. × 50–65 mins.; 1968, 3 eps. × 60 mins., 3 eps. × 90 mins.; 1970, 3 eps. × 90 mins.

Seven Deadly Sins
(Rediffusion, 9/5–27/6/66)

A series of self-contained plays produced under a theme title was the idea behind this seven-part collection in which each story illustrated one sin. An additional programme hook was that the identity of the vice was not revealed until the final credits. Contributing writers included Alun Falconer (with 'A Lion in His Way', 20/6/66) and Joe Orton ('The Erpingham Camp', 27/6/66). The scene pictured features Adam Faith and Joanna Dunham in Anthony Skene's 'In the Night' (13/6/66). Producer Peter Willes followed up with **Seven Deadly Virtues** (Rediffusion, 30/3–11/5/67) and substituted virtue for vice in a similar seven-part presentation. This drama package also featured plays by Bill Naughton ('It's Your Move', 30/3/67) and Joe Orton ('The Good and Faithful Servant', 6/4/67).

Softly, Softly
(BBC-1, 1966–70)

The work of the Regional Crime Squads was the subject of this **Z Cars** spin-off featuring Stratford Johns (*front*; as Det. Chief Supt. Barlow), Garfield Morgan (as Det. Chief Insp. Lewis), Norman Bowler (as Det. Sgt. Hawkins), and Alexis Kanner (as Det. Con. Stone); later joined by Frank Windsor (*back*) as Insp. Watt. David E. Rose and Leonard Lewis produced the 69 eps. × 50 mins. **Softly, Softly: Task Force** (BBC-1, 1970–76) followed, with Barlow made Head of Thamesford Constabulary CID and supervising officer of the Constabulary's Task Force. He was assisted by Watt and Hawkins under Chief Constable Cullen (Walter Gotell); 131 eps. × 50 mins. were produced by Lewis and Geraint Morris.

Talking to a Stranger
(BBC-2, 2–23/10/66)

Playwright John Hopkins's quartet of plays, produced by Michael Bakewell, earned him television's writer of the year award while Judi Dench was named television actress of the year for her performance as the rootless daughter Terry. The four plays that made up **Talking to a Stranger** were complete stories in themselves but were also interrelated: they dealt with a family crisis as seen, respectively, by daughter, son, father, and mother. Judi Dench (*2nd left*) and Michael Bryant (*left*) were the brother and sister, and the parents were played by Margery Mason (*2nd right*) and Maurice Denham (*right*). Christopher Morahan directed the plays as a part of the **Theatre 625** series; 3 eps. × 90 mins., 1 ep. × 95 mins.

Thirteen Against Fate
(BBC-1, 19/6–11/9/66)

Presented a series of thirteen hour-long crime stories from the pen of Maigret-creator Georges Simenon produced by Irene Shubik. 'The Lodger' (*Le Locataire*), scripted by Hugh Leonard and directed by James Ferman, starring Zia Mohyeddin and Gwendolyn Watts, opened the anthology; followed by such segments as 'Trapped' (*Cour d'Assises*), scripted by Julia Jones and directed by George Spenton-Foster, with Ronald Lewis and Keith Buckley, and 'The Traveller' (*Le Voyageur de la toussaint*), scripted by Stanley Miller and directed by Herbert Wise, with Kenneth J. Warren and Hywel Bennett. The music was provided by Tony Russell. The picture shows Marius Goring as 'The Suspect' (*Les Fiançailles de M. Hire*) (4/9/66).

This Man Craig
(BBC-2, 1966–67)

The Scottish town of Strathaird and its large comprehensive school was the setting of this drama series, built round the pupils, their parents, the teachers, and one teacher in particular—physics master Ian Craig (played by John Cairney, *left*, with Margaret Greig). Many Scottish writers contributed to the 50-minute episodes, including Jack Gerson, Tom Wright, Ian Kennedy Martin, Larry Forrester, and Jack Ronder. Peter Graham Scott produced-directed.

Till Death Us Do Part
(BBC-1, 1966–68; 1972; 1974–75)

This controversial sitcom, which shared top honours in the comedy field of the 1960s with **Steptoe and Son**, was written by Johnny Speight (with a pilot episode shown as a part of **Comedy Playhouse**, 22/7/65) and set in London's dockland. Warren Mitchell (*left*) headed the cast as the crusty and opinionated working-class father Alf Garnett who was constantly erupting in arguments with his son-in-law Mike (played by Anthony Booth; *2nd right*). Dandy Nichols (*2nd left*) was his long-suffering wife, Else, and Una Stubbs (*right*) played his daughter Rita. In 1975 Patricia Hayes and Alfie Bass joined the cast as the neighbours who look after Alf when Else decides to visit her sister in Australia. Thirty-nine episodes were produced by Dennis Main Wilson. **Till Death …** (ATV, 1981) brought back Alf (Mitchell), Else (Nichols), and Min (Hayes) in the new, sedate setting of Eastbourne; Speight scripted for director-producer William G. Stewart. The setting changed once again for **In Sickness and in Health** (BBC-1, 1985–), with Alf, Else, and Rita (Stubbs) now living in a council maisonette near West

1966

Ham football ground; Carmel McSharry, Arthur English, and Eamonn Walker later joined the cast. Speight scripted for producer Roger Race. Two feature films were also made: *Till Death Us Do Part* (1969) and *The Alf Garnett Saga* (1972) were produced by Associated London Films.

Vendetta
(BBC-1, 1966–68)

Based on an idea and format developed by writers Brian Degas and Tudor Gates, this underworld crime drama starred imported Italian actor Stelio Candelli as Danny Scipio, an ex-mafioso turned investigator of the Mafia ring in Britain. His gang-buster partner, Angelo James, was played by Neil McCallum. William Slater produced the 36 eps. × 50 mins. series. The scene pictured is from 'The Ten-Per-Cent Man' episode with (*l. to r.*) guest Kenneth Cope, Candelli, and McCallum.

Weavers Green
(Anglia TV, 1966)

Was the English village setting for this twice-weekly (initially Thursdays and Saturdays) soap series reflecting the life and drama (via BBC radio's *The Archers* and BBC1's **The Newcomers** (1965–69)) surrounding the practice of a couple of country veterinarians (later to be celebrated via BBC1's **All Creatures Great and Small**). Grant Taylor (*pictured*), Megs Jenkins, Maurice Kaufmann, Susan Field, Eric Flynn, Georgina Ward, John Moulder-Brown, Richard Coleman, Marjie Lawrence, John Glyn-Jones, Vanessa Forsyth, and Gerald Young composed the cast that barely managed to triumph over the trivial turn of events. Peter and Betty Lambda wrote the 49 eps. × half-hour series for producer John Jacobs.

World Cup Final 1966
(BBC-1; ATV, 30/7/66)

The 1966 World Cup gave Britain three weeks of almost non-stop soccer and established the television sport as family entertainment. The final between (4–2) winners England and West Germany drew 33 million viewers in Britain alone. Players Bobby Moore, Bobby Charlton, Alan Ball, and the toothless grin of Nobby Stiles became instant TV personalities and national images against the backdrop of what is considered perhaps the greatest football achievement in British history. In broadcasting terms it was the biggest sporting event ever covered by British television. The BBC TV producers were Alan Chivers and Bryan Cowgill; David Coleman presented the 3 hours and 20 minutes transmission and Kenneth Wolstenholme supplied the commentary. For ATV's networked **World of Sport** programme the ITV coverage was presented by anchorman Eamonn Andrews from Wembley. Stephen Wade produced.

All Gas and Gaiters

(BBC-1, 1967; 1969–71)

Popular comedy-in-the-cloisters series revolving around a farcical trio of Bishop (William Mervyn; *centre*), Archdeacon (Robertson Hare; *left*), and Chaplain (Derek Nimmo; *right*) as they played up clerical manners and crossed swords with the less-than-amused Dean (Ernest Clark). Derek Nimmo's zany performance as chaplain Noote, full of bumbling sincerity and round-about speech, became a national favourite. The series was created and written by the husband-and-wife writing team of Edwin Apps and Pauline Devaney; five series of 32 eps. × 30 mins. were produced by Stuart Allen (1st series only) and John Howard Davies. The programme was derived from a **Comedy Playhouse** entry ('The Bishop Rides Again', 17/5/66) credited to the pseudonymous writer 'John Wraith' and produced by Stuart Allen. When Nimmo also appeared in the series **Sorry I'm Single** (BBC-1, 1967), a Ronald Wolfe and Ronald Chesney comedy about a young man living in a converted Hampstead house with three girls, he received letters from distressed clergymen who had warmed to his innocent young chaplain character. Nimmo's accident-prone novice monk Brother Dominic, in **Oh Brother!** (BBC-1, 1968–70; 19 eps. × 30 mins.; wr. David Climie and Austin Steele, pr. Duncan Wood), was an offshoot of his clerical character, this time loose in a monastery; Felix Aylmer and Colin Gordon co-starred. **Oh Father!** (BBC-1, 1973; 7 eps. × 30 mins.) picked up where **Oh Brother!** left off, with Nimmo becoming Father Dominic and leaving the monastery to become a curate; Graeme Muir produced Climie and Steele's scripts.

At Last the 1948 Show

(Rediffusion, 1967; 13 eps. × half-hour)

Executive producer David Frost corralled four of the satire-comedy field's maddest practitioners to front (and write) this wall-to-wall sketch series. John Cleese (*foreground*), Marty Feldman (*left*), Graham Chapman (*right, background*), and Tim Brooke-Taylor (*right*) ran riot with their visually funny, almost surreal material (such as the one with the solo wrestler ending up strangling himself!). Linking the gags and sketches was little-girl voiced Aimi Macdonald (*centre*). Ian Fordyce directed.

Beggar My Neighbour

(BBC-1, 1967–68)

Developed from a **Comedy Playhouse** entry (24/5/66) written by Ken Hoare and Mike Sharland, starring (*l. to r.*) Reg Varney and Pat Coombs as the Butts and Peter Jones and June Whitfield as the Garveys. The humour sprang from the basic situation that the wives were sisters, as well as neighbours; Jones was an underpaid junior executive who was always broke while Varney was an opulent fitter. The 22 eps. × 30 mins. series was produced by David Croft and later by Eric Fawcett. Writers Hoare & Sharland later developed the sitcom **Mr Digby, Darling** (Yorkshire TV, 1969–71) which also starred Peter Jones with ex-**Rag Trade** colleague Sheila Hancock.

1967

Blandings Castle
(BBC-1, 24/2–31/3/67; 6 eps. × 30 mins.)

BBC TV continued their association with the works of P. G. Wodehouse by developing **Blandings Castle** (BBC-1, 24/2–31/3/67; 6 eps. × 30 mins.), a leisurely comedy featuring Ralph Richardson (*left*) as the put-upon Lord Emsworth, a man whose attempts at a placid existence were continually shattered. His sympathetic companions were Beach the butler (Stanley Holloway; *right*) and the Empress, the Lord's prize sow. The series (billed under **The World of Wodehouse** banner) was written by John Chapman and produced by Michael Mills.

Callan
(ABC TV, 1967; Thames TV, 1969–72)

British secret service agent/assassin David Callan (Edward Woodward; *pictured*) was first seen in an **Armchair Theatre** presentation called 'A Magnum for Schneider' (4/2/67; dir. Bill Bain), written by James Mitchell. This play established the business-like yet morally anguished Callan character, working for an unnamed government spy department (headed by a series of code-named people known as Hunter), assisted by a small-time crook called Lonely (Russell Hunter) and occasionally partnered by a supercilious fellow agent, Toby Meres (Peter Bowles in 'Magnum'; Anthony Valentine in the series). Patrick Mower appeared as agent Cross for a while but was killed off during the fourth series. Thirty-seven hour-long episodes were produced by Reginald Collin for Thames TV; Lloyd Shirley was executive producer for 6 hours for ABC TV. Magnum Films produced a feature film, *Callan*, in 1974 (wr. Mitchell from his novel *A Red File for Callan*, dir. Don Sharp) with Woodward, Eric Porter (as Hunter), and Peter Egan (as Meres). ATV recalled Callan back into service in a 90-minute TV movie, **Wet Job** (ATV, 2/9/81; wr. Mitchell, prod.-dir. Shaun O'Riordan), where the now retired, middle-aged agent was forced to take on one last mission.

Captain Scarlet and the Mysterons
(ITC/Century 21 TV Prod., 1967–68)

A puppet science fiction drama set in the twenty-first century featuring space warrior Captain Scarlet (voiced by Francis Matthews) as a universal protector against the evil campaigns launched by the mysterious Mysterons. A no-holds-barred hero, Scarlet was an indestructible force; he could survive car crashes, bullets, missiles, etc., all in the cause of high-speed visual action and fantastic storytelling. Voices for the regular characters were supplied by Donald Gray, Ed Bishop, Paul Maxwell, Gary Files, Cy Grant, Charles Tingwell, Sylvia Anderson, and Liz Morgan. Created by Gerry and Sylvia Anderson, the thirty-two half-hour episodes were produced by Reg Hill.

City '68
(Granada TV, 1967–68)

Headed a 13 eps. × hour series of 'topical dramas' about the fictional Lancashire city of Fylde. This city setting, the home of over three-quarters of a million people, was the springboard for the various stories dealing with city dwellers in different levels of conflict. The première episode, 'The Shooting War' (8/12/67) was written by H. V. Kershaw, based on an original idea by John Finch, and directed by Michael Apted. Geoffrey Hughes, George Innes, Geoffrey Palmer, and Kenneth Cranham were featured in the cast. H. V. Kershaw produced the programme. The scene pictured shows Rosalie Crutchley and John Bluthal in 'The Visitors' (5/1/68) episode.

Dee Time

(BBC-1, 1967–69)

Former BBC radio DJ Simon Dee (*pictured*) was given his own, twice a week (Tuesdays and Thursdays) series in the late 1960s, billed as 'an early evening scene'. His première studio guest line-up included Lance Percival, Libby Morris, Mike Newman, Cat Stevens, Jimi Hendrix Experience, and Kiki Dee. The 30-minute interview-entertainment series was produced by Terry Henebery. Following the BBC TV series, Dee switched to ITV and introduced **The Simon Dee Show** (LWT, 1970), a late night, 50-minute, Sunday chat show produced-directed by Bryan Izzard; jazz musician Maynard Ferguson and his 14-piece Orchestra supported in the music department.

Do Not Adjust Your Set

(Rediffusion, 1967–68; Thames TV, 1968–69)

Taking its cue from **At Last the 1948 Show** this 25-minute comedy–music series featured the crazy antics of Denise Coffey, Eric Idle (*right*), David Jason (*left*), Terry Jones (*2nd right*), and Michael Palin (*2nd left*) in a flurry of sketches and visual gags. Supporting were the equally bizarre Bonzo Dog Doo-Dah Band and the episodic mini-adventures of do-gooder 'Captain Fantastic' (portrayed by Jason; Coffey was his nemesis Mrs Black). Idle, Jones, and Palin also toiled in the writing department; Humphrey Barclay (later Ian Davidson) produced. A 50-minute Christmas special, **Do Not Adjust Your Stocking** (Thames TV, 25 / 12 / 68; dir. Adrian Cooper), was also produced.

The Forsyte Saga

(BBC-2, 7/1–1/7/67)

John Galsworthy's epic saga of Victorian respectability amounted to 21 hours of fine drama with each episode presented as an Act, standing dramatically by itself but holding situations in serial suspense. The large cast was led by Kenneth More (as Jo), Eric Porter (Soames; *left*), Nyree Dawn Porter (Irene; *right*), Margaret Tyzack (Winifred), June Barry (June), Michael York (Jolly), and Susan Hampshire (Fleur). Producer Donald Wilson dramatized the 26 eps. × 50 mins. series.

Further Adventures of Lucky Jim

(BBC-1, 1967)

An updated version of Kingsley Amis's 1954 novel, scripted by Dick Clement & Ian La Frenais, about the misadventures of a likeable Yorkshire misfit now loose in the 'Swinging London' of the late 1960s. Keith Barron (*pictured*) was Jim Dixon, a Walter Mitty-type character given to furious soliloquies about the idiotic behaviour he encounters in the garish, big city world of glossy journalism, photography, publicity, commercials, boutiques, and 'happenings'. The 7 eps. × 30 mins. series was produced by Duncan Wood; Kingsley Amis acted as story consultant. Clement & La Frenais returned the character, now played by Enn Reitel, for seven more half-hour episodes (BBC-2, 1 / 11–13 / 12 / 82) under producer-director Harold Snoad.

1967

The Golden Shot
(ATV, 1967–75)

Introduced and hosted in the early days by Jackie Rae, with the assistance of The Golden Girls (Carol Dilworth, Andrea Lloyd, and Anita Richardson, initially), and later by Bob Monkhouse, the game show featured contestants who were selected from home viewers and the studio audience. The contestants had to guide a blindfolded cameraman on the studio 'tele-bow' and instruct him when to fire at picture targets; home viewers did so by telephone, in view of their television sets, and studio audience contestants from a phone booth in the ATV studio, watching a monitor set. The show became extremely popular when it settled into its regular Sunday afternoon slot. Norman Vaughan and Charlie Williams, respectively, were the show's hosts during the later years.

Half Hour Story
(Rediffusion, 1967–68; 1971)

Provided producer (and former story editor) Stella Richman with a 30-minute series format to encourage well-known writers as well as new talent to contribute in this above-average-standard drama collection. The programme premièred with Alun Owen's 'Shelter' (19/5/67; dir. Alan Clarke), starring Wendy Craig and Colin Blakely. Later presentations included 'Myself, I've Got Nothing Against South Ken' (9/6/67; wr. Julian Bond); 'Between Men' (5/7/67; adapt. from a short story of the same name by Doris Lessing); and Edna O'Brien's 'Which of These Two Ladies Is He Married To?' (12/7/67; dir. Alan Clarke), starring Glenda Jackson and Sheila Raynor. The scene pictured shows Jill Bennett and John Osborne in 'It's Only Us' (26/6/68). The 1971 series presented some new material with repeated episodes.

Haunted
(ABC TV, 1967–68)

This late night supernatural series starred the 27-year-old Patrick Mower (*pictured*) as university lecturer Michael West who provided the continuity through eight 55-minute tales of psychic phenomena and occult happenings. Some years after the initial run (Nov.–Jan.) two further episodes were transmitted: 'The Ferryman' (23/12/74) and 'Poor Girl' (30/12/74). Michael Chapman was the series producer.

Magical Mystery Tour
(BBC-1, 26/12/67)

Was The Beatles' first venture as TV producers (creators-writers-directors), presenting a 50-minute musical series of *non sequiturs* involving a curious mixture of oddball characters journeying around the psychedelically styled countryside. Featured participants were (Beatles) Paul McCartney, John Lennon, George Harrison, and Ringo Starr; with Ivor Cutler, Jessie Robins, Mandy Weet, Nat Jackley, and Victor Spinetti. The programme was repeated in colour on BBC-2 (5/1/68).

Man in a Suitcase
(ITC, 1967–68)

Laconic Richard Bradford (*pictured*) was ex-CIA agent McGill, discharged from the secret service and becoming a somewhat reluctant troubleshooter-for-hire. A slickly produced and well-written espionage-crime drama series that gained something of a cult following through its thirty action-packed hour-long episodes. Series was created by Richard Harris and Dennis Spooner; producer was ex-Sapphire Films executive Sidney Cole. A two-part episode ('Variation on a Million Bucks', wr. Stanley R. Greenberg and dir. Pat Jackson (pt. I) and Robert Tronson (pt. II)) was re-edited as a 97-minute American TV feature, *To Chase a Million*, in 1967.

Market in Honey Lane
(ATV, 1967–69)

A soap drama set in a bustling street market populated by jovial Cockney venders with a flair for fast chatter. The main characters in this pavement jungle were played by John Bennett (*left*), Michael Golden, Ray Lonnen, Peter Birrel, Brian Rawlinson (*centre*), Anna Wing (*right*), and Pat Nye. The series was created by Louis Marks and produced by John Cooper. In September 1968, the title was changed to **Honey Lane** and the series became a twice-weekly, half-hour (Mondays and Wednesdays) afternoon serial.

Misleading Cases
(BBC-1, 1967–68; 1971)

Billed as **A. P. Herbert's 'Misleading Cases'**, the premiss of the series was drawn from Herbert's collection of legal absurdities written originally for *Punch* magazine. Alan Melville adapted the stories for television (with the assistance of Henry Cecil) which presented the irrepressible Albert Haddock (played as a doddering but astute old man by Roy Dotrice, *left*; with Richard Wattis) who skirmishes with the law and ends up defending himself in court with pleas that refer back to forgotten or outdated laws. Regular series characters included Mrs Haddock (Avice Landon), his patient wife, Sir Joshua Hoot, QC (Thorley Walters), the exasperated solicitor, and Stipendiary Magistrate Mr Swallow (Alastair Sim) who viewed Haddock's rounds of unorthodox jurisprudence with tolerant admiration. The first series of 6 eps. × 30 mins. was produced by Michael Mills; the second and third (1971) series, consisting of 13 eps. × 30 mins., was produced by John Howard Davies; the 1971 series was adapted by Michael Gilbert and Christopher Bond.

Never Mind the Quality, Feel the Width
(ABC TV, 1967–68; Thames TV, 1968–71)

The two central characters in this enjoyable sitcom were East End tailors Manny Cohen (John Bluthal; *foreground*), a Jewish jacket-maker, and Patrick Kelly (Joe Lynch; *background*), the trouser-maker. The comedy strand developed from their religious and patriotic differences; but their spiritual advisers, Rabbi Levy (Cyril Shaps) and Father Ryan (Eamon Kelly), were usually on hand to keep the peace. The series originated from a successful one-off play written by Vince Powell & Harry Driver for **Armchair Theatre** (tx 18/2/67; dir. Patrick Dromgoole), featuring Bluthal and Frank Finlay (as Patrick Kelly); Leonard White produced. The ABC TV series (of 17 eps.) were produced by Ronnie Baxter. When Thames TV later acquired the series they produced a further 22 eps. × half-hour.

News at Ten
(ITN, 1967–)

Was developed as the first ITV extended news programme (a half-hour format) with the intention of being able to cover the daily events in greater depth than before; it replaced the previous 12-minute format that had been broadcast at 8.55 p.m. The original **News at Ten** studio into-camera newsreaders were Alastair Burnet (*left*), Andrew Gardner, Reginald Bosanquet (*right*), and George Ffitch. The four major foreign correspondents were John Edwards, Alan Hart, Richard Lindley, and Sandy Gall, with their coverage backed up in the ITN studio by Gerald Seymour and others. Earlier news entries, offering daily and weekly news-footage compilations, were **Dateline** (ITN, 1961–67; 8/10 mins.), **ITN Reports** (ITN, 1964–65; half-hour), and **Reporting '66/Reporting '67** (ITN, 1966–67; half-hour), with the former presented by Reginald Bosanquet (as well as Colin Jones, John Whale, and Peter Woods) and the latter two by Andrew Gardner.

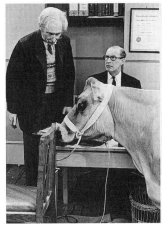

1967

No —That's Me Over Here!
(Rediffusion, 1967–68; LWT, 1970)

Gave comedian Ronnie Corbett (*left*) his start as the suburban little man who is always courting disaster. Rosemary Leach played his patient wife; his patronizing neighbour and rival was played by Henry McGee (*right*). Bill Hitchcock and (1st series) Marty Feldman produced; Hitchcock produced the later series; David Frost was executive producer. Scripts were supplied by Graham Chapman, Eric Idle, and Barry Cryer; twenty-one half-hour episodes appeared.

Not in Front of the Children
(BBC-1, 1967–70)

Wendy Craig (*left*) as the amiable yet put-upon mother of an, at times, irritable family group (husband plus three children). The 37 eps. × 30 mins. series developed from a successful, self-contained episode of **Comedy Playhouse** ('House in a Tree', 26/5/67) written by Richard Waring and produced by Graeme Muir. Carrying over from 'House in a Tree' was Paul Daneman as husband Henry, replaced in 1968 by Ronald Hines (*right*). When this series ended Wendy Craig moved smoothly into **. . . And Mother Makes Three** (Thames TV, 1971–73), another half-hour sitcom with Craig this time as a young widow with two growing sons (Robin Davies and David Parfitt), a cynical aunt (Valerie Lush), and her veterinarian boss (George Selway). The 24 eps. × half-hour series was written by Peter Buchanan and Peter Robinson (with contributions from Carla Lane and Richard Waring, among others) for producer-director Peter Frazer-Jones. That was swiftly followed by **. . . And Mother Makes Five** (Thames TV, 1974–76) in which, following her marriage to widower David (Richard Coleman), the two families move in together to begin a new series of domestic upsets; Maxine Gordon played the widower's young daughter. The twenty-six half-hour episodes were produced with Frazer-Jones once again as producer-director; the writers were Waring, Brian Cooke, Johnnie Mortimer, and 'Jonathan Marr' (Wendy Craig).

Omnibus
(BBC-1, 1967–)

A weekly programme about the creative world of music and arts, presenting such exceptional programmes as 'The World of Coppard' (15/12/67; pr.-dir. Jack Gold), featuring three stories by A. E. Coppard adapted by Kit Coppard, with music by Carl Davis; Ken Russell's 'Dante's Inferno' (22/12/67), with Oliver Reed, and 'A Song of Summer' (15/9/68); 'Whistle and I'll Come to You' (7/5/68; adapt.-pr. Jonathan Miller), the famous ghost story by M. R. James, starring Michael Hordern; 'All My Loving' (3/11/68), Tony Palmer's film of popular music; and 'Down These Mean Streets a Man Must Go' (27/4/69), a portrait of crime writer Raymond Chandler, with Tom Daly as Chandler and Edward Judd (*pictured, right*, with David Bauer and, *in background*, Robert O'Neil) as Philip Marlowe.

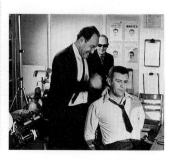

The Prisoner
(Everyman Films Prod.–ATV, 1967–68)

The enigmatic TV child of actor Patrick McGoohan (who also created the programme), **The Prisoner** (Everyman Films Prod.–ATV, 1967–68) became one of the great cult TV shows of the 1960s, despite a short run of only seventeen episodes. The McGoohan character, referred to only as Number Six, was an ex-secret agent who was kidnapped and imprisoned in a mysterious village (on location at the architecturally offbeat Welsh tourist spot of Portmeirion) and psychologically probed for information about his professional past. The jury, however, is still out on whether McGoohan's Number Six in the series was a continuation of his John Drake character from the earlier ATV series **Danger Man**; (*l. to r.*) Angelo Muscat, McGoohan, and (guest player) Leo McKern.

The Revenue Men
(BBC-2, 1967–68; 13 eps. × 50 mins., 12 eps. × 45 mins.)

An action-adventure series featuring the exploits of Customs and Excise investigators, an official department not generally known for its positive public image. The series dealt with the Investigation Branch of Customs and Excise and had the three central characters, played by Ewen Solon (*pictured*), James Grant, and Callum Mill, swoop down on drug traffickers, whisky hijackers, and major smuggling rings. Gerard Glaister produced the authentic-looking programme.

The Rolf Harris Show
(BBC-1, 1967–70; LWT, 1972–74)

Featured the bearded Australian chuckler and paint-brusher in his first prime-time entertainment series (although he had been active in children's TV programming since the early 1950s). The programme presented songs, sketches, dances, and (of course) Rolf's guess-what-it's-going-to-be paintings; the première series in January–March 1967 also featured a special 'Song for Europe' section with Sandy Shaw performing potential Eurovision Song Contest material (including the one that made it, *Puppet on a String*). Other Rolf Harris shows include **Rolf on Saturday—OK?** (BBC-1, 1977–79), **Rolf Harris Cartoon Time** (BBC-1, 1979–87), and **Rolf's Here! OK?** (BBC-1, 1981; 6 eps.).

Sanctuary
(Rediffusion, 1967–68)

The unlikely setting for this prime-time (Wednesday, 8.00 p.m.) character drama was a London convent bristling with charitable nuns. The interweaving storylines spotlighted their social work in the parish as well as the character clashes and self-doubt among the nuns themselves. The main characters were Sister Juliana (Fay Compton), the oldest nun in the community, Sister Ursula (Alison Leggatt), at odds with contemporary moral behaviour, Sister Paul (Peggy Thorpe-Bates; *right*), tough, practical, and dependable, and the young, high-spirited Sister Benedict (Joanna Dunham; *left*) who had been recalled from mission work in Tanzania and was now assigned generally unrewarding parish work. In collaboration with religious advisers, writer Philip Levene created the 26 eps. × 55 mins. series for producer John Harrison.

Sexton Blake
(Rediffusion, 1967–68; Thames TV, 1968–71)

Made his first appearance in 1893 in the boys' weekly paper called *The Halfpenny Marvel* and had his adventures penned by a wide variety of writers over the many years of the character's popularity (right up to the late 1960s). In this 64 eps. × half-hour series the consulting detective (an early literary rival to Sherlock Holmes) was played by Laurence Payne (*right*), assisted by Roger Foss (*left*) as Tinker. Ronald Marriott produced. BBC TV reintroduced the character in **Sexton Blake and the Demon God** (BBC-1, 10/9–15/10/78), a 6 parts × 30 mins. serial starring Jeremy Clyde as Blake, with Philip Davis as Tinker. Simon Raven scripted for producer Barry Letts; Roger Tucker directed.

The Short Stories of Conan Doyle
(BBC-2, 15/1–23/4/67)

Came from an idea of writer John Hawkesworth who developed the concept of the series from Conan Doyle's non-Sherlock Holmes stories, with the output ranging through many different styles and locales, and embodying the author's interest in boxing, the supernatural, and medical matters. The first of the 13 eps. × 50 mins., for instance, 'Lot 249' (adapt. Hawkesworth, dir. Richard Martin), dabbled in Egyptian mummy horror. Continuity came from a trio of undergraduates, on whom all the stories were centred: Michael Latimer played the elegant Philip Hardacre, Keith Buckley was the homely Tom Crabbe, and Christopher Matthews was the quiet Monkhouse 'Monkey' Lee. Series producer was Harry Moore. The series was also known as **Sir Arthur Conan Doyle** and **Conan Doyle**. The scene pictured shows (*l. to r.*) Matthews, Philip Manikum, and Latimer in 'Lot 249'.

The Val Doonican Show
(BBC-1, 1967–70)

Presented the Irish crooner in the popular light entertainment show in which he warbled 'middle of the road' country music (usually) from the comfort of his rocking-chair and woolly sweater. The 45-minute series was produced by John Ammonds. After a lengthy absence from regular television (he claimed that at the time there were too many lookalike shows around, in the **Cilla Black** and **The Rolf Harris Show** mode) Doonican resurfaced in a live musical show, **The Val Doonican Music Show** (BBC-1, 1977–84), produced by Yvonne Littlewood.

The Whitehall Worrier
(BBC-1, 1967)

Robert Coote's bumbling Minister, the Rt. Hon. Mervyn Pugh (*right*), was first seen in 'The Mallard Imaginaire' (5/7/66) episode of the **Comedy Playhouse** written by Alan Melville. This half-hour sitcom, which one may consider as a sort of primitive **Yes, Minister**, also featured Moria Lister (as his wife, Janet; *left*), Jonathan Cecil, and Daphne Anderson. Graeme Muir produced.

The White Rabbit
(BBC-2, 16/9–7/10/67; 4 eps. × 45 mins.)

Was the code-name for Wing Commander Yeo-Thomas (Kenneth More; *right*) who acted as a link-up with the wartime resistance in France. Dramatized by Michael Voysey, the serial was based on actual events (recorded in a biography by a Special Operations colleague, Bruce Marshall) in the life of the late Wing Commander F. F. Yeo-Thomas, GC, MC. He made two hazardous journeys into occupied France to maintain lines of communication with the Maquis but was captured by the Gestapo on the third mission and taken to Buchenwald concentration camp where he suffered constant, harrowing torture by the Nazis. Alan MacNaughton (*left*) played the Gestapo interrogator and, via flashbacks, Denise Buckley his girlfriend and Annette Crosbie his resistance worker contact in Paris. The nerve-stretching atmosphere of terror and betrayal was efficiently conveyed by director Peter Hammond and producer David Conroy.

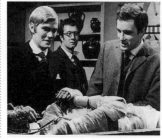

Witch Hunt
(BBC-2, 29/4–27/5/67)

A chilling serial about witchcraft in modern-day Gloucestershire, featuring Patrick Kavanagh as the newcomer to a small, eerie community inhabited by more-than-meets-the-eye characters. Cast included Anna Palk (*right*), Derek Francis, John Paul (*left*), and Sally Home. The 5 eps. × 25 mins. serial was written by Jon Manchip White; Peter Duguid directed Alan Bromly's production.

The World About Us
(BBC-2, 1967–86)

Naturalist David Attenborough started this long-running natural history series when he was in charge of BBC-2 and felt that these kinds of programme were what colour (which had begun on BBC TV's second channel in July 1967) was all about. In the early days the films came from amateur sources, then from the encouragement of more talented amateurs, and from amateurs-turned-professional before an increase in budget allowed the producers to compete with other BBC documentaries. The BBC's Natural History Unit at Bristol, which was set up in 1957 following the success of Peter Scott's **Look** series, and its Wildlife Unit developed into an important source of programmes, including **The World About Us** and eventually the blockbuster **Life on Earth**. The picture shows part of the BBC film crew's 2,000-mile trip up the Amazon and Orinoco by Hovercraft in 'The Last Great Journey on Earth'.

The Basil Brush Show
(BBC-1, 1968–80)

The furry, pointy-faced glove puppet with the aristocratic voice and 'Boom-boom!' tag line grew out of the children's slot programme **The Three Scampis** (A-R, 3/4–22/5/64), written and performed by Howard Williams, Wally Whyton, and Basil's voice and operator Ivan Owen. After a popular period with David Nixon on the magician/entertainer's BBC TV shows during the mid-1960s the character starred in his own half-hour show, introduced by Rodney Bewes, Derek Fowlds, Roy North, Howard Williams, and Billy Boyle, respectively. Johnny Downes, Ernest Maxin, Robin Nash, Brian Penders, Jim Franklin, and Paul Ciani were the foxy one's producers.

The Borderers
(BBC-2, 1968–70)

Was a 26 eps. × 50 mins. adventure series set on the Anglo-Scottish border in the sixteenth century when lawless neighbours feuded for land and cattle. Iain Cuthbertson, Joseph Brady (*left*), Michael Gambon (*right*), and Edith Macarthur starred. The programme, created by Bill Craig, was produced by Peter Graham Scott and Anthony Coburn.

The Caesars
(Granada TV, 22/9–27/10/68)

A series of six 55-minute plays, written and produced by Philip Mackie, focusing on the absolute power held by the ancient Roman emperors. 'Augustus' featured Roland Culver in the title role; 'Germanicus', Eric Flynn; 'Tiberius', André Morell; 'Sejanus', Barrie Ingham; 'Caligula', Ralph Bates; 'Claudius', Freddie Jones (*pictured*; with Nicola Pagett). Derek Bennett directed.

Cilla
(BBC-1, 1968–69; 1971–74; 1976)

Began her own weekly music/comedy show with this series usually produced by Michael Hurll (Colin Charman produced in 1974 and Hurll and James Moir co-produced in 1976). Cilla's guests in the late 1960s included Tom Jones, Donovan, and Cliff Richard (the latter with a 'Song for Europe': *Congratulations*); and in the 1970s Charles Aznavour and Sacha Distel. Perhaps with this middle-of-the-road programme, Cilla's career evolution from 'pop' (the kids) to popular (the next generation) to prime time (sanitized television: **Surprise, Surprise** and **Blind Date**) embraced the unthinkable along with the unexpectedly excellent.

Dad's Army
(BBC-1, 1968–77)

Writers Jimmy Perry and David Croft (the latter also produced) created one of BBC TV's most popular and most fondly remembered comedy series with this fun-making account of the British Home Guard during the early years of the Second World War. The setting was Walmington-on-Sea, somewhere on the south coast, and featured the mainly over-the-hill roll-call (*l. to r.*) of the pompous Captain Mainwaring (Arthur Lowe), Pte. Pike (Ian Lavender), Cpl. Jones (Clive Dunn), Sgt. Wilson (John Le Mesurier), Pte. Godfrey (Arnold Ridley), Pte. Walker (James Beck), and Pte. Frazer (John Laurie). Their misadventures came in all forms and sizes, from tackling drifting mines to runaway steam trains, and were always challenged (if not mocked) by the testy air-raid warden Hodges (Bill Pertwee); 64 eps. × 30 mins. (and two Christmas specials) were produced. A feature film, under the same title, was released in 1971.

The Expert
(BBC-2, 1968–69; 1971; 1976)

The day-to-day activities of forensic scientist Dr John Hardy (Marius Goring; *shown*) was the focus of this popular drama series. Set in Warwickshire where the crime rate of the nearby midlands cities kept Hardy busy, the clue-unravelling plots dealt with murder, robbery, sex crimes, serial killers, and medical negligence. Also appearing were Ann Morrish (as Hardy's wife, Jo) and Victor Winding (as police Insp. Fleming). The series was created by producer Gerard Glaister and writer N. J. Crisp; 62 eps. × 45/50 mins. were presented, the first BBC-2 drama series to be made in colour. An earlier BBC TV series, **Silent Evidence** (BBC-tv, 1962), had also presented a police pathologist (played by Basil Sydney) as the central character; this series had been devised by Evelyn Frazer for producer John Warrington.

Father, Dear Father
(Thames TV, 1968–73; 1978–79)

A half-hour sitcom written by Johnnie Mortimer and Brian Cooke featuring Patrick Cargill (*centre*) as a Hampstead-based novelist whose life is in constant upheaval due to the antics of his two teenage daughters (Natasha Pyne, *left*, and Ann Holloway, *right*) and the interference of his ex-wife (Ursula Howells), and occasionally her new husband (Tony Britton). The continually disrupted household also accommodated the traffic flow of his mother (Joyce Carey), his housekeeper (Noel Dyson; *background, right*), and his agent/mistress (Dawn Addams; originally played by Sally Bazely). In 1978 the Cargill character, after seeing his daughters married, moved to Australia where he 'inherited' a couple of nieces (Sally Conabere and Sigrid Thornton). During the mid-1970s, between series of **Father, Dear Father**, Cargill appeared in LWT's **The Many Wives of Patrick** (1976–78; 21 eps. × half-hour) playing a similar role, this time that of a wealthy antique dealer who has been married six times. **The Many Wives of Patrick** and the early series of **Father, Dear Father**, were produced and directed by William G. Stewart. A feature film version of *Father, Dear Father*, with most of the TV cast, was released in 1972.

The First Lady
(BBC-1, 1968–69)

Alan Plater's dramatization of the inner workings of local government presented Lancashire comedienne Thora Hird (*pictured*) with a straight role as Sarah Danby, newly elected independent member of Furness Borough Council. The crusading councillor was, at various times, aided and opposed by Will Tarrant (Robert Keegan), Deputy Leader of the Labour group on the Council, smoothie George Kingston (James Grout), Alderman and Leader of the Conservative opposition, and her schoolmaster son Tom (Henry Knowles). Despite the limitations of Town Hall machinations, and the general public's apathy towards local elections, writer-creator Plater and producer David Rose's storylining provided a finely edged series of 30 eps. × 50 mins.; Terence Dudley produced the second series.

Frontier
(Thames TV, 1968)

Was an adventure series recounting dramatic tales of a fictitious British battalion in action in Northern India during the 1880s. The stories followed the main characters—the dashing young Lt. Clive Russell (played by Gary Bond, *right*; with Patrick O'Connell), the shady political officer (James Maxwell), the crusty Lt.-Col. (John Phillips), and the uncommitted civilian reporter (Paul Eddington)—as they experienced everything from tribal uprisings to lone missions along the Russian-influenced North-West Frontier. The 8 eps. × 60 mins. series was produced by Michael Chapman, who shot the exterior scenes on location in Snowdonia, North Wales. Thames TV heralded it as the most expensive series ever mounted locally by an ITV company.

Jazz at the Maltings
(BBC-2, 1968–69)

Was a 25-minute series introduced by Benny Green from the Aldeburgh Festival Concert Hall in East Suffolk. The series featured Buddy Rich and his Orchestra (10/10/68), the Oscar Peterson Trio (17/10/68), the Dave Brubeck Quartet with Gerry Mulligan (31/10/68), the Art Blakey Sextet (7/11/68), the Dizzy Gillespie Big Band Reunion (21/11/68; *pictured*), and the Newport All-Stars, including Benny Carter (saxophone), Barney Kessell (guitar), and Red Norvo (vibraphone) (12/12/68). Terry Henebery produced.

1968

Joe 90
(Century 21–ITC, 1968–69)

Came from the Gerry and Sylvia Anderson tech-puppet factory and had as its hero a myopic 9-year-old boy whose superhero characteristics were sparked off by a special pair of spectacles. The glasses acted as a switch to release recorded adult brain patterns, absorbed by Joe after a session inside a cage called BIG RAT (Brain Impulse Galvanoscope Record and Transfer). Joe (voiced by Len Jones) was assisted in his adventures by his stepfather professor (with the voice of Rupert Davies) and his deputy (Keith Alexander). Thirty half-hour episodes were produced by David Lane.

Journey to the Unknown
(Hammer Films–20th Century-Fox TV, 1968–69)

This supernatural fantasy anthology series with science fiction elements was Hammer's second attempt in television production; there had been an unsuccessful stab at a Columbia Pictures TV co-produced **Tales of Frankenstein** series in 1957. Utilizing the written works of such genre specialists as Richard Matheson, Charles Beaumont, and Robert Bloch, producer Anthony Hinds fashioned a fairly atmospheric and moody series: Robert Heverley's 'Matakitas Is Coming' (starring American actress Vera Miles) was one of the more chilling tales. Seventeen hour-long episodes were produced in conjunction with America's ABC TV network. The scene pictured is from the episode 'Do Me a Favour and Kill Me' with Joseph Cotton and Judy Parfitt.

Late Night Horror
(BBC-2, 1968)

Despite some of the story titles, this collection of 25-minute fantasy tales presented fairly ordinary, everyday situations but with a slight distortion in their development. The series premièred with Richard Matheson's 'No Such Thing as a Vampire' (19/4/68; scr. Hugh Leonard, dir. Paddy Russell; *pictured*), then followed with 'William and Mary' (26/4/68; by Roald Dahl, dir. Richard Martin), John Burke's 'The Corpse Can't Play' (3/5/68; scr. Leonard, dir. Russell), H. Russell Wakefield's 'The Triumph of Death' (10/5/68; scr. David Campton, dir. Rudolph Cartier), Robert Aickman's 'The Bells of Hell' (17/5/68; scr. Hugh Whitemore, dir. Naomi Capon), and 'The Kiss of Blood' (24/5/68; based on a short story by Sir Arthur Conan Doyle, scr. John Hawkesworth, dir. Martin). Harry Moore produced. A similar themed collection called **Dead of Night** (BBC-2, 5/11–17/12/72) followed in later years, premièring a 7 eps. × 50 mins. series with writer-director Don Taylor's 'The Exorcism'. BBC Bristol's **Leap in the Dark** (BBC-2, 9/1–20/3/73; 19/9–10/10/75; 14/1–18/2/77; 4–12/9/80) also introduced a series of plays as investigations into the paranormal; the first three series were directed by Colin Godman, the last series by Godman and Michael Croucher.

Lulu's Back in Town
(BBC-1, 1968)

Gave singer-actress Lulu (Glaswegian Marie Lawrie) her first starring entertainment series, which was produced through the summer months (May–July) by John Ammonds. The show included such guests as Lou Rawls, the Everly Brothers, and the Alan Price Set. Her earlier TV had included appearances on the popsy youth/music show **A Whole Scene Going** (BBC-1, 1966) and as a regular with comedy series **Three of a Kind** (BBC-2, 1967; pr. John Ammonds). From **Lulu's Back in Town** she went on to **Happening for Lulu** (BBC-1, 1968–69) and **Lulu** (BBC-1, 1975), before embarking on acting elements (**The Growing Pains of Adrian Mole**) and voice-overs (**Nellie the Elephant**; Central TV-101 Film Prods., 1990–91).

Magpie
(Thames TV, 1968–80)

Half-hour (originally 40-minute) children's programme somewhat in the style of BBC TV's **Blue Peter**, with jolly presenters Tony Bastable, Peter Brady, and Susan Stranks (later Jenny Hanley, Mick Robertson, and Tommy Boyd) enthusing the post-homework brigade with unusual people, places, competitions, and animals. Also given a 5-minute slot in the programme was the zany Captain Fantastic character, held over from its origins in **Do Not Adjust Your Set**. Producers over the years were Sue Turner, David Hodgson, Randal Beattie, and Tim Jones. The title ditty ('One for sorrow | Two for joy | Three for a girl | Four for a boy') went on to haunt a generation. Pictured is presenter Susan Stranks.

A Man of Our Times
(Rediffusion, 1968)

An exact, unsentimental drama about a middle-aged man, Max Osborne (George Cole, *right*, with Thorley Walters), whose life is enmeshed in domestic and business turmoil. Jean Harvey played his separated wife, Jennifer Wilson his mistress, and Charles Tingwell and Clive Morton were his son-and-father company bosses. Stella Richman and Richard Bates produced the 13 eps. × hour series; Julian Bond was originator and chief author.

Marty
(BBC-2, 1968–69)

After many years as a successful comedy writer and group comedian Marty Feldman (*pictured*) starred in his own series of oddball sketches and clowning, assisted by John Junkin and Tim Brooke-Taylor. The series was written by Feldman and Barry Took with additional material by John Cleese, Graham Chapman, Terry Jones & Michael Palin, Donald Webster, and Philip Jenkinson. Denis Main Wilson produced. This was followed by **The Marty Feldman Comedy Machine** (ATV, 1971–72), with contributing writers Chris Allen, Rudy De Luca, Barry Levinson, Spike Milligan, Larry Gelbart (who also produced), and Feldman himself. **Marty Back Together Again** (BBC-1, 1974) returned him for more mayhem at the BBC under producer Dennis Main Wilson. Writers this time around were Johnny Speight, Ken Hoare, Barry Cryer, Graham Chapman, Tom Lehrer, and Feldman & Took.

Nearest and Dearest
(Granada TV, 1968–72)

Featured Hylda Baker (*left*) and Jimmy Jewel (*right*) as brother and sister Nellie and Eli Pledge who inherited a pickle-bottling business in this Vince Powell and Harry Driver North Country sitcom. Madge Hindle, Edward Malin, and Joe Gladwin also appeared. (The series, unluckily, premièred in the middle of a dispute between ITV and the ACTT.) Hylda Baker also appeared as a similar though tougher northern character, Nellie Pickersgill, in **Not On Your Nellie** (LWT, 1974–75) where she was a Lancashire lass who moved to London; Bryan Izzard produced-directed seventeen half-hour episodes. A feature film spin-off, *Nearest and Dearest*, was produced by Hammer / Granada in 1972.

Please, Sir!
(LWT, 1968–72)

John Alderton (*left foreground*) led the cast of this noisy sitcom as newly qualified teacher Bernard Hedges of class 5C at Fenn Street Secondary Modern school. His class featured Peter Cleall (as Duffy), Malcolm McFee (Craven), Liz Gebhardt (Maureen), Penny Spencer (as Sharon; later played by Carol Hawkins), David Barry (Abbott), and Peter Denyer (Dunstable). Noel Howlett was the weak headmaster, Joan Sanderson the assistant head, Richard Davies the Welsh teacher Price, and Derek Guyler appeared as school-keeper Potter. The 41 eps. × 45/30 mins. series was written by John Esmonde & Bob Larbey and produced-directed by Mark Stuart. A feature film version was produced in 1971 (dir. Mark Stuart). A spin-off series, **The Fenn Street Gang** (LWT, 1971–73), saw the former 5C class members in life and work after leaving school; Alderton also appeared in this series. Forty-six half-hour episodes were produced. Esmonde & Larbey supplied most of the scripts.

The Railway Children
(BBC-1, 12/5–23/6/68)

Edith Nesbit's famous 1905 children's book was produced in 1968 as a 7 eps. × 25 mins. serial by Campbell Logan, featuring (*l. to r.*) Gillian Bailey as Phyllis, Neil McDermott as Peter, and Jenny Agutter as Bobbie; in the background, Gordon Gostelow (as Perks). Set at the turn of the century, the story told of three children and their adventures with a local railway line; the central theme, however, concerned events in the life of an Edwardian family rather than just being a story about railways. Denis Constanduros adapted; Julia Smith directed. The story was filmed as a feature by Lionel Jeffries in 1970, with Agutter repeating her TV role. The first British television version of **The Railway Children** was produced (and adapted) by Dorothea Brooking and presented 6/2–27/3/51 as an 8 part × 30 mins. serial; another BBC TV version appeared in 1957. Related to the above, as based on E. Nesbit stories, was **The Treasure Seekers** (BBC-tv, 19/2–26/3/61), six 30-minute episodes about the adventures of the Bastable children during the early 1900s; adapted and produced by Dorothea Brooking. This was followed, some twenty years later, by **The Story of the Treasure Seekers** (BBC-1, 6/1–10/2/82), 6 eps. × 30 mins. produced by Paul Stone.

Rogues' Gallery
(Granada TV, 5–26/2/68; 10/5–14/6/69)

Suitably boisterous, lascivious, and splendidly squalid hour-long tales of London's Newgate Prison during the 1750s, featuring such rogues as highwaywoman Jane Rawley (played by Jane Bond), colourful thieves Jonathan Wild (Ronald Fraser) and Jack Sheppard (Paul Shelley), and the unscrupulous Lady Sarah Bellasize (Diane Cilento, *pictured*, with Jim Dale). The first four episodes were shown under Rediffusion's *Playhouse* banner. Peter Wildeblood authored and produced.

The Ronnie Barker Playhouse
(Rediffusion, 1968)

Presented a series of half-hour single comedy plays written by Johnnie Mortimer and Brian Cooke, Hugh Leonard, and Alun Owen. The programme was produced by Stella Richman and executive producer was David Frost. The plays included 'Ah, There You Are' (10/4/68) with Barker as the decrepit Lord Rustless, the character he featured in his next series, **Hark at Barker** (LWT, 1969–70). This LWT series of comedies, set in the stately home of the lecherous Lord Rustless (Barker), also starred Frank Gatliff (as Badger the butler), Josephine Tewson (as Bates the secretary), David Jason (as Dithers the gardener), Mary Baxter (as Cook), and Moira Foot (as the maid Effie). The half-hour series was written by Peter Caulfield, Chris Miller, Bill Oddie, Gerald Wiley, and Bernard McKenna; Humphrey Barclay produced. Barclay also produced **Six Dates With Barker** (LWT, 1971), a series of six comedies with Barker in a variety of themes and disguises which included 'The Odd Job' (22/1/71) by Bernard McKenna, later filmed as a feature (*The Odd Job*, 1978) starring Graham Chapman (who also co-pr.). Barker returned as Rustless in **His Lordship Entertains** (BBC-2, 1972) with his original cast in their **Hark at Barker** roles; Harold Snoad produced. The scene pictured is from 'The Incredible Mister Tanner' episode with Barker and Alec Clunes.

The Sooty Show
(Thames TV, 1968–)

The mischievous little bear glove puppet with the sooty ears and nose and attached to the end of fall guy Harry Corbett's arm has been a British TV tradition since its TV début on BBC TV **Talent Night** in 1952. The Sooty character was joined by the squeaky Sweep in 1957 and by Soo, Sooty's cute panda girlfriend, in 1964. After many years appearing on BBC TV Corbett / Sooty and company (*pictured*) moved over to Thames TV in 1968 for a long-running half-hour series produced, originally, by Daphne Shadwell; Corbett's son Matthew took over as full-time 'handler'-presenter in 1976. Harry Corbett, after almost a quarter of a century as the popular and jovial recipient of Sooty's flour-bag, water-hose, and hammer assaults, died in 1989.

Spindoe
(Granada TV, 19/4–24/5/68; 6 eps. × 60 mins.)

Ray McAnally (*pictured*) was featured in this six-part story about internecine gang warfare in London, as the ex-boss of south London's gangland who, following his release from a seven-year prison stretch (inflicted on him in the series **The Fellows (Late of Room 17)**), tries to regain his former underworld top-dog position and territory. As written by producer Robin Chapman, it was a raw and violent study of gangland struggle for power—for its time—and helped introduce a more rugged and credible dramatic form to independent television production. Colette O'Neil played Spindoe's unfaithful wife, Richard Hurndall was the north London ganglord, and George Sewell a vengeful private detective.

The Stanley Baxter Show
(BBC-1, 9/9–4/11/68; 8/1–26/2/71)

Launched a series of wildly funny half-hour shows featuring the pliable talents of Scottish comedian Stanley Baxter (*pictured*, with guest Joan Sims) in various guises. David Bell produced in 1968, Roger Race in 1971. Baxter's flair for characterization (along with the production detail under, mostly, producer Bell) scored successfully with a series of hour-long spectaculars for LWT throughout the 1970s: **The Stanley Baxter Picture Show** (LWT, 8–29/10/72), **The Stanley Baxter Big Picture Show** (LWT, 21/12/73), **The Stanley Baxter Moving Picture Show** (LWT, 7/9/74), **The Stanley Baxter Picture Show Part III** (LWT, 19/9/75; pr. Jon Scoffield), **Stanley Baxter on Television** (LWT, 1/4/79; pr. John Kaye Cooper), and the half-hour **The Stanley Baxter Series** (LWT, 1981).

Tom Grattan's War
(Yorkshire TV, 1968; 1970)

Presented the adventures of a young boy, Tom (Michael Howe, *pictured*, *right*, with Tony Selby), who was sent to Yorkshire to live on a farm during the First World War when his father was called up and his mother went to work in a munitions factory. The 24 eps. × half-hour series was written and produced by David C. Rea (the later series pr. Audley Southcott).

1968

A Touch of Venus
(BBC-2, 1968–69)

Presented a series of short plays (20 mins.) specially written by famous authors and featuring distinguished English and Continental actresses in solo performances. The monologues included (the première ep.) 'A Blue Movie of My Own True Love' (11/9/68; wr. Emlyn Williams), starring Rachel Roberts (*shown*); 'All On Her Own' (25/9/68; wr. Terence Rattigan), starring Margaret Leighton; 'Desmond' (2/10/68; wr. John Mortimer), starring Moira Lister; 'The Jewish Wife' (16/10/68; by Bertolt Brecht, transl. Eric Russell Bentley), starring Elisabeth Bergner; and 'Linda at Pulteney's' (8/1/69), by J. B. Priestley, starring Irene Worth.

Ukridge
(BBC-1, 1968)

A year after **Blandings Castle** was screened **The World of Wodehouse** programme banner presented **Ukridge** (BBC-1, 1968), another of Wodehouse's amiable eccentrics from the 1920s. Anton Rodgers played the outrageous con man Stanley Featherstonehaugh Ukridge (seen here with Julian Holloway, *left*, as Corky) in a series of 7 eps. × 30 mins. directed by Joan Kemp-Welch.

Virgin of the Secret Service
(ATV, 1968)

Was a peculiar series that was not too sure where it hovered between the uniformed, period dramatics of **Frontier** and a tongue-in-cheek spoof of the early 007 Bond films. Scheduling at prime-time 8 o'clock (on Wednesdays), instead of in the late afternoon children's slot, made it all the more weirder. Set in 1907 India, full of mystery, mysticism, and cloak-and-dagger capers, the programme followed the derring-do adventures of Royal Dragoon Captain Robert Virgin (Clinton Greyn; *right*) in his dual role as a British spy up against the enemies of the Empire. Virgin's comic book companions were the emancipated Mrs Virginia Cortez (Veronica Strong; *left*) and his batman Doublett (John Cater); Col. Shaw-Cumberley (Noel Coleman) was his superior officer and German super-spy Karl von Brauner (Alexander Dore) his constant adversary. The thirteen hour-long episodes were produced by Josephine Douglas; the series was devised by Ted Willis.

The War of Darkie Pilbeam
(Granada TV, 12–26/7/68)

Was a trilogy of hour-long plays, written by Tony Warren, about a 1940s black marketeer, played in appropriate fedora and zoot-suit fashion by Trevor Bannister (*right*). Roy Barraclough, Christine Hargreaves (*left*), and Gabrielle Daye supported. Produced and directed by Richard Everitt; episode 2 was directed by June Howson.

The World of Beachcomber
(BBC-2, 1968–69)

Featured a strip-cartoon projection of the weird characters and situations created by J. B. Morton in his 'Beachcomber' column in the *Daily Express*; adapted for TV by Barry Took and John Junkin (with additional material by Ken Hoare), and starring Spike Milligan (*pictured*). Milligan, as link-man and performer, headed the comedy line-up of George Benson, Clive Dunn, Patricia Hayes, Julian Orchard, Sheila Steafel, Frank Thornton, and Leon Thau. The 19 eps. × 35/30 mins. series was produced by Duncan Wood. In March 1969 there followed the first of Milligan's 'Q' series, **Q5** (BBC-2, 1969; 7 eps. × 30 mins., pr. Ian MacNaughton), a Milliganesque, surreal stretch of 30 minutes; then **Q6** (BBC-2, 1975; 6 eps. × 30 mins., pr. MacNaughton), **Q7** (BBC-2, 1978; 5 eps. × 30 mins., pr. MacNaughton), **Q8** (BBC-2, 1979; 6 eps. × 30 mins., pr. Douglas Argent), and **Q9** (BBC-2, 1980; 6 eps. × 30 mins., pr. Argent); all were co-written by Milligan and Neil Shand. Milligan later returned with **There's a Lot of It About** (BBC-2, 20/9–25/10/82; 6 eps. × 35 mins., prod.-dir. Alan J. W. Bell), also featuring John Bluthal and David Lodge.

The Year of the Sex Olympics
(BBC-2, 29/7/68)

Nigel Kneale's disturbingly original and enthralling play was set in the near future, in a world completely dominated and monopolized by television. In this world of total apathy where all 'problems' like war, hate, love, and loyalty had been removed, overpopulation had now become *the* problem. The answer was found in television, with applied pornography programmes to put people off sex. The new programme subjects were art-sex, sport-sex, and, this time, the year of the sex Olympics. A tiny minority, however, decided to leave for a small island where life had not been made trivial and safe. Unfortunately, the cameras were on them 24 hours a day—for the Live Life Show, a perpetual tele-peepshow. Leonard Rossiter, Suzanne Neve, Tony Vogel (*right*), Vickery Turner (*left*), Brian Cox, and George Murcell were the featured players. Michael Elliott directed the 105-minute **Theatre 625** play for producer Ronald Travers.

Big Breadwinner Hog
(Granada TV, 11/4–30/5/69)

A new-style, violent, utterly merciless London gangland villain in the form of the young and ruthlessly ambitious Hog (played by Peter Egan; *pictured*) emerged in this series. Because of the violent methods he employed in his underworld activities the long-haired and flashy Hog became a threat to the old-time, established criminal fraternity as well as a prime target for the police. Mike Newell and Michael Apted directed the eight hour-long episodes for producer-writer Robin Chapman.

The Champions
(ITC, 1969–71)

A fantasy–espionage series that featured three super-agents (*l. to r.*, William Gaunt, Stuart Damon, and Alexandra Bastedo) working for a super-secret, Geneva-based organization called Nemesis. The introductory episode saw the trio crash-land in a *Lost Horizon*-like Tibet where they were rescued by a mysterious old man who endowed them with the independent powers of telepathy, ESP, super-strength, as well as heightening their natural senses. The series was created by producer Monty Berman and Dennis Spooner; 30 eps. × 60 mins. were produced.

1969

Civilisation
(BBC-2, 23/2–18/5/69)

A milestone documentary series of thirteen 50-minute programmes in which distinguished art historian and critic Sir Kenneth Clark (*pictured*) charted the ideas and events which led from the collapse of Greece and Rome to the twentieth century and examined the values which give meaning to the term Western Civilisation. The programme, produced by Michael Gill and Peter Montagnon, took more than two years to prepare and involved filming (by lighting cameraman A. A. Englander) in thirteen countries.

Clangers
(BBC-1/Smallfilms, 1969–73)

The popular, armour-plated, mouse-like creatures who lived inside their peculiar planet and shared adventures with other curious visitors and creatures were the creation of Oliver Postgate (as writer) and Peter Firmin (who handled the puppets and settings) under their Smallfilms banner (alongside **The Pogles**/**Pogles' Wood** and **Bagpuss** productions). Vernon Elliott handled the music.

The Complete and Utter History of Britain
(LWT, 12/1–16/2/69)

Terry Jones and Michael Palin's comical overview of British history, as portrayed in various eccentric character roles by Wallas Eaton, Colin Gordon, Roddy Maude-Roxby, Melinda May, Jones, and Palin (*pictured*, as a French soldier). The six half-hour parts were directed by Maurice Murphy for producer Humphrey Barclay.

Counterstrike
(BBC-1, 1969)

An alien invasion was (once again) the theme of this short-run science fiction series starring Jon Finch (*left*) as Simon King, an alien agent dispatched by an inter-galactic council to counter the overthrow. Helped by Mary (Sarah Brackett; *pictured*), a doctor who had discovered his origin, King pursued the alien plotters (referred to as Centaurans) around the country. In all 10 eps. × 50 mins. were produced but only nine transmitted; one episode was pre-empted and never rescheduled. The series was created by Tony Williamson and produced by Patrick Alexander.

Curry and Chips
(LWT, 1969; 6 eps. × half-hour)

By forcing the controversial issues of working-class bigotry, prejudice, and racial discrimination to caricatured lengths writer Johnny Speight hoped to dampen the inflammatory subject-matter. Stars of the series were Spike Milligan (*right*) as a newly arrived Pakistani factory hand by the name of Kevin O'Grady and Eric Sykes (*centre*; with Jerold Wells) as the liberal-minded, though confused, foreman. It was as funny a sitcom as this type of material would allow, although some uneasy moments were felt (by both cast and viewers) with the over-spicing of controversial ingredients. Keith Beckett was producer-director.

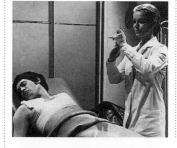

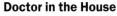

The Dave Allen Show
(BBC-1, 1969)

The relaxed, amiable Irish comedian appeared in the first of his popular comedy series for BBC TV and told amusing, somewhat sacrilegious, but rather long-winded stories intercut with single punch-line group comedy sketches. He later starred in **Dave Allen at Large** (BBC-1, 1971–73; BBC-2, 1975–76). Allen had also featured in the earlier ITV series **Tonight With Dave Allen** (ATV, 1967; LWT, 1968–69), then later in the 1970s with **Dave Allen and Friends** (ATV, 1977) and **Dave Allen** (ATV, 1978).

Dear Mother . . . Love Albert
(Thames TV, 1969; Yorkshire TV, 1970–71)

Rodney Bewes (*right*) was Albert Courtnay, a slightly bewildered lad from the North who moved to London but could not resist writing rather exaggerated letters home to his mum, in this 19 eps. × half-hour sitcom. The series was produced by Bewes & Derrick Goodwin and John Duncan. A follow-up series, **Albert!** (Yorkshire TV, 1972), continued the misadventures of Bewes's innocent-in-London; 7 eps. × half-hour were produced, again by Bewes. Both programmes were written by Bewes and Goodwin. Garfield Morgan (*left*) played Albert's boss, A. C. Strain, in the two series.

Department 'S'
(ATV/ITC, 1969)

Monty Berman and Dennis Spooner's **Department 'S'** (ATV/ITC, 1969) was a return to the counter-espionage arena, fronting three Interpol-connected agents: Jason King (played by Peter Wyngarde; *centre*), Stewart Sullivan (Joel Fabiani; *left*), and Annabelle Hurst (Rosemary Nicols; *right*). Not unlike the three leading characters in ITC's other contemporary action series **The Champions**, the trio here worked separately and as a team in assorted, way-out adventures involving double-agents, murder victims in bizarre costumes, and offbeat aviation mysteries. While tough guy Fabiani and the fetching Miss Nicols essayed their undercover roles competently but by-the-numbers it was Wyngarde's rakish, playboy author Jason King (he was a sort of 'on-call' agent) who usually stole the limelight; enough for the character to feature later in his own series, **Jason King** (ATV/ITC, 1971–72), where he became a sort of author-adventurer, penning his 'Mark Caine' novels between intrigues. Monty Berman produced both series.

Doctor in the House
(LWT, 1969–70)

Based on the popular 'Doctor' books by Richard Gordon, the series, under various headings, ran for over ten years. The series got the go-ahead when LWT's then Head of Comedy Frank Muir finally acquired the copyright to produce TV versions of the books, in consultation with the author. The format was updated to accommodate new staff and students at the famous teaching hospital of St Swithin's. The original novel's Simon Sparrow and Sir Lancelot Spratt were long gone, replaced by Michael Upton (played by Barry Evans; *3rd right*) and Professor Loftus (Ernest Clark). The other new medical students aiding Upton in the boozing and womanizing department were Paul Collier (George Layton; *3rd left*), Dick Stuart-Clark (Geoffrey Davies; *left*), and Duncan Waring (Robin Nedwell; *right*); Martin Shaw, as Welsh student Huw Evans, Simon Cuff (*2nd left*), and Jonathan Lynn (*2nd right*) also appeared occasionally. In the following series, **Doctor at Large** (LWT, 1971), Upton was a qualified MB who sought a temporary appointment at St Swithin's; Richard O'Sullivan joined the cast as prissy, by-the-book Dr Lawrence Bingham. Evans was missing from **Doctor in Charge** (LWT, 1972–73) and the focus was on the antics of Nedwell, Layton, and Davies; they carried through to **Doctor at Sea** (LWT, 1974), minus George Layton but with Ernest Clark doubling as cruise ship Captain Loftus (the Professor's brother). Nedwell and Davies continued through the last two series, **Doctor on the Go** (LWT, 1975–77) and the Australian-produced **Doctor Down Under** (1981). The LWT series were produced by Humphrey Barclay; writers included John Cleese, Graham Chapman, Grahame Garden, Bill

1969

Oddie, and Barry Cryer. In 1981 Richard Gordon and Ralph Thomas developed **Doctors' Daughters** (ATV, 1981; 6 eps. × half-hour) in which two young and attractive doctors (Lesley Duff and Victoria Burgoyne) took over the long-time family practice of three reluctantly retiring GPs (played by Jack Watling, Richard Murdoch, and Bill Fraser). (This series was originally scheduled for transmission in November 1980, but was postponed due to industrial difficulties.) BBC TV revived the series in 1991 with **Doctor at the Top** (BBC-1, 7 eps. × 30 mins.), written by George Layton and Bill Oddie, with the LWT series regulars (Nedwell, Davies, Clark, and Layton) appearing as their earlier characters but now some twenty years on. This was BBC TV's second visit to the work of Richard Gordon; they had earlier presented a 90-minute play, **Doctor in the House** (5/6/60), written by Ted Willis and directed by Wallace Douglas, starring Brian Rix (as Simon Sparrow) and Charles Cameron (Sir Lancelot Spratt).

The Doctors
(BBC-1, 1969–71)

A twice-weekly serial that featured a National Health group practice run by Dr John Somers (John Barrie; *seated*), Dr Roger Hayman (Richard Leech; *right*), and Dr Elizabeth McNeal (Justine Lord; *3rd right*); also appearing were (*l. to r.*) Lynda Marchal, Maureen O'Reilly, and (*2nd right*) Pamela Duncan. The multi-strand stories dealt with the professional and personal involvements of a typical GP's surgery. Series was produced by Colin Morris.

The Dustbinmen
(Granada TV, 1969–70)

A raucous comedy series written (and produced, 1st series) by Jack Rosenthal about the misadventures and work-evasion schemes of the crew of Thunderbird Three, a corporation garbage cart working the streets of a northern town. The crew consisted of Bryan Pringle (*2nd left*; as their leader, 'Cheese-and-Egg'), Graham Haberfield (*right*; as soccer fanatic Winston), Trevor Bannister (*2nd right*; as the dustcart Casanova, 'Heavy Breathing'), and Tim Wylton (*centre*; as dim-witted Eric); John Woodvine (*left*) was the depot manager, generally referred to as 'Bloody Delilah' (later played by Brian Wilde). The 20 eps. × half-hour series was directed by Les Chatfield; Richard Everitt produced the last two series. The series developed from a 90-minute Granada TV **Playhouse** presentation called 'There's a Hole in Your Dustbin, Delilah' (30/9/68; wr. Rosenthal, dir. Michael Apted).

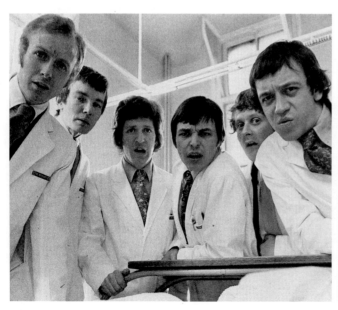

The Fossett Saga
(LWT, 1969)

Jimmy Edwards (*left*) appeared as James Fossett, an ambitious writer of penny dreadfuls in the latter part of the Victorian era. Sam Kydd (*right*) played Herbert Quince, Fossett's unpaid manservant, and June Whitfield was music-hall singer Millie Goswick. The lightweight 7 eps. × half-hour series was written by Dave Freeman and produced-directed by David Askey.

Fraud Squad
(ATV, 1969–70)

This series focused on the fraud-busting activities of Det. Insp. Gamble (Patrick O'Connell; *left*) and Det. Sgt. Vicky Hicks (Joanna Van Gyseghem; *right*) as they rooted out fraudulent crime at all levels of society from the boardroom to the bingo hall. Jack Trevor Story, Robert Holmes, and Richard Harris were among those who contributed stories. The 26 eps. × hour series was created by Ivor Jay and produced by Nicholas Palmer.

The Gold Robbers
(LWT, 1969)

The story of a multi-million bullion robbery and the CID officer who tracked down the participants was the ongoing theme of this 13 eps. × hour crime drama. Peter Vaughan (*right*; with Noel Willman, *left*, and Keith Anderson) as Det. Chief Supt. Cradock, was the linking character in each story. Guest players who were robbers or suspects included Roy Dotrice, George Cole, Katharine Blake, Alfred Lynch, Ann Lynn, and Joss Ackland. The series was written by John Hawkesworth and Glyn Jones; Hawkesworth also produced. Ex-Det. Chief Supt. Arthur Butler was the technical adviser; he had been one of the Great Train Robbery investigators.

Hadleigh
(Yorkshire TV, 1969–76)

Gerald Harper (*right*; with Jane Merrow) played James Hadleigh, the country squire and champion of the underdog who was first seen in the earlier series, **Gazette** (Yorkshire TV, 1968; 12 eps. × hour), as the owner of a local Yorkshire newspaper. **Hadleigh** was produced by Terence Williams and Jacky Stoller and featured Roland Culver, Joyce Carey, Judy Campbell, and Mary Peach. **Gazette** was created by Robert Barr and produced by Terence Williams.

Holiday 69
(BBC-1, 1969–)

The aim of this long-running series was to entertain and inform viewers planning a summer or winter holiday by offering them an honest appraisal of a variety of seasonally linked holiday resorts and travel. Cliff Michelmore (*pictured*) was the original presenter of the series, bringing his current affairs know-how to the world of getaway people. However, what the programme originally missed by dispensing free holiday advice was that it was also supplying a huge volume of free advertising for hotels, resorts, ferries, sports centres, etc. Perhaps the only element to wipe the smiles off grateful tour operators was the programme's analysis and observations of things usually left out of the brochures; the high and low season rates *plus* extras, the less savoury aspects of some locations, the travel distances between hotel and beach, the foreign exchange rates. The title of the series changed appropriately to each year of broadcast. Thames TV's **Wish You Were Here . . .?** (1976–) produced a similar format for the getaway viewer with Judith Chalmers and Chris Kelly putting the holiday habits under scrutiny. **The Travel Show** (BBC-2 / BBC Manchester, 1982–) had Isla St Clair and Desmond Lynam presenting the stories behind the scenes from the world of travel (including the extraordinary item 'Traffic Jam of the Week: where it's going to be and how to avoid it'!). In 1988 **The Travel Show** became **The Travel Show Guides**, now presented by Penny Junor and a return to the format of the original **Holiday 69**.

1969

Judge Dee
(Granada TV, 1969)

Seventh-century China was the setting for **Judge Dee** (Granada TV, 1969), an ambitious production by Granada and producer Howard Baker in an attempt to get away from the usual television crime capers and introduce a more interesting detective. Judge Dee (played by Michael Goodliffe; *2nd left*) was a travelling magistrate who not only acted as detective and prosecutor but also served as judge and jury. His travelling party consisted of three assistants, Arne Gordon, Garfield Morgan, Norman Scace, and his trio of wives. The stories, scripted by John Wiles, were based on the novels and short stories of the late Dutch diplomat Robert Van Gulik, which in turn were developed from tales of a real-life character who lived during the T'ang dynasty. Despite the unusual stories, the colourful costumes, and the excellent sets (designed by Peter Phillips) the series had only a short life; seven hour-long episodes were planned, six were produced and transmitted (8/4–13/5/69). Pictured also are Ian Ramsey (*left*) and Ursula Howells.

The Life and Times of Lord Mountbatten
(Rediffusion–Thames TV, 1/1–19/3/69)

It took producer-director Peter Morley/Rediffusion Television three years (before the company merged with ABC TV to become Thames) to make this visual record of the history of Lord Louis Mountbatten. The twelve hour-long episodes, scripted by John Terraine, covered his boyhood (as the great-grandson of Queen Victoria), his commanding role during the Second World War, becoming the last Viceroy of India, and his rise to become First Sea Lord and the Chief of Defence Staff. The wealth of film footage and rare interviews proved an outstanding feat of painstaking research by Morley's team. Alec Mango provided the narration. The production was made with the co-operation of the Imperial War Museum.

Lift Off
(Granada TV, 1969–72)

The attractive Ayshea (*left*; with guest Susan Maugham) appeared as hostess of this 'children's hour' pop music show (originally co-presented with Graham Bonney), headlining popular recording artists as well as newcomers to the 'disc scene'; rhythm-and-blues vocalist Long John Baldry was a guest on the première show. Earlier, Ayshea had hosted the similar **Discothèque** (Granada TV, 1969) before moving on to **Lift Off**, and later **Lift Off With Ayshea** (Granada TV, 1972–74).

The Liver Birds
(BBC-1, 1969–79)

Generally credited to writer Carla Lane but originally created and developed (for a 14/4/69 episode of **Comedy Playhouse**) by Lane, Myra Taylor, and Lew Schwartz. The main theme had two Liverpudlian girls sharing a bedsitter and comical adventures with boyfriends and life in general; the series resembled something of a distaff **The Likely Lads**. The cast featured Polly James (*right*) as Beryl and Pauline Collins as Dawn; Nerys Hughes (*left*) later stepped in as Sandra (after Collins) and Elizabeth Estensen came onboard as Carol (after James). The 79 eps. × 30 mins. (plus 1 ep. × 35 mins., 1 ep. × 40 mins.) were produced by Sydney Lotterby (1969–75), Douglas Argent (1975–76), and later Roger Race; early episodes were script edited by Eric Idle.

1969

The Main Chance
(Yorkshire TV, 1969–75)

A legal drama series featuring David Main (John Stride; *pictured*), a brash, calculating but brilliant young solicitor. The series of thirty-two, above-average, hour-long episodes was created by Edmund Ward and produced by David Cunliffe and John Frankau.

Man on the Moon
(ITN, 21/7/69)

And **Apollo 11—Man on the Moon** (BBC-1/BBC-2, 21/7/69) both featured live reports and live pictures of man's first landing on the moon (which attracted the largest, world-wide, TV audience ever up to that time; some 723 million in forty-seven countries). ITN followed the daily countdown to the Apollo 11 moon launch, transmitting update bulletins live every day via the TV satellite link to Cape Kennedy and TV pictures sent back to earth from the moonship. ITN's report was by their science editor Peter Fairley and former NASA official Paul Haney. The BBC TV report was by James Burke (*left*) with Patrick Moore (*right*) from the Apollo Space studio and Michael Charlton at Houston Mission Control; the programme was introduced by Cliff Michelmore (*centre*). The heroes of this intensely self-conscious moment of history were lunarnauts Neil Armstrong and Edward 'Buzz' Aldrin.

Me Mammy
(BBC-1, 1969–71)

Milo O'Shea starred as Bunjy Kennefick, an Irishman living in London with his widowed mother (played by Anna Manahan; *pictured*). The 19 eps. × 30 mins. comedy revolved around the prickly relationship between the innocent-abroad Bunjy and his sharp-tongued Mammy who was forever watchful of the devil's influence over her son, i.e. women. Yootha Joyce also appeared as Miss Argyll, Bunjy's girlfriend and Mammy's rival. Hugh Leonard scripted the series for producers James Gilbert (1969–70) and Sydney Lotterby (1971). Writer Leonard, producer Gilbert, and Milo O'Shea went on to another delightful Irish comedy series with **Tales from the Lazy Acre** (BBC-1, 10/4–29/5/72), a short-run anthology of 30-minute episodes featuring David Kelly as a feeble tramp called Dead Man who acted as a sort of commentator on the seven stories starring O'Shea. The final two episodes were co-produced by David Croft.

The Mind of Mr J. G. Reeder
(Thames TV, 1969–71)

Took its title and central character from the 1925 Edgar Wallace collection of short stories featuring the cunning yet humble J. G. Reeder (played by Hugh Burden), an investigator connected with the Public Prosecutor's office. His colleagues were department head Sir Jason Toovey (Willoughby Goddard) and assistant Mrs Houchin (Mona Bruce). Sixteen hour-long mysteries were produced by Kim Mills and Robert Love. The scene pictured shows Hugh Burden (*right*) and Frederick Schrecker (*left*) in 'The Shadow Man' episode.

1969

Monty Python's Flying Circus
(BBC-1, 1969–70; 1972–74)

Perhaps the ultimate in TV comedy craziness and absurdity, this series of bizarre characters and sketches was conceived, written, and performed by the team of Graham Chapman, John Cleese (*pictured*), Terry Gilliam, Eric Idle, Terry Jones, and Michael Palin. The rules were simply that there were no rules. Anything and everything could and did happen— either by way of live-action lunacy (the dead parrot, the Ministry of Silly Walks, Hell's Grannies, the criminal brothers Doug and Dinsdale Piranha) or through Terry Gilliam's surrealist, animated links (when Cleese was not linking sketches with 'And now for something completely different'). Carol Cleveland was also on hand to assist or perpetrate in the comic outrages. The general, and very loose, idea for the comedy show came from BBC Comedy consultant Barry Took who brought together Chapman and Cleese (then writing for **The Frost Report**) and Palin, Jones, and, later, Idle (all of whom had been appearing in **Do Not Adjust Your Set**) with the thought of setting up a late night satire show. American cartoonist Gilliam then joined the team and between themselves they turned television comedy inside out, as well as creating superb parodies of TV itself. John Howard Davies and Ian MacNaughton produced 45 eps. × 30 mins. The 1974 series was titled simply **Monty Python**. Five feature films (in a similar vein) were later produced and performed by the team.

Nationwide
(BBC-1, 1969–84)

Populist current affairs programme created by Derrick Amoore that soared through the 1970s world of miners' strikes, hot pants fashions, and glitter rock and expertly used almost every BBC TV region in the course of a single programme. Michael Barratt (*pictured*) and Frank Bough were the long-time presenters (Richard Dimbleby came on board during the latter days), supported by an enthusiastic assembly of researchers and journalists under the various editorships of Tim Gardam, Paul Corley, Richard Tait, John Gau, Michael Bunce, Paul Woolwich, Huw Williams, Ron Neil, and Roger Bolton. **Nationwide** went out in the early evening slot formerly occupied by the **Tonight** programme.

On the Buses
(LWT, 1969–73; 73 eps. × half-hour)

This sometimes vulgar sitcom focused on the comedy capers of a two-man bus crew as they dodged between their by-the-book inspector, Blake (Stephen Lewis; *centre*), and the central character's (Reg Varney; *left*) home life. Bob Grant (*right*) was his conductor side-kick in the various schemes. Doris Hare, Anna Karen, and the delightfully slow-burning Michael Robbins also appeared as family members; Doris Hare replaced Cicely Courtneidge after the first series. Ronald Wolfe and Ronald Chesney supplied the scripts for the early series; Bob Grant and Stephen Lewis and George Layton & Jonathan Lynn wrote the final two series. Stuart Allen produced the first four series; Derrick Goodwin and Bryan Izzard produced during the last three series. A year after the programme ended one of the characters, Stephen Lewis's Blake, turned up in **Don't Drink the Water** (LWT, 1974–75; 13 eps. × half-hour) where he and his spinster sister (Pat Coombs) went through a series of mishaps and misfortunes as innocents abroad who had purchased retirement property in Spain. Hammer films produced three theatrical features based on the original series, *On the Buses* (1971), *Mutiny on the Buses* (1972) and *Holiday on the Buses* (1973).

Parkin's Patch
(Yorkshire TV, 1969–70)

A rural police procedural series focusing on incidents and investigations in the life of country copper PC Moss Parkin (played by John Flanagan; *pictured*) as he dealt with such fresh-air felonies as sheep rustling, army deserters on the run, and general mayhem on the Yorkshire moors. Gareth Thomas and Heather Page co-starred. The 26 eps. × half-hour series was devised by Elwyn Jones and produced by Terence Williams. Writers Robert Barr, Allan Prior, Ian Kennedy Martin, and Jones contributed scripts; Michael Apted, Michael Newell, and Stephen Frears were among the directors.

Paul Temple
(BBC-1, 1969–71)

The adventures of novelist-detective Paul Temple and his wife Steve began in the late 1930s as a BBC radio serial, created and written by the prolific Francis Durbridge. The television series, starring Francis Matthews (*centre*; pictured with guest player Peter Miles) as Temple and Ros Drinkwater (*left*) as Steve, presented 46 eps. × 50 mins. under producers Alan Bromly, Peter Bryant, and Derrick Sherwin. Contributing writers included Wolf Rilla and Victor Canning.

Pot Black
(BBC-2, 1969–84)

Was television's first regular, colour-transmitted snooker programme, featuring (initially) the BBC-2 Knockout Snooker Competition, a single-frame series with players including Fred Davis, Rex Williams, Ray Reardon (*pictured*), and John Spencer. It was possible, for the first time, to view and follow clearly on TV the sequence of the game, with overhead cameras offering an unrestricted view of the action. The programme was produced from BBC Midland by the team of Reg Perrin, David Kenning, and Philip Lewis. Later, **Junior Pot Black** (BBC-2, 1981–) was introduced for younger viewers; originally produced by Reg Perrin from BBC Birmingham. More recently, **Pot Black Timeframe** (BBC-1 / White Rabbit, 1992) introduced a championship where the balls had to be potted against the clock; the programme was presented by Eamonn Holmes.

Randall and Hopkirk (Deceased)
(ATV, 1969–70)

Kenneth Cope (*left*; as Marty Hopkirk) and Mike Pratt (Jeff Randall; *right*) starred in this private detective series with a fantasy twist: one of the private-eye duo, Cope, returned from the dead ineptly to assist his partner as a white-suited, ghostly figure. There was comic gumshoeing with liberal doses of fist-slamming violence, plus an amusing nod to the spirit of *Blithe Spirit*. The 26 eps. × 55 mins. series was created by Dennis Spooner and produced by Monty Berman; it was transmitted in the USA as **My Partner the Ghost**. Guest player Jane Merrow (*pictured*) appeared in the 'Who Killed Cock Robin?' episode.

1969

Saturday Night Theatre
(ITV various, 1969–70)

A series of self-contained plays contributed by various ITV companies, which included Colin Welland's first TV play 'Bangelstein's Boys' (18/1/69; dir. John Mackenzie, pr. Kenith Trodd), 'MacNeil' (ATV, 1/2/69; wr. Alun Owen, dir. Charles Jarrott), with Sean Connery and Anna Calder-Marshall, 'Cornelius' (ATV, 8/2/69; wr. Alun Owen, dir. Charles Jarrott), with Michael Caine, Michael Bates, and Janet Kay, and 'Faith and Henry' (LWT, 6/12/69; wr. Julia Jones, dir. Jack Gold, pr. Kenith Trodd), with Hilary Baker and John Baron, the latter two pictured.

Scott On . . .
(BBC-2, 1969–74)

Was a 45-minute Terry Scott comedy series in which he would investigate various topics (tagged on to the end of each title) such as '. . . Habits', '. . . Superstition', '. . . the Seven Deadly Sins'. June Whitfield and Peter Butterworth were regular co-performers. Terry Scott had earlier starred in a couple of specials in the series' format: **Scott on Birds** (BBC-2, 19/12/64; wr. Marty Feldman and Barry Took, pr. Dennis Main Wilson; *pictured*, Scott with Clovissa Newcombe) and **Scott On Money** (BBC-2, 15/5/65), using the same writers and producer team.

Special Branch
(Thames TV, 1969–74)

Hard-nosed stories about the tough tactics of the Special Branch division of the police force, featuring themes concerning fanatics, anarchists, spies, and VIPs. Wensley Pithey (as Supt. Eden) and Derren Nesbitt (as Det. Chief Insp. Jordan, *left*, with guest Alastair Williamson) co-starred in this 52 eps. × hour drama. Reginald Collin, Robert Love, Geoffrey Gilbert, and Ted Childs produced the four series.

Stars on Sunday
(Yorkshire TV, 1969–79)

Was an easygoing, light entertainment showcase for a variety of top artists to perform in a religious format. Producer Jess Yates assembled a list of popular stars who sang hymns or songs requested by viewers. Harry Secombe was a regular on the programme for many years. A 1972 edition of the programme featured actress Anna Neagle reading a psalm, with co-stars Brendon O'Dowda, Noel Harrison, Patricia Cahill, and Secombe singing numbers ranging from Mozart to The Byrds. Producer Yates (*left*) is pictured with guest Terry Waite.

Stones in the Park
(Granada TV, 2/9/69)

The event was a free, open-air
concert given by the rock band
The Rolling Stones in London's
Hyde Park on a hot Saturday in
July 1969. Six camera units, under
the direction of Leslie Woodhead,
worked from dawn to dusk to
capture the atmosphere of some
500,000 colourful fans (including
camera-conscious Hell's Angels,
hippies, First Aid men, and police)
watching, listening, and dancing
to the band's dynamic
performance. Although some of
the events appeared to be shown
out of sequence, all the energy
and excitement of a huge outdoor
concert was there, intercut with
scenes of the band nervously
tuning their instruments prior to
going on and Mick Jagger
expressing his personal view of
the world in connection with the
event. Twelve hours of film was
shot (edited down to 55 mins. for
transmission by Gerry Dow) and
compiled by the production team
of Michael Darlow, Michael
Grigsby, Denis Mitchell, and John
Sheppard for producer Jo Durden-
Smith.

Strange Report
(Arena Prods.–ATV–NBC TV, 1969)

The spy-sleuth capers of Adam Strange (played by Anthony Quayle; *pictured*), a freelance forensic criminologist, were the focus of this mid-Atlantic drama series. Working out of his Paddington home-base (combination office and lab), Strange took on various, still-open-file assignments from the government with the assistance of former Rhodes scholar Hamlyn Gynt (Kaz Garas) and, often, model and artist neighbour Evelyn McLean (Anneke Wills). The series was produced (and first shown in some areas) in 1968. The sixteen hour-long episodes were produced by Buzz Berger.

Take Three Girls
(BBC-1, 1969–71)

Well-received series about the miseries and joys of three single girls sharing a London flat. Liza Goddard (*standing*; with Wendy Elms and Gary Waldhorn) played the debby cello player Victoria, Angela Down was cockney art student Avril, and Susan Jameson the actress Kate; the second series saw Victoria with two new flatmates (Avril having taken a job in Paris and Kate having headed for marriage), Jenny (Carolyn Seymour), a young journalist, and Lulie (Barra Grant), an American psychology graduate. Eleven years later **Take Three Women** (BBC-2, 21/9–12/10/82) brought the original trio (and actresses) back together in 4 eps. × 55 mins., with Victoria a widow with a young daughter, Avril owning an art gallery, and Kate sharing her life with her 13-year-old son and his teacher. The original series, devised by Gerald Savory, were produced by Michael Hayes; Savory produced the reunion four-parter. Pentangle provided the music throughout (re-forming especially for the 1982 series).

Wheel of Fortune
(Southern TV, 1969–71)

Michael Miles hosted and produced this game show in which contestants pinned their hopes on a spinning wheel which resulted in their either hitting a main prize or striking-out with a 'booby prize'. Assisting Miles with the half-hour show were announcer Bob Danvers-Walker and organist Harold Smart. Some years later an American game show called **Wheel of Fortune** (NBC/Merv Griffin Productions), which had started out in 1975 as a daytime programme, became, in 1983, the highest-rated syndicated series in American TV history. This five-nights-a-week show was hosted by Pat Sajak and featured (eventually millionairess) hostess Vanna White. Scottish TV launched a British version of the US show in 1988 hosted by Nicky Campbell (*pictured*) and assisted by Angela Ekaette (later Carol Smillie); Stephen Leahy was the show's original producer.

Who-Dun-It
(ATV, 1969)

Crime-fiction mysteries in which the viewer was invited to name the culprit before the concluding fade-out. The series of thirteen hour-long episodes appeared to hover between humour and suspense, proposing the latter but diluting it with the former. The series was created by Lewis Greifer and produced by Jack Williams. The scene pictured is from the 'Murder Goes to School' episode with Gillian Blake. Thames TV later produced a 50/45-mins. series, **Whodunnit?** (1973–78), in a similar vein; Malcolm Morris, Robert Reed, and Anthony Parker, respectively, produced. A one-off, try-out episode (35 mins.) was shown on 15/8/72; written and devised by Jeremy Lloyd and Lance Percival, directed-produced by Morris. In more recent years Granada TV's **Cluedo** (1990–), based on the famous board game, followed pretty much the same format.

Wild, Wild Women
(BBC-1, 1969)

Ronald Wolfe & Ronald Chesney
scripted this comedy series (not
too far removed from the writers'
earlier **Rag Trade** format) about a
milliner's business at the
beginning of the century. Barbara
Windsor (*centre*) starred as
budding suffragette Millie and
Paul Whitsun-Jones (*left,
background*) as the proprietor, Mr
Harcourt; (*l. to r.*) Daphne Heard,
Pat Coombs, Toni Palmer, and
Jessie Robbins were among the
sweatshop working girls. The
programme started life as an
episode (24/5/68) of **Comedy
Playhouse**. G. B. Lupino
produced.

The 1970s got under way with the Annan Committee making inquiries into the future of broadcasting. Under the chairmanship of Lord Noel Annan, two of its recommendations were crucial to the BBC:

Broadcasting services should continue to be provided as public services, and should continue to be the responsibility of public authorities. These Broadcasting Authorities should be independent of government in the day-to-day conduct of their business. (recommendation 1)

The BBC should continue to be financed from the revenue of the broadcast receiving licence. (recommendation 34)

In March 1977, the government invited comments on the conclusions and recommendations contained in Annan's final report and in due course, in July 1978, presented its own proposals in a Broadcasting White Paper. In this the government concurred with the Annan Committee's general praise of the performance of the IBA—the former ITA had become by this time the Independent Broadcasting Authority in July 1972 when the government made the Authority responsible for the establishment of Independent Local Radio. The committee saw a marked improvement in the quality of Independent Television programmes over the past decade and considered that the IBA's increased influence had been an important factor in this improvement. The White Paper proposed that there should be a fourth television channel: the IBA would run the transmission side, and the ITV companies would have an important programme involvement, but the overall administration would be the responsibility not of the IBA but of a newly created Open Broadcasting Authority (OBA).

The IBA felt that this proposal, as outlined in the White Paper, reflected a failure to understand the practicalities of running a television network, and that a fourth channel service integrated with ITV, under the IBA's more expert control, would offer the public a more effective and economic service. The ITV companies, whose contracts were due to run out in 1974 but were extended to 1976, had been lobbying strongly for an 'ITV-2' in late 1971 when a TV4 Campaign had been formed. However, in January 1972, the Minister of Posts and Telecommunications (former ITN newscaster Christopher Chataway) postponed any fourth channel decision, to the disappointment of the ITV companies and to the embarrassment of the IBA.

The year 1973 ended with the 'three-day week' and television closing down at 10.30 p.m.— ostensibly to save electricity during a nation-wide industrial dispute—until February 1974 when, with a general election looming on the horizon, the curfew was lifted. Until the energy crisis made itself felt at the turn of the year the ratio of audiences continued to divide fifty–fifty between the BBC and ITV, with the balance tipping towards the BBC at all holiday times and for just about all coverage of major events. One of the television highpoints of 1974 was the 14 November wedding of HRH Princess Anne and Captain Mark Phillips in Westminster Abbey; it was estimated that the home television audience reached some 25 million, with more than 530 million people throughout the world seeing the transmission through either live relays or recordings.

While the Coronation broadcast in 1953 boosted the sale of TV sets in this country, this Royal Wedding some twenty years later can be considered partly responsible for the increase in the sales figures of colour television. Similar colour TV sale increases were also credited to the transmissions in June 1977 of the Queen's Silver Jubilee Year, when outside broadcast cameras showed the Queen lighting a bonfire at Windsor to start a nation-wide chain of bonfires (no connection to the unfortunate events of 1992) and covered the Queen's drive to St Paul's Cathedral and her walkabout in the City of London together with other celebratory events.

In 1974 the government authorized the BBC to start a two-year experiment, regularly transmitting live 'pages' of written up-to-the-minute news and information, displayed at the viewers' request on their TV screen, either in place of, or in association with, the ordinary television picture. This CEEFAX service started on 23 September and two years later ITV introduced its own teletext, ORACLE, in July 1975.

There were also changes in schools broadcasting during the 1970s. In early 1971, programmes for schools were broadcast on BBC-1 in the morning and afternoon on weekdays during term-time. Further education programmes, including language series, and series created specially for management and industry, were televised on Saturday and Sunday mornings on BBC-1 and an educational magazine programme went out on Sunday afternoons on BBC-1; early evening education programmes, from Monday to Friday, were televised on BBC-2. Preparatory courses for the Open University were included in 1970 mid-week evening programmes on BBC-2. Also beginning in January 1971 were the BBC's programmes for the Open University's foundation courses.

The 1970s was a busy decade for TV sports. England's defence of their World Cup soccer crown in Mexico was covered by satellite all the way through to Brazil's victory in the final (1970). There were also the Commonwealth Games in Edinburgh (1970). A year later the introduction of slow-motion instant playback into sports programmes opened up the floodgates of unending controversies over refereeing decisions and bad conduct by players. Satellite links made possible same-day pictures of the Australian test cricket—a programme of highlights was beamed to BBC-2 each day.

In 1972 it was estimated that the Munich Olympic Games reached audiences of up to 17 million in the UK through 170 hours of live coverage. The BBC was the only individual European organization, apart from the German networks, to have exclusive studio facilities in Munich and to have rented a private vision circuit from Munich for its national coverage of the Games. Because of this, BBC-1 transmitted live pictures of events in the Olympic village during the nights of 5 and 6 September which were not generally available elsewhere in Europe and TV's presence enabled it to cover in detail the tragedy of the Israeli hostages. The Munich Games provided world colour television on the largest scale yet known. Some thirty Olympic locations were covered by over 160 colour TV cameras, 23 colour transmission vehicles, seven colour studios, and around 50 TV tape recorders as well as numerous rooms for cutting and editing film. These vast production facilities were provided by Deutsches Olympia Zentrum, a consortium formed by the two German networks. Two BBC Outside Broadcast units went to Munich to assist with the DOZ operation; one of them provided the Olympic boxing coverage and a BBC mobile camera was used for the cycling road race events. Fifty BBC editors, producers, production assistants, and secretaries, nearly seventy engineers, and sixteen commentators were on the spot in Munich to make this the biggest single operation ever mounted on British television.

The summer of 1974 saw the World Cup in Germany successfully covered, with some 14 million and 16 million watching Scotland's two most important games on BBC-1 alone, with the final between West Germany and Holland attracting a total UK audience of about 23 million (of which the BBC estimated its share at about 17 million). Improved coverage of the winter Test Matches in Australia was achieved as a result of a combined operation involving more extended use of satellite communication and the notable skill of video-tape engineers in London. Coverage of the Winter Olympics from Innsbruck in 1975 dominated BBC-1 schedules for a fortnight in February. Two big TV sporting occasions of 1978 were the World Cup from the Argentine and the XI Commonwealth Games from Montreal.

The increasing role of television within social life led to a growing concern over its power. An independent Programmes Complaints Commission was set up by the BBC in October 1977 to consider complaints from the public of unfair treatment in radio and television programmes. 1979 saw the completion of a study by programme makers led by Monica Sims of the BBC recommending guidelines for the portrayal of violence in television programmes. Her report was thoroughly examined by the Board of Governors after it had been endorsed by management and

discussed at length with the BBC's Consultative Group on the Social Effects of Television. The BBC working party report on Violence on Television was published in March 1979.

Original TV drama was for the most part replaced by a surge of period and novel-based serials during the 1970s, with **The Six Wives of Henry VIII** and **Elizabeth R** blazing the trail for such programmes as **Upstairs, Downstairs**, **The Onedin Line**, **Colditz**, **Jennie, Lady Randolph Churchill**, **When the Boat Comes In**, **The Pallisers**, **Edward the Seventh**, **The Duchess of Duke Street**, **I, Claudius**, and **The Glittering Prizes**.

The mainstream presentation of TV comedy took a sharp curve away from the 'Pythonesque' style of humour (and even the 1960s 'new wave' sitcoms of Johnny Speight and Galton & Simpson) to the more bland, by-the-numbers programming of **On the Buses**, **Bless This House**, **Are You Being Served?**, and **Man About the House**. However, some comedies—**Whatever Happened to the Likely Lads?**, **The Fall and Rise of Reginald Perrin**, **Fawlty Towers**, **Ripping Yarns**, and a handful of others—went some way to try and balance out this cosy, studio-bound situation comedy.

The TV documentary–drama programme excelled in the 1970s, informing and impressing viewers with such (at times, marathon) productions as **The Search for the Nile**, **The World at War**, **The Ascent of Man**, **The Family**, **The Voyage of Charles Darwin**, **Life on Earth**, and **Hollywood**. These excellent documentary studies went on to win much international acclaim and help boost British TV's standing around the world.

The early part of the 1970s, under a Conservative administration, reflected safe, reassuring, family-based programming: **Bless This House**, **For the Love of Ada**, **Queenie's Castle**, **Father, Dear Father**, **And Mother Makes Three**. Even game shows—**The Generation Game**, for example—adopted a family-focused format. During the latter half of the decade (now under Labour Prime Ministers Wilson and Callaghan) the emphasis turned in favour of the underdog (whatever their respective pursuits and motives), with such programming as **Miss Jones and Son**, **Citizen Smith**, **Rumpole of the Bailey**, and **Minder** proving popular.

1970

The Adventures of Don Quick
(LWT, 1970)

Astronaut Don Quick (Ian Hendry; *left*) was a member of the Intergalactic Maintenance Squad who saw himself as a roving Don Quixote character around the planets in this 6 eps. × hour science fiction satire. His companion was Sergeant Sam Czopanser (Ronald Lacey)! Peter Wildeblood was executive producer.

Albert and Victoria
(Yorkshire TV, 1970–71)

A comedy of Victorian era middle-class manners with Alfred Marks as the ultra-conservative father Albert Hackett ruling his large household with an affectionate fist of iron (he would not have the names of Oscar Wilde or Aubrey Beardsley mentioned in the house). Zena Walker (Barbara Murray, 2nd series) was his wife Victoria and Kika Markham (Gay Hamilton, 2nd series) his eldest daughter; other family members included Lydia (played by Petra Markham), George (John Alkin), Edward (Rufus Frampton), Arthur (John Ash), and Flora (Miriam Mann). The 12 eps. × half-hour programme was written by Reuben Ship; the first series was produced by John Nelson Burton, the second series directed-produced by Quentin Lawrence.

Aquarius
(LWT, 1970–77)

A fortnightly arts magazine programme that presented a wide range of reports on the cultural scene. Originally introduced by programme editor Humphrey Burton, later by Russell Harty and Peter Hall; Harty was also associate producer. One of the more extraordinary editions was 'Hello Dali!' (tx 11/11/73; dir. Bruce Gowers) in which surrealist Salvador Dali (*pictured*), then in his seventieth year, talked to Harty about his life and pleasures. Russell Harty's own **Eleven Plus** (LWT, 25/6–10/9/72) series, in 12 eps. × 45 mins., developed out of **Aquarius**; Harty also produced. **Eleven Plus** then gave way to **Russell Harty Plus** in October 1972.

Catweazle
(LWT, 1970–71)

Introduced an eccentric, Merlin-like wizard (played by Geoffrey Bayldon; *pictured*) who was accidentally catapulated through time from Norman England to the present day in this amusing children's adventure. He was befriended by Carrot (Robin Davies), the 14-year-old son of a farmer who lived near Catweazle's deserted water-tower hiding place. The 26 eps. × half-hour series was created and written by Richard Carpenter; produced by Quentin Lawrence (1st series) and Carl Mannin (2nd series).

Codename
(BBC-2, 1970)

Was a 13 eps. × 50 mins. spy and counter-spy thriller series featuring a spy cell which worked for a government department known as MI 17; and which used a university as their cover. Clifford Evans (*2nd left*), Anthony Valentine (*left*), and Alexandra Bastedo (*2nd right*; with Brian Peck) headed the cast. The series was created by David Proudfoot and Bill Hays; produced by Gerard Glaister.

Conceptions of Murder
(LWT, 1970)

Playwright Clive Exton took six sensational murder cases of the twentieth century and tried to re-create the minds and motives of the killers. 'The Dreams of Tim Evans' (18/9/70; dir. Graham Evans) with Hugh Burden as Christie; 'Mother and Child' (25/9/70; dir. Derek Bennett) with Angela Baddeley as Rosaline Fox; 'What Do They Know of England?' (2/10/70; dir. Evans) with Ronald Fraser (pictured, *left*, with David Webb) as Alfred Rouse; 'Peter and Maria' (9/10/70; dir. Bennett) with Nigel Green as Peter Kurten; 'Conversation Piece' (16/10/70; dir. Evans) with John Castle as Miles Giffard; and 'Tea with Major Armstrong' (23/10/70; dir. Bennett) with John Nettleton as Major Armstrong.

Crime of Passion
(ATV, 1970–73)

Each of the hour-long plays presented in this French courtroom-based series was, reputedly, based on fact, showing the dramatic events leading up to the trial via flashback. John Phillips (*left*) played Maître Lacan, Anthony Newlands (*right*) the President of the Court, and Daniel Moynihan (*top*) was Maître Savel; Bernard Archard played Maître Dubois in the final series. Cecil Clarke, Robert D. Cardona, and Ian Fordyce produced during the course of the series.

Diamond Crack Diamond
(LWT, 1970)

Presented a 6 part × hour thriller series about a Fleet Street reporter, John Diamond (played by Alan Dobie; *seated*), who had escaped from an African jail and returned to England. Stories described how he set out to expose the corruption behind the attempts of big business to exploit emerging African countries. Judy Parfitt and Iain Cuthbertson (*standing*) supported. Vincent Tilsley's scripts were produced by Andrew Brown.

1970

Doomwatch
(BBC-1, 1970–72)

Was a down-to-earth science-warning, rather than science fiction, drama series that featured a government group of scientists acting as watchdog on the new and developing forms of scientific research. The group, led by John Paul (*left*; as Dr Spencer Quist), consisted primarily of Robert Powell, Joby Blanshard (*centre*), Vivien Sherrard, and Simon Oates (*right*). Plot issues concerned irresponsible chemical waste dumping, accidents involving nuclear devices, pollution, and commercial misuse of deadly toxins. The series was created by Dr Kit Pedler and Gerry Davis; produced by Terence Dudley. A horror-slanted feature film, *Doomwatch*, was produced by Tigon British in 1972.

Drama Playhouse
(BBC-1, 1970; 1972)

Presented two series of 50-minute plays most of which were a potential source for drama series spin-offs. The programme premièred with 'The Regiment' (23/11/70), written by Robin Chapman and directed by William Slater, which was later developed into the 1972 series. Other entries included 'The Befrienders' (30/11/70), a story about the Samaritans written by Harry W. Junkin; 'The Onedin Line' (7/12/70; series); 'The Incredible Robert Baldick' (2/10/72), a science fiction tale by Terry Nation (with Julian Holloway and Robert Hardy; *pictured*); and 'Sutherland's Law' (23/8/72; series). Anthony Coburn was programme producer.

A Family at War
(Granada TV, 1970–72)

Presented the 50 eps. × hour series about the dramatic events in the life of the Ashtons, a middle-class Liverpool family, during the turbulent period of the Second World War. Featured were Colin Douglas, Shelagh Fraser, Lesley Nunnerley, Barbara Flynn, John McKelvey, Coral Atkins, and Colin Campbell. The programme was devised and edited by John Finch; Richard Doubleday and Michael Cox produced.

For the Love of Ada
(Thames TV, 1970–71)

The gentle love affair between Ada Cresswell (Irene Handl; *left*) and Walter Bingley (Wilfred Pickles; *right*) was the theme of this often amusing series from the writing team of Vince Powell & Harry Driver. The difference here was that both parties were of a senior-citizen status (Ada was a widow and Walter was the gravedigger who had buried her late husband) and as such the series hobbled awkwardly between moments of tenderness and tedium. The duo finally got hitched at the end of the first series. Barbara Mitchell (*centre*) and Jack Smethurst supported. Three series totalling 19 eps. × half-hour and one 45-minute Christmas special were produced by Ronnie Baxter. Tigon British produced a feature version under the same title in 1972 (dir. Ronnie Baxter).

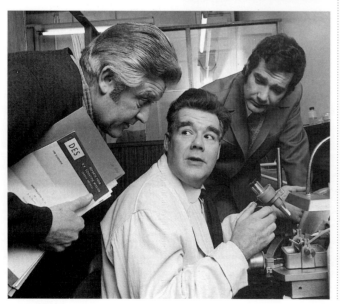

Girls About Town
(ATV, 1970–71)

Presented the comedy antics of two married women, Brenda (played by Denise Coffey; *left*) and Rosemary (Julie Stevens; *right*), who pursued various lunatic schemes in order to attract the attention of their stuffy husbands (Robin Parkinson and Peter Baldwin). The series was written by Adele Rose and produced-directed by Shaun O'Riordan, and directed by John Scholz-Conway (2nd series). Twelve half-hour episodes were produced. A half-hour pilot programme, **Girls About Town** (Thames TV, 2/10/69; wr. Rose, pr. Ronnie Baxter), was shown with Anna Quayle and Barbara Mullaney in the lead roles.

The Goodies
(BBC-1, 1970–77; 1980)

Was a wacky comedy series more in the line of a live-action cartoon, with Tim Brooke-Taylor (*right*), Graeme Garden (*left*), and Bill Oddie (*centre*) as the trio of inventive yet idiotic do-gooders. The series, of 59 eps. × 30 mins. (+ 3 specials, 30/50 mins.), was in effect an explosion of televisual special effects, incorporating fast motion, jump-cuts, step-printing, colour separation, split-screen, and reverse action. John Howard Davies and Jim Franklin produced. The series was later revived on ITV, **The Goodies** (LWT, 1982), for six half-hour episodes under director-producer Bob Spiers, with the original line-up.

Kate
(Yorkshire TV, 1970–72)

Phyllis Calvert (in her first TV series; *pictured left*) starred as Kate Graham, an agony column writer who not only found time to sort out other people's problems but also managed to support her office colleagues emotionally (including her editor, played by Jack Hedley) and smooth out her domestic life. Basil Henson and Penelope Keith (*centre*, with Tony Anholt) also appeared in the 38 eps. × hour drama series. Stanley Miller, and later Pieter Rogers, produced.

The Kenny Everett Explosion
(LWT, 1970)

The amiable loony from the radio disc world brought along his own, unique brand of humour to network television, starting off with this half-hour series (executive producer Terry Henebery) and, some years later, following this with **The Kenny Everett Video Show** (Thames TV, 1978–80), produced by David Mallet, which introduced Arlene Phillips's raunchy Hot Gossip Dancers and Everett's zany Captain Kremmen, and **The Kenny Everett Video Cassette** (Thames TV, 1981), produced by Royston Mayoh, still featuring Hot Gossip and Kremmen as well as the Everett caricatures, Sid Snot and Marcel Wave. Although he created his share of problems with not doing everything in the best possible taste, Everett went on to present the popular **The Kenny Everett Television Show** (BBC-1, 1982–88), featuring even more madcap characters (such as Beau D'Iddley of the Legion) and visual gags. Bill Wilson was the producer and the writing was by Ray Cameron, Barry Cryer, and Everett, all of whom had worked together on Everett's radio and TV shows (Neil Shand also joined them for the BBC TV series).

The Lovers
(Granada TV, 1970–71)

Were the gauche, gullible Geoffrey (Richard Beckinsale, *left*) and the naïve but instinctively scheming Beryl (Paula Wilcox; *right*). Writer-producer Jack Rosenthal charted their disruptive affair through the half-hour sitcom; Michael Apted contributed as director for the première episode. A feature film spin-off was produced by Gildor Films in 1972.

Man at the Top
(Thames TV, 1970–72)

Was a television sequel to author John Braine's popular, late 1950s novel *Room at the Top*. The 23 eps. × hour series saw the ruthless anti-hero Joe Lampton (played by Kenneth Haigh; *pictured*) older, richer, and living in the Surrey stockbroker belt with wife Susan (Zena Walker) but still as ambitious as ever. George Markstein, Lloyd Shirley, and Jacqueline Davis (2nd series) produced. John Braine also contributed scripts for the early series. A feature film based on the TV series, *Man at the Top*, was produced by Hammer/Dufton Films in 1973.

Manhunt
(LWT, 1970)

A compulsive Second World War action–drama series set in occupied France featuring the exploits of the French resistance (Beethoven's Fifth, the wartime Allied code initial, was the signature for the opening titles). The basic thread running through the series involved three characters—a French resistance fighter (Cyd Hayman; *left*), a British agent (Peter Barkworth; *right*, with guest player Andrew Keir) and a downed RAF pilot (Alfred Lynch; *2nd left*)—as they undertook the hazards of attempting to escape to England. Intelligent dialogue and plotting sustained the series throughout, drawing on the psychological and emotional dimensions of the central characters. One of the highlights was Robert Hardy's German intelligence sergeant, continually planting seeds of double-agent suspicion among the Allied escapees when not at loggerheads with Philip Madoc's sadistic SS officer. Creator Rex Firkin acted as executive producer. Eighteen years later LWT would return with a similar format, though on a broader scale, in **Wish Me Luck**.

Menace
(BBC-2, 1970; BBC-1, 1973)

A series of 23 eps. × 75-mins. thrillers, produced by Jordan Lawrence, which were intended to put the audience on the edge of their seats and keep them hooked in a style similar to ATV's **Thriller**. The series opened with Alun Richards's 'The Straight and Narrow' (29/9/70), directed by Joan Kemp-Welch and starring (*pictured, l. to r.*) Freddie Jones, Jane Hylton and, in background, Rachel Thomas. The later series presented stories by Roy Clarke ('Pick Up', with June Barry), Hugh Whitemore ('Deliver Us From Evil', with John Gielgud) and Fay Weldon ('Comfortable Words', with Sheila Hancock).

The Misfit
(ATV, 1970–71)

Ronald Fraser starred as Basil 'Badger' Allenby-Johnson, an anachronism from many years of the colonial good life in Malaya, who returned to the bewildering 1970s scene in London and his son Ted (Simon Ward) and daughter-in-law Alicia (Susan Carpenter). The comedy thread was Badger's differing reactions to Britain, 1970. Roy Clarke authored the thirteen hour-long scripts for producer Dennis Vance. Pictured (*l. to r.*) are Fraser and guests Diana Dors and Edwin Richfield.

Play for Today
(BBC-1, 1970–84)

Presented one of the most remarkable series of outstanding works for British television and opened with 'The Long Distance Piano Player' (15/10/70), written by Alan Sharp and directed by Philip Saville. Over the following fourteen years the **Play for Today** slot introduced such dramas, comedies, and fantasies as 'The Right Prospectus' (22/10/70), written by John Osborne, directed by Alan Cooke; 'The Lie' (29/10/70), the first of Swedish writer-director Ingmar Bergman's plays to be seen on British television, from a script translated by his brother-in-law Paul Britten Austin and commissioned by the Swedish Broadcasting Corporation on behalf of Eurovision members participating in **The Largest Theatre in the World**; 'The Rank and File' (20/5/71), written by Jim Allen, directed by Kenneth Loach; 'Edna, the Inebriate Woman' (21/10/71) with Patricia Hayes (*pictured*) superb as the solitary outcast, written by Jeremy Sandford and directed by Ted Kotcheff; 'Home' (6/1/72; A NET/CBC Prod.), the first TV showing in this country of the widely praised Royal Court Theatre production, written by David Storey and directed by Lindsay Anderson; 'Man Friday' (30/10/72) with Colin Blakely (as Robinson Crusoe) and Ram John Holder (as Man Friday), written by Adrian Mitchell and directed by James MacTaggart (filmed by Jack Gold in 1975); '84 Charing Cross Road' (4/11/75) with Anne Jackson (as Helen Hanff) and Frank Finlay (as Frank Doel), adapted by Hugh Whitemore from the story by Hanff, directed by Mark Cullingham (filmed by Brooksfilms for Columbia in 1987); the first appearance of John Mortimer's 'Rumpole of the Bailey' (16/12/75) with Leo McKern, directed by John Gorrie; 'Nuts in May' (13/1/76), devised and directed by Mike Leigh; Jack Rosenthal's 'Bar Mitzvah Boy' (14/9/76) exploring the emotional pulls of a traditional Jewish ceremony, directed by Michael Tuchner; 'Abigail's Party' (1/11/77) with (*pictured, l. to r.*) Harriet Reynolds, Tim Stern, Janine Duvitski, Alison Steadman, and John Salthouse, devised by Mike Leigh; Dennis Potter's 'Blue Remembered Hills' (30/1/79), about seven West Country children idling the summer away in 1943, with (*pictured, l. to r.*) Colin Jeavons,

Michael Elphick, Janine Duvitski, Colin Welland, Robin Ellis, John Bird, and Helen Mirren, directed by Brian Gibson; and the re-enactment of the Spaghetti House Siege of 'A Hole in Babylon' (29/11/79), written by Jim Hawkins and Horace Ove, with the latter also directing.

The 1980s brought 'The Flipside of Dominick Hide' (9/12/80) and later 'Another Flip for Dominick' (14/12/82), two time-warp tales starring Peter Firth, written by Jeremy Paul and Alan Gibson, the latter also directed; Trevor Griffiths's 'Country' (20/10/81) with Leo McKern and James Fox, directed by Richard Eyre; 'United Kingdom' (8/12/81) starring Colin Welland, written by Jim Allen, directed by Roland Joffe; and David Pirie's spooky 'Rainy Day Women' (10/4/84) with Charles Dance and Suzanne Bertish, directed by Ben Bolt.

Dennis Potter's devil-rape play 'Brimstone and Treacle' was due to be shown on 6/4/76 but was pulled and replaced with 'Double Dare'; it was finally transmitted on 25/8/87 and remade as a feature film by Namara Films/Alan E. Salke in 1982. Roy Minton's borstal play 'Scum' was also banned from transmission in 1977 and 1978; transmitted on 27/7/91, it was remade as a feature film by Berwick Street Films in 1979.

1970

Queenie's Castle
(Yorkshire TV, 1970–72)

Half-hour sitcom starring Diana Dors as the warlike Queenie Shepherd who ran her family group with a fist of iron and a (Yorkshire-accented) voice of fury. The cowering group consisted of (*l. to r.*) Tony Caunter, Brian Marshall, Barrie Rutter, and Freddie Fletcher; Lynne Perrie also appeared. The series was created by Keith Waterhouse and Willis Hall; Graham Evans and Ian Davidson produced the eighteen episodes. Dors also starred in the later comedy series **All Our Saturdays** (Yorkshire TV, 1973). **The Diana Dors Show** (Southern TV, 1981) featured Dors as hostess in this afternoon talk show, assisted by comedian Jack Diamond and singer Mike McKenzie; Angus Wright produced.

A Question of Sport
(BBC-1, 1970–)

Long-running quiz show featuring two panels of sports personalities competing against each other in rounds designed to test their knowledge of sports people and events other than their own field. The early series was chaired by David Vine and the first two team captains were former Heavyweight champion boxer Henry Cooper and former Welsh Rugby Union international Cliff Morgan; David Coleman took the chair from 1980. Emphasizing that it was a television rather than a radio quiz show, the questions were created from footage acquired from the BBC's enormous sports film library and were carefully selected to underline the visual (and often historical) aspects of sport. Nick Hunter was the original producer. Channel Four presented a similarly structured programme, **The Sports Quiz** (C4/Anglia TV–Action Time Ltd., 1983; originally billed as **The Sports Quiz With Steve Davis**), with then world snooker champion Davis chairing a quiz search for the person with best all-round knowledge of sport; in the première series the winning contestant was given a trip to Los Angeles for the 1984 Olympic Games. Jeremy Fox produced the half-hour series. David Vine (*centre*) is pictured with Fred Trueman and Henry Cooper.

The Roads to Freedom
(BBC-2, 4/10–27/12/70)

French philosopher and political thinker Jean-Paul Sartre's trilogy (*The Age of Reason*, *The Reprieve*, and *Iron in the Soul*) exploring personal and political freedom in a world of moral and social chaos and set against the bleak background of France on the edge of the Second World War was dramatized by David Turner in 13 eps. × 45 mins. At the centre of the complex narrative was Mathieu Delarue (played by Michael Bryant; *left*, with Rosemary Leach), the intellectual unable to commit himself to anyone or anything. The two other main characters were Brunet (Donald Burton), the committed Communist, and Daniel (Daniel Massey), the reluctant homosexual. James Cellan Jones directed for producer David Conroy.

Ryan International
(BBC-1, 14/9–16/11/70)

Kieron Moore (*pictured*) starred as the Paris-based lawyer hero Hugh Ryan in this peculiar adventure drama which called upon the Ryan character to act as a rather shadowy fixer of other people's problems or misdemeanours. Cyril Luckham, Ursula Howells, and Susan Sheers co-starred. The 10 eps. × 50 mins. series (from a format created by Moore) was produced by Eric Price.

The Six Wives of Henry VIII
(BBC-2, 1/1–5/2/70)

A highly rated 6 eps. × 90 mins. series that built its own sense of history as it progressed and featured some outstanding performances from Keith Michell (*right*; as Henry VIII), Annette Crosbie (as Catherine of Aragon), Dorothy Tutin (as Anne Boleyn), Angela Pleasance (*pictured*; as Catherine Howard) among others. The lavish series was produced by Ronald Travers, based on an idea by Maurice Cowan.

Tales of Unease
(LWT, 30/10–11/12/70)

A six-part anthology, produced by
Paul Knight, with half-hour
suspense stories based upon black
humour, 'savage irony', and
matter-of-fact menace, premièred
with 'Ride Ride', written by
Michael Hastings, and starring
Susan George. Stories included
John Burke's 'Calculated
Nightmare' with John Stratton
and Michael Culver (*pictured*), and
Andrea Newman's 'It's Too Late
Now' with Rachel Kempson.

The Tribe That Hides From Man
(ATV, 17/2/70)

The Kreen-Akrore tribe were one
of the world's last groups of
unknown people, hiding in the
deepest part of the Amazon jungle
and killing all intruders on sight.
This 75-minute documentary
presentation followed two of
Brazil's most famous explorers as
they cut a hazardous trail into the
tribe's forbidden territory. Adrian
Cowell was producer-director;
photography was by Chris
Menges, Jesco von Puttkamer,
Richard Stanley, Charles Stewart,
and Ernest Vincze. Producer-
director Cowell's **Kingdom in the
Jungle** (ATV, 14/12/71) served as
a 45-minute footnote to the above
programme.

Up Pompeii!
(BBC-1, 1970)

Featured comedian Frankie Howerd (*pictured, centre*) in this farcical,
Carry On-like series full of daft jokes, painful puns, and sexist *double
entendre* set in ancient Pompeii. Howerd played the harlequinish slave
Lurcio who related each episode's plot developments directly to
camera/studio audience. Max Adrian (later Wallas Eaton) played
Ludicrus, master of Lurcio's house, Elizabeth Larner was his wife
Ammonia, Kerry Gardner the son Nausius, and Georgina Moon the
daughter Erotica; Jeanne Mockford also appeared as Senna, the wailing
soothsayer, and William Rushton as Plautus. The 13 eps. × 35 mins.
series was written by Talbot Rothwell (hence the *Carry On* element); it
was later co-written with Sid Colin, and produced by David Croft. The
series was preceded by a 35-minute pilot try-out programme
(tx 17/9/69) written by Rothwell and produced by Michael Mills. Anglo-
EMI produced a feature film version in 1971. Howerd returned in a
similarly formatted sitcom, **Frankie Howerd in Whoops Baghdad!**
(BBC-1, 1973), playing Ali Oopla, the bondservant to the Wazir of
Baghdad (Derek Francis); the 6 eps. × 30 mins. series was written by Sid
Colin with David McKellar and David Nobbs, and others (from an idea
by Dennis Heymer). John Howard Davies produced. Howerd's Lurcio
appeared for the last time in a 45-minute Easter Monday special, **Further
Up Pompeii!** (BBC-1, 1/4/75), written by Rothwell and produced by
David Croft.

Waugh on Crime
(BBC-2, 4/12/70–8/1/71)

Shown under the series banner of **Thirty-Minute Theatre**, was a 6 eps. × 30 mins. mini-series written by Arden Winch and featuring the cases of the cerebral Det. Insp. Waugh of the CID (played by Clive Swift, *right*, with Robin Chadwick as PC White). The clue-sprinkled, Sherlock Holmes-like series of mysteries was directed by Tristan de Vere Cole and Philip Dudley for producer Innes Lloyd. The Inspector Waugh character had appeared in Arden Winch's earlier, three-part 'Something to Hide' (BBC-2, 7–14–21/10/68), also in the **Thirty-Minute Theatre** slot; Charles Gray featured as the dapper Inspector. Michael Hart directed for producer Innes Lloyd.

Barlow at Large
(BBC-1, 1971; 1973)

Detective Chief Superintendent Barlow (Stratford Johns; *pictured*) was seconded to the Home Office and to the world of diplomacy and political intrigue following his **Softly, Softly** stint at Thamesford Constabulary CID. A couple of the early stories even had him visiting such places as Amsterdam and Gibraltar. Barlow's new boss was civil servant A. G. Fenton, played by Neil Stacey; his regular assistant was Det. Sgt. David Rees (Norman Comer). Keith Williams produced 14 eps. × 50 mins. before continuing with the shorter-titled **Barlow** (BBC-1, 1974–75), still featuring Stratford Johns, assisted by Derek Newark as Det. Insp. Tucker. Williams produced a further 16 eps. × 50 mins.

Bless This House
(Thames TV, 1971–76)

Sid James (*right*) led this domestic sitcom as the perpetually confused and frustrated head of the Abbott family, with Diana Coupland (*left*) as his wife, Jean, and Robin Stewart and Sally Geeson (*centre, background*) as their teenage children, Mike and Sally; Anthony Jackson played Sid's meddlesome neighbour Trevor. The six series of 65 eps. × half-hour were produced (and directed) by William G. Stewart. Writers included Vince Powell & Harry Driver, Carla Lane & Myra Taylor, and Dave Freeman. Peter Rogers Productions produced a feature version in 1972, based on (and for the most part featuring) the TV line-up.

Brett
(BBC-1, 1971)

Featured Patrick Allen (*left*; with John Bennett) in the title role as a writer who had become a powerful and ambitious tycoon, but one with a shady past that was catching up with him. The Royston Morley-produced melodrama, of 19 eps. × 50 mins., was created by Compton Bennett and Derek Glynne; the series used generous flashback sequences to flesh out the background narrative and made location use of the Maltese countryside as a stand-in for Mexico (under director Peter Graham Scott).

Budgie
(LWT, 1971–72)

An enjoyable and well-written Soho street-life series featuring Adam Faith (*right*) as a perpetual loser with an eye on the fast money. Whatever plan, scam, or caper Budgie Bird got involved with he would always lose out to either the law or the Soho crime community's 'Mr Big', Charlie Endell (Iain Cuthbertson; *left*). As if his duck 'n' dodge life was not complicated enough, with such low-life characters as the grubby Grogan (Rio Fanning) and the dangerous Laughing Spam Fritter (John Rhys-Davies) using him, Budgie had a girlfriend, Hazel (Lynn Dalby), with his baby, his wife Jean (Georgina Hale), and his busker/con man father (George Tovey) to contend with. Written and created by Keith Waterhouse and Willis Hall, Faith's Budgie was one of television's great characters, but one who belonged strictly to the London milieu of the early 1970s; 26 eps. × hour were produced by Verity Lambert. Seven years later Scottish TV and writer Robert Banks Stewart tried to repeat the successful formula with the spin-off character of **Charles Endell Esquire** (26/4–31/5/80; 6 eps. × hour; pr. Rex Firkin), returning the former Soho kingpin (Cuthbertson) to reclaim his old haunts in Glasgow following a seven-year stretch in prison; the series was due to start in July 1979 (and two episodes were shown) but an industrial strike put ITV off the air.

Casanova
(BBC-2, 16/11–21/12/71)

Frank Finlay (shown with Gillian Hills) appeared as the eighteenth-century lover Casanova in this 6 eps. × 55 mins. series scripted by Dennis Potter. Potter related Casanova's attempted physical escape from imprisonment by the Spanish Inquisition to his sexuality and his endeavour to find mental escape from the dogmas and prohibitions of his own time. The stories followed the man from the age of 30 to his death at 73. Norman Rossington and Zienia Merton also appeared. The series was filmed in England, Scotland, and Venice. Production was designed by Peter Seddon; costumes by John Bloomfield. John Glenister directed for producer Mark Shivas.

The Comedians
(Granada TV, 1971–85)

A non-stop session of British stand-up comics battering the studio audience with wall-to-wall gags (the cleaned-up versions, of course) from the working men's club circuit. Among the top names featured during the show's lengthy run were Charlie Williams, Bernard Manning (*pictured*), Frank Carson, Mike Reid, Duggie Brown, Colin Crompton, Ken Goodwin, and George Roper. John Hamp produced the half-hour series.

Elizabeth R
(BBC-2, 17/2–24/3/71)

A compelling six-part voyage through Tudor history during the reign of Elizabeth I, from her tortuous path to the throne to her lonely death shortly after the execution of the Earl of Essex. Glenda Jackson's strong, no-frills performance in the title role was ably supported by Daphne Slater (as Mary Tudor), Robert Hardy (Earl of Leicester), and Robin Ellis (Essex). Writers John Hale (screenwriter of *Anne of the Thousand Days* and *Mary, Queen of Scots*), John Prebble, and Rosemary Ann Sisson contributed episodes; costumes were by Elizabeth Waller; settings designed by Peter Seddon. Roderick Graham produced. Pictured are Glenda Jackson and Michael Williams.

1971

The Generation Game
(BBC-1, 1971–77)

Also known as **Bruce Forsyth and The Generation Game**, the mechanics of this game show involved competitions between family tandems (father and daughter, aunt and nephew, etc.) which tested them on anything from general knowledge to physical ability. The rapid-paced show became the perfect platform for the non-stop wit (and at times irritating interference) of host Bruce Forsyth, originally assisted by glamour girl Anthea Redfern (*pictured*). Alan Tarrant, James Moir, and Alan Boyd produced, successively. In 1978 the show was revived as **Larry Grayson's Generation Game** (BBC-1, 1978–82) with camp comedian Grayson hosting the proceedings with the support of Scottish singer Isla St Clair; Alan Boyd produced. The programme returned as **Bruce Forsyth's Generation Game** (BBC-1, 1990–) with 'Brucie' back at his old station, assisted now by Rosemarie Ford; David Taylor produced.

A Ghost Story for Christmas
(BBC-1, 1971–78)

Featured a series of holiday period 30–55-minute specials based on famous horror–fantasy stories (mainly by M. R. James) and shown late night. M. R. James's 'The Stalls of Barchester' (24/12/71; adapt. and pr. Lawrence Gordon Clark) premièred the series, followed by 'A Warning to the Curious' (24/12/72) by MRJ; the chilling 'Lost Hearts' (25/12/73), also from an MRJ story, about a long-dead girl and boy (Michelle Foster and Christopher Davies, *pictured*) who materialize to torment the owner of a rambling Lincolnshire mansion; 'The Treasure of Abbot Thomas' (23/12/74) with Michael Bryant; 'The Ash Tree' (23/12/75) with Edward Petherbridge; Charles Dickens's 'The Signalman' (22/12/76) with Denholm Elliott; 'Stigma' (28/12/77) by Clive Exton; and John Bowen's 'The Ice House' (25/12/78). Some stories were also billed as **Christmas Ghost Story**. In December 1986 Robert Powell retold five spooky MRJ tales in 15-minute parts for BBC-2's **Classic Ghost Stories**.

The Guardians
(LWT, 1971)

Was a near-future fantasy about a new society run by committee and enforced by sinister police called the Guardians. The thirteen hour-long episodes told of the conflict between those representing order and those dedicated to its overthrow. Central character Tom Weston (John Collin; *left*, with Robin Ellis) was caught between the two clashing forces, used by one and hunted by the other. Gwyneth Powell, Cyril Luckham, and Edward Petherbridge supported. The series was created by Rex Firkin and Vincent Tilsley; produced by Andrew Brown.

Hine
(ATV, 1971)

Barry Ingham (*right*; with Timothy West) was Joe Hine, a freelance arms dealer and big-time businessman acting on behalf of major countries in a multi-billion dollar market-place of guns, tanks, missiles, and jet fighters. The 13 eps. × hour series was created and produced by Wilfred Greatorex.

It's Awfully Bad for Your Eyes, Darling . . .
(BBC-1, 1971)

Alternatively scatty and witty sitcom co-written by Jilly Cooper and Christopher Bond about four mindless 'dolly birds' sharing a flat and each other's underwear, and stealing each other's boyfriends. The four were (*l. to r.*) Jane Carr, Joanna Lumley, Elizabeth Knight, and Jennifer Croxton. Leon Thau produced the 6 eps. × 30 mins. series. The pilot programme was presented as a part of the **Comedy Playhouse** series (15/4/71).

Justice
(Yorkshire TV, 1971–74)

A drama series about a tough and successful lady barrister, Harriet Peterson (played by Margaret Lockwood), practising in the north of England; she moved to London for the second series. The series of thirty-nine hour-long episodes was produced by James Ormerod and (3rd series) Jacky Stoller; Peter Willes was executive producer. Willes had earlier produced a 90-minute one-off play, **Justice is a Woman** (Yorkshire TV, 4/9/69), featuring Lockwood as barrister Julia Stanford.

Last of the Mohicans
(BBC-1, 17/1–7/3/71)

A handsome production of J. Fenimore Cooper's Leatherstocking tales shot by the BBC in the west of Scotland and starring Kenneth Ives (*right*) as the pathfinder Hawkeye, with John Abineri (*left*) as Chingachgook. The setting was, like the earlier Canadian-produced series first seen in 1957, America during the Franco-British war of the 1750s. The 8 eps. × 45 mins. series was written by Harry Green for producer John McRae; it was directed by David Maloney. Two years later McRae produced **Hawkeye, The Pathfinder** (BBC-1, 18/11–16/12/73) as a five-part, 55-minute serial (in co-production with 20th Century Fox TV & ABC-TV), dramatized by Allan Prior and Alistair Bell, featuring Paul Massie in the title role and Abineri repeating his Chingachgook. Maloney again directed.

Look—Mike Yarwood!
(BBC-1, 1971–76)

Impressionist Mike Yarwood (*pictured*; in Groucho Marx routine) was one of television's successes who maintained a faithful following for many years. His impressions of British political figures (Harold Wilson, in particular) became extremely popular, as did his 'Eddie Waring' and 'Robin Day'. A prime-time Saturday evening show, **Mike Yarwood in Persons** (BBC-1, 1977–81), followed. He later signed with Thames for two series, also called **Mike Yarwood in Persons** (Thames TV, 1983; 1986); scripted by David Renwick, Barry Cryer, and, from Yarwood's early 1970s series, Eric Davidson. Director-producer for Thames was Keith Beckett.

The Old Grey Whistle Test
(BBC-2, 1971–83; 1985)

Started out as a late night Tuesday programme observing, analysing, and reflecting contemporary rock music and musicians. The programme was initially introduced by Ian Whitcomb, with Richard Williams supplying the reviews/previews; Bob Harris (*pictured*) introduced from 1972. Under producer Michael Appleton the programme became a successor to **Disco 2**; Appleton also produced **Rock Goes to College** (BBC-2, 1978–81) as a replacement between series of **OGWT**. **Rock** was a 40-minute series featuring the best of contemporary British and American rock bands, with each week's recording taking place on a college campus in front of an audience of students; Pete Drummond introduced. **OGWT** shortened its title to **Whistle Test** in 1984 (then 1986–88) for the remaining series of programmes.

1971

The Onedin Line
(BBC-1, 1971–80)

Told the dramatic story of a young man's rise to wealth and power in organizing and establishing his own shipping line in the second half of the nineteenth century. Peter Gilmore (*pictured*) starred as James Onedin; Anne Stallybrass (as his wife Anne), Jessica Benton, Brian Rawlinson, Howard Lang, and Edward Chapman also appeared. The 91 eps. × 50 mins. series was produced by Peter Graham Scott, Peter Cregeen, and Geraint Morris. The series developed from a **Drama Playhouse** entry (tx 7/12/70) written by Cyril Abraham and directed by William Slater.

Parkinson
(BBC-1, 1971–82)

Unlike most of the previous attempts at a late night talk show on British television, this 45-minute series hosted by former Yorkshire journalist Michael Parkinson went on to become a huge success and totalled over 350 episodes and 'best of' specials. Studio interview guests over the years included Pierre Salinger, John Lennon, Kenneth Tynan, Orson Welles, Trevor Howard, Jacques Tati, Jack Lemmon, Bing Crosby, Sir Robert Helpmann, Mickey Spillane, Buddy Rich, John Wayne, and Anita Loos. Parkinson (*right*) is pictured with guest Terry-Thomas in the première programme.

The Persuaders!
(Tribune Prod./ITC, 1971–72)

International action-adventure series about two wealthy playboy types, Lord Brett Sinclair (Roger Moore; *left*) and Danny Wilde (Tony Curtis; *right*), who were brought together by retired Judge Fulton (Laurence Naismith) to become his 'instruments of justice' in fighting crime and corruption. The 24 eps. × hour series was created and produced by Robert S. Baker.

Play Away
(BBC-2, 1971–84)

Studio-based children's (up to the age of 7) entertainment series demonstrating the pratfalls and buffoonery of accomplished kiddie-audience performers such as Brian Cant (*pictured*), Derek Griffiths, Toni Arthur, and, later, Julie Stevens, Tony Robinson, and Floella Benjamin. The success of the presenters' antics could often be gauged by the high-decibel squeals of pleasure from the studio audience minors (and on occasion their accompanying parents!). Music was supplied by Jonathan Cohen and the Play Away Band. The 25/30-minute series was produced by Ann Reay and Cynthia Felgate.

The Rivals of Sherlock Holmes
(Thames TV, 1971; 1973)

Was based on Hugh Greene's anthology, with episodes announcing: 'During the years 1891 to 1914, when the Sherlock Holmes stories were serialised in *Strand Magazine*, Conan Doyle's hero was not the only detective operating in London; he had rivals . . .' Producers Robert Love, Jonathan Alwyn, and Reginald Collin presented tales from such period authors as R. Austin Freeman ('A Message from the Deep Sea' with John Neville as Dr Thorndyke and 'The Moabite Cipher' with Barrie Ingham as Thorndyke; the latter pictured, *left*, with Peter Sallis); Arthur Morrison ('The Affair of the Tortoise' and 'The Case of Laker, Absconded' with Peter Barkworth as Arthur Hewitt); Jacques Futrelle ('Cell 13' and 'The Superfluous Finger' with Douglas Wilmer as Professor Van Dusen); and William Hope Hodgson ('The Horse of the Invisible' with Donald Pleasance as Carnacki the ghost hunter). Twenty-six hour-long episodes were produced.

The Search for the Nile
(BBC-2, 22/9–27/10/71)

A spectacular, historical drama-documentary series set in the middle of the last century telling the colourful and exciting story of the quest for the source of the Nile. The 6 eps. × hour drama reconstructed the adventures and hardships endured by some of the principal searchers: Samuel Baker (played by Norman Rossington), Richard Burton (Kenneth Haigh), James Grant (Ian McCulloch), John Hanning Speke (John Quentin), Dr David Livingstone (Michael Gough), and Henry Morton Stanley (Keith Buckley; *pictured*). James Mason narrated. Produced by Christopher Ralling; photography was by Brian Tufano and John Baker.

The Sky's the Limit
(Yorkshire TV, 1971–74)

Hughie Green and his old **Double Your Money** colleague, Monica Rose, hosted this travel game show in which contestants could win a travel voucher enabling them to go round the world (21,000 miles) as well as carry a pocketful (£600) of spending money. Format and research was by Vic Hallums; Peter Holmans produced.

The Snow Goose
(BBC TV–Universal TV; BBC-2 tx, 28/12/71)

Set in pre-war Britain, on the Essex coast marshes, this haunting and sensitive tale of a deformed artist loner, Philip Rhyayader (played by Richard Harris), and a wide-eyed orphan, Fritha (Jenny Agutter), who developed a kinship by healing and nurturing back to health a Canadian snow goose which had strayed off its migratory course, became one of the TV highlights of the period. The 55-minute film, adapted by Paul Gallico from his novella, was a co-production with the American Universal Television company (the US tx had been on 15/11/71 under the **Hallmark Hall of Fame** banner), produced by Frank O'Connor and directed by Patrick Garland. Ray Henman was the film cameraman and the wildlife photography was by Patrick Carey. Carl Davis supplied the music. The programme was also known as **Paul Gallico's The Snow Goose**.

1971

The Two Ronnies
(BBC-1, 1971–86)

Starring for the first time in their own joint series, the two Ronnies, Ronnie Barker (*right*) and Ronnie Corbett (*left*), presented a long-time, highly popular, often outrageously funny comedy-variety show that made excellent use of both characters' eccentricities and comedy quirks (Corbett's long-winded anecdotes, Barker's multiple characterizations, spoonerisms, and plain verbal silliness). While not actually a double act, in the Morecambe and Wise mould, the two distinctively individual performances of Corbett and Barker proved to work together very well. Terry Hughes, Peter Whitmore, Brian Penders, Paul Jackson, and Marcus Plantin, successively, held the producer's chair over the years.

UFO
(ATV/ITC/Century 21, 1971–72)

Live-action science fiction drama series from the Gerry and Sylvia Anderson studio with Ed Bishop starring as the commander of a future (1980s) organization called SHADO (Secret Headquarters, Alien Defence Organization) which had been set up to warn of alien invaders. George Sewell, Gabrielle Drake, and Peter Gordeno co-starred. Reg Hill produced the twenty-six hour-long episodes; special effects were by Derek Meddings. Pictured are Ed Bishop and Antonia Ellis.

Upstairs, Downstairs
(LWT, 1971–75)

Highly regarded and extremely popular costume serial set in an upper-crust Edwardian household and interweaving the dual narrative threads of the relationship of the downstairs servants and the upstairs Bellamy family, as well as the interconnecting lives of those in service. Among the below-stairs circle were butler Gordon Jackson (*right*), house parlourmaid Jean Marsh, cook Angela Baddeley (*left*), under-house parlourmaid Pauline Collins, footman George Innes (later Christopher Beeny), and lady's maid Patsy Smart; chauffeur John Alderton (as Thomas) later joined the working ranks. The Bellamy family and their social circle included Lord and Lady Bellamy (David Langton and Rachel Gurney; Hannah Gordon came in later as the second Lady Bellamy), son James (Simon Williams), daughter Elizabeth (Nicola Pagett), and Georgina (Lesley-Anne Down), Lord Bellamy's ward. The series was devised by actresses Jean Marsh and Eileen Atkins, and the sixty-eight hour-long episodes were produced by John Hawkesworth. A 13 eps. × hour spin-off series, **Thomas and Sarah** (LWT, 1979), featuring the adventures of the Pauline Collins and John Alderton characters, was produced by Christopher Hodson.

The View from Daniel Pike
(BBC-2, 1971–73)

The dark and squalid investigations of Glasgow private eye Daniel Pike, played in a suitably tough and terse manner by Roddy McMillan, formed the north-of-the-border/Raymond Chandler-ish background for this crime-buster series. Edward Boyd created as well as contributed scripts to the 15 eps. × 50 mins. programmes (6 eps. 1st series; 9 eps. 2nd series), produced by Anthony Coburn. McMillan is pictured (*right*) with Neil McCarthy in the première (25/11/71) episode.

Adam Smith
(Granada TV, 1972–73)

Was a religious drama series—a first for the Sunday evening sequence of religious programming—about the Revd Adam Smith (played by Andrew Keir; *pictured*) who was the parish minister of the small Scottish border village of Lammerton. The series opened with Adam Smith at a crisis point in his life following the death of his wife after a long and painful illness: should he stay in Lammerton now that his reasons for staying have died with her? He stayed, much to the spiritual benefit of the village, for 39 eps. × half-hour. Although the serial's main function was to be drama, it was drama with a built-in message. Produced by June Howson.

The Adventurer
(ITC, 1972–73)

Undercover espionage drama filmed in England and the south of France, **The Adventurer** was the story of American intelligence agent Gene Bradley (Gene Barry; *pictured*). Bradley posed as a wealthy film star travelling from one film location or pleasure resort to another on behalf of the US government. His contact man was a Mr Parminter, played by Barry Morse, who passed himself off as Bradley's producer-manager. Aimed squarely at the international TV sales market, the series failed to generate enough interest, despite the exotic locations, due to the TV spy genre fading out in the path of the 1970s cop show boom. The 26 eps. × half-hour series was produced by Monty Berman; music was by John Barry.

The Adventures of Black Beauty
(LWT–Talbot TV–Freemantle Ltd., 1972–74)

Based on Anna Sewell's famous 1877 juvenile classic of the dashing thoroughbred, with scripts written specially for the TV series, the fifty half-hour adventures featured Dr James Gordon (played by William Lucas), his daughter Vicky (Judi Bowker; later Stacy Dorning, *pictured*, as Jenny), her brother Kevin (Roderick Shaw), and their housekeeper Amy Winthrop (Charlotte Mitchell) in an exciting variety of equestrian escapades. Sid Cole produced; Charles Crichton, Alan Gibson, and Freddie Francis shared most of the first series' directing chores. Around the same time best-selling author Monica Dickens's 1963 story of a horse, *Cobbler's Dream*, formed the basis for **Follyfoot** (Yorkshire TV, 1971–73), set around a sanctuary for rescued horses run by an eccentric Colonel (Desmond Llewellyn) and his young helpers (Steve Hodson, Gillian Blake, and Christian Rodska); executive producer Tony Essex developed the 39 eps. × 30/35 mins. children's series. Producer Murray Newey returned the original Black Beauty series for another fifteen half-hour episodes (following a 55-minute première episode) as **The New Adventures of Black Beauty** (LWT–Isambard/Freemantle Production, 1/9–15/12/90). Stacy Dorning and William Lucas played their original roles, with Amber McWilliams appearing as Vicky.

America
(Time-Life Films–BBC-2, 12/11/72–4/2/73)

Author-broadcaster Alistair Cooke's personal history of the USA, from the first European explorations to contemporary times, was a handsomely mounted thirteen-part documentary series. Written and narrated by the urbane Cooke (*pictured*), an American citizen since the 1940s, the programme journeyed through his fascinating assessments of the Pilgrims and Puritans, Thomas Jefferson's attempt to protect the liberty of individuals, the Gold Rush, the Civil War, the Wild West, the European immigrants, and Roosevelt's New Deal. Sir Denis Brogan was the historical adviser; Charles Chilton the musical adviser. Ann Turner directed for producer Michael Gill. As far back as 1938 Alistair Cooke was seen on British television reporting from America with the 10-minute programme **Accent in America** (BBC tx 19/8/38) as he talked 'his way from Maine to Texas'.

1972

Arthur of the Britons
(HTV, 1972–73)

A wild and rugged version of the Arthurian legends serialized for the late afternoon children's slot. But this was no chivalric epic of Arthurian romances. Instead, producer Peter Miller created a desperate sixth-century world of feudalism and barbaric combat, with young Arthur (Oliver Tobias; *pictured*) as a warlord struggling to hold off the English invaders. The settings and scenery were often grim and grimy and the action scenes spiced with extended images of brutal combat. Michael Gothard (as Kai) and Jack Watson (as Llud) played Arthur's regular companions; Rupert Davies was his Saxon enemy, Cerdig. Terence Feely and Robert Banks Stewart were among those responsible for the gritty scripts. Pat Jackson and Sidney Hayers also contributed from the director's chair. Twenty-four half-hour episodes were produced.

Black Arrow
(Southern TV, 1972–75)

Robert Louis Stevenson's swashbuckling adventure set in fifteenth-century England in the period following the Wars of the Roses featured a mysterious masked archer known as The Black Arrow. William Squire, Glyn Owen, Simon Cuff, and John Sanderson were featured over the three series; 20 eps. × half-hour were produced by Peter Croft.

The Brothers
(BBC-1, 1972–76)

A drama series about the three Hammond brothers, Edward (Glyn Owen; *centre*), Brian (Richard Easton; *right*), and David (Robin Chadwick; *left*), who are drawn into conflict over the family haulage business following the death of their father, the founder of Hammond Transport Services. Other regulars included Jean Anderson as the founder's widow, Jennifer Wilson as the late father's mistress, and Hilary Tindall as Ann, Brian Hammond's difficult wife. The 92 eps. × 45/50 mins. series was produced by Gerard Glaister, Ken Riddington, and Bill Sellars; it was created by Glaister and N. J. Crisp.

Clochemerle
(BBC-2–Bavaria Atelier GMBH (Munich), 18/2–14/4/72)

The British fascination with lavatorial humour (as exemplified by the popular *Carry On* films) reached an almost artistic peak via this BBC TV translation of Gabriel Chevallier's 1934 folk comedy novel about the installation of a *pissoir* in the centre of a small French village. The 9 eps. × 30 mins. serial related the story of the construction of the men's 'convenience', amid powerful vocal objections from the community's more straight-laced types, which developed from a local village disturbance to a small-scale rebellion, with an army detachment being brought in to quell the revolt. The Ray Galton and Alan Simpson adaptation produced a panoramic farce that managed to sustain its humour and character interest throughout all nine instalments. Producer-director Michael Mills assembled a large Anglo-French cast (the programme was filmed in the Beaujolais country of France) that included Cyril Cusack, Roy Dotrice (*centre, foreground*), Wendy Hiller (*left, foreground*), Kenneth Griffith, Cyd Hayman, Micheline Presle, Bernard Bresslaw, Madeline Smith, Wolfe Morris, Hugh Griffith, and Georgina Moon; also pictured, Freddie Earlle (*top*) and Barry Linehan (*2nd right*). Peter Ustinov provided the voice-over continuity.

Colditz
(BBC-1–Universal TV, 19/10/72–25/1/73; BBC-1, 7/1–1/4/74)

The first 15 eps. × 50 mins. series represented one of the rare co-productions between BBC TV and an American producer-distributor; Gerard Glaister was the series producer and co-creator (with Brian Degas). Stories related the struggle by POWs to effect an escape from the bleak prison fortress of Colditz Castle in Germany during the Second World War. The leading players were Robert Wagner (*left*), David McCallum (*centre*), Jack Hedley, Edward Hardwicke, Christopher Neame, Richard Heffer (*right*), and Bernard Hepton. N. J. Crisp, Ian Kennedy Martin, and Bryan Forbes contributed scripts for the first series; Troy Kennedy Martin, Thom Keyes, Ken Hughes, and Robert Muller were among the writers for the second series of 13 eps. × 50 mins.

202

Country Matters
(Granada TV, 1972–73)

A charming woodcut of a series that based its thirteen hour-long episodes on the stories of H. E. Bates and A. E. Coppard. Under series producer Derek Granger, the plays presented a fine gallery of actors (Ian McKellan, Peter Firth, Joss Ackland, Jane Lapotaire, Jeremy Brett) among the rural tales adapted by such TV scripters as James Saunders, Hugh Leonard, and Jeremy Paul. Keith Drinkel (*pictured*) appeared in 'The Higgler' episode.

Crown Court
(Granada TV, 1972–84)

A long-running, courtroom-based drama serial which was shown as a series of three-part, half-hour stories (on three consecutive afternoons) presenting a new case each week. The fictitious Fulchester Crown Court was the setting for the often fascinating (and, at times, alarming) cases; heroin smuggling, indecent assault, illegal abortion, unlawful transfer of Official Secrets, murder, arson, and malpractice were among those featured. The series also presented a fine gallery of performers within the individual stories: Barbara Shelley, T. P. McKenna, Caroline Blakiston, Vivien Merchant, Fulton Mackay, Anthony Bate, Michael Elphick, Judy Parfitt, Thorley Walters, Michael Gough, Juliet Stevenson, and Connie Booth. The scene pictured is from the 'Murder Most Foul' episode, with (*l. to r.*) John le Mesurier, Gerald Flood, Betty Hardy, Liz Fraser, and Arthur English.

Emmerdale Farm
(Yorkshire TV, 1972–)

A domestic soap serial set in the Yorkshire Dales and revolving around the extraordinarily busy and eventful lives of the country community living in and around the village of Beckindale. Leading and original players included Sheila Mercier (as Annie Sugden), Frazer Hines (as Joe Sugden), Frederick Pyne (as Matt Skilbeck), Ronald Magill (as Amos Brearley), Arthur Pentelow (as Henry Wilks); and later Stan Richards (as Seth Armstrong) and Jean Rogers (as Dolly Skilbeck). Comedian Max Wall appeared for some episodes as the cantankerous Arthur Braithwaite in 1979. The series was created by Kevin Laffan and produced in the early days by David Goddard. The programme was retitled simply **Emmerdale** in November 1989. Pictured (*l. to r.*) are Jo Kendall, Frazer Hines, Arthur Pentelow, and Sheila Mercier.

Film 72
(BBC-1, 1972–)

BBC TV's film review flagship was originally transmitted only to the London area and the south-east and presented by journalist Irma Kurtz. Barry Norman (*pictured*), at first with Jacky Gillott, took over after a few weeks and has presented the programme ever since (except for a short break in 1982 when he moved over to present **Omnibus**), with the title changing each year accordingly. The original producer was Iain Johnstone. Norman also presented such spin-off programmes as **The Hollywood Greats** (BBC-1, 3–31/8/78; 5 parts × 50 mins.), **The British Greats** (BBC-1, 30/7–27/8/80; 5 parts × 50 mins.), and **Talking Pictures** (BBC-1, 25/1–28/3/88; 10 parts × 50/55 mins.). Another BBC TV film programme, **Now Showing** (BBC-1, 1981), with Michael Wood, reviewed the past month's new films but only ran for four half-hour editions; Jane Lush produced.

1972

The Frighteners
(LWT, 1972–73)

The thirteen half-hour suspense stories, about ordinary people threatened by situations out of control, was London Weekend Television's first series filmed entirely on location in and around London. Eric Coltart, Andrea Newman, Robert Holles, Brian Phelan, Jacques Gillies, John Burke, Douglas Livingstone, Peter Collings, Wilfred Greatorex, Maurice Edelman, and David Hodson provided scripts for directors James Goddard, John Reardon, Mike Hodges (who also scripted), Henri Safran, Gareth Davies, Graham Evans, and David Reid. Paul Knight produced. The scene pictured is from 'The Minder' episode with Warren Clarke (*left*) and Kenneth J. Warren.

The Gangster Show
(BBC-2, 7/11/72)

Was the TV listing title for **The Resistible Rise of Arturo Ui**, Bertolt Brecht's parable play of Hitler's rise to power set in gangland Chicago, performed as *Der Aufhaltsame Aufstieg des Arturo Ui* in 1958. George Tabori's 105-minute adaptation for producer Tony Garnett starred Nicol Williamson (*pictured*; as Arturo Ui) in the role of the frenzied Führer using mobster rule to gain power. Supporting players included Sam Wanamaker, Al Mancini, Jill Townsend, Bruce Boa, and Frank Middlemass. Jack Gold directed the impressive production; cameraman was Brian Tufano; Carl Davis provided the music. The BBC TV presentation coincided (was it coincidence?) with the US presidential election (Nixon v. McGovern).

General Hospital
(ATV, 1972–79)

A twice-weekly afternoon stethoscope saga set in a large, modern hospital building and following the oscillating relationships, personal and professional, of the medical staff. In 1975 the serial became an hour-long programme and was seen in peak viewing time. The original cast featured David Garth, James Kerry, Ronald Leigh-Hunt, Peggy Sinclair, Lynda Bellingham, Lewis Jones, and Carmen Munro; the scene pictured shows Tony Adams (*left*) and Patrick Ryecart (*right*). Constructed in a similar vein were the hour-long Health Centre-located stories of **The Practice** (Granada TV, 1985–86).

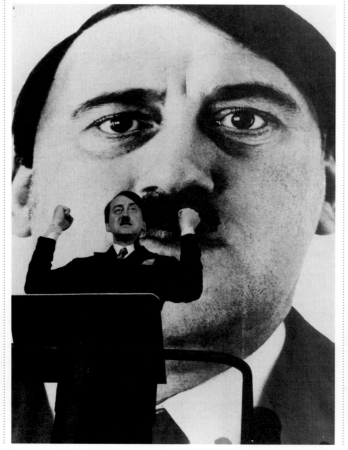

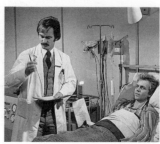

.John Craven's Newsround
(BBC-1, 1972–)

A lightweight but not patronizing regular news programme for children, generally aimed at 7 to 12 year olds, presented by journalist / editor John Craven (*pictured*). Although the programme was a part of BBC Children's TV Programmes **Newsround** drew on BBC Television News for its material and carried real news stories with very little if any restriction in subject-matter for its young audience. **Newsround Weekly** (BBC-1, 1977–78), co-presented with Lucy Mathen, and **Newsround Extra** (BBC-1, 1981–), co-presented with Paul McDowell, were later added as special weekend investigations.

Joseph and the Amazing Technicolor Dreamcoat
(Granada TV, 24/12/72)

The rock music version of the story from Genesis was presented in a 45-minute production by the Young Vic Company, featuring Gary Bond as Joseph. Music and lyrics were by Andrew Lloyd Webber and Tim Rice. Christopher Bruce was the choreographer; musical direction by Alan Doggett. The production was designed by Peter Phillips; Peter Plummer directed for producer Peter Potter.

Lord Peter Wimsey
(BBC-1, 1972–75)

Crime writer Dorothy L. Sayers's aristocratic amateur sleuth had his adventures first published during the 1920s and 1930s (a total of eleven novels and twenty-one stories). When BBC TV produced a set of mini-series based on his investigations they carefully maintained the original period setting and flavour. Ian Carmichael (*pictured*) portrayed the dapper Lord Peter; usually accompanied by his manservant Bunter (played variously by Glyn Houston and Peter Newark). The TV adventures started with 'Clouds of Witness' (5/4–3/5/72; 5 eps. × 45 mins.), adapted by Anthony Steven and directed by Hugh David, and followed up with 'The Unpleasantness at the Bellona Club' (1–22/2/73; 4 eps. × 45 mins.), directed by Ronald Wilson; 'Murder Must Advertise' (30/11–21/12/73; 4 eps. × 50 mins.), adapted by Bill Craig and directed by Rodney Bennett; 'The Nine Tailors' (22/4–13/5/74; 4 eps. × 50 mins.), adapted by Steven and directed by Raymond Menmuir; and 'Five Red Herrings' (23/7–13/8/75; 4 eps. × 50 mins.), adapted by Steven and directed by Robert Tronson. The first four serials were produced by Richard Beynon; the 1975 serial was produced by Bill Sellars for BBC Scotland. Lord Peter Wimsey later returned for three more adventures, this time played by Edward Petherbridge with Harriet Walter as companion Harriet Vane. Under the generic title of **A Dorothy L. Sayers Mystery** (BBC-2–WGBH Boston, 1987), the serials were 'Strong Poison' (25/3–8/4/87; 3 eps. × 55 mins.), 'Have His Carcass' (15/4–6/5/87; 4 eps. × 50/55 mins.), and 'Gaudy Night' (13–27/5/87; 3 eps. × 55/60 mins.).

The Lotus Eaters
(BBC-2, 1972–73)

Was a 50-minute per episode serial set around a bar in the small town of Aghios Nicholaos on the eastern coast of Crete run by Erik and Ann Shepherd (played by Ian Hendry, *pictured centre*, and Wanda Ventham, *right*). The drama series featured the crowd that floated around the bar and whose individual stories were interwoven with the Shepherds' own saga. James Kerry, Cyd Hayman, Maurice Denham, Thorley Walters, and Sylvia Coleridge were among the regular bar-flies. The series was created by Michael J. Bird and produced by Anthony Read. Karan David is pictured, *left*.

Love Thy Neighbour
(Thames TV, 1972–76)

More crude than funny sitcom series about next-door-neighbour racial intolerance, with Jack Smethurst and Kate Williams (*centre*) as Eddie and Joan Booth, a working-class couple living next door to easygoing West Indian couple Bill and Barbara Reynolds (played by Rudolph Walker, *left*, and Nina Baden-Semper, *right*). The 53 eps. × half-hour (+ 1 ep. × 45 mins. special) series was written by Vince Powell and Harry Driver; Stuart Allen, Ronnie Baxter, and Anthony Parker produced. A feature film version was produced by Hammer Films in 1973.

Mastermind
(BBC-1, 1972–)

Was not considered a mass appeal programme until a scheduling shift placed it in front of a prime-time audience and the ratings soared. The unlikely attraction stemmed more from viewer amazement at the proficiency of the specialists snap-answering a series of high-brow questions thrown at them by chief interrogator Magnus Magnusson than from the sense of armchair participation usually associated with the more traditional TV game shows. The formidable black seat and the down-beat fanfare music have become symbols of serious television.

Mr and Mrs
(HTV–Border TV, 1972–88)

Alan Taylor was the quiz-master of this popular game show in which married couples were tested on their knowledge about their partners. The half-hour, daytime show, devised by Roy Ward Dickson, had been running in the local TWW (Television Wales and West) area for a few years before it became a networked programme. Derek Batey (*pictured, left*; with contestants) was alternate quiz-master for Border TV when the two companies shared the programme from 1974. Derek Clark produced for HTV from 1972; William Cartner produced for Border TV from 1977 (Batey was producer from 1974).

My Wife Next Door
(BBC-1, 1972)

Divorced couple sitcom created by Brian Clemens and Richard Waring, starring John Alderton and Hannah Gordon (*pictured*) as the couple awaiting their absolute decree, George and Suzy Bassett, who accidentally move into adjacent cottages in the country. The 13 eps. × 30 mins. series was written by Waring and produced by Graeme Muir.

New Scotland Yard
(LWT, 1972–74)

Action-drama series about the operations of the London detective division featuring (for the first three series) John Woodvine (*right*; as Det. Chief Supt. John Kingdom) and John Carlisle (*left*; as Det. Insp. Alan Ward). They were later replaced by Michael Turner (as Det. Chief Supt. Clay) and Clive Francis (as Det. Sgt. Dexter). The 46 eps. × hour series was produced by Jack Williams.

The Pathfinders
(Thames TV, 1972–73)

A dramatized documentary series about the Pathfinder Force of the RAF during the Second World War telling the story of the aircrews who flew in advance of bombing raids to pinpoint targets for the main force. The 13 eps. × hour series starred Robert Urquhart (*right*) as W/Cdr. MacPhearson and Jack Watling (*left*) as Doc Saxon. The independently made series was produced by Gerry Brown.

Pebble Mill at One
(BBC-1, 1972–86)

Featured daily half-hour (later 45 mins.) general-viewer, magazine-style editions of people, views, and music, transmitted live, from the BBC's Pebble Mill studios in Birmingham. An easygoing alternative to midday news bulletins (the series was eventually replaced by **The One O'Clock News**), the programme offered a generally lightweight distraction for the daytime viewer from the hard news, game shows, or soap operas being broadcast around the same time. Bob Langley, Marian Foster (*2nd right*), David Seymour (*left*), and Donny MacLeod (*right*) hosted during the early years; the original editor was Terry Dobson. The programme became simply **Pebble Mill** for the period 1974–79, during which Jan Leeming (*2nd left*) also hosted. **Pebble Mill Showcase** (BBC-2, 1978; a 50-minute special had already been presented on 18/8/76) was shown for a three-month period with Norman Vaughan as host. Also **Pebble Mill on Sunday** (BBC-1, 1979) appeared for two months (Jan.–Feb.) as a seventh-day filler.

The Protectors
(Group Three Prod./ITC, 1972–74)

Featured a trio of independent crime-busters dealing with killers, smugglers, and kidnappers in a variety of exotic locations. Robert Vaughn (*left*) co-starred as London-based American Harry Rule with Nyree Dawn Porter (*right*) as English noblewoman Contessa di Contini, living in Rome; Tony Anholt, as Paris-based Paul Buchet, made up the trio. The 52 eps. × half-hour series was produced by Gerry Anderson and Reg Hill.

The Regiment
(BBC-1, 1972–73)

Traced the fortunes of the Cotswolds Regiment through the lives of two families from 1895 (and the Boer War) to 1904 India. The Gaunt family was represented by clean-cut hero Richard Gaunt (played by Christopher Cazenove; *pictured*) and the Bright family by RSM William Bright (Michael Brennan); Richard Hurndall, Richard Wordsworth, Penelope Lee, and Frederick Treves also appeared. The series of 23 eps. × 50 mins. was produced by Anthony Coburn and (2nd series) Terence Dudley. The programme developed from the première play of **Drama Playhouse** (tx on 23/11/70) written by Robin Chapman, directed by William Slater, and produced by Coburn; the series concept was by Jack Gerson and Nick McCarty.

Russell Harty Plus
(LWT, 1972–74)

Led on from **Eleven Plus** and featured Harty as a chat show host, with such studio guests as Cecil Beaton, Carol Channing, Rossano Brazzi, Omar Sharif, and Yul Brynner; Humphrey Barclay and, later, Derek Bailey produced the 60/45 mins. series. **Russell Harty Plus One** (LWT, 1973–74) was Harty having a series of late night conversations with a single guest of his choice (J. B. Priestley, Jonathan Miller, and Gloria Swanson were among his selection) in this 45-minute series produced by Bailey. Harty continued with London Weekend TV for **Russell Harty** (LWT, 1974–79), swapping stories with the fine and famous (Aznavour to Zefferelli) for over seven series; Mike Mansfield directed for producer Nicholas Barrett. Then in 1980 he shifted to BBC TV and (of course) **Russell Harty** (BBC-2, 1980–83) where his previous chat show format and familiar line-up of guests (including the infamous clash with Grace Jones; tx 13/11/80 was televised from the BBC Manchester studios and then from London's Greenwood Theatre; Ken Stephinson and Tom Gutteridge shared the producer's spot. A title and channel change produced **Harty** (BBC-1, 1983–84) but the show's theme and format remained the same. In between series of shows he featured in **Harty Goes to Hollywood** (BBC-2, 1–10/8/84) for producer Stephinson/BBC Manchester.

Sale of the Century
(Anglia TV, 1972–83)

Nicholas Parsons (*left*) was the (occasionally gruff) quiz-master of this game show where he posed questions to the contestants worth, initially, £1, £3, and £5 and which would earn the lucky entrants the right to bargains worth up to £1,000. Peter Joy and Bill Perry directed-produced the half-hour episodes. The series often featured **Celebrity Sale of the Century** whereby TV personalities became contestants, with the prizes going to charity.

Spyder's Web
(ATV, 1972)

Presented what at first appeared to be just another secret government agency with powers beyond the usual police and official authorities. Created by Richard Harris, the espionage theme (entrapment of enemy agents) and storylines tended to be as complex as the spy-thriller genre allowed for television consumption at the time. 'Spyder' was the codename given to the particular operative in the field and 'Web' referred to the clandestine unit. Patricia Cutts, Anthony Ainley (*left*; with guest Lelia Goldoni), and Veronica Carlson were the cloak-and-dagger trio who played it in the appropriate tongue-in-cheek style. The 13 eps. × hour series was produced by Dennis Vance.

The Stone Tape
(BBC-2, 25/12/72)

Nigel Kneale's chilling account of
a scientific team's attempt to
extract information from the
stone walls of a Victorian mansion
that they believe retains ancient
and traumatic memories. Michael
Bryant, Jane Asher (*pictured*), Iain
Cuthbertson, Michael Bates, and
Reginald Marsh led the cast.
Music and sound effects were by
Desmond Briscow/BBC
Radiophonic Workshop. Peter
Sasdy directed Innes Lloyd's 90-
minute production.

The Strauss Family
(ATV, 7/11–19/12/72)

Presented the nineteenth-century
story of the famous family who
created the Viennese Waltz, a new
type of music whose grace and
melodic charm matched the
elegance of the period. Eric Woofe
starred as Johann Strauss, the
father, with Stuart Wilson (*left*; as
Johann Strauss, the son), Anne
Stallybrass (as Anna), and Barbara
Ferris (as Émilie). The 90-minute
première episode was followed by
six hour-long episodes. Producer
David Reid shared directing with
David Giles.

Van der Valk
(Thames TV, 1972–73; Euston Films,
1977; Thames TV/Elmgate Production,
1991–92)

Followed the crime-busting
assignments of the Amsterdam-
based Dutch detective Van der
Valk (played by Barry Foster;
pictured) created by crime author
Nicolas Freeling and first
published in 1962. The leisurely
paced police procedurals
presented the added interest of
using the pictorial and social
aspects of Amsterdam as a fresh
background to the usual TV crime
caper. Susan Travers (later Joanna
Dunham) co-starred as the
detective's wife Arlette; Meg
Davies in the 1990s series. Michael
Chapman and Robert Love,
respectively, produced for
Thames; Geoffrey Gilbert
produced for Euston. Twenty-five
hour-long episodes were
presented. Chris Burt produced
the 2-hour episodes in the 1990s.

Villains
(LWT, 1972)

A crime drama series that
followed the exploits of nine bank
robbers, beginning at the moment
of their escape from
imprisonment. The stories of the
men, their accomplices, their
women, and the robbery were
unfolded in thirteen hour-long
episodes. Leading players included
John Kane, David Daker, Dervis
Ward, Martin Shaw, Bryan
Marshall, William Marlowe, Tom
Adams, Alun Armstrong, Michael
Culver, Bob Hoskins, and Hilary
Dwyer. Andrew Brown produced.
The scene pictured is from 'His
Dad Named Him After the
General' episode featuring Martin
Shaw and Cheryl Hall.

War and Peace
(BBC-2, 28/9/72–8/2/73)

A major 20-episode serialization
(in 45-minute instalments) of
Tolstoy's epic novel that took
some three years to produce, with
location filming in Yugoslavia and
extensive special effects work at
Television Centre. Rupert Davies
(as Count Rostov), Faith Brook (as
Countess Rostova), Morag Hood
(as Natasha), Alan Dobie (*pictured*;
as Andrei Bolkonsky), and
Anthony Hopkins (as Pierre)
starred. Dramatization was by
Jack Pulman for producer David
Conroy; John Davies directed. An
earlier TV version, though not on
such a grand scale, had been
produced and presented by
Granada TV (tx 26/3/63; 165
mins.). This English version had
been adapted by Robert David
MacDonald and directed by Silvio
Narizzano; Kenneth Griffith,
Daniel Massey, and Nicol
Williamson were featured.

1972/3

Weekend World
(LWT, 1972–88)

Was designed to fill the gap between **News at Ten** and **World in Action** and to provide a new perspective on the main domestic and international events of the week. The 90-minute midday Sunday programme was initially presented by journalists Peter Jay and John Torode. John Birt was then executive producer. The Sunday slot was later taken over by **The Walden Interview** (LWT, 1988–89) in which Brian Walden (*pictured*; with Margaret Thatcher) engaged in some lively, incisive questioning with the political and the powerful. The original series producer was John Wakefield. **Walden** (LWT, 1990–) and, for a spell, **Walden Special** (LWT, 1990) followed.

Who Do You Do?
(LWT, 1972–74)

Offered weekly face-lifts of sketches and songs by the country's top impersonators playing a number of roles. Freddie Starr and Peter Goodwright were the resident stars, supported by Margo Henderson, Roger Kitter, Barry Cryer, Faith Brown, Janet Brown, Jerry Stevens, and Dustin Gee (*pictured*) among others. The programme returned for a short series as **New Who Do You Do?** (LWT, 1975) and later **Now Who Do You Do?** (LWT, 1976). ATV produced a similar show, **Kopykats**, in 1972 under the *Saturday Variety* banner, featuring such American/Canadian performers as Frank Gorshin and Rich Little.

Are You Being Served?
(BBC-1, 1973–83)

Jeremy Lloyd & David Croft scripted this comedy series, set in a department store and featuring, in particular, the staff sharing the Ladies' Fashions and Menswear floor. The colourful cast line-up consisted of (*l. to r.*) Wendy Richard, Mollie Sugden, Frank Thornton, Arthur Brough, Nicholas Smith, Trevor Bannister, John Inman, and Larry Martyn. Harold Bennett also appeared as the ancient-yet-frisky 'young' Mr Grace, the store's owner. The 62 eps. × 30 mins. series was produced-directed by David Croft, Harold Snoad (1974 series), and, for the final series, Bob Spiers. Anglo-EMI produced a feature film spin-off in 1977. Writers Lloyd & Croft revived most of the characters in a later comedy series called **Grace and Favour** (BBC-1, 1992) in which the late Mr Grace, having used the staff's pension contributions to buy an old manor house, bequeaths the property to them. Thereafter, Sugden, Thornton, Inman, Richard, and Smith (in their original roles) try to make a living out of running the place as a country hotel. Mike Stephens directed-produced.

The Ascent of Man
(BBC-2–Time-Life Films, 5/5–28/7/73)

The late Dr Jacob Bronowski's major 13 part × 50 mins. series exploring Man's greatest discoveries and the evolution of human thought. From the development of the ideas of physics to the unravelling of the genetic code, Bronowski (*pictured*) presented a supremely educational and highly visual series of programmes that, following their US TV transmission (in 1975), led to his being hailed on American TV as a small-screen, master-class guru.

210

Billy Liar
(LWT, 1973–74)

Was the TV update of Keith Waterhouse's 1959 novel and followed the stage and screen successes. Waterhouse and Willis Hall developed a 26 eps. × half-hour series for producer-director Stuart Allen featuring Jeff Rawle (*right*) as Billy Fisher, the North Country lad with a wild imagination. Regular supporting players included George A. Cooper (*left*) as Billy's father, Pamela Vezey, his mother, Sally Watts, the girlfriend, and Colin Jeavons as his frustrated funeral parlour employer.

The Brontës of Haworth
(Yorkshire TV, 30/9–21/10/73)

A four-part serial about the lives of the Brontë family and the three famous literary sisters in particular. A doom-laden yet fascinating study, with a suitably bleak Yorkshire moorland background, of sisters Anne (Ann Penfold; *left*), Emily (Rosemary McHale; *centre*), and Charlotte (Vickery Turner; *right*), as well as their brother Branwell (Michael Kitchen; *far right*). The series (3 eps. × 75 mins., 1 ep. × 120 mins.) was scripted by Christopher Fry for producer-director Marc Miller.

The Death of Adolf Hitler
(LWT, 7/1/73)

Set entirely in the Berlin bunker, Vincent Tilsley's play moved through the last ten days of Hitler's life as his dream of a thousand-year Reich became a drugged and paranoid nightmare. The 125-minute transmission, directed-produced by Rex Firkin, featured Frank Finlay (*pictured*) as Hitler, Ed Devereaux as Martin Bormann, Oscar Quitak as Goebbels, Robert Cawdron as Goering, Michael Sheard as Himmler, and Caroline Mortimer as Eva Braun; narration was by David de Keyser.

Divorce His; Divorce Hers
(HTV, 24 and 25/6/73)

Was the television partnership début of Richard Burton and Elizabeth Taylor (*pictured*) in this John Hopkins-scripted, two-part story about a marriage under stress. Martin Reynolds (Burton) was the successful international businessman trying to keep a lid on both his marriage and boardroom politics; Jane Reynolds (Taylor) was the neglected wife searching for solace. Carrie Nye, Barry Foster, and Gabriele Ferzetti co-starred. Waris Hussein directed the two 85-minute (tx) parts for producers Terence Baker and Gareth Wigan.

Helen—A Woman of Today
(LWT, 1973)

Featured the 13 eps. × hour adventures of Helen Tulley (played by Alison Fiske; *right*), a wife with two children who leaves her husband Frank (Martin Shaw; *left*) and her home to go it alone in the cold grey world outside. The human drama with a soap serial core was produced by Richard Bates.

Jack the Ripper
(BBC-1, 13/7–17/8/73)

A documentary investigation, in 6 eps. × 50 mins., into the facts of the Whitechapel Murders of 1888 conducted by Stratford Johns (on telephone) in his role of Det. Chief Supt. Barlow and Frank Windsor (*right*) as Det. Chief Supt. Watt. The programme was written by Elwyn Jones and John Lloyd for producers Paul Bonner and Leonard Lewis.

Hunter's Walk
(ATV, 1973–76)

A local police procedural series set in the fictitious midlands town of Broadstone and featuring the police officers at Hunter's Walk. The cases tended to spring from domestic disturbances more often than serious crime capers. Ewan Hooper and Davyd Harries were the leading detectives; Duncan Preston (*pictured*) played PC Fred Pooley. Thirty-nine hour-long episodes were produced by John Cooper; the series was created by Ted Willis.

Last of the Summer Wine
(BBC-1, 1973–)

Writer Roy Clarke's dreamy, untrammelled, humorous re-creation of life in a South Yorkshire community as seen through the eyes of three elderly chums, Compo (played by Bill Owen; *left*), Clegg (Peter Sallis; *right*), and, originally, Blamire (Michael Bates; *centre*). From 1976 Brian Wilde played Foggy and then from 1986 Michael Aldridge joined Compo and Clegg as crackpot inventor Seymour; Wilde returned in 1990 when Aldridge departed. Thora Hird also came on board as Seymour's sister. The series developed from a **Comedy Playhouse** entry, tx 4/1/73. In 1988 producer-director Gareth Gwenlan presented a 45-minute one-off play called **First of the Summer Wine** (BBC-1, 3/1/88), written by Clarke, in which the three characters were shown as teenagers in 1939; David Fenwick played Clegg, Paul Wyett was Compo, and Paul McLain appeared as Seymour. Peter Sallis also appeared as Mr Clegg, the father. A half-hour series premièred in September (BBC-1, 1988–89) under producer Mike Stephens.

Man About the House
(Thames TV, 1973–76)

Johnnie Mortimer & Brian Cooke scripted this half-hour sitcom series about two girls, Chrissy (Paula Wilcox; *left*) and Jo (Sally Thomsett; *right*), who are forced to share their Earls Court flat with a boy, Robin Tripp (Richard O'Sullivan; *centre*), and, initially, conceal his presence from the snooping landlord, George Roper (Brian Murphy). Yootha Joyce played Mildred, Mrs Roper. The Ropers later moved into a new home in middle-class suburbia and their own comedy series, **George and Mildred** (Thames TV, 1976–78); Murphy and Joyce continued their original roles. O'Sullivan's Robin Tripp character also headed into his own series, **Robin's Nest** (Thames TV, 1977–81), running a bistro with live-in girlfriend Vicky (Tessa Wyatt); Tony Britton played her disapproving father. The latter two series were also from the pen of Mortimer & Cooke; director-producer Peter Frazer-Jones worked on all three programmes. A spin-off movie, *Man About the House*, was produced by Hammer Films in 1974. **George and Mildred** also went to a feature film version in 1980 (dir. Peter Frazer-Jones).

Moonbase 3
(BBC-1, 1973)

Was a short-run exploration of establishing a European scientific community on the moon in the year 2003 and featured stories harking back to the realms of speculative fiction of a decade earlier. Donald Houston (*2nd right*) was the lunar base director assisted by technicians Barry Lowe (*right*) and Ralph Bates (*left*), and psychiatrist Fiona Gaunt (*2nd left*). The 6 eps. × 50 mins. (9/9–14/10/73) series was produced by Barry Letts; Ken Hannam and Christopher Barry directed three apiece. Terrance Dicks was the script editor; BBC TV resident scientist James Burke was adviser.

New Faces
(ATV, 1973–78)

Was a talent show series modelled after **Opportunity Knocks** which presented a variety of young, and some not so young, performers trying to make their mark on television. Among the discoveries were Victoria Wood, Lenny Henry (TV debut, 1975), Marti Caine (in 1975), Jim Davidson, and Gary Wilmot. Derek Hobson was the host; the judging panel at times included Mickie Most (*2nd left*), Ed Stewart, Tony Hatch (*left*), Clifford Davies (*2nd right*), Arthur Askey (*right*), and Hilary Kingsley. Over 160 episodes were produced by Les Cocks and (later) Albert Stevenson. Central TV returned the format with **New Faces of 86** (1986) which ran through to **New Faces of 87** (1987), and to **New Faces of 88** (1988), hosted by Marti Caine. BBC TV had presented a fortnightly series, also called **New Faces** (BBC-tv, 1959), which showcased artists new to television; G. B. Lupino produced.

Sam
(Granada TV, 1973–75)

Followed the fortunes of the youngest member of a Yorkshire mining family from a 10 year old to adulthood during the bleak 1930s and 1940s. The young Sam Wilson was played by Kevin Moreton; the adult Sam by Mark McManus (*pictured*). Michael Goodliffe, Maggie Jones, and Ray Smith supported. The 39 eps. × hour series was written by John Finch and produced by Michael Cox.

Shabby Tiger
(Granada TV, 11/7–22/8/73)

A 7 eps. × hour adaptation by Geoffrey Lancashire of Howard Spring's best-selling novel of the 1930s, taking central characters Anna Fitzgerald (played by Prunella Gee; *right*) and Nick Faunt (John Nolan; *left*) from their first romantic meeting into the bohemian life in industrial Manchester. John Sharp, Sharon Mughan, and Nigel Havers also appeared. Baz Taylor directed Richard Everitt's production.

Some Mothers Do 'Ave 'Em
(BBC-1, 1973–75; 1978)

A delightfully absurd and often hilarious slapstick comedy series starring Michael Crawford (*left*) as the mac-and-beret garbed, accident-prone Frank Spencer. His hapless adventures (in the Buster Keaton/Harold Lloyd style, with Crawford performing most of his own stunts) were shared with overly understanding wife Betty (played by Michele Dotrice; *right*). The series was written by Raymond Allen, with (later) stories and numerous ad libs supplied by Crawford. The 30/35-minute episodes were produced by Michael Mills and Sydney Lotterby.

1973

Sutherland's Law
(BBC-1, 1973–76)

Iain Cutherberston (*left*) starred as John Sutherland, Procurator-fiscal (a bit like the American District Attorney) of a Highland town. His was the responsibility to investigate and prosecute cases as well as help out the defence. Maev Alexander and Don McKillop appeared in the early series; Virginia Stark was his assistant during the later series. The programme developed from a **Drama Playhouse** entry (tx 23/8/72) written and produced by Anthony Coburn, which featured Derek Francis and Gareth Thomas (*pictured, centre*, with James Giles).

That's Life
(BBC-1, 1973–94)

A popular consumer watchdog programme presented by Esther Rantzen (*centre*) and assisted over the years by a succession of male back-up reporters (pictured are George Layton, *left*, and Bob Welling). The programme developed from a similar magazine series, **Braden's Week** (BBC-1, 1968–72), in which Bernard Braden and his team (reporters John Pitman and Rantzen, and editors Desmond Wilcox and Bill Morton) took a late night overview of the events of the previous week; they also received hundreds of letters from viewers who had experienced problems with domestic appliances and customer services and who sought some form of advice/action. Esther Rantzen took these cries for help to **That's Life** and built the programme around them.

Thriller
(ATV, 1973–76)

This series of feature-length, self-contained, filmed dramas with the emphasis on suspense and last-reel twists was created, and for the most part written, by Brian Clemens. The casting was often a point of interest: Helen Mirren in 'A Coffin for the Bride' (1/6/74), George Maharis in 'Death to Sister Mary' (15/6/74), Diana Dors in 'Nurse Will Make It Better' (11/1/75), and Denholm Elliott in 'The Crazy Kill' (3/5/75). Stanley Baker is shown in the 'Who Killed Lamb?' (Yorkshire TV, 16/3/74) episode of the *Thriller* anthology.

The Tommy Cooper Hour
(Thames TV, 1973–75)

The befezzed comedian with a haphazard line in misbehaving magic tricks and panic-stricken laughter was a popular television performer in numerous series and specials covering three decades. He starred in this Thames TV series of irregular, hour-long specials produced by Royston Mayoh. One of his earliest regular TV appearances was in **It's Magic** (BBC-tv, 1952), followed by **Cooper or Life With Tommy** (A-R, 1957), **Cooper's Capers** (ATV, 1958), **Cooperama** (ABC TV, 1966), **Life With Cooper** (ABC TV, 1966–69), **Tommy Cooper** (LWT, 1970), **Cooper** (Thames TV, 1975), **Cooper—Just Like That** (Thames TV, 1978), and **Cooper's Half Hour** (Thames TV, 1980).

Warship
(BBC-1, 1973–77)

Was a drama series about the adventures of the frigate HMS *Hero* and her crew, viewed for the most part from the officers' station. The 45 eps. × 50 mins. series was devised by Ian Mackintosh and Anthony Coburn (the latter also produced; later Joe Waters). The programme featured (*l. to r.*) Brian Jameson, Don Henderson, Graeme Eton, Donald Burton, David Savile, and John Lee; Bryan Marshall and Derek Godfrey also appeared. The programme also represented an unprecedented collaboration between the navy and the BBC (with the navy supplying the use of a real warship for the production).

Within These Walls
(LWT, 1973–78)

Told the story of day-to-day prison life behind the walls of the fictitious Stone Park, HM Prison for Women. Googie Withers (*right*; with guest Frances Cuka) starred as Faye Boswell, the newly appointed Governor whose job it was to help and understand the problems of the inmates, the prison staff, and, in between the conflicts and humour, keep her personal life intact. In 1976 Helen Forrester (played by Katharine Blake) became the new Governor until, for the final series in 1978, Susan Marshall (Sarah Lawson) took over. Jack Williamson produced the hour-long series.

The Wombles
(BBC-1, 1973)

The furry creatures (with names like Great Uncle Bulgaria, *left*, Tobermory, Bungo, Orinoco, *centre*, and Wellington, *right*) who collected rubbish and lived under Wimbledon Common were the creation of author Elisabeth Beresford. Their television adventures, in 5-minute segments, were animated and directed by Ivor Wood, and told by Bernard Cribbins; Mike Batt supplied the wombly music. A few years later Lionel Jeffries directed the feature *Wombling Free* (1977) for Ian Shand Productions–Rank. The series returned years later on ITV, again as **The Wombles** (FilmFair Production/Central TV, 1990–91), to captivate a whole new generation of afternoon viewing children. A half-hour special, **The Wandering Wombles**, was presented on 20/12/91 featuring the furry ones in the gardens of Buckingham Palace.

The World at War
(Thames TV, 1973–74)

A first-rate television documentary series (26 eps. × hour) telling the story of the greatest conflict in the history of the world. The expertly researched and ambitiously produced programme, narrated by Laurence Olivier, presented a wealth of dramatic footage illustrating (between eye-witness interviews) the period from Hitler's pre-war Germany to the horrific climax at Hiroshima. The programme was produced by Jeremy Isaacs; Noble Frankland was the historical adviser, and the music was by Carl Davis.

Antony and Cleopatra
(ATV, 28/7/74)

Richard Johnson and Janet
Suzman (*pictured*) were featured in
this 3-hour ATV presentation,
directed by Jon Scoffield, of the
Royal Shakespeare Company, in
Trevor Nunn's production of
Shakespeare's famous story of
power and passion in ancient
Egypt. For the RSC production of
the previous year Janet Suzman
won critical acclaim for her
performance of the Egyptian
queen as a 'swarthy, torrid gipsy'.
Patrick Stewart, Corin Redgrave,
Mary Rutherford, Philip Locke,
Ben Kingsley, and Tim Pigott-
Smith were among the roll-call of
supporting players.

The Aweful Mr Goodall
(LWT, 1974)

Widower Jack Goodall (Robert
Urquhart; *right*) was a 55-year-old,
retired ex-MI5 Colonel who could
not quite resist getting himself
involved in intrigue and assorted
mysteries even though he had
moved away from his past life to a
comfortable flat in Eastbourne.
His former Intelligence agency,
headed by Millbrook (Donald
Churchill), had a way of drawing
him back into the dark world of
espionage agents, smugglers, and
murderers. The six hour-long
episodes (5/4–10/5/74) were
produced by Richard Bates. Jim
Goddard and John Reardon
directed three episodes apiece.
(According to the producers the
'e' in aweful is intentional.) Also
pictured is guest player Eleanor
Bron.

Catholics: A Fable of the Future
(HTV–Hemisphere Prods., 14/4/74)

Was set in a remote Irish
monastery some time in the
future and focused on the plight of
a divided man, an abbot who was
in conflict with both the Vatican
and his own inner convictions.
Trevor Howard (*pictured*) played
the abbott, supported by Raf
Vallone, Martin Sheen, Cyril
Cusack, and Andrew Keir. Brian
Moore adapted the script from his
award-winning novel; the 90-
minute transmission was directed
by Jack Gold for producer Barry
Levinson.

Don't Ask Me
(Yorkshire TV, 1974–78)

Each week three experts tackled
viewers' queries about science and
the everyday world, and a guest
celebrity put forward a question of
his or her own. The original panel,
chaired by Derek Griffiths,
consisted of nutrition expert Dr
Magnus Pike (*pictured*), botanist
David Bellamy, and doctor Miriam
Stoppard; Brian Glover and Rob
Buckman appeared in later
editions. The première producers
were Kevin Sim, David Taylor, and
Simon Welfare. Fifty-five half-
hour episodes were produced.
Don't Just Sit There (Yorkshire
TV, 1979–80), with the same panel
line-up, followed with nineteen
half-hour episodes.

Fall of Eagles
(BBC-1, 15/3–7/6/74)

This 13-part × 50 mins. series traced the collapse of the three great European dynasties, the Romanovs, the Hohenzollerns, and the Habsburgs. The series covered the nineteenth century and up until the final years of the First World War. Barry Foster appeared as Kaiser Wilhelm, Charles Kay as Tsar Nicholas, Laurence Naismith (*right*) as Emperor Franz Josef and Curt Jurgens as Bismarck; Tony Jay (as Tsar Alexander III; *left*) and Maurice Denham (as Kaiser Wilhelm I; *centre*) also appeared. Stuart Burge produced.

The Family
(BBC-1, 3/4–26/6/74)

A twelve-part documentary serial following, fly-on-the-wall style, the day-to-day life of the Wilkins family of Reading. The BBC film crew, under director Franc Roddam, caught the high notes and downsides of mother Margaret Wilkins, bus conductor father Terry, daughter-in-law Karen, her husband Gary, elder daughter Marion, her boyfriend Tom, youngest daughter Heather, and young son Christopher. Paul Watson produced; cameraman was Philip Bonham-Carter. **The Family: The After Years** (BBC-2, 10/12/83; 40 mins.) portrayed what happened to the Wilkins following their few brief weeks of fame.

Father Brown
(ATV, 1974)

A slow-moving yet graceful whodunit series based on G. K. Chesterton's famous amateur detective Father Brown, played as a wily old sleuth by Kenneth More (*left*; with Dennis Burgess). The 13 eps. × hour series was produced (by Ian Fordyce) with a careful eye to 1920s period detail and costume, but some of the drawn-out plots moved at such a leisurely pace that it was hard to understand how the hero continued to hold an interest in his step-by-step cases. A visual example of the crime literature that Americans term 'English cozies'.

Happy Ever After
(BBC-1, 1974–78)

Featured the long-term professional comedy partnership of Terry Scott and June Whitfield as Terry and June Fletcher (*pictured*), a couple with twenty-five years of marriage behind them. The series developed from a **Comedy Playhouse** segment (tx 7/5/74) written by John Chapman and Eric Merriman, and produced by Peter Whitmore. The half-hour sitcom later became **Terry and June** (BBC-1, 1979–87) and remained popular for several more years. There was also an ITV **Happy Ever After** (ATV, 1969–70), a quite different series presenting a collection of hour-long plays produced by John Cooper.

1974

It Ain't Half Hot, Mum
(BBC-1, 1974–81)

Was another successful sitcom from the writing partnership of Jimmy Perry and producer David Croft, this time featuring the characters that made up the Royal Artillery Concert Party unit of the British army stationed in India during the latter days of the Empire. The 56 eps. × 30 mins. series starred Michael Bates, with the original roll-call consisting of George Layton (*right*), Windsor Davies (*left foreground*), Melvyn Hayes (*2nd right*), Donald Hewlett, Christopher Mitchell, John Clegg, Michael Knowles, Stuart McGugan, Don Estelle, Mike Kinsey (*2nd left*), and Kenneth Macdonald (*left*).

Jennie, Lady Randolph Churchill
(Thames TV, 22/10–3/12/74)

Launched as part of the Churchill centenary celebrations, this 7 eps. × hour series followed the colourful career of American Jennie Jerome (played by Lee Remick; *centre*) from her first meeting with Randolph Churchill (Ronald Pickup; *left*) at Cowes in 1873, to her political campaigning on behalf of Randolph, the quarrel between Randolph and the Prince of Wales, the Boer War, and her launching of an ambitious literary magazine. Andrew Brown produced; Stella Richman was executive producer. Christopher Cazenove (*right*) also appeared as George Cornwallis-West.

Microbes and Men
(BBC-2, 18/9–23/10/74)

A 6-part × 55 mins. drama series on the men who challenged and conquered disease. The series opened with 'The Invisible Enemy', starring Robert Lang as Ignaz Semmelweis, and later presented 'A Germ is Life', 'Men of Little Faith', and 'Certain Death' with Arthur Lowe (*right*; with Stephen McKenna) as Louis Pasteur, and 'The Tuberculin Affair' and 'The Search for the Magic Bullet' with Milo O'Shea as Paul Ehrlich. Peter Goodchild produced.

Moody and Pegg
(Thames TV, 1974–75)

A comedy-drama series that teamed Judy Cornwell (*right*, as Daphne Pegg) and Derek Waring (*left*; as Roland Moody) as an unlikely couple forced to share a London flat; he was a recently divorced antique dealer, she a spinster and civil servant. Two series of 6 eps. × hour were produced by Robert Love and written by Julia Jones and Donald Churchill.

Napoleon and Love
(Thames TV, 1974)

A nine-part series of hour-long plays about the life and loves—such as Desirée Clary (Karen Dotrice) and Josephine (Billie Whitelaw; *left*)—of the young Napoleon Bonaparte (played by Ian Holm; *right*) as he advanced through the military and political ranks of power. Philip Mackie scripted Reginald Collin's production.

218

No—Honestly
(LWT, 1974–75)

A sprightly domestic sitcom starring husband-and-wife team Pauline Collins and John Alderton (*pictured*) as newly married, scatty couple Clara and C.D. Thirteen half-hour episodes were produced by Humphrey Barclay; Lynsey de Paul wrote and performed the theme music. The follow-up, **Yes—Honestly** (LWT, 1976–77; 26 half-hour eps.), featured Donal Donnelly as Matt, a composer, and Liza Goddard as Lily Pond, his new secretary (and later wife). Georgie Fame supplied the theme music this time; Barclay again produced. Terence Brady and Charlotte Bingham scripted both programmes.

Orson Welles Great Mysteries
(Anglia TV, 1974–76)

Offbeat tales ranging from the sinister (Conan Doyle's 'The Leather Funnel') to the mysterious (Stanley Ellin's 'Death of an Old-Fashioned Girl') and featuring a dreamy title sequence with cloak-swirling host Orson Welles. Under producer John Jacobs the 25 eps. × half-hour anthology presented stories based on works by such authors as W. W. Jacobs, Wilkie Collins, Margery Allingham, Somerset Maugham, Dorothy Sayers, and O. Henry. Featured players included Donald Pleasance, Christopher Lee, Susannah York, Peter Cushing, Joan Collins, Victor Buono, Dean Stockwell, and Claire Bloom. The scene pictured is from 'La Grande Breteche' episode with Cushing and York.

The Pallisers
(BBC-2, 19/1–29/6/74; 26/10/74 + 2/11/74)

Was a well-produced 26 eps. × 50 mins. drama series based on the novels of Anthony Trollope concerning Victorian politics and passion. Susan Hampshire (*standing centre*), Philip Latham (*standing right*), and Roland Culver starred in Simon Raven's adaptation for producer Martin Lisemore; Hugh David directed.

Porridge
(BBC-1, 1974–77)

A successful comedy series set in a prison and starring Ronnie Barker (*2nd left*) as the wily Fletcher, an old lag doing time yet again. Brian Wilde, Fulton Mackay (*left*), Richard Beckinsale (*2nd right*), and Brian Glover (*right*) also appeared. The series, created and written by Dick Clement & Ian La Frenais, stemmed from a self-contained episode of Barker's **Seven of One** (BBC-2, 1973) comedy programme called 'Prisoner and Escort' (1/4/73; wr. Clement & La Frenais, pr. Sydney Lotterby), also with Wilde and Mackay. The 18 eps. × 30 mins. series (plus two 40/45-minute specials) was produced by Lotterby. **Going Straight** (BBC-1, 1978) carried on where **Porridge** left off, with the Barker character now released from prison and trying to avoid anything illegal (or at least not getting caught at it). Richard Beckinsale (continuing as Godber) and Patricia Brake (as Fletch's daughter Ingrid) supported; 6 eps. × 30 mins. were produced by Lotterby and written by Clement & La Frenais. Black Lion Films-Witzend produced a feature version, *Porridge*, in 1979 (dir. Dick Clement).

1974

Rising Damp
(Yorkshire TV, 1974–78)

The birth-line of this amusing sitcom was in writer Eric Chappell's 1973 stage play, *The Banana Box*, a comedy about people living in a shabby tenement run by a landlord named Rooksby. This was developed into a TV pilot programme, **Rising Damp** (Yorkshire TV, 2/9/74; pr. Ian MacNaughton), starring Leonard Rossiter (now called Rigsby; *2nd left*), Richard Beckinsale (*left*), Frances de la Tour (*2nd right*), and Don Warrington (*right*), as landlord and tenants of a seedy boarding house catering mainly for students. This in turn became the 26 eps. × half-hour series (plus one half-hour special), directed-produced by Ronnie Baxter. Black Lion Films produced a feature version, also titled *Rising Damp*, in 1980 from a script by Chappell.

South Riding
(Yorkshire TV, 1974)

Set in the summer of 1932, this series delved into the lives of the people of the South Riding of Yorkshire during a period of poverty and change. Starring Dorothy Tutin (*right*), Hermione Baddeley (*left*), and Nigel Davenport (*centre*), Winifred Holtby's story was dramatized by Stan Barstow for producer-director James Ormerod; Alastair Reid directed the thirteen hour-long episodes.

Thick as Thieves
(LWT, 1974)

Superb sitcom scripted by Dick Clement & Ian La Frenais starring John Thaw (*centre*), Bob Hoskins (*left*), and Pat Ashton (*right*). Dobbs (Hoskins) was released from prison after a three-year sentence to arrive home and discover that his old friend and fellow thief, Stan (Thaw), had been living with his wife, Annie (Ashton). The trio were then forced to share an uncomfortable (but nevertheless hilarious) household. Eight half-hour episodes were directed-produced by Derrick Goodwin.

The Top Secret Life of Edgar Briggs
(LWT, 1974)

Starred David Jason (*pictured*) as counter-espionage agent Edgar Briggs, one of the Secret Service's greatest bunglers. Edgar created chaos for thirteen half-hour episodes, in a manner not unlike American TV's accident-prone agent Maxwell Smart (in the **Get Smart** series of the mid-1960s). The series was created and written by Bernard McKenna & Richard Laing (Jason wrote one ep.) and produced by Humphrey Barclay.

Zodiac
(Thames TV, 1974)

A light-hearted thriller series of six hour-long episodes featuring Anton Rodgers (*left*) as Scotland Yard detective David Gradley who teams up with a pretty, young astrologer called Esther Jones (played by Anoushka Hempel; *right*) to solve various mysteries. The series was produced by Jacqueline Davis.

Angels
(BBC-1, 1975–83)

A hospital-based drama serial following the lives of a group of student nurses as they tried to cope with their work at St Angela's hospital, their chaotic personal lives, and each other. The serial was developed by Paula Milne as a kind of gritty, semi-documentary look at the nursing profession, not unlike the form **Z Cars** took with the police. Fiona Fullerton (*3rd left*) and Julie Dawn Cole (*3rd right*) were among the first student arrivals; Shirley Cheriton, Kathryn Apanowicz and Pauline Quirke appeared in later series. Ron Craddock produced 57 eps. × 50 mins.; 97 eps. × 25 mins. were produced by Julia Smith and Ben Rea, respectively. The 25-minute episodes were transmitted twice weekly. Also pictured are (*l. to r.*) Karan David, Lesley Dunlop, Clare Clifford, and Erin Geraghty.

Arena
(BBC-2, 1975–)

Won a series of BAFTA awards for being 'Best Programme Without a Category' during the early 1980s and this term is perhaps the most suitable description for this all-arts-embracing programme. At first the two strands of theatre and art were united under the general **Arena** banner (shown as **Arena: Theatre** from 1/10/75 and **Arena: Art and Design** from 8/10/75), later joined by cinema (**Arena: Cinema** from 22/9/76), television (**Arena: Television**, 17/4/78), and contemporary music (**Arena: Rock**, 24/5/78). The various subheaded programmes were shown in rotation on Wednesday evenings; Alan Yentob was the editorial overseer for the first seven years. Comedian Alexei Sayle is pictured in 'The Private Life of the Ford Cortina' edition.

Celebrity Squares
(ATV, 1975–79; Central TV, 1993–)

Presented the simple game of noughts and crosses as a spectacular, celebrity-populated TV game show where each contestant chose a square and master of ceremonies Bob Monkhouse (*pictured*) asked the celebrity in that square a question; the contestant then had to say whether the celebrity's answer was right or wrong. The show was introduced by the wacky voice of Kenny Everett. The show's format was based on the American NBC TV version called **Hollywood Squares** which had been running since the mid-1960s. Paul Stewart Laing directed and produced the first five series, Glyn Edwards directed and produced the last series. The series was revived in the 1990s and produced by Peter Harris.

The Cuckoo Waltz
(Granada TV, 1975–77; 1980)

A 26 eps. × half-hour comedy series, written by Geoffrey Lancashire, following the fortunes of journalist Chris Hawthorne (played by David Roper) and his down-to-earth wife, Fliss (Diane Keen), as they tried to make ends meet on his meagre salary. Lewis Collins, in an early featured role, played their irritatingly well-off friend, Gavin. The four series were produced by Bill Gilmour, Brian Armstrong, and John G. Temple (last two series). Keen and Roper are pictured with their on-screen twins (played by Joanee and Christopher Oliver).

Days of Hope
(BBC-1, 11/9–2/10/75)

Told the four-part, dramatic story of the conflicts surrounding three people during the period 1916–26. The mini-series was written by Jim Allen, directed by Kenneth Loach, and produced by Tony Garnett; and is perhaps the high-water mark of the Loach and Allen school of naturalism. Paul Copley (*left*; with Alun Armstrong) played Ben Matthews, the son of a Yorkshire farming family, Pamela Brighton was his sister Sarah, and Nikolas Simmonds was her husband Philip Hargreaves. The four parts consisted of '1916: Joining Up' (11/9/75, 95 mins.), '1921' (Black Friday) (18/9/75, 100 mins.), '1924' (the first Labour government) (25/9/75, 80 mins.), and '1926: General Strike' (2/10/75, 135 mins.). Photography was by Tony Pierce-Roberts and John Else.

Edward the Seventh
(ATV, 1/4–1/7/75)

Timothy West starred in this richly mounted period piece, with scripting shared by David Butler and series' director John Gorrie, concerning the conditioning of the future king. Annette Crosbie appeared as the sympathetic Victoria and Robert Hardy was Teutonic Prince Albert. The Cecil Clarke-produced 13-hour series was based on the book *King Edward the Seventh* by Philip Magnus; the programme was retitled for American TV as **The Royal Victorians**. West, as the elderly Edward, is pictured with Moira Redmond (as Mrs Kepple).

Fawlty Towers
(BBC-2, 1975; 1979)

John Cleese's gift to television situation comedy, in two series of 6 eps. × 30/35 mins., undoubtedly stands as BBC TV's finest and funniest programme of the 1970s. Cleese (*left*), together with Connie Booth, wrote the entire series, which featured an ill-mannered Torquay hotelier with a compulsive desire verbally to brutalize his guests; he also appeared in the role of Basil Fawlty and Booth played the waitress Polly. Prunella Scales played Basil's no-nonsense wife Sybil and Andrew Sachs (*right*) was the hotel's unfortunate Spanish waiter, Manuel. The first series (19/9–24/10/75) was produced by John Howard Davies; the second series (19/2–26/3/79) was produced by Douglas Argent. The last episode of the final series was not transmitted until 25/10/79 due to an industrial dispute.

Get Some In!
(Thames TV, 1975–78)

Life in the mid-1950s RAF during the days of compulsory National Service was the theme of this sitcom series. The bunch of reluctant recruits were represented by David Janson (*left*), Gerard Ryder, Robert Lindsay (*right*; before he became **Citizen Smith**), and Brian Pettifer. Tony Selby was their barking-dog Corporal. The series was written by John Esmonde & Bob Larbey. Michael Mills directed-produced the thirty-four half-hour episodes; there was also a Christmas special, 'Christmas at the Camp' (25/12/75), directed-produced by Robert Reed.

The Good Life
(BBC-1, 1975–78)

Was one of the television comedy hits of the 1970s, featuring Richard Briers (*2nd left*) as Tom Good, a middle-aged draughtsman who gave up his comfortable job to live a self-sufficient life (utilizing his small back garden) in Surbiton. Involved in his hit-and-miss endeavours were his patient wife, Barbara (Felicity Kendal; *left*), and the class-conscious next-door neighbours, Jerry Leadbeatter (Paul Eddington; *right*) and wife Margo (Penelope Keith; *2nd right*). The series was created and written by the team of John Esmonde & Bob Larbey. John Howard Davies produced the 28 eps. × 30 mins. series; also two specials (tx 26/12/77 and 10/6/78).

The Growing Pains of PC Penrose
(BBC-1, 1975)

Was a comedy series set in a small Yorkshire town about a young, probationary police officer, PC Penrose (Paul Greenwood; *left*), who was taken under the fatherly wing of the craggy Sgt. Flagg (Bryan Pringle; *right*). The Roy Clarke-scripted series of 7 eps. × 30 mins. was produced by Douglas Argent. The Penrose character, nicknamed Rosie, returned for a further series of domestic misadventures in **Rosie** (BBC-1, 1977–81), with Paul Greenwood starring in 27 eps. × 30 mins. Clarke supplied the scripts for producer Bernard Thompson.

The Hanged Man
(Yorkshire TV, 15/2–5/4/75)

Followed the tarot card definition (and symbol) of a person being in a state of conversion, in this case one Lew Burnett (played by Colin Blakely; *shown*), whose international construction industry background had created many enemies; one or more of whom had already made three attempts on his life. At the third attempt he decided to stay 'dead' so that he could find out who was after him, and why. Michael Williams, Gary Watson, and Jack Watson were among the suspects. The series was created and written by Edmund Ward and co-produced (with Ward) by Marc Miller. Eight hour-long episodes were presented. A spin-off series, **Turtle's Progress** (ATV, 1979–80; pr. Joan Brown and Nicholas Palmer), featured two small-time crooks who had stolen a hoard of safe deposit boxes.

It's a Lovely Day Tomorrow
(ATV, 8/10/75)

A disaster drama-documentary, based on the memories of survivors, re-creating a tragic wartime (3 March 1943) incident in which 173 people died of asphyxiation when a panicked crowd stampeded and fell in a crush in London's East End Bethnal Green underground station. Bernard Kops's 70-minute script focused on the Bell family, Mario Renzullo as the son, Ray Mort and Marjorie Yates as the parents, Cheryl Kennedy the sister, and Liz Smith as the granny of the family. Anton Furst designed; photography was by Chris Menges. John Goldschmidt was director-producer.

Jim'll Fix It
(BBC-1, 1975–)

A popular children's show that claimed 'whatever your wildest dream, Jimmy Savile will try to make it come true'. The kids wrote in (in their thousands) with their requests, ranging from being a lion-tamer in a circus to piloting the Concorde, and the cigar-chomping Jimmy Savile (*pictured, left*) made it happen for them. Original producer was Roger Ordish.

Johnny Go Home
(Yorkshire TV, 22/7/75)

A 2-hour documentary on the true story of two runaway children, Annie (aged 10) and Tommy Wylie (aged 14; *pictured*), who headed for London where they ended up sleeping rough on the streets. Director-producer John Willis's documentary on the squalor of homeless young people and exposure of the people who prey on them made newspaper headlines, prompted a parliamentary debate, and set off a major investigation by the Department of Health and Social Security. Yorkshire TV followed with an updated version, **What Happened to Johnny Go Home** (18/11/75; dir.-pr. Willis), which looked forward to solving the problems of homeless children. John Fairley & Michael Deakin were executive producers.

The Naked Civil Servant
(Thames TV, 17/12/75)

This dramatized television film portrait of effeminate homosexual Quentin Crisp (played by John Hurt) was based on his autobiography and told the story of his life from the late 1920s to the mid-1970s; and of his efforts to achieve acceptance of his right to lead his life without harassment or humiliation. Liz Gebhardt, Patricia Hodge, John Rhys-Davies, and Lloyd Lamble also appeared. Quentin Crisp himself introduced the 1½-hour film. Jack Gold directed Philip Mackie's dramatization for producer Barry Hanson.

Nightingale's Boys
(Granada TV, 1975)

Derek Farr (*pictured*) starred as the ageing schoolmaster Bill Nightingale, nearing retirement, who reflects on how the high point of his career, his old class of 1949, turned out. The 7 eps. × hour series was written by Arthur Hopcraft, C. P. Taylor, Jack Rosenthal, Colin Spencer, John Finch, and Alexander Baron; and directed by Richard Everitt, Les Chatfield, Peter Plummer, Roger Tucker, and June Howson for producer Brian Armstrong.

Poldark
(BBC-1, 1975–77)

Based on Winston Graham's four Poldark novels (written in the 1940s and early 1950s), this romantic drama was set in the eighteenth century and the wilds of Cornwall, and followed ten years in the life of the young hero, Ross Poldark (played by Robin Ellis; *left*). Angharad Rees (*right*) played Demelza and Ralph Bates was George Warleggan. The 29 eps. × 50/55 mins. serial was produced by Morris Barry and Tony Coburn for BBC Birmingham.

Quiller
(BBC-1, 1975)

Was the code-name for a troubleshooter who worked for a clandestine government agency known as 'the Bureau' in this 13 eps. × 50 mins. espionage drama starring Michael Jayston (*pictured*). Supporting players were Moray Watson and Sinead Cusack. The series was based on the character created by Elleston Trevor (writing as Adam Hall) in a series of espionage novels published since the mid-1960s. The series was produced by Peter Graham Scott.

Rutland Weekend Television
(BBC-2, 1975–76)

Eric Idle's madcap, half-hour series which presented 'mini-spectacular programmes' from Britain's smallest television network. Neil Innes (who also supplied the music), David Battley (*centre*), Henry Woolf (*left*), and Gwen Taylor helped run RWT. Idle (pictured, *right*, teaching viewers to 'Ski In Your Home') scripted for producer Ian Keill. From **RWT** came **The Rutles** (BBC-2, 27/3/78; wr. Idle, dir. Gary Weiss and Idle), presenting the semi-legendary life story of the 'pre-fab four', Dirk, Nasty, Stig, and Barry. The 65-minute programme, with guests Michael Palin, Neil Innes, Mick Jagger, and Ron Wood, featured such Rutlemania hits as 'A Hard Day's Rut', 'All You Need is Lunch', and 'W. C. Fields Forever'.

Space: 1999
(ITC, 1975–77)

A sizeable fragment of the Moon is explosively cast off into deep space following a nuclear build-up, with the surviving land mass containing a colony (Moonbase Alpha) of Earth people (later also a shape-changing alien) who go on to become reluctant inter-stellar explorers. The shifting cast headlined Martin Landau (*centre*; as Moonbase Commander John Keonig), Barbara Bain (*right*), Barry Morse (*left*), Nick Tate, Zienia Merton, Anton Phillips, Catherine Schell (as alien Maya), and Tony Anholt. A series more conscious of keeping up with 1970s fashion than delivering on-screen imagination, the 48 eps. × hour were produced by Sylvia Anderson (1st series) and Fred Freiberger (2nd series), and created by Gerry and Sylvia Anderson. Director Charles Crichton was particularly active during the programme's first series.

The Squirrels
(ATV, 1975–77)

A half-hour sitcom about the in-fighting office staff in the accounts department of a television hire firm, International Rentals. Featured players were Bernard Hepton (*centre*), Ken Jones (*left*), Patsy Rowlands, Alan David, Ellis Jones, and Karin MacCarthy (*right*). The Eric Chappell scripts were produced by Shaun O'Riordan.

The Stars Look Down
(Granada TV, 4/9–27/11/75)

Was adapted by Alan Plater from A. J. Cronin's best-selling novel of the north-east, torn by the violence and industrial unrest of 1910. A large cast featured Avril Elgar (*pictured*), Norman Jones, James Bate, Rod Culbertson, Ian Hastings, Alun Armstrong, Basil Dignam, and Anne Raitt. Roland Joffe directed Howard Baker's 13 eps. × hour production.

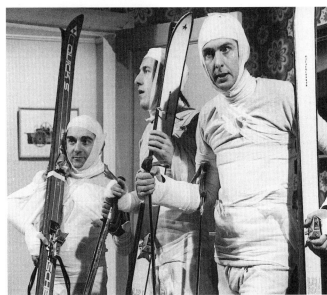

1975

The Survivors
(BBC-1, 1975–77)

Was a science-fantasy drama series about a random group of people (mainly in the middle-class bracket) who were left after a global disaster, a great epidemic, and who struggled to make contact with other surviving groups around the country. The 38 eps. × 50 mins. programme was created by Terry Nation and produced by Terence Dudley: (*l. to r.*) Lucy Fleming, Carolyn Seymour, Ian McCulloch; Stephen Dudley and Tanya Ronder were among the original group; later Denis Lill, Lorna Lewis, and John Abineri became the central characters.

The Sweeney
(Thames TV–Euston Films, 1975–76; 1978)

Screaming tyres and blasting shotguns were the mark of this crime series featuring a trio of Scotland Yard Flying Squad officers, played by John Thaw (*right*; as Det. Insp. Regan), Dennis Waterman (*left*; Det. Sgt. Carter), and, their boss, Garfield Morgan (Det. Chief Insp. Haskins). The hour-long series, full of tough language, sweeping action, and accurate location photography, developed from an **Armchair Cinema** entry ('Regan', 4/6/74) written by Ian Kennedy Martin. Fifty-three episodes were produced by Ted Childs. Two original feature films also evolved from the series: *Sweeney!* (1976) and *Sweeney 2* (1978).

Trinity Tales
(BBC-2, 21/11–26/12/75)

Alan Plater's excellent updating of Chaucer's *Canterbury Tales*, modernizing the pilgrimage into six tall stories told by a group of Rugby League supporters travelling in a minibus on their way to the final at Wembley. The travellers consisted of (*l. to r.*) Eric the Prologue (Francis Matthews), Dave the Joiner (Paul Copley), Judy the Judy (Susan Littler), Nick the Driver (Colin Farrell), Smith the Man of Law (John Stratton), Stan the Fryer (Bill Maynard), and Alice the Wife of Batley (Gaye Brown). The 6 eps. × 50 mins. were directed by Tristan de Vere Cole for David Rose's BBC Birmingham production.

Two's Company
(LWT, 1975–79)

Teamed American actress Elaine Stritch, as London-based American thriller writer Dorothy McNab, and Donald Sinden, as Robert, her extremely English butler, in this 29 eps. × half-hour sitcom which attempted to exploit the social side of the UK–USA divide. Bill MacIlwraith scripted; Stuart Allen and Humphrey Barclay produced. The title **Two's Company** had earlier headed a half-hour comedy series produced by Granada TV in 1956 and starred Libby Morris and Dick Emery with Kenneth Connor.

Wodehouse Playhouse
(BBC-1, 1975–78; 20 eps. × 30/35 mins.)

Presented three series of plays based on P. G. Wodehouse short stories, with John Alderton and Pauline Collins appearing as various characters throughout the series. The stories were adapted by David Climie and produced by David Askey (1st series), Michael Mills (2nd series), and Gareth Gwenlan (3rd series). Pictured are Alderton and Collins in 'The Truth About George' episode.

Beasts
(ATV, 1976)

A collection of six-hour-long stories of a supernatural flavour created and written by Nigel Kneale: 'Special Offer' (16/10/76), 'During Barty's Party' (23/10/76), 'Buddyboy' (30/10/76), 'Baby' (6/11/76), 'What Big Eyes' (13/11/76), and 'The Dummy' (20/11/76). Nicholas Palmer produced. The scene pictured is from the film studio-located story 'The Dummy', with Simon Oates (*left*) and Clive Swift (*right*).

Bill Brand
(Thames TV, 1976)

Trevor Griffiths's straight-to-the-point drama series about a young working-class lecturer, Bill Brand (played by Jack Shepherd; *left*), whose controversial views in community politics made his path to Westminster an uneven climb in a socially and politically closed-circuit network. Eleven one-hour episodes were produced by Stuart Burge.

Bouquet of Barbed Wire
(LWT, 9/1–20/2/76)

Was adapted from her own novel by Andrea Newman and concerned the tangled sexual relationships of a middle-class family on the verge of breaking apart. The 7 eps. × hour mini-series featured Frank Finlay (*left*), Susan Penhaligon (*right*), James Aubrey, and Sheila Allen. The series was directed-produced by Tony Wharmby. **Another Bouquet** (LWT, 7/1–18/2/77) followed as a 7 eps. × hour sequel, also scripted by Newman, with Finlay, Allen, and Aubrey resuming their earlier roles. John Frankau was director-producer.

1976

Brief Encounter
(ATV, 4/1/76)

Noel Coward's play, *Still Life*, was remade (after the 1946 feature) as a TV movie starring Sophia Loren and Richard Burton (*pictured*). The soapy romantic sufferings of a middle-aged couple trapped in boring marriages was more the stuff of daytime programming than prime-time scheduling. Jack Hedley, Rosemary Leach, and John Le Mesurier co-starred. The TV film was first telecast in 1974 under American NBC TV's **Hallmark Hall of Fame** banner. Alan Bridges directed John Bowen's 90-minute screenplay for producer Cecil Clarke. Production credits give Carlo Ponti-Cecil Clarke Prods. and FCB Prods. as producing company.

The Crezz
(Thames TV, 1976)

Featured twelve light-hearted, hour-long, soap-style plays about the inhabitants of the fictitious Carlisle Crescent in London. Joss Ackland, Isla Blair, Peter Bowles, Hugh Burden, Nicholas Ball (*pictured, right*), Janet Kay (*left*), and Elspet Gray led the cast. Writers included Clive Exton (who also devised the series), John Wells, and Willis Hall. Paul Knight produced.

The Dame of Sark
(Anglia TV, 29/12/76)

Celia Johnson (*right*) was Sybil Hathaway, the British ruler of the Channel Island of Sark, in this dramatized story of the woman who fought for the survival and the dignity of her people under German occupation during the Second World War. Peter Dyneley (*centre*; as her American husband), Simon Cadell, and Tony Britton (*left*; as Count von Schmettau, the German commandant) co-starred. The hour-long play (by William Douglas Home) was adapted by David Butler and directed by Alvin Rakoff for producer John Jacobs.

Dickens of London
(Yorkshire TV, 28/9–12/12/76)

The story of novelist Charles Dickens, from his childhood under the spell of his prodigal father to his latter years of disillusionment and ill-health. The 13 eps. × hour series, starring Roy Dotrice (*pictured, right*) as Dickens, was written by Wolf Mankowitz and directed-produced by Marc Miller. Also pictured are Simon Bell as Dickens the boy and Gene Foad as Dickens the young man.

The Duchess of Duke Street
(BBC-1, 1976–77)

Set in Edwardian London and based on the real-life Rosa Lewis of the Cavendish Hotel, producer John Hawkesworth's 31 eps. × 50/55 mins. series featured Gemma Jones (*right*) as Louisa Trotter, a Cockney kitchenmaid who rose to become a famous cook, mistress of the Prince of Wales, and proprietress of the Bentinck Hotel, Duke Street. Christopher Cazenove, Donald Burton (*left*), and John Cater also appeared. The series captured the audience that had followed Hawkesworth's earlier serial drama, **Upstairs, Downstairs**.

228

The Fall and Rise of Reginald Perrin
(BBC-1, 1976–79)

Was author David Nobbs's caricaturing of mindless habit and the business world, in this case illustrated through the hilarious actions of Reginald Perrin (Leonard Rossiter; *left*) as he quits his home, his wife, and his boring routine in a jelly factory to take to the road in a new identity. Pauline Yates (*right*) was his understanding wife Elizabeth, John Barron his dreadful self-made boss C. J., and Sue Nicholls his office secretary Joan. The three series of 21 eps. × 30 mins. were produced by John Howard Davies (1st series) and Gareth Gwenlan. The programme was based on Nobbs's own book, *The Death of Reginald Perrin*.

The Feathered Serpent
(Thames TV, 21/6–26/7/76; 3/4–8/5/78)

Murder, intrigue, and human sacrifice was the theme of these two Children's Programme series of 6 eps. × half-hour set in ancient Mexico. Patrick Troughton starred as evil priest Nasca, with Diane Keen (*pictured*) as Empress Chimalma, supported by Brian Deacon, Robert Gary, Richard Willis, and Sheila Burrell. John Kane scripted for producer-director Vic Hughes; Hughes and Stan Woodward directed.

The Fosters
(LWT, 1976–77)

Although originally billed as a 'sparkling new comedy series' about life in a typical south London black family, the format of the series (along with a generous quantity of original scripts) was acquired from a Norman Lear-produced CBS TV sitcom called **Good Times** which had premièred on American television in 1974. The LWT version, produced and directed by Stuart Allen, starred Norman Beaton and Isabelle Lucas as Samuel and Pearl Foster, Lenny Henry and Lawrie Mark as their sons Sonny and Benjamin, and Sharon Rosita as teenage daughter Shirley; Carmen Munro was their busybody neighbour, Vilma. There were 26 eps. × half-hour produced. Pictured (*l. to r.*) are Munro, Mark, Henry, Lucas (*foreground*), Beaton, and Rosita.

Gangsters
(BBC-1, 1976; 1978)

Featured some of the fastest, roughest, violent action (as stylized realism) on television in the 1970s. It also featured a stunning plot line involving a multiracial underworld network, set around the Birmingham area, of gang wars, drug and immigrant smuggling, prostitution, and undercover narcotics agents. The 12 eps. × 50/55 mins. series stemmed from Philip Martin's 110-minute play for **Play for Today** (BBC-1, 9/1/75; dir. Philip Saville, pr. Barry Hanson) starring Maurice Colbourne (*right*) as London villain John Kline, Ahmed Khalil (*left*; as agent Khan), Elizabeth Cassidy, Saeed Jaffrey, Paul Antrim, and Paul Barber. The series was produced by David Rose for BBC Birmingham and directed by Alastair Reid. Music was composed by Dave Greenslade.

1976

The Glittering Prizes
(BBC-2, 21/1–25/2/76)

Novelist Frederic Raphael's series of six outstanding television plays following a group of Cambridge students from their youthful days in the early 1950s, through individual successes and failures, to middle age in the mid-1970s. The six 80-minute plays starred Tom Conti and Barbara Kellermann (*shown*). Waris Hussein and Robert Knights directed three of the plays each for producer Mark Shivas. **Oxbridge Blues** (BBC-2, 14/11–19/12/84) was Raphael's return to multi-part TV with this series of seven plays, adapted from his own short stories, published as *Sleeps Six* and *Oxbridge Blues*; James Cellan Jones produced-directed.

I, Claudius
(BBC-2, 20/9–6/12/76)

Writer Jack Pulman's serialization of the novels of Robert Graves (*I, Claudius* and *Claudius the God*) presented a riveting history of ancient imperial Rome as told in flashback by the wily 'fool, idiot and stammerer' Claudius (portrayed by Derek Jacobi; *left*). This perception of history as a combination of dangerous farce, bloodbath, and perpetual duplicity was symbolized perfectly via the slithering snake featured over the programme's opening titles. The excellent cast also included Brian Blessed (as Caesar Augustus), Sian Phillips (as Livia), George Baker (*right*; as Tiberius), and John Hurt (*centre*; as Caligula). The twelve episodes were directed by Herbert Wise for Martin Lisemore's lively production.

Multi-Coloured Swap Shop
(BBC-1, 1976–81)

Was a Saturday morning children's show linking cartoons and pop/sports star interviews with a nation-wide swap of any item (as long as it was not a kid brother for a sister, or a budgie for a vulture!). Noel Edmonds (*right*) presented, with Keith Chegwin (*left*) and Maggie Philbin; John Craven presented a 'News Swap'. Next came **The Late Late Breakfast Show** (BBC-1, 1982–86), a 40-minute Saturday early evening programme with Edmonds presenting a mixed-bag collection of youngster interests and antics, including a hazardous stunts section which, unfortunately, resulted in the death of a 25 year old and pulled the final curtain on the programme.

The Muppet Show
(ATV/Central TV, 1976–81)

Presented a high-speed half-hour of slapstick, songs, and sketches performed by a company of ingeniously crafted puppets created by Jim Henson. Each programme spotlighted a human guest who became trapped in the Muppets' mad routines and usually ended up a foil to such crazed creatures as Kermit the Frog, Fozzie Bear, The Great Gonzo, Wayne and Wanda, Animal, Statler and Waldorf, and the highly explosive Miss Piggy. Scripts were provided by Jack Burns, Marc London, Henson, and Jerry Juhl; Jack Burns also produced. Henson followed his Muppets success with **Fraggle Rock** (TVS, 1984–89), featuring more bizarre puppet creatures known as the Fraggles, who inhabited an unknown portion of the south coast on which stood an old lighthouse kept by the Captain (played by Fulton Mackay). Duncan Kenworthy produced. Four feature films were developed from the Muppet series: *The Muppet Movie* (1979), *The Great Muppet Caper* (1981), *The Muppets Take Manhattan* (1984), and *Muppet Christmas Carol* (1992). The Kermit and Miss Piggy characters are pictured.

Open All Hours
(BBC-2, 1976; 1981–82)

Ronnie Barker (*left*) was the mean, bullying corner-shop keeper Arkwright in this comedy series written by Roy Clarke. Between cheating his customers and counting his money Arkwright found time to intimidate his youthful assistant, Granville (David Jason; *centre*), and make passes at buxom Nurse Gladys Emmanuel (Lynda Baron; *right*). Sydney Lotterby produced.

Rock Follies
(Thames TV, 24/2–30/3/76)

Writer Howard Schuman's sour-taste account of the fortunes of three girls who join together to front a rock band was, between belting out large doses of Andy Mackays's music, a cynical descent into the world of the music business. (*r. to l.*) Charlotte Cornwell (as Anna), Julie Covington (as Dee), and Rula Lenska (as 'Q') featured as the rock trio The Little Ladies; Emlyn Price appeared as their novice manager. Six hour-long episodes were produced. The Little Ladies returned the following year in **Rock Follies of '77** (Thames TV, 4–18/5/77; 22/11–6/12/77), still mired in the deep end of the rock 'n' roll biz with little hope of moving up the success slope. Andrew Brown produced both series; the sequel was transmitted in two instalments of three episodes.

Rogue Male
(BBC-2–20th Century Fox TV, 22/9/76)

An excellent television version of author Geoffrey Household's 1939 thriller about a sporty English gentleman whose failed attempt to assassinate Hitler in Austria finds him pursued back to rural England by fanatical Nazis. Peter O'Toole (*pictured*) starred as Sir Robert Hunter, the would-be assassin, with John Standing, Alastair Sim, Cyd Hayman, Harold Pinter, and Maureen Lipman filling out the cast. The 100-minute telefilm was scripted by Frederic Raphael and directed by Clive Donner for Mark Shivas's production; photography was by Brian Tufano.

Sailor
(BBC-1, 5/8–7/10/76)

A documentary series of 10 eps. × 30 mins. offering a frank account of life on the ocean wave in one of the Royal Navy's ships, in this case HMS *Ark Royal*. Photography was by Patrick Turley. John Purdie produced. In a similar vein, **Fighter Pilot** (BBC-1, 9/9–28/10/81) presented a series of 8 eps. × 30 mins. which followed the fortunes of the young men who were trained to fly the fast jets of the Royal Air Force. Colin Strong produced.

1976/7

Second Verdict
(BBC-1, 27/5–1/7/76)

Stratford Johns and Frank Windsor returned as Detective Chief Superintendents Barlow and Watt in a series of 6 eps. × 50 mins. to reinvestigate crimes from the past, using their normal techniques to collect and examine evidence. Among the great criminal mysteries they looked at were 'The Lindbergh Kidnapping' (27/5/76), 'Who Killed the Princes in the Tower?' (3/6/76), and 'Lizzie Borden' (24/6/76; with Rosemary Leach, *pictured*). Leonard Lewis produced.

The Water Margin
(BBC-2, tx 1976–78)

Was a free-wheeling, fighting-and-magic adaptation of the Chinese classic written by Lo Kuan-chung in the fourteenth century; David Weir wrote the scripts from the translations of the Japanese screenplays. The general theme was that a thousand years ago, in China, the souls of 108 knights were reborn to fight the tyranny and corruption of the government. Atsuo Nakamura (*pictured*) starred as the hero Lin Chung. In the English version, voices were dubbed by Michael McClain, Miriam Margolyes, and Burt Kwouk, among others, and Michael Bakewell directed; Toshio Masuda was the original director of the NTV, Tokyo production. Another Japanese (NTV–Kokusai Hoei) adventure production shown on BBC TV, **Monkey** (BBC-2, tx 1979–81), featured the pilgrimage of a young Buddhist priest and his companions and was based on the sixteenth-century book, itself based on an ancient Chinese legend, written by Wu Ch'eng-en. The English adaptation was by Weir and the English version was directed (for World Wide Sound London) by Bakewell; Yusuke Watanabe was the original director.

When the Boat Comes In
(BBC-1, 1976–77; 1981)

James Mitchell's saga of cobblestone life in South Shields during the economic depression of the 1920s featured James Bolam (*right*) as jack-the-lad Jack Ford and Susan Jameson (*left*) as the unworldly Jessie Seaton in this 51 eps. × 50 mins. series. Leonard Lewis, Andrew Osborn, and David Maloney produced, respectively.

The XYY Man
(Granada TV, 1976–77)

Was cat burglar Spider Scott (Stephen Yardley; *pictured*), a man with a genetic defect in his chromosomes that, theoretically, gave him criminal inclinations. The character was introduced in a three-part serial (3–17/7/76; adapted by Ivor Marshall from the novel by Kenneth Royce, dir. Ken Grieve) in which he was recruited for a job by British Intelligence. The following year Richard Everitt produced a further ten hour-long episodes, also with Yardley.

All You Need Is Love
(LWT–Theatre Projects, 12/2–4/6/77)

Ambitious 17 parts × hour survey of the history of popular music devised and directed by Tony Palmer. The programme traced pop music's social, musical, and commercial origins from its African roots to the seventeenth segment subtitled 'New Directions' (featuring, among others, Black Oak Arkansas, Manfred Mann, Stomu Yamash'ta, and Mike Oldfield). Other segments, from ragtime and jazz through to glitter rock, also presented multiple interviews and performance footage (gathered through newsreels and *March of Time* stock): Irving Berlin, Scott Joplin, Hoagy Carmichael, Charlie Parker, Bessie Smith, Billie Holiday, Edith Piaf, Judy Garland, Al Jolson, Lorenz Hart, Artie Shaw, Buddy Rich, Stevie Wonder, The Supremes, Tex Ritter, Minnie Pearl, Woody Guthrie, the Andrews Sisters, Elvis Presley, Carl Perkins, The Beatles, The Beach Boys, Frank Zappa, Jimi Hendrix (*pictured*), David Bowie, and Bob Marley and The Wailers were among those featured. The series, co-financed by EMI Films and Phonogram, was produced by Richard Pilbrow and Neville C. Thompson.

Citizen Smith
(BBC-1, 1977–80)

Robert Lindsay (*pictured*) was Wolfie Smith, the self-elected Che Guevara of the Tooting Popular Front, a small-change political movement, in this John Sullivan-scripted comedy series. Wolfie's comrades were Mike Grady, Tony Millan, George Sweeney, and Cheryl Hall as his girlfriend Shirley. In all 28 eps. × 30 mins. were produced by Dennis Main Wilson (3 series) and Ray Butt (final series). A prototype episode (12/4/77; wr. Sullivan, pr. Peter Whitmore) was shown as a part of **Comedy Special** (BBC-1, 5/4–3/5/77).

Count Dracula
(BBC-2, 22/12/77)

Bram Stoker's Gothic romance was presented as a wild, hallucinatory journey through nightmarish images bordering on the off-the-wall visual antics usually associated with rock promo productions; a surreal blending of film and video effects. Louis Jourdan (*pictured*; with Judi Bowker) was the title character, supported by Frank Finlay (as Van Helsing), Susan Penhaligon (as Lucy), Mark Burns, and Jack Shepherd (as Renfield). Gerald Savory adapted the 155-minute production; Philip Saville directed for producer Morris Barry. Production was designed by Michael Young.

Don't Forget to Write!
(BBC-2, 18/4–23/5/77; 18/1–22/2/79)

Writer Charles Wood's excellent comic-drama series about a none-too-successful playwright, Gordon Maple (George Cole; *left*), who is plagued by an assortment of trivial—on occasion not so trivial—problems in his professional life; although he appeared to make most of his money writing films which were never made he still had to deal with impossible film producers. Gwen Watford played his wife, Mabel, and Francis Matthews (*right*) was Tom Lawrence, a friend who happened to be a rather more successful playwright. Two series of 6 eps. × 50 mins. were produced by Joe Waters. The series originated from an earlier, one-off play, 'A Bit of a Holiday' (1/12/69; wr. Wood, dir. Marc Miller; also starring Cole and Watford), produced as a part of **The Root of All Evil** (Yorkshire TV, 1968–69) plays.

Dummy
(ATV, 9/11/77)

A harrowing dramatized documentary telling the true story of 'Sandra X' (played by Geraldine James; *pictured*), a young, deaf girl who, after undergoing years of special treatment, was rejected by society and forced into backstreet prostitution. The 90-minute film was written by Hugh Whitemore and directed-produced by Franc Roddam; camera work was by Chris Menges and Mike Nunn edited.

The Eagle of the Ninth
(BBC-1, 4/9–9/10/77)

Some time during AD 117, the Ninth Roman Legion, the Hispana, marched north from their station at Eburacum (where York now stands) to deal with tribal uprisings in Caledonia. They were never seen again. This 6 eps. × 30 mins. series featured a Roman soldier, played by Anthony Higgins (*pictured*), whose father had been with the Ninth, setting off in search of the legion and their eagle standard. Dramatized by Bill Craig, the series was based on Rosemary Sutcliff's 1954 book; Pharic MacLaren produced for BBC Scotland.

Hard Times
(Granada TV, 25/10–15/11/77)

Was the Charles Dickens story of young Louisa Gradgrind (Jacqueline Tong; *left*) who struggles to overcome a childhood lacking in beauty and imagination in Coketown (an amalgam of the cities of the Industrial Revolution) when a circus comes to town and draws a sharp contrast to the grim factory life. Patrick Allen (*right*), Timothy West, Edward Fox, Rosalie Crutchley, and Alan Dobie led the cast. Arthur Hopcraft adapted the four hour-long episodes for producer Peter Eckersley; John Irvin directed. The series was co-produced with WNET New York.

The Krypton Factor
(Granada TV, 1977–)

Is a contest of personality, endurance, and intelligence to find the 'Super Person of Great Britain'. With the prize of a (sort of self-congratulatory) Krypton Factor Trophy at the end of the line, presenter Gordon Burns tested the candidates for intelligence and physical ability (the latter over a military obstacle course), including observation and general knowledge. In 1988 Granada introduced a junior version, **Young Krypton**, presented by Ross King. Gordon Burns is pictured presenting the international edition, challenged in 1981 by the American version of the game show.

Marie Curie
(BBC-2, 16/8–13/9/77)

Jane Lapotaire (*left*) starred as Marie Curie and Nigel Hawthorne (*right*) as her husband, Pierre, in Elaine Morgan's 5 eps. × 55 mins. serial on the life and work of the Nobel Prize-winning discoverer of radium; the story spanned the period from 1886 to 1911. John Glenister directed for producer Peter Goodchild; incidental music was by Carl Davis.

Mind Your Language
(LWT, 1977–79)

Was a half-hour sitcom revolving around a language-school teacher, Jeremy Brown (Barry Evans; *left foreground*), and his polyglot class of national stereotypes (portrayed with good humour by Dino Shafeek, George Caliller, *right*, Kevork Malikyan, *centre*, Robert Lee, Jacki Harding, Jamila Massey, Ricardo Montez, Albert Moses, Françoise Pascal, and Pik-Sen Lim). Twenty-nine episodes were produced by Stuart Allen; Vince Powell scripted.

Murder Most English
(BBC-2, 8/5–19/6/77)

Subtitled 'A Flaxborough Chronicle', author Colin Watson's delightfully nasty sense of humour emerged in this 7 eps. × 50 mins. comic-mystery series featuring Det. Insp. Purbright (Anton Rodgers, *right*, with John Comer) of Flaxborough CID as he policed the fictitious region the author (in his books) had referred to as 'a high-spirited town . . . Like Gomorrah'. Richard Harris dramatized the stories (which Watson had been writing since the late 1950s) for producer Martin Lisemore; Ronald Wilson directed.

1990
(BBC-2, 1977–78)

Was a late 1970s production set in an imaginary future where bureaucracy has run riot and the country is under the ruthless administration of the PCD (the Department of Public Control). It was also creator-writer Wilfred Greatorex's personal, disturbing vision of a near future, beyond Orwell's *1984* gloom-casting, where such identifiable frustrations as government red tape and VAT men had evolved into an all-powerful bureaucracy. Edward Woodward (*left*; with Lisa Harrow) appeared as Jim Kyle, a subversive journalist working against the PCD, which was controlled by Herbert Skardon (Robert Lang). Prudence Fitzgerald produced the 16 eps. × 50/55 mins. series. The 1978 series of eight episodes was programmed as **Drama 2: 1990**.

The Norman Conquests
(Thames TV, 1977)

Playwright Alan Ayckbourn's successful trilogy of comedies that viewed the same weekend of domestic discord between three couples from different vantage points: 'Table Manners' (5/10/77), 'Living Together' (12/10/77), and 'Round and Round the Garden' (19/10/77). The cast consisted of (*l. to r.*) Richard Briers, Tom Conti, Penelope Wilton, David Troughton, and Penelope Keith; Fiona Walker, not pictured, also appeared. Herbert Wise directed for producers Verity Lambert and David Susskind.

Parosi
(BBC-1, 1977–78)

A series of 26 × 15 mins. programmes in Hindustani and English telling the story of two Asian families living in Britain. The première cast included (*l. to r.*) Roshan Seth, Indira Joshi, and Nabeel Gul; Soni Razdan and Paul Satvendar also appeared. The Sunday morning transmitted series was produced by Robert Clamp.

Philby, Burgess and Maclean
(Granada TV, 31/5/77)

A well-received dramatic retelling of the infamous roles played by three British double-agents in stealing A-bomb secrets from the West for the Soviets. Anthony Bate appeared as Kim Philby, Derek Jacobi (*right*) as Guy Burgess, and Michael Culver (*left*) as Donald Maclean; Richard Hurndall, Patrick Holt, Elizabeth Seal, and Arthur Lowe supported. The 90-minute play was written by Ian Curteis and directed by Gordon Flemyng.

Play of the Week
(BBC-2, 1977–79)

The opening play of this notable collection was Tom Stoppard's 'Professional Foul' (21/9/77), about an English visitor (played by Peter Barkworth, pictured with co-star Stephen Rea, *right*) to Prague who gets caught up in the struggle for human rights; directed by Michael Lindsay-Hogg. The series followed up with such outstanding contributions as 'The Sinking of HMS *Victoria*' (12/10/77), written by James Warner Bellah and Donald Macintyre, directed by Leonard Lewis; Dornford Yates's 'She Fell Among Thieves' (1/3/78), scripted by Tom Sharpe and directed by Clive Donner; and the trilogy 'The Lost Boys' (11–18–25/10/78), written by Andrew Birkin and starring Ian Holm (as J. M. Barrie); Rodney Bennett directed for producer Louis Marks. **Play of the Week** was also the title of an ITV collection of plays that was networked by Associated-Rediffusion during 1956–67. During the programme's early years feature films (such as *Under the Red Robe* and *Dark Journey*) were slotted into the series but the main stream of individual plays contained such delights as Gerald Savory's adaptation of the James M. Cain novel 'Double Indemnity' (Granada TV, 29/3/60), with Donald Pleasance (as Keyes), William Sylvester (as Walter Huff), and Madeleine Sherwood (as Phyllis), directed by Cliff Owen; John Arden's 'Serjeant Musgrave's Dance' (Granada TV, 24/10/61), with Patrick McGoohan and Freda Jackson, directed by Stuart Burge; Sidney Kingsley's 'Darkness at Noon' (A-R, 15/1/63), based on a novel by Arthur Koestler and directed and adapted by Cyril Coke; and 'Acquit or Hang!' (A-R, 6/1/64), Stanley Miller's story of the court martial of the *Bounty* mutineers, directed by Cyril Coke.

Première
(BBC-2, 1977–80)

Gave new directors the opportunity to direct their first film for television, under, originally, producer Graham Benson. The programme opened with Roger Bamford directing Alan Sillitoe's 'Pit Strike' (22/9/77) and followed with Richard O'Brien's 'A Hymn From Jim' (29/9/77) for director Colin Bucksey; Alan Bennett's 'A Little Outing' (20/10/77), directed by Brian Tufano; Alan Plater's 'Give Us a Kiss, Christabel' (27/10/77), directed by Peter Farrell, with Dennis Waterman and Jan Francis (*pictured*); and 'Something's Wrong' (25/9/78), written and directed by Frederic Raphael. The second (1978) series was also billed as **Première 2**.

The Professionals
(Avengers Mark 1 Prod./LWT, 1977–83)

The kill-or-capture activities of a special undercover section known as CI5 (for Criminal Intelligence 5) was the format for this gun-blasting, screaming-tyres drama. George Cowley (Gordon Jackson; *centre*), commander of the section, was a no-nonsense superior who drove his men to their limits to get the job done, whether it was terrorists, assassins, or mad bombers. Two of his most effective agents were ex-SAS hardcase Bodie (Lewis Collins; *right*) and the more sensitive former policeman Doyle (Martin Shaw; *left*). Excellent photography and editing during some of the more quick-fuse moments made this a superior, fast-moving series. Created by Brian Clemens, the fifty-seven hour-long episodes were produced by Sidney Hayers (1st series) and Raymond Menmuir; Albert Fennell and Clemens were executive producers; music was by Laurie Johnson.

Raffles
(Yorkshire TV, 1977)

Crime author E. W. Hornung's famous gentleman thief, Raffles, first appeared in print in 1899 and as a stage production (*Raffles, The Amateur Cracksman*) in 1903. Yorkshire TV based their TV series and pilot programme on Hornung's three short-story collections and one novel featuring the A. J. Raffles character. **Raffles—The Amateur Cracksman** (Yorkshire TV, 10/9/75) starred Anthony Valentine as Raffles and Christopher Strauli as his companion Bunny Manners. The pilot was produced by Peter Willes, adapted for TV by Philip Mackie, and directed by Christopher Hodson. The 1977 series of thirteen hour-long episodes continued with Valentine (pictured, *left*, with guest Bruce Robinson) and Strauli in their original roles, with Mackie adapting the stories for producer Jacky Stoller.

Ripping Yarns
(BBC-2, 27/9–25/10/77; 10–24/10/79)

Michael Palin and Terry Jones's hilarious liberty-taking with English literature produced two series of 30-minute episodes overflowing with wit and parody. One of the more delightfully crazy episodes, 'Across the Andes by Frog' (18/10/77; dir. Terry Hughes), featured Palin (*pictured, right*) and Denholm Elliott (*left*) in 'the epic story of one man and six frogs who tried to defy the world in the greatest gamble of all'. **Tomkinson's Schooldays** (BBC-2, 7/1/76; wr. Palin & Jones, dir. Hughes), a 30-minute parody of Thomas Hughes's Victorian era story, was the basis for the series.

Secret Army
(BBC-1, 1977–79)

A Second World War drama series about the rescue of Allied aircrews from occupied Europe through an escape organization called Lifeline. The escape line was run by a young Belgian woman known as Yvette (Jan Francis; *left*); her second-in-command was restauranteur Albert (Bernard Hepton; *right*), with RAF liaison officer Curtis (Christopher Neame). On the German side there was Luftwaffe officer Brandt (Michael Culver) and Gestapo man Sturmbahnführer Kessler (Clifford Rose). Producer Gerard Glaister devised the 42 eps. × 55 mins. series with Wilfred Greaterox. A 5 eps. × 50 mins/1 ep. × 55 mins. sequel, **Kessler** (BBC-1, 13/11–18/12/81), followed, bringing the story to date and featuring Rose's Kessler as a wanted war criminal; the series was devised by producer Glaister and John Brason.

Supernatural
(BBC-1, 11/6–6/8/77)

A mood-drenched collection of 8 eps. × 50 mins. sinister stories written by Robert Muller and Sue Lake (one episode) which revolved around tales spun by members of the Club of the Damned. 'Countess Ilona' and 'The Werewolf Reunion' (both dir. Simon Langton and starring Billie Whitelaw) and 'Night of the Marionettes' (dir. Alan Cooke) were particularly spooky entries. Pieter Rogers produced. Jeremy Brett is pictured as the title character in the episode 'Mr Nightingale'.

Target
(BBC-1, 1977–78)

Followed the door-smashing, head-banging Regional Crime Squad cases of Det. Supt. Steve Hackett (Patrick Mower; *left*). The première series moved at such a violent pace that it whipped up a minor storm over its face-cracking depiction of police tactics. Philip Madoc, Brendan Price (*pictured, right*), and Vivien Heilbron co-starred. The 18 eps. × 50 mins. series was produced by Philip Hinchcliffe.

1977/8

Wings
(BBC-1, 1977–78)

Was based on the records of the early fighter pilots and focused on the dramatic adventures of three young Royal Flying Corps pilots, played by Tim Woodward (*pictured*), Nicholas Jones, and Michael Cochrane. Peter Cregeen produced 25 eps. (in 2 series) × 50 mins.; the series was created by Barry Thomas.

All Creatures Great and Small
(BBC-1, 1978–90)

Based on the successful series of autobiographical books by the pseudonymous James Herriott about the more humorous aspects of a young, newly qualified veterinary surgeon living and working in the Yorkshire Dales during the 1930s. Christopher Timothy (*left*) starred as James Herriott, with Robert Hardy, Carol Drinkwater, and Peter Davison (*right*); Lynda Bellingham later joined the cast. The popular, long-running series was originally produced by Bill Sellars for BBC Birmingham.

The BBC Television Shakespeare
(BBC-2, 1978–85)

Presented the complete canon of Shakespeare's plays, in full performing versions and generally with actors of the highest calibre. The first year's productions were 'Romeo and Juliet' (3/12/78; dir. Alvin Rakoff; 170 mins.) with Patrick Ryecart and Rebecca Saire (*pictured*), 'Richard II' (10/12/78; dir. David Giles; 155 mins.) with Derek Jacobi, John Gielgud, Jon Finch, and Wendy Hiller, and 'As You Like It' (17/12/78; dir. Basil Coleman; 150 mins.) with Helen Mirren, Richard Pasco, James Bolam, and Angharad Rees. The following year: 'Julius Caesar' (11/2/79; dir. Herbert Wise; 165 mins.) with Richard Pasco, Charles Gray, and Virginia McKenna, 'Measure for Measure' (18/2/79; dir. Desmond Davis; 145 mins.) with Kate Nelligan and Tim Pigott-Smith, 'Henry VIII' (25/2/79; dir. Kevin Billington; 160 mins.) with John Stride, Timothy West, Ronald Pickup, and Claire Bloom, 'Henry IV', pts. 1 (150 mins.) and 2 (150 mins.) (9 and 16/12/79; dir. David Giles) with Anthony Quayle and Jon Finch, 'Henry V' (23/12/79; dir. David Giles) with David Gwillim and Alec McCowen.

Blake's Seven
(BBC-1, 1978–81)

A frantic space–adventure series about an interplanetary resistance group battling against a totalitarian government. The programme, created by Terry Nation, featured (in the première series, *l. to r.*) Michael Keating (as Vila), David Jackson (Gan), Gareth Thomas (Blake), Sally Knyvette (Jenna), Paul Darrow (Avon), and, not pictured, Jan Chappell (Cally). David Maloney produced 52 eps. × 50 mins. (three series) and Vere Lorrimer produced the fourth series.

Bless Me, Father
(LWT, 1978–81)

The sitcom adventures of the mischievous and eccentric Father Charles Duddleswell (played by Arthur Lowe; *right*) in his London suburb parish of St Jude's, Fairwater, during the early 1950s. His shy, young curate, and everlasting foil, Father Neil Boyd, was played by Daniel Abineri (*left*). The author was Peter de Rosa; David Askey directed-produced the 21 eps. × half-hour.

Botanic Man
(Thames TV, 1978)

Was a ten-part series filmed on locations around the world in which eccentric conservationist David Bellamy (*pictured*) told the story of the evolution of life on earth. The series won a BAFTA award for personal contribution and the Radio Industries Club award for best science-based programme; Randal Beattie produced. Bellamy had previously presented **Bellamy on Botany** (BBC-1, 1972), **Bellamy's Britain** (BBC-1, 1974), **Bellamy's Europe** (BBC-1, 1976), and appeared later in **Up a Gum Tree** (BBC-1, 1979–80), **Bellamy's Backyard Safari** (BBC-1, 1981), **Bellamy's New World** (BBC-1, 1983), **Discovery** (Yorkshire TV, 1985), **Bellamy's Bugle** (Yorkshire TV, 1986–88), **Bellamy on Top of the World** (Yorkshire TV, 1987), and **Bellamy's Bird's Eye View** (Yorkshire TV, 1989). In more recent years Bellamy has presented a six-part series examining the elemental cycles vital to life in **Bellamy Rides Again** (BBC-1, 13/6–18/7/91); John Percival produced.

Bruce Forsyth's Big Night
(LWT, 1978)

Was a series of entertainment specials featuring games, music, and two sitcoms, presented by Bruce Forsyth (*pictured*; with guest Juliet Prowse) and Anthea Redfern; Richard Drewett produced. One of the sitcoms was a return to the 1960s slapstick **The Worker**, starring Charlie Drake in his luckless job-hunter role, supported once again by Henry McGee; Stuart Allen directed the scripts by Drake. The other sitcom starred Jimmy Edwards, Ian Lavender, and Patricia Brake as **The Glums**, based on the original radio scripts for *Take It From Here* written by Frank Muir & Denis Norden; John Kaye Cooper directed for producer Simon Brett. The Glum family proved so popular that they reappeared in their own half-hour series of comedy double-bill routines as **The Glums** (LWT, 1979).

Butterflies
(BBC-2, 1978–83)

A Carla Lane-scripted sitcom about a woman in her early forties, married and comfortably settled, who felt she had reached an age and stage in her life at which time was passing her by. The central character, Ria, was played by Wendy Craig (*2nd right*); Geoffrey Palmer (*2nd left*) was her husband Ben, who took her for granted, Adam (Nicholas Lyndhurst; *left*) and Russell (Andrew Hall; *right*) were the teenage sons; and Bruce Montague played Leonard, a recently divorced man who fell in love with Ria. The 30-minute episodes were produced by Gareth Gwenlan.

By Alan Bennett—Six Plays
(LWT, 2/12/78–24/2/79)

Specially written for television by Alan Bennett and highlighted by his amusing observations of the quirkier side of human nature; the series included 'Me! I'm Afraid of Virginia Woolf' (2/12/78), directed and produced by Stephen Frears; 'Doris and Doreen' (16/12/78; with Prunella Scales and, *right*, Patricia Routledge), directed by Frears; 'The Old Crowd' (27/1/79), directed by Lindsay Anderson; 'Afternoon Off' (3/2/79), directed and produced by Frears, 'One Fine Day' (17/2/79), directed and produced by Frears; and 'All Day on the Sands' (24/2/79), directed by Giles Foster. Some years later Bennett wrote six monologues for **Talking Heads** (BBC-1, 19/4–24/5/88), performed by the actresses Patricia Routledge, Maggie Smith, Stephanie Cole, Julie Walters, Thora Hird, and one by Bennett himself.

1978

Clouds of Glory
(Granada TV, 1978)

Presented two films about the Lakeland Poets, William Wordsworth and Samuel Coleridge, which were filmed on location where they had lived. Both directed by Ken Russell (his first TV since 1971), the first production featured David Warner as Wordsworth in 'William and Dorothy' (9/7/78), with Felicity Kendal and Preston Lockwood; the second, 'The Rime of the Ancient Mariner' (16/7/78), featured David Hemmings (*pictured, left*) as Coleridge, with Kika Markham (*right*; as his wife, Sarah); Warner and Kendal (as Wordsworth and his sister, Dorothy) also appeared. The two hour-long films were written by Melvyn Bragg & Russell and produced by Norman Swallow. Dick Bush was cameraman, Mike Grimes designed, and Anthony Ham edited the films.

Disraeli
(ATV, 5–26/9/78)

Presented a four-part mini-series on the life and times of Benjamin Disraeli (Ian McShane; *left*), one of Britain's most opportunist and colourful prime ministers. Mary Peach (*right*), Leigh Lawson, Margaret Whiting, Mark Dignam, William Russell, and Antony Brown (as Sir Robert Peel) co-starred. The series was written by David Butler for producer Cecil Clarke and directed by Claude Whatham.

Edward and Mrs Simpson
(Thames TV, 8/11–20/12/78)

Simon Raven's scripts for this 7 eps. × hour reconstruction of the events leading up to Edward, the Prince of Wales's abdication in 1937 portrayed Edward Fox's Prince of Wales as a person easily manipulated and Cynthia Harris's Wallis Simpson as calculating, with the latter's performance being particularly memorable. Waris Hussein directed for producer Andrew Brown.

Empire Road
(BBC-2, 1978–79)

Represented a racially mixed community of West Indians and Asians living in a suburban street in Birmingham, and focused on the life of West Indian landlord Everton Bennett (played by Norman Beaton; *left*): his humorous relationship with brother-in-law Walter (Joe Marcell; *centre*) and the romantic relationship between Bennett's son Marcus (Wayne Laryea) and his Asian girlfriend Ranjanaa (Nalini Moonasar). Corinne Skinner-Carter (*right*) co-starred as wife Hortense Bennett; Rudolph Walker joined the cast for the second series. The relatively short-run series of 15 eps. × 30 mins. was, however, the first TV programme conceived and written by a black writer, Michael Abbensetts, for a black cast.

Enemy at the Door
(LWT, 1978–80)

The Second World War Nazi occupation of the Channel Islands was the theme of this 26 eps. × hour drama series. Alfred Burke (*right*; with David Waller) starred as German Major Richter, with Emily Richard, Antonia Pemberton, John Malcolm, Simon Cadell, and Simon Lack. Michael Chapman (1st series) and Jonathan Alwyn (2nd series) produced for executive producer Tony Wharmby.

240

An Englishman's Castle
(BBC-2, 5–12–19/6/78)

Featured 3 × 50 mins. plays written by Philip Mackie about the making of a successful soap opera in a state controlled television service, and of its author and producer Peter Ingram (played by Kenneth More; *pictured* with co-star Isla Blair). The plays were set in contemporary London, but in a Britain defeated in 1940 and now a satellite state of Germany. Paul Ciappessoni directed Innes Lloyd's production. 'An Englishman's Castle' was presented as a part of the **Play of the Week** (BBC-2, 1977–79) series, which had premièred a year earlier with Tom Stoppard's 'Professional Foul'.

Grange Hill
(BBC-1, 1978–)

A realistic drama series about life in a comprehensive school which provoked continuing controversy from adults yet was highly rated by the youthful audience it was aimed at. (*l. to r.*) Todd Carty, Paul McCarthy, Rene Alperstein, Linda Slater, Terry Sue Patt, George Armstrong; and Robert Morgan, Christopher Hall, Miriam Mann, Michelle Herbert, and Susan Tully were among the early Grange Hill pupils. The programme was created and originally written by Phil Redmond; Anna Home was executive producer. Todd Carty reappeared as Tucker Jenkins in **Tucker's Luck** (BBC-2, 1983–85), now grown up and facing the harsh realities of life after school with his mates Alan (George Armstrong) and Tommy (Paul McCarthy). Storylines were provided by Redmond for producer David Hargreaves.

Hazell
(Thames TV, 1978–79)

Was based on the crime novels by Gordon Williams and Terry Venables, featuring London East End private eye James Hazell (Nicholas Ball, *right*, with Peter Miles) in a 22 eps. × hour series of cynical, spoof Raymond Chandler gumshoe capers. June Roberts (later Tim Aspinall) produced in suitable *film noir* fashion which included lightweight, self-parody voice-overs by Ball.

The Hong Kong Beat
(BBC-1, 1/3–26/4/78)

Spellbinding, nine-part documentary look at the policing of what is effectively the last British colony, with producer John Purdie's camera following the hazardous, and occasionally humorous, activities of the British Colonial Force as they work among the 4.5 million Chinese packed into the densely populated colony. Photography was by Patrick Turley; edited by Arthur Solomon.

Law and Order
(BBC-2, 1978)

Writer G. F. Newman's four facets of crime and punishment (which on original transmission drew complaints from the police) presented 'A Detective's Tale' (6/4/78), with the policeman's view of crime, featuring Derek Martin (*left*; with Billy Cornelius); 'A Villain's Tale' (13/4/78), fronting the villain's point of view, with Peter Dean; 'A Brief's Tale' (20/4/78), regarding the judicial procedures, with Ken Campbell; and 'A Prisoner's Tale' (27/4/78), observing prison society. The 4 eps. × 80 mins. drama was directed by Leslie Blair for producer Tony Garnett.

Lillie
(LWT, 1978)

A 13 eps. × hour drama series about the colourful life of Lillie Langtry (played by Francesca Annis, *left*, with guest Derek Smith), the Jersey girl who had Victorian high society gossiping as the mistress of the Prince of Wales, later to be Edward VII. Director John Gorrie steered the series for producer Jack Williams. Francesca Annis had earlier played Langtry in a couple of episodes of **Edward the Seventh**.

The Mayor of Casterbridge
(BBC-2, 22/1–5/3/78)

BBC TV commemorated the fiftieth anniversary of Thomas Hardy's death with a 7 eps. × 50 mins. adaptation by Dennis Potter of Hardy's dramatic 1885 novel. The serial starred Alan Bates (*right*; as Michael Henchard), with Anna Massey (*left*), Anne Stallybrass, and Avis Bunnage. David Giles directed for Jonathan Powell's production; music was by Carl Davis.

Mixed Blessings
(LWT, 1978–80)

Presented the humorous situations faced by Thomas and Susan (played by Christopher Blake and Muriel Odunton; *pictured*), the young partners of a mixed marriage, as they tried to deal with life and, especially, their respective families. Twenty-two half-hour episodes were produced by Derrick Goodwin; Sid Green scripted.

The One and Only Phyllis Dixey
(Thames TV, 1/11/78)

Phyllis Dixey was regarded as Britain's First Lady of Striptease and was one of the biggest attractions in the heyday of London's Whitehall Theatre. Philip Purser's script took up the story from her early days as a chorus girl in the 1920s, recreating her stage performances and shows, as well as her battles with the Lord Chamberlain's office. Lesley-Anne Down (*pictured*) starred as Dixey, supported by Chris Murney, Michael Elphick, Elaine Paige, and Patricia Hodge. Michael Tuchner directed the 110-minute TV movie. Also known as **Peek-A-Boo**.

Out
(Euston Films–Thames TV, 24/7–28/8/78)

A 6 eps. × hour gritty underworld drama serial starring Tom Bell as a bank robber, Frank Ross, who after his release from prison became obsessed with finding the informer who put him away. The no-prisoners-taken gangland narrative provided many juicy roles for TV crime genre character actors in Trevor Preston's screenplay, directed by Jim Goddard for producer Barry Hanson. Pictured are (*l. to r.*) Bell, Bryan Marshall, and John Junkin.

Pennies from Heaven

(BBC-1, 7/3–11/4/78)

Dennis Potter's televisually unorthodox (with the actors miming to songs) representation of the travels and offbeat adventures of a song-sheet pedlar, Arthur Parker (played by Bob Hoskins; *left*), and the beautiful young teacher, Eileen (Cheryl Campbell; *right*), whom he meets on the road. Gemma Craven and Kenneth Colley supported. Billed as 'a play with music in six parts', the programme was produced by Kenith Trodd and directed by Piers Haggard. Potter also wrote the screenplay for MGM's 1981 feature remake with Steve Martin and Bernadette Peters in the lead roles.

The Prime of Miss Jean Brodie

(Scottish TV, 1978)

Delightful adaptation by Jay Presson Allen of Muriel Spark's novel about a schoolteacher (Geraldine McEwan; *pictured*) with radical ideas on educating young girls, set in Scotland during the early 1930s. The cast included Lucinda Bateson, Maxine Gordon, Ann Mitchell, Robert Urquhart, Anna Wing, and Tammy Ustinov. Seven hour-long episodes were produced by Richard Bates; music was by Marvin Hamlisch. Presson Allen's adaptation of Spark's novel was first filmed by 20th Century-Fox in 1968 (Maggie Smith was Jean Brodie).

Rings On Their Fingers

(BBC-1, 1978–80)

War of the sexes sitcom series about a man and woman, played by Martin Jarvis and Diane Keen (*pictured*), who had been living happily together for a long time, and had decided to get married—or rather, she had decided and he had tried to find a way around it. (He didn't!) The 18 eps. × 30 mins. series was written by Richard Waring and produced-directed by Harold Snoad.

Rumpole of the Bailey

(Thames TV, 1978–79; 1983; 1987–88; 1991–)

Was the magnificent creation of barrister-playwright John Mortimer, featuring Leo McKern (*shown*) as Horace Rumpole, the wily, mildly eccentric Old Bailey hack lawyer. McKern's Rumpole first appeared in a 65-minute play written by Mortimer for BBC TV's **Play for Today** ('Rumpole of the Bailey', 16/12/75; dir. John Gorrie, pr. Irene Shubik); Alastair Sim was reputedly up for the role before it went to McKern. Thames's **Rumpole of the Bailey** consisted of five series of 30 eps. × hour; produced, in turn, by Shubik and Jacqueline Davis. Thames TV also produced a 2-hour (tx) special, **Rumpole's Return** (30/12/80), written by Mortimer and directed by John Glenister for producer Jacqueline Davis. Regulars in the series were Peggy Thorpe-Bates (as Hilda Rumpole), Julian Curry (as Erskine-Brown), Moray Watson (as George Frobisher), Peter Bowles (as Guthrie Featherstone), and Patricia Hodge (as Phyllida).

1978

The Sandbaggers
(Yorkshire TV, 1978; 1980)

Featured the special operations team of the British espionage organization SIS. Situated in East and West Germany, the secret services drama starred Roy Marsden (*right*), Elizabeth Bennett, Richard Vernon, Ray Lonnen (*left*), Alan MacNaughtan, and, in the 1978 series, Diane Keen (*centre*). Ian MacKintosh scripted the 19 eps. × hour series for producer Michael Ferguson.

Saturday Night People
(LWT, 1978–80)

Was a 45-minute late night show regarding itself as 'journalism with laughs', which meant that it was an attempt at a TV gossip column with Russell Harty, Clive James, and Janet Street-Porter (*latter two pictured*) presenting inside stories on the powerful and the famous. Barry Cox produced.

Send in the Girls
(Granada TV, 1978)

Seven one-hour episodes following the adventures of Velma Hardy (played by Annie Ross; *pictured*) and her Girls (Diana Davies, Anna Carteret, and Floella Benjamin) whose job it was to put sex appeal into sales promotions. The short-run series was produced by June Wyndham-Davies.

The South Bank Show
(LWT, 1978–)

Continued where **Aquarius** left off, featuring a series of arts programmes, presented by Melvyn Bragg, covering the best in contemporary and traditional culture. The series alternated between interviews with prominent personalities and topical reviews of the arts scene before it went into producing more full-length studies of film-makers, musicians, authors, and artists. Original executive producer was Nick Elliott. Miles Davis, *pictured*, was the subject of a 25/4/82 edition; Nigel Wattis was director-producer.

Spearhead
(Southern TV, 1978–79)

Followed the fortunes of a group of British soldiers, Six Platoon, B Company Wessex Rangers, as they completed their tour of duty in Ulster (1st series) and later in Germany (2nd series). A third series, **Spearhead—In Hong Kong** (Southern TV, 1981), saw them stationed in the Colony to guard against illegal immigration from mainland China. Roy Holder (as Sgt. Bilinski) and Martin Jacobs (as Lt. Pickering) led the regular cast, consisting of George Sweeney, Charles Cork, Gordon Case, Peter Turner, Stafford Gordon, and Robin Davies. Nick McCarty was the scriptwriter; James Ormerod was director-producer, with Derek Martinus directing the final series.

Strangers
(Granada TV, 1978–82)

Followed the crime-busting career of Don Henderson's (*right*; with guest Leslie Schofield) Bulman (previously a police sergeant in **The XYY Man**, now Det. Sgt.) who had been drafted into the police force of a northern city. The above-average 32 eps. × hour stories, produced by Richard Everitt, also featured John Ronance, Dennis Blanch, and Frances Tomelty. Murray Smith was the principal author. Henderson/Bulman returned again in **Bulman** (Granada TV, 1985; 1987), a 20 eps. × hour series in which the now retired ex-policeman ran a clock-mending shop between freelance detective work; he was assisted by Lucy McGinty (Siobhan Redmond), an ex-colleague's daughter. Steve Hawes and Sita Williams produced.

3—2—1
(Yorkshire TV, 1978–87)

Was an hour-long game show hosted by Ted Rogers and his team of glamorous assistants/secretaries (known as 'The Gentle Secs'), backed up by a company of resident comedians and surprise guest celebrities. Whichever pair out of the three mixed couples competing for the prizes in the rather convoluted structure of this game made it to the final stage they ran the chance of winning either a brand new car or a loser's 'booby' prize of an animated garbage container, affectionately referred to as 'Dusty Bin'. The series was produced by Derek Burrell-Davis.

Top Gear
(BBC-2, 1978–)

Featured newsreader Angela Rippon as the presenter (along with Barrie Gill) of this 25-minute series tackling issues related to motoring and covering all things of interest to ordinary motorists and road users; driving stress, safety belts, drunken driving, motor offence fines, parking problems, petrol economy, car tests, and driving abroad. The programme had been tried out earlier in 1978 in the BBC Midland Region, and its success led to a networked series under producer Derek Smith. A previous BBC TV series on the ('minority'-interest) subject, **Wheelbase** (BBC-2, 1964–73), had approached it mainly from an industry point of view; it was originally produced by Brian Robins. ITV's **Drive-In** (Thames TV, 1971–78), with presenters Shaw Taylor and Tony Bastable, also looked at cars and car users with editions covering points from traffic behaviour in cities to international rallies; the producer was Jim Pople. Angela Rippon is pictured in period mood with a 1911 Belsize car.

The Voyage of Charles Darwin
(BBC-2, 31/10–12/12/78)

The story of Charles Darwin's five-year scientific expedition to South America in HMS *Beagle* was a detailed dramatization painstakingly researched, meticulously reproduced, and filmed over a period of nearly a year. The programme featured Malcolm Stoddard (*shown*; as Charles Darwin), Andrew Burt, Iain Cuthbertson, and George Cole. The 7 eps. × hour were written by Robert Reid and directed by Martyn Friend for Christopher Ralling's production.

Warrior Queen
(Thames TV, 1978)

Set in the year AD 61, this 6 part × half-hour action-drama followed the militaristic adventures of Queen Boudicca (played by Sian Phillips; *pictured*) after the death of her husband, King of the Iceni tribe (in what is now Norfolk), in her battles with the Roman Procurator, Catus Decianus (Nigel Hawthorne). Some sequences were recorded at the rebuilt Iron Age settlement at the Butser Trust, Petersfield. The script was by Martin Mellett; Neville Green and Michael Custance directed for producer Ruth Boswell.

Wilde Alliance
(Yorkshire TV, 1978)

A comedy-thriller series moving around the (exceptionally) eventful lives of detective fiction writer Rupert Wilde (John Stride; *right*) and his wife Amy (Julia Foster; *left*); Christopher Bridgewater (played by John Lee), Rupert's literary agent, often got caught up in the Wildes' wild mysteries. Thirteen hour-long episodes were produced by Ian Mackintosh.

Will Shakespeare
(ATV, 13/6–18/7/78)

A six-part drama in hour-long episodes written by John Mortimer and concentrating on the human side of Shakespeare, on the bawdy, romantic aspects of his life, and his role in the court life of Queen Elizabeth I. Tim Curry (*pictured*) starred in the title role, with Ian McShane, John McEnery, André Morell, and Simon MacCorkindale. Peter Wood directed for producer Cecil Clarke. BBC TV's earlier **The Man Shakespeare** (BBC-2, 25/4/64) was a dramatized documentary on Shakespeare's life, based on known facts and widely accepted beliefs; scripted by Ivor Brown. Roger Croucher appeared as William Shakespeare; Hugh David narrated. The 55-minute play was designed and produced by Hal Burton as a contribution to the quatercentenary celebrations of the birth of the Bard.

Agony
(LWT, 1979–81)

Hot- and cold-running comedy series about agony columnist Jane Lucas (played by Maureen Lipman; *pictured*) who writes the problem page for *Person* magazine and has her own radio phone-in programme. Most of Jane's problems, however, arose from her own life, involving psychiatrist husband Simon Williams, her boss Jan Holden, her mother Maria Charles, secretary Diana Weston, freaky DJ pal Peter Blake, and her two gay neighbours, Peter Denyer and Jeremy Bulloch. The 20 eps. × half-hour series was written by Len Richmond and Anna Raeburn (1st series), and Stan Hey and Andrew Nickolds. John Reardon produced and directed.

Antiques Roadshow
(BBC-1, 1979–)

Each week antiques specialist Arthur Negus (pictured, *centre*, with Angela Rippon) went on the road with a team of experts from Britain's leading auction houses to meet the public informally and discuss the treasured possessions brought along for their assessment. The half-hour, Sunday series was a successor to the West Region programme **Going for a Song?** (BBC-1, 1965–77) in which customers and connoisseurs explored the world of antiques (in the days before it became a national obsession); Negus and Max Robertson were part of the original team. Anglia TV's **Heirloom** (1987–) followed a similar, antiques-discussion line under producer Colin Eldred.

Blankety Blank
(BBC-1, 1979–89)

Terry Wogan (later Les Dawson) hosted this comedy quiz game in which contestants attempted to match their 'blanks' with six guest celebrities. Original producer was Alan Boyd. Pictured with Wogan (*left*) are guests John Junkin, Beryl Reid, Arthur English, Dilys Watling, Spike Milligan, and Sandra Dickinson.

Danger U.X.B.
(Thames TV–Euston Films, 1979)

Followed the hazardous assignments of a Second World War bomb disposal squad during Hitler's blitz on London. Developed, produced, and occasionally scripted by John Hawkesworth, this 13 eps. × hour series starred Anthony Andrews (*pictured*) as Brian Ash, a young officer with the Royal Engineers who was posted to the hastily assembled bomb disposal company. His team of (somewhat reluctant) Sappers included George Innes, Maurice Roeves, Kenneth Cranham, and Robert Pugh; Judy Geeson, Iain Cuthbertson, and Deborah Watling also appeared.

Dick Barton—Special Agent
(Southern TV, 1979)

Was based on the popular BBC radio detective and, in this television version, featured Tony Vogel (*kneeling left*) as Barton and Anthony Heaton as his companion Snowey. The 31 eps. × 15 mins. cliff-hanger serial, reviving the radio programme's urgent signature theme, was written by Clive Exton and Julian Bond, and directed-produced by Jon Scofield.

Dick Turpin
(Gatetarn–Seacastle Prod.–LWT, 1979–80; 1982)

The eighteenth-century adventures of celebrated highwayman Dick Turpin (played by Richard O'Sullivan; *left*) formed the basis for this 25 eps. × half-hour series produced by Paul Knight and Sidney Cole. Because of its early evening (Saturday) scheduling the hero and his escapades were more in keeping with the romantic 'gentleman of the road' theme than the notorious stand-and-deliver character of history. Turpin's accomplice was young Swiftnick (Michael Deeks; *right*) and together they harrassed the greedy, aristocratic Sir John Glutton (Christopher Benjamin) and his thief-taker Captain Nathan Spiker (David Daker). During the programme's initial run a five-part mini-serial was produced under the title **Dick Turpin's Greatest Adventure** (16/5–13/6/81; dir. Gerry Poulson) in which an American girl (Mary Crosby) travels to England to seek justice from the Attorney-General (Patrick Macnee) on behalf of colonists suffering under a corrupt governor (Wilfred Hyde-White); the cast also featured Susan Hampshire, Ed Bishop, Oliver Tobias, Alfie Bass, and Donald Pleasance. The majority of stories were scripted by Richard Carpenter; Charles Crichton was director for several episodes.

Flambards
(Yorkshire TV, 1979)

Adapted from the romantic novels by Kathleen Peyton, and set during the early part of the twentieth century, this 12 eps. × hour series followed the pains and passions of a young girl (played by Christina McKenna) as she grew up amid the turmoil of an all-male household at Flambards, the family country home. The series also featured Edward Judd, Steven Grives, Alan Parnaby, Sebastian Abineri, and Rosalie Williams. Adapting writers included Alan Plater, Alex Glasgow, William Humble, and K. M. Peyton, for producer Leonard Lewis.

Fred Dibnah, Steeplejack
(BBC-2, 6/9/79)

The high-altitude world of old factory chimneys either under repair or demolition as seen through the eyes of Lancashire steeplejack Fred Dibnah (*pictured*). Fred's stardom grew from an appearance in a 1977 news item about repairing the Bolton Town Hall clock, resulting in this 50-minute BBC Manchester documentary about his steeplejacking life and job, the 7 eps. × 30 mins. **Fred** (BBC-2, 9/9–21/10/82) and the 5 eps. × 30 mins. **A Year With Fred** (BBC-2, 9/2–9/3/87); all written and produced by Don Haworth.

Kelly Monteith
(BBC-2, 1979–84)

Was a bright, young American stand-up comedian who had a success with his own comedy sitcom series during the early 1980s. The general format moved around his predicaments with his marriage and his flat, often with witty remarks made directly to the camera. Gabrielle Drake co-starred as his wife. The series was written by Monteith and Neil Shand; James Moir was the original producer.

Kidnapped
(HTV West–Tele-Munchen, 7/4–30/6/79)

Was an ambitious serialization of Robert Louis Stevenson's epic drama of the dangerous times following the Highlanders' defeat at Culloden in 1746. David McCallum (*pictured*, *right*) starred as Alan Breck, a hero of Culloden who was fleeing for his life; German actor Ekkehardt Belle appeared as David Balfour, and French actress Aude Landry as Catriona, daughter of a Highland rebel. Patrick Magee, Bill Simpson, and Frank Windsor supported. Peter Graham Scott produced thirteen half-hour episodes.

Life on Earth
(BBC-2, 16/1–10/4/79)

Was the epic story of how species coped with succeeding problems of development and adapted to solve new situations, from the first primitive cells to the plants and animals that now live around us. A network of the world's most expert Natural History photographers were deployed to cover every continent and exploit all the techniques of microphotography, underwater photography, time-lapse photography, and photography at 3,000 frames a second. The 13 parts × 55 mins. programme was presented by David Attenborough (*pictured*) and produced by BBC Bristol; Christopher Parsons was executive producer. Followed by **The Living Planet** (BBC-1, 1984) and **The Trials of Life** (BBC-1, 1990).

The Mallens
(Granada TV, 1979–80)

A drama series developed from the best-selling novel by Catherine Cookson, adapted by Jack Russell, and set in nineteenth-century Northumberland. The first series of seven hour-long episodes (10/6–22/7/79; pr. Roy Roberts, dir. Richard Martin) featured John Hallam (*pictured*; as Squire Thomas Mallen), David Rintoul, Sue Barton, Pippa Guard, and Caroline Blakiston. A second series of six hour-long episodes, billed as **Catherine Cookson's The Mallens** (and based on the novel *The Mallen Girl*), ran from 29/5/80 to 3/7/80 and starred Juliet Stevenson, as the late Squire's illegitimate daughter Barbara, Gerry Sundquist, June Ritchie, and Blakiston. Russell again adapted for producer Roberts; Mary McMurray directed.

Minder
(Thames TV–Euston Films, 1979–85; 1988–)

Created by Leon Griffiths, this comedy-drama about a shady London car dealer and his bodyguard-for-hire partner became a national success due to its perfectly balanced sense of black humour, colourful characterization, and latent underworld menace. George Cole (*left*) was Arthur Daley and Dennis Waterman (*right*) was the 'minder', ex-boxer and former prison inmate Terry McCann. Also in the regular cast were Patrick Malahide (as Det. Sgt. Chisholm) and Glynn Edwards (as drinking-club owner Dave). Lloyd Shirley and George Taylor produced. **Minder on the Orient Express** (tx 25/12/85), a 2-hour Christmas special, written by Andrew Payne, was followed a couple of years later by the 90-minute **Minder**: 'An Officer and a Car Salesman' (tx 26/12/88), written by Tony Hoare, directed by Roy Ward Baker, and produced by George Taylor. From 1991, following Waterman's departure from the series (he went on to lead the cast of the BBC-1 sitcom **On the Up** in 1990 as self-made millionaire Tony Carpenter), Cole's Daley was joined by his nephew Ray (played by Gary Webster).

Not the Nine O'Clock News
(BBC-2, 1979–80; 1982)

A group effort comedy series full of lunatic sketches, hilarious send-ups, and pretty much anything and everything of a questionable taste. The established line-up featured (*l. to r.*) Griff Rhys Jones, Rowan Atkinson, Mel Smith, and Pamela Stephenson. The 18 eps. × 30/25 mins. were produced by John Lloyd and Sean Hardie. Original line-up (April 1979) was Atkinson, Chris Emmett, Christopher Godwin, John Gorman, and Jonathan Hyde; by October 1979 it was Atkinson, Chris Langham, Stephenson, and Smith.

1979

The Omega Factor
(BBC-1, 13/6–15/8/79)

Was an espionage thriller, but one that blended the world of parapsychology with the methods of the spy. The series featured James Hazeldine (*left*) as an investigative journalist, who also happens to be a natural psychic and who is co-opted by MI5. Louise Jameson (*right*) played Dr Anne Reynolds, a professional sceptic. The 10 eps. × 50 mins. series was written by Jack Gerson and produced by George Gallaccio for BBC Scotland.

Quatermass
(Euston Films, 24/10–14/11/79)

Author Nigel Kneale's final chapter of his Professor Quatermass saga was set in a depressive near future society where roving gangs wander the litter-strewn streets, battling each other for loot and territory. Into this great urban collapse came an elderly Professor Quatermass (played by John Mills; *pictured*), after some twenty years of seclusion in Scotland, now searching for his grandchild. Simon MacCorkindale, Barbara Kellerman, and Margaret Tyzack co-starred in Kneale's four hour-long episodes; directed by Piers Haggard for producer Ted Childs. The serial was later re-edited into a 105-minute theatrical release under the title *Quatermass Conclusion*.

Question Time
(BBC-1, 1979–)

A 60-minute programme chaired for the first ten years by the formidable Robin Day (Sir Robin from 1981) in which a panel of politicians was put through intense inquisitions on network television by Day, the studio audience, and each other. The programme's high points were scored by Day's relentless probing of truth and meaning behind a politician's evasive comments as well as his rapid-fire crosstalk with the audience. Along with this also came a wide range of criticism, from those who complained that he was rude to politicians, to those who considered him unable to see beyond life at Westminster. **Question Time** *was* Robin Day. The original producer was Barbara Maxwell. Brian Lapping Assoc. produced the programme for the BBC from 1991; Peter Sissons took the chair from 1989. Pictured (*l. to r.*) are Teddy Taylor MP, Edna O'Brien, Day, Most Revd Derek Worlock, and Michael Foot MP.

The Racing Game
(Yorkshire TV, 1979–80)

A short-run series of crime thrillers based on the stories of jockey turned writer Dick Francis. The hero, Sid Halley (Mike Gwilym; *pictured*), was a crippled ex-jockey who had turned to private detective work; Mick Ford played Halley's sidekick, Chico. The sleazy underside of the racing world was expertly navigated in scripts by Terence Feely, Trevor Preston, Leon Griffiths, and Evan Jones in six hour-long episodes produced by Jacky Stoller.

Roald Dahl's Tales of the Unexpected
(Anglia TV, 1979)

Offered a collection of weird yarns based on author Roald Dahl's short stories and introduced by Dahl himself. Episodes included 'Man from the South' (starring Jose Ferrer, *pictured*, with Michael Ontkean), 'Mrs Bixby and the Colonel's Coat' (with Julie Harris), 'Lamb to the Slaughter' (Susan George), and 'A Dip in the Pool' (Jack Weston). The series later became simply **Tales of the Unexpected** (Anglia TV, 1980–88), minus Dahl, and continued presenting the half-hour dramas with a twist in the closing moments. John Rosenberg produced both versions.

Sapphire & Steel
(ATV/Central TV, 1979–82)

An intriguing science-fantasy serial starring David McCallum and Joanna Lumley (*pictured*) as two mysterious time–space agents who appeared in the current dimension of time whenever there was a time–space dislocation (people warped into the past, or brought forward in time). This unique and delightfully offbeat, twice-weekly series, shown in cliff-hanger segments, was a riot of ghostly figures from the past intruding into the present, the dead reappearing alive, malevolent shapes transporting people into the settings of photographic images, and characters being flipped back in time. The special effects and video camerawork were made all the more striking with excellent use of suspense-triggering camera angles and lighting. A total of thirty-four half-hour episodes was produced by Shaun O'Riordan; P. J. Hammond created and scripted the serials.

Screenplay
(Granada TV, 1979)

Was a series of summer season plays that managed to help launch at least one popular series for GTV: **Cribb**, from 'Waxwork' (19/8/79) written by Pauline Macauley from a story by author Peter Lovesey with June Wyndham-Davies as director-producer. Other notable plays that came under the programme's banner were Thomas Keneally's (adaptation by Brian Gibson) 'Gossip from the Forest' (29/7/79; dir. Gibson) starring Hugh Burden, Ronald Hines, and Michael Mellinger; 'The Sound of the Guns' (12/8/79; dir. Gordon Flemyng), journalist James Cameron's first TV play, starring Freddie Jones, Kenneth Cranham, and Warren Clarke; and Victoria Wood's 'Talent' (5/8/79; dir. Baz Taylor), in which Wood also appeared with Julie Walters. Pictured are (*l. to r.*) Peter Newton, Ray Armstrong, Michael Mellinger, Ronald Hines, Hugh Burden, and John McGregor in 'Gossip from the Forest'.

The Secret Hospital
(Yorkshire TV, 22–3/5/79)

Two stark documentary reports dealing with top-security institutions. 'Part One: Rampton—The Big House' focused on disturbed criminals as well as drawing awareness to the hundreds of mentally handicapped men and women, innocent of any crime, who were confined to the bleak Rampton Hospital; 'Part Two: Eastdale—The Way Out' looked at the Eastdale experimental unit which eased patients from top-security hospitals, like Broadmoor, back into the routine of the outside world. Director-producer John Willis (*pictured*), who had created **Johnny Go Home**, investigated this social problem.

1979

Shelley
(Thames TV, 1979–89)

A situation comedy featuring the irrepressible and cynical James Shelley (Hywel Bennett), a man never easily defeated by bureaucratic bumblers. Belinda Sinclair appeared as Frances, Shelley's live-in girlfriend, and Josephine Tewson was their landlady. Peter Tilbury created the half-hour series for director-producer Anthony Parker. Bennett and Sinclair are pictured.

Shoestring
(BBC-1, 1979–80)

Easygoing gumshoe Eddie Shoestring (Trevor Eve, *pictured*, with Debbie Farrington) was presented as more of a private ear than a private eye. Set in the West Country, this Robert Banks Stewart-created character was a phone-in detective who took on cases arising out of Radio West telephone calls. His radio station boss was played by Michael Medwin; Doran Godwin and Liz Crowther also appeared. The 21 eps. × 55 mins. series was produced by Robert Banks Stewart.

Suez 1956
(BBC-1, 25/11/79)

Author Ian Curteis's mammoth 190-minute play based on one of the world's great international crises was, as Curteis openly declared, a highly subjective one. Curteis, who first took his controversial play to the BBC in 1973, claimed that it was not a drama-documentary or an attempt to 'reconstruct' real events, that all the facts shown were correct; the interpretation and guesswork, constituting about three-quarters of the play, were his own. The massive cast was led by Michael Gough (*pictured*; as Sir Anthony Eden), Robert Stephens (as President Nasser), and Peter Cellier (as Selwyn Lloyd), with Richard Vernon, Alexander Knox, Wensley Pithey, Oscar Quitak, Douglas Wilmer, and Jennifer Daniel. Michael Darlow directed Cedric Messina's production.

Telford's Change
(BBC-2, 7/1–11/3/79)

Featured a ten-episode drama series about Mark Telford (played by Peter Barkworth; *right*), an international banking hotshot, who yearns for the simple life and achieves it, against his London-based, career-carving wife's (Hannah Gordon; *centre*) wishes, by getting himself transferred to the managership of a small branch bank. Barry Davis directed Brian Clark's scripts for producer Mark Shivas.

Thundercloud
(Yorkshire TV, 1979)

Centred on life among a group of land-locked sailors operating on a shore-based station on the Yorkshire Moors at the beginning of the Second World War. The Admiralty, however, were convinced that the station was actually a destroyer in the North Sea. The thirteen half-hour comedy episodes starred Derek Waring, John Fraser, James Cosmo, and Sarah Douglas; executive producer Ian MacKintosh devised the programme. Pictured (*l. to r.*) are Fraser, Waring, and John Ringham from the 'Don't Go Near the Water' episode.

Tinker, Tailor, Soldier, Spy
(BBC-2, 10/9–22/10/79)

Superior espionage drama serial based on John le Carré's novel (dramatized by Arthur Hopcraft) and featuring retired spy-master George Smiley (played by Alec Guinness, *left*, with Patrick Stewart). The 7 eps. × 50 mins. story, concerning the unearthing of a double agent among the top ranks of the British Secret Service, also starred Bernard Hepton, Terence Rigby, Michael Aldridge, Ian Richardson, Alexander Knox, Ian Bannen, and Hywel Bennett. John Irvin directed for producer Jonathan Powell. Alec Guinness's Smiley returned for more espionage and duplicity in **Smiley's People** (BBC-2, 20/9–25/10/82), co-scripted by John le Carré and John Hopkins from le Carré's original. Eileen Atkins, Anthony Bate, and Curd Jurgens were among those appearing. The 6 eps. × hour serial was produced again by Powell; Simon Langton directed. The third outing for spy-master George Smiley came with **A Murder of Quality** (Thames TV/Portobello Prods., 10/4/91), a 2-hour production with Denholm Elliott starring as Smiley, supported by Glenda Jackson, Joss Ackland, Billie Whitelaw, and David Threlfall; Gavin Millar directed le Carré's screenplay for producer Eric Abraham.

Tiswas
(ATV/Central TV, 1979–82)

The anarchic Saturday morning children's TV show began in 1974 as a local ATV programme in the Birmingham area and was, perhaps, along with LWT's **Saturday Scene**, the earliest, live, all-morning linked package specially made for children. The rampant, madhouse antics of flan-flinging, tossing of buckets of water, and being locked in the Cage (where the guest victims were targets of custard pies, and worse) by presenters Sally James (who had also presented the earlier **Saturday Scene**), Lenny Henry, Bob Carolgees (with Spit the Dog), John Gorman, and Clive Webb, and orchestrated by producer-presenter Chris Tarrant, became a cult watched by over 5 million adults and children. Producer Tarrant, with most of his **Tiswas** team, later introduced **OTT** (Central TV, 1982) as a late night, adult version of the children's show; the initials stood for 'Over the Top', which described the format perfectly (the **Tiswas** title originally came from the initials 'Today Is Saturday'). Newcomers to Tarrant's team were Helen Atkinson-Wood and Alexei Sayle. **Saturday Stayback** (Central TV, 1983) appeared in the **OTT** slot a year later, produced and presented by Tarrant, with Atkinson-Wood, Carolgees, Tony Slattery, and Phil Cool; John Gorman was assistant producer. Chris Tarrant and Sally James are pictured, *centre*, with some of the studio kids.

1979

To the Manor Born
(BBC-1, 1979–81)

An immensely popular sitcom series built around class snobbery and starring Penelope Keith (*left*) as Audrey fforbes-Hamilton, an upper-class lady who was forced to move out of her stately home and reluctantly sell the property to *nouveau* millionaire businessman Richard DeVere (played by Peter Bowles; *right*); Angela Thorne (*centre*) was her patient friend, Marjory. The series was written by Peter Spence and produced by Gareth Gwenlan.

Tropic
(ATV, 29/7–5/8/79; 24/11–15/12/79)

Was a 6 eps. × half-hour comedy serial by Leslie Thomas, based on his book *Tropic of Ruislip*, set in the executive housing estate of Plummers Park. Most of the characters and situations were enjoyable lonely housewife parodies of the steamy station kiosk-type novels. The cast included Ronald Pickup (*left*), Hilary Tindall, Hilary Pritchard (*right*), John Clive, Ronald Lacey, and Charlotte Howard. Director-producer was Matthew Robinson.

Worzel Gummidge
(Southern TV, 1979–81)

The famous character from post-war children's fiction, created by Barbara Euphan Todd, was translated to TV by Keith Waterhouse & Willis Hall in a series (22 eps. × half-hour, plus a 60-minute Christmas special) of comedies starring Jon Pertwee as Worzel, with Una Stubbs (*pictured*) and Barbara Windsor; supported by Mike Berry, Jeremy Austin, Charlotte Coleman, and Geoffrey Baydon (as the Crowman). The series was directed-produced by James Hill. A short-run, follow-up series, **Worzel Gummidge Down Under** (UK tx C4, 1987 and 1989), was produced in New Zealand by Toti Productions, again with Pertwee and Stubbs.

Year Zero—The Silent Death of Cambodia
(ATV, 30/10/79)

Journalist John Pilger's 52-minute documentary presented the first footage to come out of that country in four years. Pilger and producer-director David I. Munro's film crew photographed some of the most repulsive, pitiable, and enraging effects of war and super-power diplomacy ever seen on television. At the end of the programme Pilger stated 'You can assume that most of the people you saw in tonight's film are now dead.' The ATV team included (*l. to r.*) cameraman Gerry Pinches (*kneeling*), Pilger, director David Munro, and sound recordist Steve Phillips; also researcher Nicholas Claxton. The world-wide response to **Year Zero** raised some £19 million in relief funds and one year later Pilger reported in **Cambodia—Year One** (ATV, 10/9/80) what had been achieved as well as pointing out how the suffering nation was being kept in the shadows by power politics. David Munro again produced-directed the 52-minute documentary. John Pilger had earlier featured in **Pilger** (ATV, 12/5–16/6/74), a 6 eps. × half-hour series in which he looked at situations ranging from Vietnam (some sixteen months after 'peace' was officially declared) to the plight of thalidomide victims, prisoners on remand, and the two worlds of a black teenager living in Newcastle; Charles Denton produced.

British television in the 1980s took off with a series of domestic 'firsts'. Channel Four, Britain's first new national television service for twenty years, was launched; a breakfast TV service was introduced; a cable and satellite TV network was established, and the use of video recorders spread from one home in seven in 1982 to 71.5 per cent of the country by 1992.

The most significant event during the early 1980s was the launch of Channel Four Television on 2 November 1982. Britain's second independent TV channel was established as a wholly owned subsidiary of the IBA and was required to 'encourage innovation and experiment'. The channel was financed by a subscription levied on the ITV companies, which in turn sold advertising time on the channel in their respective regions. Under its first chief executive, Jeremy Isaacs, Channel Four brought a new dimension to television, with its investment in films made for TV (which were also released to cinemas overseas) and the commissioning of varied and at times controversial programmes. In early 1987, for instance, Channel Four experimented with a red-bordered triangle, displayed continuously throughout films which might offend some viewers but this was eventually dropped when it became clear it actually attracted attention to controversial programmes. Alongside the opening of Channel Four, the Welsh Fourth Channel Authority—Sianel Pedwar Cymru (S4C)—was established to supply Welsh language programming.

A few months after the opening of Channel Four, TV-am won the franchise scramble to become the company to provide Britain's first independent nation-wide breakfast television service, starting in February 1983. Initially featuring a starry line-up of 'united artists', Anna Ford, David Frost, Michael Parkinson, Robert Kee, and Angela Rippon led by former British Ambassador Peter Jay, the company failed to establish itself as a TV service with 'a mission to explain' and with falling audience ratings it was soon obliged to recapture audiences with more lightweight entertainment. The BBC's morning TV service, however, had opened a month before TV-am, stealing an advantage over its ITV rival with a similar cosy, chatty format. It was later revised in October 1986 as a more hard news-based programme.

Cable TV opened up following the favourable Hunt Report of the Inquiry into Cable Expansion and Broadcasting Policy of 1982. Applications were invited for twelve franchises to operate multi-channel cable networks in 1983. A Cable Television Authority was established, with responsibility for awarding franchises and monitoring the companies' output. By 1988, with only ten cable services operational out of the twenty-five franchises then available, both public and corporate interests were still slow to take off.

In 1977 the UK was allocated five Direct Broadcasting by Satellite (DBS) channels at an international conference. In 1983 it was announced that the government would authorize the BBC to start services on two of the channels and would use a satellite built and provided by a UK consortium. The Home Secretary also announced that two satellite channels would be offered to the Independent Television Companies. January 1984 saw the start of the first commercial satellite channel, Sky Channel. In one year Sky Channel had exceeded its original target and reached 2.8 million equipped homes in Europe and 100,000 in Britain. In April 1986, the IBA advertised direct broadcasting by satellite contracts (a previous joint venture with the BBC and five independent companies having collapsed). By December of that year, British Satellite Broadcasting (BSB), a consortium which initially included Granada and Anglia TV, the Virgin Group, Amstrad, and Pearson (although Amstrad later withdrew from the group), was awarded a contract to provide a service. The franchise was for a term of fifteen years and would be the world's first privately financed national television service by DBS. By 1988 there were two competing systems: Astra (operated by the Société Européenne des Satellites in Luxembourg and backed by financial institutions along with Thames TV, Ulster TV, and TSW) and BSB. Following the successful launch of the Ariane rocket which placed the Sky satellite in orbit, the new Sky TV station began broadcasting on the Astra satellite in February 1989. Sky's original four channels consisted of Sky Channel (game shows), Sky News, Sky Films Channel, and Eurosport; Sky originally hoped to include the Disney Channel but that corporation later withdrew. November 1989 saw Sky Television celebrate its one-millionth customer. BSB began broadcasting in April 1990 with five channels, consisting of Power station (rock music), Galaxy (entertainment channel), Now Channel (news magazine), Movie Channel, and Sports Channel. Less than a year later, with BSB losing an estimated £8 million a week and Sky losing over £2 million a week, the two broadcasters merged and became BSkyB.

The Royal Wedding between HRH The Prince of Wales and Lady Diana Spencer in July 1981 was the first of the three major television events of the 1980s. The 5½-hour morning transmission followed the Carriage Procession to St Paul's Cathedral and the Marriage Service through to the Bride and Bridegroom's appearance on the Palace balcony. It was estimated that over 500 million viewers world-wide were reached by the London-based transmissions, with picture feeds supplied by BBC and ITV. Around sixty cameras were in use for the Wedding coverage on BBC, with some forty-four for the main morning coverage, including twelve in St Paul's. These cameras, apart from offering colour, were far more flexible and sensitive than those used for the 1953 Coronation, but while the equipment was more reliable, the professionalism of outside broadcast engineers and producers was tested by the greater expectations both audiences and broadcasters had of television's capabilities.

In 1982 the BBC was criticized over its reporting of the Falklands War. It was claimed to have been too 'even-handed' in its coverage of the Argentine and British forces. The BBC was obviously sensitive to criticisms of its coverage of the war, much of which was ill-informed or hasty, or a result of the difficulties caused by how the Ministry of Defence had managed the media and information. Director-General Alasdair Milne responded by saying the BBC was well aware of the responsibility it carried and of its need to maintain the balance between the public's 'right to know' and national security. The BBC gave detailed evidence about how it had handled these broadcasting problems to the House of Commons Select Committee on Defence. Subsequently, the Corporation was exonerated from the charge that BBC broadcasts had alerted Argentina to the imminence of the attack on Goose Green.

A renewed campaign to televise the proceedings of the House of Commons was launched in November 1987 by an all-party group led by former Labour Home Secretary Merlyn Rees. In spite of continued opposition from Prime Minister Margaret Thatcher, the House of Commons voted in January 1988 in favour of televising its proceedings for a six-month trial period. When the House of Commons Select Committee on Televising Proceedings of the House of Commons finally published the rules (in April 1989) under which cameras would be allowed into the Chamber, both the BBC and ITN complained that the rules were too restrictive. Under the rules, cameras would be forbidden to show MPs misbehaving and would have to focus on the Speaker's chair during any disorder. Although the Select Committee had published its rules governing the introduction of cameras in April, transmission did not begin until November 1989. In spite of the reservations held by many in the House, the initial reaction to admitting the television cameras was largely favourable. It soon became apparent, following the earlier trial period, that early guidelines, such as restricting the cameras to head and shoulder shots of MPs while speaking, needed to be modified. After the first two months, the rules were relaxed and it was also decided to permit wide-angle shots to show the reactions of groups of MPs.

Continuing government concern with the BBC's finances led to the setting up of the Peacock Committee in March 1985, primarily 'to assess the effects of the introduction of advertising or sponsorship on the BBC's home services, either as an alternative or a supplement to the income now received through the license fee'. The Peacock Report was published in July 1986. Its main recommendations were that advertisements should not be introduced into the BBC, that broadcasting should look to the twenty-first century, to take account of future developments in satellite and cable transmission, and that subscription should ultimately replace the licence fee, with broadcasters selling their products direct to the public. In a Commons debate on the future of broadcasting in November 1986, the Home Secretary supported Peacock's recommendation of an increase in independent production in broadcast services. The BBC expressed interest in commercial organizations funding programmes made by independent producers although they would not be allowed to mention particular products or lines of business since sponsored programmes are prohibited by the BBC's charter. In 1989, the Director-General of the BBC stated that subscription services would be a means of raising extra money for the BBC, although they should not substitute for the licence fee. Though the principle of publicly funded broadcasting was not under direct attack by the Conservative Government, an increasingly beleaguered BBC found itself forced to concede on a number of fronts.

The 1980s represented a period of big productions, due partly to the revived international interest in British television inherited from the critically acclaimed classic drama serials and documentaries of the previous decade. **Tenko**, **The Borgias** (despite its unintentional moments of humour), **Flame Trees of Thika**, **Brideshead Revisited**, **The Jewel in the Crown**, **Edge of Darkness**, **Lost Empires**, and **Fortunes of War** were among the big-budget productions that acquired both an appreciative audience and critical approval. The most talked-about playwright of the decade was probably Dennis Potter whose work during the 1980s (the *film noir*ish **The Singing Detective** and the sexually exploitative **Black Eyes**) had viewers split between delight and disgust.

But perhaps more interestingly it was a period noted for its steady stream of socially and politically slanted dramas (**Boys from the Blackstuff**, **Oi For England**, **Made in England**, **A Very British Coup**) and comedies (**Yes, Minister**, **Spitting Image**), which tended to reflect in one form or another the social and civil upheaval of the 'Thatcher years'. Quite possibly the 'yuppie' world of such series as **Capital City** and **Gentlemen and Players** at the close of the 1980s mirrored the inclination of the times more clearly.

Blade on the Feather
(LWT–Pennies from Heaven Ltd., 19/10/80)

Was the first of three TV films written by Dennis Potter under his own independent production banner with Kenith Trodd as producer; the other two were **Rain on the Roof** (LWT–Pennies from Heaven Ltd., 26/10/80; dir. Alan Bridges) and **Cream in My Coffee** (LWT–Pennies from Heaven Ltd., 2/11/80; dir. Gavin Millar). **Feather** starred Donald Pleasence (*right*) as a retired, Soviet-side spy heading a household containing his younger second wife, Kika Markham, his daughter, Phoebe Nicholls, and his seedy butler, Denholm Elliott. Tom Conti (*left*) played the mysterious visitor on a mission to eliminate the old man who had become a security risk. Richard Loncraine directed the 87-minute telefilm.

Bloody Kids
(Black Lion Films/ATV, 23/3/80)

A manic study of urban anarchy as two young boys, Leo (Richard Thomas) and Mike (Peter Clark), stage a knife fight at a football ground to impress and confuse the police; the joke backfires when Mike does accidentally stab his friend. Leo is rushed to hospital, although he is not badly hurt, and Mike goes on the run through the streets of the city. He joins a gang of teenagers, which includes the crazy Ken (Gary Holton, *left*, with Nula Conwell and Gwyneth Strong), as they run amok through shopping centres and precincts. Finally, Mike reaches Leo and together they precipitate an emergency evacuation of the hospital. The 90-minute TV feature (transmitted in a 105-minute slot) was written by Stephen Poliakoff for producer Barry Hanson; Stephen Frears directed. Photography was by Chris Menges; George Fenton supplied the music. Palace Pictures/BFI released the film theatrically in 1983.

Buccaneer
(BBC-1, 27/4–20/7/80)

Concerned the anxieties (both financial and physical) of a small air freight company called Red-Air which was run by pilot Tony Blair (played by Bryan Marshall; *left*) and financier Charles Burton (Clifford Rose); Pamela Salem (*pictured*) also appeared as journalist Monica Burton, the latter's wife. The 13 eps. × 50 mins. (première ep. was 55 mins.) series was created by Eric Paice and N. J. Crisp, and produced by Gerard Glaister.

Cribb
(Granada TV, 1980–81)

Author Peter Lovesey preferred to think of his Sgt. Cribb stories as Victorian police procedural novels, which is exactly what the TV series represented. Det. Sgt. Cribb (Alan Dobie; *right*) works for Scotland Yard's CID during its early days in the 1880s and most of his cases are representative of Victorian life, with the imaginative plots revolving around bare-knuckle prize-fighting, spiritualism, the seaside, Irish terrorism, and even one ('The Last Trumpet') dealing with London Zoo's sale of the legendary elephant Jumbo. Cribb's Scotland Yard superior Inspector Jowett (David Waller; *centre*) turns up to frustrate Cribb occasionally; William Simons (*left*) appears as Cribb's assistant Det. Con. Thackeray. Thirteen hour-long episodes were produced by June Wyndham-Davies; Brian Thompson, Peter and Jacqueline Lovesey, Bill Macilwraithe, and Arden Winch adapted/wrote the teleplays. The series was preceded by a 90-minute pilot episode ('Waxwork', 19/8/79; adapted by Pauline Macauley from the 1978 novel by Lovesey, pr.-dir. Wyndham-Davies) which was transmitted as part of the 1979 Granada TV **Screenplay** collection. ATV's 1963 **Sergeant Cork** series was based in the same period and developed along similar themes.

Death of a Princess
(ATV, 9/4/80)

Co-producer/director Antony Thomas's drama documentary about his investigation into the 1977 public execution of an Arabian princess and her lover made fascinating and at the same time sensational viewing. The 2-hour programme became the subject of overreaction by the (never specifically named) Saudi government and caused a political rift between the British government and the Saudi Arabian Royal Family. The film was shot in England and the Middle East, and co-produced by Martin McKeand from Thomas's script; Paul Freeman played the investigating journalist and Suzanne Abou Taleb played the unfortunate princess.

Did You See . . .?
(BBC-2, 1980–87; 1991–)

Television reviewing itself, or rather host Ludovic Kennedy (*right*; with guest Dr Jonathan Miller) exchanging comments on the previous week's TV output with his generally media-backgrounded guests (such as Janet Street-Porter, journalist Irma Kurtz, Salman Rushdie, Martin Amis) was the theme of this intelligent TV analysis programme. Producers over the early period were John Archer, Sue Mallinson, and Chris Mohr. Jeremy Paxman took over as presenter for the 1990s series. Commercial television's equivalent, in a sort of vox pop way, is **Right to Reply** (C4, 1982–86; 1988–) which allows the viewer to walk in off the street and use a 'Video Box' (a recording booth) to air their problems or pleasures about anything transmitted by Channel Four or ITV. The weekly programme then responds, with the participation of relevant programme makers, to the viewers' comments. **Right to Reply** presenters over the years have been Gus Macdonald (1982–86), Linda Agran (1988), Brian Hayes (1989–90), Rory McGrath (1991), and Sheena McDonald (1992–93).

Drake's Venture
(Westward TV, 28/12/80)

A colourful costume adventure starring John Thaw (*pictured, foreground*) as Francis Drake, dispatched by Queen Elizabeth I (Charlotte Cornwell) on a secret mission to raid the Spanish ports of South America for gold and treasure. The 110-minute TV movie was written by John Nelson Burton, photographed by David Howarth, designed by Jane Martin, and produced-directed by Lawrence Gordon-Clark. Paul Darrow also appeared, as Thomas Doughty.

The Enigma Files
(BBC-2, 15/4–22/7/80)

Tom Adams (*pictured*) starred as Det. Chief Insp. Nick Lewis whose job it was to deal with unsolved crimes, consigned to the Prisoners' Property Office. His associates were Kate Burton (Sharon Mughan), Executive Officer at the PPO, and Phil Strong (Duggie Brown), the PPO's Laboratory Technician. Derek Ingrey scripted the 15 eps. × 50 mins. series for producer Joe Waters.

Flickers
(ATV, 17/9–22/10/80)

Was set in the early days of the British cinema and featured Bob Hoskins (*2nd left*) as poverty-row showman Arnie Cole, touring his Travelling Bioscope Theatre around provincial village halls. Though his moving-picture exhibitions barely made enough money with which to survive, Arnie's personal ambition was to make comedy films rather than show them. His meeting up with the fiercely critical Maud (played by Frances de la Tour; *centre*) changed his life: he finally took a shot at movie-making. The 6 eps. × hour series was devised and written by Roy Clarke and produced by Joan Brown. Also pictured are Fraser Cains, *left*, and Andrew de la Tour.

1980

Fox
(Euston Films, 1980)

The individual and collective lives of the large south London Fox family were charted in a two-phase period as they tried to establish some sense of order and understanding within the clan leading up to and following the death of the dominant family head, Billy Fox (played by Peter Vaughan). Pictured are Elizabeth Spriggs (*seated*), Ray Winstone (*crouching*), (*standing, l. to r.*) Derrick O'Connor, Eamon Boland, Larry Lamb, Bernard Hill; and Rosemary Martin, Richard Weinbaum, and Cindy O'Callaghan made up the Fox dynasty. The thirteen hour-long episodes were written by Trevor Preston for producer Graham Benson and directed by Jim Goddard.

The Gentle Touch
(LWT, 1980–84)

Jill Gascoine starred as Det. Insp. Maggie Forbes (*pictured*, with co-star William Marlowe), a woman whose life was split between her roles as a wife (her husband was also a police officer), a mother, and being a policewoman. Kim Mills, Jack Williams, and Michael Verney-Elliott shared the producing chores over fifty-six hour-long episodes. The following year Gascoine/Forbes returned in **C.A.T.S. Eyes** (TVS, 1985–87) as the leader of a special intelligence squad (Covert Activities, Thames Section), under Home Office boss Beaumont (played by Don Warrington). Forbes's team consisted of Rosalyn Landor (later replaced by Tracy-Louise Ward) and Leslie Ash. Thirty hour-long episodes were produced; the series premièred with a 90-minute introductory story.

The Good Companions
(Yorkshire TV, 1980–81)

A 9 eps. × hour adaptation, by Alan Plater, of J. B. Priestley's famous novel about a struggling touring concert party in the 1930s. Cast included John Stratton, Judy Cornwell, Jeremy Nicholas, Vivienne Martin, Jan Francis, Frank Mills, Jo Kendall, Bryan Pringle, John Blythe, and Simon Green. Music was by David Fanshawe; Leonard Lewis produced.

Great Railway Journeys of the World
(BBC-2, 30/10–18/12/80)

Seven hour-long travel films exploring the still running famous rail routes; with Ludovic Kennedy (*pictured*) travelling New York–Los Angeles, Michael Frayn Sydney–Perth, Brian Thompson Bombay–Cochin, Michael Palin London–Kyle of Lochalsh, Michael Wood Cape Town–Victoria Falls, Miles Kington Lima–La Paz, and Eric Robson Paris–Budapest. Roger Laughton produced.

Hammer House of Horror
(ATV–Hammer Film Prod.–Chips Prod.–Cinema Arts, 1980)

A series of thirteen hour-long spine-chillers produced specially for TV by horror movie specialists Hammer Films under producer Roy Skeggs. Among the Hammer feature film directors contributing were Peter Sasdy ('The Thirteenth Reunion', 'Rude Awakening', 'Visitor from the Grave'), Alan Gibson ('The Silent Scream', 'The Two Faces of Evil'), and Don Sharp ('Guardian of the Abyss'). Peter Cushing is pictured in 'The Silent Scream' episode. **Hammer House of Mystery and Suspense** (Hammer Film Prod., 1984–85) followed a few years later, presenting a collection of thrillers in the 'Hitchcock' mould; Skeggs once again produced the 85-minutes series.

Hollywood
(Thames TV, 8/1–1/4/80)

A thirteen-part series (of hour episodes) spotlighting the Silent Era of American cinema history, focusing on the large-scale spectaculars, the film-makers (directors, cameramen, art directors), and the stars. Written, directed, and produced by Kevin Brownlow and David Gill, the expertly researched and carefully compiled series approached its silent-screen subject with just the right blend of historic data and wide-eyed wonder, aided by James Mason's low-key narration. The suitably grand theme music accompanying the series was by Carl Davis. The Brownlow–Gill team followed with **Unknown Chaplin** (Thames TV, 5–12–19/1/83), three hour-long episodes tracing the early films and working methods of Charlie Chaplin using rare out-takes and uncut rushes. Mason again narrated and Davis supplied the music. A later two-part, 2-hour documentary focused on **Buster Keaton—A Hard Act to Follow** (Thames TV, 30/9 and 7/10/87) in which the legendary comedian's early film-making life was recounted and explored through some excellent use of rarely seen footage. Lindsay Anderson narrated and Davis once again scored.

Ireland: A Television History
(BBC-2–Radio Telefis Eireann, 2/12/80–24/2/81)

The first major attempt to tell the history of a country on television, from its beginning to the present day, through eyewitness accounts and archive footage (at times in conflict with what was actually recalled). Programme writer-presenter Robert Kee (*pictured*) began his 13 eps. × 50/55 mins. story from 800 years ago when England first became involved with Ireland and took the history through to the country's most recent decade of violence. Jenny Barraclough produced; Jeremy Isaacs was series producer. Fourteen years earlier RTE had produced **Insurrection—Easter Week, 1916** (BBC-2/Telefis Eireann, 24/4–1/5/66), a dramatic reconstruction in 8 eps. × 25 mins. of the Dublin Easter Rising and fierce week-long battle for freedom and independence. The cast featured Conor Farrington, Eoin Ò Suilleabhain, Jim Norton, Ronnie Walsh, and Michael McAuliffe. The dramatization by Hugh Leonard was produced and directed by Louis Lentin. **The Troubles** (Thames TV, 5/1–2/2/81) presented a five-part documentary series on the background to the Northern Ireland problem, covering events from the British conquest of Ireland to contemporary situations. Narration was by Rosalie Crutchley. Richard Broad and Ian Stuttard produced; Taylor Downing was associate producer.

Juliet Bravo
(BBC-1, 1980–85)

Was the radio call sign of Insp. Jean Darblay (Stephanie Turner; *pictured*), the new chief in charge of the all-male Hartley Section Police Station. The series, created by Ian Kennedy Martin, dealt with the personal and professional pressures experienced by a woman holding down a top job in, traditionally, a male domain. The role of Inspector was taken over by Anna Carteret in 1983. Terence Williams and Colin Shindler produced the first two series; Jonathan Alwyn and Geraint Morris the later series.

Lady Killers
(Granada TV, 1980–81)

Robert Morley introduced this anthology of famous murder cases involving women. The first series of seven hour-long episodes featured Ruth Ellis (played by Georgina Hale in 'Lucky, Lucky Thirteen!'), Charlotte Bryant (Rita Tushingham in 'Don't Let Them Kill Me on Wednesday'), and Amelia Elizabeth Dyer (Joan Sims in 'Suffer Little Children') among the lady killers. The second series of seven hour-long plays, now screened as **Ladykillers**, premièred with 'Miss Elmore' (10/7/81; wr. Edwin Pearce, dir. Nicholas Ferguson), starring John Fraser as Dr Crippen and Hannah Gordon as Ethel Le Neve. The programme was produced by Pieter Rogers. The scene pictured is from the 'Not For the Nervous' episode with Elaine Paige. **Saturday Night Theatre** also presented a six-part series of plays about women criminals in Victorian times under the subtitle of 'Wicked Women' (14/2–21/3/70), produced-directed by David Cunliffe.

1980

Metal Mickey
(LWT, 1980–83)

Metal Mickey was a 5 ft. robot (in the R2-D2/*Star Wars* style) built by young Ken Wilberforce (Ashley Knight) to help around the oddball household inhabited by Haley (Lucinda Bateson; *left*), Steve (Gary Shail; *2nd left*), Granny (Irene Handl; *centre*), Janey (Lola Young), Mother (Georgina Melville), and Father (Michael Stainton). The half-hour, 'children's slot' series was produced by Michael Dolenz; Colin Bostock-Smith supplied the scripts.

The Nesbitts Are Coming
(Yorkshire TV, 17/4–22/5/80)

The Nesbitts were a family of roving villains who wandered from town to town and battled with law and order in this offbeat comedy series. The principal players were (*l. to r.*) Deidre Costello as Marle Nesbitt, Christian Rodska as Tom Nesbitt, Maggie Jones as Mrs Nesbitt, Clive Swift as Mr Nesbitt, and John Price as Len Nesbitt. This sitcom with music, devised and written by Dick Sharples, developed from the characters Sharples created for a two-part episode of **Z Cars** ('The Nesbitts are Back', tx 1 and 2/5/67) in the 1960s and guest starred Hylda Baker (as Mrs Nesbitt), Jack Woolgar (Mr Nesbitt), Barry Lowe (Tom), Graham James (Len), and Lynda Marchal (Marlene). The six-part Yorkshire TV series was directed-produced by Ronnie Baxter.

Newsnight
(BBC-2, 1980–)

A news and current affairs programme offering the viewer a longer and more reflective look at the day's news, at what has been going on in the world and why. Original studio line-up included reporters Peter Snow (*2nd left*), Peter Hobday, Charles Wheeler (*right*), and John Tusa; up-to-the-minute newsroom summaries came from Fran Morrison (*left*) and nightly sports news from David Davies (*2nd right*). It represented the first time that the BBC combined its news and current affairs resources to provide an in-depth programme at a regular time at the end of the evening.

Nobody's Perfect
(LWT, 1980–82)

A domestic sitcom charting the highs and lows in the lives of Bill and Sam Hooper (played by Elaine Stritch and Richard Griffiths), a middle-aged couple who had been married for eight years; it was a second marriage for both. Also appearing were Kim Braden, Moray Watson, and Ruby Head. Humphrey Barclay produced. American producer Norman Lear's **Maude** series (CBS TV, 1972–78) was the basis for this programme. Elaine Stritch is pictured with guest Carroll Baker in a 1982 episode.

Oppenheimer
(BBC-2, 29/10–10/12/80)

A powerful seven-part drama series about the rise and fall of J. Robert Oppenheimer (played by Sam Waterston; *pictured*), 'the father of the atomic bomb'. Peter Prince's scripts told the story from when Oppenheimer was the head of the US government secret laboratory at Los Alamos, New Mexico, where the bombs that fell on Hiroshima and Nagasaki (effectively ending the Pacific War) were built. When Oppenheimer, in later years, spoke out publicly against the destructive use of technology he was subjected to a security clearance hearing which amounted to a trial for treason. Also in the cast were Jana Shelden, Kate Harper, Garrick Hagon, and Peter Whitman. Barry Davis directed for producer Peter Goodchild.

Play Your Cards Right
(LWT–Talbot TV–Goodson-Todman Prod., 1980–87)

A three-stage game show with contestants using their knowledge of public opinion and skill in a card game, hosted by Bruce Forsyth (*shown*). The show was devised by Chester Feldman and produced (during the early series) by David Bell. Some seven months after its première it was retitled **Bruce Forsyth's Play Your Cards Right**. Forsyth later hosted **You Bet!** (LWT, 1988–), a large-scale, off-beat game show originally produced by Richard Hearsey; Matthew Kelly took over as host in 1991 with Linda Beadle as producer.

Staying On
(Granada TV, 28/12/80)

In a moving postscript to the story of the British Raj this drama, based on Paul Scott's award-winning novel and filmed on location in India, featured the elderly couple of Tusker and Lucy Smalley (played by Trevor Howard and Celia Johnson; *pictured*) who had chosen to 'stay on' as the sole English residents of a small Indian hill station. The 100-minute film was adapted by Julian Mitchell for producer Irene Shubik. Silvio Narizzano directed; music was by Carl Davis; photography by Wolfgang Suschitzky.

Take the High Road
(Scottish TV, 1980–)

Domestic soap serial about the changing pattern of life in rural Scotland and set around the sprawling Glendarroch Estate. Original players included Edith Macarthur (as Elizabeth Cunningham, owner of Glendarroch House), Caroline Ashley (daughter Fiona), Alec Monteath (as Dougal Lachlan), Eileen McCallum (as Isabel Blair; pictured, *right*, with Irene Sunters) and Jimmy Chisholm (as Jimmy Blair). In 1987, when the Elizabeth Cunningham character was killed off, Jan Waters and Michael Browning joined the cast as the new owners of the Estate, Lady Margaret and Sir John Ross-Gifford. Clarke Tait was the original director-producer of the half-hour serial.

Training Dogs the Woodhouse Way
(BBC-2, 7/1–10/3/80)

Barbara Woodhouse (*left*) was another delightful TV eccentric whose shrill 'Walkies!' command to her canine pupils made her a household celebrity with viewers. In this 10 eps. × 25 mins. series she demonstrated her own quick method of training domestic dogs—as well as their owners! The series was produced by Peter Riding. Later she presented **Woodhouse Roadshow** (BBC-1, 15/9–27/10/82) in which she travelled the country training dogs and ponies; Bryn Brooks produced.

Why Didn't They Ask Evans?
(LWT, 30/3/80)

Was the first of an irregular series of Agatha Christie adaptations for ITV. Based on Christie's 1934 novel, and set during that period, the 210-minute production featured the amateur sleuths Bobby Jones (James Warwick) and Lady Frances Derwent (Francesca Annis, pictured with John Gielgud) in a country estate murder mystery. John Davies and Tony Wharmby directed for producer Jack Williams. This was followed by an adaptation of the 1929 novel, **Agatha Christie's The Seven Dials Mystery** (LWT, 8/3/81), following the espionage and secret society adventures of Bundle (Cheryl Campbell) and Jimmy Thesiger (James Warwick). Pat Sandys adapted the 150-minute production for producer Jack Williams; executive producer Tony Wharmby directed.

Yes Minister
(BBC-2, 1980–82)

Hilarious comedy series featuring the Rt. Hon. James Hacker MP (played by Paul Eddington; *left*), a newly appointed Minister for Administrative Affairs, and Permanent Under-Secretary, Sir Humphrey Appleby (Nigel Hawthorne; *right*), following their respective struggles to gain and hold on to the levers of power. Creators Antony Jay and Jonathan Lynn supplied suitably convoluted plotlines embellished with excellent dialogue exchanges. When Hacker later became Prime Minister the series returned, appropriately, as **Yes, Prime Minister** (BBC-2, 1986–88), with Sir Humphrey now promoted to Cabinet Secretary; Derek Fowlds also returned as their put-upon Private Secretary Bernard Woolley.

Artemis 81
(BBC-1, 29/12/81)

A peculiar science-fantasy film involving aliens (in the shape of Roland Curram, *left*, and Sting, *right*), pagan relics, ancient curses, and a young student of the paranormal (played by Hywel Bennett). Dinah Stabb, Dan O'Herlihy, Anthony Steel, Daniel Day Lewis, and Ingrid Pitt also appeared. The 185-minute production by David Rose was written by David Rudkin and directed by Alastair Reid.

Bergerac
(BBC-1, 1981–91)

Robert Banks Stewart created and produced, initially, this detective series set on the Channel Island of Jersey. Det. Sgt. Jim Bergerac (John Nettles; *left*) was the offshore policeman who often found himself caught up in the affairs of the super-rich in the isolated millionaire's community of Jersey. Also appearing were Terence Alexander, as Bergerac's former father-in-law Charlie Hungerford, and Cecile Paoli (*right*), as one-time girlfriend Francine (later on in the series he retired from the force and shared his life with Danielle Aubry, played by Therese Liotard, between freelance detective adventures). **Bergerac** came about when Trevor Eve, star of **Shoestring**, did not want to do another series and producer Robert Banks Stewart decided to adapt the sleuth format/thriller series to Jersey. The theme music was composed by George Fenton.

Big Jim and the Figaro Club
(BBC-2, 8/7–12/8/81)

Developed from a one-off 30-minute play by Ted Walker screened under the **Turning Year Tales** (BBC-2, 24/6–5/8/79) series of seven filmed plays. The **Big Jim** stories, set during the early 1950s and featuring the humorous working-class fellowship of a gang of building tradesmen employed by a seaside council, starred Norman Rossington (as Big Jim; *driving*) and Roland Curram (as the nasty Clerk of Works). Also appearing were (*l. to r.*) David Beckett, Sylveste McCoy, David John, and Gordon Rollings, riding shotgun. Bob Hoskins narrated the 5 eps. × 30 mins. series produced by Colin Rose for BBC Bristol.

Bognor
(Thames TV, 1981)

Of the title was Simon Bognor (David Horovitch, pictured with Giselle Wolf) of the Board of Trade's investigative arm. This twice-weekly series of 18 eps. × half-hour lighthearted mysteries was based on the novels of Tim Heald (the first of which was published in 1973) and adapted by T. R. Bowen (12 eps.) and Carey Harrison (6 eps.). Ewan Roberts and Joanna McCallum were also featured. A later mini-series, **Just Desserts** (Thames TV, 9–16–23/3/82; adapt. Bowen, dir. Robert Tronson), brought Bognor back in a three-part drama in which he was assigned to investigate the world of top-class restaurants. Series producer was Bernard Krichefski; John Frankau was executive producer.

The Borgias
(BBC-2, 14/10–16/12/81)

The colourful and at times unintentionally amusing serial story of Rodrigo Borgia (Adolfo Celi; *centre*) who, in spite of his age and his many illegitimate children, set about achieving election to the papal throne by a mixture of bribery, blackmail, and political cunning. The programme was critically slammed on original screening for the actors' gabbled delivery and theatrical overplaying. The 7 eps. × 55 mins./3 eps. × 50 mins. also starred Oliver Cotton (*left*), Anne Louise Lambert, and Alfred Burke; Seretta Wilson is pictured right. Music was by Georges Delerue; Mark Shivas produced.

Brideshead Revisited
(Granada TV, 12/10–22/12/81)

Evelyn Waugh's popular novel was dramatized, for the first time, by John Mortimer as a serial story following a group of characters over three turbulent decades and moving between great English houses and scenes in Oxford, Venice, London, Paris, North Africa, and New York. Jeremy Irons (*right*), Anthony Andrews (*left*), Diana Quick, John Gielgud, Laurence Olivier, and Stephane Audran led the large cast. Charles Sturridge and Michael Lindsay-Hogg directed for Derek Granger's production.

Bullseye

(ATV, 1981; Central TV, 1982–85;
Central TV–Chatsworth TV, 1986–89;
Central TV–Phi Television, 1990–91;
Central TV, 1992–)

Jim Bowen hosted this quiz show
based on the rather quirky
combination of darts and general
knowledge, with contestants
playing in pairs and testing their
skill at scoring on the dartboard to
qualify for a round of questions to
win money and prizes. World-
ranking darts players were
brought in as guest competitors.
The series was originally
produced by Peter Holmans.
Pictured during a Christmas
special edition are (centre) guests
Les Dennis, Marti Caine, and,
wearing glasses, Jim Bowen.

The Chinese Detective

(BBC-1, 1981–82)

Was Det. Sgt. John Ho (David Yip;
right) of east London's Limehouse
district. The stories and subplots
moved between screaming-tyre
police action and the careful,
personal world of Ho, a natural
loner, as he tried to come to terms
with his life outside the strict rules
of the Chinese community. Derek
Martin played his superior, Det.
Chief Insp. Berwick, and Robert
Lee (left) was his father, Joe Ho.
The series, of 10 eps. × 50 mins.,
was created by Ian Kennedy
Martin. Terence Williams
produced.

Dangermouse

(Thames TV–Cosgrove-Hall Prod.,
1981–87)

Colourfully animated series
featuring secret agent
Dangermouse (centre), his partner
Penfold (left), and their arch-
enemy Baron Greenback.
Splendid animation work and
exciting story-lines, for the
younger set, were supported by
the character voices of David
Jason, Terry Scott, Edward Kelsey,
and Brian Trueman (the latter also
scripted). The series of 15-minute
episodes was produced by Mark
Hall and Brian Cosgrove. In 1988
Cosgrove and Hall produced the
delightful Daffy Duck-like **Count
Duckula** (Thames TV–Cosgrove-
Hall Prod., 1988–) which
followed the animated adventures
of a Bela Lugosi-resembling duck
(right); Jason also supplied the title
character's voice.

The Day of the Triffids

(BBC-1, 10/9–15/10/81)

Adapted from John Wyndham's
novel by Douglas Livingstone as a
6 eps. × 30 mins. serial, this
science-fiction tale of the world
being taken over by a species of
mobile plants following a
radiation shower from a meteor
storm was an enthusiastic attempt
to combine an end-of-the-world
thriller with special effects fantasy.
John Duttine, Emma Relph,
Maurice Colbourne, and Stephen
Yardley appeared in the David
Maloney production directed by
Ken Hannam.

A Fine Romance

(LWT, 1981–84)

A domestic comedy series, written
by Bob Larbey, about a couple of
adults fumbling their way through
to becoming a couple; Laura (Judi
Dench; 2nd left) was contented and
capable, Mike (Michael Williams;
right) was waiting for someone to
make his mind up. Real-life
husband and wife team of
Williams and Dench filled the
roles with perfect theatrical ease.
Richard Warwick (left) and Susan
Penhaligon (2nd right) supported.
James Cellan Jones and Don
Leaver produced-directed.

The Flame Trees of Thika
(Euston Films, 1/9–13/10/81)

A visually rich and colourful dramatization by co-producer John Hawkesworth of the autobiographical novel by Elspeth Huxley. The seven hour-long episodes, filmed on location in Kenya, told of young Elspeth (played by Holly Aird; *right*) and her mother Tilly (Hayley Mills; *left*) trying to adjust to their new life in Africa in the period leading up to the outbreak of the First World War. Roy Ward Baker directed; Christopher Neame co-produced.

Game for a Laugh
(LWT, 1981–85)

Targeted the studio audience and innocent members of the public (**Candid Camera** style) for its often juvenile pranks and mad games. The result was usually an uncomfortable brew of embarrassment and forced humour. The original line-up of presenters were (*l. to r.*) Matthew Kelly, Sarah Kennedy, Henry Kelly, and Jeremy Beadle. The latter continued with more candid camera stunts and situations in **Beadle's About** (LWT, 1986–90) and **Beadle's Box of Tricks** (LWT, 1989), later presenting highlights of home videos that went disastrously wrong with **You've Been Framed!** (Granada TV, 1990–).

Going Gently
(BBC-2, 5/6/81)

Thomas Ellice's psychologically and emotionally stunning play (shown under the **Playhouse** presentation banner), adapted for television from the novel by Robert C. S. Downs, featuring a pair of terminal cancer patients and their nurse in a bleak hospital ward setting. Norman Wisdom, Fulton Mackay, and Judi Dench, as patients and nurse, delivered exceptional performances for director Stephen Frears in Innes Lloyd's 70-minute production.

Going Out
(Southern TV, 1981)

Writer Phil Redmond's addictive 6 eps. × 25 mins. series following the lost and lonely lives of a group of teenagers for the first six weeks after they had left an inner-city comprehensive. The central characters were Sammy (Perry Benson; *right*), Roger (Andrew Paul; *left*), Sean (Marcus Francis; *2nd right*), Gerry (Linda Robson), Cathy (Michele Winstanley), and Dikey (Peter-Hugo Daly; *2nd left*); Gerard Kelly played the local thug, Arty Jackson. Colin Nutley was director-producer.

Hi-De-Hi!
(BBC-1, 1981–88)

The sitcom misadventures and mishaps of the entertainment staff of the fictitious Maplin's Holiday Camp, set in 1959. The cast featured Simon Cadell (as manager Jeffrey Fairbrother; later replaced by another manager played by David Griffin), Paul Shane, Ruth Madoc, Jeffrey Holland, Leslie Dwyer, Felix Bowness, Diane Holland, Barry Howard, and Su Pollard (*pictured*). The series was created and written by Jimmy Perry & David Croft (the latter also produced). A 40-minute pilot programme introducing the characters and setting was shown on 1/1/80. An hour-long pilot programme for the series **You Rang, M'Lord?** was shown on BBC-1 on 29/12/88 featuring some of the main **Hi-De-Hi!** cast (Shane, Holland, Pollard) as servants in an Edwardian household; the subsequent series (1990–93) was also a Perry & Croft collaboration.

The History Man
(BBC-2, 4–25/1/81)

Starred Antony Sher (*left*) as sociology lecturer Howard Kirk who with his wife Barbara (Geraldine James; *right*) were fashionable Watermouth University's well-known progressive couple in this satirical 2 eps. × 50 mins., 2 eps. × 60 mins. serial. Supporting players included Isla Blair, Paul Brooke, Laura Davenport, Veronica Quilligan, and Maggie Steed. The screenplay was by Christopher Hampton and was based on the novel by Malcolm Bradbury. Robert Knights directed Michael Wearing's BBC Birmingham production.

The Hitch-Hiker's Guide to the Galaxy
(BBC-2, 5/1–9/2/81)

Author Douglas Adams's marvellous satire of science-fiction concepts and conventions, featuring Simon Jones, David Dixon (*centre*), Mark Wing-Davey (*left*), Sandra Dickinson (*right*), and David Learner; with computer read-out voice-over by Peter Jones. The 6 eps. × 35 mins. serial was produced by Alan J. W. Bell.

Kinvig
(LWT, 4/9–16/10/81)

A 7-part × half-hour science fantasy sitcom written with a certain malevolent humour by Nigel Kneale and following the adventures of an electrical repair man, Des Kinvig (Tony Haygarth), who was transported to the planet Mercury by a stunningly beautiful alien called Miss Griffin (Prunella Gee). Brian Simmons co-directed the première episode with producer-director Les Chatfield. Haygarth and Gee are pictured.

Maybury
(BBC-2, 12/5–4/8/81; 24/6–5/8/83)

Was the first drama series to be set in a hospital psychiatric unit, presenting stories reflecting typical case histories. The aim was to demythologize mental illness and psychiatry in an entertaining fashion. Patrick Stewart (*right*; with Kenneth Haigh and Madhave Sharma) starred as Dr Edward Roebuck. Ruth Boswell produced the 13 eps. × 50 mins. / 7 eps. × 50 mins. series.

Nanny
(BBC-1, 1981–83)

Wendy Craig starred in this 30 eps. × 55 mins. series featuring the life and nursery work of Nanny Barbara Gray (Craig, *pictured*, with Charles Langdale) during the 1930s. David Burke, Jane Booker, and John Quayle also appeared. The programme, based on an idea by Craig, was produced by Guy Slater (first two series) and Bernard Krichefski (final series).

Never the Twain
(Thames TV, 1981–83; 1986–89)

Sitcom about two feuding antiques dealers, played by Donald Sinden (*right*) and Windsor Davies (*left*), whose children (Julia Watson and Robin Kermode) get married, despite their fathers' ongoing bickering. Johnnie Mortimer wrote the half-hour series for director-producer Peter Frazer-Jones.

Only Fools and Horses
(BBC-1, 1981–83; 1985–86; 1989; 1990–91)

The hilarious wheeling-dealing antics of south London wide boy 'Del' Trotter (played with charming ease by David Jason; *centre*), assisted by his younger, generally put-upon brother Rodney (Nicholas Lyndhurst; *left*) and Grandad (Lennard Pearce; *right*; later with Buster Merryfield as Uncle Albert). This John Sullivan-scripted sitcom was one of the comedy highlights of 1980s BBC television. Ray Butt and Gareth Gwenlan produced.

1981

Postman Pat
(BBC-1, 1981–)

Created by children's book author and former teacher John Cunliffe, this stop-frame puppet animation series featured the leisurely and amusing tales of a rural postman, Pat, 'and his black-and-white cat' called Jess, as they wound their way around the little town of Greendale. Ken Barry supplied the narration and voices; music was by Bryan Daly. Ivor Wood was the producer and designer; and later founder of Woodland Animations, which took over licensing of **Postman Pat** from the BBC in 1989. The original 13 eps. × 15 mins. were run and re-run for over ten years.

Private Schulz
(BBC-2, 6/5–10/6/81)

At the outbreak of the Second World War Schulz (played by Michael Elphick; *left*) is released from Spandau jail where he had served a sentence for fraud. His aim is to sit out the war in a safe, anonymous job far from hostilities. Instead, he is mistakenly recruited into SS Counter Espionage, where he dreams up the idea of producing forged banknotes to flood the British wartime economy. His commander, and accomplice, SS officer Major Neuheim, was played by Ian Richardson (*right*); Billie Whitelaw played the ambitious, Dietrich-like, Bertha Freyer. This wonderfully macabre farce, in 6 eps. × 50 mins., was written by the late Jack Pulman; Robert Chetwyn directed for Philip Hinchcliffe's production.

A Sense of Freedom
(Scottish TV, 17/2/81)

Drama based on the autobiography of murderer Jimmy Boyle (played by David Hayman; *pictured*), a violent criminal who reacted with equal brutality against the tough prison system. Jake D'Arcy, Alex Norton, and Fulton Mackay also appeared. The script was by Peter McDougall; John Mackenzie directed Jeremy Isaacs's 105-minute production. Music was supplied by Frankie Miller, with Rory Gallagher and his band; photography by Chris Menges.

Smuggler
(HTV–Gatetarn Prod., 1981)

Action-adventure series, set in 1802, about ex-naval officer turned smuggler Jack Vincent (Oliver Tobias; *pictured centre*) living by his wits and his sword. Paul Knight and Sidney Cole produced the thirteen half-hour episodes, written, for the most part, by Richard Carpenter. Tobias's Jack Vincent returned in a 12 eps. × half-hour sequel, **Adventurer** (Thames TV–Gatetarn–TV New Zealand, 1987), created by Carpenter (who also wrote most of the stories), Paul Knight, and Sidney Cole, with the latter also producing.

Solo
(BBC-1, 1981–82)

The plot of this Carla Lane-scripted sitcom was that 30-year-old Gemma Palmer (played by Felicity Kendal; *pictured*) decided to reinstate her independence by spring-cleaning her unsatisfactory life (dismissing her unfaithful boyfriend, quitting her job) and going it alone. The 13 eps. × 30 mins. also featured Stephen Moore (as ex-boyfriend Danny) and Elspet Gray (as mother Mrs Palmer). Gareth Gwenlan produced.

Sorry!
(BBC-1, 1981–88)

Ronnie Corbett (*left*) played the depressed hero Timothy Lumsden, a 41-year-old still living at home and dominated by his mother, in this comedy series written by Ian Davidson and Peter Vincent. Barbara Lott (*right*) co-starred as his mother. The series was produced by David Askey. Some ten years earlier Corbett had appeared in a similar sitcom, **Now Look Here!** (BBC-1, 1971–3), where he had played a mother-dominated bachelor; with Madge Ryan (as Mother). A second series saw the Corbett character married, to Laura (played by Rosemary Leach), and in his own home but still plagued by the interfering Mother (with Gillian Lind in the role). **Now Look Here!** was written by Barry Cryer and Graham Chapman; Bill Hitchcock produced the first series, Douglas Argent the second series. **Son of the Bride** (BBC-1, 6/6–11/7/73), similarly, offered a 6 eps. × 30 mins. comedy featuring Terry Scott as a man who had yet to sever the mental umbilical cord with his mother (played by Mollie Sugden); John Kane scripted for producer Peter Whitmore.

Taff Acre
(HTV, 1981)

Short-run, twice-weekly afternoon soap serial set in a present-day Welsh village, with the Johnson family (played by Richard Davies (*pictured*), Stuart Davis, Rhoda Lewis, Beth Morris, Dewi Morris, and Sue Jones Davies) at the centre of the stories. Twenty-six half-hour episodes were produced by Alan Clayton.

Tenko
(BBC-1, 1981–82; 1984)

Japanese prisoner-of-war drama featuring a group of British women fleeing from the invasion of Singapore who are captured by the Japanese forces. An intentionally gritty, grubby series starring Anne Bell, Stephanie Beacham (*pictured, centre*), Patricia Lawrence, Claire Obennan, Stephanie Cole, Emily Bolton, and Burt Kwouk (*foreground right*) as Captain Yamuchi. Lavinia Warner created the 30 eps. × 55 mins. series, produced by Ken Riddington and Vere Lorrimer. A 110-minute conclusion was shown as **Tenko Reunion** (BBC-1, 26/12/85), set in 1950 Malaya; Michael Owen Morris directed Jill Hyem's script for producer Riddington.

1981/2

Triangle
(BBC-1, 1981–83)

Covered the twice-weekly (Mondays and Wednesdays) serial fortunes of the Triangle Line, a ferry company working the geometrical route between Felixstowe, Gothenburg, and Amsterdam. The sea-borne serial, created and produced by Bill Sellars, featured Kate O'Mara (*centre*), Michael Craig (*left*), Larry Lamb (*right*), Nigel Stock, Douglas Sheldon, Nicolette McKenzie, Elizabeth Larner, Paul Jerricho, and Cindy O'Callaghan.

Winston Churchill—The Wilderness Years
(Southern TV, 6/9–11/10/81)

Was set during the period of Churchill's life when he almost sank into political oblivion, from the General Election of 1929 to the outbreak of the Second World War. Robert Hardy (*seated*) played Churchill, with Sian Phillips as Clementine and Nigel Havers as son Randolph (*pictured*). The series was devised by producer Richard Broke and Martin Gilbert. Ferdinand Fairfax directed; Mark Shivas was executive producer.

Wolcott
(ATV, 13–14–15/1/81)

George William Harris (*pictured*) starred as police detective Winston Churchill Wolcott, a tough, black, East End policeman who was moved from the uniformed branch to the CID and faced trouble and racial tension inside and outside the Force. The three-part mini-serial was scripted by Barry Wasserman and Patrick Carroll for producer Jacky Stoller; Colin Bucksey directed.

World's End
(BBC-2, 1/10–18/12/81)

A 13 part × 30 mins. serial story about an extremely varied bunch of people who all live in the London locality of World's End, that annexe of Chelsea where the most disparate of types mingle. The Mulberry pub was the crossroads where all the characters congregated; players included (*l. to r., back row*) Paul Brooke, Peter Harlowe, Pam Scotcher, Tom Marshall, Michael Angelis, Neville Smith, Harry Fowler, and (*front row*) Primi Townsend, Helen Bush, Ellen Pollock, and Catherine Neilson. The series was created and written by Ted Whitehead; Pedr James produced.

The Agatha Christie Hour
(Thames TV, 1982)

A series of ten hour-long plays based on stories by Christie: 'The Case of the Middle-Aged Wife' (7/9/82; adapt. Freda Kelsall, dir. Michael Simpson); 'In a Glass Darkly' (14/9/82; adapt. William Corlett, dir. Desmond Davis); 'The Girl in the Train' (21/9/82; adapt. Corlett, dir. Brian Farnham); 'The Fourth Man' (28/9/82; adapt. Corlett, dir. Simpson); 'The Case of the Discontented Soldier' (5/10/82; adapt. T. R. Bowen, dir. Simpson); 'Magnolia Blossom' (12/10/82; adapt. John Bryden Rogers, dir./exec. prod. John Frankau); 'The Mystery of the Blue Jar' (19/10/82; adapt. Bowen, dir. Cyril Coke); 'The Red Signal' (2/11/82; adapt. Corlett, dir./exec. prod. Frankau); 'Jane in Search of a Job' (9/11/82; adapt. Gerald Savory, dir. Christopher Hodson); 'The Manhood of Edward Robinson' (16/11/82; adapt. Savory, dir. Farnham).

Airline
(Yorkshire TV, 1982)

Set in the post-war 1940s, this action-drama series followed the hit-and-miss aviation business adventures of demobbed pilot Jack Ruskin (Roy Marsden; *right*) as he tried to make a living out of running his own, one-plane air service. Richard Heffer, Sean Scanlan, Polly Hemingway, and Terence Rigby (*centre*) also appeared. The 9 eps. × hour series was created by Wilfred Greatorex; designed by Richard Jarvis & David Crozier; and produced by Michael Ferguson.

A. J. Wentworth, BA
(Thames TV, 1982)

Was a series of six half-hour comedies about the life of a schoolmaster (played by Arthur Lowe; *centre left*, with Harry Andrews) during the 1940s. Based on H. F. Ellis's short stories, the series was adapted for television by Basil Boothroyd. Michael Mills produced and directed. The series was transmitted some four months after actor Arthur Lowe's death.

Beau Geste
(BBC-1, 31/10–19/12/82)

P. C. Wren's 1925 adventure novel of British upper-class honour mingling with life in the rough and rugged ranks of the nineteenth-century French Foreign Legion was produced by Barry Letts for the early Sunday evening audience as an 8 eps. × 30 mins. serial escapade. Despite its toning down of anything remotely 'brutal', the programme was an interesting departure from the usual BBC-1 Sunday classic format while retaining, for the most part, this programme slot's traditional quality of production. Coming in at a total cost of £600,000, the serial managed to effect the Arab–Legionnaire conflict from the filming location of a disused sandpit near Wareham, Dorset, as well as a re-created desert fort constructed from plaster and scaffolding by designer Paul Joel. Benedict Taylor (as Beau), Anthony Calf (Digby), and Jonathon Morris (John) starred in Alistair Bell's dramatization, directed by Douglas Camfield.

Bird of Prey
(BBC-1, 22/4–13/5/82)

An intriguing four-part thriller featuring innocuous civil servant Henry Jay (Richard Griffiths) who stumbled across a massive computer-based conspiracy and became a target for the 'invisible agents' behind the shadowy enterprise. The 1 ep. × 55 mins., 3 eps. × 50 mins. serial co-starred Jeremy Child, Carole Nimmons, and Jim Broadbent. Michael Rolfe directed Ron Hutchinson's screenplay for producer Michael Wearing. Hutchinson provided a sequel, **Bird of Prey 2** (BBC-1, 6–27/9/84), involving Henry Jay (Griffiths) in more computer fraud crime; Nimmons and Lee Montague also appeared. Don Leaver directed Bernard Krichefski's production.

1982

Black on Black
(C4/LWT, 1982–85)

Presented news, opinions, and events from black communities in Britain and around the world, compiled and prepared by a top team of black reporters (Simi Bedford, Kim Gordon, Julian Henriques, and Elaine Smith). Original presenter was Beverly Anderson; later presenters included (*l. to r., standing*) Trevor Phillips, Pauline Black, Victor Romero Evans, and (*foreground*) main presenter Louise Bennett. The hour-long series also offered the latest in black music, theatre, and art. Beverly Anderson presented; Trevor Phillips produced.

The Bounder
(Yorkshire TV, 1982–83)

The out-of-synch duo in this sitcom about oddball couplings were Peter Bowles (*left*) as a sophisticated rogue, just released from prison after serving time for embezzlement, who moves in with his ex-brother-in-law, George Cole (*right*). Fourteen half-hour episodes were written by Eric Chappell and produced-directed by Vernon Lawrence.

Boys from the Black Stuff
(BBC-2, 10/10–7/11/82)

This five-part black comedy-drama written by Alan Bleasdale about the individual and collective lives of a Merseyside tarmac gang was based on Bleasdale's 110-minute play **The Black Stuff** (BBC-2, 2/1/80), featuring Michael Angelis (as Chrissy), Bernard Hill (as Yosser; with his now near legendary 'Gi' us a job?' cry), Tom Georgeson (as Dixie), Alan Igbon (as Loggo), Peter Kerrigan (as George), and Gary Bleasdale (as Kev); Julie Walters, Jean Boht, and James Ellis also appeared in the serial. The play was directed by Jim Goddard for David Rose's BBC Manchester production. The serial was directed by Philip Saville for Michael Wearing's BBC Birmingham production.

Brookside
(C4/Brookside Prods. Ltd., 1982–)

Phil Redmond created this twice-weekly serial set on a housing estate on the outskirts of Liverpool and presenting half-hour instalments of the traumas and domestic dramas of modern family life. Featured among the original regular characters were Roger and Heather Huntingdon (played by Rob Spendlove and Amanda Burton); the Grant family, consisting of children Damon (Simon O'Brien), Barry (Paul Usher), and Karen (Shelagh O'Hara), and parents Sheila (Sue Johnston; *pictured right*) and Bobby (Ricky Tomlinson; *left*); the Collins family, with daughter Lucy (Katrin Cartlidge), son Gordon (Nigel Crowley), and parents Paul (Jim Wiggins) and Anabelle (Doreen Sloane); and young couple Gavin and Petra Taylor (Daniel Webb and Alexandra Pigg). Two of the characters were later given their own three-part drama, **Damon and Debbie** (C4/Mersey TV Prod., 4–18/11/87), in which Damon Grant (O'Brien) and girlfriend Debbie McGrath (Gillian Kearney) were on the run from Liverpool. The 3 eps. × hour were written by Frank Cottrell Boyce and directed by Bob Carlton. Another short-run spin-off, **South**, written by Boyce and featuring Jamie (Sean McKee) and Tracy (Justine Kerrigan) was shown during C4's morning Schools broadcast under *The English Programme* banner (tx 14 and 21/3/88); 2 eps. × 27 mins.

Clive James on Television

(LWT, 1982–84; 1988)

Presented a smirking round-up of offbeat television programmes from around the world, highlighting the eccentricities associated with, for instance, Japanese game shows (featuring the now infamous **Endurance**) and American community cable programmes. The half-hour series was produced by Nicholas Barrett. Perhaps the busiest man on television, Clive James had earlier presented **The Clive James Paris Fashion Show** (LWT, 1/5/81), **Clive James and the Calendar Girls** (LWT, 29/8/81), and **Clive James at the Movies** (LWT, 27/12/81 and the later edition, 2/4/83, both pr. Barrett) in similar style. James went on to present, with his inimitable observations, **Clive James Live in Las Vegas** (LWT, 25/7/82), **The Late Clive James** (LWT, 1983; 1985–87), **The Late Clive James Show** (LWT, 1984), **Clive James Meets Roman Polanski** (LWT, 25/1/84), **The Clive James Screen Test** (LWT, 22/4/84), **Clive James and The Great American Beauty Pageant** (LWT, 26/8/84), **Clive James Meets Katharine Hepburn** (C4/LWT, 13/4/85), **Clive James in Dallas** (LWT, 27/12/85), **Clive James on Safari** (LWT, 3/1/87), **Clive James and the Calendar Girls go to France** (LWT, 22/5/87), **Clive James at the Playboy Mansion** (LWT, 18/7/87), **Clive James and the Heroes of San Francisco** (LWT, 5/9/87), **Clive James in Japan** (LWT, 19–26/12/87), **Clive James Finally Meets Frank Sinatra** (BBC-1, 31/8/88), **Clive James—Racing Driver** (LWT, 23/12/88), **Clive James on 88** (BBC-1, 31/12/88), **Clive James—Postcard from Rio** (BBC-1, 4/1/89), **Clive James—Postcard from Chicago** (BBC-1, 11/1/89), and **Clive James—Postcard from Paris** (BBC-1, 18/1/89). **Saturday Night Clive** (BBC-2, 1989–) had James taking a critical look at what was going on in the world via satellite links and studio guests. **The Talk Show with Clive James** (BBC-2, 1990–) was exactly as the title suggested, with James meeting head to head with various studio guests, as was **The Clive James Interview** (BBC-2, 1991). James also led the audience through an autobiographical hour of his boyhood life in Australia in **The Flash of Lightning** (LWT, 10/1/82), based on his best-selling *Unreliable Memoirs*.

The Comic Strip Presents . . .

(C4/Filmworks/Comic Strip Prod./Michael White, 1982–84; 1986; 1988)

Premièring with the funny 'Five Go Mad in Dorset' (2/11/82), the Comic Strip gang (generally consisting of, *l. to r.*, Dawn French, Peter Richardson, Jennifer Saunders, Adrian Edmonson; and Rik Mayall) acted-wrote-directed a series of comic absurdities based on film or genre themes. One of their great successes was 'The Strike' (20/2/88; wr. and dir. Peter Richardson and Peter Richens), in which Hollywood mogul Goldie (Robbie Coltrane) casts Al Pacino (played by Richardson) and Meryl Streep (Saunders) as union leader Arthur Scargill and his wife in a movie about the British miners' strike. Michael White was executive producer. **The Comic Strip Presents . . .** returned in 1990 as a BBC-2 (1990–) presentation, produced by Lolli Kimpton and featuring the original line-up as well as enjoying guest performances from such folk as Lenny Henry, Leslie Phillips, Nigel Planer, and Alexei Sayle.

Countdown

(C4/Yorkshire TV, 1982–)

Was the very first Channel Four programme to be transmitted (at 4.45 p.m. on Tuesday, 2/11/82). **Countdown** was a quiz show involving the juggling of letters, numbers, and anagrams as contestants competed against the clock. Radio personality Ted Moult and his team of statisticians and wordsmiths were originally on hand for verification (one of the guest wordsmiths was Gyles Brandreth; *also pictured, left*). The programme was presented by Richard Whiteley (*seated*), with the assistance of hostesses Beverley Isherwood and Kathy Hytner (*right*); later Carol Vorderman (*centre*) took over as presenter-associate. John Meade produced the half-hour, Monday to Thursday series.

1982

East 103rd Street
(Central TV, 17/2/82)

Was director-cameraman Chris Menges's absorbing and often grim 80-minute documentary about a poor Puerto Rican-American family involved in the New York Spanish Harlem milieu of drug addiction, prostitution, and gang violence. Fly-on-the-wall story focused on the family's teenager Candy, a girl hovering somewhere between her mother's addiction and the imminent heroin addiction of her brother.

Ennal's Point
(BBC-2, 7/1–11/2/82)

A six-part drama series based on the behind-the-scenes life of the men and women of the Royal National Lifeboat Institution. Philip Madoc (*pictured*), Glyn Owen, Gerald James, and James Warrior led the cast. The series, with the technical assistance of the real Mumbles lifeboat coxswain and crew, was scripted by Alun Richards. The BBC Cymru/Wales production was by John Hefin; Gareth Davies and Myrfyn Owen directed.

The Flight of the Condor
(BBC-2, 14–28/2/82)

Was a three-part special presentation by **The World About Us** exploring the landscape of the Andes along the spine of South America. Supported by a hypnotic soundtrack of Chilean music, producer Michael Andrews (*pictured*) and his BBC Bristol team (camera, Hugh Miles, Rodger Jackman; sound, Donaldo McIver) used the geographical sweep of the magnificent condor bird as a thread through the films, following its flight path north from Tierra del Fuego to Peru. Gary Watson was the narrator for the 3 eps. × 55 mins. programme.

Foxy Lady
(Granada TV, 1982; 1984)

Was set in the year 1959 and featured Diane Keen as the plucky Daisy Jackson, the new editor of the ailing northern newspaper the *Ramsden Reminder* which was teetering on the edge of bankruptcy. Geoffrey Burridge, Patrick Troughton, Milton Johns, Alan David, and Gregor Fisher supported. The two series (6 eps., 25/10–29/11/82; 7 eps., 18/1–29/2/84) of half-hour episodes were written by Geoffrey Lancashire, for producer John G. Temple. Diane Keen is pictured with guest Sam Kelly in a scene from the 18/1/84 episode.

Harry's Game
(Yorkshire TV, 25–26–27/10/82)

A 3 parts × hour political thriller, shown on consecutive nights, about British undercover agent Captain Harry Brown (Ray Lonnen) who is assigned to track down a ruthless killer among the back streets of an ominously present IRA Belfast. Gerald Seymour adapted his own novel for producer Keith Richardson. Lawrence Gordon Clark directed. Later transmitted (18/6/83) in a 145-minute film version.

I Remember Nelson
(Central TV, 14–28/4/82 + 18/10/82)

A 4 parts × hour mini-series focusing on the life of Horatio Nelson, from his return to England in 1801 after the Battle of the Nile to his death at the Battle of Trafalgar in 1805. Kenneth Colley (*right*) starred as Lord Nelson, with Geraldine James (as Emma Hamilton), John Clements, Anna Massey (as Lady Nelson), Tim Pigott-Smith (*centre*; as Capt. Hardy), and Phil Daniels. Hugh Whitemore scripted for producer Cecil Clarke; Simon Langton directed and Patrick Gowers supplied the music. The final episode was held over due to the Falklands crisis of early 1982.

Jane
(BBC-2, 2–6/8/82)

Starred Glynis Barber (*pictured*) as the famous *Daily Mirror* cartoon-strip heroine (originally illustrated by Norman Pett) whose wartime adventures, usually resulting in the loss of some or most of her wardrobe, made her the 'darling of the forces'. Producer Ian Keill's five nightly instalments (5 eps. × 10 mins.) used live actors against drawn backgrounds to good televisual effect; a 45-minute compilation edition was shown at the weekend. Jane / Glynis Barber returned for more TV adventures in **Jane in the Desert** (BBC-2, 3–7/9/84), with another 5 eps. × 10 mins. produced by Keill from Mervyn Haisman's scripts.

A Kind of Loving
(Granada TV, 4/4–6/6/82)

Stan Barstow's 10 part × hour serial adaptation of his own novel (and its two sequels) tracing the life and loves of a West Riding miner's son, Vic Brown (played by Clive Wood), over the period 1957 to 1973. Joanne Whalley also appeared (in her first major role). The series was produced by Pauline Shaw.

The Life and Adventures of Nicholas Nickleby
(C4/Primetime TV Prod., 7–14–21–28/11/82)

Presented in four acts the Royal Shakespeare Company's epic, award-winning, 9-hour stage production directed by Trevor Nunn and John Caird (there was a simultaneous stereo broadcast from Capital Radio for London viewers). Roger Rees starred as Nickleby, with Emily Richard, Jane Downs, John Woodvine, David Threlfall, and Alun Armstrong supporting. Adaptation was by David Edgar. Jim Goddard directed the TV version for producer Colin Callender; the programme was produced in association with RM Prods. For its 100th edition, **The South Bank Show** made a 2-hour special documentary looking behind the scenes at the making of the RSC's production of *Nicholas Nickleby* called 'Nickleby & Co.' (2/8/81; dir.-pr. Andrew Snell).

1982

Living in Styal
(Granada TV, 13–14–15–16/9/82)

Presented four hour-long documentary films about HM Prison, Styal, a closed prison in rural Cheshire that contained about 250 women. The films showed three new prisoners arriving ('Comings and Goings'), their interviews with prison staff ('Assessment'), a look at the long-termers ('Like It or Lump It'), and, for the final film, the question of whether some women living in Styal should be there at all ('Bleak'). Peter Carr directed for producer Steve Morrison; photography was by Diane Tammes.

Muck and Brass
(Central TV, 1982)

A straight drama series, despite the presence of Mel Smith, about property dealer Tom Craig (Smith) and his battles against officialdom and big business. Tom Clarke's story was produced by Margaret Matheson; Peter Richardson was associate producer.

Nancy Astor
(BBC-2–Time Life Prods., 10/2–7/4/82)

Told the story of the colourful life of Nancy Langhorne, later Astor, from her early days in late nineteenth-century Virginia through her marriage to Waldorf Astor to her political activities as a Member of Parliament. Lisa Harrow (*right*) starred as Nancy, with James Fox (*left*; as Waldorf Astor), Dan O'Herlihy, Sylvia Syms, Nigel Havers, and Pierce Brosnan. The 9 eps. × 55 mins. series was written by Derek Marlowe and directed by Richard Stroud for producer Philip Hinchcliffe.

Play for Tomorrow
(BBC-1, 1982)

The world of 'speculative fiction' featured here in a series of six specially commissioned plays dealing with imaginative events in the near future. Under producer Neil Zeiger, the six 55-minute productions were: Caryl Churchill's 'Crimes' (13/4/82), starring Julia Foster and T. P. McKenna, directed by Stuart Burge; Peter Prince's 'Bright Eyes' (20/4/82), with Robin Ellis and Sarah Berger, directed by Peter Duffell; Michael Wilcox's 'Cricket' (27/4/82), with Malcolm Terris and Anne Raitt, directed by Michael Darlow; Tom McGrath's 'The Nuclear Family' (4/5/82), with Jimmy Logan and Ann Scott-Jones, directed by John Glenister; Stephen Lowe's 'Shades' (11/5/82), with Tracey Childs and Stuart MacKenzie, directed by Bill Hays; and Graham Reid's 'Easter 2016' (18/5/82), with Denys Hawthorne (*left*), Eileen Pollock (*right*), and Derrick O'Connor, directed by Ben Bolt.

Police
(BBC-1, 4/1–15/3/82)

Six-part fly-on-the-wall documentary by director Roger Graef and cameraman (and co-dir.) Charles Stewart about the routine and lives of the men and women of 'E' Division of Thames Valley Police. The controversial series (particularly over the third film, 'A Complaint of Rape') was followed by **Police: Operation Carter** (BBC-1, 16/9–21/10/82) in which Graef and Stewart observed the No. 5 Regional Crime Squad in their attempts to crack the network of top London gangs. Both documentaries came from BBC Bristol. The 90-minute drama **Closing Ranks** (Central TV–Zenith Prod., 10/1/88), written by Graef (who also dir.) and Andy Smith, told the story of the corrosive effects of a flashy, dangerous London policeman (played by Rob Spendlove) who was transferred to a country police station.

278

The Snowman
(C4/Snowman Enterprises–TVC, 26/12/82)

Produced by the same company that made The Beatles' *Yellow Submarine*, this delightful 25-minute animated film about a snowman that comes to life on Christmas Eve and treats the little boy who built him to an incredible adventure was based on a picture book by Raymond Briggs. The special flying sequence, accompanied by the voice of young Peter Auty singing *Walking in the Air*, was animated by Stephen Weston and Robin White. Jimmy Murakani was the supervising animation director; music was by Howard Blake. Diane Jackson directed for producer John Coates.

Sunday Sunday
(LWT, 1982–)

Former Ulster TV presenter Gloria Hunniford's late afternoon topical magazine show in which she focused on the London entertainment scene and interviewed celebrities in the studio. The hour-long series was produced by Charles Brand. She later presented the family game show **We Love TV** (LWT–B and E TV Prod., 1984–85) for producer Brian Welsey, and a morning magazine, **Gloria Live** (BBC-1, 1990–92; later shortened to simply **Gloria**), discussing issues of the day with studio guests and audience; Jill Dawson was the original producer of the Monday–Friday programmes.

The Tube
(C4/Tyne Tees TV, 1982–87)

Influential rock magazine show featuring live music performances from the Tyne Tees studio (the entrance to which became the programme's title) presented by Paula Yates, Jools Holland, Leslie Ash (for a short period), Gary James, and Muriel Gray. Malcolm Gerrie and Paul Corley produced the 90-minute shows. **The Tube Return Ticket** (Tyne Tees TV, 1984) presented six programmes featuring the best moments from the early series; **Tube Extra—The Great Hollywood Swindle** (C4/Tyne Tees TV, 3/10/85) was a special film report on Malcolm McLaren in Los Angeles; and **Eurotube** (C4/Tyne Tees TV, 5/7/86; pr. John Gwyn) presented a special 5-hour marathon edition that went out live throughout Europe. There were also two other 5-hour, live specials, **A Midsummer Night's Tube** (C4/Tyne Tees TV, 24–5/6/83 and 29–30/6/84), running from 8.00 p.m. Friday night to 1.00 a.m. Saturday morning.

A Voyage Round My Father
(Thames TV, 2/3/82)

Told the story of writer John Mortimer's developing years in the Mortimer household and his relationship with his blind father, Clifford Mortimer. Laurence Olivier (*left*) played the father, Alan Bates (*right*) was John Mortimer, Jane Asher his wife Elizabeth, and Elizabeth Sellars his mother. Many of the scenes for the TV version (Mortimer's play had already been a stage success) were shot at the author's Oxfordshire home. The 90-minute production was directed-produced by Alvin Rakoff.

Wagner's Ring
(BBC-2, 17/10–19/12/82)

Was divided into ten weekly parts and broadcast simultaneously by Radio 3 in stereo. Patrick Chereau's challenging Bayreuth production of Wagner's famous *Ring* cycle—all 14 hours of it from performances recorded in 1979 and 1980 at Bayreuth—provided a striking new interpretation of the century-old masterpiece. Donald McIntyre performed as Wotan, ruler of the gods, Hermann Becht as Alberich, a Nibelung dwarf, and Norma Sharp, Ilse Gramatzki, and Marga Schiml as the Rhinemaidens. Jeannine Altmeyer as Sieglinde and Peter Hofmann as Siegmund (*pictured*) also appeared. The centenary production was recorded in Wagner's own theatre under the artistic supervision of the composer's grandson, Wolfgang Wagner. Design was by Richard Peduzzi; costumes by Jacques Schmidt. The programme was a co-production of Unitel, Bavarian Television, and the Bayreuth Festival. Brian Large was television director.

We'll Meet Again
(LWT, 19/2–14/5/82)

Second World War drama focusing on the often uneasy relationship between the inhabitants of the small Suffolk town of Market Wetherby and the 525th Bomb Group of the US Eighth Air Force stationed nearby. Susannah York (*right*) starred, with Michael J. Shannon (*left*), Ray Smith, June Barry, and Ed Devereaux. Thirteen hour/90-minute episodes were produced by Tony Wharmby, with scripts by David Butler, David Crane, and John Gorrie.

Whoops Apocalypse
(LWT, 14/3–18/4/82)

Was an off-the-wall 6 part × half-hour series chronicling the outrageous events leading up to the Third World War, and featured Barry Morse as US President Johnny Cyclops, Richard Griffiths (*right*; with Geoffrey Palmer) as Soviet Premier Dubienkin, John Barron as US security adviser The Deacon, and Alexei Sayle as Commissar Solzhenitsyn. Andrew Marshall & David Renwick scripted for producer Humphrey Barclay; John Reardon directed.

Wogan
(BBC-1, 1982–92)

Started out as a late night chat and music show, presented by BBC Radio favourite Terry Wogan (also with Paula Yates), before it became the American-style evening show, stripped (Mondays, Wednesdays, and Fridays) across the week, from February 1985. The show's original producer was Marcus Plantin. Earlier, Wogan had presented **Lunchtime with Wogan** (ATV, 1972–73), a half-hour daytime series of music and chat, and **What's On Wogan?** (BBC-1, 1980), a short series of similar Saturday evening programmes produced by Alan Boyd. Terry Wogan (*right*) is pictured here with guest Clement Freud in an early show. Wogan returned in October 1992 with a late evening 'end-of-the-week conversation' series called **Terry Wogan's Friday Night** (BBC-1, 1992–), blending chat and music in a fashion similar to his original programme a decade earlier.

The Young Ones
(BBC-2, 1982; 1984)

Were four lunatic students who squatted in a rambling house and experienced bizarre comic situations which were usually unrelated to any story-line, whenever there even was one. The comic quartet with a franchise to shock and disgust were loud-mouth Cliff Richard fan Rick (Rik Mayall), dim-witted hippy Neil (Nigel Planer), stud-headed punk Vivien (Adrian Edmondson), and the peculiarly remote character Mike (Christopher Ryan). Alexei Sayle also popped up as their unscrupulous landlord. The two series of 35-minute scripts were written by Ben Elton, Rik Mayall, and Lise Mayer for producer Paul Jackson; with additional material supplied by Sayle. Producer Jackson had earlier scored with the comedy team sketches and performances of Lenny Henry, Tracey Ullman, and David Copperfield in **Three of a Kind** (BBC-1, 1981; 1983), which included script contributions from comedy writers such as Kim Fuller, Mike Radford, Bob Grant & Doug Naylor, and Ian Hislop. Edmondson, Ryan, Mayall, and Sayle are pictured, *l. to r.*

Young Sherlock—The Mystery of the Manor House
(Granada TV, 31/10–19/12/82)

A drama series for the younger set based on the life of Sherlock Holmes when he was a schoolboy. Guy Henry (*pictured*) played young Sherlock in this nine-part series of half-hour stories (eps. 1 and 2 were shown together) written by Gerald Frow and directed by Nicholas Ferguson for Pieter Rogers's production.

Agatha Christie's The Secret Adversary
(LWT, 9/10/83)

Was a 130-minute TV movie première for the following week's series, **Agatha Christie's Partners in Crime** (LWT, 1983–84), starring Francesca Annis (*centre*) as Tuppence Cowley and James Warwick (*left*) as Tommy Beresford (they later became the Beresfords); guest Gavan O'Herlihy is pictured right. Something of a TV celebration of period costumes and cars, the whodunnit mysteries focused on the usual sleuthing and clue-unearthing familiar to Christie readers and 'English cozy' buffs. **Secret Adversary** was adapted by Pat Sandys, directed by Tony Wharmby, and produced by Jack Williams; the latter also produced the series. Producer-director June Wyndham-Davies arrived later with **Agatha Christie's The Last Seance** (Granada TV, 27/9/86), starring Anthony Higgins, Norma West, and Jeanne Moreau; the hour-long drama was adapted by Alfred Shaughnessy.

Auf Wiedersehen, Pet
(Central TV–Witzend Prods., 1983–84; 1986)

Followed the darkly humorous adventures of a gang of bricklayers working on a construction site in Germany. The colourful group included (*l. to r.*) Tim Healy, Gary Holton (*background*), Christopher Fairbank, Pat Roach, Timothy Spall, Jimmy Nail, and Kevin Whately. Thirteen hour-long episodes were produced. A later series (13 eps. × hour) saw the gang journey to Spain in search of work and get involved with some expatriate villains. The series were written by Dick Clement & Ian La Frenais, from an original idea by Franc Roddam. Martin McKeand produced.

Birth of a Nation
(Central TV, 19/6/83)

Was the first of four highly
acclaimed dramas by David
Leland looking at different
aspects of education. In this first
play, directed by Mike Newell, Jim
Broadbent played a
comprehensive schoolteacher
who objects to the use of corporal
punishment. The other three
dramas that followed were **Flying
into the Wind** (Central TV,
26/6/83; dir. Edward Bennett),
featuring the problems of a family
choosing to educate their children
at home, **Rhino** (Central TV,
3/7/83; dir. Jane Howell), about a
14 year old playing truant from
school to look after a 3 year old,
and, perhaps the most impressive
of all, **Made in Britain** (Central
TV, 10/7/83; dir. Alan Clarke),
with Tim Roth (*pictured*) as the
articulate skinhead Trevor. All
four dramas were produced by
Margaret Matheson.

The Black Adder
(BBC-1, 15/6–20/7/83)

Was, initially, a rather crude, off-the-wall comedy series set during the
Middle Ages and featured the self-serving schemes of Black Adder
(played by Rowan Atkinson; *pictured*) as he tried to manipulate those
around him; Tony Robinson (as Baldrick), Tim McInnerny, and Brian
Blessed co-starred. The 6 eps. × 35 mins. were written by Richard Curtis
and Atkinson; directed by Martin Shardlow. **Blackadder II** (BBC-1,
9/1–20/2/86) followed and set Edmund Blackadder in Elizabethan
England as the bastard great, great grandson of the repulsive original;
supported by McInnerny, Robinson, Miranda Richardson (as Queen
Elizabeth I), and Stephen Fry (as Lord Melchett). This 6 eps. × 30 mins.
series was written by Curtis and Ben Elton; directed by Mandie Fletcher.
Blackadder the Third (BBC-1, 17/9–22/10/87) continued the strain
with E. Blackadder Esq. now butler to the Prince Regent (Hugh Laurie)
during the late eighteenth century; Robinson and Helen Atkinson Wood
supported. Again the 6 eps. × 30 mins. series was written by Curtis and
Elton; directed by Fletcher. **Blackadder's Christmas Carol** (BBC-1,
23/12/88) was a 45-minute special with Atkinson as Ebenezer
Blackadder, Tony Robinson as Baldrick, Robbie Coltrane as the Spirit of
Christmas, Miranda Richardson as Queen Elizabeth I, Stephen Fry as
Lord Melchett, Hugh Laurie as Prince Regent, and Miriam Margolyes as
Queen Victoria. The Curtis & Elton script was directed by Richard
Boden. The final saga, **Blackadder Goes Forth** (BBC-1, 28/9–2/11/89),
placed Captain Blackadder on the Western Front in 1917 sharing the
perils of trench warfare with Pte. Baldrick (Robinson), Lt. Colthurst St
Barley (Hugh Laurie), General Melchett (Stephen Fry), and Captain
Darling (Tim McInnerny). Again 6 eps. × 30 mins. were written by
Curtis & Elton and directed by Richard Boden. All series were produced
by John Lloyd.

Blockbusters
(Central TV, 1983–)

Britain's first daily game show in
which 16–18 year olds test their
speed and general knowledge.
The programme, presented by
the amiable Bob Holness
(*pictured*), acquired something of
a cult following among the
college set. The show was
produced in association with
Talbot Television and Freemantle
Prods.

Brass
(Granada TV, 1983–84)

Comedy (when not parody) series that followed the intertwining lives of two families, the wealthy, business-owning Hardacres and their employees, the Fairchilds. The half-hour series featured Timothy West (*pictured, left*), Caroline Blakiston (*right*), Barbara Ewing, Geoffrey Hinsliff, Robert Reynolds, James Saxon, Gail Harrison, Emil Morgan, and Gary Cady. John Stevenson and Julian Roach authored the scripts for producer Bill Podmore. The series reappeared on Channel Four in 1990 under producer Mark Robson for a short-lived six episodes (23/4–28/5/90) with players West, Blakiston, Saxon, Harrison, Morgan, Ewing, and Cady returning in their original roles. Stevenson & Roach again supplied the stories.

Breakfast Time
(BBC-1, 1983–)

Was Britain's first breakfast television programme, premièring at 6.30 a.m. on 17 January 1983. Original presenters and studio line-up were Frank Bough (*2nd right, front row*), Selina Scott (*2nd left, front row*), and Nick Ross as the link people, with newsreader Debbie Rix (*left, front row*), weatherman Francis Wilson (*left, back row*), sports reporter David Icke, keep-fit girl Diana Moran ('The Green Goddess'), astrologer Russell Grant, gossip columnist Chris Wilson, and food and cookery expert Glynn Christian. Mike Smith (*right, back row*) and Fern Britton (*right, front row*) also appeared. Programme editor was Ron Neil.

By the Sword Divided
(BBC-1, 16/10–18/12/83; 6/1–10/3/85)

Authentically re-created English Civil War romance–drama serial in 10 eps. × 55 mins. about the political rift between the Royalist Laceys and their Parliamentarian relatives. Julian Glover, Sharon Mughan, Timothy Bentick (*left; with Malcolm Stoddard*), Lucy Aston, and Bob Edwards starred. The programme was created by John Hawkesworth and produced by Brian Spiby; the second series of ten episodes was produced by Jonathan Alwyn. Brigadier Peter Young, founder of Civil War enthusiasts The Sealed Knot, was military consultant.

Charlie Muffin
(Thames TV–Euston Films, 31/8/83)

British Intelligence drama concerning a captured head of a Soviet spy network, a defecting KGB chief, and the scruffy secret agent, Charlie Muffin (David Hemmings), who was given the assignment to ferret out the facts from the fakes. Supporting players included Sam Wanamaker, Jennie Linden, Pinkas Braun, Ian Richardson, Ralph Richardson, and Clive Revill. The 2-hour TV movie was written by Keith Waterhouse, from a novel by Brian Freemantle, and directed by Jack Gold.

1983

The Cleopatras
(BBC-2, 19/1–9/3/83)

An 8 eps. × 50 mins. serial that looked at life under the Cleopatras, from the luxurious to the mildly grotesque, and was told in flashback form to the final Cleopatra (played by Michelle Newell; who also played the character's great-grandmother). Projecting the powerful queens during the period between the Pyramids of ancient Egypt and the spread of the Roman Empire were Elizabeth Shepherd (as Cleo II), Prue Clarke (Cleopatra Selene), Pauline Moran (Cleopatra Berenike), Caroline Mortimer (Cleopatra Thea), Sue Holderness (Cleo IV), and Amanda Boxer (Cleopatra Tryphaena). Philip Mackie's scripts were directed by John Frankau for producer Guy Slater. The spectacular costumes were designed by Barbara Kidd and the lush studio production was by designer Michael Young. Elizabeth Shepherd is pictured with Stephen Greif (as Demetrius).

Death of an Expert Witness
(Anglia TV, 8/4–20/5/83)

Premièred an irregular series of multi-part murder mystery stories starring Roy Marsden (*pictured*) as Scotland Yard Det. Chief Supt. Adam Dalgliesh; Herbert Wise directed Robin Chapman's dramatization. The series was based on the novels by crime author P. D. James and productions, up to the late 1980s, included **Shroud for a Nightingale** (Anglia TV, 9/3–6/4/84; dramatized by Chapman, dir. John Gorrie), **Cover Her Face** (Anglia TV, 17/2–24/3/85; dramatized by Chapman, dir. John Davies), **The Black Tower** (Anglia TV, 8/11–13/12/85; dramatized by William Humble, dir. Ronald Wilson), and **A Taste for Death** (Anglia TV, 14/10–18/11/88; dramatized by Alick Rowe, dir. John Davies). John Rosenberg served as series producer. **Devices and Desires** (Anglia TV, 4/1–8/2/91; dramatized by Thomas Ellice, dir. John Davies) was the last of the series; while the one-off, 2-hour presentation of **Unnatural Causes** (Anglia Films, 2/1/93; dramatized by Peter Buckman, dir. John Davies) saw Marsden's final appearance as Dalgliesh.

Don't Wait Up
(BBC-1, 1983–90)

Family-based sitcom series written by George Layton and featuring the highs and lows in the muddled lives of father and son doctors Toby (Tony Britton; *left*) and Tom Latimer (Nigel Havers; *right*). Tom had come through an expensive divorce and now lived in a flat while his ex-wife, Helen (Jane How), had their house. Adding insult to injury, he also had to pay her rent to use his surgery. Dinah Sheridan also appeared as Tom's mother Angela Latimer. Harold Snoad produced-directed all six series.

An Englishman Abroad
(BBC-1, 29/11/83)

Told the true story of a meeting between the actress Coral Browne (*left*), in Moscow with the Royal Shakespeare Company, and the exiled traitor Guy Burgess. Alan Bennett's 65-minute script was expertly produced (by Innes Lloyd) and directed (by John Schlesinger) on British locations that succeeded in re-creating the dreary Moscow of the 1950s. Alan Bates (*right*) co-starred as Burgess; Charles Gray, Harold Innocent, and Vernon Dobtcheff supported.

Give Us a Break
(BBC-1, 1983)

Introduced a couple of very unlikely lads, a scouser, Mo Morris (played by Paul McGann; *left*), and a cockney, Micky Noades (Robert Lindsay; *right*), who formed an unholy alliance in and around the snooker halls of London. Shirin Taylor played Micky's barmaid girlfriend and Mo's sister Tina. The Geoff McQueen-scripted series (of 50-minute episodes) led the duo through this comedy-drama with the hope that their 'big break' was just around the next corner. A 90-minute special, 'Hustle, Bustle, Toil an' Muscle' (BBC-1, 31/12/84), was produced by Terence Williams for the holiday season.

Highway
(ITV, 1983–)

Sunday evening series following host Harry Secombe's musical journey through Britain in which he talked and sang with the people he met on the way. The programme (with contributions from the various regional ITV companies) presented a lightweight blend of music, readings, hymns, prayers, and minor celebrities. Executive producer was Bill Ward. Secombe is pictured with guest Dame Vera Lynn in the edition honouring the fiftieth anniversary of the day the Second World War began.

The Irish RM
(C4/Little Bird Films–Rediffusion Films–Ulster TV–RTE/James Mitchell Prod., 1983–85)

Lively series based on the collection of comic Anglo-Irish stories written at the turn of the century by Irish cousins Edith Somerville and Martin Ross (Violet Florence Martin). Peter Bowles (*3rd right*) played the central character, Major Sinclair Yeates, a retired British Army officer who moved to the west of Ireland to become a Resident Magistrate (a Justice of the Peace who assists local magistrates). Bryan Murray (*far right*), Lise-Ann McLaughlin, Doran Godwin, Anna Manahan, Brenda Conroy, and Faith Brook co-starred. **The Real Charlotte** (Granada TV, 16–30/6/91) was a three-part all-Irish drama production based on the novel by the creators of **The Irish RM** and adapted by Bernard McLaverty; Tony Barry directed the Edith Somerville–Martin Ross script for Niall McCarthy's production. Patrick Bergin, Jeananne Crowley, and Joanna Roth headed the cast.

Jemima Shore Investigates
(Thames TV, 1983)

Based on the novels by Antonia Fraser, this short-run hour-long drama series starred Patricia Hodge (*right*) as television reporter and part-time private investigator Jemima Shore. The series was produced by Tim Aspinall. The Jemima Shore character first appeared on TV in 'Quiet as a Nun' (11–27/4/78; adapt. Julia Jones, dir. Moira Armstrong; 6 eps. × half-hour), a part of the **Armchair Thriller** series, where she was played by Maria Aitken.

1983

Just Good Friends
(BBC-1, 1983–86)

John Sullivan scripted this comedy that hovered between love and laughter and emotional failure and breakdown. The central theme concerned Vince Pinner (Paul Nicholas; *right*) and Penny Warrender (Jan Francis; *left*) in a love–hate relationship when they met up again some five years after he failed to show at their wedding. The actual thread running through the series was whether Penny and Vince would get back together again. (They did—and finally married in Paris.) Ray Butt was original producer of the twenty-two episodes.

Kennedy
(Central TV, 20–21–22/11/83)

Grand, three-part drama serial about the 35th (and youngest ever) President of the United States, John F. Kennedy (portrayed by Martin Sheen; *left*). Reg Gadney's screenplay took the story from JFK's inauguration through to the fateful day in Dallas in 1963. The enormous cast featured Blair Brown (*right*) as Jacqueline Bouvier Kennedy, John Shea as Robert Kennedy, E. G. Marshall as Joseph Kennedy, Geraldine Fitzgerald as Rose Kennedy, Vincent Gardenia as J. Edgar Hoover, Nesbitt Blaisdell as Lyndon B. Johnson, and Charles Brown as Martin Luther King. Jim Goddard directed Andrew Brown's production. Ernie Vincze was director of photography; Richard Hartley composed the music.

The Lady is a Tramp
(C4/Regent Prods., 1983–84)

May well have been a sitcom spin-off from the not so amusing 'Edna, the Inebriate Woman' (of **Play for Today** fame). This half-hour comedy series about two 'bag ladies', starring Patricia Hayes (*left*) and Pat Coombs (*right*), was written specially for Hayes (her first starring series) by Johnny Speight. William G. Stewart produced.

The Nation's Health
(C4/Euston Films Prod., 6–27/10/83)

Writer G. F. Newman's scathing four-part drama series presented his thesis that doctors, under the present system, do their patients more harm than good. He explored this through the character of Dr Jessie Marvill (played by Vivienne Ritchie), a young hospital doctor who finds her work causing her to question the attitudes of those around her and her own beliefs about the proper practice of medicine. Sebastian Shaw, Ian McDiarmid, William Boyde, Alan Thompson, P. H. Moriarty, Richard Ireson, and Julian Fox were among those supporting. The 4 eps. × 100 mins. were: 'Acute', 'Decline', 'Chronic', and 'Collapse'; all directed by Les Blair for producer Irving Teitelbaum. Pictured are (*l. to r.*) James Griffiths, Trevor Bowen, Ashley Herman, and Ritchie in the 'Acute' episode.

286

No Problem!
(C4/LWT, 1983–85)

Busy sitcom about a family of kids whose parents have returned to Jamaica leaving them the run of the house in Willesden. The series featured (*l. to r.*) Sarah Lam, Alan Igbon, Judith Jacob (*standing*), Shope Shodeinde, Trevor Thomas, Chris Tummings, Malcolm Frederick; also appearing were Victor Romero Evans and Janet Kay. Mustapha Matura and Farrukh Dhondy scripted for producer Charlie Hanson.

The Old Men at the Zoo
(BBC-2–London Films, 15/9–13/10/83)

Based on Angus Wilson's 1961 novel but updated so the action takes place in the near future, the five-part serial (1 ep. × 50 mins., 4 eps. × 55 mins.) used the setting of London Zoo with its fictional keepers and curators as a metaphor: the government and civil service of a fantasy future Britain. Featured players were Stuart Wilson, Robert Morley, Maurice Denham, Andrew Cruickshank (*pictured, centre*), Robert Urquhart, and Marius Goring. The TV adaptation was by Troy Kennedy Martin; Stuart Burge directed for producer Jonathan Powell.

Reilly—Ace of Spies
(Thames TV–Euston Films, 5/9–16/11/83)

Dashing costume-and-dagger adventures of a Russian-born British spy working against turn-of-the-century Bolsheviks starred Sam Neill (*left*) in the title role, supported by Leo McKern, Norman Rodway, Peter Egan, Jeanne Crowley, John Rhys-Davies, Tom Bell (*right*), Kenneth Cranham (as Lenin), Ian Charleston, David Burke (as Stalin), and Anthony Higgins. The 1 ep. × 75 mins., 11 eps. × hour series was written by Troy Kennedy Martin; Jim Goddard and Martin Campbell directed for producer Chris Burt. Director of photography was Peter Jessop.

Storyboard
(Thames TV, 1983–89)

An occasional series of self-contained stories acting as pilot programmes for possible series spin-off. **Storyboard** premièred with 'Inspector Ghote Moves In' (26/7/83) by H. R. F. Keating, directed by Peter Duguid; Sam Dastor is pictured as the title character. The first series also presented the introductory episodes for the series **The Bill** via Geoff McQueen's 'Woodentop' (16/8/83; dir. Peter Cregeen) and **Lytton's Diary** (30/8/83; dir. Brian Parker), written by Ray Connolly from an idea by Peter Bowles and Philip Broadley. Other successful spin-offs were **Mr Palfrey of Westminster** (Thames TV, 1984–85) from the pilot 'The Traitor' (23/8/83; wr. George Markstein, dir. Christopher Hodson), **King and Castle** (Thames TV, 1986) from the pilot 'King & Castle', with Nigel Planer and Derek Martin, *pictured right* (20/8/85; wr. Ian Kennedy Martin, dir. Richard Bramall), and **Ladies in Charge** (Thames TV, 1986) from the pilot of 27/8/85 (wr. Alfred Shaughnessy from an idea by Kate Herbert-Hunting, dir. John Davies).

Treasure Hunt
(C4/Chatsworth TV Prod., 1983–)

A frantic game show in which two contestants work together to win £1,000 if they can find the answers to five sets of clues in 45 minutes. The clues are distributed within a 50-mile radius and unearthed by the show's airborne 'runner', Anneka Rice (*pictured with her team*), acting on the instructions of contestants closeted in the studio with maps and references. Front man was Kenneth Kendall. Deviser and programme associate was Ann Meo; Malcolm Heyworth and Peter Holmans produced. **Interceptor** (Thames TV–Chatsworth TV, 1989–90), with Annabel Croft, featured a similar set-up but in reverse (with the mobile Croft directing the contestants while another person tries to 'immobilize' them!).

Vietnam
(C4/Central TV, 1983)

Was the first of two documentary series about the country and its continuing conflict presented by Channel Four. This Central TV series of twelve hour-long episodes focused on the unsteady development of the country from the colonial French period starting in 1945. Director-production team was Martin Smith, Henri de Turrene, and Judy Vecchione; executive producer was Richard Ellison. **Vietnam—The Ten Thousand Day War** (C4/Cineworld Prod., 1984–85) presented twenty-six half-hour episodes (premièring with an hour-long programme) covering the war until the final defeat in 1975, with exclusive footage from the military archives in Hanoi, balanced by film from the US. The series was produced in Canada by Michael Maclear and Ian McLeod; and written by Associated Press journalist Peter Arnett, who had been chief of AP's Saigon bureau from 1961 to 1975 and had won a Pulitzer Prize for his Vietnam dispatches. Narration was by Richard Basehart.

Widows
(Thames TV–Euston Films, 16/3–20/4/83)

A tough crime caper drama about four women who stage an armed robbery based on the plans drawn up by their deceased husbands; three of the women were widows of professional criminals. The six hour-long episodes, written by Lynda La Plante, starred (*l. to r.*) Maureen O'Farrell, Fiona Hendley, Eve Mottley, and Ann Mitchell. Ian Toynton directed for producer Linda Agran. A sequel, **Widows** [II] (Thames TV–Euston Films, 3/4–8/5/85), followed the four women (with Debbie Bishop now in the Mottley role) as they headed for a life of ease and luxury in Rio. La Plante's six hour-long scripts were directed by Paul Annett for producer Irving Teitelbaum.

The Wind in the Willows
(Thames TV, 27/12/83)

Was a 90-minute animated musical version of the classic story of the adventures of Mole, Rat, Badger, and Toad of Toad Hall set in Edwardian England. This Cosgrove–Hall production, adapted by Rosemary Anne Sisson from Kenneth Grahame's 1908 book, led to the delightful **The Wind in the Willows** (Thames TV, 1984–88) series, also produced by Mark Hall and Brian Cosgrove. The characters' voices were supplied by Michael Hordern (Badger), Richard Pearson (Mole), Peter Sallis (Rat; Ian Carmichael in the 1983 prog.), and David Jason (Toad).

The Adventures of Sherlock Holmes
(Granada TV, 1984–85)

Featured Jeremy Brett (as Holmes; *left*) and David Burke (*right*, as Watson; played by Edward Hardwicke from 1986) in a superbly produced and authentically designed series, developed for TV by John Hawkesworth. Created closely and accurately after the spirit and style of the illustrated *Strand Magazine* stories of the 1890s, Brett's interpretation of Sir Arthur Conan Doyle's famous character is now widely regarded as being the finest screen performance to date. In 1986, following the Reichenbach Falls 'death' of Holmes at the end of the second series, the programme was revived as **The Return of Sherlock Holmes** (Granada TV, 1986–88). A 2-hour version of 'The Hound of the Baskervilles' (31/8/88; dramatized by T. R. Bowen, dir. Brian Mills) was also produced. **The Casebook of Sherlock Holmes** (Granada TV, 1991) returned the detective for seven more episodes; Michael Cox produced. Then a 2-hour special, 'The Master Blackmailer', was shown on 2/1/92 (with Peter Hammond directing June Wyndham-Davies's production); followed over a year later by two 2-hour productions, 'The Last Vampyre' (27/1/93) and 'The Eligible Bachelor' (3/2/93), also under the **Sherlock Holmes** (Granada TV) banner. BBC-tv, however, were the first to produce a Sherlock Holmes series in 1951 (with Alan Wheatley as the Baker Street sleuth); two more BBC-tv series of adaptations followed, in 1965 (with Douglas Wilmer in the title role) and 1968 (with Peter Cushing).

Alas Smith and Jones
(BBC-2, 1984–87)

Led half of the former **Not the Nine O'Clock News** quartet, Mel Smith (*left*) and Griff Rhys Jones (*right*), into their own, highly popular series of 30-minute skits and sketches which featured such enjoyably bizarre fare as (the première promo listing exclaimed) 'a hard-hitting exposé of sperm banks, Samurai accountants and chiropody'. The duo's classic face-to-face rambling dialogue exchanges became one of the high points of the series, creating a wave of imitators throughout the media. Producers over the series' run were Martin Shardlow (1984), Jimmy Mulville (1985), and John Kilby (1986–87); Jamie Rix later produced a 40-minute Christmas special, **Alas Sage and Onion** (BBC-2/Talkback Prod., 21/12/88), which included Smith and Jones's guests Lindsay Duncan, Clive Mantle, Tony Slattery, and Geoff McGivern. The pair returned in a new though similar formatted series in the 1990s, **Smith and Jones** (BBC-1/Talkback Prods., 1990–), for producer Jon Plowman.

'Allo, 'Allo
(BBC-1, 1984–92)

A superb spoof of BBC TV's earlier **Secret Army** drama, set around a café in occupied France during the Second World War. The large cast featured Gorden Kaye (*centre*), Carmen Silvera (*left*), Kim Hartman, Vicki Michelle (*right*), Kirsten Cooke, Arthur Bostrom, Guy Siner, Sue Hodge, Richard Marner, Richard Gibson, John Louis Mansi, Gavin Richards (later Roger Kitter), Hilary Minster, Jack Haig (later Robin Parkinson), Kenneth Connor, and John D. Collins. The half-hour serial sitcom was created and written by David Croft (who also produced) and Jeremy Lloyd. A 35-minute pilot episode had been presented on 30/12/82.

American Caesar
(C4/Cineworld Prod., 24/5–19/7/84)

General Douglas MacArthur was the subject of this documentary study into the man and the myth, tracing his life and military career from the eve of Pearl Harbor, in 1941, to the Korean war and MacArthur's personal conflict with the then President Harry Truman. Eight half-hour episodes were produced by Ian McLeod, based on the book by journalist William Manchester. The series was hosted by John Huston and narrated by John Colicos. MacArthur is pictured signing the acceptance of the surrender of the Japanese aboard the battleship USS *Missouri* in Tokyo Bay in September 1945.

Aspel & Company
(LWT, 1984–)

Stands as London Weekend's long-time Saturday night celebrity talk show, hosted by the affable Michael Aspel (*pictured*). The series, usually with the emphasis on trivial patter, may be amusingly remembered from more recent years for guest Oliver Reed's entertaining presentation of himself as someone struggling with the after-effects of the studio hospitality room!

Big Deal
(BBC-1, 1984–86)

Starred Ray Brooks (*left*) as no-hoper gambler Robby Box and Sharon Duce (*centre*; with Lisa Geoghan) as his lover Jan in this drama series in 50-minute episodes. The general format featured Robby's London low-life circuit of pubs, bookies, all-night poker games, and cafés. The series was written by Geoff McQueen for producer Terence Williams. Brooks and Duce returned together in **Growing Pains** (BBC-1, 1992–), a drama series in 50-minute episodes about a family who foster children. Written by former schoolteacher Steve Wetton, the programme originated on radio with Brooks and Duce in the principal roles; Brooks bought the rights and helped turn it into the TV series, produced by Richard Bramall.

The Bill
(Thames TV, 1984–92; Thames TV/Yorkshire TV, 1993–)

Started out as an hour-long episode of Thames's **Storyboard** collection ('Woodentop', 16/8/83; wr. Geoff McQueen, dir. Peter Cregeen). Setting and stories featured the Sun Hill police station in London's East End and the policemen and policewomen who patrol the area. The original series of hour episodes (the programme became twice-weekly half-hours from 19/7/88) presented the cast of John Salthouse, Eric Richard, Mark Wingett, Colin Blumenau, Trudie Goodwin, Gary Olsen, Roger Leach, Christopher Ellison, Nula Conwell, Jeffrey Stewart, and Robert Hudson. Pictured are (*l. to r.*) Graham Cole, Charlie Creed-Miles, and Seeta Indrani in a late 1980s story.

The Box of Delights
(BBC-1, 21/11–24/12/84)

Presented a 6 eps. × 30/35 mins. adaptation of John Masefield's 1935 story of ancient heroes, flashing rings, and black arts starring Devin Stanfield, Patrick Troughton (*pictured*), and Robert Stephens. The £1 million budget (shared with co-production company, Lella) allowed the programme to feature some very sophisticated, for its time, special effects: colour separation overlay, electronic 'paintbox', and Quantel techniques (enabling the camera to shrink the screen image to one-twentieth of its size). Alan Seymour's dramatization was directed by Renny Rye; Paul Stone produced.

Caught in a Free State
(C4/RTE Prod., 5–26/4/84)

A four-part series dramatizing the attempt by German Intelligence to establish agents in neutral Ireland during the Second World War. Peter Jankowsky, Joan O'Hara, and Barry McGovern (*pictured*; as Irish Premier Eamon de Valera) led the cast. Brian Lynch's story was directed-produced by Peter Ormrod.

Chance in a Million
(C4/Thames TV, 1984–86)

The mix-ups and misfortunes of the hapless Tom Chance (Simon Callow; *left*) was the comedy source of this twitchy sitcom series. Brenda Blethyn (*right*) was his equally confused partner, Alison Little. Andrew Norris & Richard Fegen's 18 eps. × half-hour scripts were directed-produced by Michael Miles.

The Country Diary of an Edwardian Lady
(Central TV, 22/2–16/5/84)

Was the story of Edwardian artist Edith Holden and her private observations of wildlife in her native Warwickshire, written and illustrated as *Nature Notes for 1906*. The original diary was discovered by her great-niece who eventually got it published (in 1977), which in turn led to this 12 eps. × half-hour series. Pippa Guard (*pictured*) starred as Edith, supported by Brian Rawlinson, Elisabeth Choice, Lill Roughley, Isabelle Amyes, and Anthony Daniels. The series was adapted by Elaine Feinstein and Dirk Campbell from Holden's book; Dirk Campbell directed Patrick Gamble's production.

Crime Inc
(Thames TV, 1984)

Presented a seven-part, hour-long documentary series about the Mafia crime families, from the early Dutch Schultz rackets in New York, through Capone (*pictured*) and Luciano, to today's big business narcotics empires operating behind respectable fronts. A grisly yet almost hypnotic survey illustrated by gruesome news pictures, mobster home movies, police video, and boastful FBI informants. The programme took producer-writer-narrator Martin Short some four years to make. Former Scotland Yard organized crime expert Frank Pulley acted as consultant.

Crimewatch UK
(BBC-1, 1984–)

A 'reality' programme set to keep the public informed about serious unsolved crimes as well as hoping to get those crimes solved through viewer response. Based in part on a similar German TV programme called **File XY Unsolved** and the old **Police 5** bulletins, **Crimewatch** presented factual reconstructions of major crimes baffling police (the re-enaction of the crimes sometimes depicted quite brutally) and then opened phone lines to anyone who had information. Presenters Nick Ross and Sue Cook (*pictured, centre*) also informed viewers about crime prevention and observed forensic areas of police work. Similarly themed spin-off programmes followed: **Crimewatch GB** (BBC-1, 1984), **Drugwatch** (BBC-1, 1985), **Crimewatch Update** (BBC-1, 1986), and **Crimewatch Files** (BBC-1, 1988), the latter with Ross and Cook looking at the inside stories behind the major investigations. ITV followed the lead with their **Crime Monthly** (LWT, 1989) and **Crime Story** (ITV various, 1992–).

The District Nurse
(BBC-1, 1984; 1987)

A drama serial featuring Nerys Hughes (*pictured*) as Megan Roberts, a district nurse trying to do her job around the villages of South Wales in the 1920s and often in conflict with the hypocrisy of the tight-knit communities. In the later series, set during the early 1930s, she lived in the chaotic household of Dr Emlyn Isaacs (Freddie Jones) who practised in a Welsh seaside town. The programme of 30-minute episodes was devised by Julia Smith (who also produced) and Tony Holland.

Doctor Fischer of Geneva
(BBC-2–Consolidated Prods., 1/10/84)

Told the enjoyably macabre story of self-made millionaire Dr Fischer (played by James Mason, *right*; one of his last major screen appearances) who gathered together a collection of wealthy Geneva people to observe the levels of humiliation they would submit themselves to for additional wealth. However, he met his match with son-in-law Dr Jones (Alan Bates; *left*) when he tried to corrupt someone with no money at all. The excellent cast included Greta Scacchi, Clarissa Kaye, Hugh Burden, David de Keyser, Jacques Herlin, Cyril Cusack, and Barry Humphries. Producer Richard Broke scripted Graham Greene's story for the 96-minute telefilm directed by Michael Lindsay-Hogg.

Duty Free
(Yorkshire TV, 1984–86)

Presented an undemanding sitcom series about two couples on holiday in Spain. Pictured (*l. to r.*), Keith Barron, Joanna Van Gyseghem, Neil Stacy, and Gwen Taylor were the quartet whose adventures mostly revolved around compromising hotel-room mix-ups and misunderstandings. The series was written by Eric Chappell and Jean Warr; Vernon Lawrence produced.

Ever Decreasing Circles
(BBC-1, 1984; 1986–89)

Sitcom series featuring Richard Briers (*left*) as Martin Bryce (in a performance not unlike his Tom character in **The Good Life**), a man with a perfectly synchronized life: he is a pillar of the community, chairman of the tennis, cricket, motor, and every other club committee. His patient wife Ann's (Penelope Wilton; *centre*) only spark of unorganized light comes with the arrival of new, man-about-townish neighbour, Paul (Peter Egan; *right*), whom Martin regards as a threat in more ways than one. Stanley Lebor and Geraldine Newman supported the regular cast. The John Esmonde & Bob Larbey scripts of 27 eps. × 30 mins. were produced and directed by Sydney Lotterby (the first series) and Harold Snoad (1986–89).

The Fainthearted Feminist
(BBC-2, 19/3–16/4/84)

A 5 eps. × 30 mins. comedy series looking at the funny side of feminism based on the unsigned (but written by journalist Jill Tweedie) column called *Letters from a Fainthearted Feminist* which first appeared in the *Guardian* in 1981. Lynn Redgrave (*right*) starred as Martha, with Jonathan Newth (*left*; as her husband, Josh), Sarah Neville (Mary), and Helen Cotterill (Mo). Co-written by Jill Tweedie and Christopher Bond; Mandie Fletcher directed for producer Zanna Beswick.

The Far Pavilions
(C4/Geoff Reeve and Assoc. Prod./Goldcrest, 3–5/1/84)

Set in the turbulent nineteenth-century days of the British Raj, this was the story of a young British officer in the élite Corps of Guides who, due to his orphaned upbringing, was torn between the differing cultures of India and of Great Britain. Ben Cross (*foreground, left*) starred as Ash, the British officer; with Amy Irving, Christopher Lee, Benedict Taylor, Rossano Brazzi, Saeed Jaffrey, Robert Hardy, Sneh Gupta, Omar Sharif (*right*), and Sir John Gielgud. The epic $12 million production was based on the novel by M. M. Kaye and adapted by Julian Bond. The 1 × 2 hours and 2 × 115 mins. parts were directed by Peter Duffell for producer Geoffrey Reeve; director of photography was Jack Cardiff.

4 American Composers
(C4/Trans Atlantic Films Prod., 1984)

Peter Greenaway directed the four-part series in which he spotlighted four innovative composers: the then 70-year-old *enfant terrible* 'John Cage' (31/3/84; *pictured*), singer-dancer-composer-film-maker 'Meredith Monk' (7/4/84), the exuberant 'Philip Glass' (14/4/84), and the wry talent of 'Robert Ashley' (22/4/84). The 65-minute films were produced by Revel Guest.

1984

Fresh Fields
(Thames TV, 1984–86)

Lightweight sitcom about a middle-aged couple, Hester and William Fields (played by Julia McKenzie and Anton Rodgers; *pictured*), trying to make the most out of life before it is too late. Ann Beach played their busybody neighbour Sonia. John Chapman scripted for producer Peter Frazer-Jones. **French Fields** (Thames TV, 1989–91) saw the couple relocated to France after William was headhunted for a job. Chapman scripted with Ian Davidson; James Gilbert produced.

Freud
(BBC-2, 14/9–19/10/84)

Was a 6 part × 60 mins. dramatization of the life, work, and ideas of scientist and philosopher Sigmund Freud, the father of psychoanalysis. David Suchet (*pictured*) starred as Freud, resigned to die in exile and recalling, and analysing, the early years of his life; Alison Key appeared as Anna Freud. Moira Armstrong directed Carey Harrison's scripts for John Purdie's production.

The Front Line
(BBC-1, 6/12/84–17/1/85)

Sitcom series, of 6 eps. × 30 mins., filmed in Bristol and Cardiff about two brothers who live completely different lifestyles. Sheldon (played by Alan Igbon; *left*) was the Rasta who was always landing his more responsible, elder brother Malcolm (Paul Barber; *right*) in trouble; Malcolm was a security officer with ambitions to join the police. Roger Race directed-produced the scripts by Alex Shearer.

The Glory Boys
(Yorkshire TV–Alan Landsburg Prod., 1–2–3/10/84)

Three hour-long action dramas about urban terrorists operating in London and involving an attempt by an Arab guerrilla and an IRA activist to assassinate an Israeli nuclear scientist. Rod Steiger (*right*; as Sokarev, the scientist) and Anthony Perkins (*left*; as contract 'minder' Jimmy) starred; Gary Brown and Aaron Harris were the two ill-matched assassins. Gerald Seymour's scripts were directed by Michael Ferguson for Michael Glynn's production.

Goodbye Mr Chips
(BBC-1, 29/1–4/3/84)

James Hilton's 1934 short novel, about the memories of gentle old schoolmaster Mr Chipping of his long years at Brookfield School, was dramatized in 6 eps. × 30 mins. by Alexander Baron for the 5.15 p.m. Sunday slot. Roy Marsden (*left*) starred as Chips, with Anne Kristen (as Mrs Wickett) and Jill Meager (*centre*; as Katherine). Gareth Davies directed for producer Barry Letts.

The Invisible Man
(BBC-1, 4/9–9/10/84)

Producer Barry Letts's straight adaptation of H. G. Wells's classic fantasy featured Philip Donaghy (*pictured*) in the title role as the crazed Dr Griffin bent on power-mad murder and mayhem. The competent video production (under effects supervisor Dave Jervis) of 6 eps. × 30 mins. was written by James Andrew Hall and directed by Brian Lighthill.

The Jewel in the Crown
(Granada TV, 9/1–3/4/84)

Granada's monumental mini-series based on the late Paul Scott's famous *The Raj Quartet*, a cycle of four novels set in the closing years of British rule (1942 to 1947) in India. The story followed the fortunes of a group of characters during that turbulent period. Outstanding among the lead players were Tim Pigott-Smith (as Ronald Merrick, a superbly evil British military officer), Susan Wooldridge and Art Malik (as the tragic lovers Daphne Manners and Hari Kumar), missionary Peggy Ashcroft, aristocratic aunt Rachel Kempson, Russian exile Eric Porter, romantic hero Charles Dance (*pictured*), and alcoholic mother Judy Parfitt with Geraldine James as her strong, independent daughter. Under the personal supervision of Granada TV chairman Sir Denis Forman, the series took four years to produce and cost somewhere in the region of £5 million. The 1 ep. × 2 hours, 13 eps. × hour series was adapted for television by Ken Taylor; Christopher Morahan (who also produced) and Jim O'Brien directed alternate episodes.

The Lenny Henry Show
(BBC-1, 1984–85; 1987–88)

Gave comedian Henry (*pictured*) the chance to showcase his comedy talents in his own series, presenting an assortment of caricatures such as Delbert Wilkins, PC Ganga, the nostalgic, elderly Jamaican Deakus, Fred Dread, and Theophilus P. Wildebeeste. **Lenny Henry Tonite** (BBC-1, 1986), written by Ben Elton, presented a short-run series with a new character and situation each week in a change from the 2-minute per character sketch established with his earlier series. Geoff Posner produced and directed both programmes. A later sitcom, the six-part **Chef!** (BBC-1 / APC–Crucial Films, 28 / 1–11 / 3 / 93), featured Henry as the flamboyant and aggressive chef of a smart restaurant; Charlie Hanson produced Peter Tilbury's half-hour scripts.

The Living Planet
(BBC-1, 19/1–5/4/84)

A magnificent 'Portrait of the Earth' by and with David Attenborough (*pictured*) showing how various species earn their living on earth and interact with one another and how groups of species, including man, manage in particular environments. The 12 eps. × 55 mins. series, produced by Ned Kelly, Andrew Neal, and Richard Brock for BBC Bristol, was followed by a 40-minute special, **The Making of The Living Planet** (BBC-1, 12/4/84), presented by Miles Kington and produced by Brock. A sequel to **Life on Earth** (BBC-1, 1979); followed by **The Trials of Life** (BBC-1, 1990).

Miss Marple
(BBC-1–Arts and Entertainment Network (USA)–Network 7 (Australia), 1984–)

Agatha Christie's famous spinster crime snooper Miss Jane Marple appeared in twelve novels and multiple short stories, between 1930 and 1976, before BBC TV produced the first (irregular) series based on the character. Joan Hickson (*pictured*) starred as Miss Marple, a shrewd old lady with an eye for the obvious and a penchant for gossip, in these skilfully crafted TV adaptations: 'The Body in the Library' (26–8/12/84; scr. T. R. Bowen, dir. Silvio Narizzano), 'The Moving Finger' (21–2/2/85; scr. Julia Jones, dir. Roy Boulting), 'A Murder is Announced' (28/2–2/3/85; scr. Alan Plater, dir. David Giles), 'A Pocketful of Rye' (7–8/3/85; scr. T. R. Bowen, dir. Guy Slater), 'Murder at the Vicarage' (25/12/86; scr. T. R. Bowen, dir. Julian Amyes), 'Sleeping Murder' (11 and 18/1/87; scr. Ken Taylor, dir. John Davies), 'At Bertram's Hotel' (25/1–1/2/87; scr. Jill Hyem, dir. Mary McMurray), 'Nemesis' (8 and 15/2/87; scr. T. R. Bowen, dir. David Tucker), '4.50 from Paddington' (25/2/87; scr. T. R. Bowen, dir. Martyn Friend), and 'A Caribbean Mystery' (25/12/89; scr. T. R. Bowen, dir. Christopher Petit). The 1990s followed with 'They Do It with Mirrors' (29/12/91; scr. T. R. Bowen, dir. Norman Stone) and, her final case, 'The Mirror Crack'd from Side to Side' (27/12/92), featuring Claire Bloom and Barry Newman; Norman Stone directed T. R. Bowen's 115-minute screenplay for producer George Gallaccio.

1984

Mitch
(LWT, 1984)

Was a crime reporter (played by John Thaw; *pictured*) for a tabloid national newspaper whose door-stepping, privacy-invasion adventures made up the yarns for this drama. Roger Marshall (who also created), Jeremy Burnham, and Tony Hoare contributed script copy, Don Leaver, Gerry Mill, and Terry Green directed the stories, and Peter Cregeen directed-produced the ten hour-long editions.

Mr Palfrey of Westminster
(Thames TV, 1984–85)

Counter-espionage drama featuring Alec McCowan (*left*) as Mr Palfrey, a quiet, rather precise man working for a spy chief known as the Co-ordinator (Caroline Blakiston). The series developed from an episode of Thames TV's **Storyboard** collection: 'The Traitor' (23/8/83; wr. George Markstein, dir. Christopher Hodson). Producer for the 10 eps. × hour series was Michael Chapman.

The Price is Right
(Central TV–Talbot TV–Goodson-Todman Prod., 1984–88)

American-derived game show in which audience-selected contestants became (suddenly and inexplicably) hysterical and used their knowledge of the prices of household items in bids to win prizes, hosted by Leslie Crowther (with microphone). The live-wire contestants were chosen, apparently, on the basis of personality and enthusiasm. William G. Stewart produced.

Robin of Sherwood
(HTV–Goldcrest, 1984–86)

Superb sword-and-sorcery tales from the Greenwood created (and for the most part written) by the prolific Richard Carpenter. The main characters were Robin of Loxley (Michael Praed; *pictured*), Little John (Clive Mantle), Will Scarlet (Ray Winstone), Maid Marion (Judi Trott; *pictured*), Friar Tuck (Phil Rose), Much (Peter Llewellyn Williams), and the brooding, stylized Saracen Nasir (Mark Ryan). The Sheriff of Nottingham (Nickolas Grace) and the inept Sir Guy of Gisburne (Robert Addie) represented their usual enemy but both barbaric Lord Owen (Oliver Cotton) and the supremely sinister Druid Gulnar (played with acid-dripping delight by Richard O'Brien) came across as the most fascinating if not the most horrifying characters. Praed's Robin was killed off at the end of the second series and was replaced by Robert of Huntingdon (Jason Connery) in 1986 for the last series. Twenty-four hour-long episodes and one 2-hour episode were produced by Paul Knight and Esta Charkham; the mystical title music was supplied by Clannad.

Scully
(C4/Granada TV, 1984)

Alan Bleasdale's cocky, young Liverpudlian character Franny Scully (Andrew Schofield) appeared in this short-run series of half-hour misadventures produced by Steve Morrison. Ray Kingsley (as his pal Mooey), Mark McGann, and Richard Burke supported. Bleasdale had earlier presented the character in 'Scully's New Year's Eve' (3/1/78) as a part of the **Play for Today** series. The 75-minute play also featured Schofield as Scully and Kingsley as Mooey, with Jane Freeman as Mrs Scully; Michael Simpson directed David Rose's production. Pictured are (*l. to r.*) footballers Kenny Dalglish and Bruce Grobbelaar with Schofield.

Spitting Image
(Central TV, 1984–)

Topical comedy sketch show with hideously cruel caricatures of important (or otherwise) personalities in the world. The impertinent attacks on leading political figures, particularly the outrageously funny characterizations of British politicians, turned the skilfully crafted puppets into near mascots for their public profile targets. Peter Fluck & Roger Law created the puppets for the production team of Jon Blair, Tony Hendra, and John Lloyd.

Thomas the Tank Engine and Friends
(Clearwater Film–Britt Allcroft Ltd./Central TV, 1984–86)

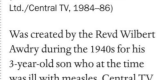

Was created by the Revd Wilbert Awdry during the 1940s for his 3-year-old son who at the time was ill with measles. Central TV turned the character into a colourful (model) animated children's TV series, shown in 10/15-minute episodes, narrated by Ringo Starr. Thomas's steam-engine adventures, which he shared with friends Terence the Tractor, Percy the Saddle Tank, Toby the Tram Engine, James the Red Engine, etc., became an instant hit with the mid-afternoon audience. David Mitton directed; executive producer was Britt Allcroft. Oliver Postgate's **Ivor the Engine** (A-R, 1962–64; BBC-1, 1976–77) shunted along similar lines, with David Edwards and Postgate; later Olwen Griffiths, Anthony Jackson, and Postgate telling thirty-nine 5-minute railway stories with illustrations by Peter Firmin.

Threads
(BBC-2, 23/9/84)

Chillingly realistic drama-documentary focusing on imagined events in the aftermath of a nuclear attack on Sheffield. Actually, Barry Hines's 115-minute scenario covered the period of the days before and the thirteen years after the attack, interweaving actors, professional extras, and volunteers, amid the desolate landscape, with computer and voice narration based on scientific consensus as to the probable consequences for all life forms. Karen Meagher and Reece Dinsdale led the large cast as a young Sheffield couple caught up in the holocaust. Mike Jackson produced and directed. Pictured are survivors David Brierley and Rita May.

The Tripods
(BBC-1, 1984–85)

Science-fiction adventure set in the twenty-first century (transmitted in the Saturday **Doctor Who** slot) featuring two teenage cousins, Will (John Shackley) and Henry (Jim Baker), who join in the battle to free Earth from alien domination, the latter visually represented by enormous, metallic Tripods. The 25 eps. × 30 mins. series was adapted by Alick Rowe from author John Christopher's (H. G. Wells-inspired) trilogy, first published in 1967, and produced by Richard Bates; a projected third series for 1986 never materialized.

1985

Albion Market
(Granada TV, 1985–86)

Twice-weekly soap serial set in a busy covered market in Manchester, launched as a sort of weekend stablemate (it went out Fridays and Sundays) to the long-running **Coronation Street**. However, the domestic and dramatic, painful and passionate events in the lives of an ethnically mixed bag of noisy characters did not spark the viewing audience and the series only notched up 100 eps. × half-hour. Leading players included David Hargreaves (*pictured back row 6th left*; as Derek, the market superintendent), Bernard Spear (*back row 4th right*), Carol Kaye (*back row 3rd right*), Burt Caesar (*back row 6th right*), Dev Sagoo (*front row 2nd left*), Paul Bhattacharjee (*front row left*), Philip Tan (*back row right*), and Pik-Sen Lim (*back row 2nd right*); Tony Booth and pop singer Helen Shapiro joined the serial in its latter days. Bill Podmore was executive producer.

The Beiderbecke Affair
(Yorkshire TV, 6/1–10/2/85)

The first of Alan Plater's three comedy-thrillers was set around mysterious characters, intriguing plots, and National Security, and featured reluctant amateur detectives Trevor Chaplin (played by James Bolam), a Bix Beiderbecke jazz buff, and girlfriend Jill Swinburne (Barbara Flynn; *pictured centre*). Six hour-long episodes were produced by Anne W. Gibbons. **The Beiderbecke Tapes** (Yorkshire TV, 13 and 20/12/87) and **The Beiderbecke Connection** (Yorkshire TV, 27/11–18/12/88) followed, both under producer Michael Glynn. Plater's earlier 4 eps. × hour serial, **Get Lost!** (Yorkshire TV, 12/6–3/7/81), served as something of a format/character source for **Beiderbecke**; two teachers (played by Bridget Turner and Alun Armstrong) get embroiled in missing-person mysteries. Michael Glynn produced.

Black Silk
(BBC-2, 7/11–26/12/85)

Rudolph Walker (*right*) played Larry Scott, a talented and socially committed barrister in an otherwise all-white London chambers who took on cases 'a lot of white barristers wouldn't touch'. Kika Markham (*left*) co-starred as his colleague and girlfriend Julie Smythe. The 8 eps. × 50 mins. series was devised by Mustapha Matura and Rudy Narayan. Ruth Boswell produced.

Blind Date
(LWT, 1985–)

A sort of TV dating service and game show, hosted by Cilla Black (*left*), in which young people question each other sight unseen to choose a partner for a blind date. The winning couple, after their expense-paid day out together (anywhere from Mumbles to Malaga), return the following week to have Cilla ring-master embarrassing footage of their date and hear what the couple really thought about each other. For the same company Cilla Black also hosted **Surprise, Surprise** (LWT, 1984–), a family entertainment show with audience participation; Christopher Biggins was Cilla's accomplice in the unpredictable encounters.

Blott on the Landscape
(BBC-2, 6/2–13/3/85)

Tom Sharpe's farcical black comedy of how Sir Giles Lynchwood (played by George Cole; *right*), a landowning MP for South Worfordshire, attempted to have a motorway built through his wife's ancestral home, Handyman Hall. Geraldine James was the wife, Maud, and David Suchet (*left*) was Blott the handyman. The story was adapted and updated by Malcolm Bradbury in 6 eps. × 50 mins.; Roger Bamford directed for producer Evgeny Gridneff.

Charters and Caldicott
(BBC-1, 10/1–14/2/85)

A 6 part × 50 mins. whodunit serial featuring the pair of lovable buffers created by Frank Launder & Sidney Gilliat in their screenplay for Hitchcock's 1938 film *The Lady Vanishes*. Keith Waterhouse's story placed the duo, played by Robin Bailey (*left*; as Charters) and Michael Aldridge (*right*; Caldicott), in a mystery involving industrial double-dealing and a trail of murder, and happily retained the pair's cautious view of a world divided into those who play cricket and those who do not. Julian Amyes directed for producer Ron Craddock.

Connie
(Central TV, 1985)

Aimed to be a part-gritty, part-caricature look at the cut-throat world of fashion from a sweatshop-floor level. The story followed the revenge-filled return of a former fashion chain owner, Connie (Stephanie Beacham; *left*), as she tried to climb back to the top of the business and settle a few old scores along the way. The series, written by Ron Hutchinson, also featured Brenda Bruce, Paul Rogers, Richard Morant, Pam Ferris (*right*), and George Costigan. Nicholas Palmer produced.

Dempsey and Makepeace
(LWT–Golden Eagle Films, 1985–86)

High adrenalin, all-action attempt at American-style TV police series set in and around London and featuring a tough ex-New York cop, Lt. Dempsey (played by Michael Brandon; *right*), and the upper-class English Sgt. Harriet Makepeace (Glynis Barber; *left*). They both worked for SI10 (a special police undercover unit) under Chief Superintendent Spikings (Ray Smith). The series was devised by Jesse Carr-Martindale but the format presented on TV was created by writer Ranald Graham when he was brought in to construct the 105-minute première episode ('Armed and Extremely Dangerous', 11/1/85; dir.-pr. Tony Wharmby) which showcased the cat-and-dog duo's violent methods of operation. Twenty-nine hour-long episodes were produced by Tony Wharmby.

1985

EastEnders
(BBC-1, 1985–)

BBC Television's high-rating, twice-weekly serial (with, later, an omnibus edition at weekends) set in inner-city London and generally situated around Albert Square in the London Borough of Walford, E20. The Beales and the Fowlers were the central families around whom most of the stories revolved. Lou Beale (played by Anna Wing) was the head of a large cockney family, with son Pete (Peter Dean), his wife Kathy (Gillian Taylforth), and their son Ian (Adam Woodyatt); and daughter Pauline Fowler (Wendy Richard) married to Arthur (Bill Treacher) and living with their children, Mark (David Scarboro; later played by Todd Carty) and Michelle (Susan Tully). Their local pub, the Queen Vic, also housed two colourful and volatile characters, shady publican Den Watts (Leslie Grantham) and his wife Angie (Anita Dobson; *pictured*). The serial was created by producer Julia Smith and script-editor Tony Holland. In 1988 BBC TV presented a 60-minute **EastEnders** special called **Civvy Street** (BBC-1, 26/12/88) which was set around Christmas 1942 and featured a young Lou (played by Karen Meagher), struggling to bring up her young family alone (her husband Albert having gone off to war), and her friend Ethel (Alison Bettles), continually in search of a man and a pair of nylons.

Edge of Darkness
(BBC-2, 4/11–9/12/85)

Appeared as Troy Kennedy Martin's tribute to television *film noir*, blending paranoid fantasy with a complicated mystery plot. Bob Peck (*pictured*) played Craven, a police detective investigating the background to his daughter's murder. Joanne Whalley was his daughter Emma and American actor Joe Don Baker was a hulking CIA agent. The 6 eps. × 55 mins. serial was directed by Martin Campbell for producer Michael Wearing.

Girls on Top
(Central TV–Witzend, 1985–86)

A frenzied comedy series about four bizarre and incompatible girls who share a flat. The sitcom featured (*l. to r.*) Dawn French, Joan Greenwood (as their equally oddball landlady), Tracey Ullman, Ruby Wax, and Jennifer Saunders. The series was written by Wax, French, and Saunders; Paul Jackson produced-directed.

Hold the Back Page
(BBC-1, 12/11/85–28/1/86)

Drama series about Fleet Street reporter Ken Wordsworth (David Warner, *left*, with guest Peter Hughes) who was forced to switch from his highbrow Sunday newspaper job to a daily tabloid in order to pay the alimony. The Andrew Nickolds & Stan Hey-scripted stories followed sports writer Ken as he moved around the various sporting events. Eric Allan, Gil Brailey, Lee Whitlock, David Horovitch, Peter-Hugo Daly, and Richard Ireson supported.

Howards' Way
(BBC-1, 1985–90)

Was a glossy drama serial set in the lush countryside of Hampshire and along the River Hamble, the wealthy world of swanky yachts, powerboats, and the marine business. The serial originally moved around Tom Howard (played by Maurice Colbourne; *2nd right*), a former aircraft designer who took his career and the family funds into the boatyard industry. Jan Harvey (*right*) played his wife, Edward Highmore (*left*) his son, and Tracey Childs (*centre*) was his daughter; Dulcie Gray (*2nd left*), Glyn Owen, Susan Gilmore, and Stephen Yardley were among the original cast members. The programme was devised by Gerard Glaister and Allan Prior.

Jenny's War
(HTV, 3–24/6/85)

Dyan Cannon (*pictured*) starred in this 4 eps. × hour mini-series about a British-resident American schoolteacher, Jenny Baines (Cannon), who travels to Nazi Germany during the early years of the Second World War to search for her son, an RAF pilot missing in action. The series was written and directed by Steven Gethers from a novel by Jack Stoneley. Robert Hardy, Elke Sommer, and Richard Todd co-starred. Peter Graham Scott produced.

Lytton's Diary
(Thames TV, 1985–86)

Peter Bowles (*centre*) appeared as the *Daily News* diary writer Neville Lytton, a man who was constantly thrashing about in the gossip-column world of scandal and personal survival. The series, written by Ray Connolly, came from an original idea by Bowles and Philip Broadley; the pilot episode was seen as part of Thames TV's **Storyboard** collection (tx 30/8/83; wr. Connolly, dir. Brian Parker). The 14 eps. × hour series was produced by Chris Burt and Derek Bennett.

Mapp & Lucia
(LWT, 1985–86)

The popular E. F. Benson stories about the social rivalry between Emmeline Lucas, affectionately known as Lucia (played by Geraldine McEwan; *left*), and the dowdy Miss Elizabeth Mapp (Prunella Scales; *right*) were dramatized by Gerald Savory for a 10 eps. × hour series. The setting was the village of Riseholme during the early 1930s. Nigel Hawthorne appeared as the foppish Georgie Pillson. Michael Dunlop produced.

1985

Max Headroom
(C4/Chrysalis, 4/4/85)

Was the name given to a computer-created character who developed out of a 65-minute science fiction telefilm starring Matt Frewer, Nickolas Grace, Amanda Pays, and Paul Spurrier; Steve Roberts's script was directed by Rocky Morton & Annabel Jankel for producer Peter Wagg. The irreverent Max then became a talking-head presenter of an MTV-like rock promo series, **The Max Headroom Show** (C4/Chrysalis, 1985–87), also produced by Wagg. There was even a 45-minute holiday special called **Max Headroom's Giant Christmas Turkey** (C4/Chrysalis, 26/12/86). American TV then turned the format back into a science fiction drama series, **Max Headroom** (ABC TV–Chrysalis–Lakeside Prods.–Lorimar, 1987; UK tx C4, 1989), with Frewer, Pays, George Coe, Chris Young, Jeffrey Tambor, and Jere Burns. The name 'Max Headroom' derives from the overhead bridge-level sign indicating maximum headroom height for tall vehicles.

The Mistress
(BBC-2, 1985; 1987)

Three years after **Solo** Felicity Kendal (*right*) returned in another Carla Lane-scripted sitcom, this time as Maxine, a woman who also lived on her own but enjoyed life as the mistress of Luke (Jack Galloway; *left*) who was married to Helen (Jane Asher). Unlike **Solo** this tended to present the solo woman/mistress in a more positive light. Gareth Gwenlan again produced and directed.

Operation Julie
(Tyne Tees TV–Chatsworth TV, 4–5–6/11/85)

Was a three-part dramatization, based on fact, about one of Britain's biggest police drug searches (making headline news in the 1970s). The screenplay by Gerry O'Hara, Keith Richardson, and Bob Mahoney was based on the book written by Colin Pratt and Dick Lee. Colin Blakely (*pictured, left*) starred as Det. Insp. Richard Lee with David Swift as Det. Supt. Gosling. Bob Mahoney directed for producers Malcolm Heyworth and Peter Holmans.

The Price
(C4/Astramead–RTE–Telepictures Corp., 10/1–14/2/85)

A 6 part × hour thriller focusing on the psychological complications of a kidnap experienced by computer magnate Geoffrey Carr (Peter Barkworth) who was forced into the position of having to raise the ransom for his captive wife and stepchild. The taut script was by Peter Ransley; Peter Smith directed for producer Mark Shivas. The scene pictured shows Derek Thompson and kidnap victim Harriet Walter.

Relative Strangers
(C4/Humphrey Barclay Prod., 1985–87)

Were Fitz (Matthew Kelly; *left*) and his teenaged son John (Mark Farmer; *right*), an 18-year-old, street-wise kid who appeared one day claiming that Fitz was his father, following a romantic one-night fling with his mother back in 1966. The half-hour sitcom was written by Laurence Marks & Maurice Gran. John Kaye Cooper and Humphrey Barclay produced.

Saint and Greavsie
(LWT, 1985–)

Had former soccer players Ian St John (*left*) and Jimmy Greaves (*right*) as an ITV Sport double act presenting their views on the vital issues in football and taking a fan's eye view of the big sporting events of the week. The midday Saturday programme was originally edited by Bob Patience; it grew out of the presenter duo's 'On the Ball' slot in **World of Sport**.

The Secret Diary of Adrian Mole, Aged 13¾
(Thames TV, 1985)

A comedy-drama series by Sue Townsend from her best-selling book about the life of a troubled teenager, Adrian Mole (played by Gian Sammarco; *left*), and his chaotic family. Also appearing were Julie Walters (as his mother), Stephen Moore (father), Beryl Reid (Grandma), and Lindsay Stagg (girlfriend Pandora; *right*). Sammarco returned as Adrian Mole in a series of half-hour stories, **The Growing Pains of Adrian Mole** (Thames TV, 1987), with the same cast, except that the part of the mother was now played by singer-actress Lulu. Contributing producer-director for both series was Peter Sasdy.

Supergran
(Tyne Tees TV, 1985–87)

Was based on the popular children's books by Forrest Wilson (adapted for TV by Jenny McDade), about a chirpy old lady who was accidentally struck by a beam from a magic ray machine and acquired magical powers. The half-hour series starred Gudrun Ure (*pictured*) in the title role, with Iain Cuthbertson as the villain, The Scunner Campbell, and Bill Shine as Inventor Black. Keith Richardson produced.

Taggart
(Scottish TV, 1985–)

An irregular series of three-part and feature-length stories featuring Mark McManus (*left*; pictured with Iain Anders) as tough Glasgow cop Det. Chief Insp. Taggart. The grim and gritty series developed from a three-part thriller called **Killer** (Scottish TV, 6–20/9/83) created and written by Glenn Chandler and directed by Laurence Moody; Neil Duncan (as Det. Sgt. Livingstone) and Tom Watson (as Supt. Murray) co-starred with McManus. Haldane Duncan, Robert Love, and Peter Barber-Fleming produced the various programmes. Later mini-serials (all Scottish TV) have been: **Dead Ringer** (2–16/7/85), **Murder in Season** (23/7–6/8/85), **Death Call** (2–16/2/86), **Knife Edge** (24/2–10/3/86), **Killing Philosophy** (15–29/4/87), **Funeral Rites** (9–23/9/87), **Cold Blood** (31/12/87), **Dead Giveaway** (7–21/9/88), **Root of Evil** (28/9–12/10/88), **Double Jeopardy** (30/12/88), **Flesh and Blood** (5–19/9/89), **Love Knot** (1/1/90), **Hostile Witness** (1–15/3/90), **Evil Eye** (4–18/9/90), **Death Comes Softly** (3–17/12/90), **Rogues' Gallery** (31/12/90), **Violent Delights** (1/1/92), **Nest of Vipers** (9–23/1/92), **Double Exposure** (30/1–13/2/92), **Hit Man** (17/9–1/10/92), **Ring of Deceit** (8–22/10/92), **Fatal Inheritance** (1/1/93), **Death Benefits** (16/2–2/3/93), **Gingerbread** (20/4–4/5/93), and **Death Without Dishonour** (11–25/5/93); most of the three-part stories have been re-edited and re-screened as 'feature' presentations.

Tender is the Night

(BBC-1–Showtime–The Movie Channel, 23/9–28/10/85)

Anglo-American mini-series adaptation of F. Scott Fitzgerald's 1934 novel centring on the mentally troubled wife (Mary Steenburgen) of a psychiatrist (Peter Strauss) during the post-First World War years in Europe. Dennis Potter adapted the six eps. × 50/55 mins. story but, instead of following Fitzgerald's form of placing the glamorous aspects (the characters' future) up front and then shading in the background (the characters' past), structured the tale in a strict chronological order (which may have made the viewing easier for some but rather moved the story out of kilter). Robert Knights directed Betty Willingale's production.

Three Up, Two Down

(BBC-1, 1985–89)

Registered the character comedy clashes (social and in-law) of the snobbish Daphne Trenchard (played by Angela Thorne; *2nd left*) and the easygoing cockney Sam Tyler (Michael Elphick; *left*); Daphne's daughter Angie (Lysette Anthony; *right*) was happily married to Sam's son, Nick (Ray Burdis; *2nd right*), and they had a baby (the Three Up). Richard Ommanney's scripts placed the bickering grandparents together sharing the downstairs flat (the Two Down) in the young couple's house as child-minders. David Askey produced.

Victoria Wood—As Seen on TV

(BBC-2, 1985–86)

Was a welcome showcase for the comic writing and performing talents of Victoria Wood, along with her stock company of Julie Walters, Celia Imrie, Duncan Preston, Susie Blake, and Patricia Routledge. The series also introduced the hilarious TV soap opera spoof 'Acorn Antiques', with its shaky antique shop setting and such characters as Miss Babs (Imrie; *right*), the pompous owner, her assistant Miss Berta (Wood; *2nd left*), handyman Clifford (Preston; *left*), and the hump-backed charlady Mrs Overall (Walters; *2nd right*), who kept missing her cues and bumping into the props. A Christmas show, **Victoria Wood Special** (BBC-2, 18/12/87), offered a behind-the-scenes 'report' on the cast and crew of 'Acorn Antiques'. Geoff Posner produced-directed. Victoria Wood's other TV credits include 'Talent' (Granada TV, 5/8/79; dir. Baz Taylor under the **Screenplay** banner), **Nearly a Happy Ending** (Granada TV, 1/6/80; dir. Taylor), **Wood and Walters: 'Two Creatures Great and Small'** (Granada TV, 1/1/81; 30 mins.; dir. Stuart Orme), 'Happy Since I Met You' (Granada TV, 9/8/81; dir. Taylor under the **Screenplay** banner), **Wood and Walters** (Granada TV, 1982) series, and the **Victoria Wood** (BBC-1, 1989) six-part series.

A Woman of Substance

(C4/Portman Artemis Prod., 2–3–4/1/85)

Barbara Taylor Bradford's marathon romantic yarn about the travails and triumphs of a Yorkshire servant girl, Emma Harte, driven by ambition. The period drama started off in 1905 after a contemporary flashback and carried on through to the First World War. Deborah Kerr was cast as Emma Harte in later years, while Jenny Seagrove (pictured with Barry Bostwick) played the younger Emma; John Mills, Diane Baker, George Baker, Gayle Hunnicutt, Nicola Pagett, and Miranda Richardson were among the supporting cast. Don Sharp directed Lee Langley's adaptation for Diane Baker's production. A 240-minute follow-up, **Hold the Dream** (Robert Bradford Prods.–Taft Entertainment TV–Bradford Portman Prods., US tx 4 and 11/11/86), was produced by Harry R. Sherman (dir. Don Sharp and wr. Barbara Taylor Bradford) with Kerr returning as the English matriarch Emma Harte.

Bluebell
(BBC-1, 12/1–2/3/86)

Carolyn Pickles (*pictured*) starred as Margaret Kelly, aka Miss Bluebell, who danced her way from the back streets of Dublin to the bright lights of pre-war, late night Paris during the time when the Folies Bergère extravaganzas made Paris and the Bluebell Girls justly famous. The 8 eps. × 50 mins. serial was written by Paul Wheeler, directed by Moira Armstrong, and produced by Brian Spiby.

Boon
(Central TV, 1986–)

Ken Boon (Michael Elphick; *pictured*) was an ex-fireman forced into early retirement due to ill health who became something of a modern-day (lone) Ranger when he placed a want-ad. for 'Anything Legal Considered'. Based in a small, edge-of-town Birmingham hotel run by his old friend Harry Crawford (David Daker), Boon accepted (and was occasionally drawn into) private assignments ranging from acting as a 'minder' to fending off protection racket gangs. Rachel Davies, Joan Scott, and Neill Gavin played his companions during the early series; Neil Morrissey and Lesley-Anne Sharpe were his sidekicks from the second (and now filmed; the earlier series had been on tape) series. The programme was created by Jim Hill and Bill Stair.

Bread
(BBC-1, 1986–)

Featured the sitcom stories of the Boswells, a Catholic, working-class Liverpool family who were all unemployed (except for one, initially) and who lived by their wits, and everything they could get out of the DHS. Created and written by Carla Lane, the series starred (*l. to r., back row*) Victor McGuire, Bryan Murray, Melanie Hill (Gilly Coman in the early series), Giles Watling, Kenneth Waller, (*front row, seated*) Ronald Forfar, Graham Bickley (Peter Howitt in the early series), Jean Boht, Nick Conway, and Jonathon Morris.

Brush Strokes
(BBC-1, 1986–91)

Featured Karl Howman (*pictured*) as Jacko, a cockney Jack-the-lad painter and decorator who womanized his way through this occasionally funny but often silly sitcom. Supporting cast included Gary Waldhorn, Elizabeth Counsell, Mike Walling, Nicky Croydon, and Howard Lew Lewis. The series was written by John Esmonde & Bob Larbey; produced originally by Sydney Lotterby. Esmonde & Larbey later created **Mulberry** (BBC-1, 1992–93) for Howman, about a mysterious 'but lovable' character hired by a cranky old spinster (played by Geraldine McEwan) to take care of her household; John B. Hobbs produced.

1986

Casualty
(BBC-1, 1986–)

An expertly produced drama series set at night in the casualty department of a busy general hospital. Episodes presented multi-strand stories and sub-plots (in the American **St Elsewhere** style) in a format created and initially scripted by Jeremy Brock and Paul Unwin. The original series featured Derek Thompson (*pictured*), Catherine Shipton, Julia Watson, Brenda Fricker, and Christopher Rozycki. Geraint Morris was première producer.

Dead Head
(BBC-2, 15/1–5/2/86)

A 4 parts × 50 mins. *film noir*ish thriller about a small-time south London crook, Eddie Cass (played by Denis Lawson, *left*, with Larrington Walker), who became innocently entwined in a gruesome murder and, as a result, a soft target of the secret state. George Baker, Lindsay Duncan, Simon Callow, Norman Beaton, and Don Henderson co-starred. Howard Brenton scripted for producer Robin Midgley; Rob Walker directed.

Dear John . . .
(BBC-1, 1986–87)

A John Sullivan-scripted comedy series about lonely divorcé John (Ralph Bates; *right*), now living in a bedsit after a losing bout in the divorce courts, who decides to join a 1–2–1 encounter group. Supporting players and members of the group were Michael Cochrane, Peter Blake (*left*), Belinda Lang (*centre*), Peter Denyer, and Rachel Bell as leader of the group. Ray Butt produced. American TV acquired the series format and presented their own **Dear John** (NBC/Ed Weinberger Prods.–Paramount TV, 1988–90) with Judd Hirsch starring in the Bates role; BBC TV later screened the series as **Dear John: USA**.

Equinox
(C4/Uden Associates Prod., 1986–)

An informative weekly series about all aspects of technology and science, ranging from the mysteries of memory to the way our image of future cities and space travel was constructed. Patrick Uden produced. The scene pictured is from the 'At the Edge' (26/11/87) edition, an Independent Communications Production, produced-directed by Chris Haws, about the history of fighter pilots and their aircraft and featured one of the Top Gun Instructors at Miramar.

Floyd on Food
(BBC-2, 23/9–28/10/86)

Presented intrepid gastronaut Keith Floyd (*pictured*) in a series of unorthodox cookery programmes (first shown locally on BBC South-West) where he introduced, with the help of available vineyard produce, a wide range of culinary delights. An earlier, networked programme had been **Floyd on Fish** (BBC-2, 14/11–19/12/85). Floyd continued with other series exploring the gastronomic regions of various cultures and countries: **Floyd on France** (BBC-2, 1/9–6/10/87), **Floyd on Britain and Ireland** (BBC-2, 30/8–4/10/88), **Floyd's American Pie** (10/10–14/11/89), **Floyd on Oz** (BBC-2/Stockley Chase, 11/4–6/6/91), **Floyd on Spain** (BBC-2/Lifetime, 18/8–29/9/92), and **Far Flung Floyd** (BBC-2/Lifetime Broadcast, 13/7–24/8/93), a tour of the Far East, for BBC South-West producer David Pritchard, always accompanied by the programme's title soundtrack performed by The Stranglers. As much a programme about camera manipulation and wine-sampling as about food preparation. Years earlier Floyd had been a regular contributor of cookery items on the afternoon magazine programme **Here Today** (HTV, 1980–82). He later took over from Clive James (**Clive James on Television**) for a short-lived series of **Floyd on TV** (LWT, 1989).

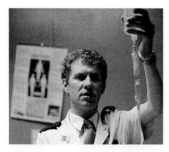

Help!
(BBC-1, 1986; 1988)

Was a roustabout comedy series following the exploits of three optimistic young Liverpudlians who were out of work and generally game for anything. The three stars were (l. to r.) David Albany (as Lennie), Stephen McGann (as Tex), and Jake Abraham (as Davva). Joe Boyle scripted for producer-director Mike Stephens/BBC Manchester.

Hot Metal
(LWT, 1986; 1988)

Was a pleasantly foolish comedy series centred on a low-life newspaper, the *Daily Crucible*, which was taken over by the tycoon owner of Rathouse International and placed under the editorship of the mysterious 'Russell Spam'. Robert Hardy (*left*) and Geoffrey Palmer (*right*) starred in this Andrew Marshall and David Renwick-scripted series for producer Humphrey Barclay.

Ladies in Charge
(Thames TV, 1986)

Six hour-long dramas featuring three young ladies who, in the London of the 1920s, were determined to help the needy. The series opened with novelist Fay Weldon's 'Zoe's Fever' (6/5/86; dir. Richard Bramall). The three ladies were played by Carol Royale, Julia Hills, and Julia Swift. Peter Duguid produced; from an idea by Kate Herbert-Hunting. Pictured (l. to r.) are Hills, Orlando Wells, Royale, and Amanda Root from the **Storyboard** pilot.

The Life and Loves of a She Devil
(BBC-2, 8–29/10/86)

A macabre black-comedy serial in four hour-long episodes which combined outrageous fantasy with some devastating truths as husband Bobbo (Dennis Waterman) informed his wife Ruth (Julie T. Wallace, pictured as one of the characters she becomes) that he had fallen in love with someone else, the glamorous novelist Mary Fisher (Patricia Hodge). The serial was dramatized by Ted Whitehead from the novel by Fay Weldon. Philip Saville directed for producer Sally Head. Later produced as a feature film, *She-Devil*, by Orion in 1989.

Lovejoy
(BBC-1/Tamariska–Witzend Prods.–McShane Prods., 1986–)

Comedy-thriller series based on the novels by Jonathan Gash and dramatized by Ian La Frenais about a shady antiques dealer who entangles himself in detective work. Original producer Robert Banks Stewart made excellent use of the colourful East Anglian settings. Ian McShane (*left*) starred as Lovejoy, supported by Phyllis Logan (*right*), Dudley Sutton, and Chris Jury.

The Monocled Mutineer
(BBC-1, 31/8–21/9/86)

Fascinating serial (of 2 eps. × 75 mins., 1 ep. × 80 mins., 1 ep. × 95 mins.) adapted from a true story about a British army mutiny led by a dashing rogue, Private Percy Toplis, on the eve of the Battle of Passchendaele in 1917. Paul McGann (*pictured*) starred as Toplis, with Cherie Lunghi as lover Dorothy and Matthew Marsh as his partner in mutiny Charles Strange. The script was by Alan Bleasdale, based on the book by William Allison and John Fairley. Richard Broke produced.

Paradise Postponed
(Thames TV, 15/9–24/11/86)

John Mortimer's 1 ep. × 90 mins. / 10 eps. × hour drama series, written especially for television (although Mortimer also wrote a novelized version in tandem with the script), chronicling English life since the late 1940s. An element of mystery gave the series its main focal point: why would a liberal parish priest leave his inheritance to a manipulative politician instead of his family? The large cast was headed by Michael Hordern (*front left*), Jill Bennett, Colin Blakely, Annette Crosbie (*front right*), Eleanor David, Peter Egan (*standing right*), Paul Shelley (*standing left*), David Threlfall, Richard Vernon, Thorley Walters, and Zoe Wanamaker. Alvin Rakoff directed Jacqueline Davis's production.

Prospects
(C4/Euston Films, 1986)

This 12 eps. × hour series set in the Isle of Dogs Enterprise Zone in London may have been viewed as something of a lower-case **Minder**. Young Billy (Brian Bovell; *right*) and Pincy (Gary Olsen; *left*) organized and launched, with great energy, one fast-money-making scheme after another only to watch each enterprise crumble in front of them. Alan Janes scripted for producer Greg Smith.

The Singing Detective
(BBC-1, 16/11–21/12/86)

A musical thriller serial in 6 eps. × 60–80 mins. featuring Michael Gambon (*pictured*) as Philip Marlow, a bed-bound pulp writer who fantasizes about his fictional detective character, his own childhood, and the people and events in his hospital ward. Co-starring were Patrick Malahide, Joanne Whalley, Janet Suzman, Jim Carter, and Alison Steadman. Jon Amiel directed for producers John Harris and Kenith Trodd. Dennis Potter's screenplay mingled fantasy and reality as his hero fought his illness (a severe attack of psoriasis) amid mounting paranoia about his ex-wife and her lover; Potter himself suffered for years with the same illness.

The Two of Us
(LWT, 1986–90)

A domestic sitcom, with occasional flashes of wonderful character interplay, about a young couple, Ashley (Nicholas Lyndhurst) and Elaine (Janet Dibley), who live together, and are in love, but have opposing outlooks on life. The half-hour series was written by Alex Shearer and produced by Marcus Plantin.

A Very Peculiar Practice
(BBC-2, 21/5–2/7/86; 24/2–6/4/88)

Related the misadventures of an idealistic young doctor, Stephen Daker (Peter Davison, *left*, with Timothy West), who joined a practice on a modern university campus. Andrew Davies's superb script observed the professional and moral deterioration of Dr Daker as he struggled his way through an ailing medical centre on a campus filled with manic feuding intellectuals. His colleagues were the boozy head of the practice Jock McCannon (Graham Crowden), Dr Bob Buzzard (David Troughton), a right-winger who did not like his patients, and Dr Rose Marie (Barbara Flynn), who believed that sickness was something men invented to impose upon women; Joanna Kanska appeared in the second series as Daker's Polish distraction Grete Grotowska. For the second series Lowlands University became a sort of high-security concentration campus when the new American Vice-Chancellor Jack B. Daniels (Michael J. Shannon), an unscrupulous asset-stripper, took over. David Tucker directed for producer Ken Riddington. Davies composed a footnote to the lives of his characters in 1992 when he scripted a 95-minute **Screen One** film titled 'A Very Polish Practice' (BBC-1, 6/9/92) and featured Davison, Kanska, and Troughton in a story set in Warsaw; Tucker once again directed Riddington's production.

The Charmer
(LWT, 18/10–22/11/87)

Ralph Gorse (Nigel Havers; *centre*) was the con man, sexual adventurer, and murderer whose self-serving, duplicitous activities with the ladies (Rosemary Leach, *pictured left*; Fiona Fullerton, Abigail McKern, and Judy Parfitt), and the Military, finally brought about his downfall. Bernard Hepton (*pictured right*) also appeared as Gorse's constant adversary Donald Stimpson. The 6 eps. × hour series, set during the late 1930s, was written by Allan Prior (from a character created by author Patrick Hamilton), directed by Alan Gibson, and produced by Philip Hinchcliffe.

Fortunes of War
(BBC-1, 11/10–22/11/87)

Alan Plater's 7 part × 60 mins. adaptation of Olivia Manning's *The Balkan Trilogy* and *The Levant Trilogy*, first published between 1960 and 1980. The serial, set during the Second World War, observed the cruelties of war and the dislocated fates of civilian Britons caught on the far side of the German advance, and in particular followed the course of a young and troubled marriage. Kenneth Branagh and Emma Thompson (*pictured*) starred as the couple, Guy and Harriet Pringle; Ronald Pickup appeared as the dilapidated emigré aristocrat Prince Yakimov. James Cellan Jones directed Betty Willingale's production.

French and Saunders
(BBC-2, 1987–88)

The original press release announced this wonderfully wacko comedy-sketch series as a 'spectacular, full of spectacularness, dangerousness, star-guestness and good old-fashioned family fun. A must.' And that about said it all. Performers Dawn French (*right*) and Jennifer Saunders (*left*) also scripted their own material. Saunders's **Absolutely Fabulous** series was developed from one of the sketches first seen in this series. Geoff Posner produced.

Inspector Morse
(Central TV/Zenith Prod., 1987–92)

Intelligent, leisurely, almost plodding police procedural series featuring the Oxford-based detective created by Colin Dexter in a popular series of novels. John Thaw starred as Morse. The **Morse** television stories (usually of a 2-hour duration) were classic, old-style whodunnits, moving from clue to suspect, red herring to culprit, at a stately pace. Morse's sidekick was the sensible, somewhat slow-witted Det. Sgt. Lewis (Kevin Whately). John Thaw is pictured with guest Sharon Maughan in a scene from the 'Deceived by Flight' episode.

Jimmy's
(Yorkshire TV, 1987–)

The fly-on-the-wall observations of real-life medical drama among the wards at St James' Hospital in Leeds, W. Yorkshire, was the theme of this popular documentary series. With the reputation of being Europe's largest general hospital, 'Jimmy's' attracted the mid-evening viewers into sharing all the joy and heartache, the skill and care, and generally the emotional highs and lows of a major medical station—in much the way that carefully constructed TV documentary series have always managed to draw in the initially reluctant. Richard Handford and Irene Cockcroft were the original production force behind the series.

Knightmare
(Anglia TV, 1987–)

Was television's first computerized adventure game show, aimed specifically at the younger set. Created by Tim Child, this half-hour virtual reality game locked teams of four youngsters in a battle of wits and survival with grotesque wizards, knights, warrior jesters, wraiths, and assorted monsters from the computer graphics imagination. Hugo Myatt was Treguard, the Dungeon Master (and host); *pictured*, facing a contestant.

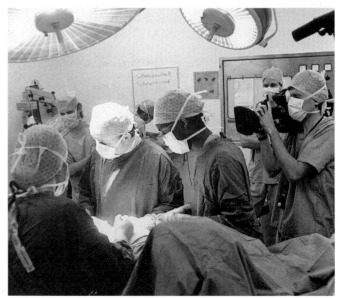

The Last Resort With Jonathan Ross
(C4/Callender Co. Prod.–Channel X, 1987–88)

This 45-minute show of chat, music, and celebrity guests was hosted by prime-time fashion elf Jonathan Ross (*pictured*). Colin Callender was the producer. In 1988 the show's title was shortened to **The Last Resort**. The following year another, longer series appeared, **One Hour With Jonathan Ross** (C4/Channel X Prod., 1989–90), produced by Katie Lander. This led to **Tonight With Jonathan Ross** (C4/Channel X Prod., 1990–92), produced by Ian Gardhouse, **Jonathan Ross Presents . . .** (C4/Channel X Prod., 1991), **Ross Meets Madonna** (C4, 21/10/92; pr.-dir. Chris Cowey) for an exclusive hour-long interview, and the enjoyably outrageous **Saturday Zoo** (C4/Channel X Prod., 1993). Earlier in his career Ross had been a member of the production team, under producers Gordon Elsbury and Katie Lander, on the **Soul Train** (Action Time Prod., 1985) segment of Channel Four's 'Friday Zone' programme slot. In 1989 he presented and co-produced the six-part **Son of the Incredibly Strange Film Show** (C4/Channel X–Sleeping Partners Prod., 29/9–27/10/89) which allowed him to meet various cult-status exploitation-market film-makers.

Life Story
(BBC-2, 27/4/87)

Was the hypnotic story of the race to the double helix of DNA, the basis of all modern genetics, and one of the greatest true detective stories of the twentieth century. Presented as a **Horizon** special, William Nicholson's 110-minute screenplay starred Jeff Goldblum (*right*) as Jim Watson, Tim Pigott-Smith (*left*) as Francis Crick, Alan Howard as Maurice Wilkins, and Juliet Stevenson as Rosalind Franklin. Director Mick Jackson's production was extensively researched and used some of the real scientists who took part in the race in the early 1950s.

The London Embassy
(Thames TV, 1987)

Paul Theroux's story (based on his book) of a young American political officer, Spencer Savage (played by Kristoffer Tabori; *centre*), assigned to a new post at the US embassy in London. The 6 eps. × hour drama series followed his experiences as he sought to familiarize himself with London, the English, and the activities of the 200-odd staff at the embassy. Richard Bates produced.

The Media Show
(C4/MSL–Beat Prods.; Wall to Wall Prod., 1987–91)

Presented a magazine programme overview of film, TV, advertising, print, and stage items, reviewing and analysing topical subjects behind the scenes of popular media. The programme started off as a fortnightly show, presented by Muriel Gray; later by Emma Freud. Andy Lipman, Kathy Myers, and Jane Root produced (later Adam Barker); Michael Jackson edited.

The New Statesman
(Yorkshire TV, 1987–)

Political comedy series featuring Rik Mayall (*left*) as Alan Beresford B'Stard, an unscrupulous politico who rode roughshod over everyone and everything to reach his personal objectives, usually of a financial and/or sexual nature. Marsha Fitzalan (as his wife Sarah) and Michael Troughton (*right*; as his assistant Piers Fletcher-Dervish) co-starred. The half-hour series was written by Laurence Marks & Maurice Gran; David Reynolds was the original producer.

Night Network
(ITV/Night Network Prod., 1987–88)

Introduced regular all-night programming (from 1.00 a.m. to 6.00 a.m.) with such nocturnal nibbles as 'Video View', with Craig Charles (*far left*) on new video releases; 'The Big Screen', with Robert Sandall (*2nd left*) on the week's cinema releases, and Mick Brown looking at videos to hire and buy; 'Pillow Talk', where Emma Freud met the rich and famous for an under-the-duvet interview; as well as various clips, competitions, **Batman** episodes, and so on. David G. Hillier directed; Jill Sinclair produced. Also pictured are (*l. to r.*) presenters Rowland Rivron, Geoffrey Cantor, Kim Newman, Angie Clarke, and Paul Thompson.

1987

Porterhouse Blue
(C4/Picture Partnership Prod., 3–24/6/87)

Four-part TV adaptation, by Malcolm Bradbury, of Tom Sharpe's best-selling novel about Porterhouse, Cambridge University's most archaic and reactionary college. David Jason (*right*) starred as Skullion, the head porter; with Ian Richardson (*left*), John Sessions, Paul Rogers, Barbara Jefford, and Griff Rhys Jones. The four hour-long episodes were directed by Robert Knights for producer Brian Eastman; photography was by Dick Pope, design by Eileen Diss.

Pulaski
(BBC-1, 2/10–20/11/87)

Satiric crime series, written by Roy Clarke, featuring New York actor David Andrews (*pictured*) as American actor Larry Summers who stars in a TV mini-series, 'Pulaski', about a Polish-American private detective and former priest. In performance, Pulaski is sober, brave, and honest; off-air, Larry Summers is a drunk, a lecher, and all-purpose bad boy. The stories have the character/actor confuse TV fiction with reality thus drawing him into (real) local crimes. Caroline Langrishe played his wife, Kate, as well as the character Briggsy in the 'TV show'. The eight-part series was produced by Paul Knight.

Rockcliffe's Babies
(BBC-1, 1987–88)

Ian Hogg (*pictured*) starred as tough, no-nonsense Det. Sgt. Alan Rockcliffe whose job it was to train an eager bunch of plain-clothes PCs who make up the Crime Squad of Victor Tango Division into full-blown detectives. The squad consisted of Bill Champion, Brett Fancy, John Blakey, Joe McGann, Alphonsia Emmanuel, Martyn Ellis, and Susanna Shelling. The series was created by Richard O'Keeffe and produced by Leonard Lewis. Ian Hogg's Rockcliffe later returned in **Rockcliffe's Folly** (BBC-1, 1988) where, minus his Babies, he moved to the West Country to investigate rural crime. Ron Craddock produced.

Scoop
(LWT, 26/4/87)

Novelist Evelyn Waugh's classic send-up of Fleet Street was turned into a £2.5 million film version by London Weekend and producer Sue Birtwistle, starring Michael Maloney (*centre*) as *Daily Beast* nature correspondent William Boot who is dispatched by mistake to cover a civil war in an African Republic. The 2-hour film was adapted by William Boyd and directed by Gavin Millar; Denholm Elliott (*right*), Michael Hordern (*left*), Herbert Lom, Nicola Pagett, and Donald Pleasence also starred. An earlier version had been produced by BBC TV as a 7 eps. × 30 mins. serial: **Scoop** (BBC-2, 8/10–19/11/72) featured Harry Worth as Boot, with Sheila Hancock and Brian Oulton supporting; Barry Took adapted for producer Michael Mills.

Secret Society
(BBC-2, 22/4–13/5/87)

Controversial for its time (on the grounds that material in it might breach national security) this documentary series spotlighted sensitive areas relating to political and military secrecy in the UK. Initially a six-part programme, two of writer-presenter Duncan Campbell's (*pictured*) editions were withdrawn by BBC TV due to pressure from certain MPs. The series was originally set for transmission in November 1986 but was 'delayed' for various internal reasons, including the banning of the 'Cabinet' episode (concerning 'election dirty tricks') and the 'Zircon' episode (about a new British spy satellite code-named Zircon). 'Cabinet' never did make it to the schedules on account of being 'out of date' but the other episode finally showed up as **The Zircon Affair** via BBC-2 on 30/9/88 in a special 75-minute programme presented by Ludovic Kennedy. The four original episodes screened were 'We're All Data Now' (on databanks held by the DHS), 'In Time of Crisis' (on emergency laws in the event of a war or national emergency), 'A Power in the Land' (on the Association of Chief Police Officers and their influence on government policies), and 'Skywatch' (reporting on Britain's radar defence network). The series was produced for BBC Scotland by Brian Barr and directed by Dennis Cosgrove.

Tutti Frutti
(BBC-1, 3/3–7/4/87)

Wildly funny 6 eps. × 60/70 mins. series featuring The Majestics, 'Scotland's Kings of Rock', as they prepared for their silver jubilee tour. Robbie Coltrane starred as Danny McGlone, a failed painter and piano bar star, who returned from New York for his big brother Jazza's funeral, bumped into an old flame, Suzi Kettles (Emma Thompson), and found himself fronting the ageing rock 'n' rollers. Also appearing were Maurice Roeves, Stuart McGugan, and Jake D'Arcy as members of the band. Written by John Byrne for BBC Scotland producer Andy Park; Tony Smith directed. The picture shows Robbie Coltrane as Big Jazza.

Wolf to the Slaughter
(TVS, 2–23/8/87)

Introduced crime writer Ruth Rendell's Inspector Wexford (played by George Baker) to television in an irregular series of stately paced mysteries dramatized from Rendell's novels and stories; **Wolf** was dramatized by Clive Exton and produced-directed by John Davies. Following serials were **A Guilty Thing Surprised** (TVS, 19/6–3/7/88; wr. Exton, dir. Mary McMurray), **Shake Hands Forever** (TVS, 23/9–7/10/88; wr. Exton, dir. Don Leaver), **No More Dying Then** (TVS, 22/10–5/11/89; wr. Geoffrey Case, dir. Jan Sargent), and **A Sleeping Life** (TVS, 12–26/11/89; wr. Roger Marshall, dir. Bill Hays; Baker is pictured with Sylvia Syms). Two telefilms were also produced during the late 1980s: **No Crying He Makes** (TVS, 23/12/88; billed as 'The Ruth Rendell Christmas Mystery'), with Mary McMurray directing Paula Milne's 90-minute adaptation, and **The Veiled One** (TVS, 17/12/89), McMurray directing Trevor Preston's 2-hour dramatization. Neil Zeiger produced from 1988. Several more two- and three-part Wexford serials (including **An Unkindness of Ravens**, **Achilles Heel**, **Means of Evil**, **The Speaker of Mandarin**, **The Mouse in the Corner**, **An Unwanted Woman**, etc.) followed into the 1990s, produced by Neil Zeiger. The programmes were also billed as 'Ruth Rendell Mysteries'.

Andy Capp
(Thames TV, 1988)

Saw Reg Smythe's *Daily Mirror* strip-cartoon character transferred from the printed page to Keith Waterhouse's TV scripts. The television crossover, played in sitcom fashion, was less than successful and only 6 eps. × half-hour were shown. James Bolam played Andy and Paula Tilbrook was Flo. The series was produced by John Howard Davies. BBC TV's **Jane**, elevated from similar origins, did not fare much better in 1982.

Campaign
(BBC-2, 6/1–10/2/88)

A fascinating 6 eps. × 50/55 mins. drama serial starring Penny Downie (*right*) as Sarah Copeland, a rising copywriter at the HFK advertising agency, who was pitching for the most prestigious account in the business. Rosalind Bennett, Robbie Engels, David Cardy, John Fortune, Gary Waldhorn (*left*), and Peter-Hugo Daly also appeared. The busy script was by Gerard Macdonald; Brian Farnham directed Ruth Boswell's production.

Christabel
(BBC-2, 16/11–7/12/88)

An extraordinary story of love and moral courage based on the autobiography (*The Past Is Myself*) by Christabel Bielenberg, an Englishwoman married to an anti-Nazi German lawyer in Hitler's Germany. Elizabeth Hurley (*left*) played Christabel, Stephen Dillon (*right*) was her husband, Peter, and Nigel Le Vaillant as would-be Hitler assassin Adam von Trott. The 4 eps. × 55/65 mins. drama was scripted by Dennis Potter and produced by Kenith Trodd. Adrian Shergold directed; Remi Adefarasin was lighting cameraman.

The Chronicles of Narnia
(BBC-1, 1988–90)

Presented a major BBC production of C. S. Lewis's epic Narnia saga, starting with 'The Lion, the Witch and the Wardrobe' (13/11–18/12/88; 6 eps. × 30 mins.; dir. Marilyn Fox) and followed with 'Prince Caspian' (19–26/11/89; eps. 1 and 2 × 30 mins.; dir. Alex Kirby), 'Voyage of the Dawn Treader' (3–24/12/89; eps. 3 to 6 × 30 mins.; dir. Alex Kirby), and 'The Silver Chair' (18/11–23/12/90; 6 eps. × 30/25 mins.; dir. Alex Kirby). The original young stars were Richard Dempsey (as Peter), Sophie Cook (as Susan), Jonathan R. Scott (as Edmund), and Sophie Wilcox (as Lucy). The White Witch was played by Barbara Kellermann (*pictured*) in the première story. Alan Seymour dramatized the stories for producer Paul Stone. During the 1960s Pamela Lonsdale produced a ten-part version of **The Lion, the Witch and the Wardrobe** (ABC TV, 9/7–10/9/67) from an adaptation by Trevor Preston; Zuleika Robson, Elizabeth Crowther, Edward McMurray, Paul Waller, and Elizabeth Wallace starred.

Colin's Sandwich
(BBC-2, 18/10–22/11/88)

Was an amusing 6 eps. × 30 mins. comedy series starring Mel Smith (*pictured*) as underachiever Colin Watkins, a wage slave at British Rail during the day and a writer at night. Louisa Rix co-starred as his girlfriend Jenny. John Kilby produced (with Jamie Rix) and directed the scripts by Paul Smith and Terry Kyan.

DEF II
(BBC-2, 1988–)

Fast and frantic early evening programme for a young audience (primarily the 15 to 25 year olds) under the executive leadership of Janet Street-Porter, following her success with the trend-setting **Network 7** at Channel Four. The Monday and Wednesday slots were filled with, for example, **Rough Guide to Europe**, an alternative travel guide presented by Magenta De Vine (*right*) and Sankha Guha (*left*), **Behind the Beat**, a black music magazine, **Open to Question**, with young people interviewing a guest celebrity, and **Dance Energy**, presented by Normski, alongside various retro American series. Street-Porter was also responsible for buying in the English version of the French music show **Rapido** (featuring the quirky presentation of Antoine de Caunes).

The Fear
(Euston Films, 17/2–16/3/88)

Presented the veneered violence of young, north London gangsterdom, as the stylish and ruthless Carl Galton (played by Iain Glen; *2nd right*) manipulated his family, friends, and the London underworld with his designer-clad muscle. His gang members consisted of (*l. to r.*) Sam Smart, Stephen Persaud, Jerome Flynn, Mario Kalli, and Jesse Birdsall; Susannah Harker played Linda, his wife. The 5 eps. × hour mini-series was written by Paul Hines; directed by Stuart Orme; designed by Andrew Mollo; produced by Jacky Stoller; with music by Colin Towns.

Game, Set & Match
(Granada TV, 3/10–19/12/88)

Adapted by John Howlett from Len Deighton's celebrated espionage trilogy (*Berlin Game, Mexico Set,* and *London Match*), this £5 million production featured Ian Holm (*centre*) as agent Bernard Samson who is caught up in a complicated international web of Cold War double-agents and triple-dealing. Also appearing were Anthony Bate, Michael Culver, Frederick Treves, Mel Martin, and Amanda Donohoe. The 1 ep. × 2 hours / 12 eps. × hour were produced by Brian Armstrong.

Hale & Pace
(LWT, 1988–)

Popular comedy series of spoofs and quick sketches featuring Gareth Hale and Norman Pace and their off-the-wall character impressions: the ineptly villainous Two Rons (*pictured*) and the manic children's programme presenters Billy and Johnny. Alan Nixon produced. They had earlier developed the Two Rons characters (a wicked parody of the Kray Twins used in their act) into a half-hour series called **The Management** (C4/LWT, 1988), produced by Charlie Hanson.

1988

Hannay
(Thames TV, 1988–89)

Period spy thriller series featuring John Buchan's officer-adventurer Richard Hannay (Robert Powell) in multiple escapades that pitted him against the various intrigues concocted by agents of Imperial Germany and Count von Schwabing (Gavin Richards) in particular. Richard Bates produced. Powell is pictured with guest Caroline Lee Johnson in a scene from the 'That Rough Justice' episode. Powell had earlier played Buchan's hero in the 1978 feature version of *The Thirty Nine Steps*. Buchan's **The Three Hostages** (BBC-1, 27/12/77) also featured Hannay (played by Barry Foster) in John Prebble's 85-minute screenplay, adapted from the 1924 novel, of this secret service thriller directed by Clive Donner for producer Mark Shivas. During the early 1950s Patrick Barr was Sir Richard Hannay in C. A. Lejeune's 6 eps. × 30 mins. adaptation of **The Three Hostages** (BBC-tv, 21/6–26/7/52), directed by Julian Amyes for producer Ian Atkins.

London's Burning
(LWT, 1988–)

As a series stemmed from a successful 2-hour TV film by Jack Rosenthal shown on 7/12/86 (dir. Les Blair) focusing on the lives of the firemen, and firewoman, on and off duty from Blue Watch B25 Blackwall. The main players (and original line-up) of this excellent drama consisted of Mark Arden (*right*; as Vaseline), James Hazeldine (Bayleaf; *centre*), James Marcus (Station Officer Tate), Sean Blowers (Sub-Officer Hallam), Rupert Baker (Malcolm), Richard Walsh (Sicknote; *left*), Gerard Horan (Charisma), Katharine Rogers (Josie), and Glen Murphy (George). Paul Knight was the original producer.

Piece of Cake
(LWT/Holmes Associates Prod., 2/10–6/11/88)

Featured the young fighter pilots of RAF Hornet Squadron based in northen France during the first year of the Second World War. The six hour-long episodes were written by Leon Griffiths, adapted from the novel by Derek Robinson. The leading players were Tim Woodward, David Horovitch, Tom Burlinson, Neil Dudgeon (*right*), Jack McKenzie, Tom Radcliffe, George Anton (*left*), Boyd Gaines (*centre*), and Nathaniel Parker. Ian Toynton directed for producer Andrew Holmes.

Red Dwarf
(BBC-2, 1988–)

Rob Grant & Doug Naylor scripted this imaginative sitcom set on the spacecraft mining ship *Red Dwarf* in which all the crew have been killed except for one, Dave Lister (played by Craig Charles; *left*). Lister's only company was the hologram of a former colleague, the irritating Arnold Rimmer (Chris Barrie; *centre*), the mutated ship's Cat (Danny John-Jules; *right*), and a speaking computer image called Holly (Norman Lovett, on screen background; later Hattie Hayridge); Robert Llewellyn as the naïve android Kryten later joined the cast. The BBC North-West–Paul Jackson Production was produced by Ed Bye, Grant, and Naylor.

Singles
(Yorkshire TV, 1988–91)

Followed the romantic comedy events in the lives of two couples (played by Roger Rees and Judy Loe, and Eamon Boland and Susie Blake) who met in a singles bar; Simon Cadell replaced Rees as a new suitor for the Loe character in 1991 (Rees having joined the cast of American sitcom **Cheers** for the 1989–90 season). Eric Chappell and Jean Warr wrote the half-hour series of on-again, off-again romances for producer-director Vernon Lawrence. The scene pictured shows (*l. to r.*) Rees, guest Sharon Duce, and Loe.

South of the Border
(BBC-1, 25/10–12/12/88)

The offbeat private-eye capers of two young women in Deptford, south-east London. Pearl Parker (played by Buki Armstrong; *left*), who had turned her back on a disastrous love affair, and Finn Gallagher (Rosie Rowell; *right*), just released from prison after two years for theft, joined forces to form a haphazard detective agency. Lawyer friend Milly (Dinah Stabb) and Pearl's ex-lover Fitz (Brian Bovell) were on hand for assistance. The 8 eps. × 60 then 50 mins. series was written by Susan Wilkins; Antonia Bird directed for producer Caroline Oulton.

The Storyteller
(C4/TVS–Jim Henson Org. Prod., 1988)

Colourfully produced series retelling the great European folk-tales and combining actors with fantasy creatures (with some excellent special effects) from Jim Henson's Creature Shop. John Hurt was the Hobbit-like Storyteller (pictured with the Storyteller's dog) for the half-hour series. Along similar lines, **Grim Tales** (Central TV–Initial Film & TV Prod., 1989–91) featured Rik Mayall presenting stories based on the tales of the Brothers Grimm with a wide range of animation and puppetry (by Emma Calder and Ged Haney of Pearly Oyster Prods.). Corinne Westacott produced.

Thin Air
(BBC-1, 8/4–6/5/88)

Was set around a commercial radio station and involved a female radio reporter, Rachel Hamilton (Kate Hardie; *centre*), in unravelling the multiple plot strands of dubious property development on a massive scale, the disruption and forced exodus of a local community, the stripping away of local authority powers, left-wing activism, and designer drugs. Also appearing were Nicky Henson (*left*), Kevin McNally (*right*), James Aubrey, Sam Kelly, Brian Bovell, and Sarah Jane Morris. The 5 eps. × 50 mins. thriller was scripted by Sarah Dunant & Peter Busby. Antonia Bird directed Caroline Oulton's moody production.

A Very British Coup
(C4/Skreba Prod., 19 and 26/6 and 3/7/88)

Three-part political thriller scripted by Alan Plater from the novel by Chris Mullin starring Ray McAnally (*pictured*) as the newly elected Prime Minister Harry Perkins, a former steelworker from Sheffield. The opposition forces, out to prove Perkins was unable to handle the position, ranged from Sir Percy Browne (Alan MacNaughtan), Head of the Secret Service, to the newspaper baron Fison (Philip Madoc). The 3 eps. × hour were directed by Mick Jackson for producers Ann Skinner and Sally Hibbin.

Wish Me Luck
(LWT, 1988–90)

Followed the hazardous missions undertaken by members of the Special Operations Executive, and the fortunes of two women agents in particular, in Nazi-occupied France during the Second World War. Liz Grainger (played by Kate Buffery) was the upper middle-class blonde and Mathilde Firman (Suzanna Hamilton) was the restless and complicated young Cockney. Col. James Cadogan (Julian Glover) and Faith Ashley (Jane Asher) were their SOE chiefs. A second series introduced two new agents (played by Lynn Farleigh and, *pictured*, Jane Snowden) to the behind-enemy-lines activities; later joined by Catherine Schell. Created by Jill Hyem and Lavinia Warner, the 15 eps. × hour series was produced by Colin Shindler and Lavinia Warner (1st series), and Michael Chaplin (2nd and 3rd series).

Agatha Christie's Poirot
(LWT–Carnival Films, 1989–)

Handsomely produced mystery-drama series featuring David Suchet (*pictured*) as the famous fictional detective Hercule Poirot. Set loosely around the mid-1930s, with a careful eye on period detail, the whodunit (and why?) plots and never-ending list of eccentric suspects were displayed as a delightful celebration of pre-Second World War English crime fiction. Series regulars were Hugh Fraser (as Poirot's often muddle-headed companion Captain Hastings), Philip Jackson (Scotland Yard Inspector Japp), and Pauline Moran (Miss Lemon, the secretary). Earlier, TVS had produced an hour-long comedy-thriller, **Murder By the Book** (TVS, 28/8/86; wr. Nick Evans, dir. Lawrence Gordon Clark) starring Ian Holm as Poirot; Peggy Ashcroft also appeared as Agatha Christie.

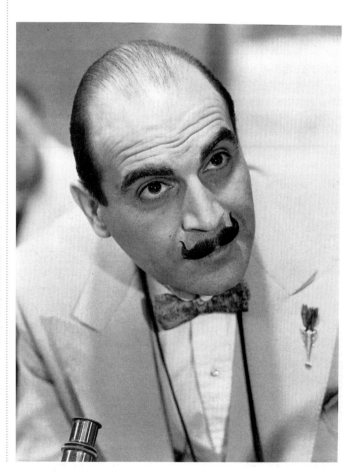

Around the World in 80 Days
(BBC-1, 11/10–22/11/89)

Fascinating and generally humorous 7 eps. × 50 mins. documentary series in which actor/writer Michael Palin (*pictured*) attempted to emulate the achievements and adventures of Jules Verne's Phileas Fogg character by circumnavigating the globe before eighty days elapsed. Roger Mills directed for series producer Clem Vallance; Nigel Meakin was film cameraman.

Birds of a Feather
(BBC-1/Alomo Prod., 1989–)

Hot and cold sitcom series starring Pauline Quirke (*centre*) and Linda Robson (*left*) as sisters Sharon and Tracy who end up living together after their criminal husbands are sent to prison. Lesley Joseph (*right*) was their man-hungry neighbour Dorien; Alun Lewis (as Darryl) and David Cardy (as Chris; later Peter Polycarpou) appeared as the inmate husbands. Created and written by the team of Laurence Marks & Maurice Gran. Esta Charkham and (in the 1990s) Nic Phillips produced.

Blackeyes
(BBC-2, 29/11–20/12/89)

Playwright Dennis Potter's directing début with his own 4 eps. × 55 mins. serial story was told in the by now expected multi-layered narrative. Michael Gough (*right*) starred as a peculiar, elderly novelist who had written a novel based on what his niece Jessica (Carol Royle) had told him of her modelling career. He went on to distort the material into a tacky piece of near pornography which, to everyone's amazement, became a fashionable success. It was called *Blackeyes* and featured a beautiful model of that name (played by Gina Bellman; *left*). Rick McCallum produced.

Campion
(BBC-1, 22/1–12/3/89)

Crime writer Margery Allingham's private detective Albert Campion (played by Peter Davidson; *pictured*) was seen in 8 eps. × 55 mins. stories re-creating the early 1930s period of the British murder mystery. Although in the novels Allingham's hero-character continued on through to the 1960s where he became a spy, these TV adaptations remain faithful to the more leisurely era of the English whodunits. Brian Glover co-starred as Campion's cockney valet, Magersfontein Lugg. Two earlier Campion serials had also been produced by BBC TV: **Dancers in Mourning** (BBC-tv, 10/8–14/9/59; 6 eps. × 30 mins.) and **Death of a Ghost** (BBC-tv, 27/6–1/8/60; 6 eps. × 30 mins.) starring Bernard Horsfall as Campion; both serials were produced by John Harrison from John Hopkins's adaptations.

Capital City
(Thames TV–Euston Films, 1989–90)

The high-pressure world of City money traders at a London merchant bank and their professional and personal pursuits was the central theme of this drama series created by Andrew MacLear. Douglas Hodge (*pictured*) played senior trader Declan McConnochie, one of the leading characters operating out of international bank Shane Longman. Dorian Healy, Rolf Saxon, William Armstrong, Joanna Kanska, and Jason Isaacs appeared as fellow dealers. The series was produced by Irving Teitelbaum. Euston Films also produced a theatrically released feature, *Dealers*, in 1989 with a setting similar to the above; the script, not surprisingly, was by Andrew MacLear.

1989

Desmond's
(C4/Humphrey Barclay Prod., 1989–)

Was Desmond's Barber Shop in Peckham where various transient characters would hang out, exchanging quips and generally criticizing each other. Occasionally, someone could be seen actually getting a haircut. Norman Beaton (*right*) played Desmond and Carmen Munroe was his wife, Shirley; Ram John Holder (*left*), Christopher Asante, Kim Walker, Justin Pickett, Robbie Gee, and Nimmy March also appeared. The half-hour sitcom was produced by Humphrey Barclay and Charlie Hanson.

Frederick Forsyth Presents
(FFS Prod.–LWT, 1989–90)

Mini-series of 115/120-minute films by popular author Frederick Forsyth, adapted and scripted by Murray Smith, dealing with MI6 activities (usually set in an East German location) regarding Libya, IRA, KGB, CIA, and the Kremlin. Original three films were 'A Casualty of War' (2/12/89; dir. Tom Clegg), 'Just Another Secret' (9/12/89; dir. Lawrence Gordon Clark; with Beau Bridges; *pictured*), and 'Pride and Extreme Prejudice' (16/12/89; dir. Ian Sharp). Executive producers were Murray Smith, Frederick Forsyth, and Nick Elliott.

The Ginger Tree
(BBC-1–NHK, 26/11–17/12/89)

An Anglo-Japanese co-production (BBC TV's first) made in 4 eps. × 60 mins. at a cost of £4 million was a sumptuous serial telling the story of a young Scots girl, Mary Mackenzie (played by Samantha Bond; *left*), who in 1903 travels to join her English fiancé in Manchuria. She finds herself trapped in a war zone and, disillusioned with her upper-crust officer husband, begins a passionate affair with a Japanese nobleman, Count Kentaro Kurihama (Daisuke Ryu; *right*). The serial also marked the first BBC drama to be shot for HDTV (High Definition Television). Screenplay was by Christopher Hampton, based on the novel by Oswald Wynd. Anthony Garner directed Tim Ironside Wood's production.

Making Out
(BBC-1, 1989–91)

Comedy drama series about a group of defiant women toiling away at Lyne Electronics, a dilapidated factory making modern technological components. Margi Clarke (*2nd right*), as the fiery Queenie, led the cast, consisting of Melanie Kilburn (*left*), Rachel Davies (*2nd left*), Shirley Stelfox (*right*), Moya Brady, Heather Tobias, Tracie Bennett, and Barbara Keogh; Keith Allen was their factory boss and Brian Hibbard was Queenie's boyfriend. The series was devised by Franc Roddam for producer John Chapman.

The Manageress
(C4/Zed Ltd. Prod., 1989–)

Hour-long drama series telling the story of what happens to a struggling football club when the owners make the appointment of a woman as the team's new manager. Cherie Lunghi (*pictured, centre*) starred as manager Gabriella Benson, originally with Warren Clarke, Tom Georgeson, Sergio Fantoni, and Mark McGann. Glenn Wilhide and Sophie Balhetchet produced.

The Paradise Club

(BBC-1/Zenith, 19/9–21/11/89; 25/9–27/11/90)

Two brothers, Frank Kane (Don Henderson; *right*) and Danny Kane (Leslie Grantham; *left*), were reunited after the death of their tyrannical mother who ruled her underworld empire with a rod of iron. Danny inherited the gangland feuds and Frank her former headquarters, the Paradise Club, a seedy dance-hall in London's docklands. Two series of 10 eps. × 50 mins. were produced by Selwyn Roberts.

Press Gang

(Central TV/Richmond Films & TV, 1989–)

A lively children's hour comedy-drama series about an enthusiastic group of teenagers who run the *Junior Gazette*, a school newspaper that the principal characters continue working on even after they appear to have left school. The series, based on an idea by Bill Moffat, presented stories and themes more on the side of 1970s American drama **Lou Grant** than the expected juvenilia of something like, say, **Adventure Weekly** (BBC-1, 1968–69); story areas dealt with questions about intrusion of privacy, press profile causing public disgrace, censorship, private and public morals, etc. Intelligent and adult dialogue (and situations) combined with cinema-style photography and editing gave this series a look and feel far above its target audience and programming slot. Regular players included Julia Sawalha (*left*; as editor Lynda Day), Dexter Fletcher (*right*; as a slightly overboard acted American kid, Spike), Lee Ross, Kelda Holmes, Lucy Benjamin, and Mmoloki Chrystie as the news staffers. Sandra C. Hastie produced.

Saracen

(Central TV, 1989)

Saracen Systems was the name of an élite private security company that specialized in bodyguard work and VIP protection. The company's top operatives were the gun-and-muscle duo of Tom Duffy (Patrick James Clarke; *left*) and David Barber (Christian Burgess; *right*). Michael Byrne, John Bennett, and Ingrid Lacey supplied the office back-up. The hour-long series was created by Chris Kelly and Ted Childs; Deirdre Keir produced.

Stay Lucky

(Yorkshire TV, 1989–91; 1993–)

Hour-long series of comedy-thrillers about two strong-willed people who by accident become a rather reluctant couple sharing a houseboat. Dennis Waterman starred as Cockney wide boy Thomas, on the run from the London underworld, and Jan Francis was the headstrong Northern gal, Sally; Susan George, for a few episodes, and then Leslie Ash came on board for the 1993 series. The series was originally presented as a three-part story (8–22/12/89) written by Geoff McQueen for producer-director David Reynolds. Pictured are (*l. to r.*) Niall Toibin, Emma Wray, Francis, and Waterman.

Surgical Spirit

(Granada TV–Humphrey Barclay Prod., 1989–)

Comedy series set around a busy hospital and featuring an excellent performance by Nichola McAuliffe (*pictured*) as Sheila Sabatini, a sharp-tongued female surgeon renowned for acerbic put-downs. Duncan Preston (*pictured*), Marji Campi, David Conville, and Emlyn Price were her hospital colleagues. Peter Learmouth wrote the half-hour series for Humphrey Barclay's production.

Traffik

(C4/Picture Partnership Prod., 22/6–17/7/89)

Intense five-part (1 ep. × 120 mins., 4 eps. × hour) drama serial telling the stories of a British politician, Jack Lithgow (Bill Paterson; *pictured*), who finds himself in conflict with the opium farmers of the North-West Frontier in Pakistan; local opium farmer Fazal (Jamal Shah) and his family, threatened by Lithgow's mission; and the wealthy Helen (Lindsay Duncan) in Hamburg following the seizure of a major drugs haul. Alastair Reid directed Simon Moore's screenplay for Brian Eastman's production.

Young Charlie Chaplin

(Thames TV, 1989)

Late afternoon programmed drama series that loosely traced the boyhood of Charlie Chaplin, who grew up under the shadow of his music-hall star father. Joe Geary (*pictured*) starred as young Chaplin, with Lee Whitlock as Sydney Chaplin, Ian McShane as Charles Chaplin Sr., and Twiggy (*pictured*) as mother Hannah Chaplin. Written by Colin Shindler, with Andrew Nickolds and Stan Hey, the series was produced by Shindler to celebrate the centenary of the birth of the great silent-film comedian.

The beginning of the 1990s, following the recession which hit industry the world over, was a turbulent time for British television. The government seemed determined to challenge the existing structures in both the public and commercial sectors, in order to introduce increased competition. The 1991 licence awards were designed to extract more government revenue from what was perceived as an advertising monopoly.

The Broadcasting Act of 1991, passed by a Conservative government in its third term, instituted a bidding procedure whereby the fifteen regional ITV franchises were awarded to those companies which, having passed a 'quality' threshold, had submitted the highest cash bid. While the outcome only directly affected four of the companies, the consequences of the act effectively destabilized the whole of the ITV network.

Television South West (TSW) and Television South (TVS) were ruled out for overbidding; the Independent Television Commission (ITC) deciding their business plans were simply unsustainable. Their respective licences were won by Westcountry Television and Meridian Broadcasting in January 1993. Both Yorkshire TV and HTV were challenged for the size of their bids: YTV had put up an enormous £37.37 million and has since merged with Tyne Tees to effect economies and HTV has since had to reduce its staff to cover overheads.

Both Thames TV and breakfast television contractor TV-am were outbid for their licences, with the latter being replaced by GMTV (Good Morning Television). The loss of Thames TV was perhaps the most surprising decision. It was replaced by Carlton, part of business executive Michael Green's huge empire. Green's other company interests include the advertising facilities house Moving Picture Company, Quantel, the Zenith group of production companies, and the Technicolor laboratories. The Carlton Group also held a 20 per cent interest in Central TV and a further 20 per cent in GMTV.

The Broadcasting Act also strengthened the position of independent production companies. Both the BBC and ITV were required by statute to commission 25 per cent of their programmes from independents. This increased reliance on independent producers and the burdens of their franchise bids forced ITV companies to become increasingly competitive and commercial; in 1992 Granada's chairman, David Plowright, left in a dispute over the company's commitment to in-house production and to what he considered to be a declining investment in high-quality programme production. The BBC launched its 'producer choice' scheme in late 1991 with the intention of saving some £50 million over four years by cutting both the costs and overheads of television production. This scheme forces direct competition with outside commercial companies for all services provided by the BBC with producers buying from either the BBC or outside sources, including ITV, and is estimated to offer them 'greater scope to make quality programmes while ensuring maximum value for money for licence payers'.

Government scrutiny and the impact of the independent production quota meant the BBC also had to rationalize its operations; an additional threat of radical changes to the Corporation's structure looms when its charter comes up for renewal in 1996. The launch in 1992 of an encoded night-time subscription service, BBC Select, which supplied a range of special interest programmes, opened up a fresh source of revenue. The BBC in partnership with Thames also premièred the UK Gold channel, consisting of archive comedies and dramas, on the Astra satellite system.

A fifth terrestrial channel to join the UK market may be Channel Five, if approved by the ITC. The proposed service has been a subject of controversy since it was first mooted in the Broadcasting Act. Its start-up costs would be prohibitive and its revenue potential dubious. The sole bidder to date has been Channel Five Holdings, a consortium led by Thames TV, producer-distributor RPTA / Primetime, and Toronto's City TV founder Moses Znaimer. With the TV companies already under commercial pressure and with Channel Four entering the field as an independent advertising market, the ITC still has to be convinced that the Channel Five Holdings' plan for a network of city stations can be made to work in the UK.

Sky Television and BSB merged in late 1990 which led the IBA to consider whether the new company, British Sky Broadcasting (BSkyB), could legally transmit via the DBS Marco Polo satellite. The merger was also controversial in that Sky had been exempt from UK restrictions on foreign and cross-media ownership. Its Astra satellite used European frequencies and therefore had been classified as a non-domestic service; it also meant that News Corporation proprietor Rupert Murdoch, who owned Sky, now controlled half of the satellite service to the UK and five national newspapers.

Following the merger, however, the European Commission ruled that Sky's agreement with the European Broadcasting Union granting exclusive rights to sporting events was unlawful, forcing the company to replace the Eurosport channel with their own Sky Sports.

Sports programming has increasingly become the object of intense competition between channels, as one of the few sure-fire ratings winners. In August 1991 ITV, having lost out to BSkyB and the BBC on Premier League and FA Cup matches, agreed to pay £40 million for a four-year contract to screen Football League and Rumbelows Cup matches. Channel Four negotiated the transmission rights to Italian league matches on Sundays and ITV also signed an agreement to screen the 1995 Rugby Union World Cup series for £10 million. In May 1992 the BBC joined BSkyB in a £304 million deal to screen matches from the new Premier Football League over a five-year period. ITV then, unsuccessfully, sought to have the arrangement overruled in the High Court because it believed that the BBC and BSkyB had unfairly increased their final bid after learning that they had offered £262 million.

As to programming trends, the 1990s has yet to discover itself. Sadly, soap operas have again captured the interest of viewers, this time embracing the juvenile audience who were immediately hooked into Australian imports, **Neighbours** and **Home and Away** and their sister productions, with something of a mindless dedication. **EastEnders** and **Coronation Street** have topped the ratings as usual, and **Eldorado** stopped being a twice-weekly Eldorado when viewers' patience with it ran out.

Another programme that has attracted large audiences throughout the early 1990s is Yorkshire TV's revival of H. E. Bates's idealistic tales of rural 1950s life in **Darling Buds of May**—definitely a boost for YTV and perhaps something of a national comforter from the point of view of the ruling political party.

Only the subversive comedy elements of **One Foot in the Grave** and **Have I Got News for You?** have so far managed to separate the shells (the reality) from the nuts (the foolish).

Chancer
(Central TV, 1990–)

Fast cars, fast bucks, and fast girls was the mainstay of this go-for-it drama featuring Clive Owen (pictured, *right*, with Susannah Harker) as sultry go-getter Stephen Crane, a young opportunist with an eye on the bottom of the deck business deal. The series was produced by Sarah D. Wilson; music was by Jan Hammer. Supporting players included Benjamin Whitrow, Lynsey Baxter, Sean Pertwee, and Harker as his girlfriend.

The Chief
(Anglia Films, 1990–)

Hour-long drama series starring Tim Pigott-Smith (*pictured*) as Chief Constable John Stafford, the no-nonsense head of the fictitious Eastland constabulary. The gritty stories explored all levels of authority and observed police procedure from the upper echelons, with Stafford often involved in head-on clashes with the Home Office and with the Police Authority, as well as with his own subordinates. Karen Archer co-starred as Assistant Chief Constable Anne Stewart. Ruth Boswell produced the series.

The Crystal Maze
(C4/Chatsworth TV, 1990–)

An adventure game in which **Krypton Factor**-like contestants pitted their wits and skills against a bizarre battery of games inside what appeared to be a live-action version of a computer-game 'dungeon'. *Rocky Horror Show* creator and performer Richard O'Brien was the maze-master (whose impish appearance tended to shroud his apparent sincerity in aiding his contestants) and the aim of the mainly physical contest was to collect as many 'time crystals' as possible within 40 minutes in order to win a prize.

Drop the Dead Donkey
(C4/Hat Trick Prod., 1990–)

Hilarious backstage sitcom set in a commercial TV newsroom loaded with eccentric characters (shades of **The Mary Tyler Moore Show**)—but with one interesting advantage over other professional-group sitcoms, as well as some excellent writing. Each half-hour episode presented elements of real-life news events of that week right up to the day of transmission (much the way **Spitting Image** operated). Writers Andy Hamilton and Guy Jenkin (they also produced the series) developed some superb newsroom caricatures: the power-yuppie newsroom boss (played by Robert Duncan; *right*), the neurotic news editor (Jeff Rawle; *centre*), the arrogant, sex-crazed anchorman (David Swift), the pompous co-presenter (Victoria Wicks), and the self-serving field news reporter (Stephen Tomkinson). Their slightly more rational colleagues included Haydn Gwynne (*pictured*) as assistant news editor (Ingrid Lacey later took over the job), and the gambling-mad news assistant/writer played by Neil Pearson. The series/episodes' topicality content was so much a part of the structure that repeat screenings demand a date-setting and contemporary news-brief introduction.

1990

The Green Man

(BBC-1–Arts and Entertainment Network, 28/10–11/11/90)

Presented a three-part (1 × 55 mins., 2 × 50 mins.) comedy-thriller ghost story adapted by Malcolm Bradbury from Kingsley Amis's novel featuring Albert Finney as drunken, womanizing country restaurant owner Maurice Allington. His restaurant, The Green Man, was reputedly haunted but although there had not been a sighting in years Maurice suddenly started experiencing supernatural phenomena; suggesting that these were in part due to the dying Gramps (cameo by Michael Hordern) and in part due to his rampant adultery—although everyone was convinced that it was the result of his hitting the bottle too often. Linda Marlowe (*right*), Sarah Berger (*left*), Nicky Henson, and Josie Lawrence supported. The clever, subdued lighting, photography, and special effects were expertly co-ordinated by director Elijah Moshinsky for producer David Snodin.

Have I Got News for You?

(BBC-2/Hat Trick, 1990–)

Uproarious comedy quiz show which vivisected the week's news and headlines from a satirical if not schoolyard humour angle. The programme (ensuring topicality by recording each edition the night before transmission) was hosted by Angus Deayton (*centre*) with resident team captains *Private Eye* editor Ian Hislop (*left*) and comedian Paul Merton (*right*) wittily assassinating the questions, the responses, each other, and even their own guests (usually from the world of journalism, humour, and politics). The more extreme elements of ribald humour had to be excised from the broadcast tape but a few seconds always managed to find its way through to transmission. Harry Thompson produced the hectic half-hours.

Jeeves and Wooster

(Granada TV/Picture Partnership Prods.–Carnival Films, 1990–93)

A welcome return to TV of P. G. Wodehouse's two most popular characters, this time in the form of comedy duo Stephen Fry and Hugh Laurie. Together with the colourful and elegant period look of the series (courtesy of production designer Eileen Diss) and the splendid scripts (adapted by Clive Exton), Laurie's non-stop socializing upper-class feather-brain Bertie Wooster and Fry's valet Jeeves, taking command with offhand charm when the need arose, were inspired choices for the parts (although Fry was less the senior figure than the literary original). Brian Eastman produced the twenty-two hour-long episodes with just the right touch of farce and frenzy; Anne Dudley's excellent period-style music was also a highlight, especially when combined with Animation City's main titles.

Keeping Up Appearances

(BBC-1, 1990–)

Writer Roy Clarke's highly amusing observations of the opinionated, judgemental, and, ultimately, vulnerable Hyacinth Bucket ('pronounced Bouquet!'), a busybody lady trying hard to assume a middle-to-upper class existence despite her own social *faux pas* and her carefree, unemployed-class relatives. The excellent Patricia Routledge (*right*) led the cast as the bossy Hyacinth, with Clive Swift (*left*) as her long-suffering husband Richard, Judy Cornwell and Shirley Stelfox as sisters Daisy and Rose (the latter character later played by Mary Millar), and Geoffrey Hughes as slob brother-in-law Onslow. Josephine Tewson was Hyacinth's nervously wrecked neighbour Elizabeth, later joined by her musician brother Emmet (David Griffin). Director-producer Harold Snoad steered this enjoyable half-hour sitcom to deserved popularity.

Maid Marian and Her Merry Men
(BBC-1, 1989–)

Ringing the changes on the established Robin Hood legend, writer and former **Blackadder** performer Tony Robinson created this amusing and clever children's series featuring Kate Lonergan's Maid Marian as the real leader of the outlaw band (more hockey captain than scourge of the greenwood), with Robin (Wayne Morris) as a cowardly wimp (he was given a yuppie persona and known as Robin of Islington). The genuinely determined but completely incompetent Merry Men included a dwarf called Little Ron (Mike Edmonds), a Rastafarian (Danny John Jules), and Rabies (Howard Lew Lewis). Richard Callanan produced the half-hour episodes.

Never Come Back
(BBC-2, 21/3–4/4/90)

A superbly *film noir*ish three-part period thriller, adapted from the 1941 John Mair novel by David Pirie, following the labyrinthine adventures of a bored writer, Desmond Thane (played by Nathaniel Parker; *pictured*), as he gets himself drawn deeper into an espionage ring in the pre-war, shadowy London of the late 1930s. Suzanna Hamilton was the mysterious Anna Raven, the sexual hook by which the hero became snagged, and James Fox supplied the smooth, upper-crust villainy. The suitably low-key photography was by John McGlashan; Ben Bolt directed Joe Waters's atmospheric production.

Nicholas Craig
(BBC-2, 1990–)

An umbrella title covering an amusing and suitably absurd series of spoof media documentaries by Nigel Planer (*pictured, centre*), playing a pompous and patronizing 'professional personality'. The general theme of Planer's Nicholas Craig actor instructing young media hopefuls in the intricate art was demonstrated via **Nicholas Craig—The Naked Actor** (22/11–20/12/90), in which he offered an in-depth examination of an actor's mind; **Nicholas Craig's Interview Masterclass** (23/6/90), on how to make a successful appearance on a chat show; **Nicholas Craig's Masterpiece Theatre** (31/8/92; shown appropriately as a part of BBC-2's 'TV Hell' evening); and **The Nicholas Craig Masterclass** (12/3–16/4/92), five programmes in which the character excelled himself in promoting fear and loathing in his craft. The programmes were written, directed, and produced by Christopher Douglas, Charles Miller, and Caroline Wright.

One Foot in the Grave
(BBC-1, 1990–)

Outrageous and hilarious 'restless retirement' sitcom from writer David Renwick featured the domestic misadventures of cranky codger Victor Meldrew (with an excellent performance by Richard Wilson) as he tried to negotiate his way through everyday avenues of illogical and perverse behaviour in the people and objects around him. A half-hour series stacked with splendid moments, situations, dialogue, and character, with deserved praise to director-producer Susan Belbin. Annette Crosbie co-starred as Victor's verge-of-breaking-point wife Margaret, Doreen Mantle was their naïve friend Mrs Warboys, and, in a later series of episodes (from 1992), Angus Deayton and Janine Duvitski became their perplexed neighbours. The series' title music was written and performed by Eric Idle.

1990

Oranges Are Not the Only Fruit
(BBC-2, 10–17–24/1/90)

Jeanette Winterson adapted her own Whitbread Prize-winning novel into this three-part (× 55 mins.) story of a young Lancashire girl, Jess (played by Emily Aston as a child, Charlotte Coleman, *right*, as a teenager), whose evangelist mother (Geraldine McEwan; *pictured*) adopted her with the sole intention of raising her to become a missionary but then discovers that she harbours lesbian feelings. Kenneth Cranham, Elizabeth Spriggs, Freda Dowie, and Margery Withers co-starred in this well-made drama; Beeban Kidron directed for producer Phillippa Giles.

The Perfect Scoundrels
(TVS, 1990–92)

Were Peter Bowles (*right*) as Guy and Bryan Murray (*left*) as Harry, a couple of elaborate confidence tricksters who joined forces and, just to be on the comfortable side of the viewer, performed their 'stings' only on shady people who deserved to be stung. The partnership of the actors stemmed from their successful teaming in **The Irish RM** series, leading Bowles and Murray to conceive the format for **Perfect Scoundrels** which was then developed by writer Ray Connolly. This easygoing series was as much a character comedy as a confidence-trick caper series; Tim Aspinall produced the sixteen one-hour episodes.

Rab C Nesbitt
(BBC-2/BBC Scotland, 1990–)

The ranting Glaswegian street philosopher (played with awesome charm by Gregor Fisher), developed out of the cult series **Naked Video** (BBC Scotland, 1986–91) which in turn was based on the popular radio show *Naked Radio*. **Naked Video** was an ensemble comedy series with gags and sketches scattergunned over all areas and targets, almost like a live-action **Spitting Image**. Under producer Colin Gilbert the team generally consisted of Ron Bain, Andy Gray, Helen Lederer, Tony Roper, Elaine C. Smith, John Sparkes, Jonathan Watson, and Gregor Fisher. Fisher's recurring character of the bloodstained-bandaged, string-vested street drunk with a powerful opinion on society eventually grew, via writer Ian Pattison, Fisher, and producer Gilbert, into his own series, **Rab C Nesbitt**. Elaine C. Smith, Eric Cullen, and Andrew Fairlie played his obstreperous family (in a household where rats are killed in the kitchen by being clubbed to death with a frying pan), and Tony Roper was Rab's drinking pal Jamesie. There had also been a 45-minute New Year's Eve special, **Rab C Nesbitt's Seasonal Greet** (BBC Scotland, 31/12/89), which featured among the cast Iain Cuthbertson, Rikki Fulton, Gerry Sadowitz, Russell Hunter, and Susan Gilmore.

The Trials of Life
(BBC-1/BBC Bristol, 3/10–19/12/90)

Following the successes of David Attenborough's **Life on Earth** (evolution) and **The Living Planet** (environment and habitat), Attenborough (*pictured*) and the BBC's Natural History Unit brought their attention to animal behaviour in this superb twelve-part series produced by Keenan Smart. Over thirty wildlife cameramen were involved in the three-year production which from episode one (asking why some young are born live, and others from eggs) to episode twelve (passing on genes to a new generation) featured some of the most colourful, stunning, and, at times, disturbing action sequences ever filmed for a television nature series.

Vic Reeves Big Night Out
(C4/Channel X, 1990–)

An off-the-wall 'entertainment' show—perhaps a spoof of all things Jonathan Ross?—in which host Vic Reeves (*pictured*) and his partner Bob Mortimer presented what was either a parody of TV interview/variety shows or simply a limp attempt at late night programme scheduling with the aim of tapping the less than discriminating elements of the post-pub trade (in a similar vein to the late night Yorkshire TV/LWT James Whale talk/phone-in shows). Despite the competent handling of on-screen affairs by director-producer Peter Orton the jury is still out on this one.

Waiting for God
(BBC-1, 1990–)

On first viewing, appeared to be about the peculiar happenings at the business-like Byview Retirement Home, run with cost-consciousness taking priority over care by the venal Harvey Bains (Daniel Hill), but soon developed into a superb showcase for the talents of Graham Crowden, as eccentric former accountant Tom, and Stephanie Cole, as down-to-earth, sarcastic former photo-journalist Diana (*both pictured*). The characters' subversive outlook on life brought zap and zest to the world of senior citizenry that **One Foot in the Grave**, in its way, approached from a domestic angle. Janine Duvitski and Dawn Hope supported the cast. The fine scripts by Michael Aitkens were directed-produced by Gareth Gwenlan.

Waterfront Beat
(BBC-1/New Media Age, 6/1–24/2/90; 2/1–20/2/91)

Two 8-parts × 50 mins. police drama series set in a location that reflected the life and crimes of London's dockland. Written and produced by Phil Redmond, the procedurals of the newly formed Inner City and Waterfront Division were similar, if not complementary, to Geoff McQueen's **The Bill** series, observing police beat life from the gritty level of those who have to touch dirt rather than simply pass the paperwork. John Ashton, Brian McCardie, Denise Stephenson, Geoffrey Leesley, Helena Little, Owen Teale, Philip Middlemiss, and Jane Hazelgrove featured in the cast.

Your Cheatin' Heart
(BBC-1, 11/10–15/11/90)

Tutti Frutti dramatist John Byrne created this delightful six-part (× 50 mins.) serial revolving around waitress Cissie Crouch (Tilda Swinton), the criminal connections of her country-and-western singer husband Dorwood (Kevin McMonagle), and the ludicrous events that ensued when she hired the help of young journalist Frank McClusky (John Gordon-Sinclair) to prove her husband's innocence in the world of narcotics trafficking. A carefully crafted drama presenting some of the small screen's great characters and (Scottish flavoured) dialogue. Michael Whyte directed Peter Broughan's excellent production. Pictured (*l. to r.*) Swinton, Katy Murphy, Eddi Reader, and Gordon-Sinclair.

1991

Ashenden
(BBC-1/Kelso Films, 17/11–8/12/91)

A four-part drama serial based on Somerset Maugham's 1928 *Ashenden* short stories about the encounters of quiet writer Ashenden (forenamed John in the serial) who was recruited into espionage work by British Intelligence and sent into Europe during the period of the First World War and the Russian Revolution. Alex Jennings (*pictured*) featured as Ashenden, with Joss Ackland as spy-master Cumming and Ian Bannen as Secret Service Controller 'R'. The four 55-minute stories were adapted by David Pirie and directed by Christopher Morahan for producer Joe Knatchbull.

The Darling Buds of May
(Yorkshire TV–Excelsior Group Prods., 1991–)

Brought to TV for the first time H. E. Bates's idealistic stories about the happy-go-lucky Larkin family, a life-loving clan consisting of Pop Larkin (played by David Jason; *left*), Ma Larkin (Pam Ferris; *2nd left*), eldest daughter Marietta (Catherine Zeta Jones; *right*); and, not pictured, youngsters Zinnia (Katherine Giles), Montgomery (Ian Tucker), Petunia (Christina Giles), Victoria (Stephanie Ralph), and Primrose (Julie Davis). Also pictured, *2nd right*, is soon-to-be son-in-law Charlie (played by Philip Franks). Set in rural Kent in the 1950s, the series took its stories from the five novels Bates wrote about the boisterous farm family (the title of the series being that of the first novel to be published in 1958); contemporary critics were at first appalled at the immoral nature of the stories (the happily unmarried Ma and Pop Larkin, etc.) but when the public started clamouring for more, and Bates went on to publish four further novels, the critics took a less censorious view. The late author's son Richard Bates also acted as executive producer on the series; respective producers were Robert Banks Stewart (1991), Richard Bates (1991), Peter Norris (1992), and Simon Lewis (1992–93). An American feature film version of the first novel was produced by MGM in 1958 as *The Mating Game*.

GBH
(C4/GBH Films, 6/6–18/7/91)

Chronicled the clash of wills between a moderate schoolteacher, Jim Nelson (played by Michael Palin), and a ruthlessly ambitious council leader, Michael Murray (Robert Lindsay; *pictured*), in this dark, political seven-part drama written by Alan Bleasdale. The cast also included Julie Walters (as Lindsay's mother), Lindsay Duncan (*pictured*), and Michael Angelis. Bleasdale had started to write the story in 1986 as a film, then turned it into a draft for a novel before finally settling on the idea of transforming it into a serialized 10-hour drama. Robert Young directed for producers Alan Bleasdale and David Jones.

The House of Eliott
(BBC-1, 1991–)

Was devised by **Upstairs, Downstairs** creators Eileen Atkins and Jean Marsh and chronicled the setting-up of a London fashion house in the early 1920s. The interlacing of the personal and professional lives of the central characters in a colourfully costumed period setting was similar in tone and style to the 1970s hit drama series; the first twelve episodes cost £6 million to produce and were filmed on location in Bristol. Stella Gonet and Louise Lombard (*the latter pictured*) starred as budding fashion house owners Beatrice and Evangeline Eliott. Jeremy Gwilt produced.

330

Murder Most Horrid
(BBC-2/TalkBack, 14/11–19/12/91)

Dawn French's solo comedy endeavour was a 6 parts × 30 mins. pastiche of the gentle English murder story with French (*seated*) performing multiple roles. With writers like Ian Hislop & Nick Newman, Paul Smith & Terry Kyan, and a decent dash of the old Ealing films comedy flavour, French and her cast (which included the likes of Bill Paterson, Timothy Spall, Jane Asher, Martin Jarvis, and Kenneth Cranham) breezed through some very funny lines and situations. Bob Spiers and James Hendrie directed for producer Jon Plowman.

Noel's House Party
(BBC-1, 1991–)

Was a 50-minute live show with host Noel Edmonds inviting celebrity guests and audience members to perform silly tricks and tasks in his stately home studio set before a childishly enthusiastic studio audience. Ingredients included candid camera-style victim celebrities receiving Noel's Gotcha Oscar for allowing themselves to be the fall guy in embarrassing set-up situations (Edmonds is pictured with guest Cheryl Baker), and the operation of a Saturday morning kiddie slot hold-over, a 'gunk tank', which caused the audience to whoop with delight. Michael Leggo was the director-producer of this incredibly popular Saturday night broadcast.

Prime Suspect
(Granada TV, 7–8/4/91)

Featured Helen Mirren as Det. Chief Insp. Jane Tennison, a career policewoman who is appointed to head a murder inquiry but also has to deal with sex discrimination in the force. Tom Bell, John Benfield, John Bowe, and Zoë Wanamaker co-starred. The award-winning 4-hour drama was written by Lynda La Plante, produced by Don Leaver, and directed by Christopher Menaul. La Plante followed up with **Prime Suspect 2** (Granada TV, 15–16/12/92) which saw Mirren's DCI Tennison pursuing another murder inquiry from the discovery of a human skeleton. Colin Salmon, John Benfield (again as her superior Supt. Mike Kernan), and Philip Wright supported. La Plante's 4-hour screenplay was directed by John Strickland for producer Paul Marcus.

Selling Hitler

(Euston Films–Warner Sisters, 11/6–9/7/91)

Was the story of the great *Sunday Times* publishing hoax. In 1983 the paper published what was to be the start of a serialization of sixty long-lost diaries allegedly written by Adolf Hitler that had apparently been found in an East German hayloft. German news magazine *Stern* journalist Gerd Heidemann (played by Jonathan Pryce; *pictured left*) was the man obsessed with tracking them down and, eventually, buying the documents for which the publishing rights were acquired by press baron Rupert Murdoch (Barry Humphries). But within days the documents were exposed as forgeries by the eleventh-hour change of mind by authenticating historian Hugh Trevor-Roper (Alan Bennett). Andrew Brown produced this five-part black comedy based on Robert Harris's book about the bizarre affair. Other featured parts were played by Alexei Sayle (as forger Conny Kujau) and Alison Steadman (as Goering's daughter Edda). Alastair Reid directed Howard Schuman's amusing script.

Spender

(BBC-1/Initial, 1991–)

Geordie actor Jimmy Nail starred in this undercover detective series created by Nail and Ian La Frenais. Set in a murky-looking Tyneside, the stories trailed the introspective and moody Spender as he pursued his investigations through the shadowy world of surveillance and street contacts. A stately paced police drama that steered clear of weapons and car chases, preferring melancholy over melodrama. Martin McKeand produced the twenty 55-minute episodes.

Absolutely Fabulous

(BBC-2, 12/11–17/12/92)

Was Jennifer Saunders's first major solo project (comedy partner Dawn French having presented **Murder Most Horrid**) and was set in the trendy, and maybe not so caricatured, world of media. Saunders (*left*) portrayed the neurotic public relations business woman Edina Monsoon, a childish harridan, and Joanna Lumley (*right*) soared as her best friend Patsy, a booze-blasted, dope-dozed fashion editor of a glossy magazine who had even forgotten the location of her own office. Edina's hard-working, sincere daughter, Saffron, constantly rebelling against her mother's wacky lifestyle, was played with calm and assurance by Julia Sawalha, and June Whitfield was the take-it-as-it-comes mother. The splendid 6 eps. × half-hour series was written by Saunders and produced by Jon Plowman (who also served in that capacity on the Dawn French series).

Between the Lines
(BBC-1, 1992–)

Addictive drama series following internal investigation operations within the police force (the world of the Metropolitan Police Complaints Investigation Bureau) and the life of ambitious detective Tony Clark (Neil Pearson) in particular. The uneasy investigations of police corruption as well as the chaotic personal life of central character Clark made up the 13 eps. × 50 mins. series; produced by Peter Norris. Pearson is pictured (*left*), with Michael Angelis (who played DI Bill Kendrick).

The Big Breakfast
(C4/Planet 24, 1992–)

Bob Geldof's Planet 24 (he's one of the company's directors) was one of thirty TV production companies to apply when Channel Four announced it was looking for a fast-paced morning show. One of the elements that appealed to Channel Four was the original idea of broadcasting from a real house instead of a studio. Spanning the a.m. hours 7.00 to 9.00, the programme's original format included 'The Geldof Interview', in which Bob 'grilled world leaders' (these, incidentally, were taped since Geldof was not an early riser), and 'Cue Paula', with Mrs Geldof, Paula Yates, discussing fashion and passion with showbiz personalities 'in her boudoir'. An additional gimmick was to have a resident real-life family help out with phone-ins and competitions. Along with Geldof and Yates the other presenters were Chris Evans, Gaby Roslin, and Mark Lamarr. Charlie Parsons was executive producer; Sebastian Scott was series editor.

Eldorado
(BBC-1/Cinema Verity–J Dy T, 1992–93)

Launched with the promotion of 'sun, sand, sangria and sex', this twice a week (with in-week repeats) Euro sunshine soap opera was heralded as the BBC's most expensive and most ambitious project from an independent producer. Created by Tony Holland and producer Julia Smith, the people behind **EastEnders**, the serial focused on the lives of a community of expatriates living in southern Spain (set in the fictitious village of Los Barcos). The large cast included Patricia Brake, Jesse Birdsall, Buki Armstrong, Roland Curram, William Lucas, Hilary Crane, Dieter Schultz, and Sandra Sandri. The multinational cast, in general, seemed a good idea but the drama failed to deliver the 'heightened reality' the setting seemed to promise. The series soon began to draw negative press comments which together with sliding ratings forced the BBC into cutting its losses and aborting the experiment. Perhaps a rather unfair demise to a British TV project that tried to be 'European' when most Brits were not prepared to be Euros.

1992

Sam Saturday

(LWT–Cinema Verity, 1992–)

With television continually
introducing detectives 'with a
difference', Det. Insp. Sam Sterne
(played by Ivan Kaye; *pictured*) was
young, Jewish, and divorced, lived
alone in a terraced house, and
looked after his widowed mother.
The hour-long series was set in
north London where, to the other
police officers in his patch, he was
known as Sam Saturday because
he also worked on Saturdays, the
Jewish Sabbath. The following-up-
leads stories always managed to
interweave Sam's personal life and
problems (with his married
brother, his two daughters who
live with his ex-wife and her
wealthy husband) with his,
usually, Golders Green-connected
investigations. Sam's partner was
the hard-working Det. Sgt. Jim
Butler (Peter Armitage). Alvin
Rakoff and Sharon Bloom
produced.

WYSIWYG

(Yorkshire TV, 1992–)

Was an afternoon children's
comedy series featuring an
intergalactic TV station and its
Earth-located reporters (played by
Nick Wilton, *left*, and Clive
Mantle). A weird blend of Monty
Python and Marty Feldman-type
humour, the series took an
extremely offbeat (and at times
darkly cynical) view of life on
Earth through its reporters'
mission to observe humans in
various surroundings and
activities. Wilton also acted as the
series script editor. The title comes
from the computer acronym
'What You See Is What You Get'.

For ease of reference and cross-reference to the text, this index incorporates titles of TV programmes, series, serials, and episodes; as well as titles of books, plays, films, and radio programmes

Individuals mentioned in more than one programme on the same page are given multiple page references

Park, Andy 313
Park, Merle 149
Parker, Anthony 180, 206, 252
Parker, Brian 287, 301
Parker, Cecil 12
Parker, Charlie 128, 232
Parker, Macdonald 22
Parker, Nathaniel 316, 327
Parker, Rhonda 99
Parkin, Leonard 41
Parkins, Barbara 140
Parkinson, Michael 123, 198, 255
Parkinson, Robin 189, 290
Parkyn, Leslie 117
Parnaby, Alan 248
Parnell, Jack 96, 99, 101
Parnell, Val 52, 91
Parr-Davies, Harry 8
Parsons, Charlie 333
Parsons, Christopher 249
Parsons, John 91
Parsons, Nicholas 55, 91, 208
Parsons, Percy 11
Pascal, Francoise 234
Pasco, Richard 238
Patch, Wally 12
Paterson, Bill 322, 331
Patience, Bob 302
Patrick, Nigel 19, 113
Patrick, Roy 102
Patt, Terry Su 241
Patterson, Dan 127
Patterson, Floyd 44
Pattison, Ian 328
Patton, Micheline 11
Paul, Andrew 268
Paul, Jeremy 191, 203
Paul, John 64, 80, 161, 188
Pauliac, Jacques 16
Paxman, Jeremy 259
Payne, Andrew 249
Payne, Laurence 45, 160
Pays, Amanda 302
Peach, Mary 173, 240
Peacock, Trevor 77
Pearce, Edwin 261
Pearce, Lennard 269
Pearl, Minnie 232
Pearson, Neil 325, 333
Pearson, Richard 68, 102, 288
Peck, Bob 300
Peck, Brian 187
Pecker, Boris 8
Pedler, Kit 188
Peduzzi, Richard 280
Peel, David 34
Peet, Stephen 121
Peisley, Frederick 94
Pelissier, Anthony 52
Pemberton, Antonia 240
Pemberton, Victor 9
Penders, Brian 161, 200
Penfold, Ann 211
Penhaligon, Susan 227, 233, 267
Penny, Malcolm 104
Pentangle 180
Pentelow, Arthur 203
Percival, John 138, 239
Percival, Lance 112, 127, 155, 180
Percy, Edward 20
Percy, Esme 5, 7
Perelman, S J 109
Perkins, Anthony 294
Perkins, Carl 232
Perkins, Syd 25
Perl, Arnold 115
Perrie, Lynne 192
Perrin, Reg 177
Perry, Anthony 78
Perry, Bill 208

Perry, Jimmy 108, 162, 218, 268
Persaud, Stephen 315
Pertwee, Bill 162
Pertwee, Jon 20, 42, 68, 115, 254
Pertwee, Michael 37, 43
Pertwee, Roland 43
Pertwee, Sean 325
Peter Knight Orchestra, the 60
Peters, Bernadette 243
Peters, Sylvia 25, 27
Peterson, Oscar 128, 163
Petherbridge, Edward 196, 196, 205
Petit, Christopher 129, 295
Petrie, Edna 95
Pett, Norman 277
Pettifer, Brian 222
Pettifer, Julian 69
Pettingell, Frank 22, 94
Petty, Cecil 44
Pevan, Barry 71
Peyton, Kathleen M 248
Phelan, Brian 204
Philbin, Maggie 230
Phillips, Anton 225
Phillips, Arlene 189
Phillips, Arthur 12
Phillips, Conrad 70
Phillips, Frank 36
Phillips, John 72, 163, 187
Phillips, Leslie 118, 275
Phillips, Nic 319
Phillips, Peter 174, 205
Phillips, Robin 142
Phillips, Sian 92, 95, 230, 246, 272
Phillips, Steve 254
Phillips, Trevor 274
Philpott, Trevor 41, 69, 138
Phoenix, Pat 89
Piaf, Edith 232
Pickett, Justin 320
Pickles, Carolyn 305
Pickles, Vivian 18, 100, 131, 149
Pickles, Wilfred 188
Pickup, Ronald 218, 238, 254, 309
Pienne, Yvette 13
Pierce, Norman 8
Pierce-Roberts, Tony 222
Pigg, Alexandra 274
Pigott-Smith, Tim 216, 238, 277, 294, 311, 325
Pike, John 72
Pike, Magnus 216
Pilbeam, Nova 14
Pilbrow, Richard 232
Pilger, John 254
Pilkington, Sir Harry 85
Pinches, Gerry 254
Pinero, Arthur Wing 121
Pinfield, Mervyn 109
Pinter, Harold 108, 133, 231
Pinto, Lt-Col Oreste 82
Piper, Frederick 9, 37
Pirandello, Luigi 83
Pirie, David 191, 327, 330
Pirie, Gordon 44
Pithey, Wensley 42, 178, 252
Pitman, John 138, 214
Pitt, Ingrid 264
Plage, G Dieter 104
Planer, Nigel 275, 281, 287, 327
Plantin, Marcus 200, 280, 309
Plater, Alan 113, 120, 163, 225, 226, 236, 248, 260, 295, 298, 309, 318
Platt, Ken 60
Platt, Victor 55
Play Away Band, the 198
Pleasence, Angela 192
Pleasence, Donald 46, 54, 95, 199, 219, 236, 247, 258, 312
Plievier, Theodore 115

Plowden, Julian 116
Plowman, Jon 289, 331, 332
Plowright, David 323
Plummer, Christopher 127
Plummer, Peter 138, 205, 224
Podmore, Bill 63, 90, 283, 298
Poe, Edgar Allan 14, 124, 150
Pohl, Frederick 140
Pointer, William 47
Polanski, Roman 117, 275
Poliakoff, Stephen 258
Pollard, Su 268
Pollock, Eileen 278
Pollock, Ellen 272
Polycarpou, Peter 319
Pontcanna Children's Choir, the 73
Ponti, Carlo 228
Pope, Dick 312
Pople, Jim 245
Porter, Eric 83, 154, 155, 294
Porter, Neil 13
Porter, Nyree Dawn 142, 149, 155, 207
Portman, Eric 10
Posford, George 14
Posner, Geoff 295, 304, 310
Postgate, Oliver 81, 170, 297
Potter, Dennis 87, 134, 146, 191, 195, 242, 243, 257, 258, 304, 308, 314, 319
Potter, Gillie 16
Potter, Martin 42
Potter, Peter 78, 205
Potter, Tommy 128
Poulson, Gerry 247
Powell, Gwyneth 196
Powell, Jonathan 42, 242, 253, 287
Powell, Lester 36
Powell, Michael 20
Powell, Robert 121, 188, 196, 316
Powell, Vince 92, 140, 145, 148, 157, 165, 188, 194, 206, 234
Power, Tyrone 54
Powley, Bryan 9
Praed, Michael 296
Pratt, Colin 302
Pratt, Mike 177
Prebble, John 124, 195, 316
Prendergast, William 83, 100, 113
Presle, Micheline 202
Presley, Elvis 232
Preston, Duncan 212, 304, 322
Preston, Trevor 242, 250, 260, 313, 314
Previn, André 101
Price, Alan 129, 164
Price, Brendan 237
Price, Dennis 63, 145
Price, Emlyn 231, 322
Price, Eric 192
Price, John 262
Price, Nancy 5
Price, Red 74
Pride, Dickie 74
Priestley, J B 15, 19, 37, 168, 208, 260
Prince, Peter 263, 278
Pringle, Bryan 172, 223, 260
Pringle, Harry 10, 13
Prior, Allan 113, 132, 177, 197, 301, 309
Pritchard, David 306
Pritchard, Hilary 8, 13, 254
Prochnik, Bruce 109
Prosser, David 132
Proudfoot, David 187
Provis, Arthur 119
Prowse, Juliet 239
Prowse, Peter 127
Pryce, Jonathan 137, 332
Pugh, Robert 247
Pughe, George 9, 12
Pullen, Gerry 79
Pulley, Frank 291
Pulman, Jack 129, 209, 230, 270

Purcell, Harold 14
Purchese, John 136
Purdie, John 231, 241, 294
Purdom, Edmund 75
Purdy, Rai 75
Purser, Philip 242
Purves, Peter 70
Pyne, Frederick 203
Pyne, Natasha 163

Quatuor Centra 21
Quayle, Anna 189
Quayle, Anthony 100, 180, 238
Quayle, John 269
Quentin, John 199
Quick, Diana 266
Quigley, Godfrey 64
Quiller-Couch, Sir Arthur 35, 95
Quilley, Denis 35
Quilligan, Veronica 269
Quinn, Louis 94
Quinn, Michael 100
Quirke, Pauline 221, 319
Quitak, Oscar 43, 211, 252

Race, Roger 96, 152, 167, 174, 294
Race, Steve 33, 128
Radcliffe, Tom 316
Radford, Mike 281
Rae, Jackie 60, 156
Raeburn, Anna 246
Raglan, Robert 19
Raikin, Arkady 86
Raine, Patricia 75
Rainer, Luise 25
Raisch, Bill 126
Raitt, Anne 225, 278
Raki, Laya 114
Rakoff, Alvin 44, 108, 132, 141, 228, 238, 279, 308, 334
Ralling, Christopher 199, 245
Ralph, Stephanie 330
Ramsey, Ian 174
Randell, Ron 66, 67
Rankin, Molly 14
Ransley, Peter 302
Rantzen, Esther 138, 214
Raphael, Frederic 100, 230, 231, 236
Rattigan, Terence 32, 36, 75, 108, 168
Rau, Santha Rama 140
Raven, Simon 116, 160, 219, 240
Rawle, Jeff 211, 325
Rawlinson, A R 128
Rawlinson, Brian 70, 157, 198, 291
Rawls, Lou 164
Ray, Johnnie 52
Ray, Josephina 53
Ray, Rene 42
Ray, Robin 135
Ray, Ted 60
Rayne, Julie 120
Raynor, Sheila 156
Razdan, Soni 235
Rea, Ben 124, 221
Rea, David C 167
Rea, Stephen 236
Read, Anthony 128, 138, 206
Read, Jan 48
Reade, Winwood 105
Reader, Eddi 329
Reardon, John 204, 216, 246, 280
Reardon, Ray 177
Reason, Rhodes 76
Reay, Ann 198
Rebel, Michele 51
Redfern, Anthea 196, 239
Redgrave, Corin 216
Redgrave, Lynn 293
Redgrave, Michael 126, 146
Redgrave, Vanessa 101, 147

359